John S. Jenkins

The New Clerk's Assistant

or, Book of practical forms: containing numerous precedents and forms for ordinary business

transactions, with references to the various statutes, and latest judicial decisions

John S. Jenkins

The New Clerk's Assistant
or, Book of practical forms: containing numerous precedents and forms for ordinary business transactions, with references to the various statutes, and latest judicial decisions

ISBN/EAN: 9783337843250

Printed in Europe, USA, Canada, Australia, Japan

Cover: Foto ©Suzi / pixelio.de

More available books at **www.hansebooks.com**

THE NEW

CLERK'S ASSISTANT,

OR

BOOK OF PRACTICAL FORMS;

CONTAINING NUMEROUS PRECEDENTS AND FORMS FOR ORDINARY BUSINESS
TRANSACTIONS, WITH REFERENCES TO THE VARIOUS STATUTES AND
LATEST JUDICIAL DECISIONS;

DESIGNED FOR THE USE OF

County and Town Officers of every Grade,

BANKERS, MERCHANTS, AUCTIONEERS, MECHANICS, FARMERS
AND PROFESSIONAL MEN,

AND ADAPTED TO THE

NEW ENGLAND, NORTHERN AND WESTERN STATES AND CALIFORNIA.

BY

JOHN S. JENKINS,

Counselor at Law.

NEW EDITION, WITH APPENDIX AND NOTES.

ALBANY, N. Y.:
W. C. LITTLE & CO., LAW BOOKSELLERS, 525 BROADWAY.
1872.

PREFACE

TO THE FOURTH EDITION.

THE object originally had in view, in the preparation of this work, was, to provide a practical form book for business men,—one that should be full and complete, and yet simple and clear in its arrangement, and easily understood. It has already passed through three large editions, and the publishers have been at length compelled to stereotype it, in order to enable them to supply the demand. It is but reasonable, therefore, to infer, that the public approve of the plan of the work and of its execution.

This work is adapted to the Eastern, Northern and Western States. It is sold very extensively in all the New England States, Pennsylvania, Ohio, Indiana, Illinois, Michigan, Wisconsin, and California. The laws of those States being similar in their general character, the Forms included herein are consequently suited to the wants of their officers and business men.

To County and Town Officers of every grade,—to business men of all classes,—to the farmer, the mechanic, and the merchant,—this book is believed to be a useful and reliable guide and director, a well in the discharge of the public duties that may devolve on them, as in the management of their own private affairs. The Chapters on Auctions, Banks and Corporations, Fees of Officers. Homestead Exemption, Mechanics' and Laborers' Lien, Plank Roads, Supervisors, Taxes, Town Auditors and Town Houses,—and the references to the Statutes and legal decisions,—are new features in a work of this character. A considerable amount of information, and a great number of forms, are also contained in each one of the different divisions, which are not to be found in any other work or publication.

No more changes have been made in this edition than were absolutely necessary. It has been the constant aim of the author and publishers, to have the book conform, in all respects, to the Laws of the State as existing at the time of the publication of each edition. This has been a leading and peculiar feature of the work. It is possible that some might deem it still more valuable, if it could remain permanent; but a moment's reflection will serve to convince them, that its highest and greatest usefulness must depend on its keeping up with the modifications and changes that may, from time to time, be made.

New Chapters,—on the Exemption of the Homestead of a family from sale on execution, Plank Roads, and the Duties of Supervisors,—have been inserted in this edition.

The third edition of the Revised Statutes having now come into general use, the references herein contained apply to the paging and section numbers of that edition. It may be proper further to state, lest any one not familiar with the plan of the work may be led into error, that the words in the forms, in Italic letter, contained in brackets, are designed to be merely directory, and those in Roman are alone to be inserted, where any variation is proper or necessary.

GENERAL CONTENTS.

THE NEW CLERK'S ASSISTANT.

CHAPTER I.

ACKNOWLEDGMENT AND PROOF OF DEEDS, MORTGAGES, AND OTHER INSTRUMENTS.—CERTIFICATES OF DISCHARGE AND SATISFACTION.

PRACTICAL REMARKS.

1. In order to entitle a deed or conveyance of land to be recorded, it is necessary that it should be previously acknowledged or proved, before the proper officer; except, that in New Hampshire and Vermont, a deed may be recorded without the acknowledgment, but it will be valid against the claims of creditors and subsequent purchasers for sixty days only. The Revised Statutes of New York require all conveyances of lands, tenements and chattels real, with the exception of leases for a term not exceeding three years, to be recorded.[1]

. 2. Deeds or conveyances, though not recorded, are valid as between the parties and their representatives, but not against judgment creditors, or subsequent purchasers in good faith. In Maryland, Virginia and North Carolina, however, it is necessary for a deed to be acknowledged and recorded, to pass the title of the grantor.

3. Officers authorized to take the proof or acknowledgment of instruments, are restricted in the exercise of their authority for such purposes, to the place or territory to which the jurisdiction of the court to which they belong extends, or to the city, county, or town in and for which they may have been appointed or elected.[2]

, 4. Justices of the Peace may take the proof or acknowledgment of conveyances or instruments, at any place within the counties in which they reside.[3]

5. Conveyances of lands within this State, and all contracts, powers of attorney, and other instruments relating to the same, may be acknowledged or proved, as follows:

---

[1] 2 R. S., (3d ed.) 40, §§ 1, 4; Id. 46, 47, §§ 40, 42, 44; 8 Wendell, 620, 15 Id., 588, 594; 6 Hill, 469.

[2] 2 R. S., (3d ed.) 40, § 4.
[3] Laws of 1840, Chap. 238.

1. In the State: before the Justices of the Supreme Court, County Judges, Mayors and Recorders of cities, Commissioners of Deeds in cities, and Justices of the Peace in the several towns.

2. Out of the State, and in the United States: before the Chief Justice and Associate Justices of the Supreme Court of the United States, District Judges of the United States, the Judges or Justices of the Supreme, Superior, or Circuit Court, of any State or Territory within the United States, the Chief Judge, or any Associate Judge of the Circuit Court of the United States in the District of Columbia, Mayors of cities in the United States, and Commissioners of Deeds appointed by the Governor of this State, in other States and Territories, and the District of Columbia.

3. Out of the United States: before a Judge of the highest Court, in Upper or Lower Canada; before any Consul of the United States, Chargé d'Affaires, Minister Plenipotentiary, or Minister Extraordinary, resident in any foreign country; before the Mayor of London, the Mayors or Chief Magistrates of Dublin, Edinburgh and Liverpool, and any person specially authorized by a commission under the seal of the Supreme Court of this State.[1]

6. The proof or acknowledgment of any conveyance or instrument, that may be recorded or read in evidence in this State, when made by any person residing out of the State, and within any other State or Territory of the United States, may be made before any officer of such State or Territory, authorized by the laws thereof to take the proof and acknowledgment of deeds. It is necessary, however, that such officer should know, or have satisfactory evidence, that the person making such acknowledgment is the individual described in, and who executed the conveyance or instrument; also, that to the certificate of the officer, there should be attached a certificate under the name and official seal of the clerk or register of the county in which he resides, specifying, that at the time of taking the proof or acknowledgment, he was duly authorized to take the same, and verifying his hand writing.[2]

7. The official title of an acknowledging officer should always be attached to his certificate, in full. If he be a Judge, he should state of what court; if a Commissioner, or Justice of the Peace; the city or county in and for which he is such Commissioner, or Justice, should be mentioned; and if a Minister Plenipotentiary, or Chargé d'Affaires, he should say from what government he is appointed, and to what government he is accredited.

8. Where a deed is proved or acknowledged before a Commissioner of Deeds, Justice of the Peace, or County Judge, not of the degree of Counsellor at law, the certificate of the County Clerk to the

---

[1] 2 R. S., (3d ed.) 40, § 4; Laws of 1840, Chap. 238; Id., 290; Laws of 1845, Chap. 109; Laws of 1847, Chap. 280.

[2] Laws of 1848, Chap. 198.

official character of the officer taking the proof or acknowledgment, and the genuineness of his signature, should be procured, if the instrument is to be recorded in another county.

9. By the laws of this State, every written instrument, except promissory notes, bills of exchange, and the last wills of deceased persons, may be proved or acknowledged, and read in evidence on the trial of any action, with the same effect, and in the same manner, as conveyances of real estate.[1]

10. Where the execution of a conveyance is acknowledged by the party in person, the officer taking the same must certify to the identity.[2]

11. Where the execution is proved by a subscribing witness, he must state his own place of residence, and that he knows the person described in, and who executed the conveyance.[3]

12. A substantial compliance with the requirements of the statute relative to the proof and acknowledgment of conveyances, and othe instruments, is all that is required: the identical language of the law need not be used.[4]

13. Whenever erasures or interlineations occur in any conveyance, they should be noted previous to the execution, or mentioned in the certificate of the officer taking the proof or acknowledgment.[5]

14. Upon the application of any grantee in any conveyance, or of any person claiming under or through him, verified by oath, representing that a subscribing witness, residing in the county where the application is made, refuses to appear and testify, any officer authorized to take proofs or acknowledgments, except Commissioners of Deeds and Justices of the Peace, may issue a subpœna, requiring such witness to appear and testify before him.[6]

15. Where the subscribing witnesses to a conveyance are dead, proof of its execution may be made before any officer authorized to take proofs or acknowledgments of deeds, other than Commissioners of Deeds, Justices of the Peace, and County Judges, not of the degree of counsel in the Supreme Court. The evidence establishing the death of the witnesses, and of the handwriting of such witnesses, or of either of them, and of the grantor, with the names and places of residence of the witnesses examined before the officer, must be set forth in his certificate. The conveyance having been thus proved and certified, may be recorded in the proper office, provided the original deed is deposited in the same office, to remain there for the inspection of all persons desiring to examine it. Such record and deposit will be constructive evidence of the execution of the said conveyance, to all subsequent purchasers, although such conveyance, nor the record thereof, nor the transcript of the record, can be read in evidence.[7]

[1] Laws of 1833, Chap. 271.
[2] 2 R. S. (3d ed.) 42, § 12; 11 Johnson, 434; 2 Cowen, 552; 4 Wendell, 561; 13 Id., 541.
[3] 2 R. S., (3d ed) 42, § 15; 7 Wendell. 364; 1 Hill, 131.
[4] 2 Barbour's Ch. Rep., 232.
[5] 8 Cowen, 71; 7 Wendell, 364.
[6] 2 R. S. (3d ed.) 43, §§ 16, 17.
[7] 2 R. S., (3d ed.) 46, §§ 30—33

FORMS.

§ 1. *Certificate of acknowledgment by party known to the officer.*

County, ss:[1]

On this first day of May, in the year of our Lord one thousand eight hundred and forty-five, before me personally came A. B., to me known to be the individual described in, and who executed the within [*or, above, or, annexed*] conveyance [*or, bond; or, letter of attorney; or, instrument in writing,*] and acknowledged that he executed the same, for the purposes therein mentioned.

G. H., County Judge of said county.

§ 2. *Certificate where identity of Party is proven to the officer.*

County, ss :

On this first day of May, &c., before me personally came A. B., proven to me satisfactorily to be the same person described in, and who executed the within conveyance, by the oath of C. D., *subscribing witness thereto,*[2] who being by me duly sworn, did depose and say, that he resided in the city of Auburn, in the county of Cayuga ; that he was acquainted with the said A. B., and that he knew him to be the same person described in and who executed the within conveyance : and, thereupon, the said A. B. acknowledged that he executed the same.

E. F., Justice of the Peace in and for said county.

§ 3. *By Husband and Wife — known to the Officer.*

County, ss :

On this first day of May, &c., before me personally came A. B., and Mary his wife, to me known to be the individuals described in, and who executed the within conveyance, and acknowledged that they executed the same ; and the said Mary acknowledged, on a private examination by me made, apart from her husband, that she executed the said conveyance freely, and without any fear or compulsion of him.

C. D., Commissioner of Deeds in and for said county.

§ 4. *By Husband and Wife —proven to the Officer.*

County, ss :

On this first day of May, &c., before me personally came A. B., and Mary his wife, both proven to me satisfactorily to be the same persons described in, and who executed the within conveyance, by

---

[1] If a conveyance or instrument is proved or acknowledged in this State, but to be used or recorded in another State, the name of the State should be inserted in the heading of the certificate as well as that of the county.

[2] If the person by whose oath the identity is established, is not a subscribing witness, the words in italic, in the above and subsequent forms must, be omitted.

the oath of John Smith, *subscribing witness thereto*, who being by me duly sworn, did depose and say, that he resided in the town of in said county; that he was acquainted with the said A. B., and Mary his wife; that he knew them to be the same persons described in, and who executed the within conveyance: and, thereupon, they severally acknowledged before me that they executed the same; and the said Mary, &c., [*as in* § 3, *to the end.*]

E. F., Justice, &c.[1]

---

§ 5. *By Husband and Wife — Husband known, and Wife proven to the Officer.*

County, ss:

On this first day of May, &c., before me personally came A. B., and Mary his wife; the said A. B. being known to me to be the same person described in, and who executed the within conveyance; and the said Mary being proven to me satisfactorily to be the same person described in, and who executed the within conveyance, by the oath of John Smith, *subscribing witness thereto*, who being by me duly sworn, did depose and say, that he resided in the town of in said county; that he was acquainted with the said Mary, the wife of the said A. B., and that he knew her to be the same person described in, and who executed the said conveyance; and, thereupon, the said A. B., and the said Mary his wife, severally acknowledged that they executed the same; and the said Mary, &c., [*as in* § 3 *to the end.*]

E. F., Justice, &c.

---

§ 6. *By two Husbands and their Wives.*

County, ss:

On this first day of May, &c., before me personally came A. B., and Mary his wife, and C. D., and Lucy his wife, known to me to be the individuals described in, and who executed the within conveyance, and severally acknowledged that they executed the same; and the said Mary and Lucy, severally, each for herself, acknowledged, on a private examination by me made, apart from her husband, that she executed the same freely, without any fear or compulsion of him.

E. F., Justice, &c.

---

§ 7. *By Wife in separate Certificate.*

County, ss:

On this first day of May, &c., before me personally came M. B., wife of A. B., described in the within conveyance, the said M. B. being known to me to be the individual described in, and who

---

[1] The official title of the officer should always be written in full, and not abbreviated.

executed the said conveyance; and she acknowledged in a private examination by me made, apart from her husband, that she executed the same freely, without any fear or compulsion of him.

E. F., Justice, &c.

---

§ 8. *By two or more Parties.*

County, ss:

On this first day of May, &c., before me personally came A. B., and C. D., to me known to be the individuals described in, and who executed the within conveyance, and they severally, each for himself, acknowledged that they executed the same.

E. F., Justice, &c.

---

§ 9. *By five persons — three known and two identified.*

County, ss:

On this first day of May, &c., before me personally came A. B., C. D., and E. F., to me known to be three of the individuals described in, and who executed the within conveyance; and also came G. H. and I. J., satisfactorily proven to me to be two of the individuals described in, and who executed the within conveyance, by the oath of M. M., *subscribing witness thereto*, who being by me duly sworn, did depose and say, that he resided in the town of in said county; that he was acquainted with the said G. H. and I. J., and that he knew them to be the two individuals described in, and who executed the within conveyance: and, thereupon, the said A. B., C. D., E. F., G. H., and I. J., severally acknowledged before me that they executed the same, for the purposes therein mentioned.

O. P., Justice, &c.

---

§ 10. *By one of several Parties.*

County, ss:

On this first day of May, &c., before me personally came A. B., to me known to be one of the individuals described in, and who executed the within conveyance, and acknowledged that he executed the same.

E. F., Justice, &c.

---

§ 11. *By an Attorney.*

County, ss:

On this first day of May, &c., before me personally came A. B., known to me to be the same person described in, and who executed the within conveyance, and acknowledged that he executed the same as the act and deed of C. D., therein described, by virtue of a power

of attorney duly executed by the said C. D., bearing date the
day of   , in the year   , and recorded in the
office of the Clerk of the county of Onondaga, in book A of Powers
of Attorney, page 39, on the   day of   , in the
year .   .   E. F., Justice, &c.

---

§ 12. *By Attorney known to the Officer.*

County, ss:

On this first day of May, &c., before me personally came A. B.,
known to me to be the Attorney in fact of C. D., the individual
described in, and who executed the within conveyance, by his said
Attorney; and the said A. B. acknowledged that he executed the
same, as the act and deed of the said C. D.

E. F., Justice, &c.

---

§ 13. *By Attorney proven to the Officer.*

County, ss:

On this first day of May, &c., before me personally came A. B.,
proven satisfactorily to me to be the same person described in, and
who executed the within conveyance, as the Attorney in fact of C.
D., by the oath of G. H., *subscribing witness thereto*, who being by
me duly sworn, did depose and say, that he resided in the town of
in said county; that he was acquainted with the said A. B., and
that he knew him to be the individual described in, and who executed the said conveyance, as the Attorney in fact of C. D. : and,
thereupon, the said A. B. acknowledged before me that he executed
the same, as the act and deed of the said C. D.

E. F., Justice, &c.

---

§ 14. *By an Executor or Trustee.*

County, ss:

On this first day of May, &c., before me personally came A. B.,
known to me to be the Executor of the last will and testament [*or*,
Trustee of the estate] of C. D., mentioned and described in the
within conveyance, and the said A. B. acknowledged before me that
he executed the same, as such Executor, [*or*, Trustee,] as aforesaid.

E. F., Justice, &c.

---

§ 15. *By a Sheriff.*

County, ss:

On this first day of May, &c., before me personally came A. B.,
Esquire, Sheriff [*or*, late Sheriff] of the county of   , to me
known to be the same person described in, and who executed the
within conveyance, and acknowledged that he executed the same.

E. F., Justice, &c.

§ 16. *By a Deputy Sheriff.*

County, ss ·

On this first day of May, &c., before me personally came C. D., to me known to be the individual described in, and who executed the within conveyance, as the general deputy of A. B., Esquire, Sheriff of the county of   , and acknowledged that he executed the said conveyance, as such general deputy as aforesaid.

E. F., Justice, &c

---

§ 17. *By a Party to confirm Deed executed during Infancy.*

County, ss:

On this first day of May, &c., before me personally came A. B., to me known to be the individual described in, and who executed the within conveyance, and thereupon duly acknowledged that the said conveyance was formerly executed by him when he was an infant under twenty-one years; that he has since arrived at full age, and is desirous of confirming his former execution thereof; and that he now acknowledges that he executed the same, as and for his act and deed.

E. F., Justice, &c.

---

§ 18. *Certificate of Proof by Subscribing Witness known to the Officer.*

County, ss:

On this first day of May, &c., before me personally came C. D., subscribing witness to the within conveyance, to me known, who, being by me duly sworn, did depose and say, that he resided in the town of   in said county; that he knew A. B., the individual described in, and who executed the said conveyance; that he was present and saw the said A. B. sign, seal, and deliver the same, as and for his act and deed; and that the said A. B. acknowledged the execution thereof: whereupon the said C. D. became the subscribing witness thereto.

E. F., Justice, &c.

---

§ 19. *By Subscribing Witness proven to the Officer.*

County, ss:

On this first day of May, &c., before me personally came M. N and C. D., and the said M. N., to me known, having been by me duly sworn, did depose and say, that he resided in the town of   in said county; that he was acquainted with the said C. D., the subscribing witness to the within conveyance, and that he knew him to be the same person, which is to me satisfactory evidence thereof and the said C. D., being by me duly sworn, &c., [*as in* § 18, *to the end.*]

E. F., Justice, &c.

§ 20. *By Subscribing Witness — Grantors residing in another State.*

County, ss:

On this first day of May, &c., before me personally came C. D., to me known, who being by me duly sworn, did depose and say, that he resided in the town of   in said county; that he knew A. B., and E. his wife, the individuals described in, and who executed the within conveyance; that they severally reside in the town of   in the State of   ; that he was present and saw them sign, seal, and deliver the said conveyance, as and for their act and deed, and that he thereupon became the subscribing witness thereto.

E. F., Justice, &c.

---

§ 21. *The same, by Subscribing Witness proven to the Officer.*

County, ss:

On this first day of May, &c., before me personally came M. N., and C. D., and the said M. N. to me known, having been by me duly sworn, did depose and say, that he resided in the town of   in said county; that he was acquainted with the said C. D., the subscribing witness to the within conveyance, and that he knew him to be the same person, which is to me satisfactory evidence thereof : and the said C. D., being by me duly sworn, on his oath, said, that he resided in the town of   in the State of   ; that he knew A. B., and E. his wife, &c., [*as in* § 20, *to the end.*]

E. F., Justice, &c.

---

§ 22. *By Subscribing Witness as to the Husband, and Acknowledgment by the Wife, both being known to the Officer.*

County, ss:

On this first day of May, &c., before me personally came C. D., to me known, who being by me duly sworn, did depose and say, that he resided in the town of   in said county; that he knew A. B., one of the individuals described in, and who executed the within conveyance; that he was present and saw the said A. B. execute the same, and that he, the said C. D., thereupon became the subscribing witness thereto. At the same time, also appeared before me E. B., the wife of the said A. B., *to me personally known,* who, on a private examination by me made, apart from her husband, acknowledged that she executed the within conveyance freely, without any fear or compulsion of her said husband.

E. F., Justice, &c.

---

§ 23. *By Subscribing Witness as to the Husband, and Acknowledgment by the Wife, both proven to the officer.*

County, ss:

On this first day of May, &c., before me personally came C. D.

2

who being by me duly sworn, &c., [*as in* § 22, *to the end, omitting the words in italic, and then add:*] And at the same time also appeared before me, M. N., to me personally known, who being by me duly sworn, did depose and say, that he resided in the town of   in the county of   ; that he knew the said C. D. to be the same person who was a subscribing witness to the within conveyance; and that he also knew the said E. B., who made the aforesaid acknowledgment, to be one of the individuals described in, and who executed the said conveyance, which is to me satisfactory evidence thereof.   E. F., Justice, &c.

---

§ 24. *By Subscribing Witness to Deed executed by an Attorney.*

County, ss:

On this first day of May, &c., before me personally came C. D., to me known, who being by me duly sworn, did depose and say, that he resided in the town of   in said county; that he knew A. B., the person described in, and who executed the within conveyance, as the Attorney in fact of M. N. therein named; that he was present and saw the said A. B. execute the same as such Attorney, and that he, the said C. D., thereupon became the subscribing witness thereto.   E. F., Justice, &c.

---

§ 25. *Proof of the execution of a Deed where the Subscribing Witnesses are dead.*

County, ss:

On this first day of May, &c., before me personally came G. H., to me known, who being by me duly sworn, and the within conveyance being shown to him, did depose and say, that he knew the parties therein described; that he was well acquainted with A. B., the grantor; that he had frequently seen him write, and knew his handwriting; and that the name of the said grantor subscribed to the said conveyance was in the proper handwriting of the said A. B.

And the said G. H. further on his oath said, that he was well acquainted with C. D., one of the subscribing witnesses to the said conveyance, and with his handwriting; that the said C. D., at the time of the date of said deed, resided in the town of   in the county of   , and has been dead about one year; and that the name of the said C. D., deceased, subscribed as a witness to said conveyance, was in his proper handwriting.

And the said G. H., further deposed and said, that at the time of the date of said conveyance, he was, and for several years had been, also acquainted with one E. F., a shoemaker, who then resided in the said town of   , in the county of   , and in the neighborhood of the said grantor; that the said E. F. died at the town of   aforesaid in the year 1844, and since the date of said conveyance; that he, the said G. H., was not acquainted with the handwriting of the said E. F.; that he has never known or heard of any other person of the name of E. F.; [*if necessary, insert,* residing in the neighborhood of said grantor,] and that he cannot say in whose handwriting the name of the said E. F. is subscribed to the said conveyance.

And I hereby certify, that the aforesaid deposition of the said G. H. is to me satisfactory evidence of the death of all the witnesses to the within conveyance, and of the handwriting of C. D., one of the said witnesses, and of the handwriting of A. B., the grantor therein named.

J. P. H., County Judge of said county.

§ 26. *Proof of Deed executed by a Moneyed Corporation.*
Cayuga County, ss:

On this first day of May, &c., before me personally came N. B., the President of the Cayuga County Bank, to me known, who being by me duly sworn, did depose and say; that he resided in the city of Auburn, in said county; that he was the President of the Cayuga County Bank; that he knew the corporate seal of the said Bank; that the seal affixed to the within conveyance was such corporate seal; that it was so affixed by order of the Board of Directors of the said Bank; and that he signed his name thereto by the like order as President of said Bank. [*If the conveyance is proven by a Cashier, or the Secretary of a Company, and executed by him and the President, substitute* Secretary, *or* Cashier, *for* President, *and the name of the Company for the Bank, in the foregoing, and then add:* And be the said N. B. further said, that he also knew C. D., the President, of the said Bank, [*or,* Company,] and that the signature of the said C. D., subscribed to the said conveyance was in the genuine handwriting of the said C. D., and was thereto subscribed, in the presence of the said N. B., by the like order of the said Board of Directors.]

E. F., Justice, &c.

§ 27. *The same, by a Religious Corporation.*
County, ss:

On this first day of May, &c., before me personally came A. B., to me known, who, being by me duly sworn, did depose and say, that he resided in the town of   in said county, and was the Clerk of the Corporation of the Rector, Churchwardens, and Vestrymen of the Protestant Episcopal Church of St. Peter's [*or,* the Corporation of the Trustees of the first Methodist Episcopal Society,] in the town of   aforesaid; that the seal affixed to the within conveyance was the corporate seal of the said corporation, and that it was affixed by order of the said corporation. [*If necessary add clause proving the handwriting of the subscribers to the conveyance.*]

E. F., Justice. &c.

§ 28. *Form of acknowledgment in New England States.*[1]

Commonwealth [*or*, State] of   , } ss:
County of   ,

Salem, May 1, 1847.

Then personally appeared before me, the within [*or*, above named A. B., and acknowledged [*or*, and C. B. his wife, and severally acknowledged] the foregoing instrument to be his [*or*, their] free act and deed.   E. F., Justice, &c.

---

§ 29. *Acknowledgment in Pennsylvania.*

State of Pennsylvania, } ss:
   Mercer County,

The first day of May, &c., before me, one of the Justices of the Peace, [*or*, one of the Judges of the Court of Common Pleas] in and for said county, personally appeared the above named A. B., and acknowledged [*or*, and C. B. his wife, and severally acknowledged] the foregoing written indenture to be his [*or*, their] act and deed, to the end that the same might be recorded according to law. [*If necessary, add:* And she, the said Caroline, being of lawful age, and being examined by me separate and apart from her husband, and the contents of said indenture being fully made known to her, did declare, that she did voluntarily, and of her own free will and accord, seal, and as her act and deed deliver, the same, without any coercion or compulsion of her said husband whatever.]

Witness my hand and seal.

E. F., Justice, &c. [L. S.][2]

---

§ 30. *Acknowledgment by Husband and Wife in Michigan.*

State of Michigan, } ss:
   Wayne County,

Be it remembered, that on this first day of May, &c., before me, a Justice of the Peace in and for the county aforesaid, appeared A. B., and Mary his wife, and severally acknowledged that they had severally executed the within instrument, for the uses and purposes therein mentioned: And the said Mary, on a private examination apart from her husband, acknowledged that she executed the within instrument freely, and without fear or compulsion from any one.* And I further certify, that the persons who made said acknowledgment are known to me to be the individuals described in, and who executed the within instrument.   E. F., Justice, &c.

---

[1] The acknowledgment may be before a Judge of a Supreme or Circuit Court, Notary Public, Mayor of a city, Commissioner appointed in another State, or a foreign Minister or Consul of the United States.

[2] A simple scroll, made with a pen, is sufficient to constitute a seal in Pennsylvania.

§ 31. *The same, in Ohio.*

State of Ohio,   } ss:
   Hamilton County,

Be it remembered, &c., [*as in* 30, *to the* *.]

E. F., Justice, &c.

---

§ 32. *The same, in Illinois.*

State of Illinois,   } ss:
   Cook County,

Be it remembered, that on the first day of May, &c., before me, the subscriber, one of the Justices of the Peace in and for said county, personally appeared A. B., and Mary his wife, to me personally known to be the individuals described in, and who executed the within deed, and severally acknowledged that they had executed the same:* And the said Mary, after I had made her acquainted with and explained to her the contents of the said deed, on an examination separate and apart from her said husband, acknowledged the same to be her act and deed, and that she executed the same voluntarily and freely, and without compulsion of her said husband, and that she does not wish to retract.   E. F., Justice, &c.

---

§ 33. *The same, in Indiana.*

State of Indiana,   } ss:
   Jackson County,

Be it remembered, &c., [*as in* § 32 *to the* *, *and then add:*] And the said Mary, on a private examination, separate and apart from, and out of the hearing of her husband, acknowledged that she executed such deed of her own free will and accord, without any coercion or compulsion of her husband.   E. F., Justice, &c.

---

§ 34. *The same, in Alabama.*[1]

State of Alabama,   } ss:
   Lowndes County,

This day, before me, G. H., Esq., Judge, &c., personally appeared A. B., and acknowledged, [*or*, and M. B. his wife, and severally acknowledged] that he [*or*, they] signed, sealed, and delivered the foregoing deed to C. D., on the day and year therein mentioned, as his [*or*, their] voluntary act and deed. [*If necessary, add:* And the said M. B., on a private examination, apart from her husband, acknowledged that she signed, sealed, and delivered the said deed, as her voluntary act, freely, and without any fear, threats, or compulsion of her husband.]

Given under my hand and seal, this   day of   , in the year eighteen hundred and   .   G. H. [L. s.]

---

[1] The acknowledgment may be taken before a Judge of any Supreme Court, Clerk of a Circuit Court, Notary Public, or Commissioner for Alabama. As in Pennsylvania, a scroll of the pen constitutes a seal.

§ 35. *Satisfaction of Mortgage and Acknowledgment, by individual known to the Officer.*

I, A. B., of the town of   in the county of   and State of   , do hereby certify, that a certain mortgage, bearing date the   day of   , in the year one thousand eight hundred and   , made and executed by C. D., of the first part, to *me, the said* A. B., of the second part, and recorded in the office of the Clerk of the County of   , in book 27 of mortgages, at pages 250 and 251, on the first day of May, A. D., 1845, [*if the mortgage has been assigned, insert the name of the assignee instead of A. B., at the commencement of the certificate; omit the words, " me, the said,"* *in Italic; and insert here:* and which said mortgage was duly assigned to me by the said A. B., the mortgagee above named, by assignment dated the   day of   , in the year   , and recorded in the office of the Clerk of the county of   aforesaid, in book 20 of mortgages, at page 9, on the tenth day of June, A. D., 1845,] is fully paid, satisfied and discharged. Dated the first day of July, 1846.   A. B.

In presence of
    G. H.

        County, ss:
On this   day of   , in the year one thousand eight hundred and forty-five, before me came A. B., known to me to be the individual described in, and who executed, the above certificate, and acknowledged that he executed the same.

                                        E. F., Justice, &c.

————

§ 36 *Certificate of Satisfaction to be written on the Mortgage.*

I, A. B., the mortgagee within named, [*or, the assignee of the within named mortgagee,*] do hereby certify that the within named mortgage is fully paid, satisfied and discharged Dated the   day of   , A. D., 18 .   A. B.
            [*Add acknowledgment, as in § 35.*]

————

§ 37. *Satisfaction by an Executor, Administrator or Trustee.*

I, A. B., executor of the last will and testament of C. D., deceased, [*or,* administrator of the goods, chattels and credits, which were of C. D., deceased; *or,* trustee of the estate of C. D., &c.,] do hereby certify that a mortgage made and executed by E. F. to the said C. D., in his lifetime, [*or,* to me as such trustee as aforesaid,] bearing date, &c. [*Follow the preceding forms, as the case may require.*]

In presence of   A. B.
    G. H.

§ 38. *Acknowledgment of Satisfaction by Individual proven to the Officer.*

County, ss:

On this first day of May, &c., before me personally came A. B., satisfactorily proven to me to be the same person described in, and who executed the above certificate, by the oath of C. D., to me known, who, being by me duly sworn, did depose and say: that he resided in the town of   in said county; that he was acquainted with the said A. B.; and that he knew him to be the same person described in, and who executed, the above certificate, which is to me satisfactory evidence thereof : and, thereupon, the said A. B. acknowledged before me, that he executed the said certificate.   E. F., Justice, &c.

---

§ 39. *Proof of Execution of Certificate, by Subscribing Witness known to the Officer.*

County, ss:

On this first day of May, &c., before me personally came C. D., subscribing witness to the above certificate, to me known, who being by me duly sworn, did depose and say, that he resided in the town of   in said county; that he was acquainted with A. B.; that he knew him to be the same person described in, and who executed the above certificate; that he saw him sign the same: that the said A. B. acknowledged the execution thereof in his presence; and that he subscribed his name as a witness thereto.

E. F., Justice, &c.

---

§ 40. *The same, by Subscribing Witness proven to the Officer.*

County, ss:

On this first day of May, &c., before me personally came L. M., to me known, and C. D.; and the said L. M. being by me duly sworn, did depose and say, that he resided in the town of   in said county; that he was acquainted with the said C. D., and that he knew him to be the same person who is the subscribing witness to the above certificate, which is to me satisfactory evidence of his identity; and the said C. D., being by me duly sworn, did depose and say, that he resided in the town of   in the county of   ; that he was acquainted with A. B. [*as in* §39, *to the end.*]   E. F., Justice, &c.

---

§ 41. *Certificate of Satisfaction by a Corporate Company, with Proof of Execution.*

I, J. S. S., President of the Bank of Auburn, do hereby certify, that a certain mortgage bearing date the first day of June, one thousand eight hundred and forty-one, made and executed by C. D., and E. his wife, to F. G., and by the said F. G. assigned to the said

Bank of Auburn, by assignment dated the tenth day of July, one thousand eight hundred and forty-three, and recorded in the office of the Clerk of the county of Cayuga, in book No. 34 of mortgages, page 99; and which said mortgage was recorded in the office of the Clerk of the county of Cayuga aforesaid, in book No. 30 of mortgages, pages 10 and 11, on the second day of June, A. D. 1841, is fully paid, satisfied, and discharged.

In witness whereof, the said Bank of Auburn has caused its corporate seal to be hereunto affixed, the first day of May, in the year one thousand eight hundred and forty-five.

　　　[L. S.]　　　　　　　　　　　J. S. S., President.

In presence of
　　C. H. M.

Cayuga County, ss:

On this first day of May, &c., before me personally came J. S. S., in the above certificate mentioned, President of the Bank of Auburn aforesaid, to me known; and the said J. S. S., being by me duly sworn, did depose and say, that he resided in the town of　　　　　,
in the said county: that the seal affixed to the above certificate was the corporate seal of the said Bank of Auburn, and was affixed thereto by the order of the Board of Directors of said Bank; and that he subscribed his name thereto by the like order.

　　　　　　　　　　　　　　　　E. F., Justice, &c.

----

§ 42. *Satisfaction of Judgment in a Justice's Court, where a Transcript is filed in the County Clerk's Office.*[1]

　　　　County Clerk's Office.

A. B.　　） Judgment rendered in favor of the plaintiff against
against　 〉 defendant, before E. F., Esq., a Justice of the Peace in
C. D.　　）and for said county, for　　　dollars and　　　cents, damages and costs.

Transcript filed and Judgment docketed, the　　　day of　　　, in the year 1845.

Satisfaction of the above mentioned judgment is hereby acknowledged.　　　　　　　　　　　　　　　　A. B.

Subscribed and acknowledged before me, the　　　day of　　　, in the year 1845, by A. B., known to me to be the plaintiff above named, [or, made known to me by the oath of E. F., to be, &c.; or known to me to be one of the plaintiffs, &c.]

　　　　　　　　　　　　　　　　E. F., Justice, &c.

----

§ 43. *Satisfaction of Judgment in a Court of Record.*[1]

Supreme Court, [*or,* County Court,]

A. B. } Of the day of January, one thousand eight
against } hundred and forty-seven.
C. D. } Satisfaction for $

Satisfaction is acknowledged between A. B., plaintiff, and C. D., defendant, for dollars. Judgment docketed the tenth day of January, one thousand eight hundred and forty-five, in the office of the clerk of county.

      A. B., [*or,* T. S., Attorney for plaintiff.]

Subscribed and acknowledged before me, the day of , 1847, by A. B., known to me [*or,* made known to me,] to be the plaintiff in the above entitled cause, [*or,* the Attorney for the plaintiff in the above entitled cause.]   E. F., Justice, &c.

---

§ 44. *Application for a Subpœna to compel a Subscribing Witness to attend before an officer, to prove the Execution of a Conveyance.*

To G. H. Esq., County Judge of county:

I, A. B., do hereby make application to you to issue a subpœna, requiring E. F., who resides in the town of in said county, to appear and testify before you, touching the execution of a certain conveyance of real estate, made and executed by I. J., to me, the said A. B., [*or, if the application is made by the heir, or personal representative of the grantee, name such grantee,*] and to which the said E. F. is a subscribing witness; the said E. F. having refused, upon my request, to appear and testify touching the execution of the said conveyance; and the same not having been proved or acknowledged, cannot be so proved or acknowledged without the evidence of the said E. F. Dated the first day of July, 1847.   A. B.

   County, ss:

A. B. the applicant above named, being duly sworn, says that the facts stated and set forth in the above application are true.

   Sworn to before me, }
 this first day of July, 1847. }
   G. H., County Judge.

---

[1] Satisfaction of Judgments in Courts of Record, may be acknowledged by the Attorney, within two years after filing the record, 2 R. S., (3d ed.) 459 § 35.

B

§ 45. *Form of the Subpœna.*[1]

County, ss:

To E. F., of the town of   in said county:

In the name of the People of the State of New York, you are hereby commanded to appear before me, at my office, [or, dwelling house,] in the town of   , in said county, on the   day of July, instant, at ten o'clock in the forenoon, then and there to testify, touching the execution of a conveyance of real estate, from I. J. to A. B., to which you are a subscribing witness, as appears by the application of the said A. B. to me made under oath. Hereof fail not at your peril. Given under my hand, this first day of July 1847.   G. H., County Judge.

---

§ 46. *Affidavit to obtain Warrant, to be endorsed on the original Subpœna.*

County, ss:

A. B., of   , being duly sworn, says, that on the first day of May, instant, at the town of   , in said county, he served the within subpœna on E. F., therein named, personally, by then and there showing him the same, and delivering to him a true copy thereof, and by paying [or, tendering] to him the sum of   for his fees for travelling to the place specified in the said subpœna, and for his attendance in pursuance thereof.   A. R.

    Sworn to before me,
this   day of   , &c.
    G. H. County Judge.

---

§ 47. *Warrant.*

County, ss:

To the Sheriff of said county, greeting:

In the name of the People of the State of New York, you are hereby commanded forthwith to apprehend E. F., in your county, and bring him before me, G. H., Esq., County Judge of said county, at my office in the town of   , in said county, to testify touching the execution of a conveyance of real estate, from I. J. to A. B., to which the said E. F. is a subscribing witness, as is said; the said E. F. having been duly subpœnaed to appear before me, to testify touching the execution of the said conveyance, and having, without reasonable cause, neglected [or, refused] to attend in pursuance

---

[1] This Subpœna is to be served by showing the original, under the hand of the officer, to the witness, and at the same time delivering to him a copy thereof, and paying or tendering him the legal fees for one day's attendance, which are fifty cents for attendance; and if the witness resides more than three miles from the place of attendance, travelling fees, at the rate of four cents per mile going and returning. 2 R. S. (3d ed.) 497, § 54; Laws of 1840, Chap. 385. If the witness refuses to appear after the service of the Subpœna, without good cause, the officer issuing the same has power to compel his attendance, by warrant directed to the Sheriff of the county. 2 R. S. (3d ed.) 498, § 55. And if he still persists in refusing to testify, or to answer a legal question, without reasonable cause, he may be committed to the common jail of the county. Id., § 5

thereof. Given under my hand and seal, the   day of July, 1847.   G. H. [L s.]

---

§ 48. *Commitment for Refusal to Testify.*

By G. H., County Judge of   county, to A. P., Sheriff of the said county, greeting:

E. F., having this day been brought before me on a warrant by me issued, to compel his attendance to testify [*where the witness appears in pursuance of the subpœna, say:* having this day appeared before me, in pursuance of a subpœna by me issued, requiring him to appear and testify] touching the execution of a conveyance of real estate, from I. J. to A. B., to which the said E. F. is a subscribing witness, as is said; and the said E. F., although required by me, having refused to answer upon oath [*if the commitment is made on account of the refusal of the witness to answer a particular question, deemed pertinent by the officer, insert here:* the following question, &c., *specifying it particularly*] touching the execution of the said conveyance. I do, therefore, in the name of the people of the State of New York, command you forthwith to convey the said E. F. to the jail of the said county, and there commit him to close custody in such jail, without bail, and without the liberties of the jail, until he shall submit to answer on oath as aforesaid, [or, the question aforesaid,] or be discharged according to law. Given under my hand and seal, the   day of July, 1847.

G. H. [L s.]

---

§ 49. *Oath to be administered to a Subscribing Witness.*[1]

You do solemnly swear, that you will true answers make, to such questions as shall be put to you, touching the execution of this deed: So help you God: [*Or,* You do swear in presence of the ever-living God, that, &c., *as above, omitting the words:.* So help you God: *or,* You do solemnly, sincerely, and truly affirm and declare, that, &c., *as above, omitting the words as aforesaid.*]

---

§ 50. *Oath to a Witness proving the identity of the Parties, or of the Subscribing Witness, to a Conveyance.*

You do solemnly swear, that you will true answers make to such questions as shall be put to you, touching the identity of the parties [*or, the subscribing witness*] to this conveyance. So help you God. [*If necessary, vary as in the foregoing form.*]

---

§ 51. *Oath to a Deponent.*

You do solemnly swear, that the contents of this affidavit, by you subscribed, are true. So help you God. [*Vary as above when necessary.*]

---

[1] For the provisions of the Statute in relation to the administration of oaths, *vide* 2 R. S. (3d ed.) 504–5.

CHAPTER II.

AGREEMENTS AND CONTRACTS.

PRACTICAL REMARKS.

1. In the following cases, every agreement is void, unless such agreement, or some note or memorandum thereof, expressing the consideration, be in writing, and subscribed by the party to be charged therewith:[1]

1. Every agreement that, by its terms, is not to be performed within one year from the making thereof;[2]

2. Every special promise to answer for the debt, default, or miscarriage of another person;[3]

3. Every agreement, promise, or undertaking, made upon consideration of marriage, except mutual promises to marry.[4]

2. Every contract for the sale of any goods, chattels, or things, for the price of fifty dollars, or more, is void, unless:

1. A note or memorandum of such contract be made in writing, and be subscribed by the parties to be charged thereby; or

2. Unless the buyer shall accept and receive part of such goods, or the evidences, or some of them, of such things in action; or

3. Unless the buyer shall, at the time, pay some part of the purchase money.[5]

3. Every contract for the leasing for a longer period than one year, or for the sale of, any lands, or any interest in lands, is void, unless the contract, or some note or memorandum thereof, expressing the consideration, be in writing, and be subscribed by the party by whom the lease or sale is to be made. An agreement to sell growing trees, with the right to enter and remove, is such an interest in lands as to require a contract in writing.[6]

4. In contracts for the sale of land, where the vendee gives notice

---

[1] 2 R. S. (3d ed.) 195, § 2.
[2] 10 Wendell, 426; 13 Id., 308; 15 Id., 345; 3 Hill, 128; 5 Id., 200; 2 Barbour's Ch. Rep. 221.
[3] 4 Wendell, 657; 9 Id., 273; 19 Id., 557; 24 Id., 35, 255; 2 Hill, 663; 3 Id., 128, 584; 4 Id., 178; 5 Id., 145, 160, 483; 2 Denio, 45.

[4] 10 Wendell, 461.
[5] 2 R. S. (3d ed.) 195, § 3; 3 Wendell, 112; 13 Id., 54; 17 Id., 333; 20 Id., 431; 23 Id., 270; 24 Id., 323; 26 Id., 341; 5 Hill, 201; 1 Denio, 51; 1 Comstock, 261; 2 Id., 258.
[6] 2 R. S. (3d ed.) 194 § 8; 2 Hill, 485, 1 Denio, 550.

of a refusal to perform the contract, no tender of a deed by the vendor is necessary in order to compel a specific performance.[1]

5. In every action upon a sealed instrument, and where a set-off is founded upon a sealed instrument, the seal thereof is only presumptive evidence of a sufficient consideration.[2]

6. In Pennsylvania, Virginia, Alabama and Georgia, a scroll of ink made with a pen constitutes a seal; but in New York and other States, wax, or some tenacious substance, is necessary, except it be the seal of a court, public officer, or corporation.[3]

7. A party signing an instrument purporting to be executed by him, with his initials only, is bound.[4]

8. The term 'agree,' does not of itself import a consideration.[5]

9. Where one party puts an end to an executory contract by a refusal to fulfil, the other party is entitled to an equivalent in damages, for the direct gains and profits which he would have realized from performance, though not for the collateral gains or profits, or remote damages. And where a person is employed at a salary and discharged before the expiration of the term of service, the damages will be reduced, if he subsequently obtained employment.[6]

10. Where an agreement to lease or sell lands, or a sealed instrument, is executed by one acting as an attorney, it must distinctly and clearly appear to be the act and deed of the principal; it must be executed in his name, and purport to be sealed with his seal.[7]

11. In all ordinary cases, where the consideration is expressed, there is no difference between an agreement under seal, and one not under seal, except that the former can be more easily proved, and is therefore to be preferred.

12. Written contracts, capable of a sensible construction, must be determined by the language itself, and not by parol proof; although courts may resort to extrinsic circumstances to discover the intentions of the parties.[8]

13. Misrepresentations of material facts, though not intended to deceive, will entitle a party to rescind a contract.[9]

14. Written contracts may be waived by parol.[10]

---

[1] 2 Comstock, 60.
[2] 2 R. S. (3d ed.) 504, § 96; 11 Wendell, 107; 16 Id., 629; 21 Id., 626; 25 Id., 107; 6 Hill, 63.
[3] 2 Hill, 227; 3 Id., 493.
[4] 1 Denio, 3, 471.
[5] 1 Denio, 226.
[6] 7 Hill, 61; 1 Denio, 317; 2 Id., 609.
[7] 4 Hill, 351, and authorities there cited.
[8] 1 Barbour's S. C. Rep., 464, 635.
[9] 1 Barbour's S. C. Rep., 471.
[10] 1 Barbour's S. C. Rep., 114, 326

FORMS.

§ 52.   *General form of Agreement — Damages fixed.*

This agreement made the   day of   , one thousand eight hundred and   , by and between A. B., of the town of   , in the county of   , of the first part, and C. D., of   , of the second part, witnesseth: The said party of the second part covenants and agrees, to and with the party of the first part, to [*state the subject matter of the agreement.*] And the said party of the first part covenants and agrees to pay unto the said party of the second part, for the same, the sum of   dollars, lawful money of the United States, as follows: the sum of   dollars, on the   day of   , 18   , and the sum of   dollars on the   day of   , 18   , with the interest on the amount due, payable at the time of each payment,

And for the true and faithful performance of all and every of the covenants and agreements above mentioned, the parties to these presents bind themselves, each unto the other, in the penal sum of   dollars, as fixed and settled damages, to be paid by the failing party.

In witness whereof, the parties to these presents have hereunto set their hands and seals, the day and year first above written.

Signed, sealed, and delivered in the }
  presence of G. H.   }   A. B. [L. s.]
              C. D. [L. s.]

---

§ 53. *Agreement on the Sale and Purchase of Personal Property.*

This agreement, by and between A. B., of, &c., and C. D., of, &c., made the   day of, &c., witnesseth: That the said C. D., in consideration of the agreement hereinafter contained, to be performed by A. B., agrees to deliver to the said A. B., at his storehouse, in the village of   , three hundred bushels of wheat, [*or*, two hundred barrels of pork, *as the case may be*,] of good merchantable quality, on or before the   day of   , 18   . And the said A B., in consideration thereof, agrees to pay to the said C. D. the sum of one dollar for each and every bushel of the said wheat, immediately upon the completion of the delivery thereof.

In witness, &c., [*as in* § 52.]

---

§ 54. *Agreement for Building a House.*

This agreement for building, made the   day of   , one thousand eight hundred and   , by and between A. B., of, &c., of the first part, and C. D., of, &c., of the second part, witnesseth: That the said party of the second part, covenants and agrees, to and with the said party of the first part, to make, erect, build and finish, in a good, substantial, and workmanlike manner, on the vacant lot of the said party of the first part, situate on   street, in the village of   , a dwelling-house, agreeable to the draft, plan, and explanation, hereto annexed, of good substantial materials, [*If the materials are to be furnished by the party of the first part, say:* of such materials as the said party of the first part shall find or provide for the same,] by the   day of   next.

And the said party of the first part covenants and agrees to pay unto the party of the second part, for the same, the sum   dollars, lawful money of the United States, as follows: the sum of   dollars in thirty days from the date hereof, and the remaining sum of   dollars, when the said dwelling-house shall be completely finished. [*If necessary, add:* And also, that he will furnish and procure the necessary materials for the said work, in such reasonable quantities, and at such reasonable time or times, as the said party of the second part shall or may require.]

And for the true and faithful performance of all and every of the covenants and agreements above mentioned, the parties to these presents bind themselves, each unto the other, in the penal sum of   dollars, as fixed and settled damages, to be paid by the failing party.

In witness, &c., [*as in* § 52.]

---

§ 55. *Agreement for Re-building Mills.*

This agreement, made the   day of, &c., between A. B., of, &c., of the first part, and C. D., of, &c., of the second part, witnesseth: That the party of the first part, for the consideration hereinafter mentioned, doth promise and agree, to and with the party of the second part, that he will, on or before the   day of   next, well and sufficiently re-build, or cause to be re-built, the mills of the said party of the second part, situate on the outlet of the   lake, in the town of   in the county of   , with such materials [*If the workmen are employed by the party of the second part, insert:* and workmen to be employed under him] as the said party of the second part shall find and provide for the same; and that he, the said party of the first part, shall not absent himself, or depart from the work and re-building aforesaid, without leave of the said party of the second part; and that if he shall absent himself without leave, he will pay to the said party of the second part, the sum of   dollars for every day of such absence, to be stopped and deducted from the wages becoming due to the said party of the first part, as hereinafter provided.

And the said party of the second part, in consideration of the premises, doth promise and agree, to and with the party of the first part, to pay to the said party of the first part, the sum of dollars, [*or,* for all such time as he shall be employed in the work of re-building aforesaid, weekly, and every week, the sum of dollars, and so in proportion for a less time than a week; and, in addition thereto, the sum of dollars,] on the completion of the work and re-building aforesaid.

In witness, &c., [*as in* § 52.]

§ 56. *Agreement for making Flour Barrels.*

This agreement, made the day of, &c., between A. B., of, &c., of the first part, and C. D., of, &c., of the second part, witnesseth: That the said A. B., for the consideration hereinafter mentioned, agrees to make, or cause to be made, for the said C. D., at the cooper-shop of the said C. D., in the town of , two thousand good, hard, well seasoned flour barrels; the staves and heading to be of white oak timber, and the hoops of black ash, either round or square, as the said C. D. shall direct. The materials are to be furnished by the said A. B., at his own proper cost and charge, and he is to have the free and uninterrupted use of the tools in the shop of the said C. D., as aforesaid, without paying any thing for the same.

In consideration whereof, the said C. D. agrees to pay to the said A. B. the sum of thirty cents, for each and every of the said two thousand barrels; such payment to be made as often as the said A. B. shall have completed one hundred barrels, in the proper proportion for the same.

In witness, &c., [*as in* § 52.]

§ 57. *Agreement to Sell and Deliver Cord-Wood, or Stone.*

This agreement, made the day of, &c., between A. B., of, &c., and C. D., of, &c., witnesseth: That the said A. B., for the consideration hereinafter mentioned, agrees to sell to the said C. D., five hundred cords of seasoned maple and beech cord-wood and to deliver, and securely pile the same, on the berm bank of the Erie Canal, immediately east of bridge, in the town of , [*or,* one thousand perches of good quarry stone suitable for building, and to deliver and cord the same, on the south side of the vacant lot of the said C. D., situate on street, in the village of ,] on or before the day of next.

In consideration whereof, the said C. D., agrees to pay to the said A. B. the sum of for each and every cord of wood, [*or,* perch of stone,] as aforesaid, upon the final and complete delivery thereof.

In witness, &c., [*as in* § 52.]

§ 58. *Agreement to sell Stock in Grocery Store.*

This agreement, made the   day of   , in the year 1845, between A. B., of, &c., and C. D., of, &c., witnesseth: That the said A. B., for the consideration hereinafter specified, agrees to sell to the said C. D., and the said C. D. agrees to buy of the said A. B., all the stock of goods and groceries, wares and merchandise, belonging to the said A. B., and now being in the grocery store occupied by him at the corner of   street, in the village of   , together with the furniture and fixtures thereunto appertaining, and also all the oats, hams, cheese, potatoes and produce, of every name and nature, bought or contracted for by the said A. B., and intended for sale in the said grocery store. The stock of goods and groceries, wares and merchandise, is to be inventoried to the said C. D. at the original cost, without including transportation expenses; and deduction is to be made for any depreciation in value on account of damage, wear or tear: the furniture and fixtures are to be inventoried at their fair cash value, and if the above parties cannot agree as to such valuation, and as to such deduction as aforesaid, the same shall be determined according to the appraisal of E. F., G. H., and I. J., of   , aforesaid, or a majority of them: the oats, hams, cheese, potatoes and produce, are to be inventoried at their original cost. Said inventory is to be completed within ten days from the date hereof, and the property above specified delivered over to the said C. D. immediately thereupon.

In consideration of the premises, the said C. D. agrees to execute and deliver to the said A. B., as and for the purchase money of the above mentioned property, and in full payment therefor, his promissory note, or notes, in such several sums as the said A. B. shall direct, payable at six months after date, at the   Bank, with interest. [*If necessary, add:* and endorsed by L. M., of   , aforesaid.]

And the said A. B. further covenants and agrees, to and with the said C. D., that he will not, at any time hereafter, engage, directly or indirectly, or concern himself, in carrying on or conducting the grocery business[1] within one mile of the premises now occupied by him as aforesaid for such purpose.

And it is expressly understood that the stipulations aforesaid are to apply to, and to bind, the heirs, executors, and administrators of the respective parties, and in case of failure, the parties bind themselves, each unto the other, in the sum of   dollars, as fixed and settled damages, to be paid by the failing party.

In witness, &c., [*as in* § 52.]

---

[1] If it is desired to bind the party not to | the words, "either as principal or agent," engage in the business, even as an agent, | should be inserted here

3

§ 59.   *Agreement to Engrave Maps.*

This agreement, made the   day of, &c., between, A. B., of, &c., and C. D., of, &c., witnesseth: That the said A. B., for the consideration hereinafter specified, covenants and agrees, to and with the said C. D., that he will provide good and proper steel plates, and will engrave thereon, separately, the map of each and every State and Territory in the United States, according to the plans, specifications and drawings, hereunto annexed; and that he will finish and complete the same in a workmanlike manner, and deliver them to the said C. D., on or before the   day of   next.

In consideration whereof, the said C. D. covenants and agrees to pay to the said A. B., upon the delivery of each and every of the said engraved plates, the sum of   dollars, in full payment and satisfaction therefor.

In witness, &c., [*as in* § 52.]

---

§ 60.   *Agreement to Freight Sloop, or Canal Boat.*

This agreement, made the   day of, &c., between L. S. & Co., factors and commission merchants, of the city of   , of the first part, and C. D., owner and master of the sloop [*or*, canal boat] Empire, of the second part, witnesseth: That the said party of the first part covenant and agree, to and with the said party of the second part, that they will lade and freight the aforesaid sloop [*or*, canal boat] Empire, for and during the ensuing season of navigation, to commence on the 20th day of   instant, when the said sloop [*or*, canal boat] is to be in readiness to receive her first lading, at the dock of the said party of the first part, [*or*, at Pier No.   ,] in the city of   , aforesaid, as well on her upward trips from the said city of   to the city of   , and the intermediate ports, as on her return trips from   to   ; and that they will pay to the said party of the second part for carrying the same, on the delivery of each and every cargo in a safe and sound condition, as hereinafter mentioned, at and after the following rates of compensation, viz:

FOR UP FREIGHT.

Salt, - - - - - - - - -	—— cents per bushel.
Merchandise, - - - - - - - -	—— do hundred.
Household Furniture, - - - - -	—— do do
Coal, - - - - - - - - - -	—— dollars per ton.
&c., &c.	

FOR DOWN FREIGHT.

Flour, - - - - - - - - -	—— cents per barrel.
Pork, - - - - - - - - -	—— do do
Hay, - - - - - - - - -	—— dollars per ton.
Wheat and Corn, - - - - - -	—— cents per bushel
Butter, - - - - - - - -	—— do firkin.
Staves and Heading, - - - - -	—— do thousand
&c. &c.	

And the said party of the second part, in consideration of the premises, covenants and agrees to and with the said party of the first part, that he will safely carry all such lading and freight as he may or shall receive from the party of the first part as aforesaid, and deliver the same in as good and sound condition as when so received, according to the respective bills of lading to be furnished to him by the party of the first part, or their agents; that he will pay all costs and charges of transportation, including towage and wharfage; [insert toll, if necessary;] that he will regularly ply between   and   , and the intermediate ports, with his sloop [or, canal boat] as aforesaid, during the entire season of navigation above mentioned; and that he will not occupy more than   days, unless hindered or delayed by some unavoidable accident, in making either an upward or downward trip.

It is also further understood and agreed between the parties, that all lading and freight shall be delivered to the party of the second part, at his sloop, [or, canal boat,] and that he shall discharge the same, on the dock, at his own cost and charge; that the party of the first part shall not, at any time, require the said party of the second part to carry, or convey, on his sloop, [or, canal boat,] any timber, or lumber, (staves and heading excepted,) any carts, cars, or vehicles, of any description whatever; or any horses, mules, cattle, swine, or animals of any name or nature; and that all the aforesaid conditions and stipulations, shall be binding upon the heirs, executors, administrators and survivors, of the respective parties.

In witness whereof, the parties have hereunto affixed their names, the day and year above written.

In presence of   }   L. S. & Co.
                                   C. D.

---

§ 61. *Agreement to Sell Shares of Stock in an Incorporated Company.*

This agreement, made the   day of, &c., between A. B., of, &c., and C. D., of, &c., witnesseth: That the said A. B. agrees to sell and convey to the said C. D., on or before the   day of   , next, one hundred shares of the capital stock of the   company, now owned and held by the said A. B., and standing in his name on the books of the said company, and to make and execute unto the said C. D. all assignments, transfers and conveyances, necessary to assure the same to him, his heirs and assigns.

In consideration whereof, the said C. D. agrees to pay unto the said A. B., for each and every share of such stock, the average cash market price of the same, for and during twenty days preceding the   day of   , aforesaid, to be determined by the sales made at the board of brokers in the city of New York.

In witness, &c., [as in § 52.]

§ 62. *Agreement of Barter.*

This agreement, made the   day of, &c., between A. B., of, &c., and C. D., of, &c., witnesseth: That the said A. B. agrees to sell and deliver to the said C. D., at his store in   , on the   day of   instant, one hundred barrels of fine salt, in good substantial barrels, suitable for packing beef and pork, and for the use of the kitchen and dairy.

In consideration whereof, the said C. D. agrees to sell and deliver to the said A. B., at the store-house of G. H., in   , on the   day of   , aforesaid, one thousand pounds of good merchantable cheese, and four hundred pounds of sweet table butter; both to be well packed, in tierces or firkins, and to be made in dairies where at least fifteen cows are kept.

In witness, &c., [*as in* § 52.]

---

§ 63. *Agreement for Towing Line of Canal Boats.*

This agreement, made the   day of, &c., between A. B., C. D., E. F., and G. H., composing the   Towing and Navigation Company, of the first part, and L. M., N. S., and T. O., owners and proprietors of the   Line of canal boats, of the second part, witnesseth: That the said party of the first part, for and in consideration of the covenants hereinafter contained, covenant and agree, to and with the said party of the second part, that they will furnish and provide fit and suitable teams, with safe and skilful drivers, and tow the boats belonging to the party of the second part, regularly plying between   and   , on the Erie Canal, and not exceeding   in number, for and during the entire season of navigation, to commence on the   day of   , 18 .

And in consideration of the premises, the said party of the second part covenant and agree, to and with the said party of the first part, to pay, or cause to be paid, to the said party of the first part, for each and every running trip so made by their boats, as aforesaid, the sum of   dollars.

It is further understood and agreed between the aforesaid parties, that two boats of the party of the second part shall leave   on the   instant, and that three shall leave   on the   instant, provided the canal shall be navigable at that time, and if not so navigable, then as soon thereafter as it shall become so: it is also agreed between the said parties, that the time or times of departure from   or   , during the remainder of the season, shall depend upon the convenience of the party of the second part; with the proviso, however, that not more than   boats shall leave either end of the route, or more than   boats pass any station on the same, during any period of twenty-four hours; that when the said boats of the party of the second part are laden to the burden of   tons, or upwards, they shall be towed not less than   miles per hour, running time; when

light, or carrying not more than   tons freight, they shall be
towed not less than   miles per hour, as aforesaid: and it is
further agreed that the party of the second part shall furnish and
provide the drivers employed by the party of the first part, when
engaged in towing their boats, with suitable meals on board, at regular hours, relieving them in the charge of their teams at such times
by one of the hands engaged on such boats; that, whenever any
boat of the party of the second part shall be detained, on account
of the negligence or carelessness of the drivers, servants, or agents
of the party of the first part, a deduction shall be made from the
compensation of the party of the first part, as aforesaid, at and after
the rate of   dollars per hour, during the time of each detention, except, that after the first day of October next, such deduction
shall be   dollars per hour; that the party of the second
part shall pay to the party of the first part, or to their regularly
authorized agent or agents, the sum of   dollars, part and
parcel of the compensation to be paid as aforesaid, on the
day of each and every month during the season of navigation, subject, however, to all necessary deductions then liable to be made on
account of detention; and that, within   days after the final
close of navigation, the aforesaid parties, by themselves, or their
agents, shall meet at the office of the said party of the second part,
in the city of   , and examine, close and settle their respective
accounts, and pay and fully discharge all balances which may be
found due and owing upon such examination and settlement, by reason of the premises.

In witness, &c., [as in § 52.]

---

§ 64. *Agreement to Cultivate Land on Shares.*

This agreement, made the '   day of, &c., between A. B., of,
&c., and C. D., of, &c., witnesseth: That the said A. B. agrees that
he will break up, properly fit, and sow with wheat, all that field
belonging to the said C. D., lying immediately north of the dwelling
house and garden of the said C. D., in the town of   , aforesaid,
and containing twenty acres or thereabouts, on or before the twenty-
fifth day of September next; that when the said crop, to be sown as
aforesaid, shall be in fit condition, he will cut, harvest, and safely
house it in the barn or barns of the said C. D.; and that he will
properly thresh and clean the same, and deliver one-half of the
wheat, being the produce thereof, to the said C. D., at the granary
near his dwelling-house, as aforesaid, on or before the   day
of   , in the year 18 .

It is understood between the parties, that one-half of the seed
wheat is to be found by the said C. D.; that the said A. B. is to
perform all the work and labor necessary in the premises, or cause
it to be done; and that the straw is to be equally divided between

the parties, within ten days after the crop of wheat shall have been threshed, as aforesaid.

In witness, &c., [*as in* § 52.]

---

§ 65. *Agreement to Sell the Copyright in a Book.*

This agreement, made the   day of, &c., between A. B., of, &c., and C. D., of, &c., bookseller and publisher, witnesseth: That the said A. B. agrees to sell, and does sell to the said C. D., all his copyright, title, interest, and property, in and to a certain book, written and compiled by the said A. B., entitled, [*give the title of the book at length,*] and entered, and copyright secured by the said A. B., in the Clerk's Office of the Northern District of New York, on the   day of   , in the year 1845; and the said A. B. also agrees to prepare and furnish a fair copy of the said work to the printer to be employed by the said C. D., and to superintend the printing, and correct the proof thereof; provided, however, that it shall be printed in the   of   , aforesaid.

In consideration whereof, the said C. D. agrees to pay unto the said A. B. the sum of   dollars, on the   day of next.

It is understood between the aforesaid parties, that the first edition of the work to be printed as aforesaid, shall not exceed copies; and that if the said C. D. shall, at any future time, determine to publish another edition of the said work, he shall pay to the said A. B., in addition to the sum agreed to be paid, as aforesaid, the sum of   dollars for each and every subsequent edition, not exceeding   copies of the same, to be due and payable immediately upon the issue thereof.

In witness, &c., [*as in* § 52.]

---

§ 66. *Agreement to Sell and Assign Bond and Mortgage.*

Whereas A. B., of the town of   , in the county of   , and State of   , and M. his wife, on the first day of May, one thousand eight hundred and forty, did execute a certain indenture of mortgage, and a bond bearing even date therewith, to C. D., of the town of, &c., which said mortgage, and the bond accompanying the same, were executed for the purpose of securing the payment of the sum of four hundred dollars, in four years from the tenth day of May (then) instant, with interest annually from the day last aforesaid; and which said mortgage was recorded in the office of the Clerk of the county of   , aforesaid, in book 16 of mortgages, at pages 286 and 287, on the second day of May, 1840, at 12 o'clock, M.: Now, therefore, this agreement, made and executed between C. D., aforesaid, of the first part, and E. F., of the town of, &c., witnesseth: That the party of the first part, for the considerations hereinafter mentioned, doth covenant and agree, to and with the party of the second part, to sell, transfer, assign, and set over, unto the said party of the second part, the indenture of mortgage above described, and the bond accompanying the same, whenever the payments hereinafter specified to be made by the said party of the second part, to the party of the first part, shall be fully made and completed: To have and to hold the said bond and mortgage, and all the moneys due or to become due thereon, and all the interest conveyed by the said mortgage, in and to the lands therein described, unto the party of the second part, from the time of the completion of such sale, transfer, and assignment, as aforesaid, forever. And the said party of the first part doth further covenant and agree, to and with the party of the second part, that he hath good right to assign and set over the bond and mortgage aforesaid, to the said party of the second part; and that the sum of four hundred dollars of principal, and twenty-one dollars of interest, is due upon the same at the day of the date hereof.

And the said party of the second part, in consideration of the premises, doth covenant and agree, to and with the party of the first part, that he will pay or cause to be paid unto the said party of the first part, the sum of four hundred dollars, in manner following, viz: fifty dollars on the ensealing and delivery of these presents, and the remaining sum of three hundred and fifty dollars, in two equal annual payments from the day of the date hereof, with annual interest.

And it is further agreed, by and between the aforesaid parties, that if the party of the second part shall, at any time, elect to pay the whole sum agreed to be paid, as aforesaid, to the party of the first part, with the lawful interest due thereupon, he shall have the right so to do, and the said party of the first part shall, immediately upon such payment, transfer, assign, and set over, unto the said party of the second part, the bond and mortgage above mentioned; and also, that the covenants and agreements aforesaid are to apply to, and to bind the representatives of the respective parties to these presents.

In witness whereof, the aforesaid parties have hereunto set their hands and seals, the day and year above written.

Signed, &c., [as in § 52.]

------

§ 67. *Agreement to Change Mortgage Security.*

This agreement, made the   day of, &c., between A. B., of, &c., and C. D., E. F., and G. H., of, &c., witnesseth: That whereas the said A. B. hath this day sold and conveyed unto the said C. D., E. F., and G. H., by warranty deed duly executed, four acres of land, situate, lying, and being on the south-east corner of   and   streets, in the village of   , for the price, or consideration, of one thousand dollars; and, in order to secure the payment of the sum of eight hundred dollars, parcel thereof, the said C. D., E. F., and G. H., have executed and delivered to the said A.

B. a mortgage upon the aforesaid premises, together with their joint bond, conditioned for the payment of the said sum of eight hundred dollars, in eight equal annual payments from this date, with annual interest: and whereas it is the intention of the said C. D., E. F., and G. H., to divide the said premises conveyed to them into village lots, and to sell and dispose of the same upon such terms as shall seem meet and advantageous: Now, therefore, the said A. B., in considera-ration of the premises, doth, for himself, his heirs, executors, administrators, and assigns, covenant and agree, to and with the said C. D., E. F., and G. H., their executors, administrators, and assigns, that they, the said C. D., E. F., and G. H., their executors, administrators, and assigns, shall and may, at all times hereafter, have the right of changing the security above mentioned, by substituting, instead of the same, or of any part thereof, not less than one hundred dollars, the like security, on other real estate of at least equal value; and that he, the said A. B., his heirs, executors, administrators, or assigns, shall and will, upon request to him or them made, forthwith execute and deliver to the said C. D., E. F., and G. H., their executors, administrators, or assigns, good and sufficient releases and discharges of the said mortgage, or of the lien upon any portion of the premises therein described, whenever the said C. D., E. F., and G. H., their executors, administrators, or assigns, shall furnish the said A. B., or his representatives, as aforesaid, with such other security as above mentioned.

In witness, &c., [*as in* § 52.]

---

§ 68. *Agreement respecting Party Wall.*

This agreement, made the   day of, &c., between A. B., of, &c., and C. D. of, &c., witnesseth: That whereas the said A. B. is the owner of the lot and store known as number   Genesee street, in the city of Auburn; and the said C. D. is the owner of the lot adjoining the same, on the northerly side thereof, on which last mentioned lot the said C. D. is about to erect a brick store: Now, therefore, the said A. B., in consideration of the sum of   dollars, to him in hand paid, the receipt whereof is hereby acknowledged, doth, for himself, his heirs, executors, administrators, and assigns, covenant, grant, promise, and agree, to and with the said C. D., his heirs, executors, administrators, and assigns, that he, the said C. D., his heirs and assigns, shall and may, in the erection of the brick store about to be built, as aforesaid, freely and lawfully, but in a workmanlike manner, make use of the northerly gable end wall of the said A. B., or so much thereof as the said C. D., his heirs or assigns, may desire, as a party wall, to be continued and used as such forever.

And the said A. B. and C. D. do hereby mutually covenant and agree for and with themselves, and their respective heirs and assigns that if it shall hereafter become necessary to repair or re-build the whole, or any portion of the said party wall, the expense of such repairing or re-building shall be borne equally by the said A. B. and C. D., their respective heirs and assigns, as to so much and such portion of the said wall as the said C. D., his heirs and assigns, shall or may use for the purposes aforesaid; and that whenever the said party wall, or any portion thereof, shall be re-built, it shall be erected on the same spot where it now stands, and be of the same size, and the same or similar materials, and of like quality, with the present wall.

It is further mutually understood and agreed between the aforesaid parties, that this agreement shall be perpetual, and at all times be construed into a covenant running with the land; and that no part of the fee of the soil upon which the wall of the said A. B., above described, now stands, shall pass to, or be vested in, the said C. D. his heirs and assigns, in or by these presents.

In witness, &c., [*as in* § 52.]

---

§ 69. *Agreement of Purchaser at Auction Sale.*

This agreement, made the   day of, &c., between A. B., of, &c., and E. F., of, &c., by C. D., his agent, witnesseth: That whereas the said A. B. hath this day become the purchaser, at public auction, of the following described property, viz: all that piece or parcel of land, &c., [*describe the premises sold,*] at the consideration price of   dollars; and the said A. B. hath also paid to the said E. F., by the said C. D., his agent, as aforesaid, the sum of   dollars, part and parcel of the purchase money of the said premises: Now, therefore, the said A. B. agrees to pay the remaining sum of   dollars unto the said E. F., his agent, or attorney, on the   day of   next: and the said E. F., by his agent as aforesaid, agrees, that he, the said E. F., will execute and deliver to the said A. B. a good and sufficient warranty deed, with full covenants, for the premises above described, immediately upon the payment of the said sum of   dollars last above specified.

In witness, &c., [*as in* § 66.]

---

§ 70. *Agreement with a Clerk or Workman.*

This agreement, made the   day of, &c., between A. B., of, &c., and C. D., of, &c., witnesseth: That the said C. D. covenants and agrees, faithfully, truly, and diligently, to write [*or,* work] for the said A. B. as his clerk, [*or,* journeyman,] in the office [*or,* shop, *or,* store] of the said A. B., at   , aforesaid, from the   day of   instant, for and during the space of   years: In consideration of which service so to be performed, the said A. B. covenants and agrees to pay to the said C. D. the sum of   dollars annually, in four equal quarterly payments.

And it is understood and agreeb between the aforesa.d parties, that the death of either of them occurring prior to the expiration of the said term of   years, this agreement shall thereupon terminate.

In witness, &c., [*as in* § 52.]

---

§ 71. *Agreement, or Subscription, for Raising Money to Build a Church, or Bridge.*[1]

We, the undersigned, do hereby severally promise and agree to pay to A. B., C. D., and E. F., the Trustees of the First Presbyterian Society in the town of   , [*or, the Commissioners of Highways of the Town of   ,*] the sums set opposite to our respective names, on demand, [*or as the terms of payment may be,*] for the purpose of building a church or place of worship for the said society in the town of   , aforesaid; [*or, for the purpose of constructing a bridge over the   river, on the road leading from   , to   ;*] and we request the said Trustees [*or, Commissioners*] to contract for the building of such church or place of worship, and to build the same, [*or, for the construction of such bridge, and to construct the same,*] and to apply the sums of money hereto subscribed in payment therefor.

Witness our hands, this   day of   , 1850.

NAMES.		AMOUNT.
G. H.	- - - - - - - - - - - - -	$100 00
L. M.	- - - - - - - - - - - - -	75 00

---

§ 72. *Agreement with a Mason, for Plastering a House, Laying Brick, &c.*

This agreement, made the   day of, &c., between A. B., of, &c., and C. D., of, &c., witnesseth: That the said C. D., for the consideration hereinafter mentioned, promises and agrees, to and with the said A. B., that he will do and perform, by himself or persons in his employ, in a good and workmanlike manner, and with materials to be furnished by the said A. B., all the work to be done and performed by the bricklayer and plasterer, in and about the erecting and building a new dwelling house on the vacant lot of the said A. B., on   street, in the city of   , according to the plans and specifications hereto annexed; and also, that he will use the utmost care in working up the materials to be furnished by the said A. B., as aforesaid, to the best advantage for the said A. B., and that

---

[1] In an agreement, or subscription, of this kind, according to the recent decisions of the New York Courts, it is necessary that there should be a request to the Trustees, Commissioners, or Committee of Citizens, if one be selected to perform the work, or to carry the object for which the money is raised into effect; otherwise, the agreement will be void for want of consideration. See, 2 Denio, 403 · 1 Comstock, 581.

he will complete the said work on or before the   day of
next.

And the said A. B., in consideration of the premises, agrees to
furnish and provide good and sufficient materials for the said work,
at such time or times as the said C. D. may request; and to pay the
said C. D. for all such work as shall be performed by him or his
servants in and about the said new dwelling house, ornamental work
excepted, on the completion of the same, at and after the rate of
   per yard of three feet square, and the sum of   dollars
for all the ornamental work done or performed in and about the said
dwelling house,—it being expressly understood and agreed, that no
extra charge is to be demanded or allowed, for corners, arches, jams,
joints, fire places, or any other kind of work not strictly ornamental,
but all the work is to be measured as plain, except the ornamental
work to be paid for, as aforesaid, in gross.

In witness, &c., [*as in* § 52.]

------

§ 73. *Agreement to Sell Land.*

This agreement, made and entered into the   day of, &c.,
between A. B., of, &c., of the first part, and C. D., of, &c., of the
second part, witnesseth: That the said party of the first part, in
consideration of the covenants and agreements hereinafter contained,
agrees to sell unto the said party of the second part, all that piece
or parcel of land bounded and described, &c., [*insert description of
premises,*] for the sum of   dollars: And the said party of
the second part, in consideration of the premises, agrees to pay to
the said A. B. the sum of   dollars, in manner following,
viz: dollars on the execution of these presents;
dollars, on the   day of   , next; and the remaining
sum of   dollars, on the   day of   , A. D., 1846,
with the lawful interest from this date, on each payment, at the time
of making the same.

And the said party of the first part also agrees, that on receiving
the said sum of   dollars, at the time and in the manner
above mentioned, he will execute and deliver to the said party of
the second part, at his own proper cost and expense, a good and
sufficient deed, for the conveying and assuring to him, the said party
of the second part, the fee simple of the said premises, free from
all incumbrance; which deed shall contain a general warranty, and
the usual full covenants.* And it is understood that the stipulations
aforesaid are to apply to, and to bind, the heirs, executors, administrators and assigns, of the respective parties; and that the party of
the second part is to have immediate possession of the premises

In witness, &c., [*as in* § 52.]

§ 74. *The Same, executed by an Attorney.*

This agreement, made, &c., between A. B., of, &c., of the first part, by E. F., his Attorney, and C. D., of, &c., of the second part, witnesseth: That the said party of the first part, &c., [*as in § 73 to the words,* In witness, *&c., and then add:*]

In witness whereof, the said parties have hereunto set their hands and seals, the day and year first above written.   A. B. [L. s.]

In presence of }
G. H.   }   By E. F., his Attorney.
                                                  C. D. [L. s.]

———

§ 75. *The Same, with Covenants as to Possession, Taxes, and Forfeiture.*

This agreement, made, &c., [*as in § 73 to the *, and then add:*] and it is further agreed between the parties to these presents, that the party of the first part is to have and retain possession of the premises until the   day of   next, when the same shall be delivered up to the party of the second part, upon his compliance with the agreements herein above contained; that the said party of the second part shall pay all taxes and assessments, becoming chargeable to, and upon the said premises, after the delivery of the possession thereof to him as aforesaid; and that, if default be made in fulfilling this agreement, or any part thereof, on the part and behalf of the said party of the second part, then, and in such case, the said party of the first part shall be at liberty to consider this contract as forfeited and annulled; and if the said party of the second part shall be in the possession of the said premises, at the time of making such default, the party of the first part shall have full and ample right to proceed against the said party of the second part, and remove him therefrom, in the manner now provided by law for the removal of persons forcibly entering into the possession of, and detaining, any lands or other possessions.

It is also agreed between the said parties, that the above stipulations shall apply to, and bind, their respective heirs, executors, administrators, and assigns.

In witness, &c., [*as in § 52.*]

CHAPTER III.

APPRENTICES AND SERVANTS.

PRACTICAL REMARKS

1. Every male infant, and every unmarried female under the age of eighteen years, with the consent of the persons or officers hereinafter mentioned, may, of his or her own free will, bind himself, or herself, in writing, to serve as clerk, apprentice, or servant, in any profession, trade, or employment; if a male, until the age of twenty-one years, and if a female, until the age of eighteen years, or for any shorter time: such binding will be as valid and effectual as if the infant were of full age at the time of making the engagement.[1]

2. Such consent must be given:

1. By the father of the infant. If he be dead, or be not in a legal capacity to give his consent, or if he shall have abandoned and neglected to provide for his family, and such fact be certified by a Justice of the Peace of the town, and endorsed on the indenture, then,

2. By the mother. If the mother be dead, or be not in a legal capacity to give such consent, or refuse, then,

3. By the guardian of such infant duly appointed. If such infant have no parent living, or none in a legal capacity to give consent, and there be no guardian, then,

4. By the Overseers of the Poor, or any two Justices of the Peace of the town, or any County Judge of the county where such infant shall reside.[2]

3. Such consent must be signified in writing, by the person entitled to give the same, by a certificate at the end of, or endorsed upon, the indentures.[3]

4. The executors of any last will of a father, who shall be directed in such will to bring up his child to some trade, or calling, may bind such child to service, in like manner as the father might have done. The County Superintendents of the Poor may, in like manner, bind

---

[1] 2 R. S. (3d ed.) 215, § 1; 6 Johnson, 274; 8 Id., 328; 14 Id., 374; 19 Id., 113; 5 Cowen, 363. 527.

[2] 2 R. S. (3d ed.) 215, § 2.
[3] 2 R. S. (3d ed.) 215, § 3; 10 Johnson, 89; 5 Cowen, 170; 2 Hill, 596.

out any child, under the ages above specified, who shall be sent to a county poor house, or who may or shall, or whose parents may or shall, become chargeable to any county, to be clerks, apprentices, or servants. The Overseers of the Poor of any town or city, possess the like power in such town or city, with the consent, in writing, of any two Justices of the Peace of the town, or of the Mayor, Recorder, and Aldermen, of any city, or of any two of them. No child of an Indian woman, however, can be bound as an apprentice, under the foregoing provisions, except in the presence and with the consent of a Justice of the Peace, whose certificate of consent must be filed by the Clerk of the•town in which the indenture of apprenticeship shall be executed.[1]

5. The age of every infant bound as aforesaid, must be inserted in the indenture, and will be taken to be the true age, without further proof thereof; and public officers who act in such cases, should inform themselves fully of the infant's age. Every sum of money paid, or agreed for, in relation to the binding out of any clerk, or apprentice, must also be inserted in the indenture.[2]

6. Whenever any child is bound out by the County Superintendents of any county, or the Overseers of the Poor of any town, the person to whom the child may be bound, must enter into an agreement, to be inserted in the indentures, that he will cause such child to be instructed to read and write, (if a male, to be also instructe[1] in the general rules of arithmetic,) and that he will give su... apprentice, at the expiration of his or her service, a new bible. The counterpart of any indentures executed by the County Superintendents, must be deposited in the office of the Clerk of their county; the Overseers of the Poor will deposit a counterpart of any indentures executed by them, in the Clerk's office of their city or town.[3]

7. Any person coming from any foreign country beyond sea, may bind himself to service, if an infant, until the age of twenty-one years, or for any shorter term. Such contract of service, if made for the purpose of raising the passage money, may be for the term of one year, although such term may extend beyond the time when he will be of full age; but shall in no case be for a longer term. No contract made, as aforesaid, will bind the servant, unless it be acknowledged by him before some Mayor, Recorder, or Alderman of a city, or some Justice of the Peace; nor unless a certificate of such acknowledgment, and that the same was made freely, on a private examination, be endorsed thereupon. Any such contract may be assigned by the master, by an instrument in writing, endorsed thereon, executed in the presence of two witnesses, if such assignment be approved of, in writing, by any magistrate, as aforesaid, whose certificate of approbation must also be endorsed.[4]

---

[1] 2 R. S. (3d ed.) 215, §§ 4–7; 13 Johnson, 270.   [3] 2 R. S. (3d ed.) 216, §§ 10, 11.
[2] 2 R. S. (3d ed.) 215–16 §§ 8, 9.   [4] 2 R. S. (3d ed.) 216, §§ 12–14

8. No indenture, or contract, for the service of any apprentice, is valid, as against the person whose services may be claimed, unless made in the manner above prescribed.[1]

9. The master is entitled to all the earnings of the apprentice.[2]

10. A guardian is liable, although the apprentice has gone off and left his master.[3]

11. An apprentice is not assignable, although the assignment would be valid as a covenant for the services of the apprentice.[4]

12. An apprentice cannot recover of an assignee, on an implied promise, where service has been voluntarily rendered.[5]

13. Our laws recognize no general authority in a father to dispose of his children, except for some specific and temporary purpose, such as apprenticeship during the father's life, or guardianship after his death.[6]

14. If any person lawfully bound to service, as above mentioned, willfully absent himself without leave, he must serve double the time of such absence, unless he shall otherwise make satisfaction, but such additional term of service cannot extend beyond three years next after the expiration of the original term.[7]

15. If any person refuses to serve, any Justice of the Peace of the county, or the Mayor, Recorder, or any Alderman of the city, where he shall reside, has the power to commit him to jail.[8]

16. If any apprentice be guilty of any misdemeanor or ill behavior; or if any master be guilty of any cruelty, misusage, of refusal of any necessary provisions or clothing, or of a violation of the terms of the indenture; complaint may be made to any two Justices of the Peace of the county, or to the Mayor, Recorder, and Aldermen of the city, or any two of them, who will summon the parties before them and examine into the grounds of complaint; and if the same prove to be well founded, they must either commit the apprentice to solitary confinement in the common jail of the county, for a term not exceeding one month, there to be employed at hard labor; or discharge the offending apprentice from his service, and the master from his obligations; or, in case of ill usage by the master, discharge the apprentice from his obligation of service.[9]

17. The above statutory provisions in relation to apprentices willfully absenting themselves, refusing to serve, or being guilty of any misdemeanor or ill behavior; and masters guilty of ill usage, &c., do not extend to those cases where the master or mistress has received, or is entitled to, any sum of money as a compensation for instruction.[10]

---

[1] 2 R. S. (3d ed.) 218, § 26; 8 Johnson, 328.
[2] 6 Johnson, 274.
[3] 14 Johnson, 374; 5 Cowen, 170.
[4] 19 Johnson, 113.
[5] 2 Barbour's S. C. Rep., 208.
3 Hill, 399.

[7] 2 R. S. (3d ed.) 218, § 28.
[8] 2 R. S. (3d ed.) 219, § 29.
[9] 2 R. S. (3d ed.) 219, §§ 30–32; 13 Johnson, 270.
[10] 2 R. S. (3d ed.) 219, § 33.

18. In cases where money has been paid, or agreed to be paid, and Justice of the Peace of the county, or any Mayor, Recorder, or Alderman of the city, in which the apprentice resides, has the power of inquiring into all disputes in relation thereto, and of making such order and direction as the equity of the case may require. If the difficulty cannot be reconciled, the master or the apprentice may be recognized, in such sureties as the officer shall approve, for his appearance at the next Court of Sessions, and such Court, on hearing the parties, may either discharge the apprentice from service, or order the sum of money to be paid, or to be refunded; or, if not paid, discharge the same, and direct the securities to be canceled; or punish the apprentice by fine, or imprisonment, or both, as for a misdemeanor.[1]

19. No person can accept from any journeyman or apprentice. any contract or agreement, nor cause him to be bound by oath or otherwise, that after his term of service shall have expired, such journeyman or apprentice will not set up his trade, profession, or employment, in any particular place, shop, house or cellar; nor can any person exact from any journeyman or apprentice, after his term of service shall have expired, any money or other thing, for using and exercising his trade, profession or employment, in any place. Every security given contrary to the foregoing provisions will be void; any money paid, may be recovered back by the person paying the same, with interest; and every person accepting such agreement, causing such obligation to be entered into, or exacting money or other thing, as aforesaid, forfeits one hundred dollars to the apprentice, or journeyman, from whom the same shall have been received.[1]

20. Upon the death of any master, to whom any person may have been bound to service, as clerk, apprentice, or otherwise, by the County Superintendents of the Poor, or by the Overseers of the Poor, the executors or administrators of such master may, with the consent of the person bound to service, signified in writing, and acknowledged before a Justice of the Peace, assign the contract of such service to any other person; which assignment will vest in such assignee all the rights of the original master, and render him subject to all his obligations. If the person so bound to service refuses to give such consent, such assignment may be made under the sanction of an order of the Court of Sessions of the county, after fourteen days' notice of an application to that effect, served on the apprentice, his parent, or guardian, if there be any in the county; and when so made, such assignment will be as valid and effectual as if the consent had been given in the manner aforesaid.[3]

21. The above provisions apply as well to mistresses, female guardians, apprentices and wards, respectively, as to masters, male guardians, apprentices and wards.[4]

[1] 2 R. S. (3d ed.) 219, 220, §§ 34-36; Laws of 1847, chap. 280, art. v.
[2] 2 R. S. (3d ed.) 220, §§ 39, 40
[3] 2 R. S. (3d ed.) 220, §§ 41, 42.
[4] 2 R. S. (3d ed.) 221, § 43.

FORMS.

§ 76. *Apprentice's Indenture.*

This indenture witnesseth: That C. B., of the town of   , in the county of   , and State of   , now aged fourteen years, by and with the consent of A. B., his father [*or,* mother, his father being dead, *or,* being legally incapacitated, *or,* having abandoned or neglected to provide for his family] endorsed hereupon, hath voluntarily, and of his own free will and accord, put and bound himself apprentice to E. F., of the town of, &c., to learn the art, trade, and mystery of a hatter; and as an apprentice to serve from this date, for, and during, and until the full end and term of, five years next ensuing, [*or,* until the said C. B. shall have attained the age of twenty-one years, which will be on the   day of   , in the year 18 ,] during all which time the said apprentice shall serve his master faithfully, honestly, and industriously; his secrets keep, and lawful commands every where readily obey; at all times protect and preserve the goods and property of his said master, and not suffer or allow any to be injured or wasted. He shall not buy, sell, or traffic, with his own goods, or the goods of others, nor be absent from his said master's service, day or night, without leave; but in all things behave himself as a faithful apprentice ought to do, during the said term. And the said master shall clothe and provide for the said apprentice in sickness and in health, and supply him with suitable food and clothing; and shall use and employ the utmost of his endeavors to teach, or cause him, the said apprentice, to be taught or instructed, in the art, trade, or mystery of a hatter; and also cause the said apprentice, within such term, to be instructed to read and write, and in the general rules of arithmetic; and at the end of the said term, give the said apprentice a new bible. [*If necessary, insert here:* And the said E. F. acknowledges that he has received, with the said C. B., from A. B., his father, [*or,* mother,] the sum of   dollars, as a compensation for his instruction, as above mentioned; *or:* And the said E. F. further agrees to pay to the said C. B. the following sums of money, viz: for the first year of his service   dollars; for the second year of his service   dollars; and for every subsequent year, until the expiration of his term of service,   dollars; which said payments are to be made on the first day of January in each year.]

And for the true performance of all and singular the covenants and agreements aforesaid, the said parties bind themselves, each unto the other, firmly by these presents.

In witness whereof, the parties aforesaid have hereunto set their hands and seals, the   day of   , in the year one thousand eight hundred and   .

Signed, sealed, and delivered, ⎞
     in presence of   ⎬
         G. H.   ⎠

C. B. [L s.]
E. F. [L s.]

---

§ 77. *Consent of Father or Mother.*

I do hereby consent to, and approve of, the binding of my son, C. B., as in the above [*or*, within] indenture mentioned. Dated the day of   , in the year 18   .

A. B.

---

§ 78. *Justice's Certificate, where Mother gives consent.*

I, G. H., a Justice of the Peace of the town of   , in the county of   , do certify, that A. B., the father of the infant named in the within indenture, is dead, [*or*, is not in legal capacity to give his consent thereto; *or*, has abandoned and neglected to provide for his family.] Dated the   day of   , 18   .

G. H., Justice of the Peace.

---

§ 79. *Consent of Guardian.*

I, S. T., the guardian, duly appointed, of C. B., in the within indenture named, do certify, that the father and mother of the said C. B. are dead, [*or*, that the father of the said C. B. is dead, and that the mother of the said C. B. refuses her consent to the said indenture of apprenticeship; *or*, is not in legal capacity to give her consent to the said indenture of apprenticeship;] and that I do hereby consent, as his guardian, that he, the said C. B., may bind himself in and by the said indenture.

Dated the   day of   , 18   .

S. T., Guardian of the said C. B.

---

§ 80. *Certificate of Consent of the Overseers of the Poor, two Justices of the Peace of the town, or County Judge of the county in which the Infant resides.*

We, the undersigned, Overseers of the Poor of the town of   *or*, two Justices of the Peace of the town of   ; *or*, I, the undersigned, County Judge of   county,] where the within named C. B. resides, do certify, that the said C. B. has no parent living, [*or*, no parent in legal capacity to give consent to the within indenture; *or*, no father living, and his mother is not in legal capacity to give consent to the within indenture,] and that he has no guardian, and that we, the said Overseers, [*or*, Justices;

or, I, the said Judge,] do consent that the said C. B. may bind himself in and by the said indenture.

G. H.
M. P.

§ 81. *Agreement of the Father, where he intends to bind himself to answer in Damages.*

This indenture, made the   day of   , in the year one thousand eight hundred and   , between A. B., of, &c., and E. F., of, &c., witnesseth: That the said A. B., in consideration of the covenant and agreement hereinafter mentioned, doth, by these presents, put and bind his son C. B., to the said E. F., to learn the art, trade, and mystery, of a hatter, and as an apprentice to serve from this date, for, and during, and until the full end and term of, five years next ensuing, to the best of his power and skill, faithfully and honestly, in all lawful business and matters that the said E. F. may direct; and the said A. B. doth hereby covenant and agree with the said E. F., that the said C. B. shall in all things well and truly serve the said E. F., during the said term, according to the conditions of the indenture this day executed by the said C. B. and E. F., with my written consent thereupon endorsed, and now on file in the office of the Clerk of the town of   ; and the said E. F. doth covenant and agree with the said A. B., to pay to the said A. B. the sum of   dollars, on the first day of   , in each and every year during the term aforesaid.

In witness whereof, the said parties to these presents have hereunto set their hands and seals, the day and year first above written.

Sealed and delivered ⎫
in presence of   ⎬
G. H.   ⎭

A. B. [L. s.]
E. F. [L. s.]

§ 82. *The Same, Endorsed upon the Indenture.*

In consideration of the covenants and agreements to be performed by E. F., to and with my son C. B., specified and contained in the within indenture, I do hereby bind myself to the said E. F., for the true and faithful performance and observance, by the said C. B., of the matters and things by him to be performed and observed in and by the said indenture; and I do hereby covenant to and with the said E. F., that the said C. B. shall, in all things, well and truly perform and observe the same.

In witness whereof, I have hereunto put my hand and seal, the day of, &c.

In presence of ⎫
G. H.   ⎬

A. B. [L. s.]

§ 83. *Servant's Indenture.*

This indenture witnesseth: That M. B., of the town of, &c., now aged thirteen years, by and with the consent of A. B., of the town aforesaid, her father, [*or,* mother, &c., *as in* § 76,] has voluntarily and of her own accord, put and bound herself to E. F., as a domestic servant, to serve from the date hereof, for and until the full end and term of five years next ensuing; [*or,* until she shall have attained the age of eighteen years, which will be on the   day of   , 18   ;] during all which time the said servant shall serve her master faithfully, honestly and industriously; all lawful commands every where readily obey; and protect and preserve the goods and property of her said master, and not suffer or allow any to be injured or wasted: she shall not be absent from service without leave; and in all things, and at all times, shall behave as a faithful servant ought to do. And the said E. F. shall and will furnish and provide the said servant, during the continuance of the said term, with suitable and sufficient food and clothing; and cause her, within the said term, to be instructed to read and write; and, at the expiration of the said term, shall give her a new bible, and the sum of   dollars. And for the true performance of all and singular the covenants and agreements aforesaid, the said parties bind themselves, each unto the other, firmly by these presents.

In witness, &c., [*as in* § 76, *and consent of father or mother, as in* § 77.]

---

§ 84. *Contract to Bind to Service a Minor, coming from a Foreign Country beyond Sea, and Acknowledgment.*[1]

This indenture, made the   day of, &c., between C. B., an infant under the age of twenty-one years, to wit: of the age of nineteen years, on the   day of   last, coming from the city of Dublin, in Ireland, a foreign country beyond sea; and E. F., of the city of New York, witnesseth: That the said C. B., in pursuance of the statute in such case made, and in consideration of the covenants hereinafter contained, binds himself to serve the said E. F. from the day of the date hereof, until the full end and term of two years; [*or,* until the said C. B. shall be twenty-one years of age, which will be on the   day of   , in the year   ;] during which term the said C. B. shall well and faithfully serve the said E. F., and his assigns, in all such lawful business as he shall be put to by the said E. F., or his assigns, to the utmost of the power and ability of the said C. B.; and, at all times, behave himself honestly and obediently to the said E. F., and his assigns.

---

[1] The execution of the contract should be acknowledged before a Mayor, Recorder, Alderman, or Justice of the Peace.

And the said E. F. covenants on his part, and agrees to and with the said C. B., that he, the said E. F., will find and allow to the said C. B. suitable and sufficient food and clothing, and all other necessaries, during the said term.

In witness whereof, the parties have hereto set their hands and seals, the day and year above written.   C. B. [L. S.]
                  E. F. [L. S.]

State of New York, } ss:
   County, }
  On the   day of   , in the year   , personally came before me C. B., to me known to be the person who executed the within contract, and, on a private examination before me, acknowledged that the said contract was made and executed by him freely, for the purposes therein mentioned.

        G. H., Justice of the Peace.

---

§ 85. *Assignment of foregoing Indenture.*[1]

Know all men by these presents, that I, the within named E. F., for and in consideration of the sum of   dollars, have assigned and set over, and by these presents do assign and set over, the within indenture, and the servant [*or,* apprentice] therein named, unto C. D., of , his executors, administrators, and assigns, for the residue of the term within mentioned; he and they performing all and singular the covenants therein contained, on my part to be kept and performed, and indemnifying me from the same.

In witness, &c., [*as in* § 82.]
  In presence of }
   G. H.   }
   L. M.   }   E. F. [L. S.]

---

§ 86. *Approval of the Assignment, by a Mayor, Recorder, Alderman, or Justice of the Peace.*

I hereby approve of the foregoing assignment of the within indenture.

     W. V. B., Mayor of the city of New York.

---

§ 87. *Certificate of Consent to the Binding of the Child of an Indian Woman.*

I, G. H., a Justice of the Peace of the town of   , in said county, do certify, that R. M., the male child of S. M., an Indian woman, in my presence and with my consent, was bound as an

---

1 Two witnesses are required to the assignment.

apprentice to E. F., of   , by indenture, dated this day, and duly executed in the town of   , aforesaid; and that I subscribed my name as a witness thereto.

Dated the   day of   , 18   .

G. H., Justice of the Peace.

---

§ 88. *Complaint by Master against Apprentice for Refusing to Serve.*

To G. H., a Justice of the Peace of the County of   :

I, E. F., of the town of   , in said county, hatter, hereby make complaint to you, that C. B., an apprentice lawfully bound to serve me, the said E. F., whose term of service is still unexpired, and with whom I have not received, nor am I entitled to receive, any sum of money as a compensation for his instruction, refuses to serve me, as by law and the terms of his indenture of apprenticeship he is required.

Dated the   day of   , 18   .

County, ss:

E. F., the person named in the foregoing complaint, being duly sworn, deposes and says, that the facts and circumstances stated and set forth in the said complaint are true.

Sworn to before me, this
     day of   , 18   .   E. F.

G. H., Justice of the Peace.

---

§ 89. *Warrant on the foregoing Complaint.*

County, ss :

To any Constable of said County, greeting:

Complaint has been made to me, G. H., one of the Justices of the Peace of said county, upon the oath of E. F., of   , in said county, hatter, that C. B., an apprentice lawfully bound to serve the said E. F., whose term of service is still unexpired, and with whom the said E. F. hath not received, nor is entitled to receive, any sum of money as a compensation for his instruction, refuses to serve the said E. F., as by law and the terms of his indenture of apprenticeship he is required: Now, therefore, you are hereby commanded forthwith to apprehend the said C. B., and bring him before me, at my office in   , to answer to the said E. F. and be dealt with according to law.

Given under my hand, this   day of   , 18   .

G. H., Justice of the Peace.

§ 90. *Commitment of an Apprentice Refusing to Serve.*

County, ss:

To any Constable of said county, greeting:

Complaint on oath was made to me, the undersigned G. H., a Justice of the Peace of said county, by E. F., of   , in said county, hatter, that C. B., an apprentice lawfully bound to serve the said E. F., whose term of service was still unexpired, and with whom the said E. F. had not received, nor was entitled to receive, any sum of money as a compensation for his instruction, refused to serve the said E. F., as by law and the terms of his indenture of apprenticeship he was required: And the said C. B., by virtue of my warrant thereupon issued, has been brought before me to be dealt with according to law; and whereas, after due proof before me of the facts as above stated and set forth, the said C. B. still persists in such refusal to serve the said E. F.: Now, therefore, you are hereby commanded, in the name of the People of the State of New York, to take and convey the said C. B. to the common jail of said county, and deliver him to the keeper thereof, who is commanded to receive the said C. B. into the said common jail, there to remain until he shall consent to serve the said E. F. according to law.

Given, &c., [*as in* § 89.]

---

§ 91. *Complaint to two Justices concerning any Misdemeanor or Ill Behavior of Apprentice.*

To G. H. and S. T., Esquires, Justices of the Peace of the county of   :

I, E. F., of the town of   , in said county, hatter, hereby make complaint to you, that C. B., an apprentice lawfully bound to serve me, the said E. F., whose term of service is still unexpired, and with whom I have not received, nor am I entitled to receive, any sum of money, as a compensation for his instruction, has been guilty of misdemeanors and ill behavior toward me, the said E. F., as follows, viz: [*describe the particulars of the complaint.*]   E. F.

County, ss:

E. F. the person named in the foregoing complaint, being duly sworn, &c., [*as in* § 88.]

---

§ 92. *Warrant on foregoing Complaint.*

County, ss:

To any Constable of said county, greeting:

Complaint has been made to us, the undersigned, Justices of the Peace in and for the said county, upon the oath of E. F., of in said county, hatter, that C. B., an apprentice lawfully bound to serve the said E. F., whose term of service is still unexpired, and with whom the said E. F. hath not received, nor is entitled to receive, any sum of money as a compensation for his instruction, has been guilty of misdemeanors and ill-behavior toward him, the said E. F., as follows, viz: [*give the particulars, as in the complaint.*] Now, therefore, you are hereby commanded forthwith to apprehend the said C. B., and bring him before us, at the office of G. H., in the town of   , that we may hear, examine into, and determine the said complaint, and deal with the said C. B. according to law.

Given under our hands, this   day of   , 18   .

         G. H., Justice of the Peace.
         S. T., Justice of the Peace.

---

§ 93. *Commitment of Apprentice on foregoing Complaint.*

County, ss:

To any Constable of said county, greeting:

Complaint on oath was made to us, the undersigned G. H. and S. T., Justices of the Peace in and for the said county, by E. F., of   , in said county, hatter, that C. B., an apprentice lawfully bound to serve the said E. F., whose term of service was still unexpired, and with whom the said E. F. had not received, nor was entitled to receive, any sum of money as a compensation for his instruction, had been guilty of misdemeanors and ill-behavior toward him, the said E. F., as follows, viz: [*as in the complaint;*] and the said C. B., by virtue of our warrant thereupon issued, has been brought before us, and upon due examination of the proofs and allegations of the parties, it satisfactorily appears to us, that the said C. B. is guilty of the premises charged against him, as aforesaid:* Now, therefore, you are hereby commanded, in the name of the People of the State of New York, to take and convey the said C. B. to the common jail of said county, and deliver him to the keeper thereof, who is commanded to receive the said C. B. into the said common jail, there to remain in solitary confinement, and to be employed at hard labor, for the term of one month.

Given, &c., [*as in § 92.*]

---

§ 94. *Discharge of the Apprentice from Service, and the Master from his Obligations.*

County, ss:

Complaint on oath was made to us, &c., [*as in § 93 to the *, and then add:*] Now, therefore, we do hereby discharge the said C. B. from the service of the said E. F., and the said E. F. from all and every of his obligations incurred under and by virtue of the indentures of apprenticeship of the said C. B.

Given, &c., [*as in § 92.*]

§ 95. *Complaint by the Apprentice to two Justices, for the Cruelty or Misusage of his Master, or his Refusal to furnish him with Necessary Provisions, or Clothing.*

To G. H. and S. T., Esquires, two of the Justices of the Peace of the county of   :

I, C. B., apprentice to E. F., of the town of   , in said county, hatter, hereby make complaint to you, that the said E. F., to whom I am lawfully bound by indentures of apprenticeship, the term of service in which hath not yet expired, and who hath not received, nor is entitled to receive, any sum of money as a compensation for my instruction, has cruelly beat, bruised, and wounded me, the said C. B. , being his apprentice, as aforesaid; [or, has misused and ill treated me, the said C. B., being his apprentice, as aforesaid, by refusing to furnish me with necessary provisions and clothing;] to wit, at   , aforesaid, on the   day of   , 18

C. B.

County, ss:

C. B., the person named in the foregoing complaint, being duly sworn, &c., [*as in* § 88.]

---

§ 96. *Summons on the foregoing Complaint.*

County, ss :

To any Constable of said county, greeting:

Complaint has been made to us, the undersigned, Justices of the Peace, in and for the said county, upon the oath of C. B., apprentice of E. F., of   , in said county, hatter, that the said E. F., to whom the said C. B. is lawfully bound by indentures of apprenticeship, the term of service in which hath not yet expired, and who hath not received, nor is entitled to receive, any sum of money as a compensation for the instruction of the said C. B., has cruelly beat, &c., [*as in* § 95, *substituting* him *for* me:] Now, therefore, you are hereby commanded to summon the said E. F. and C. B. to appear before us, at the office of G. H., in the town of   , on the   day of   instant, at two o'clock in the afternoon of that day, that we may hear, examine and determine the said complaint.

Given, &c., [*as in* § 92.]

---

§ 97. *Discharge of Apprentice on foregoing Complaint.*

County, ss:

Complaint on oath was made to us, the undersigned, G. H. and S. T., Justices of the Peace in and for the said county, by C. B., apprentice to E. F., of   , in said county, hatter, that the said E. F., to whom the said C. B. was lawfully bound by indentures of apprenticeship, the term of service in which was still unexpired, and who had not received, nor was entitled to receive, any sum of money as a compensation for the instruction of the said C. B., had cruelly beat, &c., [*as in* § 96;] and the said E. F., by virtue of our summons thereupon issued, has been brought before us, and upon due examination of the proofs and allegations of the parties, it satisfactorily appears to us, that the said E. F. is guilty of the premises so charged against him, as aforesaid: Now, therefore, we do hereby discharge the said C. B. from the service of the said E. F., any thing in his indentures of apprenticeship, as aforesaid, to the contrary, notwithstanding.

Given, &c., [*as in* § 92.]

---

§ 98. *Complaint by Apprentice against the Master, where Money has been paid, or agreed to be paid.*

To G. H., a Justice of the Peace of the county of   :

I, C. B., apprentice to E. F., of the town of   , in said county, hatter, hereby make complaint to you, that the said E. F., to whom I am lawfully bound by indentures of apprenticeship, the term of service in which hath not yet expired, and who hath received the sum of fifty dollars, [*or,* who is entitled to receive the sum of fifty dollars, on the   day of   , 18 ,] as a compensation for my instruction, has cruelly beat, bruised, and wounded me, the said C. B., being his apprentice, as aforesaid, [*or,* has misused and ill treated me, &c., *as in* § 95.]

County, ss :

C. B., the person named in the foregoing complaint, being duly sworn, &c., [*as in* § 88.]

---

§ 99. *Summons on foregoing Complaint.*

County, ss:

To any Constable of said county, greeting:

Complaint has been made to me, one of the Justices of the Peace in and for the said county, upon the oath of C. B., apprentice to E. F., of   , in said county, hatter, that the said E. F., to whom the said C. B. is lawfully bound by indentures of apprenticeship, the term of service in which hath not yet expired, and who hath received the sum of fifty dollars, [*or, as in* § 98,] as a compensation for the instruction of the said C. B., has cruelly beat, bruised and wounded him, the said C. B., being his apprentice, as aforesaid, [*or,* has misused and ill treated him, &c., *as in* § 95.] Now, therefore, you are hereby commanded to summon the said E. F. and C. B. to appear before me, at my office, in the town of   , in said county, on the   day of   instant, at two o'clock in the afternoon of that day, that I may hear, examine into, and determine the said complaint.

Given, &c., [*as in* § 89.][1]

---

§ 100. *Recognizance of Master and Surety, on foregoing Complaint.*

State of New York, } ss:
    County, }

We, E. F. and L. M., of   , in said county, acknowledge ourselves to be severally indebted to the People of the State of New York, that is to say: The said E. F. in the sum of   dollars, and the said L. M., in the sum of   dollars, to be well and truly paid, if default shall be made in the condition following:*

Complaint on oath having been made to the undersigned, G. H., a Justice of the Peace of the said county, by C. B., an apprentice, against E. F., his master, above named, the parties were summoned and appeared before the said Justice, and after due examination into the premises, the difficulty between the said parties could not be compounded or reconciled: Now, therefore, the condition of this recognizance is such, that if the said E. F. shall personally appear at the next Court of Sessions, to be held in and for said county, then and there to answer to the complaint aforesaid, and to do and receive what shall, by the court, be then and there enjoined upon him, and shall not depart the court without leave, then this recognizance shall be void, otherwise of force.

Taken, subscribed, and acknowledged, }
    the   day of   , 18 , before me, }
           G. H., Justice of the Peace.

E. F. [L. S.]
L. M. [L. S.]

---

§ 101. *Order of Court of Sessions on the Complaint.*

State of New York, } ss:
    County, }

At a Court of Sessions of the county of   , held at   in and for said county, on the   day of   , 18   ·
Present, N. O., County Judge; G. H., and S. T., Justices of the Peace:

Complaint on oath having been made to G. H., a Justice of the Peace of the said county, by C. B., an apprentice, against E. F., his master, who had received the sum of fifty dollars [*or, who was entitled to receive, &c., as in* § 98,] as a compensation for the instruction of the said C. B., that the said E. F. had cruelly beat,

---

[1] If the Justice decides to make such order and direction in the premises *as the equity of the case seems to require,* forms § 94, or § 97, may be varied for the purpose. If the difficulty cannot be compounded or reconciled, forms § 100, etc., will be found applicable.

bruised, and wounded him, the said C. B., being his apprentice, as aforesaid, [or, had misused and ill treated him, the said C. B., being his apprentice, as aforesaid, by refusing to furnish him with necessary provisions and clothing,] the said parties were summoned and appeared before the said Justice; and, after due examination into the premises, the difficulty between the two parties could not be compounded or reconciled: Whereupon the said E. F. was recognized personally to appear at this Court of Sessions of the said county, to answer to the complaint aforesaid, &c.: And now, the said parties having been heard by their respective counsel, it is ordered and decreed by this court, that the indentures of apprenticeship of the said C. B. be, and the same are, hereby canceled, and declared of none effect; and that the said C. B. be, and is, forever discharged from the same: And it is further ordered, that the said E. F. refund to A. B., [or, to the personal representatives of A. B.,] the father, [or, to M. B., the mother, or, guardian, *as the case may be*,] of the said C. B., the sum of fifty dollars, [or, the sum of   dollars, being part of the aforesaid sum of   dollars,] paid by the said A. B. to the said E. F., as a compensation for the instruction of the said C. B.: [or: And it is further ordered, that A. B., or the personal representatives of A. B.,] the father [or, M. B., the mother, or, guardian, *as the case may be*] of the said C. B., be, and he [or, she] is hereby forever discharged of and from his [or, her] agreement to pay to the said E. F. the aforesaid sum of   dollars, on the   day of   , 18   , as a compensation for the instruction of the said C. B., and that the securities given therefor be forthwith delivered up or canceled.]   L. M., Clerk.

---

§ 102. *Complaint by Master against Apprentice Refusing to Serve, where Money has been paid, or agreed to be paid.*

To G. H., a Justice of the Peace of the county of   :

I, E. F., of the town of   , in said county, hatter, hereby make complaint to you, that C. B., an apprentice lawfully bound to serve me, the said E. F., whose term of service is still unexpired, and with whom I have received the sum of   dollars, [or, with whom I am entitled to receive the sum of   dollars, on the   day of   , 18   ,] as a compensation for his instruction, refuses to serve me, as by law and the terms of his indenture of apprenticeship he is required. Dated, &c., [*as in* § 88 *with the verification.*]

---

§ 103. *Summons on the foregoing Complaint.*

County, ss:

To any Constable of said County, greeting:

Complaint has been made to me, G. H., one of the Justices of the

Peace of said county, upon the oath of E. F., of   , in said
county, hatter, that C. B., an apprentice lawfully bound to serve the
said E. F., whose term of service is still unexpired, and with whom
the said E. F. hath received the sum of   dollars, [*or*, with
whom the said E. F. is entitled to receive the sum of   dollars,
on the   day of   , 18   ,] as a compensation for his
instruction, refuses to serve the said E. F., as by law and the terms
of his indenture of apprenticeship he is required: Now, therefore,
you are hereby commanded, &c. [*as in* § 99.]

---

§ 104. *Recognizance of Apprentice and Surety on foregoing*
Complaint.

State of New York, }
      County, } ss:

We, C. B., and R. B., of, &c., [*as in* § 100 *to the**, *and then add:*]
Complaint on oath having been made to the undersigned, G. H., a
Justice of the Peace of the said county, by E. F., the master, against
C. B., his apprentice above named, the parties were summoned, &c.,
[*as in* § 100 *to the end, substituting the name of the apprentice for*
that of the master.]

---

§ 105. *Order of Court of Sessions on the foregoing Complaint.*

State of New York, }
      County, } ss:

At a Court of Sessions of the county of   , held at   ,
    in and for said county, on the   day of   , 18   :
    Present, N. O., County Judge; G. H., and S. T., Justices of
the Peace:

Complaint on oath having been made to G. H., a Justice of the
Peace of said county, by E. F., the master, against C. B., his apprentice, with whom the said E. F. had received the sum of
dollars, [*or*, with whom the said E. F. was entitled to receive the
sum of   dollars, on the   day of   , 18   ,] as a compensation for his instruction, that the said C. B. refused to serve the
said E. F., as by law and the terms of his indenture of apprenticeship he was required, the said parties were summoned and appeared
before the said Justice: and after due examination into the premises,
the difficulty between the said parties could not be compounded or
reconciled: Whereupon the said C. B. was recognized personally to
appear at this Court of Sessions of the said county, to answer to the
complaint aforesaid, &c.: And now, the said parties having been
heard by their respective counsel, and the said C. B. being found
guilty of the premises, it is ordered and decreed that the said C. B.
.e fined in the sum of   dollars, [*or*, that the said C. B. be

imprisoned in the common jail of said county of   , there
to remain in solitary confinement until he shall consent to serve the
said E. F.; or, *if necessary, include both fine and imprisonment,
or follow* § 101, *according to the order of the Court.*][1]

---

[1] Where the master complains against the apprentice, for any misdemeanor, or ill behavior, forms § 102, etc., will require but little alteration to meet the case.

CHAPTER IV.

ARBITRATION AND AWARD.

PRACTICAL REMARKS.

1. All persons, except infants and married women, and persons of unsound mind, may, by an instrument in writing, submit to the decision of one or more arbitrators, any controversy existing between them which might be the subject of an action at law, or of a suit in equity; any claim to an interest for a term of years, or for one year, or less, in real estate; or any controversy respecting the partition of lands between joint tenants, or tenants in common, or concerning the boundaries of lands, or the admeasurement of dower. No claim to real estate, in fee or for life, can be thus submitted. The parties to any such admission may agree, that a judgment of any court of law and of record, to be designated in such instrument in writing, as aforesaid, shall be rendered upon the award made in pursuance thereof.[1]

2. The arbitrators must appoint a place and time for the hearing, otherwise their award will be void; and they have the power to adjourn from time to time, or, for good cause shown, to postpone the hearing to any time not extending beyond the day fixed for rendering their award. Before proceeding to take testimony, they must take the prescribed oath. Such oath may be administered by any Judge, of any Court of Record, or by any Justice of the Peace, or by any Commissioner of Deeds. The attendance of witnesses may be compelled by subpœna, to be issued by any Justice of the Peace. The oaths to witnesses and other persons examined before arbitrators, may be administered by such arbitrators, or any, or either of them.[2]

3. All the arbitrators must meet together, and hear all the proofs and allegations of the parties; but an award by a majority will be

---

[1] 2 R.S. (3d ed.) 628, §§ 1, 2; 1 Hill, 44.   chap. 187; 1 Hill, 489; 3 Barbour's S. C.
[2] 2 R. S. (3d ed.) 629, §§ 3-6; Laws of 1843,   Rep., 276.

valid, unless the concurrence of all be expressly required in the submission. The award must be in writing, subscribed by the arbitrators, and attested by a subscribing witness.[1]

4. An award made without notice to the parties of the hearing, and without their being present, or having an opportunity to be heard, is absolutely void.[2]

5. Upon proving the submission and the award, by the affidavit of the subscribing witness, or by the affidavit of the arbitrators, within one year after making such award, the court designated in such submission shall, by rule, in open court, confirm the award made in pursuance thereof, unless the same be vacated or modified, or a decision thereon be postponed.[3]

6. Any party complaining of such award, may move the court designated in the submission, to vacate the same, upon the ground that it was produced by fraud or corruption; or that the arbitrators were guilty of misconduct in refusing to postpone the hearing, or rejecting proper testimony; or that they exceeded their powers.[4]

7. Such award may be modified or corrected, in like manner, where there is an evident miscalculation of figures; where the arbitrators have decided some matter not submitted to them; or where the award is imperfect. All applications to vacate, or modify an award, must be made at the next term of the court after the publication of such award.[5]

8. Judgments entered up, in pursuance of any award and confirmation thereof, may be set aside, in the same manner as judgments in other cases, and are subject to the same provisions of law.[6]

9. Whenever a party revokes the submission to arbitration before the publication of the award, he will be liable to the adverse party for all the costs, expenses, and damages, the latter may have incurred. If the submission so revoked be contained in the condition of the bond, suit may be commenced thereon by the obligee (the revocation being assigned as the breach thereof,) who will be entitled to recover the costs, expenses, and damages he may have incurred.[7]

10. Where a judgment, entered in pursuance of any award, as aforesaid, requires a party to perform some act, other than the payment of money, and he refuses to do the same, he may be proceeded against, as in other cases of contempt.[8]

11. A submission to arbitrators, of the subject matter of a pending suit, and an award thereon, puts an end to the suit; and the plaintiff's remedy is on the award.[9]

[1] 2 R. S. (3d ed.) 629, §§ 7, 8; 2 Hill, 75; 4 Barbour's S. C. Rep., 250.
[2] 3 Barbour's S. C. Rep., 275.
[3] 2 R. S. (3d ed.) 629, § 9; 5 Wendell, 102; Id., 520; 4 Hill, 561; 6 Id., 303.
[4] 2 R. S. (3d ed.) 629, § 10; 17 Johnson, 405; 10 Wendell, 589; 17 Id., 412; 1 Hill, 319, 489.
[5] 2 R. S. (3d ed.) 629, 630, §§ 11, 12; 5 Wendell, 520; 10 Id., 589; 17 Id., 412; 1 Paige, 293.
[6] 2 R. S. (3d ed.) 630, §§ 13–17.
[7] 2 R. S. (3d ed.) 631, §§ 23, 24; 16 Johnson, 205; 5 Paige, 578.
[8] 2 R. S. (3d ed.) 631, § 18.
[9] 12 Wendell, 503; 1 Hill, 69; 2 Id., 387; 6 Id., 610; 3 Barbour's S. C. Rep., 275.

12. If the arbitration bond requires the award to be in writing, ready for delivery to the parties on or before a given day, the award is a nullity, unless a counterpart of the award delivered to the prevailing party is prepared for the other party.[1]

13. If an agent enter into a submission in his own name, or if a person on behalf of himself and others, but without authority, enter into such submission, he will be personally bound to perform the award.[2]

14. A submission to arbitrators is valid, though by parol ; but the award made in pursuance thereof, cannot be enforced in the manner prescribed by the statute.[3]

15. Where the submission to arbitrators contains an express condition, the award must comply with it strictly.[4]

16. It is immaterial what the form of a submission may be, provided the intention of the parties appears.[5]

17. The award must be confined to the submission.[6]

18. Where a submission is verbal, and there is no agreement that the award shall be in writing, it may be by parol.[7]

19. Where the submission is made to two arbitrators, with the power of choosing an umpire in case of disagreement, the award of the umpire, when made, is final and conclusive.[8]

20. The power of arbitrators is confined to the parties submitted, and if they exceed that limit, their award will, in general, be void.[9]

21. Oral testimony may be given, either in law or equity, to invalidate an award, even though the submission and award be in writing, and under seal.[10]

22. An agreement to pay a certain sum, in case of not abiding by an award, is a penalty, and the opposite party can only recover the sum awarded.[11]

23. No provision is made in the statute for the compensation of arbitrators, but suit may be maintained by them separately, for a reasonable sum in payment for their services.[12]

24. Arbitrators are not obliged to deliver their award till their fees are paid.[13]

25. By the amended constitution of New York, tribunals of conciliation are authorized to be established. No definite action has yet been had in the Legislature on the subject; but should such tribunals be established, they will be found to differ very slightly in character from our present courts of arbitration, and the forms used in the one can readily be adapted to the other.[14]

---

[1] 1 Hill, 321.
[2] 5 Hill, 419.
[3] 2 Hill, 471.
[4] 3 Barbour's S. C. Rep., 56.
[5] 1 Barbour's S. C. Rep., 584.
[6] 1 Barbour's S. C. Rep., 325.
[7] 2 Barbour's Ch. Rep., 430.
[8] 17 Johnson, 405 ; 1 Hill, 489.
[9] 7 Hill, 329.
[10] 7 Hill, 329.
[11] 1 Denio, 464.
[12] 1 Denio, 183.
[13] 3 Barbour's S. C. Rep., 275.
[14] Amended Constitution, (1846,) Art. vi., § 23.

FORMS.

§ 106. *Special Submission to Arbitrators.*

Whereas a controversy is now existing and pending, between A.
B., of, &c., and C. D., of, &c., in relation to an exchange of horses,
made by and between the said parties, at the town of   , aforesaid,
on the   , day of   last past: Now, therefore, we, the undersigned A. B. and C. D., aforesaid, do hereby submit the said controversy to the arbitrament of E. F., L. M., and S. T., of, &c., or any
two of them; and we do mutually covenant and agree, to and with
each other, * that the award to be made by the said arbitrators, or
any two of them, shall, in all things, by us, and each of us, be well
and faithfully kept and observed; provided, however, that the said
award be made in writing, under the hands of the said E. F., L. M.,
and S. T., or any two of them, and ready to be delivered to the said
parties in difference, or such of them as shall desire the same, on the
         day of   next.

Witness our hands and seals, this   day of   , A. D. 18   .
   In presence of }
     G. H.   }   A. B. [L. s.]
                                   C. D. [L. s.]

---

§ 107. *General Submission.*

Whereas differences have for a long time existed, and are now
existing and pending, between A. B., of, &c., and C. D., of, &c., in
relation to divers subjects of controversy and dispute: Now, therefore, we, the undersigned A. B. and C. D., aforesaid, do hereby
mutually covenant and agree, to and with each other, that E. F., L.
M., and S. T., of, &c., or any two of them, shall arbitrate, award,
order, judge, and determine, of and concerning all and all manner
of actions, cause and causes of actions, suits, controversies, claims,
and demands whatsoever, now pending, existing, or held, by and
between us, the said parties: and we do further mutually covenant
and agree, to and with each other, [as in § 106, *from the * to the
end.*]

---

§ 108. *Short Form of General Submission.*

We, the undersigned, hereby mutually agree to submit all our
matters in difference, of every name or nature, to the award and
determination of E. F., L. M., and S. T., for them to hear and determine the same, and make their award in writing, on or before the
         day of   next.

Witness our hands, this   day of   , 18   .
   In presence of }
     G. H.   }   A. B.
                                     C. D

§ 109. *Agreement for Judgment, to be inserted in the Submission, if necessary.*

And it is hereby further agreed between the said parties, that judgment in the Supreme Court of the State of New York [*or*, County Court of   county,] may be rendered upon the award to be made pursuant to this submission, to the end that all matters in controversy between them [*if the submission be special, insert here*, in that behalf,] shall be finally concluded.

---

§ 110. *Arbitration Bond.*[1]

Know all men by these presents: That I, A. B., of the town of   , in the county of   , am held and firmly bound unto C. D., of the town of   , in the county of   , in the sum of five hundred dollars, lawful money of the United States, to be paid to the said C. D., or to his certain attorney, executors, administrators, or assigns; for which payment, to be well and faithfully made, I bind myself, my heirs, executors, and administrators, firmly by these presents.

Sealed with my seal; dated the   day of   , A. D., 18 .

The condition of this obligation is such: That if the above bounden A. B., shall well and truly submit to the decision and award of E. F., L. M., and S. T., named, selected, and chosen arbitrators, as well by and on the part and behalf of the said A. B., as of the said C. D., to arbitrate, award, order, judge, and determine, of and concerning all and all manner of actions, cause and causes of actions, suits, controversies, claims and demands, whatsoever, now depending, existing, or held, by and between the said A. B. and the said C. D.; so that the said award be made in writing, under the hands of the said E. F., L. M., and S. T., or any two of them, and ready to be delivered to the said parties, or such of them as shall desire the same, on or before the   day of   , 18 ; then this obligation to be void, or else to remain in full force. [*Where there is no submission in writing, separate from the bond, the following clause may be inserted here:* And the above bounden A. B. hereby consents and agrees, that judgment in the Supreme Court of the State of New York [*or*, County Court of   county] shall be rendered upon the award to be made, as aforesaid, to the end that all matters in controversy between the said parties [*or*, the above mentioned matter in controversy] may be finally concluded.]

Signed and sealed }
  in presence of   }   A. B. [L. S.]
    G. H.   }

---

1 Each party should have a bond. The obligor in one will be the obligee in the other.

§ 111. *Condition of Bond on a Special Submission.*

The condition of the above obligation is such: That if the above bounden A. B. shall well and truly submit to the decision of E. F., L. M., and S. T., named, selected, and chosen arbitrators, as well by and on the part and behalf of the said A. B., as of the said C. D., between whom a controversy exists, to hear all the proofs and allegations of the parties, of and concerning a certain exchange of horses, made by and between them, at the town of , aforesaid, on the day of, &c., and all matters relating thereto; so that the award of the said arbitrators be made, &c., [*as in* § 110.]

§ 112. *Notice to Arbitrators of their Appointment.*

To E. F., L. M., and S. T., Esquires:

You are hereby notified, that you have been nominated and chosen arbitrators, as well on the part and behalf of the undersigned A. B., of, &c., as of C. D., of, &c., also undersigned, to arbitrate, award, &c., [*as in the submission or bond, specifying the time within which the award must be made;*] and you are requested to meet the said parties at the house of O. R., in the town of , aforesaid, on the day of, &c., at ten o'clock in the forenoon of that day, for the purpose of fixing upon a time and place when and where the proofs and allegations of the said parties shall be heard. Dated the day of, &c.

              A. B.
  Yours, &c.,   C. D.

§ 113. *Arbitrator's Oath.*

We, the undersigned, arbitrators, appointed by and between A. B. and C. D., do swear that we, respectively, will faithfully and fairly hear and examine the matters in controversy between the parties above named, and will make a just award therein, according to the best of our understanding.

Sworn to, this day of ,   E. F.
  18 ., before me.   L. M.
    G. H., Justice of the Peace.   S. T.

§ 114. *Notice of Hearing for opposite Party, if necessary.*

In the matter of an arbitration, of and concerning certain matters in difference between A. B., of the one part, and C. D., of the other part.

Sir: You will please take notice that a hearing in the matter above specified, will be had before the arbitrators, at the house of O. R., in the town of, &c., on the day, of &c. Dated the day of, &c.   Yours, &c.,   A. B.
  To C. D.

§ 115. *Oath on Application to a Justice of the Peace for a Subpœna.*[1]

You do swear that you will true answers make to all such questions as I shall put to you, touching the necessity and propriety of my issuing a subpœna upon your present application for the same.

---

§ 116. *Subpœna to appear before Arbitrators.*

Town of , } ss:
County,

The People of the State of New York, to N. P., R. S., and J. O., Greeting:

We command you, and each of you, personally to appear and attend at the house of O. R., in the town of , in said county, on the day of instant, at ten o'clock in the forenoon of that day, before E. F., L. M., and S. T., arbitrators chosen to determine a controversy, [*or, certain matters in controversy,*] between A. B. and C. D., then and there to testify in relation thereto, before said arbitrators, on the part of the said A. B. Hereof fail not at your peril.

Given under my hand, this day of , 18 .

G. H., Justice of the Peace.

---

§ 117. *Oath of Witness before Arbitrators.*

You do solemnly swear, that the evidence you shall give to the arbitrators here present, on a controversy, [*or, on certain matters in controversy,*] between A. B. and C. D., shall be the truth, the whole truth, and nothing but the truth: So help you God. [*The oath may be varied according to form § 49, if required.*]

---

§ 118. *Revocation.*

To E. F., L. M., and S. T., Esquires:

Take notice, that I do hereby revoke your powers as arbitrators under the submission made to you by C. D. and myself, in writing. [*or as the case may be,*] on the day of 18 .

A. B.[2]

---

§ 119. *Notice of Revocation.*

To C. D..

You are hereby notified that I have this day revoked the powers of E. F., L. M., and S. T., arbitrators chosen to settle the matters in

---

[1] The statute does not in terms render it necessary for a Justice of the Peace to require a party to an arbitration, applying for a subpœna, to be sworn, but it is always best to administer the oath

[2] If the submission is under seal, the instrument revoking it should likewise be under seal.

controversy between us; and that the following is a copy of such revocation: [*Insert the Revocation.*] Dated the   day of
18   .   Yours, &c.,   A. B.

---

§ 120. *Award.*

To all to whom these presents shall come, or may concern:

Send greeting, E. F., L. M., and S. T., to whom were submitted, as arbitrators, the matters in controversy existing between A. B., of, &c., and C. D., of, &c., as by their submission in writing [*or, by the condition of their respective bonds of submission, executed by the said parties, respectively, each to the other,*] and bearing date the   day of   , A. D. 18   , more fully appears: Now, therefore, know ye, that we, the arbitrators mentioned in the said submission, [*or, bonds,*] having been first duly sworn according to law, and having heard the proofs and allegations of the parties, and examined the matters in controversy by them submitted, do make this award in writing ; that is to say: The said C. D. shall make, execute, and deliver, to the said A. B., on or before the   day of   instant, a good and sufficient assignment of a certain bond and mortgage, executed, &c., to the said C. D., &c. ; and the said A. B. shall pay, or cause to be paid, to the said C. D., the sum of   dollars, immediately upon the execution and delivery of the said assignment; [*or:* The said C. D. shall pay, or cause to be paid, to the said A. B., the sum of   dollars, within ten days from the date hereof, in full payment, discharge, and satisfaction, of and for all moneys, debts and demands, due, or owing from him, the said C. D., to the said A. B.; *or:* The said C. D. shall henceforth forever cease to prosecute a certain suit commenced by him, against the said A. B., in the Supreme Court of the State of New York, now pending and undetermined in the said court; and the said A. B. shall pay, or cause to be paid, to the said C. D., on or before the   day of, &c., the sum of   dollars, in full satisfaction of the costs, charges and expenses, incurred by the said C. D., in and about the prosecution of his suit, as aforesaid.] And we do further award, adjudge and decree, that the said A. B. and C. D. shall, and do, within ten days next ensuing the date hereof, seal and execute unto each other, mutual and general releases, of all actions, cause and causes of action, suits, controversies, claims and demands whatsoever, for, or by reason of, any matter, cause, or thing, from the beginning of the world down to the date of the said bonds of arbitration, [*or,* the said submission.]

In witness whereof, we have hereunto subscribed these presents, this   day of   , one thousand eight hundred and

In the presence of }
   G. H.   }   E. F
                                                     L. M.
                                                     S. T.

§ 121. *Release to be executed by Party to an Arbitration, when required in the Award.*

Know all men by these presents: That I, A. B., of the of   , for and in consideration of the sum of one dollar to me in hand paid by C. D., of   , and in pursuance of an award made by E. F., L. M., and S. T., arbitrators between us, the said A. B. and C. D., and bearing date the   day of   , one thousand eight hundred and   , do hereby release, and forever discharge, the said C. D., his heirs, executors, and administrators, of and from all actions, cause and causes of action, suits, controversies, claims and demands whatsoever, for, or by reason of, any matter, cause, or thing, from the beginning of the world down to the   day of   , one thousand eight hundred and   . [*Insert the date of the bonds of arbitration, or of the submission.*]

In witness whereof, I have hereunto put my hand and seal, this   day of   , one thousand eight hundred and   .

In presence of }
G. H.   }   A. B. [L. S.]

---

§ 122. *Affidavit of the Execution of the Arbitration Bond.*

County, ss:

G. H., of said county, being duly sworn, deposes and says: that he was present, and saw A. B. sign, seal, and, as his act and deed, deliver the bond hereunto annexed; that the name A. B., subscribed to the said bond, is the proper and genuine signature of the said A. B.; and that this deponent set his name as a subscribing witness to the same, at the time of its execution and delivery by the said A. B., as aforesaid: and further says not.   G. H.

Sworn to, &c., [*as in* § 113.]

---

§ 123. *Affidavit of the Execution of the Award.*

County, ss:

G. H., of said county, being duly sworn, deposes and says: that he was present, and saw E. F., L. M., and S. T., sign, publish, and declare, their final award and arbitration in writing, between A. B., of, &c., and C. D., of, &c., bearing date the   day of, &c., and hereunto annexed; that the names E. F., L. M., and S. T., subscribed to the said award, are the proper and genuine signatures of the said E. F., L. M., and S. T.; and that this deponent set his name as a subscribing witness to the said award, at the time of its execution and publication, as aforesaid: and further says not.   G. H.

Sworn to, &c., [*as in* § 113.]

CHAPTER V.

ASSIGNMENTS.

PRACTICAL REMARKS.

1. In order to render an assignment valid, when made in good faith, it is only necessary that it should contain sufficient words to convey all the right, title and interest, of the assignor, to the assignee, and assure to the latter the full and entire possession and enjoyment thereof.

2. All transfers, or assignments, of goods, chattels, or things in action, made in trust, for the use of the person making the same, are void as against the creditors, existing or subsequent, of such person.[1]

3. Every assignment of any estate, or interest, in lands, or in goods or things in action, or of any rents or profits issuing therefrom, made with the intent to hinder, delay, or defraud, creditors or other persons, is void.[2]

4. An insolvent debtor may give a preference to one creditor, to the exclusion of all others, provided it be done in good faith; and this, even after suit commenced against him by another creditor.[3]

5. If the assignor reserve to himself the power to revoke the conveyance; or to change the trusts, by giving a preference to other creditors at a future time; or if he direct the surplus, after paying the preferred creditors, to be returned to him; the conveyance will be void. The doctrine is well established, that the debtor must make an unconditional surrender of his effects, for the benefit of those to whom they rightfully belong.[4]

6. An assignment, made by an insolvent debtor, of all his property, in trust to pay certain specified creditors, and then, without making provision for the remaining creditors, in trust to re-convey or re-assign the residue to the debtor, is void on its face as to the creditors

---

1 2 R. S. (3d ed.) 195, § 1 ; 6 Hill 438.
2 2 R. S. (3d ed.) 197, §§ 1–3.
3 5 Johnson, 355 ; 6 Cowen, 287.

4 14 Johnson, 458 ; 5 Cowen, 547 ; 11 Wendell, 187. ; 6 Hill, 438

not provided for; and proof that there would be no surplus will not make it good.[1]

7. General assignments by an insolvent debtor, giving preferences to certain creditors, are upheld reluctantly by our courts, and they must be executed in perfect good faith, and an entire and absolute surrender of the debtor's property must be made for the payment of his debts.[2]

8. An assignment by an insolvent debtor, in trust to pay preferred creditors, should not authorize the trustees named therein to sell property on credit.[3]

9. An assignment for the benefit of creditors, authorizing the assignee, in his discretion, to change the order of preference of the creditors, is fraudulent and void.[4]

10. Assignments of the property or effects of a limited partnership, made by such partnership when insolvent, or in contemplation of insolvency, and giving a preference to creditors, are void.[5]

11. Where an assignment is made for the benefit of creditors, it must be accompanied by immediate delivery, either actual or implied.[6]

12. Voluntary conveyances in trust for creditors are regarded with jealousy, but the question of fraudulent intent is always one of fact, and not one of law.[7]

13. No higher rates of compensation should be given to trustees or assignees, by an assignment, than those allowed to executors, administrators, and guardians, for similar services.[8]

14. An action brought by an assignee of a chose in action, will be without prejudice to any set-off, or other defence, existing at the time of, or before notice of the assignment.[9]

15. Every assignment of any interest in land must be in writing.[10] Assignments of mortgages should be acknowledged and recorded, in the same manner as direct conveyances of real estate.

16. An assignment of a mortgage by an individual, or by a corporation, without a seal, is a valid transfer of the mortgage debt, though not of the mortgage itself.[11]

17. An assignment of a policy of insurance should always receive the assent of the insurers; to be signified in writing, if a company, by the President or Secretary.

18. The assignee of an insurance policy cannot recover for any loss in his own name, unless there be an express promise on the part of the company to be responsible; even though the assignment be made with their consent.[12]

[1] 4 Barbour's S. C. Rep., 456; 2 Comstock, 365.
[2] 6 Hill, 438; 10 Paige, 229.
[3] 9 Paige, 405; 2 Comstock, 365.
[4] 4 Barbour's S. C. Rep., 546.
[5] 2 R. S. (3d ed.) 51, § 20.
[6] 1 Barbour's S. C. Rep., 210.
[7] 2 R. S. (3d ed.) 198, § 4; 8 Cowen, 406; 4 Wendell, 30?; 7 Id., 438; 8 Id., 375; 11 Id., 251; 12 Id., 297; 15 Id., 212, 628; 16 Id., 520; 17 Id., 54, 492; 19 Id., 183, 514, 524; 20 Id., 118, 507; 23 Id., 653; 24 Id., 117; 25 Id., 396, 615; 26 Id., 511; 1 Hill, 347, 439, 467; 4 Id., 271; 6 Id., 433, 438; 3 Paige, 557; 2 Barbour's S. C. Rep., 9.
[8] 2 Comstock, 365.
[9] Laws of 1849, part II., title III., § 112.
[10] 2 R. S. (3d ed.) 47, § 44. Id., 194, § 6
[11] 1 Denio, 520.
[12] 3 Hill, 88.

D

FORMS.

§ 124. *Assignment to be Endorsed on an Instrument.*

In consideration of the sum of   dollars, to me in hand paid, by C. D., of, &c., the receipt whereof is hereby acknowledged, I do hereby transfer, assign and set over, to the said C. D., his heirs and assigns, all my right, title and interest, in and to the within instrument ; and I do hereby constitute the said C. D., my attorney, in my name, or otherwise, but at his own cost and charge, to take all legal measures which may be proper or necessary, for the complete recovery and enjoyment of the assigned premises.

Witness my hand and seal, this   day of   , 18 .
In presence of }
    G. H.   }   A. B. [L. S.]

---

§ 125. *Assignment by a Firm, for the Benefit of Creditors.*

This indenture, made the   day of   , in the year   , between A. B. and C. D., copartners, under the name, style, or firm, of B. & D., of the first part, and E. F., of, &c., of the second part :

Whereas the said copartnership is justly indebted in sundry considerable sums of money, and has become unable to pay and discharge the same with punctuality, or in full; and the said parties of the first part are now desirous of making a fair and equitable distribution of their property and effects among their creditors: Now, therefore, this indenture witnesseth, that the said parties of the first part, in consideration of the premises, and of the sum of one dollar to them in hand paid, by the party of the second part, the receipt whereof is hereby acknowledged, have granted, bargained and sold, released, assigned, transferred and set over, and by these presents do grant, bargain and sell, release, assign, transfer and set over, unto the said party of the second part, and to his heirs and assigns, forever, all and singular, the lands, tenements and hereditaments, situate, lying and being within the State of New York, and all the goods, chattels, merchandise, bills, bonds, notes, book accounts, claims, demands, choses in action, judgments, evidences of debt and property, of every name and nature whatsoever, of the said parties of the first part, more particularly enumerated and described in the schedule hereto annexed, marked " Schedule A"; to have and to hold the same, and every part and parcel thereof, with the appurtenances, to the said party of the second part, his heirs, executors, administrators and assigns:

In trust, nevertheless, and to and for the following uses, intents and purposes; that is to say: that the said party of the second part shall take possession of all and singular the lands, tenements and hereditaments, property and effects, hereby assigned, and sell and dispose of the same, upon such terms and conditions as in his judgment may appear best, but not upon credit, and convert the same into money; and shall also collect all and singular the said debts, dues, bills, bonds, notes, accounts, claims, demands and choses in action, or so much thereof as may prove collectible; and thereupon execute, acknowledge, and deliver, all necessary conveyances and instruments, for the purposes aforesaid: And by and with the proceeds of such sales and collections, the said party of the second part shall first pay and disburse all the just and reasonable expenses, costs, charges and commissions, of executing and carrying into effect this assignment, and all rents, taxes and assessments, due or to become due, on the lands, tenements and hereditaments, aforesaid, until the same shall be sold and disposed of; and by and with the residue, or net proceeds and avails, of such sales and collections, the said party of the second part shall,

First, Pay and discharge, in full, the several and respective debts, bonds, notes and sums of money, due, or to grow due, from the said parties of the first part, or for which they are liable, to the said party of the second part, and the several other persons and firms designated in the schedule hereto annexed, marked "Schedule B," together with all interest moneys due, or to grow due thereon; and, if said net proceeds and avails shall not be sufficient to pay and discharge the same, in full, then such net proceeds and avails shall be distributed *pro rata*, share and share alike, among the said several persons and firms named in said Schedule B., according to the amount of their respective claims; and,

Secondly, By and with the residue and remainder of the said net proceeds and avails, if any there shall be, the said party of the second part shall pay and discharge all the other copartnership debts, demands, and liabilities, whatsoever, now existing, whether due, or hereafter to become due, provided such remainder shall be sufficient for that purpose; and, if insufficient, then the same shall be applied *pro rata*, share and share alike, to the payment of said debts, demands and liabilities, according to their respective amounts; and,

Thirdly, By and with the residue and remainder of the said net proceeds and avails, if any there shall be, the said party of the second part shall pay and discharge all the private and individual debts of the parties of the first part, or either of them, whether due, or to grow due, provided such remainder shall be sufficient for that purpose; and, if insufficient, then the same shall be applied *pro rata*, share and share alike, to the payment of the said debts, according to their respective amounts; and,

Lastly, The said party of the second part shall return the surplus of the said net proceeds and avails, if any there shall be, to the said parties of the first part, their executors, administrators, or assigns.

And, for the better execution of these presents, and of the several trusts hereby reposed, the said parties of the first part do hereby make, nominate and appoint, the said party of the second part, and his executors, administrators and assigns, their, and each of their true and lawful attorney, irrevocable, with full power and authority to do, transact and perform, all acts, deeds, matters and things, which can, or may, be necessary in the premises, as fully and completely as the said parties of the first part, or either of them, might or could do, were these presents not executed; and attorneys, one or more, under him to make, nominate, and appoint, with full power of substitution and revocation; hereby ratifying and confirming all, and every thing whatsoever, that our said attorney, and his attorneys, shall do, or cause to be done, in the premises.

In witness whereof, the said parties of the first part have hereunto set their respective hands and seals, the day and year above written.[1]

Signed, sealed and delivered,   A. B. [L. s.]
     in the presence of   C. D. [L. s.]
       G. H.

---

§ 126. *General Assignment.*

Know all men by these presents: That I, A. B., of, &c., for value received, have sold, and by these presents do grant, assign, and convey, unto C. D., of, &c., all the notes, accounts, dues, debts, and demands, specified in the schedule hereunto annexed, marked "Schedule A," to have and to hold the same unto the said C. D., and his executors, administrators, and assigns, forever, to and for the use of the said C. D.; hereby constituting and appointing the said C. D. my true and lawful attorney, irrevocable, in my name, place, and stead, for the purpose aforesaid, to ask, demand, sue for, attach, levy, recover and receive, all such sum and sums of money which now are, or may hereafter become due, owing and payable, for, or on account of, all or any of the notes, accounts, dues, debts and demands, above assigned; giving and granting unto my said attorney, full power and authority, to do and perform all and every act and thing whatsoever, requisite and necessary, as fully, to all intents and purposes, as I might or could do, if personally present, with full power of substitution and revocation; hereby ratifying and confirming all that the said

---

[1] The above form may be readily varied, if the assignment is intended to be made for the general benefit of creditors, without preference; or if there are to be two or more classes of preferred debts. In order to save trouble and expense, in passing the title of real estate, deeds regularly acknowledged and executed, ought to accompany an assignment embracing real property.

attorney, or his substitute, shall lawfully do, or cause to be done, by virtue hereof.

In witness whereof, I have hereunto set my hand and seal, the day of   , one thousand eight hundred and   .

Signed, sealed, and delivered, ⎫
   in the presence of   ⎬
      E. F.   ⎭   A. B. [L. S.]

---

§ 127. *Assignment of Bond.*

Know all men by these presents: That I, A. B., of, &c., of the first part, for and in consideration of the sum of   dollars, lawful money of the United States of America, to me in hand paid by C. D., of, &c., of the second part, the receipt whereof is hereby acknowledged, have bargained, sold, and assigned, and by these presents do bargain, sell, and assign, unto the said party of the second part, his executors, administrators, and assigns, a certain written bond or obligation, and the condition thereof, bearing date the   day of   , one thousand eight hundred and   , executed by E. F. to the said A. B., and all sum and sums of money, due, or to grow due thereon: And I do hereby covenant with the said party of the second part, that there is now due on the said bond or obligation, according to the condition thereof, for principal and interest, the sum of   dollars; and I hereby authorize the said party of the second part, in my name, to ask, demand, sue for, recover, and receive, the money due, and that may grow due thereon, as aforesaid.

In witness, &c., [*as in* § 126.]

---

§ 128. *Assignment of Judgment.*

This indenture, made the   day of   , one thousand eight hundred and   , between A. B., of, &c., of the first part, and C. D., of, &c., of the second part: Whereas the said party of the first part, on the   day of July, one thousand eight hundred and   , recovered by judgment, in the Supreme Court of the State of New York, against E. F., of, &c., the sum of   dollars and   cents, damages and costs, [*or,*   dollars of debt, and   dollars for damages and costs:] Now, therefore, this indenture witnesseth, that the said party of the first part, in consideration of   dollars, to him duly paid, hath sold, and by these presents doth assign, transfer, and set over, unto the said party of the second part, and his assigns, the said judgment, and all sum and sums of money that may be had, or obtained, by means thereof, or any proceedings to be had thereupon. And the said party of the first part doth hereby constitute and appoint the said party of the second part, and his assigns, his true and lawful attorney, and attorneys, irrevocable, with power of substitution and revocation, for the use, and at the proper cost and charge of the said party of the second part, to ask, demand, and receive, and to sue out executions, and take all lawful ways for the recovery of the money due, or to become due, on the said judgment; and on payment, to acknowledge satisfaction, or discharge the same; hereby ratifying and confirming all that his said attorney or attorneys shall lawfully do, or cause to be done, in the premises. And the said party of the first part doth covenant, that there is now due on the said judgment the sum of   dollars, and that he will not collect or receive the same, or any part thereof, nor release or discharge the said judgment, but will own and allow all lawful proceedings therein; the said party of the second part saving the said party of the first part harmless, of and from any costs and charges in the premises.

In witness whereof, the party of the first part hath hereunto set his hand and seal, the day and year first above written.

Sealed and delivered in the }
    presence of   }
        G. H.   }   A. B. [L s.]

---

§ 129. *The Same, in a Shorter Form.*

Supreme Court:

A. B.   }   Judgment for $1000 on a bond, dated first May,
against }   1845. · Conditioned for the payment of $500 and
E. F.   }   interest—costs taxed at $21,50. Judgment docketed
August 2, 1845, in   County Clerk's Office.

In consideration of   dollars, to me paid, I do hereby sell, assign, and transfer, to C. D., the judgment above mentioned, for his use and benefit; hereby authorizing him to collect and enforce payment thereof, in my name, or otherwise, but at his own costs and charges: and covenanting that the sum of   dollars, with the interest from the   day of   , in the year   besides the costs, is due thereon.

In witness, &c., [*as in* § 126.]

---

§ 130. *The Same, in Another Form.*

County Court:

A. B.   }   Judgment docketed 31st July, 1847, for $210,
against }   27, damages and costs.
E. F.   }   For value received, I do hereby assign, transfer
and set over, the above mentioned judgment, to C. D., for his use, and at his risk, costs and charges, in all respects.

Dated the   day of   , 18 .   A. B.

§ 131. *Assignment of Bond and Mortgage:*

Know all men by these presents: That I, A. B., of, &c., of the first part, in consideration of the sum of   dollars, lawful money of the United States, to me in hand paid by C. D., of, &c., of the second part, the receipt whereof is hereby acknowledged, have granted, bargained, sold, assigned, transferred, and set over, and by these presents do grant, bargain, sell, assign, transfer and set over, unto the said party of the second part, a certain indenture of mortgage, bearing date the   day of   , one thousand eight hundred and   , made and executed by E. F., and M. his wife, of, &c., to the said party of the first part, together with the bond or obligation therein described, and the money due or to grow due thereon, with the interest: to have and to hold the same, unto the said party of the second part, his executors, administrators, and assigns, for their use and benefit; subject only to the proviso in the said indenture of mortgage mentioned: And I do hereby make, constitute and appoint, the said party of the second part, my true and lawful attorney, irrevocable, in my name, or otherwise, but at his own proper costs and charges, to have, use, and take, all lawful ways and means, for the recovery of the said money and interest; and, in case of payment, to discharge the same, as fully as I might, or could do, if these presents were not made: And I do hereby covenant, to and with the said party of the second part, that there is now due and owing upon the said bond and mortgage, the sum of   dollars, with interest from the   day of   , 18   ; and that I have good right to sell, transfer and assign, the same, as aforesaid.

In witness, &c., [*as in* § 126.]

---

§ 132. *The Same, in a Shorter Form.*

E. F., and M., his wife, }   Mortgage dated the   day of,
             vs.   } &c., executed by E. F., and M., his wife,
      A. B.   :   } to A. B., on certain premises described therein, being part of lot No.   , in the town of   , in the county of   ; recorded in   County Clerk's office, in book No.   of Mortgages, pages   , &c.

Bond bearing date the day aforesaid, executed by E. F., to A. B., aforesaid, in the penal sum of   dollars, conditioned for the payment of   dollars, secured by the above mortgage, on the   day of   , 18   , with interest.

In consideration of   dollars, to me paid, by C. D., of, &c., I do hereby assign, transfer and set over, unto the said C. D., the mortgage above described, and the bond accompanying the same, as aforesaid, for his use and benefit; hereby authorizing him to collect and enforce payment thereof, in my name, or otherwise, but at his own costs and charges. And I do hereby covenant that the sum of   dollars, with interest from the   day of   last past, is now due and owing on the said bond and mortgage; and that I have good right to sell and assign the same.

In witness, &c., [*as in* § 126.]

---

§ 133. *The Same, Endorsed on Mortgage.*

In consideration of   dollars, to me in hand paid, by C. D., of, &c., I do hereby sell, assign, transfer, and set over, unto the said C. D., the within indenture of mortgage, together with the bond accompanying the same, for his use and benefit; hereby authorizing him [*as in* § 132, *to the end.*]

---

§ 134. *Assignment of Bond and Mortgage, as Collateral Security.*

This indenture, &c., [*or,* In consideration of, &c., *as in either of the forms immediately preceding, and then add:*] But this indenture [*or,* this assignment] is, nevertheless, made upon this express condition, that if the said A. B., his heirs, executors or administrators, shall well and truly pay, or cause to be paid, unto the said C. D., his heirs, executors, administrators, or assigns, the sum of   dollars, on or before the   day of   , 18 , with interest from the date hereof, this indenture [*or,* this assignment] shall be void and of no effect; it being made for the purpose of securing the payment of the said sum of   dollars, with interest, as aforesaid, and for no other purpose whatever: And in case the said C. D., his heirs, executors, administrators, or assigns, shall collect and receive the money due on said mortgage hereby assigned, he, or they, shall, after retaining the sum of   dollars, with the interest thereon, and his, or their, reasonable costs and charges in that behalf expended, pay the surplus, if any there be, to the said A. B., his heirs, executors, administrators, or assigns.

In witness whereof, the said parties have hereto set their respective hands and seals, the day and year first above written, [*or,* the day of   , 18 .]

Signed, sealed and delivered, }
 in presence of }
  G. H.

A. B. [L. S.]
C. D. [L. S.]

---

§ 135. *Assignment of Lease.*

Know all men by these presents: That I, A. B., of, &c., for and in consideration of the sum of   dollars, lawful money of the United States, to me paid, by C. D., of, &c., have sold, and by these presents do grant, convey, assign, transfer and set over, unto the said C. D., a certain indenture of lease, bearing date the   day of   , in the year one thousand eight hundred and   , made by L. M., of, &c., to me, the said A. B., of a certain dwelling-house and lot, situate in, &c., with all and singular the premises therein mentioned and described, and the buildings thereon, together with the appurtenances; to have and to hold the same unto the said C. D., his heirs, executors, administrators, and assigns, from the day of   next, for and during all the rest, residue, and remainder, of the term of   years mentioned in the said indenture of lease; subject, nevertheless, to the rents, covenants, conditions, and provisions, therein also mentioned: And I do hereby covenant and agree, to and with the said C. D., that the said assigned premises now are free and clear, of and from all former and other gifts, grants, bargains, sales, leases, judgments, executions, back rents, taxes, assessments and incumbrances, whatsoever.

In witness, &c., [*as in* § 126.]

---

§ 136. *The same, by Endorsement.*

In consideration of the sum of   dollars, to me in hand paid, by C. D., of, &c., the receipt whereof I hereby acknowledge, I have bargained, sold, assigned and set over, and by these presents do bargain, sell, assign and set over, unto the said C. D., his heirs and assigns, the within written indenture of lease, and all my estate, right, title, interest, claim, property and demand, of, in and to, the lands, tenements, hereditaments and premises, therein mentioned, which I now have, by means of the said indenture, or otherwise; subject, nevertheless, to the rents and covenants in the said indenture contained.

In witness, &c., [*as in* § 126.]

---

§ 137. *Assignment of Contract for the Sale of Real Estate.*

Know all men by these presents: That I, A. B., of, &c., for and in consideration of the sum of   dollars, lawful money of the United States, to me paid, by C. D., of, &c., have sold, and by these presents do sell, transfer, assign and set over, unto the said C. D., a contract for the sale of certain real estate, being part of lot No.   in the town of   , in the county of   , aforesaid, [*or*, situate in, &c., and described as follows: *giving the description in full;*] which said contract was made and executed by E. F., of, &c., to the said A. B., and bears date the   day of   , 18   : to have and to hold the same unto the said C. D., his heirs, executors, administrators and assigns, for his and their use and benefit, forever; subject, nevertheless, to the covenants, conditions and payments, therein mentioned: And I hereby fully authorize and empower the said C. D., upon his performance of the said covenants and conditions, to demand and receive of the said E. F. the deed covenanted to be given in the said contract, in the same manner, to all intents and purposes, as I myself might, or could do, were these presents not executed.

In witness, &c., [*as in* § 126.]   6

§ 138. *The Same, by Endorsement.*

In consideration of the sum of   dollars, to me in hand paid, by C. D., of, &c., the receipt whereof I hereby acknowledge, I have bargained, sold, assigned and set over, and by these presents do bargain, sell, assign and set over, unto the said C. D., his heirs and assigns, the within contract, and all my estate, right, title, interest, claim, property and demand, of, in and to, the same, and the premises therein described; subject, nevertheless, &c., [*as in* § 137, *to the end.*]

---

§ 139. *Assignment of Bail Bond.*

Know all men by these presents: That I, A. P., the Sheriff within named, do assign and set over, to A. B., the plaintiff therein named, at his request, the within bail bond, or obligation, pursuant to the statute in such case made and provided. Dated   , this   day of   , 18   .

Signed, sealed and delivered,)
   in the presence of   }   A. P., Sheriff. [L. S.]
   G. H.

---

§ 140. *Assignment of Partnership Property by one Partner to another, to Close the Concern.*

Whereas, a copartnership has heretofore existed, between A. B. and C. D., both of the town of   , in the county of   , under the firm name of B. & D., which said copartnership is hereby dissolved and determined:

Now, therefore, this indenture, made this   day of   , in the year   , by and between the said A. B. of the one part, and the said C. D. of the other part, witnesseth: That the said A. B. doth hereby sell, transfer, assign and set over, unto the said C. D., his moiety of all the stock in trade, goods, merchandise, effects and property, of every description, belonging to, or owned by, the said copartnership, wherever the same may be; together with all debts, choses in action, and sums of money, due and owing to the said firm, from any and all persons whomsoever, to hold the same to the said C. D., and his assigns, forever, in trust, for the following purposes, namely: That the said C. D. shall sell and dispose of all the goods, property, and effects, belonging to the said firm, at such time and in such manner as he may think prudent; and shall, with reasonable diligence, collect all the debts and sums of money due and owing to the said firm; and shall, out of the proceeds of the said sales, and with the moneys thus collected, pay and discharge all the debts and sums of money now due and owing from the said firm, as far as the proceeds of said sales, and the sums of money collected, will go; and after fully satisfying all demands against the said firm, if there be any surplus, shall pay over one moiety thereof to the said A. B., or his representatives.

And the said A. B. doth hereby constitute and appoint the said C. D., his attorney, irrevocable, in his, the said C. D.'s, own name. or in the name of the said firm, to demand, collect, sue for and receive, any and all debts and sums of money due and owing to the said firm; to institute and prosecute suits for the recovery of the said debts, or to compound the same, as he may judge most expedient; to defend any and all suits against the said firm; to execute all such discharges, releases and acquittances, as may be necessary; and, generally, to do all such acts and things as may be necessary or proper, for the full and complete settlement of all business and concerns of the said copartnership.

And the said C. D., for himself, and his heirs, executors and administrators, hereby covenants, to and with the said A. B., and his representatives, that he will sell and dispose of all the partnership property and effects, to the best advantage; that he will use his best diligence and endeavors to collect all debts and sums of money due and owing to the said firm; and that he will truly and faithfully apply the proceeds of said sale, and the moneys collected, to the payment, discharge and satisfaction, of all debts and demands against the said firm, as far as the same will go; and after discharging all such debts, will pay over to the said A. B., or his representatives, one moiety of any surplus that may remain; and further, that he will keep a full and accurate account of all moneys received by him, for goods sold, or debts collected, as well as of all moneys paid out, and will render a just, true, and full account thereof, to the said A. B., or his representatives.

And the said A. B., for himself, his heirs, executors and administrators, covenants to and with the said C. D., his heirs, &c., that if it shall be found that the debts due and owing from the said firm exceed the amount of moneys received from the sale of the said partnership property and effects, and the debts collected, he will pay unto the said C. D., or his assigns, one moiety of any balance that may then be found due and owing from the said firm.

In witness, &c., [as in § 134.]

---

§ 141. *Assignment by a Sheriff, to his Successor in Office.*

This indenture, made this   day of, &c., between G. H. C., Esq., former Sheriff of the county of   , of the first part, and A. P., Esq., the present Sheriff thereof, of the second part, witnesseth: That the said G. H. C., the said former Sheriff, doth, by and with these presents, deliver to the said A. P., his said successor, the jail of the said county, with its appurtenances, with the property of the said county therein, all the prisoners confined therein, all process, orders, rules, commitments, and all other papers and documents, in the custody of the said G. H. C., as former Sheriff, as aforesaid, authorizing or relating to the confinement of such prisoners, and each and every of them: and in those cases where any such process shall have been returned, a statement in writing of the contents thereof, and when returned; all writs, summonses, and complaints, to be served, and all mesne process, and all precepts and other documents for summoning of a grand or petit jury, now in the hands of the said G. H. C., Esq., and which have not yet been fully executed by him; all executions, attachments, and final process, now in the hands of the said G. H. C., except such as he has executed, or has begun to execute, by the collection of money thereon, or by a levy on property, in pursuance thereof. The delivery is made under and in pursuance of the Revised Statutes in that behalf enacted; and the said G. H. C. doth also herein and hereby recite and certify the property, process, documents and prisoners, delivered, specifying herein the process, or other authority, by which each of those prisoners was committed and is detained, and whether the same be returned or delivered to the said A. P., the said present Sheriff, (who hath on the duplicate hereof, acknowledged in writing, the receipt of such property, process, documents and prisoners, herein specified;) that is to say:

1. The property herewith delivered is as follows: [*under each head give the particulars and details, dates, names of parties, description of process, courts, accounts, &c.*]

2. The process herewith delivered is as follows:

3. The documents herewith delivered are as follows:

4. The prisoners herewith delivered are as follows: [*name them, with the dates of commitment, offences, &c.*]

In witness whereof, as well the said former, as the said present Sheriff, have hereunto interchangeably set their hands and seals, the day and year first above written.[1]

Sealed and delivered ⎱   G. H. C. [L. S.]
 in presence of ⎰   A. P. [L. S.]
   C. D
   E. F

---

§. 142. *Assignment of a Debt, or Wages.*

Know all men by these presents: That I, A. B., of, &c., for and in consideration of the sum of   dollars, to me paid, by C. D., of, &c., the receipt whereof is hereby acknowledged, have sold, and by these presents do sell, assign, transfer and set over, unto the said

---

[1] The receipt endorsed on the duplicate, may be as follows: "I hereby acknowledge that I have received of G. H. C., late Sheriff, of, &c., the property, process, documents and prisoners, specified in the within instrument. Dated, &c.

 A. P., Sheriff of the county of "
 See, 2 R. S. (3d ed.) 534, § 87

C. D., a certain debt due me from E. F., amounting to the sum of
        dollars, for goods sold and delivered, [*or,* work, labor and
services,] with full power to sue for, collect and discharge, or sell and
assign the same, in my name, but at his own costs and charges:
And I do hereby covenant, that the said sum of   dollars, is
justly due as aforesaid, and that I have not done, and will not do,
any act to hinder, or prevent, the collection of the same by the
said C. D.

In witness, &c., [*as in* § 126.]

---

§ 143. *Assignment of Policy of Insurance.*

Know all men by these presents: That I, A. B., of, &c., in the
annexed policy named, for and in consideration of the sum of one
dollar, to me in hand paid by C. D., of, &c., the receipt whereof is
hereby acknowledged, have sold, assigned, transferred and set over,
and by these presents do sell, assign, transfer and set over, unto
the said C. D., the annexed policy of Insurance, and all sum and
sums of money, interest, benefit and advantage, whatsoever, now
due, or hereafter to arise, or to be had or made, by virtue thereof;
to have and to hold the same unto the said C. D. and his assigns,
forever.*

In witness, &c., [*as in* § 126.]

The above assignment is approved.
               M. R., President [*or,* Secretary]
               of the   Insurance Company.

---

§. 144. *Assignment of Policy, as Security.*

Know all men, &c., [*as in* § 143 *to the* *, *and then add:*] upon
the condition, however, that if a certain promissory note, for the sum
of   dollars, bearing date the   day of   , given by
the said A. B., to the said C. D., is well and truly paid, according
to the terms thereof, then this assignment is to be void.

In witness, &c., [*as in* § 126; *adding the approval in* § 143,
if necessary.]

CHAPTER VI.

AUCTIONS.

PRACTICAL REMARKS.

1. Any citizen of the State of New York may become an auctioneer, and may legally transact the business, and perform the duties of an auctioneer, in the county in which he resides, on executing, and depositing with the Comptroller, within ten days after such execution, an approved bond, with two sufficient freeholders as his sureties, in the penalty of ten thousand dollars; conditioned for the faithful performance of the duties of his office, and for the payment of the duties imposed by law, and that shall accrue on all sales made by him; and that the bond shall be forfeited, in case the obligor shall not render a true and accurate account, semi-annually, of all goods sold, or struck off, by him. Such bond, if executed by an auctioneer residing in a city, must be taken and approved of by the Mayor or Recorder; in other cases, by the County Judge of the county in which the auctioneer resides. The bond must be renewed annually, on or before the first day of January. In the city of New York, within ten days after the execution of the bond, a copy thereof, and of the certificate of approval, certified by the officer taking the same, must be filed with the Clerk of the city and county, under a penalty of one hundred dollars.[1]

2. In case of the inability of an auctioneer to attend to his duties, by sickness, by his duty as a fireman, by reason of military orders, or by his necessary attendance in a court of justice, or on account of temporary absence, he may employ a copartner, or clerk, to act in his name; such copartner, or clerk, having previously taken an oath, to be filed with the Clerk of the county, fully and faithfully to perform the duties incumbent on him by the provisions of Title 1, of Chapter 17, of Part I., of the Revised Statutes; which oath must also state the connection between him and the auctioneer.[2]

---

[1] 1 R. S. (3d ed.) 646, 647, §§ 11–18; Laws of 938, chap. 52; Laws of 1846, chap. 62.

[2] 1 R. S. (3d ed.) 646, § 8; Laws of 1835, chap. 62.

3. Auctioneers are required to make out in writing a semi-annual account, on the first Monday of July and January, in every year, in which account must be stated—the sums for which any goods or effects have been sold by him; the days on which such sales were made, and the amount of each day's sale, designating those made by himself, or in his presence, and those made in his absence, by a partner or clerk, and specifying the causes of such absence; the amount of all private sales made on commission, and the days on which they were made; the amount of duties chargeable according to law; and the amount of all goods struck off but not actually sold. Such account must be verified by the oath of the auctioneer, before the Mayor or Recorder of a city, or the County Judge of the county, and the account exhibited to such officer, within twenty days after the day on which it is dated. If any partner, or clerk, or other person connected in business with such auctioneer, shall have made any sales contained in said account, the person making such sale must also take and subscribe an oath, to be endorsed on the account, that he believes the same to be just and true in every particular; and must also set his name, or initials, opposite each sale made by him.'

4. Every auctioneer, within ten days after exhibiting his account, must pay for the use of the State, the duties accruing on the sales mentioned therein, as follows: on all wines and ardent spirits, foreign or domestic, one dollar on every hundred dollars; on all goods, wares, merchandise and effects, imported from any place beyond the Cape of Good Hope, fifty cents; and on all other goods, wares, merchandise and effects, which are the production of any foreign country, seventy-five cents. The duties are to be calculated on the sums for which the goods are struck off, and are to be paid by the person making the sale. Ships and vessels, utensils of husbandry, horses, neat cattle, hogs and sheep, articles of the growth, produce, or manufacture of the United States, except distilled spirits, are exempt from auction duties. Goods and chattels, otherwise liable to such duties, are exempt from the same, if they belong to the United States, or this State; if sold under any judgment or decree of any court of law or equity, or under any seizure by a public officer, on account of any forfeiture or penalty; if they belong to the estate of a deceased person, and are sold by an executor or administrator, or other person duly authorized; if they be the effects of a bankrupt or insolvent, and be sold by his assignees; or if they be goods damaged at sea, and are sold within twenty days after being landed, for the benefit of the owners or insurers. But in order to entitle damaged goods, or importations, to such exemption, a certificate of the board of Port Wardens of the port of New York, stating that the goods had been examined by one of the board at a proper

---

1 1 R. S. (3d ed.) 649, 650, §§ 31–35; Laws of 1835, chap. 62; Laws of 1838, chap. 62, Laws of 1846, chap. 62.

time, and that they were damaged on the voyage, so as to be entitled to exemption, and sold as damaged goods; and also a statement, on oath, of the President, or Secretary, of the Marine Insurance Company in the city or county of New York, in which the goods were insured, where insurance has been made, stating the fact of the insurance and the amount insured, must be publicly exhibited at the sale, by the auctioneer, on the demand of any Port Warden, or any person interested in the said goods, or the sale thereof.[1]

5. No auctioneer can demand, or receive, a higher compensation for his services, than a commission of two and a half per cent. on the amount of any sales made by him, unless in pursuance of a previous agreement in writing.[2]

6. Where a false return of the amount of goods sold is made by an auctioneer, he and his sureties are liable to be prosecuted by the Comptroller, to recover the duties unlawfully withheld.[3]

7. In the city of New York, public notice must be given of all auction sales, in one or more public newspapers printed in such city; and if the auctioneer is connected with any other person or firm, his name must precede, separately, the name of such person, or the title of the firm.[4]

8. All goods, wares, and merchandise, and every species of property, except ships, vessels, real or leasehold estate, exposed for sale at auction in the city of New York, and struck off by the auctioneer, to the previous owner or owners, or to any person or persons bidding in his or their behalf, or to any fictitious person or persons, or in any other manner than as an actual sale and purchase, are subject, each and every time they are so struck off, to duties, at the rate of five dollars on every hundred dollars. Any person offending against this provision is liable to a fine, not exceeding one hundred dollars, or to imprisonment not exceeding one month, or to both fine and imprisonment. The semi-annual report of the auctioneer must contain a statement of all merchandise bought in by, or on account of, the owners, the time of sale, and the amount thereof.[5]

---

[1] 1 R. S. (3d ed.) 644, 645, §§ 1, 3, 4, 5; Laws of 1835, chap. 62; Laws of 1843, chap. 85; Laws of 1846, chap. 62.
[2] 1 R. S. (3d ed.) 648, § 27.
[3] Laws of 1849, chap. 399.
[4] 1 R. S. (3d ed.) 648, § 25; Laws of 1835 chap. 62.
[5] Laws of 1847, chap. 242.

FORMS.

§ 145. *Auctioneer's Bond.*

Know all men by these presents: That we, A. B., C. D., and E. F., of, &c., are held and firmly bound unto the people of the State of New York, in the penal sum of ten thousand dollars, to be paid to the said people; for which payment, well and truly to be made, we bind ourselves, our heirs, executors, and administrators, jointly and severally, firmly by these presents. Sealed with our seals. Dated the   day of   , A. D. 18   .

The condition of this obligation is such, that if the above bounden A. B. shall well and faithfully perform the duties of an auctioneer, in and for the city [*or*, county] of   , and pay, or cause to be paid, the duties that are, or shall be, imposed by law, and that shall accrue on all sales made by him, or under his direction, as such auctioneer; and shall render a true and accurate account semi-annually, of all goods sold or struck off by him, then the above obligation shall be void; else to remain in full force and virtue.

Signed and sealed, in the   }   A. B. [L. s.]
presence of   C. D. [L. s.]
G. H.   E. F. [L. s.]

---

§ 146. *Certificate of Officer Taking and Approving the Bond.*

State of New York, } ss:
County, }

On this   day of   , 18   , personally appeared before me, A. B., C. D., and E. F., known to me to be the persons described in, and who executed the foregoing bond, and they acknowledged that they executed the same: and I hereby certify that I approve of the said bond, as sufficient for the purposes therein mentioned.

G. H., Mayor of the city of   ,
[*or*, County Judge of   county.]

---

§ 147. *Certificate to Copy.*

State of New York, } ss:
City and County of New York, }

I do hereby certify, that the within [*or*, annexed] is a true copy of a bond taken and approved by me, according to the statute, and of the certificate endorsed thereupon at the time of such taking and approval. Dated the   day of   , 18   .

G. H., Mayor of said city and county.

§ 148. *Oath of Copartner, or Clerk.*

I, S. T., do solemnly and sincerely swear, [*or*, affirm,] that I am the copartner [*or*, clerk] of A. B., an auctioneer duly authorized to act as such, in and for the city [*or*, county] of   ;* and that I will fully and faithfully perform the duties incumbent on me by the provisions of Title 1 of Chapter 17 of Part I. of the Revised Statutes of the State of New York.

Taken and subscribed before me, }   S. T
this   day of   , 18 . }
G. H., Mayor, &c.

§ 149. *Oath of Auctioneer on Exhibiting his Account.*

I, A. B., do solemnly and sincerely swear, [*or*, affirm,] that the account now exhibited by me, and to which I have subscribed my name, contains a just and true account of all the goods, wares, merchandise and effects, sold or struck off, or struck off and not actually sold, or bought in by me, at public sale, or sold by me at private sale on commission, whether subject to duty or not, or sold, struck off, or bought in, as aforesaid, by others in my name, or under my direction, or for my benefit, within the time mentioned in the within account; and of the days upon which the same were respectively sold; and that I have attended, personally, such of the said public sales as are not stated in the said account to have been made without my attendance; and that the causes therein mentioned of my absence from such sales as I did not attend, are truly stated; that I have examined the entries of all the sales mentioned in said account, in the book kept by me for that purpose, and fully believe this account to be in all respects correct; and further, that I have, during the time therein mentioned, conformed, in all things, to the true intent and meaning of the laws regulating sales by auctioneers, according to the best of my knowledge, information and belief.   A. B.

Taken, &c., [*as in* § 148.]

§ 150. *Oath of Copartner or Clerk, to be Endorsed on the Account.*

I, S. T., do solemnly and sincerely swear, &c., [*as in* § 148 *to the* *, *and then add:*] that I believe the account of sales within rendered by the said A. B., to be just and true in every particular; that the sales therein mentioned, opposite to which my name is set, [*or*, my initials are set,] are all the sales liable to auction duties, public or private, made by me within the time mentioned in said account; and that the account of such sales so therein stated, is just and true; that such sales were made by me in the absence of said A. B., who was unable to attend, from the causes specified 'n his account; and that in all acts performed by me, in behalf of such auctioneer, during the time aforesaid, I have endeavored to conform to the true intent and meaning of the laws regulating sales by auctioneers.

Taken, &c., [*as in* § 148.]

---

§ 151. *Certificate of Board of Port Wardens.*

State of New York, ss:

We, the undersigned, composing the Board of Port Wardens of the Port of New York, do hereby certify, that the goods mentioned and described in the annexed invoice, part of the cargo of the brig Mary Ann, on her voyage from   to   , which terminated on the   day of   , 18   , were duly examined by A. B., one of the undersigned, at a suitable and proper time; to wit: on the   day of   , 18 ; and that the said goods were damaged on the voyage aforesaid, so as to be entitled to exemption from auction duties, and to be sold as damaged goods, according to the provisions of the statute in such case made and provided.

Given under our hands, at the Port of New York, this   day of   , 18 .

A. B.,
C. D., } Port Wardens.
&c., &c.,

---

§ 152. *Affidavit of President, or Secretary, of Insurance Company.*

State of New York,   } ss:
City and County of New York, }

G. B., being duly sworn, says: That he is the President [or, Secretary] of the   Insurance Company in said city and county; and that the goods mentioned and described in the annexed invoice, and referred to in the certificate of the Board of Port Wardens thereunto attached, were insured in the said Company, by L. M., the owner [or, consignee] thereof, for the sum of   dollars; and further says not.

Sworn to, before me, this   } G. B.
day of   , 18 .}

G. H., Commissioner of Deeds.

CHAPTER VII.

BANKS AND CORPORATIONS.

PRACTICAL REMARKS.

1. The general laws of this State, in relation to turnpike and moneyed corporations,—their powers, privileges, liabilities, etc.—may be found, in detail, in Chapter 18 of Part I. of the Revised Statutes, (*Volume I., p.* 710, *et seq., 3d ed.*)

2. The duties and liabilities of banks, and the authority of directors to give discretionary powers to officers, in making loans and discounts, are reviewed at length, in the case of *The Bank Commissioners, vs. the Buffalo Banks,* (6 *Paige,* 499.)

3. Chapter 437 of the Laws of 1849, requires every company or association, including every individual doing business alone, incorporated or organized, or doing business under any law of this state, to publish annually, on or before the first of September, for six successive weeks, in one public newspaper, printed in the county in which the company or association may be located, a true and accurate statement, verified by the oath of the cashier, treasurer, or presiding officer, of all deposits, dividends, and interest, unclaimed for two years then next preceding.

4. For other special provisions in relation to banking corporations, see Laws of 1837, chap. 20; Id. chap. 235; Laws of 1839, chap. 355; Laws of 1840, chap. 18; Id., chap. 202; Laws of 1842, chap. 247; Laws of 1843, chap. 218; Laws of 1845, chap. 114; Laws of 1847, chap. 160; Id., chap. 419; Laws of 1848, chap. 344.

5. No special charter can be granted for banking purposes; but corporations, or associations, may be formed for such purposes under general laws. No law can be passed, sanctioning the suspension of specie payments by any person, association, or corporation, issuing bank notes of any description; and in case of the insolvency of any bank, or banking association, the billholders will be entitled to preference in payment over all other creditors.[1]

---

[1] Amended Constitution of New York, Art. viii., §§ 4, 5, 8.

6. After the first day of January 1850, the stockholders in every corporation, or association for banking purposes, issuing bank notes, or paper credits, to circulate as money, will be individually liable, to the amount of their respective shares of stock, for all debts and liabilities contracted subsequent to that day.[1]

7. The General Banking Law is contained in chap. 260, Laws of 1838; amended in chap. 363, Laws of 1840; chap. 46, Laws of 1841; chap. 160, Laws of 1847; Id., chap. 419; and chap. 340, Laws of 1848. In the volume of Session Laws for 1841, at page 351, the original law may be found, as amended by subsequent enactments, together with other statutes affecting associations formed under it. Associations formed under this law are liable to taxation.[2]

8. The provisions of law applicable to religious incorporations, are contained in volume III of the Revised Statutes, (3d ed.,) p. 244, et seq. The treasurer of every religious corporation singly, or the trustees or persons entrusted with the care and management of the temporalities of a church, congregation, or religious society, already incorporated, in the cities of New York, Albany, or Schenectady, or a majority of them, are required by the act of 1813, (section 10,) to exhibit triennially to one of the Justices of the Supreme Court, or a Judge of the Court of Common Pleas, or County Judge of the county in which the church, congregation, or society is situated, an account and inventory of all the corporate estate, and of the annual revenue arising therefrom; and if this duty be neglected for the space of six years, and if the account and inventory are not then exhibited, and the certificate of the officer, to whom the same is presented, endorsed thereupon, that the real and personal estate of the corporation does not, or has not, for the preceding six years, exceeded the sum which it is entitled by law to receive, the trustees, or persons entrusted as aforesaid, cease to be a body corporate.

9. County Courts have the power to permit the mortgage or sale of the real property of a religious corporation, situated within the county, on the application of such corporation, and to authorize the appropriation of the proceeds thereof.[3]

10. The general law providing for the incorporation of bridge companies, may be found at chap. 259, Laws of 1848.

11. The act to authorize the formation of corporations for manufacturing, mining, mechanical or chemical purposes, is contained in the Session Laws of 1848, chap. 40.

12. Chap. 319, Laws of 1848, authorizes the incorporation of benevolent, charitable, scientific and missionary societies.

13. Under the new Constitution of this State, no corporation ex-

---

1 Amended Constitution of New York, Art. viii., § 7.
2 22 Wendell, 9; 23 Id., 103; 1 Hill, 616;
2 Id., 241; 3 Id., 389; 4 Id., 442; 7 Id., 504; 1 Denio, 9; 2 Id., 380.
3 Laws of 1849, (Code of Practice,) chap. 438, § 30, sub. 9.

cept for municipal purposes, can be created by special act, where the objects of the corporation can be attained under a general law. Hereafter corporations may sue or be sued, like natural persons.[1]

14. After the dissolution of a corporation, the stock cannot be transferred so as to pass the title.[2]

15. Certificates of the incorporation of religious societies may be proved, or acknowledged, before any officer authorized to take acknowledgments, or proofs of conveyances of real estate.[3]

16. Whenever any church, congregation, or religious society, shall omit to choose officers, the old officers may hold over until others are chosen, provided an election, to supply such omission, be held within one year after its occurrence.[4]

17. A "call" from a Presbyterian congregation, drawn in the manner prescribed by the discipline of that church, and signed by three elders and a trustee, does not bind them to pay the salary, but is the act of the congregation.[5]

18. The seal of a corporation may be affixed, or impressed, directly on paper, without the use of wax or a wafer.[6]

19. It is not necessary that the proceedings of a corporation, at a corporate meeting, should be authenticated by seal.[7]

FORMS.

§ 153. *Transfer of Stock in a Bank, Company, or Corporation.*

Know all men by these presents: That I, A. B., of, &c., for value received, have bargained, sold, assigned and transferred, and by these presents do bargain, sell, assign and transfer, unto C. D., of, &c., twenty shares of capital stock, standing in my name, on the books of the   Bank: [*or,*   Company, *as the case may be:*] and I do hereby constitute and appoint the said C. D., my true and lawful attorney, irrevocable, in my name or otherwise, but to his own use and benefit, and at his own costs and charges, to take all lawful ways and means for the recovery and enjoyment thereof.

In witness whereof, I have hereunto set my hand and seal, the   day of   , A. D., 18

Sealed and delivered }
  in the presence of }
    G. H.

A. B. [L s.]

---

[1] Amended Constitution of New York, Art. viii., §§ 1–3.
[2] 2 Denio, 574.
[3] Laws of 1844. chap. 158, §§ 1, 2.
[4] Laws of 1844, chap. 158, § 3.
[5] 6 Hill, 630.
[6] Laws of 1848, chap. 197.
[7] 1 Barbour's S. C. Rep., 584.

§ 154. *Power to Transfer.*

Know all men by these presents: That I, A. B., of, &c., ao hereby constitute and appoint E. F., of, &c., my true and lawful attorney, for me, and in my name and behalf, to sell, assign and transfer to C. D., of, &c., the whole, or any part of, one hundred shares of capital stock, standing in my name, on the books of the Bank, [or, Company,] and for that purpose to make and execute all necessary acts of assignment and transfer.

In witness, &c., [*as in* § 153.]

---

§ 155. *Proxy.*

Know all men by these presents: That I, A. B., of, &c., do hereby constitute and appoint E. F., of, &c., my attorney and agent, for me, and in my name, place and stead, to vote as my proxy, at any election of directors of the   Bank, [or, Company,] according to the number of votes I should be entitled to vote, if then personally present.

In witness, &c., [*as in* § 153.]

---

§ 156. *Affidavit of Stockholder, to be made before any Officer authorized to administer Oaths, and attached to the Proxy.*

I, A. B., do solemnly and sincerely swear, [*or*, affirm,] that the shares on which my attorney and agent, in the above proxy, is authorized to vote, do not belong, and are not hypothecated to, the [*name the corporation for which the election is to be held;*] and that they are not hypothecated, or pledged to, any other corporation, or person, whatever; that such shares have not been transferred to me, for the purpose of enabling me to vote thereon at the ensuing election, and that I have not contracted to sell or transfer them, upon any condition, agreement, or understanding, in relation to my manner of voting at the said election.

Sworn to, this   day of   , }   A. B.
  18   , before me,   }
      G. H. Commissioner of Deeds, &c.

---

§ 157. *Inspector's Oath.*

I do solemnly swear [*or*, affirm] that I will execute the duties of an Inspector of the election now to be held, with strict impartiality and according to the best of my ability.

Taken and subscribed before me, }   L. M.
  this   day of   , 18   , }
      G. H., Justice of the Peace.

§ 158. *Oath of Stockholder when Challenged, to be administered by an Inspector.*

You do swear, [*or,* affirm,] that the shares on which you now offer to vote, do not belong, and are not hypothecated to, the [*name the corporation for which the election is held;*] and that they are not hypothecated, or pledged to, any other corporation, or person, whatever; that such shares have not been transferred to you, for the purpose of enabling you to vote thereon, at this election; and that you have not contracted to sell or transfer them, upon any condition, agreement, or understanding, in relation to the manner of voting at this election.

---

§ 159. *Oath of Proxy when Challenged, to be administered as in § 158.*

You do swear, [*or,* affirm,] that the facts stated in the affidavit annexed to the proxy, upon which you now offer to vote, are true, according to your belief; and that you have made no contract or agreement, whatever, for the purchase or transfer of the shares, or any portion of the shares, mentioned in such proxy.

---

§ 160. *Affidavit of President, or Cashier, to Statement of unclaimed Dividends or Deposits.*

State of New York, } ss:
      County, }

J. N. S., of said county, being duly sworn, deposes and says, that he is the cashier [*or,* president] of the   Bank, and that the above [*or,* annexed] statement of dividends [*or,* deposits] remaining unclaimed in the said bank for the space of two years next preceding the first day of September instant, is in all respects just and true, according to the best of the knowledge and belief of this deponent.   J. N. S.

Sworn to, &c., [*as in* § 156.]

---

§ 161. *Power to Receive Dividend.*

Know all men by these presents: That I, A. B., of, &c., do authorize, constitute, and appoint, E. F., of, &c., my attorney, to receive from the   Bank, [*or,* company,] the dividend now due on all stock standing in my name on the books of the said bank, [*or,* company,] and receipt for the same; hereby ratifying and confirming all that may lawfully be done in the premises, by virtue hereof.

Witness my hand and seal, this   day of   , 18   .

Signed, sealed, and delivered, }
    in presence of   }
      G. H.   A. B. [L. s.]

§ 162. *Certificate of Association Formed under the General Banking Law.*

State of New York, ⎱ ss:
    County, ⎰

We, whose names are hereunto annexed, do hereby certify: That we have associated together, for the purpose of establishing an office of discount, deposit, and circulation; that the name assumed to distinguish such association, and to be used in its dealings, is "The   ;" that the operations of discount and deposit, of such association, are to be carried on at the village of   , in the said county; that the amount of the capital stock of the same is two hundred thousand dollars, and is divided into two thousand shares; and that the following are the names and places of residence of the shareholders, and the number of shares held by each of them, respectively: A. B., of   , one hundred shares, C. D., of   , one hundred shares; E. F., of   , one hundred shares; &c. &c.:

And we do further certify, that such association will commence its operations on the first day of May next, and that it will terminate on the first day of May, in the year 18 .

Witness our hands and seals, this   day of   18 .

Signed and sealed in ⎱
   the presence of ⎰
      S. T.

A. B [L. s.]
C. D. [L. s.]
E. F. [L. s.]
&c., &c.

---

§ 163. *Proof of the Execution of the foregoing Certificate.*

   County ss:

On this   day of   , 18 , personally appeared before me S. T., to me known, who being by me duly sworn, did depose and say: That he resided in the town of   , in said county; that he was acquainted with A. B., C. D., E. F., &c., &c., and knew them to be the persons who executed the above certificate; that he was present and saw them, and each of them, sign, seal, and execute the same, and that they, each and every of them, acknowledged the execution thereof to him: whereupon he became the subscribing witness thereto.

7   G. H., Justice of the Peace.

§ 164. *Certificate of the Formation of a Manufacturing Corporation, to be Made, Signed, and Acknowledged, before any Officer competent to take the Acknowledgment of Deeds.*[1]

State of New York, }
County, } ss:

We, whose names are hereunto annexed, do hereby certify, that we have associated together as a manufacturing corporation, to continue in existence till the   day of   , 18   , [*not to exceed fifty years,*] for the purpose of carrying on, and conducting, the manufacture of glass, [*or, cotton and linen goods, &c., &c.:*] that the corporate name of the said company is "The   ;" that the amount of the capital stock thereof is one hundred thousand dollars, and is divided into one thousand shares; that the number of trustees of the said company is nine; and that the following are the names of the trustees who will manage its concerns for the first year, to wit: A. B., C. D., E. F., &c., &c. And we do further certify, that the manufacturing operations of the said company will be carried on at the city [*or, town*] of   , in the county of   , aforesaid. Dated this   day of   , 18   .

Signed and acknowledged before   A. B.
me, by the said A. B., C. D.,   C. D.
E. F., &c., &c., each and every   E. F.
of them, this   day of   ,   &c., &c.
18   .

     G. H., County Judge of   county.

§ 165. *Certificate of Incorporation of an Episcopal Church.*

To all whom these presents may concern: We, whose names and seals are affixed to this instrument, do hereby certify, that on the   day of   , in the year 18   , the male persons of full age worshiping in the school house of school district number   , in the town of   , in the county of   , and State of New York, [*or, in their house of public worship, in the town of   , in the county of   , called St John's Church; or, as the fact may be,*] in which congregation divine worship is celebrated, according to the rites of the Protestant Episcopal Church in the State of New York, and which is not already incorporated, met at their place of worship, aforesaid, for the purpose of incorporating themselves as a religious society, under the acts of the Legislature of the State of New York, and in pursuance of notice duly given to the said congregation, in the time of morning service, on two Sundays previous to such meeting, that the male persons of full age belonging to said congregation, would meet at the time and place aforesaid, for the purpose of incorporating themselves, and of electing two Church

---

[1] The original must be filed in the Clerk's office of the county in which the business is to | be carried on, and a duplicate in the office of the Secretary of State.

Wardens and eight Vestrymen: And we further certify, that the Reverend A. B., being Rector of said Church, presided at the said meeting, [or, *if there be no Rector, say:* there being no Rector of the said congregation, or church, the undersigned, L. M., was, by a majority of the said persons so met, called to the chair, and presided at the said meeting:] And we further certify, that at the said meeting, C. D. and E. F. were duly elected Church Wardens of the said congregation and church, and O. P., S. T., &c., [*name eight persons,*] were duly elected Vestrymen; that   Tuesday in Easter Week, [*or, as the case may be,*] was, by the said meeting, fixed on as the day on which the said offices of Church Wardens and Vestrymen should annually thereafter cease, and their successors in office be chosen; and that the said meeting determined and declared that the said church and congregation should be known in the law by the name of "The Rector, Church Wardens, and Vestrymen of St John's Church, in the town of   , in the county of   ."

In testimony whereof, we, the said A. B., Rector, [or, L. M.,] who presided at the said election of Wardens and Vestrymen, and R. F. and S. T., who were present and witnessed the proceedings aforesaid, have hereunto subscribed our names, and affixed our seals, this   day of   , in the year of our Lord one thousand eight hundred and   .[1]

Signed and sealed }	A. B., Rector. [L. S.]
in presence of }	R. F. [L. S.]
G. H.	S. T. [L. S.]
M. N.	

---

§ 166. *Certificate of Incorporation of other Religious Societies.*

State of New York, }
          County, } ss:

We, the undersigned, two of the elders, [*or,* two of the members,] of the church [*or,* congregation; *or,* religious society] hereafter mentioned, do hereby certify, that on the   day of   instant, the male persons of full age, belonging to a church [*or,* congregation; *or,* religious society] in which divine worship is celebrated, according to the rites of the   church, and not already incorporated, met at the place of public worship heretofore occupied by the said church, [*or, as aforesaid,*] in the town of   , in said county, for the purpose of incorporating themselves, and did then and there elect, by plurality of voices, A. B., C. D., and E. F., [*not less than three, nor more than nine,*] as trustees of the said church, [*or, as aforesaid;*] and the said persons did then and there also determine by the like plurality of voices, that the said trustees and

---

[1] The certificate must be acknowledged, or proved, before a Justice of the Supreme Court, or Judge of the county in which the place of worship is situated. For the forms, see chapter I., and § 163, *ante.*

their successors should forever hereafter be called and known by the name, or title, of " The Trustees of the   ."

Witness our hands and seals, this   day of   , 18   [1]

Signed and sealed in the }   L. M. [L. s.]
        presence of   }   G. H. [L. s.]
        S. T.   }

---

§ 167. *Triennial Report of a Religious Corporation.*

To the Hon. J. W. E., one of the Judges of the Supreme Court of the State of New York:

The undersigned, the Rector, Church Wardens, and Vestrymen of St. Mark's Church, [*or*, the Trustees of the First Baptist Society of   ,] a religious corporation, situate in the city of   , in the State of New York, respectfully report, that the following is a faithful, true, and correct account and inventory of all the estate, both real and personal, belonging to said church [*or*, congregation; *or*, society,] at the time of the exhibition of this report, to wit:

One church edifice, and lot on which the same is situate, known by the street numbers 67 and 69, on   street, in said city of   , and valued at   dollars.

One parsonage and lot, known as No. 50   street in said city of   , and valued at   dollars.

[*Insert here all the parcels and items of the real and personal estate.*]

And the undersigned further report that the following is a just and correct account of the annual revenue arising from the real and personal estate aforesaid, from the   day of   , 1847, to the   day of   , 1850, to wit: [*Insert here the revenue for each year separately.*]

Dated at   , the   day of   , 1850.
                        C. S. R., Rector.
                        R. F., }
                        J. R., } Church Wardens.
                        B. J., }
                        S. T., } Vestrymen.
                        &c. &c. }

State of New York,   }
City and County of New York, } ss:

C. S. R., R. F., &c., &c., being duly sworn, depose and say, and each for himself deposeth and saith, that he has read [*or*, heard read] the foregoing report by him signed, and that the same is in all respects faithful, just and true, to the best of his knowledge and belief.

Sworn [*or*, affirmed] to, this   day }   C. S. R.,
of   , 18, before me,   }   &c. &c.
                J. W. E., Judge of the Supreme Court.

---

[1] For form of a certificate of acknowledgment, see chapter I., end § 163, *ante*

§ 168. *Application for permission to Mortgage or Sell the Real Estate of a Religious Corporation.*

To the County Court of   County:

The undersigned, trustees of the   Society of the town of   , in said county, [*or, as the style or name of the corporation may be,*] respectfully represent, that [*here state concisely the reasons for making the application, and the manner in which the proceeds are intended to be appropriated.*]

Wherefore, the undersigned request that an order may be made and entered by this honorable court, authorizing them to mortgage [*or,* sell] the property aforesaid, upon the terms and in the manner aforesaid, and that the proceeds of such mortgage [*or,* sale] may be appropriated as above specified.

Dated at   , the   day of   , 1850.

A. B.,
C. D.,   } Trustees of the   Society
&c. &c. } of the town of   .

State of New York, } ss:
     County,   }

A. B., C. D., &c., &c., being duly sworn, depose and say, and each for himself deposeth and saith, that he has read [*or,* heard read] the foregoing application by him signed, and that the facts and circumstances therein stated and set forth are just and true, to the best of his knowledge, information and belief.

Sworn [*or,* affirmed] to, this   day }   A. B.
of   1850, before me,   }   C. D.
     J. P. H., County Judge.   &c. &c.

---

§ 169. *Order of the County Court.*

State of New York, } ss:
     County,   }

At a County Court, held at   , in and for said county, on the   day of   , 18   : Present, S. P., Esq., County Judge.

Application having been made by the trustees of the   Society of the town of   , in said county, in due form of law, for permission to mortgage [*or,* sell] all that [*describe the property*] belonging to the said Society, and to apply the proceeds to the [*as in the application;*] on motion of Mr. A. B., of counsel for the applicants, it is hereby ordered, that the said trustees of the   Society of the town of   , be authorized to mortgage [*or,* sell] the real estate aforesaid, and to appropriate the proceeds to the [*as ordered by the Court.*]

L. M., County Clerk.

CHAPTER VIII.

BILLS OF EXCHANGE AND PROMISSORY NOTES.

PRACTICAL REMARKS.

1. A bill of exchange is a written order, or request, made by one person to another, for the payment of money. It should not be drawn payable out of a particular fund, but must be for money absolutely. Bank checks are bills of exchange; so also an endorsement, payable to order, on a note or bond, is a bill of exchange.[1]

2. A written order, or request, addressed by one person to another, for the payment of a specified sum, to a third person, absolutely, is a bill of exchange, and the acceptance of it must be in writing.[2]

3. Bills of exchange must be presented for acceptance, within a reasonable time. If the drawee destroy a bill presented for acceptance, or refuse to return it for twenty-four hours, he will be deemed to have accepted it.[3]

4. Damages are allowed, and required to be paid, upon the usual protest for non-payment, or non-acceptance, of bills of exchange, drawn or negotiated in this State, at and after the following rates: If the bill be drawn upon any person, or persons, in either of the States of Maine, New Hampshire, Vermont, Massachusetts, Rhode Island, Connecticut, New Jersey, Pennsylvania, Ohio, Delaware, Maryland, or Virginia, or in the District of Columbia, three dollars per hundred dollars, upon the principal sum of the bill; if upon any person, or persons, in either of the States of North Carolina, South Carolina, Georgia, Kentucky, or Tennessee, five dollars per hundred; if upon any person, or persons, at any other place in the United States, (Territories included,) or on, or adjacent to, this continent, north of the equator, or in any British or other foreign possessions in the West Indies, or elsewhere in the Western Atlantic ocean, ten dollars per hundred; and if upon any person, or persons, in any port or place in Europe, ten dollars per hundred. Such damages will be in lieu of interest, charges of protest, and all other charges incurred

---

[1] 9 Johnson, 259; 6 Cowen, 484; 7 Id., 174; 1 Wendell, 522.
[2] 7 Hill 577
[3] 2 R. S. (3d ed.) 63, § 11; 6 Cowen, 484; 7 Id., 705.

previous to, and at the time of giving notice of non-payment or non-acceptance; but the holder will be entitled to interest on the aggregate amount of the principal sum and damages, from the time of the protest for non-acceptance or non-payment. There is no reference to the rate of exchange, in ascertaining such damages, when the bill is payable in the money of the United States; otherwise, if payable in the money of account, or currency, of any foreign country.[1]

5. A negotiable bill of exchange, or promissory note, must be for a fixed sum payable in money; and the time fixed for the payment must be such as will certainly come, though it may depend on a contingency.[2]

6. No precise form of words is necessary to constitute a valid promissory note. A promise to account for a certain sum, or an acknowledgment of indebtedness for value received, is sufficient. Any thing valuable is a good consideration for the promise, or acknowledgment.[3]

7. A note commencing, "I promise to pay, &c.," and signed by two parties, is joint and several; so also, where one signs a note as surety for another.[4]

8. A promissory note given by an infant, even for necessaries, is void.[4]

9. A guaranty of the collection of a promissory note, without expressing any consideration, is void; otherwise, with a guaranty of payment, if there be in fact a new and distinct consideration, though not expressed.[5]

10. A general guaranty of payment, upon a note payable to bearer, as, "I guaranty the payment of the within note," is, in law, a general endorsement of the note, and any subsequent holder may recover of the guarantor, on proof of demand and notice.[6]

11. A party may become an endorser of a bill, or note, by any mark, whether his initials, or other figure or sign, if it be substituted for his name, and he intend to be bound by it.[7]

12. The endorsement of a bill, or note, in blank, is a mere agreement to pay, on the usual conditions of demand and notice.[8]

13. If a note be made payable to the order of several persons, not copartners, it must be endorsed by each person. If an endorser wishes to free himself from all liability, the words, "without recourse," should be written before his name.

14. Where cross notes are given, each holder is a purchaser for value, and has the same rights as the payee of an ordinary note.[9]

15. Bills, or promissory notes, negotiable or otherwise, payable at a certain day; as, so long after date, after demand, or on any other

---

1 2 R. S. (3d ed.) 54, 55, §§ 18–23.
2 3 Denio, 428.
3 5 Johnson, 237; 2 Cowen 536; 10 Wendell, 675; 1 Hill, 256; 7 Id., 253; 3 Barbour's S. C. Rep., 374.
4 10 Johnson, 141; Id., 349.
5 15 Wendell, 343; 24 Id., 35; 26 Id., 425.

Barbour's S. C. Rep., 51; 6 Denio, 284; 2 Comstock 225; Id., 533; Id., 653.
6 4 Hill, 420; 6 Id., 639.
7 6 Hill, 443; 1 Denio, 471.
8 7 Hill, 416; 1 Denio, 608.
9 2 Denio, 621; 3 Id., 187.

Thanksgiving day, are to be treated and considered as Sunday, in New York, for all purposes whatsoever, as regards the presenting for payment or acceptance, and the protesting and giving notice of dishonor, of bills of exchange, bank checks, and promissory notes, made or drawn after the 7th day of April, 1849.[2]

17. Bills, or notes, payable on demand, given due, or on the face of which there is no time of payment expressed, are immediately due, without grace.[3]

18. A note payable in specific articles, "when called for," or without mentioning any time for the payment, is payable on demand, at the place where the articles are sold, or manufactured, by the maker; but demand must be made within reasonable hours.[4]

19. In order to hold an endorser liable, a demand of payment on bills, or notes, must be made on the third day of grace. If the third day falls on Sunday, or on any great holiday, demand must be made on Saturday, or the day preceding the holiday. The demand must be made at the place of business of the maker, or acceptor, within business hours, or at the place of payment, where it is specified. If the party has absconded, no demand is necessary; and where he has no place of business, it may be made at his dwelling-house. It is competent for any person, who has arrived at years of discretion, though not a Notary, to make the demand, if authorized by the holder. An endorsed note, payable on demand, must be presented within a reasonable time. In Massachusetts, sixty days has been held reasonable.[5]

20. Where a note, not payable at any particular place, is made and endorsed in New York, and both the maker and endorser reside in a foreign country, it must be duly presented to the maker, if the place of his residence be known, and notice given to the endorser, in order to charge the latter.[6]

21. A person becoming surety on a note, must be treated and charged as an endorser.[7]

22. An endorser may waive demand and notice before maturity of the bill or note endorsed, without any consideration for such waiver.[8]

23. The dating of a promissory note at a particular place does not make that the place of payment, and authorize a demand to be made there to charge the endorser; though it is presumptive evidence that the place mentioned is the residence of the maker.[9]

---

[1] 8 Cowen, 203.
[2] Laws of 1849, chap. 261.
[3] 8 Johnson, 189, Id., 374; 3 Denio, 12.
[4] 2 Denio, 145.
[5] 4 Hill, 129.
[6] 1 Barbour's S. C. Rep., 158; 1 Comstock 321.
[7] 7 Hill, 416.
[8] 1 Comstock, 186.
[9] 3 Denio, 145.

24. Where a note is assigned after maturity, the assignee takes it subject to all equities and set-offs, between the assignor and the maker.[1]

25. One who makes or endorses an accommodation note is a surety for the party accommodated, and the latter is liable to refund the costs of a suit for collection brought against such maker or endorser.[2]

26. In all cases where notice of non-acceptance, or non-payment, of a bill or note, or other negotiable instrument, may be given by mail, it will be sufficient if such notice be directed to the city, or town, where the person sought to be charged resided, at the time of making, drawing, or endorsing the same, unless at the time of such making, drawing, or endorsing, he shall specify thereon the post office to which he may require the notice to be addressed.[3]

27. A notice of protest should be sent to the post office at which the person to whom it is directed is accustomed to get his letters, where his address is not endorsed on the bill or note.[4]

28. No precise form of words is necessary to constitute a sufficient notice of protest. The identity of the note, and the fact of the demand and non-payment, must be brought home to the party sought to be charged, and the notice may be either oral or written.[5]

29 The certificate of the Notary need not state, by whom the service of notice, and deposit in the post office, was made.[6]

30. A sealed note is a specialty, and is not barred by the statute of limitations.

FORMS.

§ 170. *Bill of Exchange.*[7]

$2000.   BUFFALO, May 1, 1845.

Thirty days after sight, pay to the order of Messrs. B. M. & Co. two thousand dollars, and charge the same to account of

A. B.

To Messrs. T. R. & Co., New York.

---

[1] 11 Wendell, 404.
[2] 3 Barbour's S. C. Rep., 634.
[3] 2 R. S. (3d ed.) 55, § 24; Laws of 1835, chap 141.
[4] 4 Barbour's S. C Rep., 324.
   Comstock, 413.
[5] 7 Hill, 444.
[6] The usual form of accepting, is to write the word "Accepted," with the name of the acceptor, across the face, or on the back of the bill or draft.

§ 171. *A Set of Bills.*

No. 139. — Ex. £250 stg.   NEW YORK, May 1, 1845.

Thirty days after sight of this, my first of exchange, (second and third unpaid,) pay to Messrs. G. W. & Co., or order, two hundred and fifty pounds sterling, value received, and charge the same to account of   A. B.

To Messrs. T. W. & Co., London.

No. 139. — Ex. £250 stg.   •   NEW YORK, May 1, 1845.

Thirty days after sight of this, my second of exchange, (first and third unpaid,) pay to Messrs. G. W. & Co., or order, two hundred and fifty pounds sterling, value received, and charge the same to account of   A. B.

To Messrs. T. W. & Co., London.

No. 139. — Ex. £250 stg.   NEW YORK, May 1, 1845.

Thirty days after sight of this, my third of exchange, (first and second unpaid,) pay to Messrs. G. W. & Co., or order, two hundred and fifty pounds sterling, value received, and charge the same to account of   A. B.

To Messrs. T. W. & Co., London.

---

§ 172. *Promissory Note, Negotiable.*[1]

$100.   Thirty days after date, I promise to pay C. D., or bearer, [*or,* order,] one hundred dollars, for value received.

         A. B.

Albany, May 1, 1847.

---

§ 173. *The Same, Joint and Several.*

$200.   Ninety days from date, for value received, we, or either of us, promise to pay C. D., or bearer, [*or,* order,] two hundred dollars.   A. B.

Albany, May 1, 1847.   E. F.

---

§ 174. *Note, not Negotiable.*

$50.   Three months after date, I promise to pay C. D. fifty dollars, for value received.

         A. B.

Albany, May 1, 1847.

---

[1] Where a note is to be on interest, the words, "with interest," may be added to this and the following forms. The rule of law in regard to interest, where none is mentioned. is, that notes on time draw interest after due, and notes on demand, after the demand be made

§ 175. *Note, Payable on Demand.*

$50. On demand, I promise to pay C. D., or bearer, [or, order,] fifty dollars, for value received.

A. B.

Albany, May 1, 1847.

---

§ 176. *Note, Payable at Bank.*

$500. Sixty days after date, for value received, I promise to pay C. D., or order, five hundred dollars, at the Mechanics' and Farmers' Bank.

Albany, May 1, 1847.   A. B.

---

§ 177. *Note, Payable by Instalments.*

$500. For value received, I promise to pay C. D., or bearer, [or, order,] five hundred dollars, in the following manner: one hundred dollars in three months, one hundred dollars in six months, one hundred dollars in one year, and two hundred dollars in two years from date, with interest on the several sums, as they become due, [or, with annual interest.]

A. B.

Albany, May 1, 1847.

---

§ 178. *Note, Payable in Specific Articles.*

$50. One year after date, for value received, I promise to pay C. D., or bearer, [or, order,] fifty dollars, in second quality pine lumber, at the current price.

A. B.

Albany, May 1, 1847.

---

§ 179. *Memorandum Note for Money Lent.*

$100. Borrowed of C. D., one hundred dollars, payable on demand.

A. B.

Albany, May 1, 1847.

---

§ 180. *Note, with Surety.*

$100. One year from date, I promise to pay E. F., or bearer, [or, order,] one hundred dollars, for value received.

A. B.
C. D., Surety.

Albany, May 1, 1847

§ 181. *Due Bill, Payable in Goods.*

Due C. D., or bearer, ten dollars in goods, for value received, payable on demand.

A. B.

Albany, May 1, 1847

---

§ 182. *Order for Goods.*

Mr. A. B.: Please pay E. F., or bearer, ten dollars in merchandise, and charge the same to the account of

C. D.

Albany, May 1, 1847.

---

§ 183. *The Same, in another Form.*

Mr. A. B.: Please deliver to E. F., such goods as he may want, amount not to exceed twenty dollars, and charge the same to the account of

C. D.

Albany, May 1, 1847.

---

§ 184. *Order for Money.*

Mr. A. B.: Please pay E. F., or bearer, fifty dollars, and charge the same to the account of

Albany, May 1, 1847.   C. D

---

§ 185. *Guaranty of Payment, to be Endorsed on Note.*

Pay to the bearer, and, [*the foregoing words are necessary, only when the note is payable to order,*] for value received, I guaranty the payment of the within note.

C. D.

May 1, 1845.

---

§ 186. *Guaranty of Collection.*

For value received, I guaranty the collection of the within note

C. D.

May 1, 1845.

---

§ 187. *Protest of Bill for Non-Acceptance.*

United States of America, ⎱ ss:
  State of New York, ⎰

On the   day of   , 18   , at the request of A. B., [*insert the name of the holder, or endorser, or endorsee,*] I, J. N. S., a Notary Public, duly admitted and sworn, dwelling in the city of

Auburn, in the State aforesaid, did present the original bill of exchange, hereunto annexed, to E. F., the drawee therein named, for acceptance, who refused to accept the same: Whereupon I, the said Notary, at the request aforesaid, did protest, and by these presents do publicly and solemnly protest, as well against the drawee, [*add, and endorsers, if necessary*,] of the said bill, as against all others whom it doth or may concern, for exchange, re-exchange, and all costs, damages, and interest, already incurred, and to be hereafter incurred, for want of acceptance of the same. [*Vary as in the following form, if necessary.*]

Thus done and protested, in the city of Auburn aforesaid.

    In testimonium veritatis,

[L. S.]   J. N. S., Notary Public.

---

§ 188. *Protest of Bill, or Note, for Non-Payment.*

United States of America, } ss:
  State of New York,   }

On the   day of   , 18   , at the request of A. B., [*insert the name of the holder, endorser, endorsee, or cashier,*] I, J. N. S., a Notary Public, duly admitted and sworn, dwelling in the   of   , in the State aforesaid, did present the original bill of exchange, [*or, note,*] hereunto annexed, to E. F., the acceptor [*or, maker*] of the said bill, [*or, note,*] and demanded payment, who refused to pay the same: [*or, did present the original note [or, check,*] hereunto annexed, at the   Bank, where the same is made payable, [*or, at the place of business of E. F., the acceptor [or, maker*] of the said bill, [*or, note,*] he being absent therefrom, [*or, at the dwelling-house of E. F., &c., his place of business being closed, and he being absent from his said dwelling-house,*] and demanded payment of the same, which was refused:] [*or, did make diligent inquiry for the said E. F., and his place of business, or dwelling-house, in the said   of , where the said bill [or, note*] was made payable, [*or, purported to be drawn,*] but was unable to find the said E. F., or his place of business, or dwelling-house, in said   , in order to demand payment of the said bill [*or, note:*] Whereupon I, the said Notary Public, at the request aforesaid, did protest, and by these presents do solemnly and publicly protest, as well against the drawer and endorsers of the said bill, [*or, note; or, check,*] as against all others whom it doth or may concern, for exchange, re-exchange, and all costs, damages, and interest, already incurred, and to be hereafter incurred, for want of payment of the same.

    Thus done and protested in the   of   aforesaid.

    In testimonium veritatis,

[L. S.]   J N. S., Notary Public.

§ 189. *Notice of Protest for Non-Acceptance.*

Mr A. B.: Sir—You will take notice, that your bill for $2,00J, at thirty days from sight, dated May 1, 1847, drawn on C. D., has this day been protested for non-acceptance. Dated Auburn, May 5, 1847.

Yours, &c.   J. N. S., Notary Public.

---

§ 190. *Notice of Protest for Non-Payment.*

Mr A. B.: Sir—You will take notice, that your bill for $2,000, at thirty days from sight, dated May 1, 1847, drawn on and accepted by C. D., has this day been protested for non-payment: [*or*, that the bill of ·A. B. for $2,000, at thirty days from sight, dated May 1, 1847, endorsed by you, [*or*, by A. B., E. F., &c., &c.,] and drawn on and accepted by C. D., has, &c., *as above; or,* that the note of A. B. for $1,000, dated May 1, 1847, payable at the   Bank, sixty days after date, and endorsed by E. F. and G. H., has, &c., *as above.*] Dated   , July 3, 1847.

Yours, &c.,   J. N. S., Notary Public.

---

§ 191. *Certificate of Service of Notice.*

United States of America, ⎫
   State of New York, ⎬ ss.

I, C. H. M., a Notary Public, duly admitted and sworn, dwelling in the   of   , do hereby certify, that on the   day of   , 18   , notice of the protest of the before mentioned bill, [*or*, note; *or*, check,] was served upon C. D., the drawer of the said bill, [*or*, G. H., S. T., and L. M., the several endorsers of the said note,] personally, [*or*, by letters, respectively addressed to them at their reputed places of residence, and the post offices nearest thereto, and deposited in the post office in the   of   , aforesaid.]

In testimonium veritatis,

[L. S.]   C. H. M., Notary Public.

---

§ 192. *General Form of a Notarial Certificate.*

United States of America, ⎫
   State of New York, ⎬ ss:

By this public instrument be it known, to all whom the same doth or may in any wise concern: That I, A. B., a Public Notary in and for the State of New York, by letters patent, under the great seal of said State, duly commissioned and sworn, dwelling in the city of New York, do hereby certify, that [*state the subject matter of the certificate.*]

In testimony whereof, I have subscribed my name, and [L. s.] caused my notarial seal of office to be hereunto affixed the   day of   , A. D., 18   .

A. B., Notary Public.

CHAPTER IX.

BILLS OF SALE AND CHATTEL MORTGAGES

PRACTICAL REMARKS.

1. A bill of sale is a written contract, or agreement, transferring and assigning the ownership of personal property, or any interest in the same. If fraudulent, as against third persons, it is void.

2. Every sale made by a vendor, of goods and chattels in his possession, or under his control, and every assignment of goods and chattels, by way of mortgage or security, or upon any condition whatever, unless the same be accompanied by an immediate delivery, and be followed by an actual and continued change of possession, of the things sold, mortgaged, or assigned, is presumed to be fraudulent and void, as against the creditors of the vendor, or the creditors of the person making such assignment, or subsequent purchasers in good faith; and will be conclusive evidence of fraud, unless it shall be made to appear, on the part of the person claiming under such sale or assignment, that the same was made in good faith, and without any intent to defraud such creditors or purchasers. The term "creditors," as herein used, is to be construed so as to include all the creditors of the vendor, or assignor, at any time whilst such goods and chattels remain in his possession, or under his control.[1]

3. Continued possession in the vendor, or assignor, is not conclusive evidence of fraud, where the use of the goods and chattels sold, or assigned, or mortgaged, is necessary to such vendor, or assignor, in order to enable him to provide for himself or family, or obtain the means for the payment and satisfaction of his debts. The question of good faith in the transaction, arising from continued possession, i⸱

[1] 2 R. S. (3d ed.) 195, 196, §§ 5, 6 ; 8 Wendell, 375 ; 12 Id., 297; 15 Id., 212, 628 ; 15 Id., 620; 17 Id., 54, 492 ; 19 Id., 183, 514, 524 ; 20 | Id., 118, 507 ; 23 Id.. 653 ; 24 Id., 117 ; 25 Id., 396, 615; 26 Id., 511 ; 1 Hill, 347, 438, 467 ; 4 Id., 271 ; 6 Id., 433, 438.

one for a jury to determine; and they have the right, in their discretion, to excuse possession in the vendor, or mortgagor.[1]

4. Proof of a valuable consideration, or a true debt, is essential to show good faith; and if such proof be not made, the sase will not be given to the jury.[2]

5. Every mortgage, or conveyance intended to operate as a mortgage, of goods and chattels, which shall not be accompanied by an immediate delivery and continued change of possession of the things mortgaged, is absolutely void as against the creditors of the mortgagor, and as against subsequent purchasers and mortgagees in good faith, unless the mortgage, or a true copy thereof, be filed in the town or city where the mortgagor therein, if a resident of this State, resides at the time of the execution thereof; and if not a resident, then in the city or town where the property so mortgaged may be, at the time of such execution. In the city of New York, such instruments are to be filed in the office of the Register; in the other cities and county towns of this State, in the office of the County Clerk; and in all other towns, in the office of the Town Clerk thereof. The actual and continued change of possession above mentioned, must be literal, and not a mere legal, or fictitious change, in order to comply with the statute.[3]

6. Clerks of towns and counties, in whose offices chattel mortgages are required to be filed by law, must enter the names of the mortgagors and mortgagees in every such instrument, in books to be provided by them for the purpose, at the expense of their respective towns or counties, under the head of mortgagors and mortgagees, in each of such books respectively. It is also the duty of the said clerks to number every mortgage or copy so filed, by endorsing the number on the back thereof, and to enter such number in a separate column in the books in which such mortgages are entered, opposite to the name of every party thereto, also the date, the amount secured thereby, when due, and the date of the filing.[4]

7. Every mortgage, filed according to the foregoing requisitions, ceases to be valid, as against the creditors of the person making the same, or subsequent purchasers or mortgagees in good faith, after the expiration of one year from the filing thereof; unless, within thirty days next preceding the expiration of the said term of one year, a true copy of such mortgage, together with a statement exhibiting the interest of the mortgagee in the property thereby claimed by him, by virtue thereof, be again filed in the office of the Clerk, or Register, aforesaid, of the town or city where the mortgagor then resides. A copy of such instrument, or any statement therein made, certified by the Clerk, or Register, as aforesaid, is only

[1] 23 Wendell, 653; 26 Id., 511; 1 Hill, 438, 473; 4 Id., 271; 1 Comstock, 496.
[2] 1 Hill, 438; 4 Id., 271.
[3] 2 R. S. (3d ed.) 196, §§ 9, 10: 17 Wendell,
492; 19 Id., 514, 524; 23 Id., 653; 2 Hill 628; 4 Id., 271; 1 Denio, 580; 10 Paige, 127
[4] Laws of 1849, chap. 69.

8

evidence of the time of receiving and filing the same, as specified in the indorsement of such Clerk, or Register.[1]

8. The words "re-filed and renewed," with the date and signature of the Clerk, endorsed on a chattel mortgage, are not sufficient to continue it as against the claims of creditors. The interest claimed by the mortgagee must be distinctly stated.[2]

9. In Massachusetts, a chattel mortgage must be recorded by the Clerk of the town where the mortgagor resides, and also by the Clerk of the town where he transacts his business. The right of the mortgagor, or his assigns, to the property, is not forfeited, until sixty days after the mortgagee, or his assigns, gives written notice to the person holding the property, of the intention to foreclose, and files a copy of the notice in the Clerk's office where the mortgage is recorded. In Maine, a chattel mortgage must be recorded by the Clerk of the town where the mortgagor resides, and the mortgaged property must be delivered to the mortgagee, and retained in his possession.

10. After default in the payment of a chattel mortgage, the mortgagee's title to the property mortgaged becomes absolute at law, and he is entitled to the immediate possession; and he does not waive such right of possession, by filing a copy of the mortgage, with a statement exhibiting the interest claimed by him by virtue thereof, subsequent to such default. Where a chattel mortgage contains a provision that, in case of default, the mortgagee *may* sell the property at public or private sale, and out of the proceeds satisfy the debt, and return the surplus, the title of the mortgagee becomes complete, on default, without any sale being made. For the protection of the mortgagor, therefore, a clause of this character, if inserted at all, should be imperative on the mortgagee.[3]

11. Until forfeiture by non-performance of the conditions of a chattel mortgage, the interest of the mortgagor in the property mortgaged may be levied on, and sold, under an execution.[4]

12. A chattel mortgage, cannot, perhaps, be given on growing trees, fruit, or grass, while parcels of the real estate, or on produce not actually in existence; yet growing grass may be transferred in this manner, provided it actually belongs to the mortgagor.—as in the case of a tenant occupying a farm.[5]

---

[1] 2 R. S., (3d ed.) 196, §§ 11, 12; 20 Wendell, 18.
[2] 1 Denio, 163.
[3] 23 Wendell, 667; 1 Hill, 473; 2 Denio, 170.
[4] 1 Barbour's S. C. Rep., 542.
[5] 1 Denio, 550; 1 Barbour's S. C. Rep., 542; 1 Comstock, 90.

FORMS.

§ 193. *Common Bill of Sale.*

Know all men by these presents: That I, A. B., of the town of , in the county of , and State of New York, of the first part, for and in consideration of the sum of dollars, lawful money of the United States, to me paid by C. D., of, &c., of the second part, the receipt whereof is hereby acknowledged, have bargained and sold, and by these presents do grant and convey, unto the said party of the second part, his executors, administrators and assigns, the one equal, undivided half, of six acres of wheat, now growing on the farm of E. F., in the town of , aforesaid, one chestnut horse, and twenty sheep belonging to me, and now in my possession, at the place last aforesaid:[1] to have and to hold the same unto the said party of the second part, his executors, administrators and assigns, forever. And I do, for myself, my heirs, executors and administrators, covenant and agree, to and with the said party of the second part, his executors, administrators and assigns, to warrant and defend the sale of the said property, goods and chattels, hereby made, unto the said party of the second part, his executors, administrators and assigns, against all and every person and persons whomsoever.*

In witness whereof, I have hereunto set my hand and seal, this day of , one thousand eight hundred and .

Signed, sealed and delivered, }
   in presence of   }   A. B. [L. S.]
    G. H.

---

§ 194. *Bill of Sale in consideration of Maintenance.*

This indenture, made on the day of, &c., between A. B., of &c., of the first part, and C. B., of the same place, of the second part, witnesseth: That the party of the first part, in consideration of the covenants hereinafter contained, to be performed by the party of the second part, and of the sum of one dollar, to him in hand paid, by the said party of the second part, the receipt whereof is hereby acknowledged, has bargained and sold, and by these presents does grant and convey, &c., [*as in the preceding form to the *, changing the several pronouns to the third person, and substituting;* And the said party of the first part does, *for And I do, and then add:*]

---

[1] If the property conveyed consists of a great number of articles, it is as well to refer to them, in the bill of sale, as "all the goods, wares and merchandise, chattels and effects, mentioned and described in the schedule hereto annexed, marked schedule A;'"— and they should then be particularly enumerated in the schedule. The delivery is essential, where it can be made, in order to make a bill of sale valid; and the subscribing witness should be able to testify positively, as well in relation to that, as to the consideration of the sale. A bill of sale of a ship at sea, or in a foreign port, is good without delivery; but the purchaser must take possession as soon as practicable.

And in consideration of the premises, the party of the second part doth hereby covenant and agree, to and with the party of the first part, his executors, and administrators, that he will support and maintain, and comfortably and sufficiently clothe, the party of the first part, and in all respects care and provide for him, for and during the rest, residue and remainder, of his natural life; and that he, the said party of the second part, will pay unto the said party of the first part, the sum of   dollars, on the first day of January, in each and every year during the said time: provided, however, that the said party of the second part shall be forever released and discharged from the covenants above contained, on his part to be performed, if the said party of the first part shall refuse to reside in the county of   , aforesaid, except such refusal be occasioned by inability to obtain comfortable and sufficient board, lodging and maintenance, in the said county.

In witness whereof, the said parties have hereunto set their hands and seals, the day and year first above written.

Signed, sealed and delivered,   }   A. B. [L. S.]
    in presence of   }   C. D. [L. S.]
    G. H.

---

§ 195. *Bill of Sale of Registered or Enrolled Vessel.*

Know all men by these presents: That I, A. B., of, &c., owner of the brig, or vessel, called the "Isabella," of the burden of   tons, or thereabouts, now lying at the port of   , for and in consideration of the sum of   dollars, lawful money of the United States, to me paid, by C. D., of the place aforesaid, the receipt whereof I hereby acknowledge, have bargained and sold, and by these presents do bargain and sell, unto the said C. D., his executors, administrators and assigns, all the hull or body of said brig, or vessel, together with the masts, bowsprit, sails, boats, anchors, cables, spars, and all other necessaries thereunto appertaining and belonging; the certificate of the registry of which said brig, or vessel, is as follows, to wit: [*copy certificate of registry:*] To have and to hold the said brig or vessel, and appurtenances thereunto belonging, unto the said C. D., his executors administrators and assigns, to his and their proper use, benefit and behoof, forever. And I do, for myself, my heirs, executors and administrators, covenant and agree, to and with the said C. D., his executors, administrators and assigns, to warrant and defend the said brig, or vessel, and all the before mentioned appurtenances, against all and every person and persons whomsoever.

In witness, &c., [*as in* § 193.]

---

§ 196. *Bill of Sale and Chattel Mortgage.*

Know all men by these presents: That I, A. B., of, &c., in consideration of one dollar to me paid, by C. D., of. &c., the receipt whereof I hereby acknowledge, have, and by these presents do grant, bargain. sell, assign, transfer and set over, unto the said C. D. and his assigns, forever, the following goods, chattels and property, to wit: [*specify the articles, or refer to them in the schedule annexed, as directed in the note to* § 193:] Whereas I, the said A. B., am justly indebted to the said C. D., in the sum of one hundred and ten dollars, on account, for money had and received, and goods sold and delivered, [*or*, on a promissory note, dated, &c., and due months from date,] to be paid to the said C. D., or his assigns, on the   day of   , 18   , with the legal interest thereon from the day of the date hereof :

Now the condition of the above bill of sale is such, that if the said A. B. shall well and truly pay to the said C. D., or to his agent, attorney, or assignee, the above mentioned demand, [*or*, demands,] at the time, and in the manner and form above expressed, and shall keep and perform the covenants and agreements above contained, on his part to be kept and performed, according to the true intent and meaning thereof, then the above bill of sale shall be void: Otherwise, on the neglect and failure of the said A. B. to pay the said demand, [*or*, demands,] or to keep and perform the said covenants and agreements as above expressed, then, and in that case, the said C. D. and his assigns, are hereby authorized and empowered to sell the above described goods, chattels and property, [*or*, the goods, &c., described in the schedule hereunto annexed, as aforesaid,] or any part thereof, at public or private sale, at his or their option, and to retain from the proceeds of such sale, in his or their hands, sufficient to pay and satisfy the whole amount of the above mentioned demand, [*or*, demands,] with the legal interest thereon which shall be due at the time of such sale, and all costs, charges and expenses, incurred by the said C. D., or his assigns, in consequence of the neglect and failure of the said A. B., as aforesaid; rendering the overplus, if any, to the said A. B., or to his heirs, executors, administrators, or assigns, on demand. [The said C. D. and his assigns, are hereby authorized, for further security, to take the said goods, chattels, and property, into his or their possession, at any time he or they may think proper.]

In witness, &c., [*as in* § 193.]

---

§ 197. *Common Chattel Mortgage.*

This indenture, made the   day of, &c., between A. B., of, &c., of the first part, and C. D., of, &c., of the second part, witnesseth: That the said party of the first part, in consideration of the sum of   dollars, to him duly paid, hath sold, and by these presents doth grant and convey, to the said party of the second part, and his assigns, the following described goods, chattels and property, [*describe them particularly, or refer to them in the schedule, as directed in the note to* § 193,] now in my possession, at the   of

, aforesaid; together with the appurtenances, and all the estate, title and interest, of the said party of the first part therein.* This grant is intended as a security for the payment of one hundred and ten dollars, with interest, on or before the expiration of one year from the date hereof; and the additional sum of one hundred and forty dollars, with interest, on the   day of   , 18 ; which payments, if duly made, will render this conveyance void. [*The sentence near the close of* § 196 *included in* [ ] *may be added, if necessary.*

In witness whereof, the said party of the first part hath hereunto set his hand and seal, the day and year first above written.

Signed, sealed and delivered, }
    in presence of   }   A. B. [L. s.]
    G. H.

---

§ 198. *Chattel Mortgage to Secure a Note.*

This indenture, made, &c., [*as in* § 197 *to the *, and then add:*] Provided, nevertheless, that if the said party of the first part shall well and truly pay unto the said party of the second part, or his assigns, at maturity, the full amount, principal and interest, of a certain promissory note, executed by the said party of the first part, for the sum of   dollars, bearing date the   day of   , 18 payable three months after date, and now held by the said party of the second part, then this conveyance shall be void; otherwise to remain in full force and effect. [*Add clause in regard to default, and possession, if necessary.*]

In witness, &c., [*as in* § 197.]

---

§ 199. *Chattel Mortgage to Secure Endorser.*

This indenture, made, &c., [*as in* § 197 *to the *, and then add:*] Provided, nevertheless, that if the said party of the first part shall well and truly pay, at maturity, the full amount, principal and interest, of a certain promissory note, executed by him, and endorsed by the party of the second part, for the sum of   dollars, bearing even date herewith, payable one year from date, and now held by E. F., of, &c., then this conveyance shall be void; otherwise to remain in full force and effect.

In witness, &c., [*as in* § 197.]

---

§ 200. *Chattel Mortgage Requiring Sale to be Made.*

This indenture, made, &c., [*as in* § 197 *to the words,* "In witness whereof, &c.," *and then add:*] But if default shall be made in the payment of the principal or interest above mentioned, or any part thereof, then the said party of the second part, and his assigns, are hereby required to sell the goods, chattels and property, above granted, at public auction, after giving notice thereof in the manner provided by law for constable's sales, and out of the proceeds to satisfy the amount then due to the party of the second part, or his assigns, with the costs and expenses incurred by reason of such default, and return the surplus, if any there be, to the said party of the first part, or his personal representatives.

In witness, &c., [*as in* § 197.]

---

§ 201. *Conditional Clause as to Possession.*

Provided, nevertheless, [*or,* And provided also,] that, until default by the party of the first part, in the performance of the conditions aforesaid, it shall and may be lawful for him to keep possession of the property above mentioned and described, and to use and enjoy the same; but if the said party of the first part shall attempt to sell the same, or any part thereof, or to remove the same out of the county of   , without notice to the said party of the second part, or his assigns, and without his, or their, assent to such sale or removal, to be expressed in writing, then it shall be lawful for the said party of the second part, or his assigns, to take immediate possession of the whole of said property, to his, or their, own use.

---

§ 202. *Chattel Mortgage to Secure a Debt.*

Whereas I, A. B., of the town of   , in the county of   , and State of   , am justly indebted unto C. D., of, &c., in the sum of   dollars, on account, to be paid on or before the   day of   next, with interest from this date: Now, therefore, in consideration of such indebtedness, and in order to secure the payment of the same, as aforesaid, I do hereby sell, assign, transfer and set over, unto the said C. D., the property mentioned and described in the schedule hereinunder written; Provided, however, that if the said debt and interest be paid, as above specified, this sale and transfer shall be void; and this grant is also subject to the following conditions:

The property hereby sold and transferred is to remain in my possession until default be made in the payment of the debt and interest aforesaid, or some part thereof, unless I shall sell, or attempt to sell, assign, or dispose of, the said property, or any part thereof, or suffer the same unreasonably to depreciate in value; in which case the said C. D. may take the said property, or any part thereof, into his own possession.

Upon taking said property, or any part thereof, into his possession, either in case of default, or as above provided, the said C. D. shall sell the same at public or private sale; and after satisfying the aforesaid debt and the interest thereon, and all necessary and reasonable costs, charges and expenses, incurred by him, out of the proceeds of such sale, he shall return the surplus to me or my representatives.

Witness my hand and seal, this   day of   , 18   .

                                        A. B. [L. S.]

SCHEDULE ABOVE REFERRED TO.

[*Insert the articles, and let the mortgagor sign his name at the foot of the list.*]

---

§ 203. *Statement to be Filed with the Copy, within thirty days next preceding the expiration of the year.*

            County, ⎱ ss:
Town of   , ⎰

I, C. D., the mortgagee, [*or*, E. F., the assignee of C. D., the mortgagee,] named in the within [*or*, annexed] instrument, do hereby certify, that the sum of ninety-seven dollars and ten cents is claimed by me to be due thereupon, at the date hereof ; which sum constitutes the amount of my interest in the property therein mentioned and described. Dated the   day of   , 18   .

In presence of ⎱
        F. E. ⎰

            C. D., Mortgagee,
            [*or*, E. F., Assignee.]

---

§ 204. *Notice of Sale on Chattel Mortgage.*[1]

MORTGAGE SALE.

By virtue of a chattel mortgage executed by A. B. to C. D., dated the   day of   , 18   , and filed in the office of the Register of the city of   , [*or*, the County Clerk of the county of   ; *or*, the Town Clerk of the town of   ,] on the   day of   , in the year aforesaid, and upon which default has been made, I shall sell the property therein mentioned and described, viz: [*mention the articles*,] at public auction, at the house of   , in the city [*or*, town] of   , aforesaid, on the   day of   instant, [*or*, next,] at ten o'clock in the forenoon of that day. Dated at   , the   day of   , 18   .

                        C. D., Mortgagee,
                        [*or*, E. F., Assignee.]

---

[1] Where no time is specified in the mortgage, five or six days' notice of the sale will be sufficient.

CHAPTER X.

BONDS.

PRACTICAL REMARKS.

1. A bond is the acknowledgment of a debt, duty, or obligation; and it is immaterial what mode of expression is used, provided the language be sufficient to establish an acknowledgment of a debt. All persons legally capable of making a contract, may bind themselves in a bond.

2. Every bond, in itself, imports a consideration; and a failure of the consideration is not a good defence to an action brought on the bond.[1]

3. Fraud, or an illegal consideration, will invalidate a bond.

4. Wax, or some other tenacious substance, is necessary to constitute a seal in this State, except it be the seal of a court, public officer, or corporation.[2]

5. Payment may be pleaded in an action on a bond for the payment of money, though not made strictly according to the condition; and if the amount due thereon be paid after the commencement of suit, and before judgment, the action will be discontinued.[3]

6. The sum equitably due, by virtue of the condition of a bond, may be set off in any action where a set-off is allowed.[4]

7. An action may be brought in a Justice's court on a bond, the penalty of which exceeds one hundred dollars, provided the amount required by the condition does not exceed the sum of one hundred dollars.[5]

8. A bond required by law to be given, will be deemed sufficient, if it conform substantially to the form thereof prescribed by the statute, and do not vary in any matter, to the prejudice of the rights of the party to whom, or for whose benefit, such bond shall be given.[6]

---

[1] 2 Johnson, 177; 13 Id., 430; 1 Denio, 226.
[2] 2 Hill, 227; 3 Id., 493; Laws of 1848, chap. 197.
[3] 2 R. S. (3d ed.) 449, §§ 30, 31; 19 Wendell, 107.

[4] 2 R. S. (3d ed.) 450, § 39, sub. 1; 15 Wendell, 51.
[5] Laws of 1840, chap. 317.
[6] 2 R. S. (3d ed.) 641, § 34; 7 Paige 50 · 26 Wendell, 502.

F

9. The amount of the judgment rendered on a bond conditioned for the payment of money, is the penal sum, which is usually double the amount of the condition, in order to cover interest and costs.

10. A bond conditioned for the performance of a specific act, is broken on the failure to do it; but where the obligee is indemnified against damage or molestation, they must first be sustained, before a recovery can be had.[1]

11. A joint and several bond and warrant of attorney, signed by three persons, will not authorize a separate judgment against one, but only a joint judgment against all.[2]

12. An action on a sealed instrument must be brought within twenty years after a right of action accrues.[3]

13. A *bottomry* bond is an obligation founded on the joint security of a ship and its owners, and given for money borrowed, which is to be repaid on the successful termination of a voyage. At home, the bond is executed by the owners, or the master, as their agent. In a foreign country, the master has full authority to bind the owners, and pledge the ship and cargo, by a bottomry bond, in cases of necessity. Any amount of interest may be exacted, so long as the sea risk continues, irrespective of the usury laws; but when that terminates, the obligation will only draw legal interest. *Respondentia* is a contract similar to *bottomry*, except that the loan is made upon the chance of the safe arrival of the cargo. Like bottomry, it is used in cases of emergency.

14. An alteration of a bond, or other sealed instrument, in a material part, without the consent of the obligor, by any party claiming to recover under it, renders it void; otherwise, if the alteration be made by a stranger, provided the true contents can be made to appear by testimony, though the burden of proof will then be thrown on the party claiming under the instrument.[4]

FORMS.

§ 205. *Common Bond, with Condition.*

Know all men by these presents: That I, A. B., of the town of   , in the county of   , and State of New York, am held and firmly bound unto C. D., of, &c., in the sum of one

---

[1] 1 Comstock, 550.
[2] 5 Hill, 497.
[3] Laws of 1849, (Code of Practice,) chap 438, § 90.
[4] 2 Barbour's Ch. Rep., 119

thousand dollars, lawful money of the United States, to be paid to the said C. D., his executors, administrators, or assigns; for which payment, well and truly to be made, I bind myself, my heirs, executors, and administrators, firmly by these presents.

Sealed with my seal.   Dated the   day of   , one thousand eight hundred and   .

The condition of the above obligation is such, that if the above bounden A. B., his heirs, executors, or administrators, shall well and truly pay, or cause to be paid, unto the above named C. D., his executors, administrators, or assigns,* the just and full sum of five hundred dollars, in five equal annual payments, from the date hereof, with annual interest, then the above obligation to be void; otherwise to remain in full force and virtue.

Sealed and delivered, ⎱   A. B. [L. S.]
    in presence of ⎰
        G. H.

---

§ 206. *Bond of Two Obligors.*

Know all men by these presents: That we, A. B. and E. F., of, &c., are held and firmly bound, unto C. D., of, &c., in the sum of one thousand dollars lawful money of the United States, to be paid to the said C. D., his executors, administrators, or assigns; for which payment, well and truly to be made, we bind ourselves, our and each of our heirs, executors and administrators, jointly and severally, firmly by these presents.

Sealed with our seals.   Dated this   day of   , one thousand eight hundred and   .*

The condition of the above obligation is such, that if the above bounden A. B. and E. F., or either of them, their or either of their heirs, executors, or administrators, shall well and truly pay, or cause to be paid, unto the above named C. D., &c., [*as in* § 205 *to the end.*]

Sealed and delivered, ⎱   A. B. [L. S.]
    in presence of ⎰   E. F. [L. S.]
        G. H.

---

§ 207. *Bond — Several Payments.*

Know all men by these presents: &c., [*as in* § 205 *to the* *, *and then add:*] the just and full sum of five hundred dollars; in manner following, that is to say: the sum of one hundred dollars on the tenth day of   next; the sum of two hundred dollars on the   day of   , 18   ; and the remaining sum of two hundred dollars in one year from the said last mentioned date, together with the legal interest on the whole sum remaining unpaid, at the time of each payment; then the above obligation to be void; else to remain in full force and virtue.

Sealed, &c., [*as in* § 205.]

---

§ 208. *Bond, with Interest Condition.*

Know all men by these presents: &c., [*as in* § 205 *to the* *, *and then add:*] the just and full sum of five hundred dollars, on the   day of   , in the year of our Lord, 18   , and the legal interest thereon, to be computed from the day of the date hereof, and to be paid semi-annually, on the second day of January, and the first day of July, in each and every year; then the above obligation to be void; else to remain in full force and virtue. And it is hereby expressly agreed, that should any default be made in the payment of said interest, or of any part thereof, on any day whereon the same is made payable, as above expressed, and should the same remain unpaid and in arrear, for the space of sixty days, then, and from thenceforth, that is to say, after the lapse of the said sixty days, the aforesaid principal sum of five hundred dollars, with all arrearages of interest thereon, shall, at the option of the said C. D., his executors, administrators, or assigns, become and be due and payable, immediately thereafter, although the period above limited for the payment thereof may not then have expired; any thing herein before contained to the contrary thereof, in any wise notwithstanding

Sealed, &c., [*as in* § 205.]

---

§ 209. *Bond to a Corporation.*

Know all men by these presents: That I, A. B., of, &c., am held and firmly bound, unto the   Insurance Company, in the sum of one thousand dollars, lawful money of the United States, to be paid to the said   Insurance Company or assigns; for which payment, well and truly to be made, I bind myself, my heirs, executors and administrators, firmly by these presents.

Sealed with my seal. Dated the   day of   , one thousand eight hundred and   .*

The condition of the above obligation is such, that if the above bounden A. B., his heirs, executors, or administrators, shall well and truly pay or cause to be paid, unto the above named   Insurance Company, or assigns, the just and full sum of, &c., [*as in* § 205 *to the end.*]

---

§ 210. *Bond to Executors.*

Know all men by these presents: That I, A. B., of, &c., am held and firmly bound, unto E. F. and L. M., of, &c., executors of the last will and testament of S. T., deceased, late of, &c., in the sum of one thousand dollars, lawful money of the United States, to be paid to the said E. F. and L. M., executors as aforesaid, the survivors, or survivor, or his or their assigns; for which payment, well and truly to be made, I bind myself, my heirs, executors and administrators, firmly by these presents.

Sealed with my seal. Dated the   day of   , one thousand eight hundred and   .

The condition of the above obligation is such, that if the above bounden A. B., his heirs, executors, or administrators, shall well and truly pay, or cause to be paid, unto the above named E. F. and L. M., executors as aforesaid, the survivors, or survivor, or his or their assigns, the just and full sum of, &c., [*as in* § 205 *to the end.*]

----

§ 211. *Legatee's Bond.*

Know all men by these presents: That we, A. B. and O. P., of, &c., are held and firmly bound unto E. F. and L. M., of, &c., executors of the last will and testament of S. T. deceased, late of the town of   , in the sum of one thousand dollars, lawful money of the United States, to be paid to the said E. F. and L. M., executors, as aforesaid, the survivors, or survivor, or his or their assigns; for which payment, well and truly to be made, we bind ourselves, our and each of our heirs, executors and administrators, jointly and severally, firmly by these presents.

Sealed with our seals. Dated the   day of   , one thousand eight hundred and   .*

Whereas, in and by the last will and testament of the said S. T., deceased, a legacy of one hundred dollars is bequeathed to the said A. B., which has been paid to him by the said E. F. and L. M., executors as aforesaid:

Now the condition of this obligation is such, that if any debts against the deceased, above named, shall duly appear, and which there shall be no other assets to pay, and if there shall be no other assets to pay other legacies, or not sufficient, that then the said A. B. shall refund the legacy so paid, or such rateable proportion thereof, with the other legatees of the deceased, as may be necessary for the payment of such debts, and the proportional parts of other legacies, if there be any, and the costs and charges incurred by reason of the payment of the said A. B.; and that if the probate of the will of the said deceased be revoked, or the will declared void, then the said A. B. shall refund the whole of the legacy, with interest, to the said E. F. and L. M., their executors, administrators, or assigns.

Sealed, &c., [*as in* § 205.]   A. B. [L. s]
                                  C. D. [L. s]

§ 212. *Bond of Legatee, or Representative, before Suit.*

Know all men by these presents: &c., [*as in* § 211 *to the* *, *and then add:*] Whereas the said A. B. is about to commence a suit in the Supreme Court of the State of New York, against the said E. F. and L. M., as such executors, as aforesaid, for the purpose of recovering the amount of a certain legacy bequeathed to him, in and by the last will and testament of the said S. T., deceased: [*or,* for the purpose of recovering the distributive share of the property of the said S. T., deceased, due to him, the said A. B., as one of the sons and heirs of the said S. T., deceased:]

Now the condition of this obligation is such, that if any debts owing by the said deceased shall hereafter be recovered, or duly made to appear, for the payment of which there shall be no assets other than the said legacy, [*or,* distributive share,] that then the said A. B. shall refund the amount that may be recovered in any action by him against the said executors, or such rateable part thereof, with the other legatees [*or,* representatives] of the deceased, as may be necessary for the payment of the said debts, and the costs and charges incurred by a recovery against the said executors, in any suit therefor: [*If the bond is given by a legatee, the following clause must be added:*] And also, if no sufficient assets shall remain, after the payment of said legacy, to pay any other legacy which may be due, that then the said A. B. shall refund such rateable part or proportion thereof, with the other legatees, or representatives, of the deceased, as may be necessary for the payment of such other legacy.

Sealed, &c., [*as in* § 205.]

———

§ 213. *Indemnity Bond to Sheriff.*

Know all men by these presents: That we, A. B., C. D., and H. R., are held and firmly bound unto C. D., Sheriff of the county of   , &c.; [*as in* § 206 *to the* *, *and then add:*] Whereas the above bounden A. B. did obtain a judgment in the Supreme Court of the State of New York, on the   day of   , 18   , against E. F., for   dollars and   cents, damages and costs, whereupon execution has been issued, directed, and delivered to the said C. D., Sheriff, as aforesaid, commanding him, that of the goods and chattels of the said E. F., he should cause to be made the damages and costs aforesaid. And whereas certain goods and chattels that appear to belong to the said E. F. are claimed by L. M., of, &c.: Now, therefore, the condition of this obligation is such, that if the above bounden A. B. shall well and truly keep and bear harmless, and indemnify the said C. D., Sheriff as aforesaid, and all and every person and persons aiding and assisting him in the premises, of and from all harm, let, trouble, damages, costs, suits, actions, judgments, and executions, that shall, or may, at any time arise, come, or be brought, against him, them, or any of them, as well for the levying and making sale, under and by virtue of such execution, of all or any goods and chattels which he or they shall or may judge to belong to the said E. F., as for entering any shop, store, building, or other premises, for the taking of any such goods and chattels, then this obligation to be void; else to remain in full force and virtue.

[Sealed, &c., *as in* § 205.]

---

§ 214. *Bond, with Warrant of Attorney to Confess Judgment.*

Know all men, &c.: [*as in* § 205 *to the* *, *and then add:*] the just and full sum of five hundred dollars, on demand, then the above obligation to be void; else to remain in full force and virtue.

Sealed, &c., [*as in* § 205.] A. B. [L. s.]

Whereas I, A. B., of, &c., am held and firmly bound unto C. D., of, &c., by a certain bond or obligation, of this date, in the penal sum of one thousand dollars, conditioned for the payment of five hundred dollars, on demand: Now, therefore, I do authorize and empower any attorney, in any court of record in the State of New York, to appear for me at the suit of the said obligee, or his representatives, in an action of debt, and confess judgment against me upon the said bond or obligation, or for so much money borrowed, of any term, or vacation of term, antecedent or subsequent to this date; and to release to the said obligee all errors that may intervene in obtaining said judgment, or in issuing execution on the same. Signed and sealed this   day of   , A. D. 18 .

In presence of }
   G. H.   }   A. B. [L. s.]

---

§ 215. *Bond to Execute a Conveyance.*

Know all men, &c., [*as in* § 205, *to the condition, and then add:*] The condition of the above obligation is such, that if the above bounden A. B., on or before the   day of   next, or, in case of his death before that time, if the heirs of the said A. B., within three months after his decease, (if such heirs shall then be of full age, or, if within age, then within three months after such heirs shall be of full age,) shall and do, upon the reasonable request, and at the cost and charge of the said C. D., his heirs or assigns, make, execute, and deliver, or cause so to be, a good and sufficient warranty deed, in fee simple, free from all incumbrance, and with the usual covenants, of the following described premises, to wit: all, &c.; [*describe premises:*] then the above obligation to be void; else to remain in full force and virtue.[1]

Sealed, &c., [*as in* § 205.]

---

[1] The above form may be readily varied, if the condition should be to procure an heir at law to convey, when of age; and a clause may be added to warrant and defend the obligee, in the quiet enjoyment of the premises. until such conveyance be executed.

§ 216. *Bond to discharge Bond and Mortgage.*

Know all men &c.: [*as in* § 205 *to the condition, and then add:*] Whereas the said C. D. and E. his wife, have this day conveyed to the said A. B., by warranty deed, duly executed, and bearing even date herewith, the following described premises, to wit: all, &c., [*describe premises conveyed;*] subject, however, to the covenants and conditions contained in a certain indenture of mortgage, bearing date the   day of   , 18   , executed by the said C. D., and E., his wife, to S. V. R., of the city and county of Albany, for the purpose of securing the payment of the sum of   dollars, in five years from the day of the date thereof, with semi-annual interest, as covenanted to be paid by the conditions of a bond, of like date therewith, executed by the said C. D. to the said S. V. R., which said mortgage is a lien upon the premises aforesaid, and was recorded in the office of the clerk of the county of   , on the   day of   , 18   , at pages 217 and 218 of book O. of mortgages, at 10 o'clock A. M., and upon which there is now remaining due and unpaid, the said principal sum of   dollars, with interest from the   day of   , last past: Now, therefore, the condition of the above obligation is such, that if the said A. B., his heirs, executors, or administrators, shall well and truly pay, or cause to be paid, unto the said S. V. R., or his assigns, all such sum and sums of money as are, or may hereafter become due, on the said bond and mortgage, executed by the said C. D., and the said C. D., and E., his wife, as aforesaid, and forever satisfy and discharge the same, saving the said C. D., his heirs, executors, and administrators, harmless, of and from all and all manner of costs, charges, and expenses, in the premises, then the above obligation to be void; else to remain in full force and virtue.

Sealed, &c., [*as in* § 205.]

---

§ 217. *Bond of an Officer of a Bank, or Company.*

Know all men, &c.: [*as in* § 209 *to the* *, *substituting the name of the bank for that of the company, if necessary, and then add:*] Whereas the above bounden A. B. has been chosen and appointed cashier, [*or,* teller; *or,* treasurer, *as the case may be,*] of the   Company; [*or,* bank;] by reason whereof divers sums of money, goods and chattels, and other things, the property of the said company, [*or,* bank,] will come into his hands: Now, therefore, the condition of the above obligation is such, that if the said A. B., his executors, or administrators, at the expiration of his said office, upon request to him or them made, shall make or give unto the said company, [*or,* bank,] or their agent, or attorney, a just and true account of all such sum or sums of money, goods and chattels, and other things, as have come into his hands, charge, or possession, as cashier, [*or,* teller; *or,* treasurer,] as aforesaid, and shall and do pay and deliver over, to his successor in office, or any other person duly authorized to receive the same, all such balances, or sums of money, goods and chattels, and other things, which shall appear to be in his hands, and due by him to the said company; [or, bank;] and if the said A. B. shall well and truly, honestly and faithfully, in all things, serve the said company, [or, bank,] in the capacity of cashier, [or, teller; or, treasurer,] as aforesaid, during his continuance in office, then the above obligation to be void; else to remain in full force and virtue.

Sealed, &c., [as in § 205.]

---

§ 218. *Bond of Indemnity to a Surety in a Bond.*

Know all men, &c.: [as in § 206 *to the condition, and then add:*] Whereas the said C. D., at the special instance and request of the above bounden A. B., has bound himself, together with the said A. B., unto one E. F., of, &c., in a certain obligation, bearing even date herewith, in the penal sum of one thousand dollars, lawful money of the United States, conditioned for the payment of the sum of five hundred dollars, due and owing by the said A. B. to the said E. F., on, &c.: [as in the bond; *or, if a bail bond be referred to, say* — conditioned for the appearance of the said A. B., &c.; *or,* conditioned that the said A. B. shall put in special bail, &c.:] Now, therefore, the condition of the above obligation is such, that if the said A. B. shall well and truly perform and fulfill the condition of the said bond executed to the said E. F., in manner and form as he is therein required to do, and at all times hereafter save harmless the said C. D., his heirs, executors and administrators, of and from the said obligation, and of and from all actions, costs and damages, for or by reason thereof, then this obligation to be void; else to remain in full force and virtue.

Sealed, &c., [as in § 205.]

---

§ 219. *Bond of Indemnity on Paying Lost Note.*

Know all men, &c.: [as in § 206 *to the* *, and then add:*] Whereas the said C. D., on the   day of   , 18 , did make, execute and deliver, unto the above bounden A. B., for a valuable consideration, his promissory note, for the sum of one hundred dollars, written due and payable, on or before the   day of   , then next, with interest, which said promissory note the said A. B., since the delivery of the same to him, as aforesaid, has in some manner, to him unknown, lost out of his possession; and whereas the said C. D. hath this day paid unto the said A. B. the sum of   dollars, the receipt whereof the said A. B. doth hereby acknowledge, in full satisfaction and discharge of the said note, upon the promise of the said

9

A. B. to indemnify and save harmless the said C. D. in the premises, and to deliver up the said note, when found, to the said C. D., to be canceled: Now, therefore, the condition of this obligation is such, that if the above bounden A. B., his heirs, executors, or administrators, or any of them, do and shall, at all times hereafter, save and keep harmless the said C. D., his heirs, executors and administrators, of, from, and against, the promissory note aforesaid, and of and from all costs, damages and expenses, that shall or may arise therefrom; and also deliver, or cause to be delivered up, the said note, when found, to be canceled, then this obligation to be void; else to remain in full force and virtue.

Sealed, &c., [*as in* § 205.]

A. B. [L. S.]
E. F. [L. S.]

---

§ 220. *Bond for Performance, to be Endorsed on a Contract, or Agreement.*

Know all men, &c.: [*as in* § 206 *to the condition, and then add:*] The condition of this obligation is such, that if the above bounden A. B., his executors, administrators, or assigns, shall, in all things, stand to and abide by, and well and truly keep and perform, the covenants, conditions and agreements, in the within instrument contained, on his or their part to be kept and performed, at the time, and in the manner and form therein specified, then the above obligation shall be void; else to remain in full force and virtue.

Sealed, &c., [*as in* § 205.]

---

§ 221. *Bottomry Bond.*

Know all men by these presents, that I, A. B., master, and one-third owner, of the ship Isabella, for myself and C. D., who owns the other two-thirds of said ship, am held and firmly bound, unto E. F., in the penal sum of two thousand dollars, lawful money, for the payment of which to the said E. F., his heirs, executors, administrators, or assigns, I hereby bind myself, my heirs, executors and administrators, firmly by these presents.

Sealed with my seal. Dated the   day of   , A. D. 18 .

Whereas the above bounden A. B., hath taken up and received, of the said E. F., the just and full sum of one thousand dollars, which sum is to run at respondentia, on the block and freight of the said Isabella, whereof the said A. B. is now master, from the port of   , on a voyage to the port of   , having permission to touch, stay at, and proceed to call, at all ports and places within the limits of the voyage, at the rate or premium of   per cent. for the voyage: In consideration whereof, usual risks of the sea, rivers, enemies, fires, pirates, &c., are to be on account of the said E. F. And for further security of the said E. F., the said A. B. doth, by these presents, mortgage and assign over, to the said E. F., his heirs, executors, administrators and assigns, the said ship Isabella and her freight, together with all her tackle, apparel, &c.: And it is hereby declared, that the said ship Isabella, and her freight, is thus assigned over, for the security of the respondentia taken up by the said A. B., and shall be delivered to no other use or purpose whatever, until payment of this bond is first made, with the premium that may become due thereon.

Now, therefore, the condition of this obligation is such, that if the above bounden A. B., his heirs, executors, or administrators, shall and do well and truly pay, or cause to be paid, unto the said E. F., or to his attorneys, legally authorized to receive the same, his or their executors, administrators, or assigns, the just and full sum of one thousand dollars, being the principal of this bond, together with the premium which shall become due thereon, at or before the expiration of twenty days after the arrival of the said ship Isabella at the port of   ; or, in case of the loss of the said ship, such an average as by custom shall have become due on the salvage, then this obligation is to be void; otherwise to remain in full force and virtue.

Having signed to three bonds of the same tenor and date, the one of which being accomplished, the other two to be void and of no effect.

Sealed and delivered, }
  in presence of   }   A. B., for self and C. D. [L s.]
    G. H.

CHAPTER XI

CLERKS AND CRIERS.

PRACTICAL REMARKS.

1. Clerks of counties are elected to serve for three years, and must reside in the county, or city, in which the duties of the office are required by law to be executed.[1]

2. The Clerks of counties, and of all courts in this State, are required to keep their offices open for the transaction of business, every day in the year, except Sundays and the fourth of July: in the city of New York, from nine o'clock in the forenoon to four o'clock in the afternoon, and in all other parts of the State, from nine to twelve o'clock in the forenoon, and from two to five o'clock in the afternoon.[2]

3. Any Clerk of a Court of Record may administer oaths, and take affidavits, in any cause, matter or proceeding, except where the law requires the same to be administered, or taken, before particular officers.[3]

4. Every County Clerk is required to appoint, in writing, some proper person to be deputy clerk of his county, to hold during his pleasure, who must take the constitutional oath of office. Whenever the County Clerk is absent from his office, or is unable to attend to his duties, the deputy is authorized to act in his stead, except in deciding on the sufficiency of sureties for any officer. The deputy may perform *all* the duties where the office of the County Clerk becomes vacant.[4]

5. Clerks of counties are, by virtue of their offices, clerks of all Circuit Courts, Courts of Oyer and Terminer, and County Courts, held within their respective counties.[5]

---

1 Amended Constitution of New York, Art. x, § 1; 1 R. S. (3d ed.) 105, § 17; 11 Wendell, 511.
2 2 R. S. (3d ed.) 384, § 61.
3 2 R. S. (3d ed.) 383, § 56 7 Wendell, 516; 4 Paige, 548.

4 1 R. S. (3d ed.) 431, §§ 81–84; Laws of 1831, chap. 237.
5 Laws of 1847, chap. 280; Id., chap. 470 Laws of 1849, chap. 438.

6. Two constables, selected by the Sheriff of the county in which any term of the Court of Appeals or Supreme Court is held, act as the Criers of such Court.[1] Criers of other Courts are appointed by the respective Courts of which they are officers.[2]

FORMS.

§ 222. *Proclamation on Opening Court.*

Hear ye, hear ye, hear ye: All manner of persons that have any business to do at this Circuit Court and Court of Oyer and Terminer, held in and for the county of   , let them draw near and give their attendance, and they shall be heard.

§ 223. *For Sheriff to Return Process.*

Sheriff of the county of   : Return the writs and precepts to you directed and delivered, and returnable here this day, that the court may proceed thereon.

§ 224. *Before Calling Grand Jury.*

You, good men, who are here returned to inquire for the people of the State of New York, for the body of the county of   : answer to your names, every man, at the first call, and save your fines. [*Call them one by one in their order.*]

§ 225. *For Silence on Charging Grand Jury.*

All persons are strictly charged and commanded to keep silence, while the court is giving the charge to the grand jury, on pain of imprisonment.

§ 226. *To return Recognizances, &c.*

All Justices of the Peace, Coroners, Sheriffs, and other officers, who have taken any recognizances, examinations, or other matters: return the same to the court here, that they may proceed thereon.

§ 227. *Before Calling Petit Jury.*

Hear ye, hear ye, hear ye: You, good men, who are here returned, to try the several issues to be tried at this Circuit Court and Court of Oyer and Terminer, held in and for the county of   , answer to your names at the first call, and save your fines.

---

[1] Laws of 1847, chap. 429. | [2] Laws of 1842, chap. 202.

§ 228. *For Imposing Fines.*

Hear ye, hear ye, hear ye: The court have imposed a fine of dollars, upon each of the following persons, for non-attendance as grand jurors, [*or*, petit jurors; *or*, constables,] at this court, to wit: A. B., of , &c. &c.

---

§ 229. *For Persons to Appear on Recognizances.*

Hear ye, hear ye, hear ye: All manner of persons who are bound by recognizances to prosecute, or prefer, any bill of indictment, against any prisoner or other person, let them come forth and prosecute, or they will forfeit their recognizances.

---

§ 230. *For Persons Bound to Answer.*

Hear ye, hear ye, hear ye: A. B., come forth and answer to your name, and save yourself and bail, or you will forfeit your recognizance.

---

§ 231. *For Bail to Produce Principal.*

Hear ye, hear ye, hear ye: C. D. and E. F., bring forth A. B., your principal, whom you have undertaken to have here this day, or you will forfeit your recognizance.

---

§ 232. *For Discharge of Persons against whom no Bills are found.*

Hear ye, hear ye, hear ye: If any man can show cause why A. B. should stand longer bound, [*or*, imprisoned,] let him come forth, and he shall be heard, for he stands upon his discharge.

---

§ 233. *Discharge.*

Hear ye, hear ye, hear ye: No cause being shown why A. B. should longer remain in custody of the Sheriff of the county of , he is discharged.

---

§ 234. *For Jury in a Civil Cause.*

Hear ye, hear ye, hear ye: You, good men, who are here empannelled and returned, to try this issue, joined between A. B., plaintiff, and C. D., defendant, answer to your names as you are called, and save your fines.

---

§ 235. *For Defendant on an Inquest.*

C. D., come forth and make your challenges, or you will lose your challenges, and inquest will be taken against you by default.

§ 236. *For Plaintiff to Appear and Prosecute.*

A. B., appear and prosecute your action, or your default will be entered.

---

§ 237. *For Adjournment.*

Hear ye, hear ye, hear ye: All manner of persons who have any further business to do at this Circuit Court, and Court of Oyer and Terminer, may depart hence, and appear here again to-morrow morning, at   o'clock, to which time these courts are adjourned.

---

§ 238. *For Opening Court after Adjournment.*

Hear ye, hear ye, hear ye: All manner of persons who have been adjourned over to this hour, and have any further business to do at this Circuit Court, and Court of Oyer and Terminer, may draw near, and give their attendance, and they shall be heard.

---

§ 239. *Calling a Witness to answer on a Subpœna.*

D. M., come forward and testify in this issue, joined between A. B. plaintiff, and C. D., defendant, according to the command of a subpœna therein served on you, or your default will be entered.

---

§ 240. *Oath of a Witness to give Evidence.*

You do swear, that the evidence you shall give in this matter in difference, between A. B., plaintiff, and C. D., defendant, shall be the truth, the whole truth, and nothing but the truth.   So help you God.[1]

---

§ 241. *The Same, by the Uplifted hand.*

You do swear, in the presence of the ever-living God, that, &c., [*as in* § 240 *to the end.*]

---

§ 242. *Affirmation of Witness.*

You do solemnly, sincerely, and truly declare and affirm, that, &c., [*as in* § 240 *to the end.*]

---

[1] Where an oath is administered to a Jew, *Jehovah* should be substituted for *God.*

§ 243. *Oath of the Foreman of the Grand Jury.*

You, as foreman of this grand inquest, shall diligently inquire, and true presentment make, of all such matters and things as shall be given to you in charge; the counsel of the people, of your fellows, and your own, you shall keep secret: you shall present no one from envy, hatred, or malice; nor leave any one unpresented, for fear, favor affection, reward, or the hope of reward; but you shall present all things truly, as they come to your knowledge, according to the best of your understanding. So help you God.

§ 244. *Oath of Grand Jurors.*

The same oath your foreman has taken on his part, you and each of you shall truly observe and keep on your part. So help you God.

§ 245. *Of Petit Jurors in Civil Causes.*[1]

You, and each of you, shall well and truly try the several issues which you shall have in charge at this Circuit Court, and true verdicts give in them, respectively, according to evidence. So help you God.

§ 246. *Of Triers in a Civil Cause, upon a Challenge for favor.*

You shall well and truly try, and truly find, whether E. F., the juror challenged, stands indifferent between A. B., plaintiff, and C. D., defendant, in the issue about to be tried. So help you God.

§ 247. *Of Witness on a Challenge.*

You shall true answers make, to such questions as shall be put to you touching the challenge of E. F., a juror. So help you God.

§ 248. *Of Witness in a Civil Cause.*

The evidence you shall give in this issue, joined between A. B., plaintiff, and C. D., defendant, shall be the truth, the whole truth, and nothing-but the truth. So help you God.

---

[1] Where the juror affirms, or swears by the uplifted hand, this oath and the succeeding one, (§ 244,) should be administered as follows, viz : " You do solemnly, sincerely, and truly declare and affirm, that as foreman of this grand inquest, you will diligently inquire &c· ' or, " You do swear in the presence of the ever-living God, that the same oath your foreman has taken on his part, you [and each of you] will, &c."

[2] This and the succeeding forms should be varied, if necessary, in the manner pointed out in the note to § 243.

§ 249. *Of Interpreter.*

You shall truly interpret between the court, the jury, the counsel, and the witness, in this issue joined between A. B., plaintiff, and C. D., defendant. So help you God.

---

§ 250. *Of Interpreter to a Deaf and Dumb Witness.*

You shall well and truly interpret between the court, the jury, the counsel, and the witness, E. F., here produced in behalf of A. B., in this issue joined between A. B., plaintiff, and C. D., defendant. So help you God.

---

§ 251. *Voire Dire.*

You shall true answers make to such questions as shall be put to you, touching your interest in the event of this cause. So help you God.

---

§ 252. *Oath of Party, or Interested Witness, to Admit Evidence of the Contents of a Paper not Produced.*

You shall true answers make to such questions as shall be put to you, touching the power or control you have over any paper, [or, the loss or destruction of any paper,] which would be proper evidence in this cause. So help you God.

---

§ 253. *Of a Party, or Interested Witness, Preliminary to Proving the Hand Writing of a Subscribing Witness.*

You shall true answers make to such questions as shall be put to you, touching your [or, the plaintiff's; or, defendant's] ability to procure the attendance of G. H., a subscribing witness to this paper, [or, the paper in question.] So help you God.

---

§ 254. *Of Constables, on Retiring with a Jury, or Jurors, on leave.*

You shall retire with such jurors as have leave of absence from this court; you shall not speak to them yourself in relation to this trial, nor suffer any person to speak to them: and you shall return with them without delay. So help you God.

---

§ 255. *Of Constables, to Keep Jury on an Adjournment.*

You shall retire with the jury to some convenient room, to be furnished by the Sheriff; you shall not suffer any person to speak to them, nor speak to them yourself in relation to this trial, and return with them at the order of the court. So help you God.

§ 256. *Of Constable who Attends the Jury, when they retire to consider of the Verdict in Civil and Criminal Cases.*

You shall well and truly keep every person sworn on this jury, in some private and convenient place, without meat or drink, water excepted; you shall not suffer any person to speak to them, or speak to them yourself, without leave of the court, except it be to ask them whether they have agreed on their verdict, until they have agreed on their verdict. So help you God.

§ 257. *Oath on Application to Excuse, or Discharge, a Juror or Constable.*

You shall true answers make to such questions as shall be put to you, touching your application [*or*, the application for and in behalf of E. F.,] to be discharged [*or*, excused] from attendance as a juror [*or*, constable] at this court. So help you God.

§ 258. *On Application of Juror, or Constable, for a Remission of Fine.*

You shall true answers make to such questions as shall be put to you, touching your application [*or*, the application for and in behalf of E. F.] for the remission of your [*or*, his] fine, for default in attending as a juror, [*or*, constable,] at this [*or*, the last] term of this court. So help you God.

§ 259. *Oath of Poor Witness, on Application for Expenses.*

You shall true answers make to such questions as shall be put to you, touching your application for the expenses of your attendance at this court, as a witness in behalf of the people of this State. So help you God.

§ 260. *Of Applicant for Pension.*

You shall true answers make to such questions as shall be put to you, touching your application for a pension. So help you God.

§ 261. *Of Witness, on Application for a Pension.*

You shall true answers make to such questions as shall be put to you, in the matter of the application of R. S., for a pension. So help you God.

§ 262. *Of Witness on the Trial of a Justice, on Charges.*

The evidence you shall give between the people of the State of New York and G. H., on charges made against him as a Justice of the Peace, shall be the truth, the whole truth, and nothing but the truth. So help you God.

----

§ 263. *Proclamation of Arraignment for Felony.*

All persons are strictly charged and commanded, to keep silence, while the court proceed to arraign the prisoners on indictments for felony.

----

§ 264. *Proclamation for Petit Jury on the same.*

You, good men, who are here returned to inquire between the people of the State of New York, and A. B., the prisoner at the bar, answer to your names as you are called, and save your fines.

----

§ 265. *Clerk's Address to the Prisoner, before calling the Jury.*

A. B.: These good men that you shall now hear called, are the jurors who are to pass between the people of the State of New York and you; [or, *if a capital case*, to pass upon your life and death;] if, therefore, you will challenge them as they come to the book to be sworn, and before they are sworn, you shall be heard. [*The crier then calls the jurors, one at a time, as they are drawn by the Clerk; and when the juror comes to the stand, and is ready to be sworn, the Clerk says:* Juror, look upon the prisoner — Prisoner, look upon the Juror.]

----

§ 266. *Juror's Oath on a Trial for Felony.*

You shall well and truly try, and true deliverance make, between the people of the State of New York, and A. B., the prisoner at the bar, whom you shall have in charge, and a true verdict give, according to the evidence. So help you God.

----

§ 267. *Trier's Oath on a Challenge to the Favor.*

You shall well and truly try and find, whether C. D., the juror challenged, stands indifferent between the people of the State of New York and the prisoner at the bar. So help you God.

----

§ 268. *Finding of the Triers.*

The finding is; that he stands indifferent, [or, not indifferent.]

§ 269. *Oath of a Witness before the Triers.*

You shall true answers make to such questions as shall be put to you, touching the challenge of E. F., as a juror. So help you God.

---

§ 270. *Proclamation Requiring a Witness under Recognizance, to Appear and Testify.*

Hear ye, hear ye, hear ye: G. H., who is bound by recognizance to give evidence against A. B., the prisoner at the bar, come forth, answer to your name, and give evidence, or you will forfeit your re cognizance.

---

§ 271. *Oath of a Witness on a Trial for Felony.*

The evidence you shall give between the people of the State of New York, and A. B., the prisoner at the bar, shall be the truth, the whole truth, and nothing but the truth. So help you God.

---

§ 272. *Proclamation before Sentence Pronounced.*

Hear ye, hear ye, hear ye: All manner of persons are commanded to keep silence, while judgment is given against the prisoner at the bar, upon pain of imprisonment.

---

§ 273. *Proclamation before calling Jury on a Misdemeanor.*

You, good men, who are here returned to try this issue of traverse, between the people of the State of New York, and A. B., the defend-ant, answer to your names as you are called, and save your fines.

---

§ 274. *Juror's Oath, on a Trial for a Misdemeanor.*

You shall well and truly try this issue of traverse between the people of the State of New York, and A. B., the defendant, and a true verdict give therein, according to the evidence. So help you God.

---

§ 275. *Oath of a Witness on a Trial for a Misdemeanor.*

The evidence you shall give in this issue of traverse, between the people of the State of New York, and A. B., the defendant, shall be the truth, the whole truth, and nothing but the truth. So help you God.

---

§ 276. *Clerk's Address on Taking Recognizance of Prisoner.*

You, and each of you, acknowledge yourselves to be indebted to the people of the State of New York, to wit: You, A. B., in the sum of one hundred dollars: and you, C. D., in the sum of one hundred dollars, to be levied of your, and each of your goods and chattels, lands and tenements, to the use of the said people, if default shall be made in the condition following, to wit: The condition of this recognizance is such, that if A. B. shall appear at the next court [*or*, from day to day during the sitting of this court,] of [*state the court*,] to be held in and for the county of ` , then and there* to answer and stand trial upon a certain indictment against him for felony, [*or, whatever may be the offence;*] not to depart the court without leave, and to abide its order and decision, then this recognizance to be void; otherwise to remain in full force and virtue.   Are you and each of you content?

---

§ 277. *The Same, on Recognizance of Witness.*

You, &c., [*as in* § 276, *to the* *, *and. then add:*] to testify on the trial of a certain indictment against E. F., for felony, [*or, whatever may be the offence;*] not to depart the court without leave, &c., [*as in* § 276.]

---

§ 278. *The Same on Recognizance to Keep the Peace, or for Good Behavior.*

You, &c., [*as in* § 276, *to the* *, *and then add:*] to answer and stand trial upon a certain indictment against him, for [*state the offence;*] and shall also in the meanwhile keep the peace towards S. T., and all the other good people of this State, [*or*, and shall also in the meanwhile be of good behavior,] then, &c., [*as in* § 276.]

---

§ 279. *Commencement of Address where there is no Surety.*

You acknowledge yourself to be indebted to the people of the State of New York, in the sum of one hundred dollars, to be levied of your goods, &c., [*as in either of the preceding forms.*]

---

§ 280. *Calling Constables.*

Constables of the County of : Answer to your names, every man, at first call, and save your fines.

---

§ 281. *Clerk's Entry on Issuing Attachment against a Witness.*

The People, ⎞ On reading and filing an affidavit of the due ser-
 against ⎬ vice of a subpœna on E. F., to appear here this day
 A. B. ⎠ as a witness on the trial of this indictment, and he being called and not appearing, on motion of E. W. A., Esq., District Attorney, it is ordered that an attachment issue against the said E. F.

§ 282. *Arraignment of a Party indicted, after reading Indictment.*
Do you demand a trial on this indictment?

---

§ 283. *Taking Verdict on a Trial for Felony, or Murder.*
Gentlemen of the jury: Please answer to your names. [*Call them one by one.*] Have you agreed upon your verdict? [*After the answer, say:*] Jurors, look upon the Prisoner. Who shall say for you? [*The foreman rises.*] How say you; do you find the prisoner at the bar guilty of the felony [and murder, *if necessary,*] whereof he stands indicted; or not guilty? [*The foreman answers:* guilty; *or,* not guilty. *Then the Clerk adds:*] Hearken to your verdict, gentlemen, as the court has recorded it: You say, you find the prisoner at the bar guilty [*or,* not guilty] of the felony [and murder, *if necessary,*] whereof he stands indicted; and so you say all.

---

§ 284. *Polling Jury in the Same.*
[*When the polling of the jury is demanded, the Clerk will begin with the first name on the panel:*] A. B., how do you find the prisoner at the bar; guilty or not guilty? [*When the foreman has answered, call the next juror as follows:*] C. D., is that your verdict? [*Then proceed in the same manner, through the whole panel, and when all have answered, say:*] Then, gentlemen of the jury, hearken to your verdict as the court has recorded it. You say you find the prisoner at the bar* guilty of the felony [and murder, *if necessary,*] whereof he stands indicted, and so you say all.

---

§285. *Taking Verdict in other Criminal Cases.*
Gentlemen of the jury: Please answer to your names. [*Call them one by one.*] Have you agreed upon your verdict? [*After the answer, or affirmative assent, is given, say:*] Who shall say for you? [*The foreman rises.*] How say you; do you find the prisoner at the bar guilty of the misdemeanor [*or,* assault and battery, and riot; *or,* riot; *or,* offence; *or,* crime] whereof he stands indicted; or not guilty? [*The foreman answers:* guilty; *or,* not guilty. *Then the Clerk adds:*] Hearken to your verdict, gentlemen, as the court has recorded it. You say you find the prisoner at the bar guilty [*or,* not guilty] of the misdemeanor [*or,* assault and battery, and riot; *or,* riot; *or,* offence; *or,* crime] whereof he stands indicted· and so you say all.

§ 286. *Polling Jury in the Same.*

[*Proceed as in* § 284 *to the* *, *and then add:*] guilty of the misdemeanor [*or,* assault and battery, and riot; *or,* riot; *or,* offence; *or* crime] whereof he stands indicted; and so you say all.

---

§ 287. *Taking Verdict in a Civil Cause.*

Gentlemen of the jury: Please answer to your names. [*Call them one by one.*] Have you agreed upon your verdict? * How do you find? [*The foreman states the finding of the jury; the Clerk then enters the verdict, and continues:*] Gentlemen, listen to your verdict as it stands recorded. You say you find, &c., [*as the finding may be;*] and so you say all.

---

§ 288. *Entry of Verdict.*

Supreme Court,

A. B.	County of . At a Circuit Court held
against	held in and for said county, on the day
C. D.	of , 18 , before J. M., Esquire, Justice.

JURORS.

[*Insert names.*]

WITNESSES.

[*Insert names.*]

Verdict for defendant, [*or,* verdict for plaintiff, damages $; *or,* verdict for plaintiff against defendant, C. D., damages $, and verdict for the defendant E. F.; [*or, if it be a special verdict, insert the same at length.*]*   E. B. C., Clerk.

---

§ 289. *Entry of Verdict, with Assessment of Value of Personal Property.*

Supreme Court,

A. B.	County of, &c., [*as in the preceding form, to*
against	*the* *, *and then add:*] and the jury assess the
C. D.	value of the said [*mention the property in question*] at dollars: [*If necessary, add:* and they further assess

the damages of the said defendant by occasion of the delivery and detention of the said property, at   dollars.]
                E. B. C., Clerk.

---

§ 290. *Entry of Judgment.*

Supreme Court,

A. B.	Judgment,
against	January 1, 1849.
C. D.	This cause being at issue upon the facts, and a

trial by jury having been had, on which a verdict was found for the plaintiff, that, &c., [*state the finding; or, if there was no jury, say:* and the same having been submitted to the court, verdict was rendered, &c.]

Now, on motion of G. H., attorney for the plaintiff, it is ordered and adjudged by the said court, that, &c., [*as the verdict may be.*]

E. B. C., Clerk.

---

§ 291. *Taking Verdict where Personal Property is in Question.*

Gentlemen of, &c., [*as in* § 287, *to the* *, *and then add:*] How do you find? [*The foreman answers:* We find the title of the horse in question to be in the plaintiff, and assess the value thereof at one hundred dollars. *The Clerk enters the verdict, and then adds:*] Gentlemen, listen to your verdict as it stands recorded. You say you find, &c., [*as above;*] and so you say all.

---

§ 292. *Taking Verdict in Actions for Damages.*

Gentlemen of, &c., [*as in* § 287 *to the* *, *and then add:*] How do you find? [*The foreman answers:* We find for the defendant; *or,* We find for the plaintiff one hundred dollars damages and six cents costs. *The Clerk enters the verdict, and again repeats the finding, and makes the inquiry, as in* § 287.]

---

§ 293. *Taking Verdict in Cases of Lunacy, &c.*

Gentlemen of, &c., [*as in* § 287 *to the* *, *and then add:*] How do you find? [*The foreman answers:* We find that A. B. is a lunatic, of unsound mind, and incapable of managing or conducting his affairs; *or,* that A. B. was of unsound mind, at the time of the execution of the will, [*or,* deed,] in question, to wit: on the   day of   , 18 , and incompetent to execute the same; *or,* that A. B. was of unsound mind, and incompetent to contract matrimony, at the time of the solemnization of the marriage to E. D., to wit: on the   day of   , 18 . *After entering the verdict, the Clerk makes the inquiry, as in other cases.*]

---

§ 294. *Taking Verdict in Action for Recovery of Real Property*

Gentlemen of, &c., [*as in* § 287 *to the* *, *and then add:*] How do you find? [*The foreman answers:* We find the title of the land in question to be in the plaintiff; *or,* defendant: *If there is a claim for the mesne profits, add:* and assess the damages for withholding the said premises, against the defendant, at   dollars and six cents costs. *The Clerk enters the verdict, &c., as in the preceding forms.*]

§ 295. *Polling Jury in Civil Actions.*

[*Begin with the first name on the panel, as in criminal actions.*]
A. B., you say you find [*as the verdict may be: after the answer is given, then call the next juror,*] C. D., is that your verdict? [*Proceed in this manner through the list, and when all have answered, say:*] Then, gentlemen of the jury, hearken to your verdict, as the court has recorded it. You say you find [*as the verdict may be,*] and so you say all.

---

§ 296. *Certificate of Money paid into Court by Sheriff.*

Supreme Court,

A. B.	I herby certify, that A. R., Sheriff of the
against	County of , has this day paid into court
C. D.	in this action, the sum of dollars, to be

applied pursuant to the statute.
Dated the day of , 18 .

E. B. C., Clerk of
said County of

---

§ 297. *Entry of Judgment on Submission.*

Supreme Court,

A. B.	Judgment,
against	January 1, 1849.
C. D.	The above named parties, A. B. and C. D.,

having submitted the controversy between them without action, and a trial by the court being had thereon, the court decided [*state the decision.*]

Now, on motion of G. H., attorney of the said A. B., it is hereby adjudged, &c., [*as the decision may be.*]

E. B C., Clerk of
said County of

---

§ 298. *Confession of Judgment without Action.*[1]

County ss:

I, A. B., of the town of , in said county, hereby confess myself indebted to C. D., of the same place, [*or, as the case may be,*] in the sum of , and authorize the said C. D., or his executors, administrators, or assigns, to enter a judgment against me, in the Supreme Court of the State of New York, for that amount.*

The said sum of money is due on a promissory note, made by me, and dated the day of, &c., [*describe the note, or set forth in detail, the origin or cause of the indebtedness.*]

---

[1] See Laws of 1849, chap. 438—Part II., Title xii., chap. 3.
G

c

And I hereby state, that the sum by me above confessed is justly due [or, will justly become due] to the said C. D., in pursuance of the facts above set forth.

A. B.

Dated the   day of   , 18 .

§ 299. *Affidavit to verify Confession, and to be annexed thereto.*

In Supreme Court, } ss:
         County, }

A. B., above named and described, being duly sworn, says, that the above statement, by him signed, is true.

Sworn to, this   day of }
    , 18 , before me, }   A. B.
       G. H., County Clerk.
      [*Or any officer authorized to administer oaths.*]

§ 300. *Confession to secure against a Contingent Liability.*

       County, ss:

I, A. B., of, &c., [*as in* § 298 *to the* *, *and then add:*]

The following is a statement of the facts showing a contingent liability of the said C. D., for me, the said A. B., and to secure him against which, the above confession is made, viz: [*set forth the facts in detail.*]

And I hereby state, that the sum above confessed does not exceed the liability incurred by the said C. D., under the circumstances above described.

Dated, &c., [*conclude, as in* § 298, *and append the affidavit of verification,* (§ 299.)]

§ 301. *Entry of Judgment on Confession.*

In Supreme Court,
     C. D.   }   Judgment,
    against   }   January 1, 1849.
     A. B.   }   The above named A. B., having confessed a judgment to the above named C. D., for the sum of   dollars, it is hereby adjudged, that the said C. D. recover against the said A B. the sum of   dollars, aforesaid, with five dollars costs.

E. B. C., Clerk.

§ 302. *Clerk's Certificate of filing Notice of Lis Pendens.*

State of New York, } ss:
       County, }

I, E. B. C., Clerk of the said county, do hereby certify, that a notice, of which the above [or, within] is a copy, was filed in the clerk's office of said county, on the   day of   , 18   .

Dated the   day of   , 18   .

E. B. C.

---

§ 303. *Certificate of Authentication to the Acknowledgment, or Proof, of a Conveyance.*

State of New York, }
        County, } ss:

I, L. M., Clerk of the said county, do certify, that G. H., the person subscribing the within [or, annexed] certificate of acknowledgment, [or, proof,] was, at the date thereof, a Justice of the Peace of said county, and duly authorized to take acknowledgments and proofs of conveyances, to be recorded in this State; and that I am well acquainted with the handwriting of the said G. H., and verily believe that the name G. H., subscribed to the said certificate, is his proper and genuine signature.

In testimony whereof, I have caused the seal of the County
[L. S.]   Court of said county to be hereunto affixed, this
        day of   , 18   .

L. M.

---

§ 304. *Certificate of Official Character.*

State of New York, }
        County, } ss:

I, L. M., Clerk of the said county, do hereby certify, that G. H., the person subscribing the foregoing deposition, [or *whatever the instrument may be,*] and before whom the same was taken, [or, acknowledged,] was, on the   day of   , 18 , therein mentioned, the Judge of   County Court, [or, *as the case may be,*] a court of record of the said county of   ; [or, *as the proper title of the officer may be; and then add the clause in relation to the genuineness of the signature, if necessary.*]

[L. S.]   In testimony whereof, &c., [*as in* § 303.]

§ 305. *Transcript of Judgment and Clerk's Certificate.*

Supreme Court,
        A. B.   }   Damages, $253,87; Costs, $15,30.   Docketed
        against   }   , August   , 18   , at   A. M.
        C. D.   }   R. F., Attorney.

State of New York,   County, } ss:
        Clerk's Office, August   , 18   . }

I certify, that the preceding is a true copy of the docket of an original record of judgment remaining on the files of this office.

L. M., Clerk.

§ 306. *Certificate to Copy of a Record, or Paper, on File in the Clerk's Office.*

State of New York,   County, } ss:
 .   Clerk's Office, May , 18 . }

I do hereby certify, that I have compared the foregoing copy of a [*name the instrument,*] and of the endorsements thereupon, with the original records of the same remaining in this office, [or, with the originals now remaining on file in this office,] and that the same are correct transcripts therefrom, and of the whole of said original records, [*or, originals.*]

[L. S.]   In testimony whereof, &c., [*as in* § 303.]

---

§ 307. *Clerk's Certificate on Transcript of Judgment before Justice of the Peace.*

State of New York, } ss:
      County, }

I, L. M., Clerk of the said county, do certify, that G. H., the person subscribing the within [or, annexed] transcript, was, at the date of the judgment therein mentioned, viz: on the   day of   , 18 , a Justice of the Peace of the said county, and that I am well acquainted, &c., [*as in* § 303, *substituting* transcript *for* certificate.]

CHAPTER XII.

CONVEYANCES BY DEED AND MORTGAGE.

PRACTICAL REMARKS.

1. All instruments under seal are deeds; but the term 'deed,' is generally understood as applying to conveyances of land.

2. Every person capable of holding lands, (except idiots, persons of unsound minds, and infants,) seized of, or entitled to, any estate or interest in lands, may alien such estate or interest, at pleasure, subject to the restrictions and regulations provided by law.[1]

3. No purchase, or contract, for the sale of lands, in this State, made since the fourteenth day of October, 1775, with the Indians residing in the State, is valid, unless made under the authority and with the consent of the Legislature.[2]

4. Every grant in fee, or of a freehold estate, in New York, must be subscribed and sealed by the person from whom the estate or interest conveyed is intended to pass, or his lawful agent; if not duly acknowledged before its delivery, its execution and delivery must be attested by at least one witness; and if not so attested, it will not take effect as against a purchaser, or incumbrancer, until so acknowledged. A grant will not take effect, so as to vest the estate or interest intended to be conveyed, except from the time of its delivery. Almost any act of the party executing a deed, importing an intention to deliver it, will be sufficient; or it may be delivered as an *escrow*, on conditions, and will take effect, on the performance of such conditions, from the time of the delivery.[3]

5. No estate or interest in lands, other than leases for a term not exceeding one year, nor any trust, or power, over or concerning lands, or in any manner relating thereto, can be created, granted, assigned, surrendered, or declared, unless by act or operation of law, or by a deed, or conveyance in writing, subscribed by the party creating,

---

[1] 2 R. S. (3d ed.) 3, § 10.
[2] 2 R. S. (3d ed.) 3, § 11.
2 R S. (3d ed.) 22, §§ 137, 138; 13 John-son, 285; 11 Wendell. 240; 2 Hill, 659; 1 Barbour's S. C. Rep., 500.

granting, assigning, surrendering, or declaring, the same, or by his lawful agent thereunto authorized by writing.[1]

6. A contract for the sale of growing trees, with the right to enter and remove them, must be reduced to writing, in order to be valid.[2]

7. The term 'heirs,' or other words of inheritance, are not requisite to create or convey an estate in fee; and every grant of real estate, or any interest therein, will pass all the estate or interest of the grantor, unless the intent to pass a less estate or interest appears, by express terms, or is necessarily implied in the terms of the grant.[3]

8. No covenant can be implied in any conveyance of real estate, whether such conveyance contain special covenants or not. Deeds of bargain and sale, and of lease and release, may continue to be used, and will be deemed grants, and, as such, subject to the provisions of law concerning grants.[4]

9. No greater estate or interest will be construed to pass by any conveyance, than the grantor himself possessed at the delivery of the deed, or could then lawfully convey, except that every grant is conclusive as against the grantor, and his heirs, claiming from him by descent; and also, as against subsequent purchasers from such grantor, or from his heirs, claiming as such, except a subsequent purchaser in good faith, and for a valuable consideration.[5]

10. Every grant of lands will be absolutely void, if at the time of the delivery thereof, such lands be in the actual possession of a person claiming under a title adverse to that of the grantor; except as against the grantor and his heirs. But every person having a just title to lands, of which there is an adverse possession, may execute a mortgage on such lands; and such mortgage, if duly recorded, will bind the lands from the time the possession thereof may be recovered, by the mortgagor or his representatives, and will have preference over subsequent mortgages, judgments, or other instruments.[6]

11. Where the grantor in a deed has no title to the premises conveyed, the covenants of seizure and power to convey, if inserted in the deed, are broken immediately upon its execution.[7]

12. A deed should be founded on a sufficient consideration, and executed by persons able to contract and be contracted with; the subject matter must be set forth in sufficient words to describe the agreement, and bind the parties; and it should be read by or to the grantor, previous to the execution, unless the reading is expressly waived. The consideration of a deed may be either good or valuable: it must not partake of any thing immoral, illegal, or fraudulent.

---

[1] 2 R. S. (3d ed.) 194, § 6; 6 Wendell, 461; 10 Id., 436; 13 Id., 481; 16 Id., 25, 28; 2 Hill, 485.

[2] 1 Denio, 550.

[3] 2 R. S. (3d ed.) 33, § 1.

[4] 2 R. S. (3d ed.) 22, §§ 140, 142; 14 Wendell, 38; 8 Paige, 593

[5] 2 R. S. (3d ed.) 23, §§ 143, 144.

[6] 2 R. S. (3d ed.) 23, §§ 147, 148; 7 Wendell, 377; 9 Id., 516; 15 Id., 164; 21 Id, 98; 2 Hill, 626.

[7] 2 Barbour's S. C. Rep., 300.

Every deed, or contract, is void, when made for any fraudulent purpose, or in violation of law. A *good* consideration is founded upon natural love and affection between near relations by blood: a *valuable* consideration is founded on something deemed valuable, as money, goods, services, or marriage. An equitable liability is sufficient to uphold an express covenant or promise.[1]

13. Where the consideration is expressed in a deed, any averment to the contrary cannot be made, although it may be inquired into, for all purposes, except to impeach the deed as between the parties; nor will the validity of a deed depend on the amount of the consideration.[2]

14. The rule in relation to the description of premises conveyed by metes and bounds is, that known and fixed monuments control courses and distances; and the certainty of metes and bounds will include all the lands within them, though they vary from the quantity expressed in the deed. Where natural and fixed objects are wanting, and the course and distance cannot be reconciled, the one or the other may be preferred, according to circumstances.[3]

15. In the construction of every instrument granting or conveying, or authorizing the creation or conveyance of, any estate or interest in lands, it is the duty of courts of justice to carry into effect the intent of the parties, so far as such intent can be collected from the whole instrument, and is consistent with the rules of law. Material erasures or interlineations in a deed, should always be noted before the execution.[4]

16. A quit-claim deed, purporting to convey one's " right of expectancy," or possibility of inheritance, will not affect the grantor's title as heir, subsequently acquired.[5]

17. When a deed is executed by an attorney, for several principals, one seal is sufficient, provided it appear that the seal affixed was intended to be adopted as the seal of all.[6]

18. An action will lie for fraudulent representations as to the territorial extent of right in real estate conveyed or leased.[7]

19. Where land is conveyed by metes and bounds, if the description contains positive language as to quantity, it is to be regarded as descriptive only, and not as a covenant of quantity.[8]

20. If a grantor has no title, his covenant of seizin is broken immediately on the execution of his deed; but where there are covenants of warranty and quiet enjoyment only, there must be an eviction, before a recovery can be had.[9]

[1] 4 Kent's Commentaries, (2d ed.) 464; 2 R. S. (3d ed.) 193, §§ 1, 2; 2 Hill, 659; 7 Id., 253; 1 Denio, 520.
[2] 1 Johnson, 139; 4 Id., 23; 16 Id. 47; 4 Cowen, 430; 9 Id., 69; 9 Wendell, 611; 16 Id., 460; Denio, 226. 2 Barbour's Ch. Rep., 232.
[3] 4 Kent's Commentaries (2d ed.) 466; 3 Barbour's S. C. Rep., 215.
[4] 2 R. S. (3d ed.) 33, § 2; 2 Barbour's S. C Rep. 229: 1 Comstock, 96.
[5] 2 Hill, 641.
[6] 4 Hill, 351.
[7] 1 Comstock, 305.
[8] 3 Barbour's S. C. Rep., 353.
[9] 1 Comstock, 509.

21. No mortgage will be construed as implying a covenant for the payment of the sum intended to be secured; and where there is no express covenant for such - payment contained in the mortgage, and no bond or other separate instrument given, the remedies of the mortgagee will be confined to the lands mentioned in the mortgage.[1]

22. The wife of a grantor, or mortgagor, must unite with her husband in a conveyance, in order to release her right of dower, except in the case of a mortgage for the purchase money. A deed conveying any interest of a married woman in lands, except her separate estate, or unless under her power, must be executed by herself and husband: but a married woman who is an infant, cannot bind herself by deed so as to bar her right of dower.[2]

23. Where, upon the sale and purchase of land, a deed is executed by the vendor, and a mortgage given by the purchaser, and both are acknowledged and recorded at the same time, it will be presumed that the mortgage was given to secure the purchase money, though the same be executed to a third person, instead of the vendor, by direction of the latter.[3]

24. Where it is evidently the intention of the parties to a paper that the same shall be regarded as a mortgage, no form of words will defeat such intention.[4]

25. A mortgage is a lien, or security for a debt, but does not give title in, or to, real estate; and the interest of the mortgagee is a mere chattel interest.[5]

26. A mortgage conditioned for support and maintenance is good.[6]

27. If a deed be given, and the purchaser execute a mortgage, the presumption will be that they were executed at the same time, and the vendee will acquire only the equity of redemption.[7]

28. Where lands are mortgaged, and a part thereof subsequently sold by the mortgagee, the part remaining unsold is the primary · fund for the payment of the debt, and if different parcels are sold, they are to be charged with the debt in the inverse order of alienation.[8]

29. A release of a part of mortgaged premises does not impair · or destroy the lien as to the residue between the original parties.[9]

30. The mere recording of an assignment of a mortgage is not such a notice to the mortgagor as will invalidate a payment made by him, subsequent to the assignment, to the assignor.[10]

31. A mortgage discharged of record, without actual satisfaction, in consequence of fraudulent representations by the mortgagor, may be revived.[11]

---

[1] 2 R. S. (3d ed.,) 22, § 139.
[2] 1 Barbour's S. C. Rep., 399; 4 Id., 407; Id., 546.
[3] 1 Barbour's S. C. Rep., 399.
[4] 2 Barbour's S. C. Rep., 29.
[5] 3 Denio, 232; 2 Barbour's Ch. Rep., 119; 3 Barbour's S. C. Rep., 305.
[6] 2 Comstock, 360.
[7] 3 Barbour's S. C. Rep., 128.
[8] 2 Comstock, 289.
[9] 3 Barbour's S. C. Rep., 128.
[10] 2 Barbour's Ch. Rep., 82.
[11] 1 Barbour's S. C. Rep., 392.

32. A certificate of the sale of real estate on an execution, must contain: a particular description of the premises sold; the price bid for each distinct lot, or parcel; the whole consideration money paid; and the time when such sale will become absolute, and the purchaser be entitled to a conveyance, pursuant to law. The deed is to be executed by the officer making the sale.[1]

33. Two witnesses are required at the execution of a deed, in New Hampshire, Vermont, Rhode Island, Connecticut, Pennsylvania, Georgia, Ohio, Indiana, Illinois, Michigan, and Wisconsin. In Delaware, Tennessee, and North Carolina, two witnesses are required where a deed is to be proved by witnesses. In the other States, one witness is sufficient to render a deed valid, as between the parties. In this State, proof of the execution of a deed by one witness, or its acknowledgment before the proper officer, will entitle it to be recorded.

34. Mortgages of real estate may be foreclosed by advertisement, by the party holding the same, in person, where default has been made in any condition of such mortgage, and no other legal proceedings are then pending thereupon.[2]

35. In order to foreclose a mortgage, a notice, specifying the names of the mortgagor and mortgagee, and assignee, if any; the date of the mortgage, and where recorded; the amount claimed to be due at the time of the first publication of the notice; and a description of the mortgaged premises, conforming substantially with that contained in the mortgage; must be published for twelve weeks, successively, at least once in each week, in a newspaper printed in the county where the premises to be sold are situated; or, if they are situated in two or more counties, in either of them.[3]

36. A copy of the notice of foreclosure must be affixed, at least twelve weeks prior to the time designated for the sale, on the outward door of the building where the county courts are directed to be held, in the county where the premises are situated; or, if there are two or more such buildings, on the outward door of that one nearest the premises. A copy of such notice must also be served, at least fourteen days prior to the time specified therein for the sale, on the mortgagor or his personal representatives, and on the subsequent grantees and mortgagees whose conveyances or mortgages were on record at the time of the first publication of the notice, and on all persons having a lien, by judgment or decree, on the mortgaged premises, subsequent to such mortgage; such service may be made personally, or by leaving the notice at the dwelling-house of the person to be served, in charge of some one of suitable age, or by depositing a copy of such notice, at least twenty-eight days prior to

---

[1] 2 R. S. (3d ed.) 467, § 44; 20 Wendell, 416; 7 Hill, 476, 616.

[2] 2 R. S. (3d ed.) 632, §§ 1, 2; 7 Wendell, 453; 4 Paige, 58; 7 Id., 257.

[3] 2 R. S. (3d ed.) 632, 3; §§ 3, 4; 1 Hill, 10.

the time specified therein for the sale, in the post office, properly folded and directed to said person at his place of residence.[1]

37. The sale of the mortgaged premises may be postponed from time to time, by inserting a notice thereof, as soon as practicable, in the newspaper in which the original advertisement was published, and continuing such insertion until the time to which the sale was postponed.[2]

38. The sale must be made at public auction, in the day time, in the county where the mortgaged premises, or some part of them, are situated. If the premises consist of distinct farms or lots, they must be sold separately; and no more can be sold than will be sufficient to pay the amount due on the mortgage at the time of the first publication of the notice, with interest, and the costs and expenses allowed by law. The mortgagee, his assigns, or his or their legal representatives, may, fairly and in good faith, purchase the premises, or any part of them, at the sale.[3]

39. A sale of mortgaged premises, in pursuance of the foregoing directions, will be a bar of all claim or equity of redemption of the mortgagor, or his representatives, or of any person claiming under him or them, by virtue of a title subsequent to the mortgage foreclosed; and also, of any person having a lien on the premises, or any part thereof, by or under any judgment or decree, subsequent to such mortgage, who has been served with a copy of the notice of sale.[4]

40. An affidavit of the facts and circumstances of the sale must be made by the person who officiated as auctioneer; an affidavit of the publication of the notice, by the printer of the newspaper in which the same was inserted, or his foreman; and an affidavit of affixing the notice, and, also, an affidavit of serving the same, by the person, or persons, performing such duty; which affidavits may be taken by any judge of a court of record, supreme court commissioner, or commissioner of deeds, and may be filed and recorded in the clerk's office of the county in which the sale took place. Such affidavits will constitute the evidence of the sale, and foreclosure of the equity of redemption, without any conveyance; although it is better for the purchaser, when not a mortgagee or assignee, to take a deed, with the usual covenants of warranty, &c., of such mortgagee, or assignee, where there is the least possible doubt in regard to the title.[5]

41. The purchaser of lands, on foreclosure and sale under a mortgage, is entitled to the growing crops sown by the mortgagor.[6]

---

[1] 2 R. S. (3d ed.,) 632, § 3; Laws of 1842, chap. 271; Laws of 1844, chap. 346.
[2] 2 R. S. (3d ed.,) 633, § 6; 4 Denio, 104.
[3] 2 R. S. (3d ed.,) 633, §§ 6, 7; 4 Cowen, 266.; 1 Paige, 52.
[4] 2 R. S. (3d ed.,) 633, § 8; 10 Johnson, 185; 4 Paige, 59, 631; 1 Hill, 107; 6 Id., 65
[5] 2 R. S. (3d ed.,) 634, §§ 9–14; 4 Denio, 41.
[6] 2 Denio, 174.

FORMS.

§ 308. *Simple Deed.*

This indenture, made the   day of   , in the year of our Lord one thousand eight hundred and   , between A. B., of, &c., of the first part, and C. D., of &c., of the second part, witnesseth: That the said party of the first part, for and in consideration of the sum of   dollars, to him in hand paid by the said party of the second part, the receipt whereof is hereby acknowledged, hath bargained and sold, and by these presents doth bargain and sell, unto the said party of the second part, and to his heirs and assigns, forever, all, &c., [*here describe the premises;*] together with all and singular the hereditaments and appurtenances thereunto belonging, or in any wise appertaining; and the reversion and reversions, remainder and remainders, rents, issues and profits, thereof; and also all the estate, right, title, interest, claim, or demand whatsoever, of him, the said party of the first part, either in law or equity, of, in and to, the above bargained premises, and every part and parcel thereof:*

In witness whereof, the said party of the first part has hereunto set his hand and seal, the day and year first above written.

> Sealed and delivered, }
>   in presence of   }
>   G. H.   A. B. [L. s.]

---

§ 309. *Quit-Claim Deed.*

Know all men by these presents: That we, A. B., of, &c., and E. his wife, in consideration of the sum of   , to us in hand paid by C. D., of, &c., the receipt whereof we do hereby acknowledge, have bargained, sold and quit-claimed, and by these presents do bargain, sell and quit-claim, unto the said C. D., and to his heirs and assigns, forever, all our and each of our right, title, interest, estate, claim and demand, both at law and in equity, and as well in possession as in expectancy, of, in and to, all that certain piece or parcel of land, situate, &c., [*description;*] with all and singular the hereditaments and appurtenances thereunto belonging.

In witness whereof, we have hereunto set our hands and seals, the day and year first above written.

Sealed, &c., [*as in* § 308.]

> A. B. [L. s.]
> E. B. [L. s.]

§ 310. *Quit-Claim, with Covenant against Acts of Grantor.*

This indenture, made the   day of   , in the year one thousand eight hundred and   , between A. B., of, &c., of the first part, and C. D., of, &c., of the second part, witnesseth: That the said party of the first part, for and in consideration of the sum of   dollars, to him in hand paid by the said party of the second part, at or before the ensealing and delivery of these presents, the receipt whereof is hereby acknowledged, hath remised, released and quit-claimed, and by these presents doth remise, release, and quit-claim, unto the said party of the second part, and to his heirs and assigns, forever, all [*description;*] together with all and singular the tenements, hereditaments and appurtenances, thereunto belonging, or in any wise appertaining; and the reversion and reversions, remainder and remainders, rents, issues, and profits thereof: And also, all the estate, right, title, interest, [*insert*, dower and right of dower, *if necessary,*] property, possession, claim and demand whatsoever, as well in law as in equity, of the said party of the first part, of, in, or to, the above described premises, and every part and parcel thereof, with the appurtenances. And the said party of the first part, for himself and his heirs, executors and administrators, doth covenant, promise and agree, to and with the said party of the second part, his heirs, executors, administrators and assigns, that he hath not made, done, committed, executed, or suffered, any act or acts, thing or things, whatsoever, whereby, or by means whereof, the above mentioned and described premises, or any part or parcel thereof, now are, or at any time hereafter shall, or may be, impeached, charged or incumbered, in any manner or way whatsoever.

In witness, &c., [*as in* § 308.]

---

§ 311. *Warranty Deed — Short Form.*

To all people to whom these presents shall come, greeting:

Know ye, that I, A. B., of, &c., for the consideration of   dollars, received to my full satisfaction, of C. D., of, &c., do grant, bargain, sell and confirm, unto the said C. D., his heirs, and assigns, all, [*description;*] To have and to hold the above granted and bargained premises, with the appurtenances thereof, unto the said C. D., his heirs and assigns, to his and their own proper use and behoof forever. And I do, for myself, and my heirs, executors and administrators, covenant with the said C. D., his heirs and assigns, that at and until the ensealing of these presents, I am well seized of the premises, as of a good and indefeasible estate in fee simple, and have good right to bargain and sell the same, in manner and form aforesaid; and that the same is free from all incumbrance whatsoever. And further, I do by these presents bind myself, and my heirs, to warrant and forever defend the above granted and bargained premises, unto the said C. D., his heirs and assigns, against all claims and demands whatsoever.

In witness whereof, I have hereunto set my hand and seal, the   day of   , in the year one thousand eight hundred and   .

Sealed, &c., [*as in* § 308.]

---

§ 312. *Warranty Deed.*

This indenture, made the   day of   , in the year one thousand eight hundred and   , between A. B., of, &c., of the first part, and C. D., of, &c., of the second part, witnesseth: That the said party of the first part, for and in consideration of the sum of   dollars, lawful money of the United States, to him in hand paid by the said party of the second part, at or before the ensealing and delivery of these presents, the receipt whereof is hereby acknowledged. hath granted, bargained, sold, aliened, remised, released, conveyed and confirmed, and by these presents doth grant, bargain, sell, alien, remise, release, convey and confirm, unto the said party of the second part, and to his heirs and assigns, forever, all [*description;*] together with all and singular the tenements, hereditaments and appurtenances, thereunto belonging, or in any wise appertaining, and the reversion and reversions, remainder and remainders, rents, issues, and profits thereof: And also, all the estate, right, title, interest, [*insert here*, dower and right of dower, *if necessary*,] property, possession, claim and demand, whatsoever, as well in law as in equity, of the said party of the first part, of, in, or to, the above described premises, and every part and parcel thereof, with the appurtenances:* To have and to hold all and singular the above mentioned and described premises, together with the appurtenances, unto the said party of the second part, his heirs and assigns, forever.   And the said A. B., for himself, and his heirs, the said premises in the quiet and peaceable possession of the said party of the second part, his heirs, and assigns, against the said party of the first part, and his heirs, and against all and every person whomsoever, lawfully claiming or to claim the same, shall and will warrant, and by these presents forever defend.

In witness, &c., [*as in* § 308.]

---

§ 313. *Full Covenant—Short Form.*

This indenture, made the   day of   , one thousand eight hundred and   , between A. B., of, &c., of the first part, and C. D., of, &c., of the second part, witnesseth: That the said party of the first part, in consideration of the sum of   dollars, to him duly paid, hath sold. and by these presents doth grant and convey.

to the said party of the second part, and his heirs and assigns, for ever, all [*description;*] together with the appurtenances, and all the estate, title and interest, of the said party of the first part therein. And the said A. B., for himself and his heirs, doth hereby covenant and agree, that at the delivery hereof he is the lawful owner of the premises above granted, and seized of a good and indefeasible estate of inheritance therein, clear of all incumbrance whatever, of every name or nature; and that he will warrant and defend the above premises, in the quiet and peaceable possession of the said party of the second part, his heirs and assigns, forever.

In witness, &c., [*as in* § 308.]

————

§ 314. *Full Covenant Deed — the usual Form.*

This indenture, &c., [*as in* § 312 *to the* *, *and then add:*] To have and to hold the above granted, bargained and described premises, with the appurtenances, unto the said party of the second part, his heirs and assigns, to his and their own proper use, benefit and behoof, forever. And the said A. B., for himself and his heirs, executors and administrators, doth covenant, grant and agree, to and with the said party of the second part, his heirs and assigns, that the said party of the first part, at the time of the sealing and delivery of these presents, is lawfully seized in his own right, [*or, as the case may be,*] of a good, absolute, and indefeasible estate of inheritance, in fee simple, of and in, all and singular the above granted and described premises, with the appurtenances, and hath good right, full power, and lawful authority, to grant, bargain, sell and convey the same, in manner aforesaid: and that the said party of the second part, his heirs and assigns, shall and may, at all times hereafter, peaceably and quietly have, hold, use, occupy, possess and enjoy, the above granted premises, and every part and parcel thereof, with the appurtenances, without any let, suit, trouble, molestation, eviction, or disturbance, of the said party of the first part, his heirs or assigns, or of any other person or persons lawfully claiming or to claim the same. And that the same now are free, clear, discharged and unincumbered, of and from all former and other grants, titles, charges, estates, judgments, taxes, assignments and incumbrances, of what nature or kind soever.* And, also, that the said party of the first part, and his heirs, and all and every person or persons whomsoever, lawfully or equitably deriving any estate, right, title, or interest, of, in, or to, the herein granted premises, by, from, under, or in trust for, him or them, shall and will, at all time or times, hereafter, upon the reasonable request, and at the proper costs and charges in the law of the said party of the second part, his heirs and assigns, make, do and execute, or cause to be made, done and executed, all and every such further and other lawful and reasonable acts, conveyances and assurances, in the law, for the better and more effectually vesting and confirming the premises hereby granted, or so intended to be, in and to the said party of the second part, his heirs and assigns, forever, as by the said party of the second part, his heirs or assigns, or his or their counsel, learned in the law, shall be reasonably advised, devised, or required: And the said A. B., for himself and his heirs, the above described and hereby granted and released premises, and every part and parcel thereof, with the appurtenances, unto the said party of the second part, his heirs and assigns, against the said party of the first part and his heirs, and against all and every person and persons whomsoever, lawfully claiming, or to claim the same, shall and will warrant, and by these presents forever defend.

In witness, &c., [*as in* § 308.]

---

§ 315. *Deed of Land subject to Mortgage.*

This indenture, &c., [*as in* § 312 *to the* *, *and then add:*] subject, however, to the payments, conditions and agreements, specified and contained in a certain indenture of mortgage, executed by the said A. B., to E. F., on the   day of   , A. D. 18 , and recorded in   County Clerk's office, in book No.   of mortgages, at pages   , &c., on the   day of   , A. D. 18   , at o'clock A. M.; and which said mortgage was given for the purpose of securing the payment of the sum of   dollars, at the time and in the manner therein specified, and upon which there is now due and payable, [*or*, there is yet to become due and payable, on the   , day of   , 18 ,] the sum of   dollars, with interest from the   day of   , 18   : To have and to hold, &c., [*as in* § 312 *to the end; or as in* § 314; *in the latter case, however, insert after the * the words:* except as aforesaid.]

In witness, &c., [*as in* § 308.]

---

§ 316. *Corporation Deed.*

This indenture, made the   day of   , in the year one thousand eight hundred and   , between the bank of   , [*or*, the   insurance company,] of the first part, and C. D., of, &c., [*as in* § 312 *to the* *, *and then add:*] To have and to hold the above granted, bargained, and described premises, with the appurtenances, unto the said party of the second part, his heirs and assigns, to his and their own proper use and benefit, forever.   And the said bank of   , [*or*,   insurance company,] the said premises, &c., [*as in* § 312 *to the end; or*, doth covenant, grant, and agree, &c., *as in* § 314.]

In witness whereof, the said party of the first part hath hereunto caused their corporate seal to be affixed, and these presents to be sub scribed by their president and cashier, [*or*, secretary; *or, as the case may be.*]

Sealed and delivered, ⎫
  in presence of ⎬   N. B.,   [L. s.]
     G. H.   ⎭   President of the Bank of   .

---

§ 317. *Deed of Mortgaged Premises, on Foreclosure by Advertisement.*

This indenture, made the   day of   , in the year of our Lord one thousand eight hundred and   , between C. D., of, &c., of the first part, and E. F., of, &c., of the second part: Whereas, A. B., by a certain indenture of mortgage, bearing date the   day of   , one thousand eight hundred and   , for the consideration of the sum of   dollars, did bargain, sell and convey, unto C. D., his heirs and assigns, forever, all that certain piece or parcel of land, hereinafter particularly described, with the appurtenances, subject to a proviso, in the said indenture of mortgage contained, that the same should be void on the payment, by the said C. D., his heirs, executors, administrators, or assigns, of the sum of   dollars, in the manner particularly specified in the condition of a certain bond or obligation, bearing even date with the said indenture of mortgage: with a special power in the said indenture of mortgage contained, authorizing the said C. D., his heirs, executors, administrators, or assigns, if default should be made in the payment of the said sum of money mentioned in the condition of the said bond or obligation, with the interest, or of any part thereof, to sell and dispose of the mortgaged premises, or any part thereof, at public auction; and to make and deliver to the purchaser, or purchasers, thereof, good and sufficient deed, or deeds, of conveyance in the law, for the same, in fee simple: And, whereas, the said indenture of mortgage has been duly recorded according to law, as by the said indenture of mortgage, and the record thereof, and of the power therein contained, reference being thereunto had, may more fully and at large appear: [*If necessary, say:* and the same hath been duly assigned to the party of the first part, by the said C. D., as by the record of the said assignment, &c., *as above:*] And whereas, default having been made in the payment of the money intended to be secured by the said indenture of mortgage, the mortgaged premises hereinafter particularly described, were, on the   day of   , one thousand eight hundred and   , sold at public auction, to the said party of the second part, for the sum of   dollars, being the highest sum bid for the same, public notice having been previously given of such sale, by advertisement, inserted and published for twelve weeks, once in each week, successively, in a public newspaper, entitled the   , printed in the town of   , in the county in which the mortgaged premises are situated, a copy of which advertisement was, for twelve weeks prior to the time therein specified for such sale, duly affixed on the outward door of the court house in the town of   , being the building in which the county courts are directed to be held; and the said party of the first part, having caused a copy of said printed notice, or advertisement, to be duly served on all persons having any claim upon the said premises, as required by the act passed May 7th, 1844.   Now, therefore, this indenture witnesseth: that the party of the first part, for and in consideration of the sum so bid, as aforesaid, to him in hand paid by the said party of the second part, at the time of the ensealing and delivery of these presents, the receipt whereof is hereby acknowledged, hath granted, bargained, sold, aliened, released and confirmed, and by these presents doth grant, bargain, sell, alien, release and confirm, unto the said party of the second part, and to his heirs and assigns, forever, all [*description;*] together with all and singular, the tenements, hereditaments, and appurtenances, thereunto belonging, or in any wise appertaining, as the same is des cribed and conveyed, in and by the said indenture of mortgage; and also, all the estate, right, title, interest, property, claim and demand, whatsoever, both in law and equity, of the said A. B., as well as of the said party of the first part, of, in and to, the above described premises, with the appurtenances, as fully, to all intents and purposes, as the said party of the first part hath power and authority to grant and sell the same, by virtue of the said indenture of mortgage, and of the statute in such case made and provided, or otherwise: To have and to hold the said above mentioned and described premises, with their and every of their appurtenances, unto the said party of the second part, his heirs and assigns, to the sole and only proper use, benefit and behoof, of the said party of the second part, his heirs and assigns, forever.

In witness, &c., [*as in* § 308.]

§ 318. *Deed by Guardian.*

To all persons to whom these presents shall come: E. F., of   , guardian of C. B. and E. B., minors, and children of A. B., late of said   , deceased, sends greeting: Whereas, by an order of the Probate Court, holden at   , within and for the county of   , on the   day of.   , in the year   , the said E. F., in his capacity of guardian, as aforesaid, was empowered and licensed to make sale of the whole of the said minors' interest, being one undivided twelfth part each, in the real estate hereinafter described; and whereas, the said E. F. having given the bond, and taken the oath by law required, before fixing on the time and place of sale, and also given public notice of the said sale, by causing a notification thereof to be inserted and printed   weeks, successively in the newspaper called   , printed at   , did, the

11

day of   ·, in the year   , cause the said minors' interest to be exposed for sale, pursuant to the said notice, at public vendue, on the premises, and the same was then and there struck off to S. T., of, &c., for the sum of   dollars, he being the highest bidder therefor: Now, know, ye that I, the said E. F., in my capacity of guardian, as . aforesaid, by virtue of the license aforesaid, and in consideration of the sum of   dollars, to me paid by S. T., aforesaid, (the receipt whereof I hereby acknowledge,) do hereby grant, bargain, sell and convey, unto the said S. T., his heirs and assigns, two undivided twelfth parts of a certain tract or parcel of land, situate in   , bounded and described as follows, viz: [*description,*] being the shares of the said minors therein, with all the privileges and appurtenances thereunto belonging: To have and to hold the above granted premises, to him, the said S. T., his heirs and assigns forever.   And I, the said E. F., for myself, my executors and administrators, do covenant with the said S. T., his heirs and assigns, that in making the said sale, I have in all things observed the rules and directions of the law; and that I will, and my heirs shall, warrant and defend the above granted premises to the said S. T., his heirs and assigns, against the lawful claims and demands of the said minors and their heirs, and all persons claiming the same by, through, or under them, or either of them.

In testimony whereof, I, the said E. F., have, &c., [*as in* §311.]

----

§ 319. *Deed by Administrator, Empowered to sell by Surrogate.*

To all to whom these presents shall come: I, A. B., of   , in the county of   , in the State of   , administrator of the goods and estate which were of C. D., late of   , &c., deceased, intestate, send greeting: Whereas, by an order of the Surrogate of the county of   , made at a Probate Court held at   , within the county of   , on the   day of   last past, I, the said A. B., was licensed and empowered to sell and pass deeds, to convey the real estate of the said C. D., hereinafter described; and whereas, I, the said A. B., having given public notice of the intended sale, by causing a notification thereof to be printed and inserted   weeks, successively, in the newspaper called the   , printed in   , agreeably to the order and direction of said court; and having given the bond and taken the oath, by law in such cases required, previous to fixing upon the time and place of sale, did, on the   day of   instant, pursuant to the license and notice aforesaid, sell by public auction, the real estate of the said C. D., hereinafter described, to E. F., of   , in the county of   , for the sum of   dollars, he being the highest bidder therefor: Now, therefore, know ye, that I, the said A. B., by virtue of the power and authority in me vested, as aforesaid, and in consideration of the aforesaid sum of   dollars, to me paid by the said E. F., (the receipt whereof is hereby acknowledged,) do hereby grant, bargain, sell and convey, unto the said E. F., his heirs and assigns, all [*description:*] To have and to hold the above granted premises, to the said E. F., his heirs and assigns, to his and their use and behoof, forever. And I, the said A. B., for myself, my heirs, executors and administrators, do hereby covenant with the said E. F., his heirs and assigns, that in pursuance of the license aforesaid, I took the oath and gave the bond, by law required, and gave public notice of said sale, as above set forth.

In witness whereof, I, the said A. B., have, &c., [*as in* § 311.]

---

§ 320. *Executors' Deed.*

This indenture, made the   day of   , in the year   , between E. F., of, &c., and L. M., of, &c., executors of the last will and testament of A. B., deceased, late of the town of   , in the county of   , and State of   , of the first part, and C. D., of, &c., of the second part, witnesseth: That the said parties of the first part, by virtue of the power and authority to them given, in and by the said last will and testament, and for and in consideration of the sum of   dollars, lawful money of the United States, to them in hand paid, at or before the ensealing and delivery of these presents, by the said party of the second part, the receipt whereof is hereby acknowledged, have granted, bargained, sold, aliened, released, conveyed and confirmed, and by these presents do grant, bargain, sell, alien, release, convey and confirm, unto the said party of the second part, his heirs and assigns, forever, all [*description:*] Together with all and singular, the hereditaments and appurtenances, to the same belonging, or in any wise appertaining; and the reversion and reversions, remainder and remainders, rents, issues, and profits thereof: And also, all the estate, right, title, interest, claim and demand, whatsoever, both in law and equity, which the said testator had in his lifetime, and at the time of his decease, and which the said parties of the first part, or either of them, have, or hath, by virtue of the said last will and testament, or otherwise, of, in and to, the same, and every part and parcel thereof, with the appurtenances: To have and to hold the aforegranted premises, to him, the said C. D., his heirs and assigns, to his and their use and behoof, forever. And we, the said E. F. and L. M., do covenant with the said C. D., his heirs and assigns, that we are lawfully the executors of the last will and testament of the said A. B., and that we have not made or suffered any incumbrance on the hereby granted premises, since we were appointed executors of said A. B.; and that we have in all respects acted, in making this conveyance, in pursuance of the authority granted to us, in and by the said last will and testament of the said A. B.

In testimony whereof, the said parties of the first part have hereunto set their hands and seals, &c., [*as in* § 308.]

---

§ 321. *Deed of Commissioners in Partition.*

This indenture, made, &c., between A. B., C. D., and E. F., all of, &c., commissioners in partition, duly appointed as hereinafter mentioned, of the first part, and L. M., of, &c., of the second part: Whereas, S. T., and R. T., of, &c., in the town of　　　　, in the year one thousand eight hundred and　　, did exhibit to the County Court of the county of　　, a petition for a division and partition of certain premises therein mentioned, according to the respective rights of the parties interested therein, and for a sale of such premises, if it should appear that a partition thereof could not be made without great prejudice to the owners, pursuant to the statute relating to the partition of lands owned by several persons; in which petition it was, amongst other things, set forth, that the said petitioners, [*state names of parties and their respective interests, as in the petition:*] All which, together with the respective interests of each of the said parties in and to the said premises, will more fully appear from the said petition, now on file in the office of the clerk of the said court; and whereas, such proceedings were thereupon had, in the said court, that judgment was duly rendered, that partition of the said premises should be made according to the several rights and interests of the said parties: And thereupon, to make such partition, the parties of the first part to these presents being qualified, were by the said court appointed commissioners: And whereas, such proceedings were afterwards had in the said court upon the said petition, that the said commissioners, so appointed, as aforesaid, were, by a rule of said court, ordered and directed to sell the said premises, with the appurtenances, at public auction, to the highest bidder; giving notice, according to law, of the time and place of such sale; and that they should make report thereof to the said court, as by the records of the said court does more fully and at large appear. And whereas, the said commissioners, pursuant to the said order and direction, after giving public notice of the time and place of such sale, did, on the　　　　day of　　, 18　, at the town of　　　　, in said county of　　, expose to sale at public auction, all and singular the said premises, with the appurtenances; at which sale the said premises, [*or, a part of the said premises,*] as follows, viz: all [*description,*] were sold to the said party of the second part, for the sum of　　　　dollars, that being the highest sum bid for the same: And whereas, the proceedings of the said commissioners in the premises were duly reported to the said court, and the sale approved and confirmed, on the　　day of　　, one thousand eight hundred and　　, as by the records of the said court more fully appears; and the said commissioners were thereupon, by the said court, directed to execute to the said party of the second part, a conveyance of said premises, pursuant to the sale so made as aforesaid. Now this indenture witnesseth: that the said parties of the first part, pursuant to the direction and authority to them given, and for and in consideration of the sum of money so bid as aforesaid, to them in hand paid by the said party of the second part, at or before the ensealing and delivery of these presents, the receipt whereof is hereby acknowledged, have bargained, sold, aliened, conveyed and confirmed, and by these presents do bargain, sell, alien, convey and confirm, unto the said party of the second part, all the estate, right, title, interest, claim and demand, of the said parties of the first part, and also all the right, title, interest, claim and demand, of all and singular, the several and respective parties to the proceedings in partition aforesaid, of, in and to, all and singular the said premises above particularly described as purchased by the said party of the second part; together with all and singular the hereditaments and appurtenances, to the same belonging, or in any wise appertaining, and the reversion and reversions, remainder and remainders, rents, issues, and profits thereof, and of every part thereof: To have and to hold the said above bargained premises, with the appurtenances, and every part thereof, unto the said party of the second part, his heirs and assigns, to his and their only proper use and behoof, forever, in as full and ample a manner, as the said parties of the first part ought to do, pursuant to the statute and the authority as aforesaid.

In witness whereof, the said parties have hereunto interchangeably set their hands and seals, the day and year first above written.

Sealed and delivered, ⎫   A. B. [L. s.]
  in presence of ⎬   C. D. [L. s.]
     G. H. ⎭   E. F. [L. s.]
                     L. M. [L. s.]

---

§ 322. *Deed with Trust Habendum Clause.*

This indenture, made, &c., [*as in* § 308, *or* § 312, *to the* *, *and then add:*] To have and to hold all and singular the said hereinbefore granted and described premises, with the appurtenances, unto the said C. D., upon the trusts, nevertheless, and to and for the uses, interests and purposes, hereinafter limited, described and declared; that is to say, upon trust to receive the issues, rents and profits, of the said premises, and apply the same to the use of E. F., during the term of his natural life, and, after the death of the said E. F., to convey the same by deed, to G. H. in fee.

In witness, &c., [*as in* § 308.]   A. B. [L. s.]

§ 323. *Deed by Trustees of an Absconding Debtor.*

To all to whom these presents shall come: We, A. B., C. D. and E. F., of the county of   , and State of New York, Trustees of the estate of G. H., an absconding debtor, late of   , in the said county, send greeting:

Whereas, by an order of J. P. H., Esquire, County Judge of said county of   , an attachment was issued against the estate, both real and personal, of the said G. H., on the   day of   , 18   , directed to the Sheriff of the said county of   , who, by virtue of the same, attached all the property, both real and personal, of the said G. H. in the county of   ; and due notice of said attachment having been published for the time, and in the manner, required by the statute in such case made and provided, afterwards, to wit, on the   day of   , 18   , by order of J. P. H., Esquire, aforesaid, we, the said A. B., C. D. and E. F., were duly appointed Trustees of the estate of the said G. H., and for all his creditors, with such powers concerning the estate, real and personal, of the said G. H., as are given by statute in case of an absconding debtor: and we did on that day each of us take the oath required by statute, for the faithful discharge of the trust reposed in us as Trustees, and cause notice of our appointment to be published, according to law: and whereas, we, the said A. B., C. D. and E. F., having given public notice of the intended sale, by causing notice thereof to be printed and inserted two weeks, successively, in the   , a newspaper printed in the said county of   , and having caused notice of the same to be posted up in four public places in said county, we did, on the   day of   , 18   , pursuant to the issuing of said attachment, the appointment and notice aforesaid, sell by public auction, the real estate of the said G. H., hereinafter described, to L. M., of   , for the sum of   dollars; he being the highest bidder therefor, and that being the highest sum bid for the same.

Now, therefore, know ye, that we, the said A. B., C. D. and E. F., by virtue of the power and authority in us vested, as aforesaid, and in consideration of the aforesaid sum of   dollars to us paid by the said L. M., the receipt whereof is hereby acknowledged, do hereby grant, bargain, sell and convey, unto the said L. M., his heirs and assigns, all the interest which the said G. H. had on the   day of   , 18   , [*insert the day on which the attachment issued,*] to all that certain piece or parcel of land, &c., [*describe the premises:*] To have and to hold the above granted and described premises to the said L. M., his heirs and assigns, forever.

In testimony whereof, &c., [*as in § 320.*]

§ 324. *Sheriff's Certificate of the Sale of Real Estate, on an Execution.*

Supreme Court,

A. B.   I, A. P., Sheriff of the county of   , do
against   hereby certify, that by virtue of an execution in the
E. D.   above cause, tested the   day of   , in the
year   , by which I was commanded to make, of the goods and chattels of E. D., in my bailiwick,   dollars, which A. B. had recovered against him in the said court, for his damages, which he had sustained, as well by reason of the not performing certain promises, [*or*, for the detention of a certain debt; *or, as the cause of action may be,*] as for his costs and charges; and if sufficient goods and chattels could not be found, that then I should cause the said damages to be made of the real estate which the said E. D. had, on the   day of   , in the year   , or at any time afterwards, in whose hands soever the same might be; as by the said writ of execution, reference being thereunto had, more fully appears: I have levied on, and this day sold, at public auction, according to the statute in such case made and provided, to E. F., who was the highest bidder, for the sum of   dollars, which was the whole consideration of such sale, the real estate described as follows, to wit: all [*description:*] And that the sale will become absolute at the expiration of fifteen calendar months from this day, to wit, on the   day of   , A. D. 18 , and E. F., or his assigns, be entitled to a conveyance, pursuant to law, unless the said lands shall be redeemed.

Given under my hand, this first day of   , 18 .

A. P., Sheriff of the County of   .

---

§ 325. *Affidavit to Entitle a Creditor to Redeem, to be Endorsed on a Certified Copy of the Docket of his Judgment*

State of New York, } ss:
     County, }

L. M., [*or*, S. T., attorney, *or*, agent, of L. M.,] a judgment creditor of C. D., named in the copy of the docket of judgment hereunto annexed, being duly sworn, says, that the true sum due on said judgment, at the time of claiming the right to acquire the title of E. F., the original purchaser at the Sheriff's sale of the real estate of C. D., is   dollars and   cents.

Sworn to, this   day of   , }   L. M.
A. D. 18 , before me,   }
     G. H., Justice of the Peace.

§ 326. *Sheriff's Deed, where Land is Sold under an Execution*

This indenture, made, &c., between A. P., Esquire, Sheriff, [*or* late Sheriff,] of the county of   , of the first part, and E. F., of, &c., of the second part: Whereas, by virtue of a certain execution issued out of and under the seal of the Supreme Court of the State of New York, tested the   day of   , in the year 18 , at the suit of A. B., plaintiff, against C. D., defendant, directed and delivered to the said Sheriff, commanding him that of the goods and chattels of the said defendant, he should cause to be made certain moneys, in the said writ specified, and if sufficient goods and chattels could not be found, that then he should cause the amount so specified to be made of the real estate which the said defendant had on a day in the said writ mentioned, or at any time afterwards, in whose hands soever the same might be, the said Sheriff did levy on and seize, all the estate, right, title and interest, which the said defendant so had, of, in and to, the premises hereinafter conveyed and described; and on the   day of   , one thousand eight hundred and   , sold the said premises at public vendue, at the house of   , in the town of   , in the said county; having first given public notice of the time and place of such sale, by advertising the same according to law; at which sale the said premises were struck off to E. F., for the sum of   dollars, he being the highest bidder, and that being the highest sum bidden for the same.* And whereas, the said premises, after the expiration of fifteen months from the time of said sale, remained unredeemed, and no creditor of the said C. D. hath acquired the right and title of the said purchaser, according to the statute in such case made and provided.* [*If the deed is given to a redeeming creditor, substitute the name of such creditor for E. F., as aforesaid, and instead of the words between the two *s, say:* And whereas, the said premises, after the expiration of one year from the time of said sale, remained unredeemed, by any person entitled to make such redemption within that time; and whereas, L. M., a creditor of the said C. D., having in his own name [*or, as assignee; or, representative; or, trustee*] a judgment in the Supreme Court, &c., against the said C. D., for the sum of   dollars, in an action of   , rendered before the expiration of fifteen months from the time of such sale, and which is a lien and charge on the premises so sold, hath acquired all the rights of the said E. F., the original purchaser to said premises, within the time, and in the manner and form prescribed by the statute in such case made and provided; and no other creditor of the said C. D. hath acquired the said rights from or against the said E. F.] Now this indenture witnesseth: that the said party of the first part, by virtue of the said writ, and in pursuance of the act in such case made and provided, and in consideration of the sum of money so bidden as aforesaid, to him duly paid, hath sold, and by these presents doth grant and convey, unto the said party of the second part, all the estate, right, title and interest, which the said defendant had on the said day of , one thousand eight hundred and , or at any time afterwards, of, in and to, all [*description:*] To have and to hold the said above mentioned premises, unto the said party of the second part, his heirs and assigns, forever, as fully and absolutely as the said party of the first part, as Sheriff aforesaid, can, or ought to, by virtue of the said writ and the law relating thereto.

In witness whereof, the said Sheriff has, &c., [*as in* § 308.]

§ 327. *Sheriff's Deed in Partition, where Sale is Ordered.*[1]

This indenture, made, &c., between A. P., Esquire, Sheriff of the county of , in the State of New York, of the first part, and C. D., of, &c., of the second part: Whereas, in and by a certain decree, made at a County Court held at the town of , in and for said county, before J. P. H., Esquire, County Judge, on the day of , one thousand eight hundred and , in a certain cause there pending in the said court, between E. B., complainant, and A. B., C. B., and D. B., defendants, it was, among other things, ordered, adjudged and decreed,* that the said Sheriff do sell, in such separate parcels as he shall deem most for the benefit of the said parties, according to the rules and practice of the said court, and according to the statute in such case made and provided, all and singular the several pieces or parcels of land and premises therein mentioned, whereof partition is sought by the complainant's bill of complaint filed in the above cause, at public auction, at the town of , in the said county of , after giving six week's previous notice of the time and place of such sale, in one of the public newspapers published in the said county of , and in such other manner as required by law; that the said Sheriff, after such sale, make report thereof to the said court; and after such report of sale shall have been duly confirmed, and the said decree shall have been enrolled, that the said Sheriff execute and deliver deeds of conveyance for the said premises, in fee simple, to the purchasers thereof, at the said sale; and whereas, the said Sheriff, in pursuance of said decree, and having given due notice of the time and place of sale, agreeably to the said decree, did, on the day of , A. D. 18 , sell at public auction, at the town of , aforesaid, the premises in the said decree mentioned; at which sale, the premises hereinafter described, were struck off and sold, to the said party of the second part, for the sum of dollars, that being the highest sum bidden for the same; and such sale having been reported by the said Sheriff to the said court, and duly confirmed,

---

[1] Sheriffs may sell any lands in their respective counties, ordered to be sold by a decree of any court of record, and give conveyances thereof, in the same manner, and with like effect, as was formerly done by a Master in Chancery. (Laws of 1847, chap. 280, art. VI, § 77.) The Sheriff receives his disbursements for printing, and fees for selling. See, chapter XVIII.

H

and the said decree having been also enrolled: Now this indenture witnesseth: that the said Sheriff, in order to carry into effect the sale so made by him, as aforesaid, in pursuance of the said decree of the said court, and in conformity to the statute in such case made and provided, and also in consideration of the premises, and of the said sum of money so bidden, as aforesaid, being first duly paid to him by the said party of the second part, the receipt whereof is hereby acknowledged, hath granted, bargained, sold and conveyed, and by these presents doth grant, bargain, sell and convey, unto the said party of the second part, his heirs and assigns, forever, all [*description.*] To have and to hold all and singular the premises above mentioned and described, and hereby conveyed, or intended to be, unto the said party of the second part, his heirs and assigns, to his and their own proper use, benefit and behoof, forever.

In witness whereof, the said Sheriff has, &c., [*as in* § 308.]

---

§ 328. *Sheriff's Deed on Foreclosure.*

This indenture, &c.: [*as in* § 327 *to the* *, *and then add:*] That all and singular the mortgaged premises mentioned in the complaint in said cause, and in said decree described, or so much thereof as might be sufficient to raise the amount due to the complainant, for principal, interest, and costs, in said cause, and which might be sold separately, without material injury to the parties interested, be sold at public auction, according to the course and practice of this court, and under the direction of the said Sheriff, party of the first part; that the said sale be made on the   day of   , then next, at   o'clock in the forenoon of that day, at the court house in the town of   , in the county of   , aforesaid; that the said Sheriff give public notice of the time and place of such sale, according to the course and practice of said court, and that any of the parties in said cause might become a purchaser, or purchasers, on such sale; that the said Sheriff execute to the purchaser, or purchasers, of the said mortgaged premises, or such part or parts thereof as should be sold, a good and sufficient deed, or deeds, of conveyance, for the same; and whereas the said Sheriff, in pursuance of the order and decree of the said court, did, on the said   day of   , A. D. 18   , sell at public auction, at the court house in the town of   , aforesaid, the premises in the said order mentioned, due notice of the time and place of such sale being first given, agreeably to the said order; at which sale, the premises hereinafter described were struck off to the said party of the second part, for the sum of   dollars, that being the highest sum bidden for the same. Now this indenture witnesseth: [*as in* § 327 *to the end.*][1]

§ 329. *Deed of Right of Way.*

This indenture, made, &c., between A. B., of, &c., of the first part, and C. D., of, &c., of the second part: Whereas the said party of the second part hath this day granted, sold, and conveyed unto the said party of the first part, his heirs and assigns, by warranty deed, executed by the party of the second part to the party of the first part, and bearing even date herewith, a certain piece or parcel of land, described in said deed, as follows, to wit: all [*description:*] And whereas the said party of the second part is still owned and possessed of certain lands lying in the rear of the above described premises: Now, therefore, this indenture witnesseth: that the said party of the first part, in consideration* of the grant, sale, and conveyance, as aforesaid, and* of the sum of   dollars, to him in hand paid by the said party of the second part, the receipt whereof is hereby acknowledged, doth hereby grant, bargain, sell, and confirm, unto the said party of the second part, and to his heirs and assigns, forever, a right of way in and over a certain strip of land on the east side of the dwelling house on the above described premises, conveyed to the party of the first part, as aforesaid, for the said party of the second part, his heirs and assigns, and his and their servants and tenants, at all times freely to pass and repass, on foot, or with horses, oxen, cattle, beasts of burden, wagons, carts, sleighs, or other vehicle or carriage whatsoever, from the highway to the lands of the said party of the second part, as aforesaid, and from the said lands of the party of the second part to the highway, as aforesaid, the said certain strip of land being of the width of two rods, and running from the south boundary of the premises above conveyed to the party of the first part, to the said lands belonging to the party of the second part, situate in the rear thereof, and the said way is, and shall be, forever, of the dimensions of the said strip of land, as aforesaid: To have and to hold the said easement and privilege to the said party of the second part, his heirs and assigns, forever, as appurtenances belonging to his and their lands, as aforesaid. [*If necessary, insert covenants of seizin, warranty, &c.*]

In witness, &c., [*as in* § 308.][1]

---

§ 330. *Deed of a Water Course.*

This indenture, made, &c., between A. B., of, &c., of the first part, and C. D., of, &c., of the second part: Whereas the said parties, at the time of the sealing and delivery of these presents, are respectively seized in fee, of and in two contiguous tracts, pieces, or parcels, of

---

[1] If the right of way is granted for a money consideration solely, omit the words in the foregoing form, from *Whereas*, in the second line, to *Indenture*, in the tenth line; and also those between the two *&*.

land, with the appurtenances, in the town of   , aforesaid, and
whereas there is a dam and race, or water course, erected and made
in and upon a certain stream of water known as   , within the
land of the said party of the first part, for the purpose of furnishing
water for a flouring mill, erected on the land of the said party of the
first part, and owned by him: Now, therefore, this indenture witnesseth: that the party of the first part, for and in consideration of the
sum of   dollars, to him in hand paid by the party of the second
part, at or before the sealing and delivery hereof, (the receipt whereof
he does hereby acknowledge,) has granted, bargained, sold, released,
and confirmed, and by these presents does grant, bargain, sell, release,
and confirm, unto the said party of the second part, his heirs and
assigns, all the water of the said stream of water, which may or can
be led and conveyed from the easterly side of the said dam, in a race,
or flume, to be constructed at the cost, charge, and expense of the
party of the second part, four feet in width, and four feet in depth,
measuring from the surface of the embankment forming the said
dam: To have and to hold all and singular the said easement, &c.,
[*as in* § 329.]

––––––––

§ 331. *Deed of Confirmation.*

This indenture, made, &c., between A. B., of, &c., of the first part,
and C. D., of, &c., of the second part: Whereas, by a certain deed
of bargain and sale, bearing date on or about the, &c., and made
between C. B. and A. B., of the one part, and the said C. D. of the
other part, for the consideration of   dollars, the premises
therein mentioned and hereinafter intended to be released and confirmed, are thereby granted and conveyed, or intended so to be, unto
and to the use of the said C. D., his heirs and assigns, forever; as by
the said indenture of bargain and sale, relation being thereunto had,
may more fully appear. And whereas, the said A. B., at the time of
the date and making the said in part recited indenture of bargain
and sale, was not of the age of twenty-one years, but hath since
attained to such age, and hath this day, and before the execution of
these presents, duly sealed and delivered the said in part recited indenture of bargain and sale: Now this indenture witnesseth: that, as
well in the performance of a covenant for further assurance in the
said indenture of bargain and sale contained, as also for and in consideration of the sum of   dollars, to him, the said A. B.,
in hand paid by the said C. D., the receipt whereof the said A. B.
doth hereby acknowledge, he, the said A. B., hath remised, released,
aliened and quit-claimed, and by these presents doth absolutely remise, release, alien and forever quit-claim and confirm, unto the said
C. D., in his actual possession now being, by virtue of the before
mentioned indenture of bargain and sale, and to his heirs and assigns,

all [*description:*] To have and to hold the above mentioned premises to the use of the said C. D., his heirs and assigns, forever. [*Insert such covenants as may be necessary.*]

In witness, &c., [*as in* § 308.]

§ 332. *Confirmation of Deed by Endorsement.*

Be it known, that the within indenture was executed by A. B., therein named, while under the age of twenty-one years, who has now attained his full age of twenty-one years; and that the said A. B. has, on this   day of   , sealed and delivered this present indenture as his own act and deed.

In witness whereof, the said A. B. has hereunto set his hand and seal, the day and year above written.

Sealed, &c., [*as in* § 308.]

§ 333. *Conveyance by Lease and Release.*[1]

[LEASE.]

This indenture, made, &c., between A. B., of, &c., of the first part, and C. D., of, &c., of the second part, witnesseth: That the said A. B., for and in consideration of the sum of one dollar, to him in hand paid by the said C. D., at or before the ensealing and delivery of these presents, the receipt whereof is hereby acknowledged, hath granted, bargained and sold, and by these presents doth grant, bargain and sell, unto the said C. D., his executors, administrators and assigns, all, [*description,*] and the reversion and reversions, remainder and remainders, rents, issues and profits, of all and singular the said premises, and every part and parcel thereof, with the appurtenances: To have and to hold the said lands, hereditaments and premises, above granted, bargained and sold, and every part and parcel thereof with the appurtenances, unto the said C. D., his executors, administrators and assigns, from the day before the day of the date hereof, for and during, and until, the full end and term of one whole year, from thenceforth next ensuing, and fully to be completed and ended, yielding and paying therefor, at the expiration of the said year, one farthing, if the same shall be lawfully demanded; to the intent that, by virtue of these presents, and by force of the statute made for the transferring of uses into possession, he, the said C. D., may be in the actual possession of all and singular the said premises above bargained and sold, with the appurtenances, and be thereby enabled to

---

[1] The lease should precede the release, and should be dated the day before the latter. Any covenants that may be required, can be inserted before the *in testimonium* clause in the release.

take, and accept of, a grant and release of the reversion and inheritance thereof, to him and his heirs, to, for and upon, such uses, intents and purposes, as in and by the said grant, or release, shall be thereof   directed or declared.

In witness, &c., [*as in* § 308.]

[RELEASE.]

This indenture, made, &c., betwen A. B., of, &c., of the first part, and C. D., of, &c., of the second part, witnesseth: That the said A. B., for and in consideration of the sum · of   dollars, to him, the said A. B., in hand paid, at or before the ensealing and delivery of these presents, the receipt whereof he, the said A. B., doth hereby acknowledge, hath granted, bargained, aliened, released and confirmed, and by these presents doth grant, bargain, alien, release and confirm, unto the said C. D., (in his actual possession now being, by virtue of a bargain and sale to him thereof made, for one whole year, by indenture bearing date the day next before the ensealing of these presents, and by force of the statute made for transferring uses into possession,) and to his heirs and assigns, all [*description,*] and the reversion and reversions. remainder and remainders, rents, issues and profits, of all and singular the said premises, and every part and parcel thereof, with the appurtenances; and also, all the estate, right, title, interest, property, claim and demand, whatsoever, in law or equity, of him, the said A. B., of, in and to, all and singular the said premises above mentioned, and of, in and to, every part and parcel thereof, with the appurtenances: To have and to hold all and singular the said premises above, in and by these presents, released and confirmed, and every part and parcel thereof, with the appurtenances, unto the said C. D., his heirs and assigns, to his and their only proper use and behoof, forever; [*or*, to and for such uses, intents, and purposes as are hereinafter mentioned, to wit; &c.]

In witness, &c., [*as in* § 308.]

---

§ 334. *Deed of Exchange of Lands.*

This indenture, made, &c., between A. B., of, &c., of the first part, and C. D., of, &c., of the second part, witnesseth: That the said A. B. hath given and granted, and by these presents doth give and grant, unto the said C. D., his heirs and assigns, all [*description,*] with all and every of the appurtenances, in exchange of and for the lands hereinafter mentioned, of the said C. D.; To have and to hold the said premises, with the appurtenances, to the said C. D., his heirs and assigns, forever.   And the said A. B. doth covenant, &c. [*Insert such covenants as may be necessary.*]   And the said C. D. hath likewise, on his part, given and granted, and by these presents doth give and grant, unto the said A. B., his heirs and assigns, all [*description*,] with all and every of the appurtenances, in exchange of and for the premises first above described: To have and to hold the above granted premises, with the appurtenances, to the said A. B., his heirs and assigns, forever, as aforesaid. And the said C. D. doth covenant, &c., [*as above.*]

In witness whereof, the said parties have hereunto set their hands and seals, &c., [*as in* § 308.]

---

§ 335. *Deed of a Pew in a Church.*

Know all men by these presents: That we, A. B., C. D., E. F., &c., &c., the Trustees of the First Methodist Episcopal Society of the town of   , in the county of   , and State of   , [*or, as the corporate style, or title, of the church may be,*] in consideration of the sum of   dollars, to us in hand paid, by L. M. of, &c., the receipt whereof is hereby acknowledged, do hereby sell and convey unto the said L. M., a certain pew, being number   , situate in the church occupied by the said First Methodist Episcopal Society of the town of   , [*or,* situate in the church on   street, in the city of,   , aforesaid, occupied, &c.:] To have and to hold the same unto the said C. D., his heirs, executors, administrators and assigns, forever; subject to all liabilities and incumbrances now legally existing, and to such taxes and assessments as may from time to time be laid thereon; provided, however, that no alteration shall be made in said pew, nor shall the same be sold or transferred, by deed of sale, or mortgage, without the written consent of the trustees of said society, [*or as the title of the officers may be,*] for the time being; and further, that if, at any time, there shall be owing from said pew, a sum equal to one year's taxes, this conveyance shall be wholly void, and all the right, title and interest, of the said L. M., his heirs, executors, administrators and assigns, in and to the said pew, shall revert to the said society, [*or,* church.]

In witness whereof, we have hereunto set our hands, and the corporate seal of said society, [*or,* church] this   day of   , A. D., 18 .

Sealed and delivered, }   A. B.   } Trustees
  in presence of }   C. D.   } of, &c.   [L. s.]
    G. H.   &c., &c., }

---

§ 336. *Mortgage.*[1]

This indenture, made the   day of   , in the year of our Lord one thousand eight hundred and   , between A. B., of,

---

[1] A mortgage given for the purchase money of the premises therein described, or any part thereof, has priority over all other liens, founded on any demand against the mortgagor or his assigns, whether precede it or subsequent to such mortgage.

&c,, of the first part, and C. D., of, &c., of the second part, witness
eth: That the said party of the first part, for and in consideration of
the sum of   dollars, doth grant, bargain, sell and confirm, unto
the said party of the second part, and to his heirs and assigns, all
[description;] together with all and singular the hereditaments and
appurtenances, thereunto belonging, or in any wise appertaining.
This conveyance is intended as a mortgage, to secure the payment
of the sum of   dollars, in three years from the day of the date
of these presents, with annual interest, according to the condition of
a certain bond, dated this day, and executed by the said A. B. to the
said party of the second part; and these presents shall be void if
such payment be made.   But in case default shall be made in the
payment of the principal, or interest, as above provided, then the
party of the second part, his executors, administrators and assigns,
are hereby empowered to sell the premises above described, with all
and every of the appurtenances, or any part thereof, in the manner
prescribed by law; and out of the money arising from such sale, to
retain the said principal and interest, together with the costs and
charges of making such sale; and the overplus, if any there be, shall
be paid by the party making such sale, on demand, to the party of
the first part, his heirs or assigns.*
  In witness, &c., [as in § 308.]

---

§ 337. Mortgage for Part of Purchase Money.

  This indenture, &c., [as in § 336 to, and including, the description, and then add:] being the same premises this day conveyed to
the said A. B., by the said C. D., and E., his wife: and these presents are given to secure the payment of part of the consideration
money of the said premises; together with, &c., [as in § 336 to the
end.]

---

§ 338. Mortgage, with Covenant for Payment.

  This indenture, &c., [as in § 336 to the *, and then add:] And
the said party of the first part, for himself, his heirs, executors, and
administrators, doth covenant and agree, to pay unto the party of the
second part, his executors, administrators, or assigns, the said sum of
money and interest, as above mentioned, and expressed in the condition of the said bond. [If there be no bond accompanying the mortgage, the reference to it herein, and in § 336, may be omitted.]
  In witness, &c., [as in § 308.]

---

§ 339. Mortgage, with Fire Clause.

  This indenture, &c., [as in § 336 to the *, and including the
covenant in § 338, if necessary, and then add:] And it is also

εgreed, by and between the parties to these presents, that the party of the first part shall and will keep the buildings erected, and to be erected, upon the lands above conveyed, insured against loss by fire, and assign the policy, and certificates thereof, to the said party of the second part, his executors, administrators, or assigns; and in default thereof, it shall be lawful for the said party of the second part, his executors, administrators, and assigns, to effect such insurance, and the premium and premiums paid for effecting the same, shall be a lien on the said mortgaged premises, added to the amount of the said bond, or obligation, and secured by these presents.

In witness, &c., [*as in* § 308.]

---

§ 340. *Mortgage, with Interest Clause.*

This indenture, &c., [*as in* § 336, *to the words:* " But in case default,*" and instead thereof, continue as follows:*] And if default shall be made in the payment of the said sum of money above men-tioned, or of any part thereof, or if the interest that may grow due thereon, or of any part thereof, shall remain due and unpaid at the expiration of sixty days after the same shall become due and payable, according to the condition of the said bond, that then, and from thenceforth, it shall be lawful for the said party of the second part, his executors, administrators, and assigns, to consider the whole of the principal sum, as aforesaid, as immediately due and payable, and to enter into and upon all and singular the premises hereby granted, or intended so to be, and to sell and dispose of the same, and all benefit and equity of redemption of the said party of the first part, his heirs, executors, administrators, or assigns, therein, at public auction, accord-ing to law: And as the attorney of the said party of the first part, for that purpose by these presents duly authorized, constituted, and appointed, to make and deliver to the purchaser or purchasers thereof, a good and sufficient deed or deeds of conveyance in the law, for the same, in fee simple; and out of the money arising from such sale, to retain the principal and interest which shall then be due and owing on said bond or obligation, together with the costs and charges of the sale of the said premises, rendering the overplus of said purchase money, if any there shall be, unto the said party of the first part, his heirs, executors, administrators, or assigns; which sale, so to be made, shall forever be a perpetual bar, both in law and equity, against the said party of the first part, his heirs and assigns, and all other persons claiming, or to claim, the premises, or any part thereof, by, from, or under him, them, or either of them. [*Add insurance clause, if necessary.*]

In witness, &c., [*as in* § 308.

§ 341. *Mortgage by Husband and Wife.*

This indenture, made, &c., between A. B., and M. his wife, of, &c., of the first part, and C. D., of, &c., of the second part, witnesseth: That the party of the first part, for and in consideration of the sum of   dollars, to them in hand paid, the receipt whereof is hereby acknowledged, have bargained, sold, aliened, released, conveyed, and confirmed, and by these presents do bargain, sell, alien, release, convey, and confirm unto the said party of the second part, his heirs and assigns, forever, all [*description;*] together with the tenements, hereditaments, and appurtenances thereunto belonging, or in any wise appertaining; and also all the estate, right, title, interest, dower, and right of dower, property, possession, claim, and demand whatsoever, of the said party of the first part, of, in, and to the same, and the reversion and reversions, remainder and remainders, rents, issues, and profits thereof: To have and to hold the herein before granted, bargained, and described premises, with the appurtenances, unto the said party of the second part, his heirs and assigns, to his and their own proper use, benefit and behoof, forever. This conveyance is intended as a mortgage to secure the payment of the sum of   dollars, in five years from the day of the date hereof, with semi-annual interest, payable on the second day of January and the first day of July in each and every year, according to the condition of a certain bond, bearing even date herewith, executed by the said A. B. to the said party of the second part; and these presents shall be void if such payment be made. But in case default shall be made in the payment of the principal, or interest, as above provided, then the party of the second part, his executors, administrators, and assigns, are hereby empowered to sell the premises above described, with all and every of the appurtenances, or any part thereof, in the manner prescribed by law, and out of the money arising from such sale, to retain the said principal and interest, together with the costs and charges of making such sale; and the overplus, if any there be, shall be paid by the party making such sale, on demand, to the party of the first part, their heirs or assigns. And the said A. B., for himself, his heirs, executors, and administrators, doth covenant and agree to pay unto the said party of the second part, his executors, administrators, or assigns, the said sum of money and interest, as above mentioned, and as expressed in the condition of the said bond. [*Add insurance clause, if necessary.*]

In witness whereof, the said party of the first part have hereunto set their hands and seals, the day and year first above written.

Sealed, &c., [*as in* § 308.]   A. B. [L. S.]
                                            M. B. [L. S.]

§ 342. *Mortgage by Corporation.*

This indenture, made, &c., between A. B., E. F., L. M., &c., the
trustees of the first society of the   church, in the town of,
&c., of the first part, and E. F., of, &c., of the second part, witnesseth,
&c., [*as in* § 336, *to the words* "according to the condition of a
certain bond," *and instead thereof continue as follows:*] according to
the condition of a certain bond bearing even date herewith, executed
by the said party of the first part, to the said party of the second
part; and the said Trustees of the first society of the
church, in, &c., for themselves and their successors, do covenant and
agree to pay, unto the said party of the second part, his executors,
administrators, or assigns, the said sum of money, and interest, as
above mentioned, and as expressed in the condition of the said bond;
and if default shall be made in the payment of the said sum of
money as above mentioned, or the interest that may grow due thereon,
or of any part of either the said principal or interest, that then, and
from thenceforth, it shall be lawful for the said party of the second
part, his executors, administrators and assigns, to enter into and upon,
all and singular the premises hereby granted, or intended so to be,
and to sell and dispose of the same, and all benefit and equity of redemption of the said party of the first part, their successors, or assigns,
therein, at public auction, according to the act in such case made
and provided: And as the attorney of the said party of the first part,
for that purpose by these presents duly authorized, constituted and
appointed, to make and deliver to the purchaser or purchasers thereof,
a good and sufficient deed, or deeds of conveyance, in the law, for the
same, in fee simple; and out of the money arising from such sale, to
retain the principal and interest which shall then be due on the said
bond or obligation, together with the costs and charges of the sale of
the said premises, rendering the overplus of the purchase money (if
any there shall be) unto the said party of the first part, their successors or assigns; which sale, so to be made, shall forever be a perpetual bar, both in law and equity, against the said party of the first
part, their successors and assigns, and against all other persons claiming, or to claim, the premises, or any part thereof, by, from, or under
them, or any of them. [*Add insurance clause if necessary.*]

In witness whereof, the said parties of the first part have hereunto
set their hands and affixed their corporate seal, the day and year
first above written.

Sealed, &c., [*as in* § 308.]

A. B.,
E. F.,   } Trustees
L. M.,   } of, &c.,   [L. s.]
&c., &c.,)

§ 343. *Mortgage to Corporation.*

This indenture, made, &c., between A. B., of, &c., of the first part,
and the Trustees of the village of   , &c., [*or,* the Mayor
Alderman and Commonalty, of the city of   , &c.,] of the
second part, witnesseth: That the said party of the first part, for and
in consideration of the sum of   dollars, to him in hand paid
by the said party of the second part, the receipt whereof is hereby
acknowledged, hath granted, bargained, sold, aliened, released, conveyed and confirmed, and by these presents doth grant, bargain, sell,
alien, release, convey and confirm, unto the said party of the second
part, their successors and assigns, forever, all [*description;*] together
with the tenements, hereditaments and appurtenances, thereunto belonging, or in any wise appertaining; and also, all the estate, right,
title, interest, property, possession, claim and demand, whatsoever, of
the said party of the first part, of, in and to, the same; and the reversion and reversions, remainder and remainders, rents, issues and
profits thereof: To have and to hold the hereinbefore granted and described premises, with the appurtenances, unto the said party of the
second part, their successors and assigns, to their only proper use,
benefit and behoof, forever. This conveyance is intended as a mortgage, to secure the payment of the sum of   dollars, in manner
following, to wit: &c.; according to the condition of a certain bond
bearing even date herewith, executed by the said party of the first
part to the party of the second part, and these presents shall be void
if such payment be made. But in case default shall be made in the
payment of the principal or interest aforesaid, as above provided, then
the party of the second part, their successors and assigns, &c., [*as in*
§ 330, *to the* *, *and then add :*] And the said party of the first part
doth covenant, promise and agree, to and with the said party of the
second part, their successors and assigns, that he, the said party of
the first part, shall and will, well and truly pay to the said party of
the second part, their successors and assigns, the said sum of money
with the interest thereon, at the time, and in the manner, hereinbe
fore mentioned, according to the condition of the said bond.

In witness, &c., [*as in* § 308.]

---

§ 344. *Mortgage on Note.*

This indenture, made, &c., [*as in* § 336 *to, and including, the de-
cription, and then add:*] This conveyance is intended as a mortgage,
to secure the payment of a certain promissory note, now held by the
party of the second part, given by the party of the first part, for the
sum of   dollars, dated the   day of   last past, and
payable to L. M., or bearer, one year from the date thereof, with use;
and if the amount of the said note, principal and interest, shall be
paid at maturity, then these presents shall become void, and the estate hereby granted shall cease and utterly determine; but if default

shall be made in the payment of the said sum of money, or the interest, or of any part thereof, at the time herein before specified for the payment thereof, the said party of the first part, in such case, ioth hereby authorize, and fully empower the said party of the second part, his heirs, executors, administrators and assigns, to sell the said hereby granted premises at public auction, and convey the same to the purchaser, in fee simple, agreeably to the act in such case made and provided, and out of the money arising from such sale, to retain the principal and interest which shall then be due on the said note, together with all costs and charges, and pay the overplus (if any) to the said party of the first part, his heirs, executors, administrators, or assigns.

In witness, &c., [*as in* § 308.]

------

§ 345. *Mortgage to Secure Endorser.*

This indenture, made, &c., [*as in* § 336 *to, and including. the description, and then add:*] Whereas the said party of the second part, at the request, and for the benefit and behoof of the said party of the first part, hath, on the day of the date hereof, endorsed a certain promissory note, made by the said party of the first part, for the sum of   dollars, bearing even date herewith, and payable ninety days after date, to the order of G. H., at the   Bank: Now, therefore, this conveyance is intended to secure the party of the second part for all principal and interest money, costs, charges and expenses, which he may be compelled to pay, in consequence of the failure of the said party of the first part to pay and take up the said note, at maturity; and if the amount of the said note, principal and interest, shall be paid by the party of the first part, at maturity, then these presents shall become void, and the estate hereby granted shall cease and utterly determine: but if default shall be made by the said party of the first part in the payment of the said sum of money, or the interest, or of any part thereof, at the time herein before specified, and the same be paid by or collected of the party of the second part, the said party of the first part doth hereby authorize and empower the party of the second part, his heirs, executors, administrators and assigns, to sell the said premises hereby granted, at public auction, and convey the same to the purchaser, in fee simple, agreeably to the act in such case made and provided, and out of the money arising from such sale, to retain such sum, or sums, of money, as may have been paid by or collected of the said party of the second part, as above mentioned, together with all costs and charges, and pay the overplus (if any) to the said party of the first part, his heirs, executors, administrators, or assigns.

In witness, &c., [*as in* § 308.]

§ 346. *Mortgage to Executors.*

This indenture, made, &c., between A. B., of, &c., of the first part, and L. M., and S. T., both of, &c., executors of the last will and testament of E. F., deceased, of the second part, witnesseth: That the said party of the first part, for and in consideration of the sum of   dollars, to him in hand paid by the party of the second part, at or before the ensealing and delivery of these presents, the receipt whereof is hereby acknowledged, hath granted, bargained, sold, aliened, released, conveyed and confirmed, and by these presents doth grant, bargain, sell, alien, release, convey and confirm, unto the said party of the second part, and the survivors and survivor, and his and their assigns, forever, all [*description:*] together with all and singular the tenements, hereditaments and appurtenances, thereunto belonging, or in any wise appertaining, and the reversion and reversions, remainder and remainders, rents, issues, and profits thereof: and also, all the estate, right, title, interest, property, possession claim and demand whatsoever; as well in law as in equity, of the said party of the first part, of, in and to, the same, and every part and parcel thereof, with the appurtenances: To have and to hold the above granted, bargained and described premises, with the appurtenances, unto the said party of the second part, the survivors and survivor, and his and their assigns, to their only proper use, benefit and behoof, forever. This conveyance is intended as a mortgage to secure the payment of the sum of   dollars, in manner following, to wit: &c., according to the condition of a certain bond, bearing even date herewith, executed by the said party of the first part to the party of the second part; and these presents shall be void if such payment be made. And the said party of the first part, for himself and his heirs, executors and administrators, doth covenant and agree to pay unto the said party of the second part, and the survivors and survivor, or his or their assigns, the said sum of money, and interest, as above mentioned, and as expressed in the condition of the said bond; and if default shall be made in the payment of the said sum of money above mentioned, or the interest that may grow due thereon, or of any part thereof, that then, and from thenceforth, it shall be lawful for the said party of the second part, the survivors or survivor, and his or their assigns, to enter into and upon all and singular, the premises hereby granted, or intended so to be, and to sell and dispose of the same, and all benefit and equity of redemption of the said party of the first part, his heirs, executors, administrators or assigns, therein, at public auction, according to the act in such case made and provided: And as the attorney, or attorneys, of the said party of the first part, for that purpose by these presents duly authorized, constituted and appointed, to make and deliver to the purchaser or purchasers thereof, a good and sufficient deed, or deeds, of conveyance in the law, for the same, in fee simple: and out of the money arising from such sale, to retain the principal and interest which shall then be due on the said bond or obligation, together with the costs and charges of advertisement and sale of the premises, rendering the overplus of the purchase money, (if any there shall be,) unto the said party of the first part, his heirs, executors, administrators, or assigns; which sale, so to be made, shall forever be a perpetual bar both in law and in equity, against the said party of the first part, his heirs and assigns, and all other persons claiming, or to claim, the premises, or any part thereof, by, from or under, him, them, or any of them. [*Add insurance clause, if necessary.*]

In witness, &c., [*as in* § 308.]

---

§ 347. *Mortgage on Lease, by an Assignee.*

This indenture, made, &c., between A. B., of, &c., of the first part, and C. D., of, &c., of the second part: Whereas, E. F. did, by a certain indenture of lease bearing date the   day of   , in the year one thousand eight hundred and   , demise, release, and to farm let, unto G. H., and to his executors, administrators and assigns, all and singular the premises hereinafter mentioned and described, together with the appurtenances, for and during and until the full end and term of ,   years, from the   day of   , in the year 18   , and fully to be complete and ended, yielding and paying therefor, unto the said E. F., and to his executors, or assigns, the yearly rent or sum of   dollars; which said indenture of lease and term of years therein mentioned and demised, have been duly assigned to the said A. B.   And whereas, the said party of the first part is justly indebted unto the said party of the second part, in the sum of   dollars, secured to be paid by his certain bond or obligation, bearing even date with these presents, in the penal sum of ·   dollars, lawful money, as aforesaid, conditioned for the payment of the said first mentioned sum, with interest: Now this indenture witnesseth, that the said party of the first part, for the better securing the payment of the said sum of money mentioned in the condition of the said bond, or obligation, with interest thereon, according to the true intent and meaning thereof, and also for and in consideration of the sum of   dollars to him in hand paid by the said party of the second part, at or before the ensealing and delivery of these presents, the receipt whereof is hereby acknowledged, hath granted, bargained, sold, assigned, transferred and set over, and by these presents doth grant, bargain, sell, assign, transfer and set over, unto the said party of the second part, all [*description;*] with all and singular the privileges and appurtenances thereunto belonging, or in any wise appertaining; and also all the estate, right, title, interest, term of years to come and unexpired, property, possession, claim and demand whatsoever, as well in law as in equity, of the said party of the first part, of, in and to, the said demised premises, and every part and parcel thereof, with the appurtenances; and also, the said indenture of lease, and every clause, article and condition, therein expressed and contained: To have and to hold the said indenture of lease, and other hereby granted premises, unto the said party of the second part, his executors, administrators and assigns, to his and their only proper use, benefit and behoof, for and during all the rest, residue and remainder, of the said term of years yet to come and unexpired; subject, nevertheless, to the rents, covenants, provisions and conditions in the said indenture of lease mentioned: Provided always, that these presents are upon this express condition, that if the party of the first part shall well and truly pay unto the said party of the second part, the said sum of money mentioned in the condition of the said bond, or obligation, and the interest thereon, at the time and manner mentioned in the said condition, according to the true intent and meaning thereof, that then and from thenceforth these presents, and the estate hereby granted, shall cease, determine, and be utterly null and void; any thing herein before contained to the contrary in any wise notwithstanding. And the said party of the first part doth hereby covenant, grant, promise and agree, to and with the said party of the second part, that he will well and truly pay unto the said party of the second part, the sum of money mentioned in the condition of the said bond, or obligation, and the interest thereon, according to the condition thereof; and that the said premises hereby conveyed now are free and clear of all incumbrance whatsoever, and that he hath good right and lawful authority to convey the same, in manner and form as the same are hereby conveyed: And if default shall be made in the payment of the said sum of money above mentioned, or in the interest which shall accrue thereon, or of any part of either, then, and from thenceforth, it shall be lawful for the said party of the second part, and his assigns, to sell, transfer and set over, all the rest, residue, and remaining term of years, then yet to come, and all other the right, title and interest, of the said party of the first part, of, in and to, the same, at public auction, according to law; and as the attorney, &c., [*as in* § 346, *to the end.*]

---

§ 348. *Notice of Sale, on Foreclosure of Mortgage by Advertisement.*

MORTGAGE SALE.

Default has been made in the payment of the sum of   dollars and   cents, which is claimed to be due at the date of this notice, on a certain mortgage bearing date the   day of   , 18   , executed by A. B. and Mary his wife, of the town of   , in the county of   , and State of   , to C. D., of the same place, [*or, as the fact may be,*] and recorded in the office of the Clerk of the county of   , in book number 75 of mortgages, page 300, &c., on the   day of   , A. D., 18   , at twelve o'clock, meridian: [*If the mortgage is foreclosed by an assignee, insert here:* which said mortgage has been duly assigned to the subscriber:]

Now, therefore, notice is hereby given, that, in pursuance of a power of sale contained in said mortgage, and of the statute in such case made and provided, the premises described in and covered by said mortgage, to wit: "all, &c., [*give description of the premises;*] will be sold at public auction, at the court house, [or, at the house of O. P.] in the city [or, town] of   , in the county of   , on the   day of   next, at ten o'clock in the forenoon.

Dated the   day of   , 18   . [*The date should be that of the first publication of the notice.*]   C. D., Mortgagee,
[*or, Assignee.*]

---

§ 349. *Affidavit of Publication of the Notice.*

State of New York, } ss:
County, }

                             E. F., of said county, being duly sworn,
[*Attach here a*   says, that he is, and, during the whole time
printed copy of   hereinafter mentioned, has been, the publisher
the notice of   and proprietor, [or, foreman,[1] in the publish-
sale.]   ing office,] of the   Gazette, a newspaper
                printed and published in the county of   ,
aforesaid; and that the annexed printed notice of sale was inserted and published in the said newspaper twelve weeks, successively, at least once in each week; the said publication commencing on the   day of   18   , and terminating on the   day of   18   .   E. F.

Sworn to, before me, this }
    day of   , 18   . }
        G. H., Justice of the Peace.

---

§ 350. *Affidavit of Affixing Notice of Sale on the Outward Door of the Court House.*[2]

State of New York, } ss:
County, }

                       C. D., of said county, being duly sworn
[*Attach here a*   says, that on the   day of   , 18   ,
printed copy of   he affixed a notice of which the annexed
the notice of   printed notice is a just and true copy, on the
sale.]   outward door of the building where the
                county courts are directed to be held in the
county of   , aforesaid.   C. D.

Sworn, &c., [*as in* § 349.]

---

[1] The affidavit of publication may also be made by the principal clerk of the publisher.
[2] Where the printer, or the person serving the notice of sale, affixes the notice, the sub-
                be incorporated in the affidavit of publication, or of service.

§ 351. *Affidavit of Serving copy of Notice of Sale, on Person having a Lien or Incumbrance.*

State of New York, ⎱ ss:
    County, ⎰

[*Attach here a printed copy of the notice of sale.*]

M. B., of said county, being duly sworn, says, that on the   day of   , 18   , he did personally serve A. B., E. F., and G. H., &c., with a notice of sale of which the annexed printed notice is a copy, by delivering a just and true copy of said notice to each of them individually; [*or*, he did serve A. B., with a notice of sale, of which the annexed printed notice is a copy, by delivering a just and true copy of said notice to the wife, [*or*, daughter, aged eighteen years, or thereabouts,] of the said A. B., at his dwelling house, he being at the time absent therefrom; *or*, he did serve A. B., &c., &c., with a notice of sale, of which the annexed printed notice is a copy, by depositing a just and true copy of said notice in the post office in   , properly folded and directed to each one of them, at his place of residence.]
M. B.

Sworn, &c., [*as in* § 349.]

---

§ 352. *Affidavit of the Auctioneer.*[1]

State of New York, ⎱ ss:
    County, ⎰

[*Attach here a printed copy of the notice of sale.*]

G. H., of said county, being duly sworn, says, that he sold the premises described in the annexed printed notice, at public auction, at the time and place of sale therein mentioned, to wit: on the   day of   , 18   , at ten o'clock in the forenoon, at the court house, [*or*, house of O. P.] in the city [*or*, town] of   , in the county of   , aforesaid; and that C. D. then and there purchased the same, for the price of   dollars; he being the highest bidder, and that being the highest sum bidden for the same.

And this deponent further saith, that said sale was made in the day time, and, in all respects, honestly, fairly, and legally conducted, according to his best knowledge and belief; and, also, that the said C. D. purchased the said premises fairly and in good faith, as he verily believes.
G. H.

Sworn, &c., [*as in* § 349.]

---

[1] The party foreclosing the mortgage may act as auctioneer, if he chooses to do so. For the form of a deed on the sale of mortgaged premises, see § 317, ante.

§ 353. *Notice to accompany Copy of Notice of Sale served on Parties having any Lien or Incumbrance on the Mortgaged Premises.*

Sir: Take notice, that the above is a copy of a notice that the mortgage therein mentioned will be foreclosed by a sale of the mortgaged premises, pursuant to the statute in such case made and provided, at the time and place therein specified.

Dated   , the   day of   , 18   .

C. D., Mortgagor,

[*or*, Assignee.]

CHAPTER XIII.

CORONERS.

PRACTICAL REMARKS.

1. One Coroner in the city and county of New York, and four Coroners in each of the other counties in the State, are chosen at general elections held therein, to serve for three years.[1]

2. Whenever the Sheriff of a county is a party to a suit, all process in such suit, except when otherwise provided by law, must be executed by the Coroner, who has the same authority, and is subject to the same provisions and liabilities, prescribed in respect to Sheriffs in similar cases. If the Sheriff, on being arrested by a Coroner, refuses or neglects to give bail; or if he is arrested on an execution against the body, or on attachment; the Coroner is required to confine him in some house within the liberties of the jail of the county; which house thereupon becomes the jail of the county, for the use of the Coroner, and the latter is liable for any escape, and may take bonds for the liberties, in the same manner as the Sheriff in other cases.[2]

3. Where the Coroner arrests a person, at the suit of the Sheriff, he may confine the prisoner in the common jail of the county, but he will not be liable for any escape therefrom. The bond for the liberties, in such cases, must be given to the Coroner, who then becomes liable for the escape of the prisoner.[3]

4. Whenever a Coroner receives notice that any person has been slain, or has suddenly died, or has been dangerously wounded, it is his duty to go to the place where such person shall be, and forthwith summon not less than nine, nor more than fifteen persons. qualified by law to serve as jurors, and not exempt from such service. to appear before him forthwith, at such place as he shall appoint, to make inquisition concerning such death or wounding. Whenever six, or

---

[1] Amended Constitution of New York, Art. x., § 1; Laws of 1847, chap. 240.

[2] 2 R. S. (3d ed.,) 538, 539, §§ 109-116; Id., 621, § 67.

[3] 2 R. S. (3d ed.,) 539, 540, §§ 117-120.

more, of the jury appear, they are to be sworn by the Coroner. He has the power to issue subpœnas for witnesses, returnable forthwith, or at such time and place as he shall appoint; and it is his duty to cause some surgeon, or physician, to be subpœnaed to appear as a witness on the inquest. Witnesses duly subpœnaed are liable to the same penalties, and their attendance may be enforced in the same manner, as in Justices' courts.[1]

5. The jury, upon the inspection of the person dead or wounded, and after hearing the testimony, are to deliver to the Coroner their 'nquisition in writing, signed by them; in which they must state all the circumstances attending such death or wounding, and who were guilty thereof, either as principal or accessory, and in what manner. If the jury find that any murder, manslaughter, or assault, has been committed, the Coroner is required to bind over the witnesses to appear at the next criminal court to be held in the county, at which an indictment can be found; and he has the power to issue process for the apprehension of persons charged with any such offences, and to examine them, in the same manner as Justices of the Peace. The testimony of all witnesses examined before a Coroner, is to be reduced to writing, and returned by him, with the inquisition, and all recognizances and examinations taken by him, to the next criminal court of record held in the county.[2]

6. In case of the absence, or inability to attend, from sickness or any other cause, of the Coroner of the city and county of New York, any Alderman, or special Justice, of the city, may perform any duty appertaining to the office of such Coroner, in regard to the holding of inquests.[3]

7. No Coroner can hold an inquest in any state prison, upon the body of any deceased convict, unless requested so to do by the agent, physician, or chaplain of the prison; or by any of the state prison inspectors. It is the duty of every agent, however, to call a Coroner, in all cases of the death of a convict other than from ordinary sickness.[4]

8. The Coroners of the several counties of this State are required to deliver over to the respective County Treasures, all moneys, or other valuable things, found with or upon the bodies of deceased persons; or when inquests are held, if the same be unclaimed by the legal representatives of such person or persons, within sixty days after holding such inquest. Before auditing and allowing the accounts of the Coroners, the Supervisors of the county are to require from them respectively, a statement in writing, verified by oath, or affirmation, of all money or other valuable things, found, as aforesaid, and of the disposition of the same.[5]

---

2 R. S. (3d ed.) 827, §§ 1—4; Laws of 1847, chap. 118.
2 2 R. S. (3d ed.) 827, 828, §§ 5—8; 24 Wendell, 520.
3 2 R. S. (3d ed.) 828, § 9.
4 2 R. S. (3d ed.) 859, § 100.
5 Laws of 1842, chap. 155.

FORMS.

§ 354. *Oath to be Administered to the Foreman of a Coroner's Jury.*

You do swear that you will well and truly inquire how, and in what manner, and when and where, the person lying here, [*or, as the case may be*,] came to his death, [*or*, was wounded,] and who such person was, and into all the circumstances attending such death, [*or*, wounding,] and by whom the same was produced, and that you will make a true inquisition thereof, according to the evidence offered to you, or arising from the inspection of the body. So help you God.

---

§ 355. *Oath of other Jurors.*

The same oath which A. B., the foreman of this inquest, hath on his part taken, you, and each of you, do now take, and shall well and truly observe and keep, on your parts. So help you God.

---

§ 356. *Oath of Witness on Coroner's Inquest.*

The evidence you shall give upon this inquest, touching the death of C. D., [*or*, the person whose body has been viewed,] shall be the truth, the whole truth, and nothing but the truth. So help you God.

---

§ 357. *Inquisition of Murder.*

State of New York, ⎱ ss:
    County, ⎰

An inquisition taken for the people of the State of New York, at the house of R. F., in the town of   , in said county of on the   day of   , A. D., 18   , before me, G. H., one of the Coroners in and for said county, upon the view of the body of C. D., [*or*, a person unknown,] then and there lying dead, upon the oaths of A. B., E. F., L. M., &c. &c., good and lawful men of the said county, who, being duly sworn to inquire, on the part of the people of the State of New York, into all the circumstances attending the death of the said C. D., [*or*, person unknown,] and by whom the same was produced; and in what manner; and when and where the said C. D. [*or*, person unknown] came to his death, do say, upon their oaths, as aforesaid, that* one O. P., of [*or*, late of] the town of   , in the county of   , aforesaid, [*or, as the case may be*,] on the   day of   , in the year 18 , at   o'clock in the afternoon of that day, with force and arms, did, at   , in the county of   , aforesaid, then and there, feloniously, violently, and of his malice aforethought, make an assault in and upon the body of the aforesaid C. D., [*or*, person unknown,] then and there present; and that the aforesaid O. P., then and there, with a certain sword made of iron and steel, [*or*, with a certain instrument made of, &c., to them unknown; *or, as the case may be*,] which he, the said O. P., then and there held in his right hand, violently, feloniously, and of his malice aforethought, inflicted a mortal wound, [*or*, wounds] upon the left breast [*or, as the case may be*] of the said C. D., of which said mortal wounds the said C. D., then and there instantly, [*or*, on the   day of, &c.,] died; and so the said jurors do say that the said O. P. did then and there feloniously kill and murder the said C. D., against the peace of the people of this State, and their dignity.

[*If necessary, add:* And the said jurors further say, upon their oaths, as aforesaid, that C. P., of, &c., and R. M., of, &c., were feloniously present with loaded pistols, [*or*, drawn swords; *or, as the case may be*,] at the time of the felony and murder aforesaid, in form aforesaid committed, that is to say, on the   day of   , 18   , aforesaid, at the town of   , aforesaid, in the said county of   , at   o'clock in the afternoon of that day; and that the said C. P., and R. M., did then and there comfort, aid and abet, the said O. P., in doing and committing the felony and murder aforesaid, in the manner aforesaid, against the peace of the people of this State, and their dignity.]

In witness whereof, as well the said Coroner, as the jurors, aforesaid, have to this inquisition set their hands and seals, on the day of the date of this inquisition, as aforesaid.

G. H., Coroner.	[L. S.]
A. B.	[L. S.]
E. F.	[L. S.]
L. M.	[L. S.]
&c. &c.	

---

§ 358. *Inquisition where Murderer is Unknown.*

State of New York, } ss:
        County,   }

An inquisition, &c.; [*as in* § 357 *to the* *, *and then continue as follows:*] a certain person unknown, on the   day of, &c., [*as in* § 357, *to the end, substituting* "certain person unknown" *for* "O. P.," *in all cases; and, if necessary, add the following:* And the said jurors, upon their oaths aforesaid, further say, that the said certain person unknown, who committed the felony and murder aforesaid, after he had committed the same, in manner aforesaid, did flee away to parts unknown, against the peace of the people of this State, and their dignity.]

In witness, &c., [*as in* § 357.]

§ 359. *Inquisition on a Person who has Committed Suicide.*

State of New York, }
     County, } ss:

An inquisition, &c.; [*as in* § 357, *to the* *, *and then continue as follows:*] the said C. D. [*or*, person unknown] did, on the day of   , 18   , at the town of   , in said county of   , voluntarily, and of his own malice aforethought, inflict a mortal wound, [*or*, wounds,] in and upon the body of him, the said C. D., [*or*, person unknown,] of which said mortal wounds the said C. D., [*or*, person unknown,] then and there instantly died; [*or, as the case may be;*] and so the jurors aforesaid, upon their oaths aforesaid, say that the said C. D., [*or*, person unknown,] did, then and there, in manner aforesaid, and at the place aforesaid, voluntarily, and of his own malice aforethought, kill and murder himself, the said C. D., [*or*, person unknown,] against the peace of the people of this State, and their dignity.

In witness, &c., [*as in* § 357.]

---

§ 360. *Inquisition where One has been Wilfully Poisoned.*

State of New York, }
     County, } ss:

An inquisition, &c., [*as in* § 357, *to the* *, *and then continue as follows:*] one O. P., of, &c., [*or*, late of, &c.,] on, &c., at   o'clock in the forenoon of that day, with force and arms, did, at   in the county of   , aforesaid, then and there feloniously, willfully, and of his malice aforethought, mix and mingle a certain quantity of white arsenic, the said O. P. then and there knowing the said white arsenic to be a deadly poison, in a certain quantity of coffee, [*or, as the case may be;*] and the said O. P., afterwards, to wit: on the same day and year last aforesaid, at the time and place last aforesaid, contriving and intending the said C. D. [*or*, person unknown,] with poison feloniously to kill and murder, did, feloniously, wilfully, and of his malice aforethought, offer and give the poison aforesaid, so mixed and mingled as aforesaid, to him, the said C. D., [*or*, person unknown,] to take, drink and swallow; and that the said C. D., [*or*, person unknown,] not knowing the poison aforesaid to have been mixed and mingled as aforesaid, afterwards, to wit: on the same day and year last aforesaid, and at the time and place last aforesaid, by the procurement and persuasion of the said O. P., did take, drink and swallow the said poison, so as aforesaid mixed and mingled by the said O. P.; and thereupon the said C. D., [*or*, person unknown,] by reason of the taking, drinking, and swallowing, the poison as aforesaid, became then and there sick, and distressed in his body; and the said, C. D., [*or*, person unknown,] on the   day of   , 18 .

did die of the poison aforesaid, given and taken as aforesaid, and of the sickness and distemper thereby occasioned; and so the said jurors say, that the said O. P. did feloniously, wilfully, and of his malice aforethought, and in the manner, and by the means aforesaid, poison, kill and murder, the said C. D., [or, person unknown,] against the peace of the people of this State, and their dignity.

In witness, &c., [as in § 357.]

---

§ 361. *Inquisition where One Poisons Himself*

State of New York, ⎱
    County, ⎰ ss:

An inquisition, &c., [as in § 357, *to the *, and then continue as follows:*] the said C. D., [or, person unknown,] on the   day of, &c., at, &c., in the county aforesaid; did voluntarily, [or, when in a deranged state of mind,] mix and mingle a certain quantity of white arsenic, the said C. D. then and there knowing the said white arsenic to be a deadly poison, [or, through mistake, the said C. D. not knowing that the said white arsenic was a deadly poison,] in a certain quantity of coffee, [or, *as the case may be ;*] and the said C. D. did then and there, at the time and place aforesaid, drink and swallow the poison aforesaid, so as aforesaid mixed and mingled, whereby and by reason of which, he became sick and distressed in his body ; and the said C. D., on the   day of   , 18 , did die of the poison aforesaid, so taken as aforesaid, and of the sickness and distemper thereby occasioned: And so the jurors aforesaid, upon their oaths aforesaid, say that the said C. D. did voluntarily, [or, when in a deranged state of mind; or, through mistake,] kill himself in manner and form as aforesaid.

In witness, &c., [as in § 357.]

---

§ 362. *Inquisition where One Drowns Himself.*

State of New York, ⎱
    County, ⎰ ss:

An inquisition, &c., [as in § 357, *to the *, and then continue as follows:*] the said C. D., [or, person unknown,] on the   day of &c., at, &c., in the county aforesaid, voluntarily, and of his own malice aforethought, drowned himself in the   river, situate in the town of   , aforesaid: and so the jurors aforesaid, upon their oaths aforesaid, say that, &c., [as in § 361, *to the end.*]

§ 363. *Inquisition where One is Drowned by Accident.*

State of New York, }
        County, } ss:

An inquisition, &c., [*as in* § 357, *to the* *, *and then continue as follows:*] the said C. D., [*or*, person unknown,] on the   day of, &c., at, &c., in the county aforesaid, went into the   river, situate in the town of   , aforesaid, to bathe, and then and there casually, accidentally, and by misfortune, was suffocated and drowned in the water of the said river, of which suffocating and drowning the said C. D., [*or*, person unknown, then and there died; and so the jurors aforesaid, upon their oaths aforesaid, do say that the said C. D., [*or*, person unknown,] in the manner and by the means aforesaid, casually, accidentally, and by misfortune, came to his death and not otherwise.

In witness, &c., [*as in* § 357.]

---

§ 364. *Inquisition on a Person who has Died a Natural Death.*

State of New York, }
        County, } ss:

An inquisition, &c., [*as in* § 357 *to the* *, *and then continue as follows:*] the said C. D., [*or*, person unknown,] on the   day of, &c., at, &c., in the county aforesaid, was found lying dead on the highway, near the house of A. B., in the town of   , [*or, as the case may be:*] and that he had no marks of violence appearing on his body; and so the said jurors, upon their oaths as aforesaid, do say that the said C. D., [*or*, person unknown] died by the visitation of God, in a natural way, and not otherwise.

In witness, &c., [*as in* § 357.]

---

§ 365. *Inquisition on a Person Found Dead, with Marks of Violence.*

State of New York, }
        County, } ss:

An inquisition, &c., [*as in* § 357 *to the* *, *and then continue as follows:*] the said C. D., [*or*, person unknown,] on, &c., at, &c., was found lying dead on the highway, &c., [*or, as the case may be:*] and that the body of the said C. D., [*or*, person unknown,] when so found, as aforesaid, appeared to have been stabbed twice, with some sharp or pointed instrument, to the said jurors unknown, in or near the left breast thereof, and to have been bruised or beaten with clubs, sticks, or the fists of some person, or persons, to the said jurors unknown; and the said jurors, upon their oaths as aforesaid, do say that the said C. D. [*or*, person unknown] came to his death by the said wounds and bruises, appearing on his body, as aforesaid, and not otherwise.

In witness, &c., [*as in* § 357.]

---

§ 366. *General Form of an Inquisition.*

State of New York, }
County, } ss:

An inquisition indented and taken, for the people of the State of New York, at the house of R. F., in the town of   , in said county of   , on the   day of   , A. D. 18   , before me, G. H., one of the Coroners in and for said county, upon the view of the body of a female infant, then and there lying dead, upon the oaths of A. B., E. F., L. M., &c., &c., good and lawful men of the said county, who being duly sworn to inquire, on the part of the people of the State of New York, into all the circumstances attending the death of the said female infant, and by whom the same was produced, and in what manner, and when, and where; the said female infant came to her death, do say, upon their oaths as aforesaid, that the said female infant was found lying entirely naked and dead, in a certain inclosure of A. B., in the town of   , aforesaid, near the public highway, known as the   , on the   day of   , &c.; that the said female infant, when so found, as aforesaid, appeared, &c.; [*here state the appearance of the body, and whether there were marks of violence, or otherwise;*] that the said female infant was, at the time of her death, of the age of   years, or thereabouts, and that the parents or guardians of the said infant are to the jurors unknown; and so the jurors aforesaid, upon their oaths as aforesaid, do say, that the said female infant came to her death as aforesaid, &c. [*State the finding of the Jury as to the cause of the death.*]

In witness, &c., [*as in* § 357.]

---

§ 367. *Inquisition on the Body of a Lunatic who has Killed Himself.*

State of New York, }
County, } ss:

An inquisition, &c., [*as in* § 357 *to the* *, *and then continue as follows:*] the said C. D., [*or*, person unknown,] on, &c., at, &c., and at the time of his death, was a lunatic, and a person of insane mind; and that the said C. D. [*or*, person unknown] being a lunatic, and a person of insane mind, as aforesaid, did, on, &c., at, &c., [*state the facts.*]

In witness, &c., [*as in* § 357.]

§ 368. *General Form of Warrant, to be issued by the Coroner,*
upon an Inquisition.[1]

County, ss:

To any Constable of the said County, [*or,* the Sheriff, Constables,
or other officers of the peace of the said County, whom these
may concern: *or,* To John Doe, a citizen of the said County,]
greeting:

Whereas, O. P. is charged upon the inquisition of A. B., E. F.,
L. M., &c. &c., good and lawful men of the said county, indented
and taken, upon their several oaths, before me, G. H., one of the
Coroners in and for said county, at the house of R. F., at, &c., on,
&c., with having feloniously killed and murdered C. D., of, &c., on
the   day of, &c., at, &c.

You are, therefore, hereby commanded, in the name of the people of the State of New York, forthwith to take the said O. P., and
bring him before me, to be dealt with according to law. Hereof fail
not at your peril.

Given under my hand, this   day of   , 18 .
G. H., Coroner.

---

§ 369. *Form of Examinations, &c., Taken before the Coroner.*

The People of the State of New York, ⎫
          against   ⎬   County, ss:
          O. P.   ⎭

Examination of witnesses, taken at the house of R. F., in the town
of   , in said county, on the   day of, &c., before G.
H., one of the Coroners in and for the said county, in the matter of
a complaint made upon the oath of J. D. against O. P., for feloniously killing and murdering C. D., on, &c., at, &c., [*or,* made against
O. P., of felony and murder, who is charged, upon the inquisition
of A. B., &c. &c., with having feloniously killed and murdered C. D.,
on the   day of, &c., at, &c.] [*Insert the testimony of the*
witnesses, in the same manner as in cases before Justices of the
Peace.]

I do hereby certify, that the foregoing is a correct statement and
account of an examination taken by and before me, as above stated,
and of the testimony of the several witnesses produced, sworn and
examined thereupon.

Given, &c., [*as in* § 368.]

---

[1] For different forms of warrants, subpœnas, recognizances, &c., see Chapter **XXV**

§ 370. *Examination before Coroner and Jury.*

State of New York, }
      County, } ss:

Examination of witnesses produced, sworn and examined, on, &c., at, &c., before me, G. H., one of the Coroners in and for the said county, and A. B., E. F., L. M., &c. &c., good and lawful men of the said county, duly sworn upon their oaths to inquire into all the circumstances, &c., [*as in* § 357, *to the words* "do say," *and then proceed with the testimony of the witnesses.*]

I do hereby certify, that the foregoing is a correct statement and account of an examination taken by and before me, and the jurors aforesaid, at the time and place aforesaid, and of the testimony, &c., [*as in* § 369.]

---

§ 371. *Statement of Coroner, to be made to the Board of Supervisors.*

Statement and inventory, of all moneys, and other valuable things, found with, or upon, all persons on whom inquests have been held, by and before G. H., one of the Coroners in and for the county of   , for and during the year commencing on the   day of   , 18   :

Upon whom found.	Articles.	Disposition thereof.
C. D.	One gold watch, chain, and key; two gold finger rings; and twelve dollars in specie.	Delivered to the Treasurer of the county of .
M. B.	One coat; one hat; &c.	Delivered to the legal representatives of the said M. B.

    County, ss:

G. H., of said county, coroner, as aforesaid, being duly sworn, says: that the foregoing statement and inventory, of all moneys, and other valuable things, found with, or upon, all persons on whom inquests have been held, by and before him, within the time specified in said statement and inventory, and of the disposition thereof, is in all respects just and true, to the best of his knowledge and belief; and that the moneys and other articles mentioned in such statement and inventory, have been delivered to the Treasurer of the county of   , [*or*, to the legal representatives of the persons therein mentioned.]

    Sworn to, this   day of   , }   G. H.
A. D. 18   , before me, }
        S. T., Justice of the Peace.

CHAPTER XIV.

COVENANTS.

PRACTICAL REMARKS.

1. A covenant is an agreement, by which one person obliges himself to do something beneficial, or abstain from doing something which, if done, might be prejudicial to another, and can only be created by deed indented, or by deed poll. No particular form of words is necessary to create a covenant, but the instrument containing it must be under seal.[1]

2. The words "covenant, promise and agree," or " covenant, agree, &c." or "covenanted, conditioned, concluded and agreed upon," or " I agree to do, &c.," or "yielding and paying," or " I oblige myself to pay, &c.," are sufficient to constitute a covenant.

3. Covenants are sometimes implied; as a lease for years, rendering rent, implies a covenant to pay the rent; but no covenant can be implied in any conveyance, under the Revised Statutes of New York, whether it contain special covenants or not.[2]

4. Covenants real, are those connected with lands, or other real property: covenants of warranty, for quiet enjoyment and future assurance, that neither the grantor nor his heirs shall make any claim to the land conveyed, by a tenant to repair, to pay rent, or that no building shall be erected upon a common or public square owned by a grantor in front of premises conveyed, are all covenants running with an estate in land.[3]

5. A covenant of warranty runs with the land till broken by the eviction of the purchaser or his assignee, when a right of action accrues; the covenant then takes the character of a chose in action, and may be released by the covenantee or assignee.[4]

---

[1] 6 Cowen, 445.
[2] 2 R. S. (3d ed.) 22, § 140; 14 Wendell, 88; 8 Paige, 598; 2 Barbour's Ch. Rep., 559.
[3] 13 Johnson, 236; 5 Cowen, 137; 8 Id., 206;

[3] 7 Wendell, 281; 10 Id., 180; 17 Id., 148; 21 Id., 120; 2 Hill, 105; 6 Id., 599; 3 Denio, 284; 4 Paige, 510.
[4] 1 Barbour's S. C. Rep., 399.

6. If a grantor has no title, his covenant of seizin is broken immediately on the execution of his deed; but where there are covenants of warranty and quiet enjoyment only, there must be an eviction, before a recovery can be had.[1]

7. A covenant for quiet enjoyment in a lease of land for life is binding upon a subsequent grantee in fee of the premises.[2]

8. Personal covenants are those which affect only the covenanter during life, or are merely collateral to the title to land; as covenants that the grantor is well seized, that he has good right to convey, and that the premises are unincumbered.[3]

9. If a day be appointed for the performance of any act, which is to happen, or may happen, before the performance of the act, which is the consideration of the first mentioned act, then the covenants are several and independent, and an action may be brought without averring performance of the consideration: the same rule applies where there is no fixed time for the consideration. But when the day appointed for the payment of the money, or performance of an act, is to happen after the thing, which is the consideration, is to be performed, the covenants are dependent, and no action will lie before the performance of the consideration. Where a covenant goes only to a part of the consideration, it is an independent covenant. But where the covenants go to the whole consideration on both sides, they are mutual conditions, and dependent. Where two acts are to be done at the same time, neither party can maintain an action, without showing performance, or an offer to perform, on his part.[4]

10. Covenants are to be construed according to their spirit and intent; and where, from the subject matter of the covenant, it is the evident intent of the parties that they should be taken severally, they may be so taken, although there be no express words to that effect.[5]

11. A covenant must be construed by itself, and cannot be controlled by a verbal agreement.[6]

FORMS.

§ 372. *General Form of Covenant by one Person.*

And I, the said A. B., for myself and my heirs, executors and administrators, do hereby covenant, to and with the said C. D., his heirs and assigns, that, &c.

---

[1] 1 Comstock, 509.
[2] 3 Barbour's S. C. Rep., 391.
[3] 4 Johnson, 72; 3 Hill, 134; 3 Denio, 284.
[4] 17 Johnson, 293; 6 Cowen, 296; 2 Wendell, 407; 5 Id., 496; 8 Id., 615; 1 Denio, 59; 3 Id., 73.
[5] 6 Johnson, 49; 1 Wendell, 228.
[6] 5 Wendell, 153.

§ 373. *Joint and Several Covenant.*

And we, the said A. B. and C. D., for ourselves and our heirs, executors and administrators, do hereby jointly and severally covenant, to and with the said E. F., his heirs and assigns, that, &c.

---

§ 374. *Several Covenant.*

And we, the said A. B. and C. D., do hereby severally, and not jointly, but each for himself and his heirs, executors and administrators, covenant, to and with the said E. F., that, &c.

---

§ 375. *Covenant by Husband, for himself and his Wife.*

And the said A. B., for himself and his heirs, executors and administrators, and for and on behalf of his wife, the said M. B., and her heirs, &c., doth covenant with the said E. F., that, &c.

---

§ 376. *Covenant of Seizin.*

And the said A. B., for himself, and his heirs, &c., doth hereby covenant, to and with the said C. D., his heirs and assigns, that he is lawfully seized, as of a good and indefeasible estate of inheritance in the law, in fee simple, of and in the above granted premises, &c.

---

§ 377. *Several Covenant of Seizin.*

And the said A. B., E. B. and C. B., do hereby, severally, and not jointly, and each for himself, and for his heirs, executors and administrators, covenant, to and with the said C. D., that he is lawfully seized of the one-third part, of, &c.

---

§ 378. *Covenant by Several Grantors, where Each Confines his Covenant to his own Portion of the Estate.*

And the said A. B., for himself, his heirs, &c., and for the estate, right, title, quiet enjoyment, and further assurance, of the one-third part of the above granted premises; and the said E. B., for himself, &c., and for the estate, &c., of one other third part of the said premises; and the said C. B., for himself, &c., and for the estate, &c., of one other, and the remaining third part of the said premises, do, and each and every of them doth, severally, but not jointly, covenant, to and with, &c.

---

§ 379. *Covenant that Premises are Unincumbered.*

And the said A. B., for himself, &c., doth hereby covenant, to and with the said C. D., his heirs and assigns, that the said premises hereby granted, are free and clear, of and from all incumbrance, of every name and nature whatsoever.

§ 380. *Covenant for Further Assurance.*

And further, the said A. B., for himself, &c., doth hereby covenant, to and with the said C. D., his heirs and assigns, that he, the said A. B., for himself and his heirs, and all and every other person or persons, lawfully claiming, or to claim, by, from, or under, him, or them, shall and will, from time to time, and at all times hereafter, upon the reasonable request, and at the cost and charge of the said C. D., his heirs and assigns, make and execute, or cause and procure to be made and executed, all and every such further, and other lawful and reasonable deed, or deeds, whatsoever, for the further, better, and more perfect and absolute, assurance of the said premises hereby granted, or intended so to be, with their appurtenances, unto the said C. D., his heirs and assigns, as by him or them, or by his or their counsel, learned in the law, shall be reasonably advised, devised, or required.

§ 381. *Joint Covenant against Incumbrance.*

And the said A. B. and C. D., for themselves, their heirs, &c., do severally, and not jointly, nor one for the other, or for the act or deed of the other, but each for his own acts only, covenant, promise, grant and agree, to and with the said E. F., his heirs and assigns, by these presents, that they, the said A. B. and C. D., have not heretofore done, or committed, any act, matter, or thing, whatever, whereby the premises hereby granted, or any part thereof, are, or shall be, charged, in title, estate, or otherwise.

§ 382. *Covenant for Quiet Enjoyment.*

And the said A. B., for his heirs, &c., doth covenant, promise and and agree, to and with the said C. D., his heirs and assigns, by these presents, that he, the said C. D., his heirs and assigns, shall and lawfully may, from time to time, and at all times hereafter, peaceably and quietly have, hold, occupy, possess and enjoy, the said premises, &c., hereby granted, or intended so to be, with the appurtenances, without the lawful hindrance, or molestation of the said A. B., his heirs and assigns, or of any other person or persons whatsoever, by or with his or their act, consent, privity, or procurement.

§ 383. *Covenant by Tenant for Life, and Tenant in Fee of the Reversion.*

And we, the said A. B., and A. B., junior, for ourselves respectively, and our respective heirs, do severally, and not jointly, covenant and agree, to and with the said C. D., his heirs and assigns, that we are lawfully seized in fee of the aforegranted premises, in manner following, that is to say: that the said A. B. is seized thereof for his life, and as tenant by the courtesy; and that the said A. B., junior, is seized in fee simple of the reversion, or remainder thereof, expectant upon the determination of the said estate by the courtesy, &c.

---

§ 384. *Mutual and Dependent Covenant.*

And the said A. B., for himself, &c., doth hereby covenant and agree, to and with the said C. D., his heirs and assigns, that he will pay to the said C D., his heirs or assigns, the sum of   dollars, on the   day of   next; and in consideration thereof, the said C. D., for himself, &c., doth covenant and agree, to and with the said A. B., his heirs and assigns, that he will make and execute to the said A. B., &c., a good and sufficient warranty deed, &c., on the payment of the said sum of money as aforesaid.

---

§·385. *Independent Covenants.*

And the said A. B., for himself, &c., doth hereby covenant and agree, to and with the said C. D., his heirs and assigns, that he will pay unto the said C. D., &c., the sum of   dollars, on or before the expiration of one year from the date of these presents, with legal interest thereon. And the said C. D., for himself, &c., doth covenant, &c., to and with the said A. B., &c., that he will sell, transfer, and convey, to the said A. B., &c.,   shares of the capital stock of the bank of   , on or before the expiration of ninety days from the date hereof.

CHAPTER XV.

DEBTOR AND CREDITOR.

PRACTICAL REMARKS.

1. Every insolvent debtor may obtain a discharge from his debts, under the provisions of the Revised Statutes of this State, upon executing an assignment of all his estate for the benefit of his creditors. The petition for that purpose must be signed by the debtor, and by so many of his creditors residing in the United States, as have debts in good faith, owing to them by such debtor, and amounting to two-thirds of all his debts owing to creditors residing in the United States. Corporations, executors, and administrators, like other persons or firms, may become petitioning creditors. The petition must be accompanied by the affidavits of the debtor and petitioning creditors, forms of which are hereinafter given. Annexed to the petition there must be a schedule, containing a full and true account of all the creditors of the petitioner; the place of residence of each creditor, if known; and if not known, the fact must be stated; the sum owing to each creditor, and the nature of each debt or demand, whether on written security, account, or otherwise; the true cause and consideration of indebtedness in each case, and the place where it accrued; and a full and true inventory of all the estate, both real and personal, in law and equity, of the insolvent; of the incumbrances existing thereon; and of all the books, vouchers, and securities, relating thereto.[1]

2. The officer receiving the petition of an insolvent debtor, is required to make an order for all the creditors of the insolvent, to show cause why he should not make an assignment, and be discharged from his debts. Notice of the order is to be published in the State paper, and in a newspaper printed in the county, and also in one printed in the city of New York, provided one-fourth in amount of

---

[1] 2 R. S. (3d ed.) 76, §§ 1–5; Id., 92, § 7, et seq.; 20 Johnson, 21; 1 Wendell, 156; 2 Paige, 602; 3 Id., 338

the debts accrued in that city. If all the creditors reside within one hundred miles of the place where cause is to be shown, the notice is to be published once in each week, for six weeks successively; if any of the creditors reside over one hundred miles from such place, the notice is to be published ten weeks. It is also necessary that the creditors of the insolvent, provided they reside in the United States, and their places of residence are known, should be served with a copy of the notice of the order to show cause, either personally or by mail. If the service be personal, it must be made at least twenty days before the time fixed for the discharge, and if by mail, at least forty days. Where the notice is sent by mail, it should be folded and directed like a letter.[1]

3. At the time of the hearing, proof must be presented of the due service of notice of the order to show cause on creditors residing in the United States.[2]

4. On the day fixed for the hearing, the officer proceeds to hear the proofs and allegations of the parties: if there be no opposition, an order is entered requiring the debtor to make an assignment; and when due proof of the execution of such assignment, and the transfer of the property of the debtor to the assignee, is presented to the officer, a discharge is granted. Creditors may, however, demand a jury in the premises, when the same proceedings are had as on the trial of other causes. Fraudulent preferences, or concealments, or collusion with creditors, or wrongful interference with property transferred to the assignee, if made to appear on the hearing, will prevent the petitioner from obtaining a discharge.[3]

5. A discharge granted in pursuance of a petition presented as aforesaid, will exonerate the insolvent from all debts due at the time of the assignment, or contracted before that time, though payable afterwards, founded upon contracts made since the 12th of April, 1813, within the State, or to be executed within this State, and from all debts owing to persons resident within this State, at the time of the first publication of the notice above mentioned; or owing to persons not residing in this State, who united in the petition for a discharge, or who shall accept a dividend from the insolvent's estate; and from all liabilities incurred by such insolvent, by making or endorsing any promissory note, or bill of exchange, previous to his assignment. Such discharge will also operate upon a previously existing judgment, obtained against the debtor for *tort*.[4]

6. Petitions in the case of an insolvent debtor, must be presented to a Justice of the Supreme Court, County Judge, or Recorder of a city. In the city of Schenectady, the petition may be presented to

1 2 R. S. (3d. ed.) 77, §§ 8–11; Laws of 1847, chap. 366; 1 Wendell, 90.
2 Laws of 1847, chap. 366.
3 2 R. S. (3d. ed.) 18, § 12, et seq.; 13 Johnson, 385; 6 Wendell, 632; 7 Id., 240.

4 2 R. S. (3d. ed.) §§ 30, 31; 9 Johnson, 127; 10 Id., 63, 289; 20 Id., 208; 2 Wendell, 457; 9 Id.; 313; 12 Id., 102; 19 Id., 150, 629; 5 Hill, 242; 3 Paige, 338.

the Mayor. In the city of New York, application may be made to any one of the Justices of the Superior Court, or Judges of the Court of Common Pleas. The officer to whom the petition is presented, must reside in the same county with the insolvent debtor. If there be no officer in the county authorized to act in the premises, the application can be made to an officer in any other county: the place appointed for the hearing, however, must be in the county where the debtor resides.[1]

7. Any person against whom any suit shall have been commenced in a court of record, in which such person cannot be arrested or imprisoned, may present a petition to a Justice of the Supreme Court, or County Judge in the same county; or, in the city of New York, to any one of the Justices of the Superior Court, or Judges of the Court of Common Pleas, praying that his property may be assigned. Fourteen days' notice of the presentation of the petition is required to be given. The notice is to be served with a copy of the petition, account, and inventory, forms of which are hereinafter given, on the plaintiff, or plaintiffs, by whom the defendant shall be prosecuted, their personal representatives, or attorney; and proof of such service must be made at the time of presenting the petition. The subsequent proceedings upon such petition, are similar to those in the case of an insolvent debtor, as above mentioned. The discharge granted in pursuance thereof, will exonerate the debtor from being proceeded against by any creditor entitled to a dividend of the estate of such petitioner.[2]

8. An assignment executed by an insolvent debtor, under the foregoing provisions, of all his estate, real and personal, passes the title to all lands he may own, without further description, and whether such lands are mentioned in the inventory or not. A re-conveyance to him will not be presumed.[3]

9. Whenever any debtor is imprisoned in the State Prison, for any term less than his natural life; or in any penitentiary, or county jail, for a criminal offence, for any term more than one year; application may be made to any of the officers to whom the petition of an insolvent may be presented, by any creditor of such debtor, or by any of his relatives, or by any relative of his wife, for the appointment of trustees to take charge of the estate of such debtor. A copy of the sentence of conviction of such debtor, duly certified by the Clerk of the court, under his seal of office, together with an affidavit of the applicant, that such debtor is actually confined under the sentence, and that he is indebted, (in any sum whatever,) must be presented to the officer, who thereupon proceeds to appoint two or

---

[1] 2 R. S. (3d. ed.) 91, 92, §§ 1–6.
[2] Laws of 1831, chap. 300, § 12, et seq.;
[3] R. S. (3d ed.) 110, § 13, o seq.; 3 Hill, 109
[4] Id., 581, 606.
[5] 2 Denio, 61.

more fit persons, as trustees of the estate of the debtor. Whenever the imprisoned debtor is lawfully discharged from imprisonment, the trustees are bound to surrender up to him all his real and personal estate, and all moneys belonging to him, in their hands, after retaining sufficient for their expenses and lawful commissions.[4]

10. Assignees, or trustees, of insolvent or imprisoned debtors, may be appointed to fill vacancies, by the officer before whom the former proceedings were had, or his successor in office, or any other officer residing in the same county with the original assignee or trustee, to whom the petition might, in the first instance, have been presented. The appointment must be certified, and filed in the Clerk's office of the county.[5]

FORMS.

§ 386. *Letter of License to a Debtor.*

To all to whom these presents shall come: We, E. F., of, &c., and G. F., of, &c., [*name the several creditors,*] whose names are under-written, and seals affixed, creditors of A. B., now or late of   , send greeting: Whereas, the said A. B., on the day of the date hereof, is indebted unto us, the said creditors, in divers sums of money, which, by reason of great losses and misfortunes, he is not at present able to pay and satisfy, without respite of time be given him for that purpose: Know ye, therefore, that we, the said creditors, and every one of us, do, by these presents, severally give and grant unto the said A. B., free license, liberty and leave, to come, go and resort, unto us, and every of us, his said creditors, to compound and take order with us, and every one of us, for our and every of our debts; and also go about his other business and affairs, at his free will and pleasure, from the day of the date hereof, until the full end and term of   months next ensuing, without any let, suit, trouble, arrest, attachment, or other disturbance whatsoever, to be offered or done unto him, the said A. B., his wares, goods, money, or merchandise, whatsoever, by us, or the assigns of us, or any or either of us, or by our or any of our means or procurement; and we, the said creditors, severally and respectively, each for himself, his executors and administrators, do severally, and not jointly, covenant and agree, to and with the said A. B., his executors, adminis-

----

[1] 2 R. S. (3d ed.) 74, 75, §§ 1-5; 15 Wendell, 250.   [2] Laws of 1846, chap. 153

trators, and every of them, by these presents, that if any trouble, vexation, wrong, damage, or hinderance, shall be done unto him, the said A. B., either in his body, goods, or chattels, within the said term of   months, from the date of these presents, by us, or any of us, contrary to the tenor and effect of this our license, that then he, the said A. B., his executors and administrators, shall be acquitted and discharged towards and against him and them, of us, his and their executors, administrators, partners and assigns, and every of them, by whom and by whose means he shall be vexed, arrested, troubled, imprisoned, attached, grieved, or damnified, of all manner of actions, suits, quarrels, debts, dues and demands, either in law or equity, whatsoever, from the beginning of the world to the day of the date of these presents: provided always, nevertheless, and it is the true intent and meaning of these presents, and of the said parties hereunto, that if all the said parties shall not subscribe and seal these presents, then, and in such case, the liberty and license hereby given and granted, and every clause, covenant, matter and thing, herein contained, shall cease and be utterly void, to all intents and purposes; any thing hereinbefore contained, to the contrary thereof, in any wise notwithstanding.

In witness whereof, the said parties to these presents have hereunto set their hands and seals, the   day of   , 18 .

. Signed, sealed and delivered }
   in presence of   }
     G. H.

E. F. [L. s.]
&c., &c.

---

§ 387. *Composition with Creditors.*

To all to whom these presents shall come: We, whose names are hereunder written, and seals affixed, creditors of A. B., of, &c., send greeting: Whereas, the said A. B. does justly owe, and is indebted unto us, his said several creditors, in divers sums of money; but by reason of sundry losses, disappointments, and other damages, happened unto the said A. B., he is become unable to pay and satisfy us of our full debts, and just claims and demands, and therefore we, the said creditors, have resolved and agreed to undergo a certain loss, and to accept of   cents, for every dollar owing by the said A. B., to us, the several and respective creditors aforesaid, to be paid in full satisfaction and discharge of our several and respective debts: Now, know ye, that we, the said creditors of the said A. B., do, for ourselves, severally and respectively, and for our several and respective heirs, executors and administrators, covenant, promise, compound and agree, to and with the said A. B., by these presents, that we, the said several and respective creditors, shall and will accept, receive and take, of and from the said A. B., for each and every dollar that the said A. B. does owe and is indebted to us, the said several and respective creditors, the sum of   cents, in

full discharge and satisfaction of the several debts and sums of money that the said A. B. does owe and stand indebted unto us; to be paid unto us, the said several and respective creditors, within the time or space of ᴏ months next after the date of these presents; and we, the said several and respective creditors, do severally and respectively covenant, promise and agree, to and with the said A. B., that he, the said A. B., shall and may from time to time, and at all times within the said time or space of　　　months next ensuing the date hereof, assign, sell, or otherwise dispose of all his goods and chattels, wares and merchandise, at his own free will and pleasure, for and towards the payment and satisfaction of the said
cents for every dollar the said A. B. does owe and is indebted unto us, as aforesaid; and that neither we, the said several and respective creditors, nor any or either of us, shall or will, at any time or times hereafter, sue, arrest, molest, or trouble, the said A. B., or his goods and chattels, for any debt or other thing, now due and owing to us or any of us, his respective creditors: so as the said A. B. well and truly pay, or cause to be paid, the said sum of　　　cents for every dollar he does owe and stand indebted to us, respectively, within the said time or space of　　　months next ensuing the date hereof; and all and every of the grants, covenants, agreements and conditions, herein contained, shall extend to and bind our several executors, administrators and assigns.

In witness whereof, we, the undersigned, have hereunto set our, &c., [*as in* § 386.]

———

§ 388. *Petition of Insolvent and his Creditors under the Two-Third Act.*

To the Hon. J. P. H., County Judge of　　　County : [*or, as the case may be.*]

The petition of A. B., of the town [*or*, city] of　　　, an insolvent debtor, and others, whose names are hereunto subscribed, creditors of the said insolvent, residing within the United States, respectfully showeth : That the said insolvent, from many unfortunate circumstances, has become insolvent, and utterly incompetent to the payment of his debts ; wherefore he, and your other petitioners, are desirous that the said insolvent's estate should be distributed among his creditors in discharge of their debts, so far as the same will extend ; and for that purpose pray, that all his estate, real and personal, may be assigned over and delivered up to J. K., of, &c., and L. M., of, &c., as assignees, appointed by the said creditors, having debts in good faith owing to them by the said insolvent, now due, or hereafter to become due, and amounting to at least two thirds of all the debts owing by the said insolvent, to creditors residing within the United States : And further, that the said insolvent may be discharged from his debts, agreeably to the direction of the statute of the State of New York, concerning "Voluntary assignments, made pursuant to the application of an insolvent and his creditors."

Dated the   day of   , 18 .

A. B.

E. F., $,) *[Insert the amount due to*
G. H., $, } *each creditor, opposite the*
S. T., & Co., $,) *signature.]*

§ 389. *Affidavit of Residence of Petitioner.*

I, L. M., do swear, that A. B., in the annexed petition named, is an inhabitant actually residing within the county of   , and State of New York.   L. M.

Sworn to before me, the   day }
     of   , 18 . }

J. P. H., County Judge; [*or any officer authorized to take affidavits to be read in a court of record.*]

§ 390. *Affidavit of Creditor.*

State of New York, } ss:
     County, }

E. F., of the said county, one of the petitioning creditors of A. B., an insolvent debtor, being duly sworn, doth depose and say, that the sum of   dollars, lawful money of the United States, being the sum annexed to the name of this deponent, subscribed to the petition, is justly due to him from the said insolvent, on account, for [*or, on a promissory note given for*] goods, wares, and merchandise, sold and delivered by him to the said insolvent; [*or, as the case may be; stating the nature of the demand—whether on written security or otherwise,—and the general ground and consideration of the indebtedness;*] and that neither he, nor any person to his use, hath received from the said insolvent, or any other person, payment of any demand, or any part thereof, in money, or in any way whatever, or any gift or reward whatsoever, upon any express or implied trust or confidence, that he should become a petitioner for the said insolvent.

Sworn, &c., [*as in* § 389.]   E. F.

§ 391. *Affidavit of one of a Firm, who are Creditors.*

State of New York, } ss:
     County, }

S. T., of the said county, partner of the firm or copartnership of S. T. & Co., who, as one of the copartners, and in their behalf, hath subscribed to the petition the name or firm of their said copartnership, as petitioning creditors of A. B., an insolvent debtor, being duly sworn, doth depose and say, that the sum of dollars, lawful money of the United States, being the sum annexed to the name of the said copartnership subscribed to the petition, is justly due to them from the said insolvent, for [*state the nature of the demand, whether owing on written security, or otherwise, with the general ground and consideration of the indebtedness;*] and that neither he, nor any person to his or their use, hath received from the said insolvent, or any other person, payment of any part thereof, in money, or in any other way whatever, or any gift or reward whatsoever, upon any express or implied trust or confidence, that he or they should become a petitioner or petitioners for the said insolvent.

Sworn, &c., [*as in* § 389.]

---

§ 392. *Schedule of Petitioner.*

The Schedule of A. B., an insolvent, annexed to and delivered with his petition, to the Hon. D. W., Recorder of the city of   , [*or, as the case may be,*] and containing a full and true account of all the creditors of the said A. B., with the place of residence of each; the sum owing to each of them by the said insolvent; the nature of each debt, with the true cause and consideration thereof; and the place where the same accrued.

Creditors.	Residence.	Amount.		Nature of debt, with true cause and consideration thereof.	Accrued at
		Dolls.	Cts.		
L. M.	New York.	562	39	On account, for goods, wares, and merchandise, sold and delivered to the said A. B.	New York.
S. T. & Co.	Albany.	1182	14	On promissory note, given on purchase of bill of goods, wares, and merchandise.	Albany.
N. B.	Auburn.	1000	00	On a bond, given as collateral security for payment of the sum of $, secured to be paid by a certain mortgage, executed by the said A. B., to the said N. B., the original consideration of which was money lent to the said A. B.	Auburn.

Also a full and true inventory of all the estate, both real and personal, in law and equity, of the said A. B., an insolvent debtor; of the incumbrances existing thereon, and of all the books, vouchers, and securities, relating thereto, as follows, to wit:

Ten acres of land, situate in, &c., subject to a certain mortgage, given, &c.; twenty shares of the capital stock of the bank of   , two horses; one lumber wagon; one two-horse carriage; one sofa, &c., &c. Dated the   day of   18 .

A. B.

§ 393. *Oath of Insolvent.*

I, A. B., do swear, that the account of my creditors, and the inventory of my estate, which are annexed to my petition, and herewith delivered, are in all respects just and true; and that I have not at any time, or in any manner whatsoever, disposed of, or made over, any part of my estate, for the future benefit of myself and family, or in order to defraud any of my creditors; and that I have, in no instance, created or acknowledged a debt, for a greater sum than I honestly and truly owed; and that I have not paid, secured to be paid, or in any way compounded with, any of my creditors, with a view fraudulently to obtain the prayer of my petition.

Sworn &c., [*as in* § 389.] A. B.

---

§ 394. *Order for Creditors to Show Cause, and for Publication.*

Ordered, That all the creditors of A. B., an insolvent debtor, be required to show cause, if any they have, before me, on the day of   next, at   o'clock in the   noon, at my office in the town of   , why an assignment of the said insolvent's estate should not be made, and he be discharged from his debts, pursuant to the provisions of the statute for the discharge of an insolvent from his debts, notice for which is to be published for six [*or,* ten] weeks, successively, in the state paper, and the newspaper printed in the county of   , entitled the   . Dated the day of   , 18 .

D. P. Justice of the Supreme Court.

---

§ 395. *Notice to be Published.*

Notice of application for the discharge of an insolvent from his debts, pursuant to the provisions of the third article of the first title of the fifth chapter of the second part of the Revised Statutes:

A. B., of the town of   , in the county of   , an insolvent debtor: [*or, if the applicant be a member of an insolvent firm, say:* A. B., of the city and county of New York, an insolvent debtor, individually, and as one of the firm, [*or,* late firm] of B. & Y.;] Notice first published, July 1, 1847. Creditors to appear before Hon. J. P. H., County Judge of said county of   , at his office in the town of   , on the   day of   next, at ten o'clock in the forenoon, to show cause, if any they have, why an assignment should not be made of said insolvent's estate, and he be discharged from his debts.

§ 396. *Notice to be served on the Creditors Residing in the United States, with the Notice of the Order to Show Cause.*

Sir:—You will please take notice, that the foregoing [*or,* the within,] is a copy of a notice to show cause, before the Hon. J. P. H., County Judge of   county, at the time and place therein specified, why I should not make an assignment of my estate, and be discharged from my debts, &c.

Dated the   day of   , 18   .

To L. M.   Yours, &c.,   A. B.

---

§ 397. *Proof of Service of Notice on Creditors Residing in the United States.*

State of New York, }
          County, } ss:

[*Attach here a printed copy of the notice,* § 395.] A. B., of said county, being duly sworn, says, that on the   day of   instant, [*or,* last past,] he served the notice, of which the annexed printed notice is a copy, on C. D., L. M., &c., &c., by delivering a copy of the same to each of them personally, [*or,* by depositing a copy of the same, properly folded and directed to each of them, at his usual place of residence, in the post office at   .]

Sworn, &c., [*as in* § 389.]   A. B.

---

§ 398. *Order for Assignment.*

Whereas, A. B., of   .   , in the county of   , an insolvent debtor, did, in conjunction with so many of his creditors residing within the United States as have debts in good faith owing to them by the said insolvent, amounting to at least two-thirds of all the debts owing by him to creditors residing within the United States, present a petition to me, for the purpose of being discharged from his debts, pursuant to the provisions of the third article of the first title of the fifth chapter of the second part of the Revised Statutes; upon hearing which, it satisfactorily appeared to me that the said insolvent is justly and truly indebted to the petitioning creditors in the sums by them respectively mentioned in their affidavits annexed to the petition; that such sums amount in the aggregate to two-thirds of all the debts owing by him at the time of his presenting his petition to creditors residing within the United States, and that he has honestly and fairly given a true account of his estate, and has in all things conformed to the matters required of him by the said article: I do, therefore, direct that an assignment be made by the said insolvent, to J. K., of, &c., and L. M., of, &c., assignees nominated by the said creditors, of all his estate, both in law and equity, in posession, reversion, or remainder, excepting from the articles mentioned in his inventory, such articles of wearing apparel and bedding, as is reasonable and necessary for the said insolvent and his family to retain, and also his arms and accoutrements. Dated the   day of , 18 .

J. P. H., County Judge of   County.

---

§ 399. *Assignment.*

Know all men by these presents: That I, A. B., having become insolvent, did, in conjunction with so many of my creditors, residing within the United States, whose debts, in good faith, amount to two-thirds of all the debts owing by me to creditors residing within the United States, present a petition to the Hon. J. P. H., County Judge of   county: [*or, as the case may be,*] praying for relief, pursuant to the provisions of the statute authorizing an insolvent debtor to be discharged from his debts; whereupon the said Judge ordered notice to be given to all my creditors to show cause, if any they had, before him, at a certain day and place, why the prayer of the petitioner should not be granted; which notice was duly published: and no good cause appearing to the contrary, he being satisfied that the proceedings were just and fair, and that I had in all things conformed to those matters required by the said statute, directed an assignment of all my estate to be made by me for the benefit of all my creditors.

Now, therefore, know ye, that in conformity to the said direction, I have granted, released, assigned and set over, and by these presents do grant, release, assign and set over, unto J. K., of, &c., and L. M., of, &c., assignees nominated to receive the same, all my estate, real and personal, both in law and equity, in possession, reversion, or remainder, and all books, vouchers and securities, relating thereto, to hold the same unto the said assignees, to and for the use of all my creditors.

In witness whereof, I have hereunto set my hand and seal, this   day, of   , in the year one thousand eight hundred and

Sealed and delivered, }   A. B.   [L. S.]
    in presence of }
      G. H.

---

§ 400. *Acknowledgment of Assignment.*

State of New York, } ss:
        County, }

On the   day of   , in the year one thousand eight hundred and   , before me came A. B., to me known, [*or*, proven to me by the oath of G. H., the subscribing witness to the above assignment,] to be the individual described in and who executed the above [*or*, said] assignment, and the said A. B. acknowledged that he executed the same.

S. T., Justice of the Peace.

§ 401. *Oath of Assignee.*

I, L. M., having been appointed assignee of A. B., an insolvent debtor, do swear, that I will well and truly execute the trust by that appointment reposed in me, according to the best of my skill and understanding.

Sworn, &c., [*as in* § 389.]   L. M.

§ 402. *Notice of Assignment, to be inserted Three Weeks.*

Pursuant to the provisions of the first title of the fifth chapter of the second part of the Revised Statutes, notice is hereby given, that the undersigned have been appointed assignees of A. B., an insolvent debtor. All persons indebted to the said debtor are required to render an account of all the debts and sums of money owing by them respectively, to the said assignees, by the   day of   next, at the office of the said L. M., in the town of   , and to pay the same; and all persons having in their possession any property or effects of the said debtor, are required to deliver the same to us, by the day above specified. All the creditors of the said debtor are also required to deliver their respective accounts and demands to the said L. M., at his office as aforesaid, by the   day of   next. Dated the   day of   , 18 .

J. K.
L. M.

§ 403. *Certificate of the Assignees.*

We do certify, that A. B., an insolvent debtor, has this day granted, conveyed, assigned and delivered, to us, for the use and benefit of all his creditors, all his estate, real and personal, both in law and equity, in possession, reversion, or remainder, and all books, vouchers and securities, relating to the same, except such articles of wearing apparel and bedding, as are reasonable and necessary for the said insolvent and his family to retain, and also his arms and accoutrements.

In witness whereof, we have hereunto set our hands and seals, this   day of   , in the year one thousand eight hundred and   .

Executed in presence of ⎫
R. F.   ⎬   J. K. [L. s.]
M. B.   ⎭   L. M. [L. s.]

§ 404. *Affidavit of Execution of Certificate.*

State of New York, ⎫ ss:
     County, ⎭

R. F., of, &c., being duly sworn, deposes and says, that he did, on the   day of   last past, [*or, instant,*] see J. K., of, &c., and L. M., of, &c., to him personally known, sign and seal the within [*or, annexed*] certificate; and that he, this deponent, subscribed his name thereto as one of the subscribing witnesses.

Sworn, &c., [*as in* § 389.]   R. F.

§ 405. *Certificate of County Clerk that Assignment has been Recorded.*

State of New York, ⎫ ss;
     County. ⎭

I, P. V., Clerk of the county of   , do hereby certify, that the assignment made by A. B., an insolvent debtor, of all his estate, both in law and equity, in possession, reversion, or remainder, (except as is excepted by the statute,) to J. K., of, &c., and L. M., of, &c., bearing date the   day of, &c., has been duly recorded in my office.

In testimony whereof, I have hereunto set my hand, the   day of   , 18 .   P. V.

----

§ 406. *Discharge.*[1]

To all to whom these presents shall come or may concern: I, J. P. H., County Judge of   County, [*or, as the case may be,*] send greeting: Whereas, A. B., of, &c., an insolvent debtor, residing within said county, did, in conjunction with so many of his creditors residing within the United States, as have debts in good faith owing to them by the said insolvent, amounting to at least two-thirds of all the debts owing by him to creditors residing within the United States, present a petition to me, praying that the estate of the said insolvent might be assigned for the benefit of his creditors, and he be discharged from his debts, pursuant to the provisions of the statute authorizing an insolvent debtor to be discharged from his debts; whereupon I ordered notice to be given to all the creditors of the said insolvent, to show cause, if any they had, before me, at a certain time and place, why an assignment of the said insolvent's estate should not be made, and he be discharged from his debts; proof of the publication whereof hath been duly made. And whereas, it satisfactorily appearing to me that the doings on the part of the creditors were just and fair, and that the said insolvent has conformed in all things to those matters required of him by the said

----

[1] For the security of the insolvent, it is well to have the discharge signed in duplicate; one copy to be filed in the County Clerk's office, and the other retained in his own possession.

statute, I have directed an assignment to be made by the said insolvent, of all his estate, real and personal, both in law and equity, in possession, reversion, or remainder, to J. K., of, &c., and L. M., of, &c., assignees nominated by the creditors to receive the same; and the said insolvent having, on the   day of   , made such assignment, and produced to me a certificate thereof, executed by the said assignees, and duly proved; and also a certificate of the Clerk of this county, that such assignment is duly recorded in his office: Now, therefore, know ye, that by virtue of the power and authority in me vested, I do hereby discharge the said insolvent from all his debts, pursuant to the provisions of the said statute.

In witness whereof, I have hereunto set my hand and seal, the   day of   , in the year of our Lord one thousand eight hundred and   .

J. P. H., County Judge, &c. [L. S.]

---

§ 407. *Petition Under Non-Imprisonment Act, after Action Commenced.*

To the Hon. C. P. D., Judge, &c.; [*or, as the case may be.*]

The petition of A. B., of the town of   , in the county of   , respectfully showeth: That an action has been commenced against him in a court of record, in which, by the provisions of the act to abolish imprisonment for debt, and to punish fraudulent debtors, he cannot be arrested or imprisoned. Your petitioner, therefore, prays, that his property may be assigned, and that he may have the benefit of the provisions of the said act; and in conformity thereto, sets forth and states: that the said action is brought by C. D., in the Supreme Court of the State of New York, and was commenced by summons, served upon the said petitioner on the   day of   last past, [*or, instant,*] and that the following is a just and true account of all his estate, real and personal, in law and equity, and of all the charges affecting the same, as the same exist at the time of preparing this petition, according to the best of his knowledge and belief, to wit: Real estate [*describe the same, if any; if otherwise, say:* None:] Personal estate, one span of horses, &c., &c.: The charges affecting the same are as follows, to wit: a chattel mortgage executed by the said A. B., to L. M., of, &c., on the   day of   , 18 , for the purpose of securing the payment of the sum of   dollars, due and owing to the said L. M., by the said A. B.: His necessary wearing apparel, bedding and furniture, for himself and family, his arms and accoutrements, and other articles, exempt by law from execution, are as follows, to wit: [*specify the articles:*] and his tools, or instruments of his trade, necessary to the carrying on of the same, not exceeding twenty-five dollars in value, are as follows, to wit: [*specify the articles.*]

And your petitioner further states, that the following is a just and true account of the deeds, securities, books and writings, whatsoever, relating to the said estate, and the charges thereon, and the names, and places of abode of the witnesses to such deeds, securities, and writings, according to the best of his knowledge and belief, to wit. [*state the details:*] and that there is no other account of any real estate, or personal estate, in law or equity, or any other charges affecting the same, as the same estate exists at the time of preparing this petition; nor any other deeds, securities, books, or writings, whatsoever, relating to the same; nor any other names, or places of abode, of any witnesses to such deeds, securities, or writings, so far set forth, as his knowledge extends concerning the same.

Dated the   day of   , 18 .

A. B., Defendant

---

§ 408. *Affidavit of Petitioner, to be endorsed on the Petition.*

I, the within named petitioner, do swear: That the within petition, and the account of my estate, and of the charges thereon, are in all respects just and true; and that I have not, at any time, or in any manner, disposed of or made over any part of my property, with a view to the future benefit of myself or my family; or with an intent to injure or defraud any of my creditors.   A. B.

Sworn to, &c., [*as in* § 389.]

---

§ 409. *Notice of Presenting Petition.*

Supreme Court,
  C. D.
  against
  A. B.

Sir: Please to take notice that the within is a true copy of a petition, with an account of my creditors, and an inventory of my estate thereunto annexed, which I intend to present to the Hon. J. P. H., &c., at his office in the town of   , on the   day of   , 18 , at   o'clock in the   noon, or as soon thereafter as the same can be heard.   Yours, &c.

A. B., Defendant.

To C. D., [*or*, A. W., attorney of]
    the plaintiff in the above suit.

J

› § 410. *Affidavit of Service of Notice.*

Supreme Court,

    C. D.

    against   County, ss:

    A. B.

O. P., of the said county, being duly sworn, doth depose and say that on the   day of   last past, [*or, instant,*] he, this deponent, served C. D., of the town of   , the plaintiff in this cause, with a notice of the above named defendant's intention of presenting the within petition to the Hon. J. P. H., &c., [*or, as the case may be,*] on the   day of   next, [*or, instant,*] at   o'clock in the   noon of the same day; and also, with a true copy of the account of the said defendant's estate as within set forth, by delivering the said notice and account; [*state the manner of service, whether personal or otherwise;*] and that the notice and account so delivered were signed by the above named defendant in this cause.   O. P.

Sworn, &c., [*as in* § 389.]

---

§ 411. *Order for Assignment.*

Whereas, A. B. did, on the   day of   , 18 , present a petition to me praying that his property might be assigned, and that he might have the benefit of the provisions of the act to abolish imprisonment for debt, and to punish fraudulent debtors; upon the hearing of which, I, being satisfied that the proceedings on the part of the petitioner are just and fair, and that he has conformed in all things to the provisions of the said act, do therefore order that an assignment of all his estate be made by him to M. P., of, &c., the assignee appointed by me to receive the same, excepting such articles as are by law exempt from execution.

Dated the   day of   , 18   .

                 J. P. H., County Judge, &c.

---

§ 412. *Assignment.*

Know all men by these presents: That I, A. B., of, &c., did present a petition to the Hon. C. P. D., one of the Judges, &c., praying that my property might be assigned, and that I might have the benefit of the provisions of the act to abolish imprisonment for debt; whereupon, such proceedings were had, that the said Judge, after hearing the said petition, ordered that an assignment should be made by me of all my property, except such articles as were by law exempt from execution: Now, therefore, know ye, that in conformity to the said order, I have released, and by these presents do grant and assign, all my estate, real and personal, both in law and equity, in possession, reversion and remainder, and all books, vouchers and securities, relating to the same, to M. P., of, &c., the assignee appointed to receive the same, except such articles as are by law exempt from execution.[1]

§ 413. *Certificate of Assignment.*

I do hereby certify, that A. B. has this day made and delivered to me an assignment of all his property mentioned in the inventory accompanying his petition, pursuant to an order made by the Hon. C. P. D., one of the Judges, &c., and that all the property specified in said inventory has been delivered to me.

In witness, &c., [*as in* § 403.]²

§ 414. *Discharge.*

To all to whom these presents shall come: I, C. P. D., one of the Judges, &c., send greeting: Whereas, A. B., against whom an action has been commenced in a court of record, in which action by the provisions of the act to abolish imprisonment for debt, and to punish fraudulent debtors, he cannot be arrested or imprisoned, did present a petition to me, praying that his property might be assigned and that he might have the benefit of the said act; which petition contained an account of his creditors, and an inventory of his estate, verified by an affidavit thereunto annexed, subscribed by him, and duly sworn to before me. He also produced satisfactory proof that a copy of the said petition, account and inventory, had been served on the creditors in the said petition named, with notice of the time and place of presenting the same to me, as required by law; and I being satisfied, on hearing the petition, that the proceedings on the part of the petitioner were just and fair, and that he had conformed to the provisions of the said act, ordered that the said petitioner make an assignment of all his property, except such articles as are by law exempt from execution, to M. P., of, &c., the assignee appointed by me; and the said petitioner having made such assignment, and produced evidence that the assignment so made was recorded in the office of the Clerk of this county, and also produced a certificate of the assignee that the property of the petitioner, specified in his inventory, had been delivered to the said assignee: Now, therefore, know ye, that by virtue of the power and authority in me vested, and in pursuance of the provisions of the said act, I do grant this

---

[1] For the form of acknowledgment, see § 400; and certificate of Clerk, see § 405.

² For Affidavit of Execution, see § 404.

discharge, to exonerate the said petitioner from being proceeded against by any creditor entitled to a dividend of his estate.

Given under my hand and seal, the   day of   one thousand eight hundred and   .

C. P. D., Judge of, &c

---

§ 415. *Affidavit of Person applying for the Appointment of Trustees for estate of Debtor confined for Crime; to Accompany the Copy of the Sentence, and Certificate of the Clerk.*

State of New York, }
            County, } ss:

A. B., of said county, being duly sworn, says, that C. D., the person named in the annexed [*or, within*] copy of sentence of conviction, is now actually imprisoned in the State prison at   , [*or, in the penitentiary of, &c.; or,* the county jail of the county of   ,] in the State of New York, under and in pursuance of the said sentence of conviction; and that the said C. D. is indebted to this deponent [*or, to L. M., of, &c.*] in the sum of   dollars, on account, [*or, as the case may be,*] for goods, wares and merchandise, sold and delivered to the said C. D., by this deponent, [*or, by the said L. M.;*] and this deponent therefore makes application for the appointment of Trustees of the estate of the said C. D., according to the statute.   A. B.

Sworn, &c., [*as in* § 389.]

---

§ 416. *Appointment of Trustees, on the Foregoing Affidavit and Application.*[1]

By the Hon. D. P., one of the Justices of the Supreme Court of the State of New York; [*or, as the case may be,*] Whereas, A. B., a creditor [*or, a relative*] of C. D., [*or, a relative of M. D., wife of C. D.,*] a debtor confined for crime, did, on the   day of   last past, [*or, instant,*] make application to me for the appointment of Trustees to take charge of the estate of the said C. D.; and did also produce a copy of the sentence of conviction of the said C. D., duly certified by P. V., Esq., Clerk of the Court of [*specify the court before which the conviction was had,*] under his seal of office, by which said court of   the said sentence of conviction was passed;

---

[1] The Trustees appointed to take charge of the estate of a debtor confined for crime, have the same rights and powers as Trustees of the estates of absconding debtors. From the time of their appointment, the real and personal estate of the debtor is vested in them; and they are clothed with full power to sue for and collect all demands, to sell and dispose of the property of the debtor, and apply the proceeds in payment of his debts. Before proceeding to the discharge of their duties, it is necessary to take and subscribe the oath, (§ 417,) which must be filed with the officer appointing them.

together with an affidavit of the said A. B., that the said C. D. is actually imprisoned under the said sentence, and is indebted to the the said A. B., [*or*, to L. M.,] of, &c., in the sum of   dollars: Now, therefore, I, the said Justice, as aforesaid, do, in pursuance of the authority to me given by the statute concerning "Attachments against debtors confined for crimes," appoint M. N. and O. P., two fit persons, to be Trustees of the estate of the said C. D., with such powers concerning the estate of the said C. D., as are conferred by the said statute.

Given under my hand and seal, this   day of, &c.

D. P. [L. S.]

§ 417. *Oath of Trustees of the Estates of Debtors.*

We, M. N. and O. P., appointed Trustees of the estate of C. D., a debtor confined for crime, [*or, as the case may be,*] do swear, and each for himself doth swear, that he will well and truly execute the trust, by his appointment reposed in him, according to the best of his skill and understanding.   M. N.

Sworn, &c., [*as in* § 389.]   O. P.

CHAPTER XVI.

DOWER.

PRACTICAL REMARKS.

1. A widow is entitled to dower of the third part of all lands whereof her husband was seized of an estate of inheritance, at any time during the marriage. In case of divorce, for misconduct of the wife, dower is forfeited; it is also barred by a pecuniary provision, made for the benefit of an intended wife, and in lieu of dower, if assented to by her; and where an estate in lands is conveyed to a person and his intended wife, for the purpose of creating a jointure for her, with her assent, to be signified by becoming a party to the conveyance; or, if an infant, by joining with her father or guardian, in such conveyance; such jointure will be a bar to any right or claim of dower, in any lands of the husband. So also a devise, or legacy, in lieu of dower, which is accepted, is a good bar.[1]

2. A testamentary provision in favor of a wife, where the intention of the testator is doubtful, may be accepted without forfeiting dower.[2]

3. Where a mortgage of lands is executed by the husband before marriage, unless it be for the purchase money, the widow is entitled to dower as against all persons except the mortgagee and those claiming under him; if a mortgage be executed after marriage, for the purchase money, the widow will not be entitled to dower as against the mortgagee or those claiming under him, except that where the premises are sold by virtue of the mortgage, after the death of the husband, and there be surplus moneys left after satisfying the mortgage, she will be entitled to the interest or income of one-third of such surplus during her life.[3]

---

[1] 2 R. S. (3d ed.) 26, § 1; Id., 27, §§ 8—11; 1 Johnson, 307; 10 Id., 30; 7 Cowen, 287; 10 Wendell, 486; 11 Id., 692; 16 Id., 61; 24 Id., 193; 3 Hill, 95; 6 Id., 482; 1 Paige, 534; 2 Id., 559; 7 Id., 259.

[2] 2 Denio, 430.
[3] 2 R. S. (3d ed.) 26, §§ 4, 5; Id., 27, § 6; 1 Barbour's S. C. Rep, 399.

4. A widow is not entitled to dower in lands conveyed to her husband by way of mortgage, unless he acquire an absolute estate therein, during the marriage.[1]

5. A woman who has obtained a divorce *a vinculo matrimonii*, for the adultery of her husband, is not entitled to dower in his real estate, after his death.[2]

6. No act of the husband alone subsequent to marriage, will affect the right of dower of his widow, but subsisting liens or incumbrances have the preference over her right.[3]

7. Where a husband exchanges lands, in which he is seized of an estate of inheritance, for other lands, his widow is not entitled to dower in both, but must make her election in one year; otherwise, it will be presumed that she elects to take her dower of the lands received in exchange.[4]

8. The widow of any alien, who, at the time of his death, was entitled to hold any real estate, if she be an inhabitant of this State at the time of such death, is entitled to dower of such real estate.[5]

9. Any woman, being an alien, who has married, or may marry, a citizen of the United States, will be entitled to dower in the real estate of her husband within this State, in the same manner as if she were a citizen of the United States.[6]

10. In a doubtful case, where the right to dower depends upon the possession of the husband, the actual possession must be shown, and it must appear that he claimed to be the owner of the premises, and exercised acts of ownership.[7]

11. A married woman under the age of twenty-one years, cannot bind herself by deed so as to bar her right of dower.[8]

12. A widow of a mortgagor is dowable of the equity of redemption, except where the time of redemption is past before the marriage takes place.[9]

13. Where lands have been alienated by the husband, in his lifetime, the widow is entitled to so much as shall be equal in value to one-third of the value of the lands at the time of the conveyance by the husband.[10]

14. A widow may release her right of dower, but she cannot convey or assign the same, before the assignment be made. The heirs or owners may, on the other hand, assign her dower, without instituting any legal proceedings.[11]

---

[1] 2 R. S. (3d ed.) 27, § 7.
[2] 4 Barbour's S. C. Rep., 192.
[3] 3 Barbour's S. C. Rep., 319.
[4] 2 R. S. (3d. ed.) 26, § 3.
[5] 2 R. S. (3d. ed.) 26, § 2; 1 Johnson's Cas., 27; 1 Cowen, 89; 12 Wendell, 66; 4 Kent's Commentaries, (2d ed.) 36.
[6] Laws of 1845, chap. 115.

[7] 6 Cowen, 301; 17 Wendell, 164; 2 Hill, 303, 341.
[8] 1 Barbour's S. C. Rep., 399.
[9] 6 Cowen, 316; 14 Wendell, 233; 19 Id., 162; 4 Kent's Commentaries, (2d ed.) 44, 45.
[10] 2 Johnson, 484; 11 Id., 51; 13 Id., 179; 10 Wendell, 485; 4 Kent's Commentaries, (2d ed.) 64, 70.
[11] 1 Barbour's S. C. Rep., 399; 3 Id. 319.

15. Any widow who shall not have had her dower assigned ⌐ ⌐ ⌐; within forty days after the decease of her husband, may apply by petition, to the Supreme Court, or the County Court of the county in which the lands lie, or to the Surrogate of the same county, for the admeasurement of her dower. A copy of such petition, with notice of the time and place when it will be presented, must be served, at least twenty days previous to its presentation, upon the heirs of the husband, or upon the owners of the land subject to dower, claiming a freehold estate therein; or upon the guardians of such heirs, or owners, as are minors. Such notice may be served personally: or, in case of the temporary absence of the party to be served, by leaving the same with any person of proper age, at the last residence of such party. If any heir or owner reside out of the State, the notice may be served upon the tenant occupying the lands; or, if there be no tenant, by publishing the same for three weeks successively, in some newspaper printed in the county where such lands are situated.[1]

16. The Court or Surrogate may, on application, appoint guardians for minors, if necessary; and notice of the application must be served on the guardian, whether the infant reside in this State or not.[2]

17. After the expiration of forty days from the death of the husband, his heirs, or the owners of land subject to dower, may, by notice in writing, require the widow to make demand of her dower, within ninety days after the service of such notice. If this notice be disregarded, and no proceedings be instituted by the widow for the recovery of her dower; or if no such proceedings be had within one year after the husband's death, where no notice has been given; the heirs or owners, as aforesaid, may apply, by petition, for the admeasurement of her dower, to the Supreme Court, County Court, or Surrogate. A copy of such petition, with notice of the time and place of its presentation, must be personally served on the widow, twenty days before the presentation.[3]

18. Upon such application being made, either by a widow, or by an heir or owner, or by the guardian of such heir or owner, the Court, or the Surrogate, to whom the same is made, may order an admeasurement of the widow's dower; and shall thereupon appoint three reputable and disinterested freeholders, as commissioners for the purpose of making such admeasurement. After taking the required oath, the commissioners so appointed will proceed to admeasure and lay off the one-third part of the lands embraced in the order, as the dower of the widow, designating such part with posts, stones, or other permanent monuments. In making such apportionment, the commissioners must take into consideration any permanent

[1] 2 R. S. (3d ed.) 582, §§ 1-3; Laws of 1849, chap. 438, Part 1, title 1, § 30, sub. 4; 4 Wendell, 630; 12 Id., 138.

[2] 2 R. S. (3d ed.) 583, §§ 4, 5.
[3] 2 R. S. (3d ed.) 583, §§ 6-8.

improvements made since the death of the husband, by any heir, owner, or guardian; and, if practicable, award such improvements within that part of the lands not allotted to the widow; and if not practicable, they shall make a proportionate reduction therefor, from the lands so allotted to her. The commissioners are also required to make a full and ample report of their doings, to the Court or Surrogate appointing them; in which report, the quantity, courses, distances, posts, stones and other permanent monuments, of the premises, must be particularly described and set forth. They may employ a surveyor, with necessary assistants, to aid them in the admeasurement.[1]

19. Within thirty days after the confirmation of the admeasurement by a County Court, or Surrogate, any party aggrieved may appeal to the Supreme Court, on giving a bond, to be approved by the County Judge, or Surrogate, in the penal sum of one hundred dollars; and the Supreme Court shall then proceed to hear and determine the said appeal, and to review all the proceedings upon the application, and do therein what shall be just.[2]

20. Real estate assigned to a widow as dower cannot be sold under the order of a Surrogate, for the payment of debts owing by her deceased husband.[3]

FORMS.

§ 418. *Assignment of Dower.*

This indenture, made the   day of, &c., between R. B., son and heir of A. B., late of, &c., of the one part, and M. B., who is the widow of the said A. B., [*or,* C. D., and M., his wife, (late M. B.,) who was the widow of the said A. B.,] of the other part: Whereas, the said A. B. was, in his lifetime, and at the time of his death, seized in his demesne, as of fee, of and in divers lands and tenements in   , in the county aforesaid, which, upon the decease of the said A. B., descended unto the said R. B.: Now, therefore, this indenture witnesseth, that the said R. B. hath endowed and assigned, and by these presents doth endow and assign, unto the said M. B., [*or, as aforesaid,*] the third part of the said lands and tenements, to wit: [*description:*] To have and to hold the said premises unto the said M. B., [*or, as aforesaid,*] for and during the natural life

---

[1] 2 R. S. (3d ed.) 583, 584, §§ 9–17; 1 Cowen, 476; 4 Wendell, 630; 8 Id., 460; 10 Id., 430; 2 Hill, 544.

[2] 2 R. S. (3d ed.) 585, 586, §§ 18–27; 2 Hill, 544.

[3] 2 Comstock, 246.

of the said M., in severalty, by metes and bounds, in the name of dower, and in recompense and satisfaction of all the dower which the said M. ought to have, of or in the said lands and tenements which were of the said A. B., in   , aforesaid.

In witness whereof, the said R. B. hath hereunto set his hand and seal, the   day of   , in the year eighteen hundred and   .

Sealed, signed and delivered, ⟩
in presence of   ⟩   R. B. [L. S.]
G. H.

---

§ 419. *Release of Dower to the Heir.*

Know all men, &c.: That I, M. B., &c., relict of A. B., late of, &c., as well for and in consideration of the sum of   dollars, to me paid, by my son, R. B. of, &c., as for the love and affection which I have to my said son, have granted, remised, released, and forever quit-claimed, and by these presents do grant, remise, release and quit-claim, unto the said R. B., his heirs and assigns, forever, all the dower and thirds, right and title of dower and thirds, and all other right, title, interest, property, claim and demand, whatsoever, in law and in equity, of me, the said M. B., of, in and to, [*descrip-tion;*] so that neither I, the said M. B., my heirs, executors, or administrators, nor any other person or persons, for me, them, or and of them, shall have, claim, challenge, or demand, or pretend to have, claim, challenge, or demand, any dower or thirds, or any other right, title, claim, or demand, of, in, or to, the said premises, but thereof and therefrom shall be utterly debarred and excluded forever, by these presents.

In witness whereof, I have hereunto set my hand and seal, the day of, &c., [*as in* § 418.]

---

§ 420. *Petition for Dower.*

To the Supreme Court of the State of New York: [*or,* To the County Court of the County of, &c.; *or,* To the Surrogate of the County of ·   :]*

The petition of M. B., of, &c., widow of A. B., of, &c., deceased, respectfully showeth, that her said husband died on the   day of   , 18   , at, &c., leaving an estate in fee belonging to him when he died, in and to [*describe the real estate;*] that she has not had her dower therein assigned to her, within forty days after the decease of her said husband, nor at any time since. Wherefore, she respectfully applies to this honorable Court, [*or,* to the said Surro-gate] for the admeasurement of her said dower. Dated. &c.

                                                  M. B.

B. F. H., Attorney.

§ 421. *Notice to be Annexed to Petition.*

To [*insert the names of the heirs or owners:*]

Please take notice that a petition of which the above is a copy, will be presented to [*name the Court or Surrogate,*] on the day of , 18 , at, &c., and that a motion will then and there be made to grant the same. Dated, &c.

M. B.

R. F., Attorney.

---

§ 422. *Notice by Heirs or Owners, if Widow does not Apply.*

To M. B., widow of, &c.: [*or if she has a second husband, address it to both:*]

Please take notice, that the subscribers, who, as heirs of A. B., deceased, [*or, as owners,*] claim a freehold estate in and to the following real estate, [*description,*] require you to demand your dower therein, within ninety days after the service of this notice. Dated, &c. [*Signatures.*]

---

§ 423. *Petition by Heirs or Owners.*

To, &c., [*as in § 420, to the *, and then continue as follows:*]

The petition of, &c., [*naming the heirs,*] heirs of A. B., deceased, late of, &c., [*or, owners of the real estate hereinafter mentioned, formerly belonging to A. B., of, &c.,*] respectfully showeth: That the said A. B., died on, &c., at, &c., leaving an estate in fee belonging to him when he died, in and to all, [*description;*] in which said premises M. B., the widow of the said A. B., is entitled to dower; that the said M. B., has not had her dower therein assigned to her within ninety days after the decease of her said husband, nor at any time since; nor has she made any application, or instituted any proceedings, for the recovery of the said dower: wherefore, the undersigned petitioners respectfully apply to this honorable Court [*or, to the said Surrogate*] for the admeasurement of the dower of the said M. B. Dated, &c. [*Signatures.*]

---

§ 424. *Order for Admeasurement of Dower.*

On hearing Mr. D. W., for M. B., widow of, &c., and Mr. C. M., in opposition thereto, and on reading and filing the petition of, &c., and the notice accompanying the same, and an affidavit of the due service of the said petition and notice on [*name the persons;*] this court doth order admeasurement to be made of the dower of the said M. B., in and to [*describe the lands;*] and C. D., E. F., and L. M., three reputable and disinterested freeholders, are hereby appointed commissioners for the purpose of making the admeasurement herein directed, and are required to make report of their proceedings therein to this court, with all convenient speed.

.D. W., for the widow.
C. M., in opposition.

---

§ 425. *Oath of Commissioners.*

We, C. D., E. F., and L. M., appointed commissioners by a rule, [*or,* order,] a copy whereof is hereunto annexed, do swear that we will faithfully, honestly and impartially, discharge the duty, and execute the trust reposed in us by the said appointment.

Sworn to, this   day of   ,⎫   C. D.,⎫
       18   , before me,   ⎬   E. F., ⎬ Commissioners.
       G. H., Justice of the Peace. ⎭   L M., ⎭

---

§ 426. *Report of the Commissioners.*

To [*the Court, or Surrogate:*]

We, the undersigned, appointed commissioners, under and by virtue of a rule, [*or,* order,] a copy whereof is hereunto annexed, do respectfully report, that we proceeded to admeasure and lay off, as speedily as possible, after the said rule or order, the one-third part of the lands embraced in the order for our appointment, as the dower of M. B., named therein, designating such part with posts, [*or,* with stones; *or,* with permanent monuments;] and in doing so, we took into view the permanent improvements made on the said lands by any heir, guardian of minors, or other owners, since the death of the husband of the said M. B., [*or,* since the alienation thereof by the [first] husband of the said M. B.,] and we found it [not] practicable to award such improvements within that part of the said lands not allotted to the said M. B.: [*If not practicable, add:* and therefore we made from the lands allotted to the said M. B., a deduction proportionate to the benefit she will derive from such part of the said improvements as is included in the portion assigned to her.] We further report, that we employed O. P., a sworn and skillful surveyor, with necessary assistants, to aid us in making the said admeasurement; and we further report, that [*insert a full and ample statement of the proceedings, with the quality, courses and distances, of the land admeasured and allotted to the widow, a description of the posts, stones, or other permanent monuments thereof, and the items of the commissioners' charges.*]

Given under our hands, at, &c., on, &c.

[*Signatures and seals.*]

§ 427. *Appeal to Supreme Court.*

To [*the County Court, or Surrogate:*]

Please to take notice, that I hereby appeal to the Supreme Court of the State of New York, from [*state the order at large.*]

Dated, &c.

M. B., [*or, as the case may be.*]

G. U., Attorney.

---

§ 428. *Bond on Appeal.*

Know all men by these presents: That I, M. B., of the town of   in the county of   , and State of New York, am held and firmly bound unto C. B., of the same place, in the sum of one hundred dollars, lawful money of the United States, to be paid to the said C. B., his executors, administrators, or assigns; for which payment, well and truly to be made, I bind myself, my heirs, executors and administrators, firmly by these presents.

Sealed with my seal. Dated the   day of   , one thousand eight hundred and   .

The condition of this obligation is such, that if the said M. B. shall dilligently prosecute a certain appeal from [*here describe the order, &c., appealed from;*] and shall pay all costs which may be adjudged by the Justices of the Supreme Court of the State of New York, against the said M. B., on such appeal, then this obligation to be void; otherwise, to remain in full force and virtue.

Sealed and delivered, }
  in presence of   }   M. B.   [L. S.]
    G. H.
    E. F.

The security in this bond is approved. Dated, &c.

J. P. H., County Judge, &c., [*or, Surrogate.*]

CHAPTER XVII.

EXCISE.

PRACTICAL REMARKS.

1. The Supervisor of every town, and the Justices of the Peace resident therein, are Commissioners of Excise for their town; three of them, consisting of the Supervisor, and and two of the Justices, are competent to execute the powers vested in the board. If the office of Supervisor be vacant, then any three of the Justices may form a board. If there be not two Justices in the town, then any two Justices of a neighboring town may be associated by the Supervisor with him.[1]

2. The Commissioners of Excise are to meet on the first Monday of May, in each year, in their respective towns, and on such other days as the Supervisor shall appoint, at such place as shall be designated by him; or, in case his office be vacant, on such other days, and at such places, as the Justices of the Peace of the town may appoint.[2]

3. Boards of Excise are required to keep a book of minutes of their proceedings, in which shall be entered every resolution granting a license to any person; which minutes shall be verified by their signatures, and filed with the Town Clerk within five days.[3]

4. The Board of Excise of any town, or city, has the power to grant licenses to keepers of inns and taverns, being residents of their town, or city, to sell strong and spirituous liquors and wines, to be drank in their houses respectively; and to grocers, being such residents, licenses to sell such liquors or wines, not to be drunk, however, in their shops, houses, out-houses, or gardens.[4]

5. Licenses to keep taverns may also be granted, without including a license to sell strong or spirituous liquors, wines, or alcoholic drinks: and in all such cases the restriction must be expressed on the face of the license.[5]

---

[1] 1 R. S. (3d ed.,) 852, § 1; 1 Johnson, 500; 2 Johnson's Cas. 346.
[3] 1 R. S. (3d ed.,) 852, § 2
[2] 1 R. S. (3d ed.,) 852, § 3; 1 Hill, 655.
[4] 1 R. S. (3d ed.,) 852, § 4; 15 Wendell, 260
[5] Laws of 1843, chap. 97.

6. Commissioners of excise are not allowed to receive any fee whatsoever, from applicants for licenses.[1]

7. Ale and strong beer are included in the terms "strong and spirituous liquors," as used in the Revised Statutes.[2]

8. Before any license can be granted, the applicant must execute a bond to the people of this State, in the penal sum of one hundred and twenty-five dollars, and with a sufficient surety, to be approved by the board, conditioned as in one of the forms hereinafter given, which bond is to be filed in the office of the Town Clerk, within five days after the execution thereof. Where a license is to be granted to any person to sell strong and spirituous liquors and wines, to be drank in the house of the seller, the board must be satisfied that he is of good moral character; that he is of sufficient ability to keep a tavern; that he has the necessary accommodation for travelers; and that a tavern is absolutely necessary for the actual accommodation of travelers, at the place where such applicant resides, or proposes to keep the same; all which must be stated in every such license.[3]

9. A board of excise, under the laws now in operation, until the actual entry of a resolution to grant a license, have a large discretion to exercise on the subject of granting or refusing licenses, with which our courts will not interfere.[4]

10. It is not necessary, where the Supervisor and two Justices form a board of excise, that all should sign a license; if signed by any two Commissioners, at a regular meeting of the board, the license is valid.[5]

11. When a license is duly granted and issued, it continues in force, unless sooner revoked, till the day after the first Monday in May in the succeeding year.[6]

12. No person, who has not at the time a license to keep a tavern, can erect, put up, or keep up, any sign indicating that he keeps a tavern, without subjecting himself to the penalty of one dollar and twenty-five cents for every day such sign shall be kept up.[7]

13. A person who sells liquor without a license, in violation of the excise law, cannot recover payment for the same of the purchaser.[8]

14. The sale of spirituous liquors, or intoxicating drinks, to any Indian residing in the State of New York, is expressly forbidden by the laws thereof; and any person violating the same is guilty of a misdemeanor, and liable to be punished by fine and imprisonment.[9]

[1] Laws of 1843, chap. 97.
[2] 3 Denio, 43.
[3] 1 R. S. (3d ed.) 853, §§ 7, 8; Id., 854, § 15; 14 Johnson, 231; 8 Cowen, 130; 1 Hill, 655.
[4] 1 R. S. (3d ed.,) 853, § 4; 15 Wendell, 260; 1 Hill, 655; 1 Denio, 540.
[5] 1 Johnson, 500.
[6] 1 R. S. (3d ed.,) 853, § 5; 11 Johnson, 179; 2 Johnson's Cas., 346; 1 Denio, 149.
[7] Laws of 1843, chap. 97.
[8] 3 Denio, 226.
[9] Laws of 1849, chap. 420.

FORMS.

§ 429. *Notice of Supervisor for Special Meeting of the Commis·
sioners of Excise.*[1]

To H. R. F., Esq., one of the Justices of the Peace of the town
of   :

You are hereby notified, that a meeting of the Commissioners of
excise of said town, will be held at my office, [*or,* at the house of H
C.,] on the   day of   instant, at ten o'clock in the
forenoon, for the purpose of acting upon such business as may be
brought before them. Dated   , July 10, 1847.

Yours, &c.,   E. W., Supervisor.

---

§ 430. *Form of Minutes of Board of Excise.*

At a meeting of the Commissioners of excise of the town of   ,
in the county of   , held on the   day of   ,
18   : Present A. B., Supervisor of the town.

G. H.,
S. T., } Justices of the said town.

Resolved, That licenses be granted to the following persons, to
retail strong and spirituous liquors and wines; and that the sum to
be paid for each license, be the sum put opposite the name of such
person, to wit:

L. M., as a Tavern Keeper.
O. P., as a Grocer.
[*Insert the sums opposite each name.*]

Resolved, That licenses be granted to the following persons to keep
taverns, under the provisions of the act entitled " An act authorizing
licenses to keep taverns, without including a license to sell spirits,
and to abolish fees for the same," passed April 12, 1843, to wit:

C. D., as a Tavern Keeper.
E. F.,   do.   do.

In witness whereof, we, the said Commissioners, have hereunto
subscribed our names, the day and year above written.

A. B., Supervisor.
G. H.,
&c., &c., } Justices.

In most of the incorporated villages in this State, the boards of Trustees are, *ex officio,* commissioners of excise Special meetings are called by the President of the board, and the proceedings are conducted in the same manner as in towns. The form herein given may be readily made applicable, by changing the official designation of the members of the board. In cities, licenses are granted by the Mayors and Aldermen.

§ 431. *License for Tavern Keeper to Sell Spirituous Liquors.*

We the undersigned, forming a board of Commissioners of excise for the town of   , in the county of   , having been applied to by L. M., a resident of the said town, who purposes to keep an inn or tavern at   , in the said town of   , for a license to sell strong and spirituous liquors and wines, to be drank in his [or, her] house; and being satisfied that he [or, she] is of good moral character, and of sufficient ability to keep a tavern, and that he [or, she] has the necessary accommodations to entertain travellers, and that a tavern is absolutely necessary for the actual accommodation of travellers, at the place where he [or, she] purposes to keep the same; and for which he [or, she] has paid a duty of   dollars, determined by us; we do therefore grant this license, and authorize him [or, her] to sell strong and spirituous liquors and wines, to be drank in the inn or tavern to be kept at the place above mentioned. This license is to be in force until the day after the first Monday in May next.

In witness whereof, we have hereunto subscribed our names, the   day of   , 18   .   .   A. B., Supervisor.

G. H., }

&c., &c., } Justices.

---

§ 432. *Bond of Tavern Keeper, on License to Sell Spirituous Liquors, with Certificate.*

Know all men by these presents: That we, L. M. and E. F., of, &c., are held and firmly bound unto the people of the State of New York, in the sum of one hundred and twenty-five dollars, to be paid to the said people; for which payment, well and truly to be made, we bind ourselves, our and each of our heirs, executors and administrators, jointly and severally, firmly by these presents.

Sealed with our seals. Dated the   day of   , one thousand eight hundred and   .*

Whereas, the said L. M. intends keeping an inn or tavern, at   , in the town of   , in said county of   , and has applied for a license to sell strong and spirituous liquors and wines, to be drank in the said inn or tavern, to be kept as aforesaid: Now, therefore, the condition of this obligation is such, that if the said L. M., during the time he shall keep an inn or tavern, will not suffer it to be disorderly, or suffer any cock-fighting, gaming, or playing with cards or dice, or keep any billiard table, or other gaming table, within the tavern by him so kept, or in any out-house, yard, or garden, belonging thereto, then this obligation to be void; else to remain in force.

Signed, sealed and delivered, }   L. M. [L. s.]

in presence of }   E. F. [L. s.]

G. H.

&c., &c.

We, the undersigned, forming a board of Commissioners of excise for the town aforesaid, approve of the security to the above bond, as sufficient for the purposes intended.

A. B., Supervisor.
G. H.,   ⎱
&c., &c., ⎰ Justices.

---

§ 433. *License for Tavern Keeper, under Act of* 1843.

We, the undersigned, forming a board of Commissioners of excise for the town of   , in the county of   , having been applied to by C. D., a resident of said town, who purposes to keep an inn or tavern at   , in the said town, for a license to keep such tavern, without including a license to sell strong or spirituous liquors, wines, or alcoholic drinks; and being satisfied that he is of good moral character, and of sufficient ability to keep a tavern, and that he has the necessary accommodations to entertain travellers, and that a tavern is absolutely necessary for the actual accommodation of travellers, at the place where he purposes to keep the same; we do therefore grant this license, and authorize him to keep an inn or tavern at the place above mentioned; provided, however, that no strong or spirituous liquors, wines, or alcoholic drinks, shall be sold by the said C. D., under or by virtue hereof. This license is to be in force until the day after the first Monday in May next.

In witness, &c., [*as in* § 431.]

---

§ 434. *Bond for Obtaining License, under Act of* 1843.

Know all men, &c., [*as in* § 432 *to the* *, *and then add*:] Whereas, the said L. M. has applied for a license to keep an inn or tavern in the town of   , in the said county of   , without including a license to sell strong or spirituous liquors, wines, or alcoholic drinks, in such inn or tavern:

Now, therefore, the condition of the obligation is such, that, &c., [*as in* § 432, *to the end.*]

---

§ 435. *Grocer's License.*

We, the undersigned, forming a board of Commissioners of excise for the town of   , in the county of   , having been applied to by O. P., a resident of said town, who purposes to keep a grocery at   , in the said town, for a license to sell strong and spirituous liquors and wines, in quantities less than five gallons, and for which he has paid a duty of   dollars, determined by us; and being satisfied that he is of good moral character; we do therefore grant this license, authorizing him to sell strong and spirituous liquors and wines, in quantities less than five gallons, but not to be drank in his shop, house, out-house, yard or garden, and it is expressly declared, that this license shall not be deemed to authorize such sale of any liquors or wines, to be drank in the house or shop of the said O. P., or in any out-house, yard, or garden, appertaining thereto, or connected therewith. This license is to be in force until the day after the first Monday in May next.

In witness, &c., [*as in* § 431.]

---

§ 436. *Grocer's Bond.*

Know all men, &c., [*as is* § 432 *to the* *, *and then add:*] Whereas, the said O. P. has applied for a license to sell strong and spirituous liquors and wines, at his grocery, in the town aforesaid: Now, therefore, the condition of this obligation is such, that if, during the term for which his license shall be granted, he will not suffer his grocery to become disorderly; that he will not sell, or suffer to be sold, any strong or spirituous liquors or wines, to be drank in his shop, or house, or in any out-house, yard or garden, appertaining thereto; and that he will not suffer any such liquor, sold by virtue of such license, to be drank in his shop or house, or in any out-house, yard, or garden, belonging thereto, then this obligation to be void; else, to remain in force.[1]

Signed, sealed, &c., [*as in* § 432.]

---

[1] For the certificate of approval, see § 422.

CHAPTER XVIII.

FEES OF OFFICERS.

PRACTICAL REMARKS.

1. No judicial officer, except Justices of the Peace, can receive, to his own use, any fees or perquisites of office.[1]

2. No officer, or other person, to whom any fee or compensation is allowed by law for any service, can take, or receive, any other, or greater fee or reward, for such service, but such as is or may be allowed by law. No *legal* fee or compensation can be demanded, or received, by any officer or person, for any service, unless such service was actually rendered by him; but any officer may demand the fee allowed to him by law for any service, for which he is entitled to require payment, before rendering the same.[2]

3. County Judges and Surrogates are forbidden to perform any official services, unless upon prepayment of the fees and perquisites imposed by law.[3]

4. No fee can be charged by any officer for administering the oath of office to any member of the Legislature, to any Inspector of Elections or to any town officer; and no more than twelve and a half cents can be charged for administering such oath to any other officer.[4]

5 Upon the settlement of any execution by a defendant, or upon settling any suit or demand, the Sheriff, or Attorney, claiming any fees which shall not have been taxed, may be required by the defendant, on his paying the expense thereof, to have his fees taxed by some proper officer of the court in which the action may be pending, or from which the execution shall have been issued; otherwise, such fees are not collectible.[5]

6. If a Justice render judgment for a greater amount of costs than is allowed by law, or for any item of costs, or fees, improperly

---

[1] Amended Constitution of New York, Art. VI, § 29.
[2] 2 R. S. (3d ed.) 741, §§ 5, 6; 5 Cowen, 661; 15 Wendell, 45; 23 Id., 57; 26 Id., 451; 1 Denio, 653; 2 Paige, 475.
[3] Laws of 1849, chap. 95.
[4] 2 R. S. (3d ed.) 742, § 17.
[5] 2 R. S. (3d ed.) 748, §§ 1, 2.

and the same be collected, the person paying the same may recover of the party who shall have received such costs, or fees, the amount thereof, with interest.[1]

7. All Clerks and Registers of counties, claiming any fees by virtue of their respective offices, upon being required in writing by the party liable to pay the same, his agent or attorney, and on payment of the expense thereof, must have their fees taxed by some officer authorized to tax costs in the Supreme Court; and either party may appeal from such taxation to the Supreme Court. No Clerk or Register can collect any fees, after having been required as aforesaid, without the same are taxed.[2]

8. In order to entitle a Sheriff, or Constable, to his poundage upon an execution, he must levy the money, or take the body of the defendant, except he be prevented by the act of the plaintiff, or the operation of law.[3]

9. A Sheriff, or Constable, can only charge mileage for the actual travel, where there are several defendants in one process, who reside at the same place.[4]

10. Witnesses who do not attend in obedience to a subpœna, are not entitled to fees, and the party paying them can recover back the money.[5]

11. No town officer is entitled to be allowed any per diem compensation for his services, unless expressly provided by law.[6]

12. No travel fees for travelling to subpœna a witness beyond the limits of the county in which the subpœna was issued, or of an adjoining county, will be allowed, unless it is made to appear to the board auditing the account, by satisfactory proof, that such witness could not be subpœnaed, without additional travel; nor will any travel fees for subpœnaing witnesses be allowed, except such as the board shall be satisfied were absolutely necessary.[7]

FORMS

§ 437. *Arbitrator's Fees.*

No provision is made by statute for the fees of Arbitrators. The usual custom, however, is to charge the same fee allowed to referees

1 2 R. S. (3d ed.) 361, § 235.
2 Laws of 1844, chap. 127.
3 5 Johnson, 252; 2 Cowen, 421.
4 1 Wendell, 104.
5 5 Wendell, 107; 3 Hill, 457; 4 Id., 595.
6 Laws of 1845, chap. 180, § 23.
7 Laws of 1845, chap. 180, § 27; 1 Denio, 658.

appointed by a court of record, viz: for each day necessarily spent in the business of the reference, three dollars to each referee, to be paid on making the report, or award, by the prevailing party. A different compensation, however, may be agreed on, in writing, by the parties.

§ 438. *Assessor's Fees.*

For each day actually and necessarily devoted to the service of the town, one dollar and twenty-five cents.

§ 439. *Auctioneer's Commission.*

Not exceeding two and one-half per cent. on the amount of any sales, unless in pursuance of a previous agreement, in writing, between the auctioneer and the owner, or consignee, of the goods or effects sold.

§ 440. *Broker's Fees.*

Fifty cents for brokage, soliciting, driving, or procuring, the loan or forbearance of one hundred dollars for one year, and in that proportion for a greater or lesser term.

Thirty-eight cents for making or renewing any bond, bill, note, or other security, given for such loan or forbearance, or for any counter bond, bill, note, or other security, concerning the same.

§ 441. *County Clerk's Fees.*

For a trial fee, to be paid by the party bringing on an action, one dollar.

For entering judgment by filing transcript, six cents.

For entering judgment in a civil action, fifty cents, except in courts where the clerk is a salaried officer, and in such cases one dollar.

For copies of all papers and proceedings in civil actions, five cents for every one hundred words.

For every certificate, twelve and a half cents; but not to be allowed for certifying a paper to be a copy, for the copying of which he shall be entitled to compensation.

Recording conveyances of real estate, and all other instruments which by law may be recorded, ten cents for each folio.

Filing every certificate of the satisfaction of a mortgage, and entering such satisfaction, twenty-five cents.

Entering a minute of a mortgage being foreclosed, ten cents.

Entering in a book the bond of every Collector, twelve and a half cents; searching therefor, six cents; entering satisfaction, twelve and a half cents.

Receiving and filing every paper deposited with him for safe keeping, three cents; searching therefor, three cents for each paper examined.

Receiving and filing the papers of any insolvent, or relating to the proceedings against any absent, concealed, absconding, or imprisoned debtor, twelve and a half cents in each case; and such papers are not to be charged as having been separately filed: Searching for such papers, six cents for each year for which searches shall be made.

Searching and certifying the title of, and incumbrances upon, real estate, ten cents for each conveyance and incumbrance certifiyed by him, instead of fees; provided that such fees shall in no case amount to less than fifty cents, nor more than five dollars.

Searching the docket of judgments and decrees, five cents a year, and twelve and a half cents for the certificate. (See 3 Denio, 171.)

Searches preparatory to making the loans authorized by the act providing for the loan of certain moneys belonging to the United States deposit fund, three dollars; except where the regular fees would be less than that sum.

Filing each chattel mortgage, or copy, six cents; six cents each party, for entering; searching for such papers, six cents each; and the same fees for certified copies, as for copies of records.

To the Clerk of the county of Rensselaer, six cents for filing a chattel mortgage, or copy, and six cents each name for docketing.

Filing and entering a specification, or copy of a contract, in the mechanics' and laborers' lien docket, eighteen cents.

For an execution issued under the mechanics' and laborers' lien law, one dollar.

For services upon the first application of an alien, including the oath or affirmation of intention to become a citizen, record and certificate thereof delivered to him, twenty cents.

For all the services requisite upon the completion of the proceedings of an alien to become a citizen, including the record and a certificate, fifty cents.

Determining and certifying the sufficiency of the sureties of any Sheriff, fifty cents.

For every report upon the title of the parties in partition, pursuant to a reference for that purpose, one dollar.

For every report respecting the incumbrances upon the estate or interest of any party in partition, pursuant to a rule or order for that purpose, one dollar.

Investing the proceeds of the sale of any estate, under proceedings in partition, pursuant to the order of the court, one-half of one per cent. upon any sum not exceeding two hundred dollars, and one-quarter of one per cent. for any excess.

Receiving the interest on such investments, and paying over the same to the persons entitled, one-half of one per cent. .

For attendance in canvassing the votes given at any election, two dollars.

Drawing all necessary certificates of the result of such canvass, eighteen cents for each folio; and nine cents each folio for the necessary copies thereof.

Recording such certificates, the same fees as are allowed for recording deeds.

For making and transmitting certified copies of the returns of Town Superintendents of common schools, six cents for each folio, to be paid by the county.

Giving notice to the Governor, of persons who have taken the oath of office, three cents for each name.

Giving such notice of persons who have neglected to take the oath of office, or to file or renew any security, within the time required by law, and of any vacancy created by any officer dying or removing out of the county or place for which he was appointed, and of all other vacancies in the county, six cents for each name reported.

Notifying every person appointed to office, twenty-five cents; and all expenses actually and necessarily incurred in giving any notice, which the Comptroller shall deem reasonable.

Searching for a bail piece, and annexing it to the recognizance roll, twelve and a half cents.

Recording every certificate of incorporation, authorized by law to be recorded, seventy-five cents.

Entering in the minutes of a court a license to keep a ferry, and for a copy thereof, one dollar; and for taking and entering the recognizance, twenty-five cents.

For administering an oath or affirmation, in cases where no fee is specially provided, and the certificate, twelve and a half cents.

Swearing a witness in the Court of Oyer and Terminer, and Court of Sessions, six cents.

Entering, or respiting a recognizance in said Courts, twelve and a half cents.

Calling and swearing a jury in the same, nineteen cents.

Entering a sentence in the minutes, twelve and a half cents; and the like fee for every certified copy thereof, and for a transcript thereof for the Secretary of State.

For copies of records, indictments, and other proceedings, the like fees as are allowed in civil cases for copies of papers filed in his office.

For taking the acknowledgment of satisfaction of a judgment in the County Court, thirty-seven and a half cents.

----

§ 442. *Clerk of the Board of Supervisors.*

A reasonable compensation for his services, to be fixed by the board, and to be paid by the county.

For a certified copy of any account on file in his office, six cents for every folio of one hundred and twenty-eight words.

---

§ 443. *Commissioners to take Testimony, to be read in Justices' Courts*

For taking and returning the testimony on a commission, whether issued to one or more commissioners, one dollar.

For every subpœna, or oath, six cents.

For serving subpœnas to appear before commissioners, the same fees as are allowed in Justices' Courts.

---

§ 444. *Commissioners to make Partition, or to Admeasure Dower.*

For every day's actual and necessary service, two dollars to each commissioner.

---

§ 445. *Commissioner of Deeds.*

For administering an oath or affirmation, and certifying the same when required, twelve and a half cents.

For taking the acknowledgment of bail in the Supreme Court, and in any County Court, or Mayor's Court, twenty-five cents.

Taking the acknowledgment of satisfaction of a decree or judgment, in the Supreme Court, any County Court, or Mayor's Court, thirty-seven and a half cents.

Taking and certifying the acknowledgment, or proof, of any conveyance or mortgage of real estate, or any instrument concerning real estate, which by law may be recorded,— for one person, twenty-five cents, and for each additional person, twelve and a half cents; (Laws of 1847, chap. 339;) but when a lease and release of the same premises executed at the same time, they must be considered as one conveyance.

Taking an acknowledgment of a power of attorney to appear in a Justice's Court, twenty-five cents.

---

§ 446. *Commissioners of Excise.*

One dollar and twenty-five cents to each Commissioner, for one day's attendance only, at the Board of Excise, during any one year; to be allowed and paid, as other town charges.

---

§ 447. *Commissioners of Highways.*

For each day actually and necessarily devoted to the service of the town, one dollar.

K

§ 448. *Commissioners to Loan United States Deposit Fund.*

Such Commissioners may retain, out of the interest moneys coming into their hands, the following per centage on the money committed to their charge, as a compensation for their services: upon twenty-five thousand dollars, or a less sum, three-quarters of one per cent.; upon the further sum of twenty-five thousand dollars, or less, half of one per cent.; and where the whole sum shall exceed fifty thousand dollars, half of one per cent., except in the city and county of New York, in which city and county the commissioners shall, upon all sums exceeding fifty thousand dollars, be permitted to retain only one-quarter of one per cent.

------

§ 449. *Constables' Fees.*

For serving a warrant or summons, twelve and a half cents.

For a copy of every summons delivered on request, or left at the dwelling of the defendant, in his absence, nine cents.

Serving an attachment, fifty cents; for a copy thereof, and of the inventory of the property seized, left at the last residence of the defendant, fifty cents.

Serving an execution, or levying any fine or penalty pursuant to any warrant, five cents for every dollar collected, to the amount of fifty dollars; and two and a half cents for every dollar collected over fifty dollars.

For every mile, going only, more than one mile, when serving a summons, warrant, attachment, or execution, six cents: to be computed from the place of abode of the defendant, or where he shall be found, to the place where the precept is returnable.

Notifying the plaintiff of the service of a warrant, twelve and a half cents; and for going to the plaintiff's residence, or where such notice was served, six cents for every mile more than one.

Summoning a jury, fifty cents.

Serving a subpœna, twelve and a half cents for each witness served; but no allowance will be made in any judgment, for service upon more than four witnesses in any cause.

Serving a summons in special proceedings in civil cases, twelve and a half cents; serving a warrant, nineteen cents; mileage, for going only, six cents for each mile.

Advertising and selling any property distrained doing damage; or levying any fine, penalty, or sum, pursuant to any warrant; the same fees as are allowed on executions from Justices' Courts.

Arresting and committing any person, pursuant to process in special proceedings in civil cases, fifty cents; and mileage, for going only, six cents.

Attending any court, pursuant to a notice from the Sheriff, one dollar and fifty cents a day in the city of New York, and one dollar and twenty-five cents a day in each of the other counties of this State, to be paid by the county.

Serving a warrant, or other process, for the arrest of any person, in criminal cases, fifty cents; and the same fees for mileage as are allowed on warrants in civil cases.[1]

Taking a defendant in custody on a mittimus, twelve and a half cents.

Conveying a person to the magistrate or court before whom he is to be brought, or to jail, twelve and a half cents, if within one mile; and for every other mile, going only, six cents.

For traveling to subpœna witnesses on behalf of the people, such fees as the board auditing the account shall be satisfed were indispensably nesessary.

For other services in criminal cases, for which no compensation is specially provided by law, such sum as the board of Supervisors of the county shall allow.

For summoning a jury under the provisions of the Revised Statutes in relation to the assignment of the estates of non-resident, absconding, insolvent, or imprisoned debtors, one dollar and twelve and a half cents.

For summoning a jury to re-assess the damages for laying out, altering, or discontinuing a road, if from the same town, one dollar; if otherwise, two dollars.

For other services, not enumerated above, which may be rendered by a Constable, the same fees as are allowed by law to Sheriffs for similar services.

For serving a summons in the city of Albany on one defendant, and notifying the plaintiff of trial, thirty-seven and a half cents; and twenty-five cents more for service of summons on every other defendant named in the same summons; serving a warrant in a civil suit in the same city, on one defendant, and notifying plaintiff, fifty cents; and thirty-seven and a half cents for every additional defendant named in the same warrant.

---

§ 450. *Coroner's Fees.*

For holding an inquest, and the necessary incidental expenses, such compensation as shall be allowed by the board of Supervisors of the county.

For all other services rendered by them, the same fees as are allowed to Sheriffs for similar services.

For confining a Sheriff in any house, on civil process, two dollars

---

[1] A Constable is not entitled to mileage, unless the party is arrested, even though he case not be found. (1 Denio. 658.)

for each week, to be paid by such Sheriff before he shall be entitled to be discharged.

---

§ 451. *County Judges, in Special Cases.*[1]

For every day employed in the hearing and decision of appeals in relation to highways, two dollars, to be paid by the party appealing, where the determination of the Commissioner, or Commissioners, shall be affirmed.

Taking the acknowledgment of a satisfaction of judgment, thirty-seven and a half cents.

Taking a bond in any case required or authorized by law, thirty-seven and a half cents.

Deciding on the sufficiency of sureties, and certifying such sufficiency when it shall appear, fifty cents.

Administering an oath or affirmation, and certifying the same when required, twelve and a half cents.

Taking the acknowledgment of bail, twenty-five cents.

Taking and certifying the acknowledgment, or proof, of any conveyance or mortgage of real estate, or any instrument concerning real estate which by law may be recorded, the same fees as are allowed to Justices of the Peace for similar services. (Laws of 1847, chap. 339.)

Receiving and filing every petition, and the affidavits, schedules and papers, accompanying the same, upon any application made pursuant to the provisions of the statute in relation to the assignment of the estates of absconding, concealed, non-resident, insolvent, or imprisoned debtors, two dollars.

For every order, warrant, certificate, or appointment, of trustees or assigns, in such proceeding, thirty-seven and a half cents.

Presiding at and conducting any trial by a jury, swearing such jury, receiving and entering their verdict, or discharging them, two dollars; but not to extend to any trial or inquest in any action at law.

Deciding on the propriety of directing an assignment of the estate of any insolvent, or imprisoned, absent, concealed or absconding debtor, two dollars.

Signing the discharge of any insolvent or imprisoned debtor, one dollar.

For every order, warrant, or attachment, made or issued in any special proceeding authorized by law, thirty-seven and a half cents.

---

[1] The fees received by the County Judge, after deducting his salary, are to be paid over to the County Treasurer, on the first Monday of May, and November; (Laws of 1847, chap. 277, §§ 8, 9; Laws of 1849, chap. 95,) and an account thereof, verified by affidavit, is to be rendered to the board of Supervisors at their annual meeting.

For every notice to any party, officer, or person, required to be given by law, twenty-five cents.

For services under the non-imprisionment act, the same fees as are allowed by law in proceedings against absconding, concealed, or non-resident debtors.

For attendance upon any special matter, where no fee is specially provided for the service rendered, twenty-five cents.

Admitting any person to prosecute as the next friend, or to defend as the guardian, of an infant, nineteen cents.

Every necessary order upon any special application, twenty-five cents.

For attendance on taking any depositions, upon any inquiry instituted by the Governor, relating to the official misconduct of any officer, two dollars for each day necessarily occupied.

Issuing any summons or process of subpœna, to compel the attendance of any witness in any proceeding before such Judge, twenty-five cents.

For every attachment, or warrant of commitment, against a witness or any other person, in a civil proceeding, twenty-five cents.

For warrant of restitution, or to put any party in possession of lands, thirty-seven and a half cents.

Taking an acknowledgment of a power of attorney to appear in a Justice's Court, twenty-five cents.

For services in criminal cases, not specially provided for, the same fees as are allowed to Justices of the Peace for similar services.

---

§ 452. *County Sperintendents of the Poor.*

Such sum, for their actual attendance and services, as the board of Supervisors of their county shall deem reasonable.

---

§ 453. *County Treasurer's Fees.*

Such commission, for receiving and paying out all moneys, as the board of Supervisors may fix, not exceeding one-half of one per cent., for receiving, and the same for paying; but the gross amount shall in no case exceed five hundred dollars per annum. This restriction does not extend to the counties of New York, Albany and Kings. The treasurer of Monroe county receives an annual salary, to be fixed by the board of Supervisors, not exceeding the half of one per cent. for receiving, and the half of one per cent. for disbursing, or eight hundred dollars in the aggregate.

For receiving moneys on securities transferred to him by the clerk of the court of appeals, one half of one per cent., and for paying out the same, one half of one per cent.

For services as administrator, in the cases provided by law, his reasonable expenses necessarily incurred; and double the commis sions allowed to executors and administrators.

For every warrant issued under the act taxing the rents of land-lords, in certain cases, one dollar.

---

§ 454, *Crier's Fees.*

For attendance upon the Supreme Court, two dollars for each day, to be certified by the Clerk of the Court.

Attendance upon other court, one dollar and fifty cents for each day, to be certified by the Clerk.

---

§ 455. *Executors' and Administrators' Fees.*

A reasonable compensation for the services of the appraisers appointed upon their application, to be allowed by the Surrogate.

For receiving and paying out all sums of money not exceeding one thousand dollars, five per cent. on every dollar.

For receiving and paying out all sums exceeding one thousand, and not less than five thousand dollars, two and a half per cent.

For receiving and paying out all sums exceeding five thousand dollars one per cent.[1]

For every deed prepared and executed by them, on the sale of any real estate made by order of the Surrogate, two dollars; and a compensation not exceeding two dollars a day, for the time necessarily occupied in such sale.

Such allowance for all actual and necessary expenses as shall be just and reasonable.

---

§ 456. *Fence Viewer's Fees.*

For every mile of travel by a Fence Viewer, from his house to the place where the strays are kept, six cents; and twenty-five cents for a certificate of the charges; to be paid by the owner of the strays, or the person applying for the certificate.

Such compensation for all other services required by law, as may be fixed by the town meetings of their respective towns.

---

§ 457. *Juror's Fees.*

For attending to serve as such, in a Justice's Court, although not sworn, six cents; for attending and trying a cause, twelve and a half cents.

---

[1] If there be more than one Executor or administrator, the allowances are to be apportioned among them by the Surrogate, according to the services rendered by them respectively. (Laws of 1849, chap. 160.)

To each juror impanneled to try a cause in any Circuit Court, County Court, or Mayor's Court, twenty-five cents for each cause, to be paid by the party noticing the cause for trial; or if noticed by both parties, to be paid by such party as the court shall direct; except that in the county of Albany, the fees of the jury are to be paid to the County Clerk.

For attending the courts of record in any county, either as a grand or petit juror, such allowance to each juror as the board of Supervisors may direct, not exceeding one dollar per day, and three cents per mile for traveling, in coming to and returning from such courts, to be paid by the County Treasurer, on the certificate of the Clerk.

To each petit juror in the county of Albany, who shall be sworn and serve as such, for attending any Circuit Court, Court of Oyer and Terminer, County Court, or Court of Sessions, one dollar per day for every day's attendance, and seventy-five cents for every twenty miles travel: grand jurors in the county of Albany are entitled to the same compensation as in other counties of the State.

To each juror in the city of New York, twelve and a half cents, for every action in which he is sworn as such in any court of record.

To each juror sworn before any officer in any special proceeding allowed by law, or before any Sheriff upon any writ of inquiry, or to try any claim to personal property, twelve and a half cents.

To each juror sworn in any proceeding authorized by the provisions of the statute in relation to absconding, concealed, non-resident, insolvent, or imprisoned debtors, twenty-five cents.

To each juror attending and serving on a jury to re-assess damages for laying out, altering, or discontinuing, a highway, if from the same town, fifty cents; if from an adjoining town, one dollar.

To each juror attending, in pursuance of a summons, but not serving on a jury, to re-assess the damages for laying out, altering, or discontinuing a highway, if from the same town, twenty-five cents; if from an adjoining town, fifty cents.

---

§ 458. *Justices of the Peace.*

For a summons, nine cents; but no more than two summons to be included in the costs in a judgment against any defendant.

For a warrant in civil actions, twelve and a half cents, an attachment or execution, nineteen cents.

Every adjournment, except when made by the Justice on his own motion, nine cents.

For a subpœna, six cents; administering an oath, six cents.

For filing every paper required to be filed with him, three cents; but not to be allowed for filing any written complaint, pleading, or process, in any cause.

For a *venire*, nineteen cents; swearing a jury, twelve and a half cents.

Entering a judgment, twenty-five cents; for a transcript thereof, twenty-five cents.

Taking every bond or other written security in civil actions, if drafted by the Justice, twenty-five cents.

For making a return upon an appeal, one dollar.

For a warrant in criminal cases, nineteen cents; to be paid by the complainant, before issuing any warrant for assault and battery, if required by the Justice.

For a bond or recognizance, twenty-five cents.

Commitment for want of bail, nineteen cents.

For a venire to summon a jury before a Court of Special Sessions, twenty-five cents; swearing such jury, twenty-five cents; trial fee or attendance, one dollar; warrant of commitment on conviction, twenty-five cents; drawing a record of conviction and filing the same, seventy-five cents; but all such charges shall not exceed five dollars in any one case.

Taking security from any person to prosecute a certiorari, upon a conviction made by a Court of Special Sessions, twenty-five cents; making a return to such certiorari, two dollars, to be paid by the county.

For every order for a commission to examine witnesses, attending, settling, and certifying interrogatories, to be annexed to the commission, fifty cents.[1]

Taking the acknowledgment of any written authority to appear by attorney in a Justice's Court, twenty-five cents.

For a copy of the process, pleadings and proofs, in any cause wherein judgment was rendered by default, and in the absence of the party against whom the same was rendered, when required by any person interested therein, twenty-five cents for the transcript, and six cents a folio for the residue thereof.

Administering an oath or affirmation, in special cases, and certifying the same when required, twelve and a half cents.

Taking the acknowledgment of bail in the Supreme Court, and in any County Court, or Mayor's Court, twenty-five cents.

Taking the acknowledgment of satisfaction of a decree in Chancery, or of a judgment in the Supreme Court, County Court, or Mayor's Court, thirty-seven and a half cents.

Taking the proof or acknowledgment of a written instrument to be read in evidence, or of a conveyance or mortgage of real estate, and certifying the same, for one person, twenty-five cents; and for each additional person, twelve and a half cents.

---

[1] The costs of a commission are to be included in the costs of the suit, though the gross amount exceed five dollars.

For swearing each witness on taking such proof or acknowledgment, six cents.

Endorsing a warrant issued from another county, twelve and a half cents.

For a summons for any offence relating to the internal police of this State, or in any special proceedings to recover possession of land, or otherwise, twenty-five cents.

For a precept to summon a jury in special cases, thirty-seven and a half cents; swearing such jury, twenty-five cents.

Hearing the matter concerning which such jury is summoned, fifty cents; receiving and entering their verdict, twelve and a half cents.

For a view of premises alleged to be deserted, fifty cents.

For one day's attendance upon the Board of Excise, one dollar and twenty-five cents.

For attendance at town meetings, one dollar and twenty-five cents.

For other services performed by Justices of the Peace, not specially provided for by law, such compensation as may be allowed by the board auditing their accounts.

For attending the Courts of Oyer and Terminer and Sessions, two dollars each day, and six cents per mile travel fee in going and returning. But one allowance of travel is to be made at any one term.

---

§ 459. *Notary's Fees.*

For the protest, for non-payment, of any note, or for the non-acceptance or non-payment of any bill of exchange, check or draft, and giving the requisite notices and certificates of such protest, including the notarial seal, if affixed thereto, seventy-five cents; and Notaries are required to furnish, under seal, the certificate authorized to be introduced as presumptive evidence in actions at law, free of expense.

Drawing and copy of every other protest, seventeen cents for every folio; and for sealing the same, twenty-five cents.

Taking an oath or affirmation, and certifying the same, twelve and a half cents.

Drawing any affidavit, or other paper or proceeding, not otherwise provided for, twenty-five cents for each folio; and twelve and a half cents per folio for a copy thereof.

---

§ 460. *Overseers of the Poor.*

For every day actually and necessarily devoted to the service of the town, one dollar to each Overseer; and all such necessary expenses as may be incurred in the discharge of their duties, to be allowed by the board auditing their accounts.

§ 461. *Overseers of Highways.*

For any excess of work over and above his assesment, performed by an Overseer of Highways, seventy-five cents per day.

---

§ 462. *Poundmaster's Fees.*

For taking into the pound and discharging therefrom, every horse, ass, or mule, and all neat cattle, twelve and a half cents each; for every sheep or lamb, three cents; and for every hog, six cents.

For feeding any beasts distrained doing damage, his reasonable charges, not exceeding six cents for each beast for every twenty-four hours.

---

§ 463. *Printer's Fees.*

For publishing notices of any application by an insolvent, under the provisions of the fifth chapter of the second part of the Revised Statutes, and furnishing the evidence of such publication for six weeks, one dollar and sixty-seven cents; if published ten weeks, two dollars.

Publishing any other notice, or any order, citation, summons, or any other proceeding or advertisement, required by law to be published in any newspaper, not more than fifty cents per folio for the first insertion, and twenty cents per folio for each subsequent insertion after the first.

Posting a copy of a notice of mortgage sale on the door of the court house, one dollar.

---

§ 464. *Referees' Fees.*

For each day necessarily spent in the business of the reference, three dollars to each, to be paid on making their report, by the prevailing party. Parties, however, may agree, in writing, on a different compensation. (Laws of 1849, chap. 438, Part II, Title X., § 313.)

Referees, to whom any question in regard to the laying out, altering, or discontinuing a highway, is referred, are entitled to two dollars per day each; to be paid by the party appealing, if the decision of the commissioner is sustained, but if reversed, by the county.

---

§ 465. *Register of Deeds in the City of New York.*

The same fees as are allowed by law to County Clerks, for similar services performed by them.

For filing a chattel mortgage, or a copy thereof, six cents; for entering the same, six cents for every party to such instrument; searching for each paper, six cents; and the like fees for certified copies of such papers as are allowed to County Clerks for copies of records.

---

§ 466. *School District Collector's Fees.*

One per cent. on all taxes voluntarily paid in, during the first two weeks after receiving a tax list and warrant; and five per cent. on all sums collected after that time.

Where a levy and sale is made, the Collector is entitled to traveling fees at the rate of six cents per mile, computing the distance from the school house in the district.

---

§ 467. *Sealers of Weights and Measures.*

For sealing and marking every beam, twelve and a half cents.

Sealing and marking measures of extension, at the rate of twelve and a half cents per yard, not to exceed fifty cents for any one measure.

Sealing and marking every weight, three cents.

Sealing and marking liquid and dry measures, if the same be of the capacity of a gallon, or more, twelve and a half cents; if the same be of less than a gallon, three cents.

Reasonable compensation for making such weights and measures conform to the standard.

---

§ 468. *Sheriff's Fees.*

For serving a writ, summons, complaint, or demand, by which a suit shall be commenced in a court of law, fifty cents.

Traveling in making any such service, six cents per mile, for going only, to be computed in all cases from the court house of the county; and if there be two or more court houses, to be computed from that which shall be nearest to the place where the service shall have been made, except, that in the county of Oneida such travel shall be computed from the court house in Whitestown.

Taking a bond on the arrest of a defendant, or taking his endorsement of appearance, or for taking a bond in any other case, where he is authorized to take the same, for which no fee is otherwise provided, thirty-seven and a half cents; and for a certified copy of such bond, twenty-five cents.

Returning a process, twelve and a half cents.

Serving an attachment for the payment of money, or an execution for the collection of money, or a warant for the same purpose, issued by the Comptroller, or by any County Treasurer, for collecting the sum of two hundred and fifty dollars, or less, two cents and five mills per dollar; and for every dollar collected, more than two hundred and fifty dollars, one cent and two and a half mills.

Advertising goods or chattels, lands or tenements, for sale, on any execution, two dollars; and if the execution be stayed or settled, after advertising and before sale, one dollar; and all legal fees paid for publishing an advertisement or postponement of the sale of real estate.

For drawing every certificate on the sale of real estate, by virtue of an execution, twenty-five cents per folio; for two copies thereof, twelve and a half cents per folio; and the Clerk's fee for filing one of such certificates.

Drawing and executing a deed, pursuant to a sale of real estate, on an execution, one dollar; to be paid by the grantee in such deed.

Serving a writ of possession or restitution, putting any person entitled into the possession of premises, and removing the tenant, one dollar and twenty-five cents; and the same compensation for traveling to serve the same, as is allowed on the service of a summons.

Taking a bond for the liberties of the jail, thirty-seven and a half cents.

Summoning the jury to attend any court, fifty cents in each cause noticed for trial at such court, or placed on the calendar thereof for trial.

Summoning a jury in any case where it shall become necessary to try the title to any personal property, attending such jury, and making and returning the inquisition, one dollar and fifty cents.

Summoning a foreign or special jury, pursuant to a *venire* for that purpose, and returning the panel, one dollar and twelve and a half cents.

Summoning a jury, pursuant to any precept or summons of any officer in any special proceeding, one dollar; and for attending such jury, when required, fifty cents.

Bringing up a prisoner upon a *habeas corpus*, to testify or answer in any court, one dollar and fifty cents; and for traveling, twelve and a half cents for each mile from the jail.

Attending before any officer with the prisoner, for the purpose of having him surrendered in exoneration of his bail; or attending to receive a prisoner so surrendered, who was not committed at the time; and receiving any such prisoner into his custody, in either case, one dollar.

Attending a view, one dollar eighty-seven and a half cents per day; going and returning, one dollar and twenty-five cents per day

Serving an attachment against the property of a debtor, under the provisions of the statute concerning absconding, concealed, non-resident, and fraudulent debtors, or against a ship or vessel, fifty cents, with such additional compensation for his trouble, and expenses in taking possession of and preserving the property attached, as the officer issuing the process shall certify to be reasonable; and where the property attached shall afterwards be sold by the Sheriff, he shall be entitled to the same poundage on the sum collected, as if the sale had been made under an execution.

Making and returning an inventory and appraisal, such sum for the appraisers as the officer issuing the attachment shall certify to be reasonable, not exceeding one dollar per day to each appraiser.

Drawing such inventory, twenty-five cents per folio; and twelve and a half cents per folio for the copy thereof.

Selling any property so attached, and advertising such sale, the same allowance as for sales on executions.

Executing any warrant to remove any person from lands belonging to the people of this State, or to Indians, such sum as the Comptroller shall audit and certify to be a reasonable compensation.

Giving notice of any general or special election, to the Supervisor, or one of the Assessors, of the different towns and wards of his county, one dollar for each town or ward, and the expenses of publishing the notice as required by law, to be paid by the county.

For any services which may be rendered by a Constable, the same fees as are allowed to Constables for such services.

For any person committed to prison, and every person discharged therefrom, in civil cases, twenty-five cents for receiving, and twenty-five cents for discharging, to be paid by the plaintiff in the process.

Summoning Constables to attend the Supreme Court, or any other court, fifty cents for each Constable.

Attending the Supreme Court, two dollars per day.[1]

For mileage on every execution, six cents per mile for going only, to be computed from the court house.

For serving executions issued by the Clerk of the County, upon a judgment rendered by a Justice of the Peace, the same fees as are allowed to Constables in the like cases.

Taking into his possession any wrecked property, and selling the same at public auction, his reasonable expenses, to be settled and allowed by the Judge making the order of sale.

Summoning a jury in any case, under the provisions of the statute relating to absconding, concealed, non-resident, insolvent, or imprisoned debtors, one dollar and twelve and a half cents, to be paid by the creditors.

Making the report required by law, after the adjournment of any Criminal Court of Record in his county, a reasonable compensation, to be allowed by the Board of Supervisors.

For every person committed to prison in criminal cases, thirty-seven

---

[1] A Sheriff is not entitled to a per diem compensation, for attending either the Circuit, Oyer and Terminer, County Court, or Court of Sessions, in his own county. (2 Hill, 411.)

and a half cents; for every prisoner discharged, thirty-seven and a half cents.

Summoning a grand jury for a Court of Oyer and Terminer, or Court of Sessions, ten dollars.

For conveying a single convict to the State Prison, or houses of refuge, for each mile from the county prison from which such convict shall be conveyed, thirty-five cents.

For conveying two convicts for each mile aforesaid, forty-five cents; three convicts, fifty cents; four convicts, fifty-five cents; five convicts, sixty cents; and for all additional convicts, such reasonable allowance as the Comptroller may think just; which said allowance, with one dollar per day for the mainteinance of each convict, whilst on the way to the State Prison, but not exceeding one dollar for every thirty miles travel, will be in full of all charges and expenses in the premises.

For selling land and executing conveyances, in pursuance of the decree of a Court of Record, the same fees as upon sales by execution; but such fees are in no case to exceed ten dollars. If the party, in whose favor the decree is made, bids the whole amount of the sale, or any part of it, or if the whole amount, or any part, be credited on the decree, the fees of the Sheriff must be estimated on the surplus, over and above the sum so bid, or credited; but if the fees in such case would be less than five dollars, and if estimated on the whole amount bid on the sale would have exceeded that sum, the Sheriff will he entitled to five dollars.[1]

------

§ 469. *Supervisor's Fees.*

For one day's attendance upon the Board of Excise in his town, one dollar and twenty-five cents.

When associated with the Town Superintendent in the erection or alteration of a school district, one dollar and twenty-five cents per day.

Two dollars per day to each Supervisor, for attending the meetings of the board.

For all necessary travel in the discharge of his official duties, eight cents per mile.

For making a copy of the assessment roll of the town, and making out the tax bill to be delivered to the Collector, three cents each name, for the first one hundred names; two cents per name for the second hundred names; and one cent per name for each name over two hundred. But a Supervisor is not entitled to the per diem allowance, while employed in copying the assessment roll, and making out the tax bill.

------

[1] See Laws of 1847. chap. 280, § 77.

§ 470. *Surrogate's Fees.*[1]

Drawing proof of a will when contested, or any other proceeding before him, for which no specific compensation is provided, fifteen cents for every folio.

Drawing every petition in any proceeding before him, not otherwise provided for, including the affidavit of verification, fifty cents.

Every certificate of the proof of a will, when contested, endorsed thereon, including the seal, fifty cents; and for any certificate upon exemplifications of records or papers filed in his office, or upon the papers transmitted upon appeal, including the seal, fifty cents.

Drawing, copying, and approving of every bond required by law, fifty cents.

Drawing, copying, and recording, every necessary paper, and drawing and entering every necessary order, and for rendering every other service necessary to complete proceedings on the appointment of a general guardian for a minor, three dollars; and for like services in appointing the same person guardian for any other minor of the same family, at the same time, one dollar and fifty cents.

Drawing, entering, and filing a renunciation, in cases where the same may be made by law, twenty-five cents.

A citation or summons, in cases not otherwise provided for, to all parties in the same proceeding, residing in any one county, including the seal, fifty cents; and for a citation to all parties in any other county, twenty-five cents.

A subpœna for all witnesses in the same proceeding, residing in one county, including the seal, twenty-five cents.

For every copy of a citation and subpœna furnished by a Surrogate, twelve and a half cents; and every such copy of citation shall be signed by the Surrogate.

A warrant of commitment or attachment, including the seal, fifty cents.

A discharge of any person committed, including the seal, fifty cents.

For drawing and taking every necessary affidavit, upon the return of an inventory, fifty cents.

For serving notice of any revocation, or other order or proceeding required by law to be served, twenty-five cents.

For swearing each witness, in cases where a gross sum is not allowed, twelve and a half cents.

For searching the records of his office for any one year, twelve and a half cents; and for every additional year, six cents; but no

---

[1] The fees received by the Surrogate, after deducting his salary, are to be paid over to the County Treasurer, on the first Monday of May and November, (Laws of 1847, chap. 277; §§ 8, 9; Laws of 1849, chap. 95;) and an account thereof, verified by affidavit, is to be rendered to the Board of Supervisors. at their annual meeting.

more than twenty-five cents shall be charged or received for any one search.

Recording every will, with the proof thereof, letters testamentary letters of administration, report of commissioners for admeasurement of dower, and every other proceeding required by law to be recorded, including the certificate, if any, when the recording is not specially provided for by this act, ten cents for every folio.

For the translation of any will from any other than the English language, ten cents for every folio.

Copies and exemplifications of any record, proceeding, or order, had or made before him, or of any papers filed in his office, transmitted on an appeal, or furnished to any party on his request, six cents for every folio, to be paid by the person requesting them.

For making, drawing entering, and recording, every order for the sale of real estate, and every final order or decree on the final settlement of accounts, one dollar and fifty cents; and for the confirmation of the sale of real estate, seventy-five cents; and for making, drawing, entering, and recording, any other order or decree, when the same is not otherwise provided for, twenty-five cents.

Hearing and determining, when the proof of a will, or the right to administration, or apppointing a guardian, is contested, two dollars.

Taking, stating and determining, upon an account rendered upon a final settlement, or determining and deciding the distribution of personal estate, if contested, two dollars for each day necessarily spent therein, not exceeding three days.

For hearing and determining any objections to the appointment of an executor or administrator, or any application for his removal, or for the removal of any guardian, or any application to annul the probate of a will, two dollars.

For hearing and determining upon an application to lease, mortgage, or sell; real estate, two dollars.

For drawing and recording all necessary papers, and drawing and entering all necessary orders on applications for letters of administration, when not contested, and for all services necessary to complete the appointment of administrators, and for the appointment of appraisers, five dollars: but in cases where a citation is necessary, seventy-five cents in addition.

For investing for the benefit of any minor, any legacies, or the distributive shares of the estate of any deceased person, in the Stocks of this State, or of the United States, one per cent. for a sum not exceeding two hundred dollars, and for any excess, one-quarter of one per cent.; for investing the same on bond and mortgage of real estate, one-half of one per cent., for a sum not exceeding two hundred dollars, and one-quarter of one per cent. for any excess.

For receiving the interest on such investments, and paying over the same for the support and education of such minor, one-half of one per cent.

Appointing a guardian to defend any infant who shall be a party to any proceeding, fifty cents; but where there is more than one minor of the same family, and the same guardian is appointed for all, twenty-five cents for each additional minor; and no greater or other fee shall be charged for any service in relation to such appointment.

Hearing and determining upon the report of Commissioners for the admeasurement of dower, one dollar.

For distributing any monies brought into his office on the sale of real estate, two per cent.; but such commission shall not in any case exceed twenty dollars for distributing the whole money raised by such sale.

But no fee shall be taken by any Surrogate in any case where it shall appear to him, by the oath of the party applying for letters testamentary or of administration, that the goods, chattels, and credits, do not exceed fifty dollars, nor shall he take any fee for copying any paper drawn by him, or filed in his office, except as above provided.

For drawing and recording all necessary petitions, depositions, affidavits, citations and other papers, and for drawing and entering all necessary orders and decrees, administering oaths, appointing guardians *ad litem*, and apointing appraisers, and for rendering every other necessary service in cases of proof of will, and issuing letters testamentary, when not contested, and the will does not exceed fifteen folios, Surrogates shall receive twelve dollars; and where the will exceeds fifteen folios, ten cents per folio for recording such excess, and six cents per folio for the copy of such excess, to be annexed to the letters testamentary.

For all fees on filing the annual account of any guardian, where the Surrogate shall draw and take the affidavit of the guardian, and for examining such accounts, fifty cents; but where the same shall not be drawn nor taken by him, he shall charge no fees.

For any necessary travel required under the law of 1837, concerning the proof of wills, &c., (Laws of 1840, chap. 460, § 69,) Surrogates are entitled to ten cents per mile, going and returning.

No fees for filing any paper in the Surrogate's office can be required; neither can any charge be made for drawing, copying, or recording his bill of fees, in any case.

---

§ 471. *Surveyor's Fees.*

For actual service in surveying, laying out, marking and mapping, any real estate, of which partition shall be made pursuant to law, or of which dower shall be admeasured, two dollars and fifty cents per day.

17

For each of his necessary chain and flag bearers, and other necessary assistants, one dollar per day.

---

§ 472. *Town Clerk's Fees.*

For filing every chattel mortgage, or copy thereof, six cents; for entering the names and numbering, six cents; searching for such papers, six cents each; and the same fees for certified copies thereof as are allowed to Clerks of counties for copies of records.

Filing and entering a certificate of marriage, twenty-five cents; and ten cents for a copy of the certificate, or of the entry.

Entering a note of strays, six cents each for all neat cattle and horses, and three cents for each sheep; to be paid by the person delivering the note.

For services as Clerk of the town meeting, one dollar and twenty-five cents per day.

When associated with the Supervisor and Town Superintendent, in the erection or alteration of a school district, one dollar and twenty-five cents per day.

Such compensation for his services in behalf of the town, including those performed as Clerk of the Town Superintendent, as the board auditing his account shall allow.

For drawing a jury to re-assess damages for laying out, altering, or discontinuing a highway, fifty cents.

The same fees for advertising and selling drifted lumber unclaimed, as are allowed to Constables making sales on executions issued out of Justices' Courts.

To the Clerk of the town of Queensbury, for entering every mark of lumber, twenty-five cents.

---

§ 473. *Town Collector's Fees.*

For collecting and receiving taxes, one per cent. on every dollar, and one cent on every amount of tax under one dollar, if paid within thirty days from the first posting of the notice required by law; where the aggregate amount to be collected does not exceed two thousand dollars, the collector is entitled to two per cent. as his fees, on all voluntary payments made within thirty days.

On all taxes remaining unpaid after the expiration of the said thirty days, such compensation as may be voted by the electors at town meeting, not exceeding five, nor less than three per cent. For collecting all unpaid taxes, five per cent., and for returning unpaid taxes, two per cent., to be allowed by the County Treasurer.

To the Collector of the town of Minerva, in the county of Essex, for travel fees from his place of residence to the office of the County Treasurer, thirty-seven and a half cents per mile; to the Collectors of the towns of Keene and Schroon, in said county, for the same, twenty-five cents per mile; but the sum to be paid to either of said Collectors, shall in no case exceed the sum of four per cent. upon the amount of the tax on the lands of non-residents, returned by such Collector.

---

§ 474. *Trustees of Absconding, Concealed, Non-Resident, or Insolvent Debtors.*

A commission of five per cent. on the whole sum which shall have come into their hands, and all the necessary disbursments made by them in the dischage of their duty.

---

§ 475. *Witnesses' Fees.*

To each witness in a Justice's Court, from the same county, subpœnaed and attending before a Justice, or before Commissioners appointed by him, twelve and a half cents; from any other place than the same county, twenty-five cents for every day's actual attendance.

For each witness, fifty cents for each day while attending any court or officer, (including Canal Appraisers,) except as otherwise provided; and if the witness resides more than three miles from the place of attendance, traveling fees, at the rate of four cents per mile, going and returning.

For every witness who shall appear and testify before any Justice of the Peace taking depositions to be used in courts in other States, fifty cents.

To any person attending a Court of Oyer and Terminer, or a court of Sessions, as a witness in behalf of the people, upon the request of the public prosecutor, or upon a subpœna, or by virtue of a recognizance, who is poor, or has come from any other State or Territory of the United States, or from any Foreign country, such reasonable sum for his expenses as the court may direct.

CHAPTER XIX.

FENCE VIEWERS.

PRACTICAL REMARKS.

1. The Assessors and Commissioners of Highways elected in any town, are, by virtue of their offices, Fence Viewers of such town.[1]

2. Whenever any stray has not been claimed and redeemed, within the time prescribed by law, it is the duty of one of the Fence Viewers, on receiving notice, to ascertain, according to the best of his knowledge and judgment, the reasonable charges of keeping such stray; a certificate whereof is to be given to the person applying for the same.[2]

3. In case the person detaining a stray, and the owner thereof, cannot agree as to the charges to be paid, at the time of redeeming such stray, the same may be ascertained and certified by two of the Fence Viewers of the town, to be selected by the former.[3]

4. When two or more persons have lands adjoining, each of them must make and maintain a just proportion of the division fence between them, except the owner or owners of either of the adjoining lands choose to let such land lie open. When a person has chosen to let his land lie open, if he afterwards encloses it, he must refund to the owner of the adjoining land, a just proportion of the value at that time of any division fence that may have been made by such adjoining owner, or build his proportion of such division fence. The value of such fence, and the proportion thereof to be paid by such person, and the proportion of the division fence to be built by him, in case of his enclosing his land, are to be determined by any two of the Fence Viewers of the town. If disputes arise between the owners of adjoining lands, concerning the proportion of fence to be maintained, or made, by either of them, such disputes may be settled by any two of the Fence Viewers of the town. When any of

---

[1] 1 R. S. (3d ed.) 388, § 8.
[2] 1 R. S. (3d ed.) 401, § 23.

[3] 1 R. S. (3d. ed.) 401, § 21.

the above mentioned matters are submitted to Fence Viewers, each party may choose one; and if either neglect, after eight day's notice, to make such choice, the other party may select both. The Fence Viewers must examine the premises, and hear the allegations of the parties. In case of their disagreement, they may select another Fence Viewer to act with them, and the decision of any two will be final upon the parties to such dispute, and upon all parties holding under them. The decision of the Fence Viewers must be reduced to writing, and contain a description of the fence, and of the proportion to be maintained by each, and forthwith filed in the office of the Town Clerk.[1]

5. If any person liable to contribute to the erection or reparation of a division fence, neglects, or refuses, to make and maintain his proportion of such fence, or permits the same to be out of repair, he cannot maintain any action for damages incurred, but will be liable to pay to the party injured all such damages as may accrue to his lands, and to the crops, fruit trees, and shrubbery thereon, and fixtures connected with the said land, to be ascertained and appraised by any two Fence Viewers of the town, and to be recovered with costs of suit; which appraisement must be reduced to writing, and signed by the Fence Viewers making the same, but will be only *prima facie* evidence of the amount of the damages. If such neglect or refusal be continued for the period of one month, after request in writing to make or repair such fence, the party injured may make or repair the same, at the expense of the party so neglecting or refusing, to be recovered from him, with costs of suit.[2]

6. If any person who has made his proportion of a division fence, be disposed to move his fence, and suffer his lands to lie open, he may, at any time between the first day of November in any year, and the first day of April following, but at no other time, give ten days' notice to the occupant of the adjoining land, of his intention to apply to the Fence Viewers of the town for permission to remove his fence; and if, at the time specified in such notice, any two of such Fence Viewers, to be selected as aforesaid, determine that such fence may with propriety be removed, he may then remove the same. If any such fence be removed without such notice and permission, the party removing the same will be liable to pay to the party injured, all such damages as he may sustain thereby, to be recovered with costs of suit. Whenever a division fence is injured or destroyed, by floods or other casualty, the person bound to make and repair such fence, or any part thereof, must make or repair the same, or his just pro-

[1] 1 R. S. (3d ed.) 402, 403, §§ 30-36; 4 Johnson, 414; 9 Id., 136; 17 Wendell, 330.

[2] 1 R. S. (3d ed.) 403, §§ 37-39; Laws of 1838, chap. 261; 11 Wendell, 40; 16 Id., 213; 3 Hill, 38.

portion thereof, within ten days after he shall be thereunto required by any person interested therein; such requisition shall be in writing, and signed by the party making it. If such person refuse or neglect to make or repair his proportion of such fence, for the space of ten days after such request, the party injured may make or repair the same, at the expense of the party so refusing or neglecting, to be recovered from him, with costs of suit.[1]

7. Witnesses may be examined by the Fence Viewers, on all questions submitted to them, and they have power to issue subpœnas for, and to administer oaths to witnesses.[2]

8. When any distress is made of any beasts doing damage, the person distraining, within twenty-four hours after such distress, unless the same was made on a Saturday, in which case, before the Tuesday morning thereafter, must apply to two Fence Viewers of the town, to appraise the damage, who are required immediately to repair to the place and view the damage done; and they may administer oaths and take the testimony of competent witnesses, in order to enable them to ascertain the extent of such damage. The Fence Viewers then certify under their hands the amount of the damage, with their fees; and if any dispute arise, touching the sufficiency of any fence around the premises where the damage was done, they may in like manner inquire into the same, and determine such dispute; which decision will be conclusive.[3]

9. The owner of any sheep or lambs that may be killed or injured by any dog, may apply to any two Fence Viewers of the town, who shall inquire into the matter, and view the sheep injured or killed, and may administer oaths and take testimony on such inquiry. If they are satisfied that the sheep or lambs were killed or hurt by dogs, and in no other way, they must certify such fact, the number of sheep killed or hurt, and the amount of the damage sustained by the owner, together with the value of the sheep killed or hurt.[4]

10. If the parties cannot agree as to the amount of the damage sustained by the owner, or possessor, of land on which floating timber or lumber has drifted, either of them may apply to any two Fence Viewers of the town in which such timber or lumber may be found, whose duty it will be, after hearing the proofs and allegations of the parties, to determine the amount of such damage, at the expense of the owner of the timber or lumber; and their decision will be conclusive. The Fence Viewers may, in such cases, issue process for witnesses on behalf of either party, and administer oaths on taking their testimony.[5]

[1] 1 R. S. (3d ed.) 403, 404, §§ 40–43; 3 Wendell, 142.
[2] 1 R. S. (3d ed.) 404, § 44.
[3] 2 R. S. (3d ed.) 507, 508, §§ 1–3; 10 Johnson 253, 369; 15 Id., 220; 19 Id., 498.
[4] 1 R. S. (3d ed.) 885, § 10.
[5] 1 R. S. (3d ed.) 877, §§ 2, 3.

FORMS.

§ 476. *Fence Viewer's Certificate, where Stray has not been Claimed or Redeemed.*

County, } ss:
Town of ,

I, the undersigned, one of the fence viewers of said town, do hereby certify, that upon the application of A. B., of said town, upon whose enclosed lands the following stray animals, to wit: [*name them,*] came, on or about the   day of   , 18 , and which strays have since that time been kept by the said A. B., and now remain unclaimed and unredeemed, I have ascertained, according to the best of my knowledge and judgment, and upon due inquiry and examination, the reasonable charges of keeping such strays, and that the same amount to the sum of   dollars and   cents: and that the fees for my service amount to   dollars.

Given under my hand, this   day of   , 18 .

E. F., Fence Viewer.

---

§ 477. *Certificate where Parties cannot Agree upon the Charges for Keeping Strays.*

County, } ss:
Town of ,

Whereas, a dispute has arisen between A. B. and C. D., of said town, concerning the reasonable charges of keeping the following strays, to wit: [*name them,*] which came upon the enclosed lands of the said A. B., on or about the   day of   , 18 . and have been kept by him since that time until the date hereof, and which are now claimed by the said C. D.: Now, therefore, we, the undersigned, two of the Fence Viewers of said town of   , do hereby certify, that we have ascertained the reasonable charges of keeping said strays, after due inquiry and examination, and that the same amount to   dollars and   cents; and that the fees for our service amount to   dollars.

Given under our hands, this   day of   , 18 .

E. F. }
G. H. } Fence Viewers.

---

§ 478. *Certificate of Value of Fence Built by an Adjoining Owner.*

County, } ss:
Town of ,

Whereas, A. B. and C. D. were, and are, the owners of certain lands adjoining, in said town of   , and on the   · day of

, 18   , or thereabouts, the said A. B. erected a division fence between the land belonging to him and that of the said C. D., who had chosen to let the same lie open; and whereas, the said C. D. has, since that time, enclosed the said land belonging to him, and a dispute has arisen between the said parties, concerning the proper proportion of the value of the said division fence, to be paid for by the said C. D.: Now, therefore, we, the undersigned, two of the Fence Viewers of said town of   , do hereby certify, that we have made due inquiry into the facts, and examined the premises; that the following is a correct description of the fence so built by the said A. B., as aforesaid, to wit: [*give description;*] that the value thereof, at the time of building the same, was   dollars; and that the proper proportion of said value, to be paid by the said C. D. to the said A. B., is   dollars: And we also certify, that the fees for our service amount to   dollars

Given, &c., [*as in* § 477.]

------

§ 479. *Certificate upon Hearing Dispute between Owners of Adjoining Lands.*

County, } ss:
Town of   ,

Whereas, A. B. and C. D. are the owners of certain lands adjoining, in the said town of   , and a dispute has arisen between them, concerning the respective proportions of a division fence to be maintained, [*or*, made,] by them. Now, therefore, we, the undersigned, Fence Viewers of said town, do hereby certify, that upon the application of the said parties, we proceeded to examine the premises and hear the allegations of the said parties; and that we do determine that said division fence be built as follows, to wit: [*give description;*] that one-third part of said fence is the proper proportion thereof to be built by the said A. B.; and that the remaining two-thirds is the proper proportion thereof to be built by the said C. D.: And we also certify, that our fees for our service amount to   dollars.

Given, &c., [*as in* § 477.]

------

§ 480. *Certificate of Damages where Division Fence is out of Repair.*

County, } ss:.
Town of   ,

We, the undersigned, two of the Fence Viewers of said town, do hereby certify, that upon the application of A. B., the owner of land adjoining the land of C. D., in said town, to ascertain and appraise certain damages alleged to have been incurred by the said A. B., in consequence of the neglect [*or*, refusal] of the said C. D. to make [*or,* maintain] his proportion of a division fence between the aforesaid lands, we proceeded to examine the premises; and, after due inquiry, and examination by us made, we do determine that the said A. B. has sustained damages to his land, crops, fruit trees, and shrubbery [*add* fixtures, *if necessary,*] in consequence of the neglect [*or,* refusal] of the said C. D. to make [*or,* maintain] his proportion of such · division fence as aforesaid; which said damages we have ascertained, and do appraise at   dollars.

[Given, &c., *as in* § 477.]

---

§ 481. *Certificate where Cattle are Distrained Doing Damage.*

County, } ss:
Town of   , }

We, the subscribers, Fence Viewers of said town, having been applied to by A. B., of said town, to appraise the damages done by [*give the number and description of beasts, as near as may be,*] distrained by him doing damage on his lands, and having been to the place, and viewed and ascertained the damages, do hereby certify the amount thereof to be   dollars and   cents, and that the fees for our services are $. And a dispute having arisen between the said A. B., on the one part, and C. D., on the other part, touching the sufficiency of the fence along the east side of the orchard on the premises of the said A. B., which fence was shown to us by the said parties; and having heard their allegations, and examined witnesses in relation thereto, we decide that the said fence is good and sufficient [*or,* bad and insufficient.]

Given, &c., [*as in* § 477.]

---

§ 482. *Notice and Certificate of Consent to Remove Division Fence.*

To Mr. A. B. :

Take notice, that I shall make application to E. F. and G. H., two of the Fence Viewers of the town of   , on the   day of   next, [*or,* instant,] for permission to remove the division fence between the land occupied by you in said town, and that owned and occupied by me, lying adjacent thereto.¹   C. D.

Dated the   day of   , 18.

---

¹ If a portion only of the division fence is to be disturbed, it should be particularly designated in the notice.

L

County, } ss:

Town of
      ,

We, the undersigned, two of the Fence Viewers of said town, do hereby certify, that upon the application of C. D., made in accordance with a notice, of which the above is a copy, duly served upon A. B., therein mentioned, more than ten days before this day, we have examined the premises where the division fence named in said notice is situate, and do determine, that the same may, with propriety, be removed.

Given, &c., [*as in* § 477.]

---

§ 483. *Certificate that Sheep, or Lambs. were Killed by Dogs.*

County, } ss:

Town of
      ,

We, the undersigned, two of the Fence Viewers of said town, do hereby certify, that upon the application of A. B., the owner of sheep, [*or, lambs,*] alleged to be killed by dogs, we proceeded to inquire into the matter, and to view the sheep [*or, lambs,*] killed, and examined witnesses in relation thereto; and that we are satisfied that sheep [*or, lambs,*] belonging to the said A. B., were killed by dogs, and in no other manner; and we also certify, that the amount of damages sustained by the said A. B., in consequence of the killing of said sheep, [*or, lambs,*] as aforesaid, is   dollars and   cents; and that the value of said sheep [*or, lambs*] is   dollars and   cents.

Given, &c., [*as in* § 477.]

CHAPTER XX.

FERRIES.

PRACTICAL REMARKS.

1. The County Court in each of the counties of this State may grant licenses for keeping ferries in their respective counties, to as many suitable persons as they think proper; which licenses will continue in force for a term to be fixed by the court, not exceeding three years. No such license can be granted to any person other than the owner of the land through which the highway adjoining to the ferry shall run, unless such owner neglect to apply for such license, after notice has been given to him, at least eight days before the sitting of the court, of the intention of such person to make the application.[1]

2. Every person applying for a license, before the same be granted, must enter into a recognizance to the people of this State, in open court, in the sum of one hundred dollars; which recognizance is to be forthwith filed with the Clerk of the county. Every license so granted, must be entered in the book of minutes of the court, kept by the Clerk, and a copy thereof, attested by him, delivered to the person licensed.[2]

3. Whenever the waters over which any ferry may be used, divide two counties, a license obtained in either will be sufficient to authorize the person obtaining the same, to transport persons, goods, wares, and merchandise, to and from either side of said waters.[3]

4. If any person (except within the counties of Essex and Clinton, the counties of Orange, Rockland, and Westchester, and the counties in the first Senate District) use any ferry for transporting across any

---

[1] R. S. (3d. ed.) 642, 643, §§ 1–3 ; 11 Wendell 590.

[2] 1 R. S. (3d. ed.) 643, §§ 4, 5.
[3] 1 R. S. (3d. ed) 643, § 6..

river, stream, or lake, any person, or any goods, chattels or effects, for profit or hire, unless authorized in the manner above provided, such person will be considered guilty of a misdemeanor; and, on conviction, be subject to such fine, for the use of the county, as the Court may adjudge; not exceeding twenty-five dollars for each offence. Where any offence is committed on waters dividing two counties, the person so offending may be proceeded against in each of said counties; but the fine imposed cannot exceed twelve dollars and fifty cents in each case.[1]

5. The foregoing provisions of the statute do not affect or alter the ferries granted by charter to the corporations of Albany and Hudson, or alter or impair any grants made by this State, or any legal right or privilege whatever, belonging to any individual or corporation, by virtue of any laws of this State, or otherwise.[2]

6. The owner of a ferry cannot use the land on the other side of the stream, unless he is himself the owner thereof, for the purpose of embarking and disembarking passengers.[3]

7. The public have an interest in a ferry; and the owners thereof are liable to answer in damages, if they should refuse to transport an individual without reasonable excuse, upon being paid or tendered the usual rate of fare.[4]

8. A County Court has power to grant a license to keep a ferry on a river, although the jurisdiction of the State extends only to the centre of the river[5]

FORMS.

§ 484. *Application for a Ferry.*

To the Hon., the County Court of   County:

The application of A. B., of the town of   , in said county of   , respectfully showeth: That he is [or, that C. D. is] the owner of the lands in said town through which the public highway runs, leading from   to   , over and across the   lake, [or,   river;] and that a ferry ought to be established, for the convenience and accommodation of the public, upon the said lake

---

1 1 R. S. (3d. ed.) 643, §§ 8, 9; 5 Johnson, 175; 11 Wendell, 590.
2 1 R. S. (3d ed.) 643, § 10.
3 3 Kent's Commentaries (2d ed.) 421
4 3 Paige, 45.
5 11 Wendell, 590

or, river:] Wherefore, the undersigned A. B., hereby makes application to the said court to grant him a license to establish such ferry, on his compliance with the provisions of the statute in such case made and provided; [*If the application be made by some person other than the owner of the land, insert here:* the said C. D., the owner of the land through which the highway runs, as aforesaid, having neglected.to apply for such license, after due service of the notice required by law, as appears by a copy of said notice and the affidavit of service, which are hereunto annexed.]

Dated the day of , 18 .   A. B.

---

§ 485. *Notice to the Owner, and Affidavit of Service,*

To Mr. C. D.:

Sir: You will take notice that I shall apply to the County Court of County, at the next term of said court, to be held at the court house in said county, on the day of next, for a license to be granted to me to keep a ferry upon the lake, [*or,* river,] from the termination of the highway running through your land, &c.: [*give a particular description of the site of the ferry.*]

Dated, &c.   Yours, &c.,

             A. B.

  County, ss:

A. B., of said county, being duly sworn, says, that on the day of instant, [*or,* last past,] he personally served C. D. with a notice, of which the above is a copy, by delivering the same to him.

Sworn to before me, this   A. B.
day of , 18 .
  G. H., Justice of the Peace.

---

§ 486. *Recognizance.*

State of New York,   ss:
  County,

Be it remembered, that I, A. B., of the town of , in said county, do hereby acknowledge myself to be indebted to the people of the State of New York, in the sum of one hundred dollars, to be well and truly paid, if default shall be made in the condition following:

Whereas, the said A. B. has this day applied to the County Court of the said county of , for a license to keep a ferry upon the lake, [*or,* river,]in the town of , in said county: Now, therefore, the condition of this recognizance is such, that if the said A. B. shall faithfully keep and attend the said ferry, provided a license shall be granted for that purpose, as aforesaid, with such and so many sufficient and safe boats, and so many men to work the same, as shall be deemed necessary, together with sufficient implements for said ferry, during the several hours in each day, and at such several rates, as the court granting said license shall from time to time order and direct, then this recognizance shall be void; else to remain of force.

Subscribed and acknowledged in }
    open court, this   day of   ,
        18 , before me.
            P. V., Clerk of   County Court.

.A. B. [L s.]

---

§ 487. *License.*

At a County Court held in and for the county of   , at the court house in said county, on the   day of   , A. D. 18 : Present, J. P. H., County Judge:

It is hereby ordered and determined, upon the application of A. B., for that purpose made to this court, that this license be granted to the said A. B., to keep a ferry upon the   lake, [*or, river,*] in the town of   , in said county of   , at or near the south-west corner of lot number   , in said town, [*or, as the case may be, describing the place where it is proposed to have the ferry,*] for the term of   years from the   day of   instant. [*If necessary add:* And it is further ordered, that the said A. B. be allowed to collect and receive ferriage for the transportation of travellers, property and effects, over and across the said ferry, at and after the following rates, viz.: [*give the prescribed rates;*] and that he shall not take, or require, any greater sum for such transportation.]

P. V., Clerk.

---

§ 488. *Certificate of Clerk to Annex to the Copy.*

State of New York, }
        County, } ss:

I, P. V., Clerk of   County Court, do hereby certify, that I have compared the foregoing [*or,* annexed] copy of a license with the original, this day entered upon the records of the said court; and that the same is a correct transcript therefrom, and of the whole of such original.

In testimony whereof, I have hereunto affixed my name, and the seal of the said court, this   day of   , A. D. 18 .

[L. s.]   P. V., Clerk.

CHAPTER XXI.

GIFTS.

PRACTICAL REMARKS.

1. Free gifts, or voluntary conveyances, made understandingly, and without fraud, will be upheld.

2. There are two kinds of gifts known in law, viz: gifts *inter vivos*, or those made between living persons; and gifts *causa mortis*, or those made in contemplation of death.[1]

3. Delivery is essential, both at law and in equity, to the validity of every gift. If the thing given be not capable of delivery, the title must be passed by some act equivalent to it, as by assignment, or other instrument in writing.[2]

4. Gifts of goods and chattels, as well as of lands, made with intent to delay, hinder, or defraud, creditors, are void as against any person who may be prejudiced thereby. Voluntary settlements of property, upon the wife or children of the party making the same, are also void as to existing creditors.[3]

5. Gifts made in expectation of death, will not be allowed to defeat the just claims of creditors, and are void as against such creditors, even though there be no fraudulent intent.[4]

6. A gift of personal property may be made by parol; it is a safer course, however, to have it done by a written instrument.[5]

---

[1] 2 Kent's Commentaries, (2d ed.) 438.
[2] 2 Johnson, 52.
[3] 2 R. S. (3d ed.) 195, § 1; Id., 197, §§ 1-3;

[4] 5 Cowen, 87; 8 Id., 406; 4 Wendell, 300; 6 Hill, 438.
[5] 2 Kent's Commentaries, (2d ed.) 443.

FORMS.

§ 489. *Gift of Personal Estate, by Deed.*

Know all men by these presents: That I, A. B., of, &c., in consid eration of the natural love and affection which I have and bear for my sister, C. B., and also for divers other good causes and considera tions, me, the said A. B., hereunto moving, have given, granted and confirmed, and by these presents do give, grant and confirm, unto the said C. B., all and singular my goods, chattels and personal es tate, of every name and nature, in whose hands, custody, or posses sion, soever, they be: [*or, the following goods and chattels, viz, &c.; describing them:*] To have and to hold all and singular the said goods, chattels, and personal estate aforesaid, [*or, goods and chattels,*] unto the said C. B., her executors, administrators and assigns, to the only proper use and behoof of the said C. B., her executors, admin istrators and assigns, forever. And I, the said A. B., all and singu lar the said goods, chattels, and personal estate aforesaid, [*or, goods and chattels,*] to the said C. B., her executors, administrators and assigns, against me, the said A. B., my executors, and administrators, and all and every other person or persons whatsoever, shall and will warrant, and forever defend.

In witness whereof, I have hereunto set my hand and seal, this day of   , A. D. 18   .

Sealed, signed and delivered, ⎱   A. B.   [L. S.]
   in presence of   ⎰
      G. H.

---

§ 490. *The Same, of Real Estate.*

This indenture, made, &c., between A. B., of, &c., of the one part, and R. B., son of the said A. B., of the other part, witnesseth: That the said A. B., as well for and in consideration of the natural love and affection which he, the said A. B., hath and beareth unto the said R. B., as also for the better maintenance, support and liveli hood of him, the said R. B., hath given, granted and confirmed, and by these presents doth give, grant and confirm, unto the said R. B., his heirs and assigns, all, &c., [*description:*] Together with all and singular the hereditaments and appurtenances thereunto belonging, or in any wise appertaining; and the reversion and reversions, re mainder and remainders, rents, issues and profits thereof, and all the estate, right, title, interest, property, claim and demand, whatsoever, of him, the said A. B., of, in and to, the said premises, and of, in and to, every part and parcel thereof, with the appurtenances: To have and to hold all and singular the premises hereby granted and confirmed, or mentioned, or intended so to be, with the appurtenances, unto the said R. B., his heirs and assigns, to the only proper use and behoof of him, the said R. B., his heirs and assigns, forever. And the said A. B., for himself, his heirs, executors, and administrators, doth covenant, &c.: [*For the necessary covenants, see forms of conveyances and covenants.*]

In witness whereof, the party of the first part hath hereunto set his hand and seal, the day and year above written.

Sealed, &c., [*as in* § 489.]

A. B. [L s.]

CHAPTER XXII.

HIGHWAYS.

PRACTICAL REMARKS.

1. The electors of each town in this State have the power, at their annual town meeting, to determine, by resolution, whether there shall be chosen one, or three, Highway Commissioners: if only one be chosen, he possesses all the powers, and discharges all the duties, of Commissioners, as provided by law. Whenever three Commissioners are chosen, they are to be divided by lot, by the canvassers, into three classes, to be numbered one, two, and three, who hold their offices, respectively, for one, two, and three years; and one Commissioner only will thereafter be annually elected, who will hold his office for three years, and until a successor be duly elected, or chosen.

But in case any Commissioner be elected to fill a vacancy, he will hold the office, only for the unexpired term; or, if appointed, only until the ensuing town meeting. Vacancies in the office of Commissioners are to be supplied until the next succeeding annual town meeting, by an appointment in writing, under the hands of any three Justices of the Peace, or two Justices and the Supervisor of the town. Where there are two vacancies to be filled at any town meeting, the canvassers must determine by lot, after the canvass, the terms for which they shall respectively hold.[1]

2. Whenever any town has determined on having three Commissioners, but desires to return two, or have but one, it has the power to do so, by a resolution adopted at an annual town meeting; and when such resolution has been adopted, no other Commissioner can be elected or appointed, until the terms of those in office at the time of adopting the resolution, expire or become vacant. Such Commissioners will be authorized to act until their respective terms become vacant or expire, as fully as if the three Commissioners continued in office.[2]

---

[1] Laws of 1845, chap. 180, § 2; Laws of 1847, chap. 455.   [2] Laws of 1847, chap. 455.

3. Every Commissioner of Highways hereafter to be elected, or appointed, before entering upon his duties, and within ten days after notice of his election or appointment, must execute to the Supervisor of his town, a bond, with two sureties, to be approved by the Supervisor, by an endorsement thereupon, and filed with him, in the penal sum of one thousand dollars.[1]

4. The general powers and duties of Commissioners of Highways are as follows, viz:

1. To give directions for the repairing of the roads and bridges, within their respective towns.[2]

2. To regulate the roads already laid out, and to alter such of them as they, or a majority of them, deem inconvenient:

3. To cause such of the roads used as highways, as shall have been laid out, but not sufficiently described, and such as shall have been used for twenty years, but not recorded, to be ascertained, described, and entered of record, in the Town Clerk's office:[3]

4. To cause the highways, and the bridges which are or may be erected over streams intersecting highways, to be kept in repair:[4]

5. To divide their respective towns into so many road districts as they may judge convenient, by writing, under their hands, to be lodged with the Town Clerk, and by him to be entered in the town book; such division to be made annually, if they think it necessary, and in all cases to be made at least ten days before the annual town meeting:

6. To assign to each of the said road districts such of the inhabitants liable to work on highways as they think proper, having regard to proximity of residence as much as may be:[5]

7. To require the Overseers of Highways, from time to time, and as often as they deem necessary, to warn all persons assessed to work on highways, to come and work thereon, with such implements, carriages, cattle, or sleds, as the said Commissioners, or any one of them, may direct:

8. To lay out, on actual survey, such new roads in their respective towns as they may deem necessary and proper; and to discontinue such old roads and highways, as shall appear to them, on the oaths of twelve freeholders, of the same town, to have become unnecessary. (They cannot, however, lay out a road, without the consent of the owner, through any orchard of the growth of four years, or more; nor over a garden cultivated four years; nor through any buildings, or any fixtures or erections for the purpose of trade or manufactures, or any yards or enclosures necessary for their use; nor through any enclosed, improved, r cultivated lands, without the consent of the owner, or on the oath of ʾwelve freeholders:)[6]

9. To render to the board of town auditors, at their annual meeting, ʾ account in writing, stating the labor assessed and performed in their

[1] Laws of 1845, chap. 180, § 3.
[2] 1 R. S. (3d. ed.) 616, § 1; 9 Johnson, 349; Id., 452; 2 Hill, 467; 6 Id., 463.
[3] 2 Johnson, 424; 24 Wendell, 491.
[4] 17 Johnson, 451; 7 Wendell, 474; 2 Hill, 9.
[5] 4 Hill, 593.
[6] 1 R. S. (3d. ed.) 628, § 69, et seq.; 4 Paige, 523; 6 Id., 83; 4 Cowen, 190; 5 Wendell, 380; 6 Id., 461; 7 Id., 264; 13 Id., 310; 20 Id., 324, 360; 2 Hill, 443; 3 Id., 458.

respective towns; the sums received by them for fines and commutations, and all other monies received under Title 1 of Chapter 16 of Part I. of the Revised Statutes; the improvements which have been made on the roads and bridges, and an account of the state thereof; and a statement of the improvements necessary to be made:[1]

10. To deliver to the Supervisor of their respective towns a statement of the improvements necessary to be made on the roads and bridges, together with the probable expense thereof, which is to be laid by him before the board, at their next meeting:[2]

11. To administer oaths to witnesses or jurors, in proceedings had by or before them.[3]

12. To cause mile boards, or stones, to be erected, where not already erected, on the post roads, and on such other public roads as they may think proper, at the distance of one mile from each other, and with such fair and legible inscriptions as they may direct:[4]

13. To cause guide posts, with proper inscriptions and devices, to be erected at the entersections of all the post roads in their town, and at the intersections of such other roads therein as they may deem necessary.[5]

5. The Overseers of Highways are required to repair, and keep in order, the highways within their respective districts; to warn all persons assessed to work thereon; to cause the noxious weeds on each side of the highway to be cut down or destroyed, out of the highway work, twice in each year — once before the first day of July, and again before the first day of September; and to collect all fines and commutation money, and to execute all lawful orders of the Commissioners. It is also the duty of Overseers to make another assessment, in addition to that made by the Commissioners, on the actual residents in their respective districts, whenever they may deem the same necessary, in order to keep the roads in repair; such assessment must be in the same proportion, as near as may be, and not exceeding one-third of the number of days assessed by the Commissioners. It is the further duty of every Overseer, once in each month, from the first day of April until the first day of December, to cause all the loose stones lying on the beaten track of every road within his district, to be removed; to keep up and renew the monuments erected as the boundaries of highways; to maintain and keep in repair, at the expense of the town, such guide posts as may have been erected by the Commissioners; and whenever the moneys received from commutations and fines are not sufficient to defray the expense of procuring scrapers and plows, or either of them, when directed by the Commissioners, to assess the deficiency upon the inhabitants of the district, according to the last assessment roll of the town. Vacancies in the office of Overseer are to be filled by the Commis-

1 1 R. S. (3d ed.) 617, § 3.
2 1 R. S. (3d ed.) 617, § 4; 1 Hill, 50.
3 Laws of 1845, chap. 180, § 2.
4 1 R. S. (3d ed.) 617, § 5.
5 1 R. S. (3d ed.) 618, § 10.

sioners, under a warrant to be filed in the office of the Town Clerk, who is required to give notice to the person appointed. If an Overseer neglects or refuses to perform his duty, the Commissioners are required to prosecute him for the same: if a complaint be made by a person resident in the town, such person must give, or offer, sufficient security to indemnify the Commissioners against costs, who are thereupon forthwith to prosecute the Overseer for the offence complained of.[1]

6. Every person owning, or occupying land, in the town in which he or she resides; every male inhabitant above the age of twenty-one years, residing in the town where an assessment is made; and all moneyed or stock corporations which appear on the last assessment roll of their town to have been assessed therein; are to be assessed to work on public highways in such town: the lands of non-residents are also to be assessed for highway labor.[2]

7. Each Overseer of Highways is required to deliver to the Clerk of the town, within sixteen days after his election or appointment, a list, subscribed by him, of the names of all inhabitants in his road district, liable to work on highways.[3]

8. The Commissioners of Highways are to meet within eighteen days after their election, at the place of holding the town meeting, on such day as they may agree on, and afterwards, at such other times and places as they may think proper. The lists of the Overseers are to be delivered to them by the Town Clerk; and at their next, or some subsequent meeting, they are to ascertain, estimate and assess, the highway labor to be performed in their town the then ensuing year, as follows: The whole number of days' work to be assessed in each year must be at least three times the taxable number of inhabitants in the town; every male inhabitant, being above the age of twenty-one years, (excepting ministers of the gospel and priests of every denomination, paupers, idiots and lunatics,) must be assessed at least one day; the residue of the work is to be apportioned upon the real and personal estate of every inhabitant, as the same may appear in the last assessment roll of the town; and upon each tract, or parcel of land, owned by non-residents: all deficiencies in the number of days' work are to be assessed in the same manner. The Commissioners must also affix the number of days' work assessed, to the name of each person mentioned in the lists furnished by the Overseers, and to the description of each tract, or parcel, of non-resident lands; such lists, when completed, are to be filed with the Town Clerk, who is re-

---

[1] 1 R. S. (3d. ed.) 617, 618, §§ 6–8; Id., 618, §§ 10–12; Id., 619, § 17; 10 Johnson, 470; 11 Id., 432; 17 Id., 439; 18 Id., 407; 1 Cowen, 260; 3 Wendell, 193; 7 Id., 181; 11 Id., 667; 9 Id., 50; 5 Hill, 216.

[2] 1 R. S. (3d. ed.) 620, § 19; Laws of 1837 chap. 431; 12 Wendell, 39.

[3] 1 R. S. (3d. ed.) 620, § 21.

quired to make copies of each list, to be subscribed by the Commissioners, and delivered to the Overseers.[1]

9. At the first, or any subsequent meeting, of the Commissioners, they are required to make out a list and statement of all lots, pieces, or parcels of land, owned by non-residents in their several towns; describing each lot, in the same manner as is required from Assessors; and giving the value affixed to such lot in the last assessment roll of the town, or, if not separately valued in such roll, then the proportionate value thereof. Lands of non-residents occupied and improved by the owner or owners, or his or their servants or agents, are liable to the same assessment for highways as if the owner or owners were residents. Whenever any non-resident owner conceives himself aggrieved by the assessment of the Commissioners of Highways, an appeal may be made by such owner, or his agent, within thirty days after such assessment, to three Judges of the county in which the land is situated, who are required, within twenty days thereafter, to convene, and decide on such appeal: Notice of the meeting is to be given by the owner, or agent, to the Commissioners, and the decision of the Judges, or of any two of them, will be final.[2]

10. It is the duty of Commissioners of Highways to credit persons living on private roads, and working the same, so much on their assessments as such Commissioners may deem necessary to work such private roads; or to annex the same to some of the highway districts.[3]

11. Every person liable to work on highways, except an Overseer, may commute for the whole, or any part of the number of days assessed to him, at the rate of sixty-two and a half cents for each day, to be paid within twenty-four hours after being notified to appear and work.[4]

12. Overseers are required to give twenty-four hours, notice to persons assessed to work on highways. No person, being a resident of a town, can be required to work on any highway, except in the district where he resides, unless, upon his application, the Commissioners consent that he may apply his work in some district where he has land. Overseers may require from persons having the same, who are assessed, and have not commuted, a team; or a cart, wagon, or plow, with a pair of horses, or oxen, and a man to manage them; and the person furnishing the same will be, entitled to a credit of three days, for each day's service therewith.[5]

13. The fine for a refusal, or neglect, to appear and work when notified by the Overseer, is one dollar for each day; and twelve and

---

1 R. S. (3d. ed.) 620, §§ 20, 23, 24; Id., 622, § 36; Laws of 1835, chap. 164.
2 1 R. S. (3d. ed.) 620, § 22, et seq.; Id., 445, §§ 11—13.

3 1 R. S. (3d. ed.) 623, § 38; Laws of 1835. chap. 154.
4 1 R. S. (3d. ed.) 624, §§ 44, 45.
5 1 R. S. (3d. ed.) 624, §§ 41, 46.

a half cents for every hour any person or his substitute may be in default. Every person, or substitute, remaining idle, or not working faithfully, or hindering others from work, is liable to be fined one dollar for each offence. If a person, required to furnish a team, carriage, man, or implements, neglects or refuses to comply, he may be fined three dollars for each day, for wholly omitting to comply with the requisition; and one dollar for each day, for omitting to furnish a cart, wagon, or plough, or a pair of horses, or oxen, or a man to manage the team. Overseers are required to make complaint on oath, to one of the Justices of the Peace of the town, within six days after any person assessed shall be guilty of any refusal or neglect, for which a penalty or fine is prescribed, unless some satisfactory excuse be rendered.[1]

14. The Commissioners of Highways are required to present a statement to the Supervisors of their respective towns, showing the amount of money necessary to be raised for improving the roads and bridges: this statement is to be laid before the Board of Supervisors, who are directed to assess, levy and collect, the amount therein specified, not exceeding two hundred and fifty dollars in any one year, in the same manner as other town charges. The electors of any town may direct an additional sum of two hundred and fifty dollars, in any one year, to be raised, if the Commissioners deem it to be necessary, and make application for that purpose at the annual town meeting; notice of which application must be given by the Commissioners, at least four weeks preceding the town meeting, to be posted up in at least five of the most public places in the town. The vote directing the last mentioned sum to be raised, must be recorded in the minutes, and the Town Clerk is required to deliver a copy of the resolution to the Supervisor, to be laid by him before the board, and the amount specified therein is to be collected as above provided. The Board of Supervisors may also cause to be levied, collected, and paid, in like manner, such sum of money, in addition to the two sums above mentioned, not exceeding five hundred dollars in any one year, as a majority of the qualified voters of any town may have voted, at any legal town meeting, to be raised in their town, for constructing roads and bridges therein: a written notice of the application to raise such amount, must be posted on the door of the house where the town meeting is to be held, and at three public places in the town, for two weeks before the town meeting, and also be openly read to the electors present, immediately after the opening of the meeting. The Board of Supervisors of any county, also, have the power to authorize a town, by a vote of such town, to borrow any sum of money, not exceeding four thousand dollars in one year, to build or repair any

---

[1] 1 R. S. (3d. ed.) 625, § 47, et seq. 1 Johnson 515; 3 Id., 474; 5 Id., 125; 10 Id., 470.

roads or bridges in such town, and prescribe the time for the payment of the same, which time shall be within ten years, and for assessing the principal and interest thereof on such town.[1]

15. Whenever any damages are allowed to be assessed by law, when any road or highway shall be laid out, altered, or discontinued, in whole or in part, such damages shall be assessed by not less than three Commissioners, to be appointed by the County Court of the county in which such road or highway shall be, on the application of the Commissioner or Commissioners of the town; and the Commissioners so appointed shall take the oath of office prescribed by the constitution, and shall proceed, on receiving at least six days' notice of the time and place, to meet the Highway Commissioners, and take a view of the premises, and hear the parties, and such witnesses as may be offered before them; and they shall all meet and act, and shall assess all damages which may be required to be assessed on the same highway, and shall be authorized to administer oaths to all witnesses produced before them. When all the Commissioners shall have met and acted, the assessment agreed to by a majority of them will be valid; and when made, it is to be delivered to a Commissioner of Highways of the town, who is required to file it within ten days after receiving it, in the office of the Town Clerk. Any person conceiving himself aggrieved, or the Commissioner or Commissioners of Highways of the town, feeling dissatisfied by reason of any such assessment, may, within twenty days after the filing thereof, as aforesaid, signify the same by notice in writing, and serving the same on the Town Clerk and on the opposite party, that is, the persons for whom the assessments were made, or the Commissioner or Commissioners of Highways, as the case may be, asking for a jury to re-assess the damages, and specifying a time, not less than ten, nor more than twenty days from the time of filing the said assessment, when the jury will be drawn at the Clerk's office of an adjoining town of the same county, by the Town Clerk thereof. The notice must be served upon the opposite party, as aforesaid, within three days after the service upon the Town Clerk, and may be served personally, or by leaving the same at the dwelling house of the party, with some person in charge thereof, or, if there be no such person, or the house be closed, then by affixing the same to the outer door of the said dwelling house.[2]

16. Three days' previous notice that a jury is to be drawn, must be served by the person or party asking a re-assessment, on the Town Clerk of the adjoining town; and at the time and place specified in such notice, said Clerk will deposit in a box the names of all persons then resident of the town, whose names are on the last jury list, and

[1] 1 R. S. (3d. ed.) 617, § 4; Laws of 1832, chap. 274; Laws of 1838, chap. 314; 1 Hill, 50; Laws of 1849, chap. 194.

[2] Laws of 1845, chap. 180; Laws of 1847, chap. 455.

who are not interested in the lands through which such road shall be located, nor of kin to either or any of the parties, and draw therefrom the names of twelve jurors. The Clerk is required to make a certificate of the drawing, setting forth the names, and the purposes for which they are drawn, which is to be delivered to the party asking for the re-assessment.[1]

17. The party receiving the certificate as aforesaid, must deliver the same, within twenty-four hours thereafter, to a Justice of the Peace of the town wherein the damages are to be assessed, by whom a summons is to be forthwith issued to one of the constables of the town, directing him to summon the persons named in the certificate of the Town Clerk, and specifying a time and place for them to meet, which must not be within twenty days from the time of filing the original assessment in the office of the Town Clerk. On the appearance of the persons summoned, the Justice who issued the summons will draw by lot six of those attending, to serve as a jury, and the first six drawn, who are free from legal exceptions, shall constitute such jury. The jurors are to be sworn, well and truly to determine and re-assess such damages as shall be submitted to their consideration; they are to take a view of the premises, hear the parties, and such witnesses as may be produced, who are to be sworn by the Justice, and render their verdict in writing under their hands. Such verdict will be certified by the Justice, and delivered to the Commissioners of Highways of the town; and the same will be final.[2]

18. In all cases of assessments under the foregoing provisions, the costs thereof will be paid by the town in which the damages shall be assessed; and in cases of re-assessments by a jury, on the application of the Commissioners of Highways, if the first assessment be reduced, the costs of such first assessment will be paid by the party claiming the damages, but if not reduced, then by the town. Where a re-assessment is had on the application of a party claiming damages, if the damages be increased, the costs shall be paid by the town, but if not, they shall be paid by such party. Where several persons become liable for costs, they are so liable in proportion to the amount of damages respectively assessed to them by the first assessment.[3]

19. When applications are made by two or more persons for a jury to re-assess damages, such jury will be drawn and summoned in accordance with the notice first served upon the Clerk of the town in which the damages are to be assessed.[4]

20. Any person conceiving himself aggrieved by any determination of the Commissioner of Highways, either in laying out, altering or discontinuing any road, or in refusing to lay out, alter or discon-

---

[1] Laws of 1847, chap. 455.
[2] Laws of 1847, chap. 455.
[3] Laws of 1847, chap. 455.
[4] Laws of 1847, chap. 445.

tinue, any road, may, at any time within sixty days after such determination shall have been filed in the office of the Town Clerk, appeal to the County Judge of the county. Such Judge, or, if he be a resident of the town, or be interested in the lands through which the road is laid out, or of kin to any of the persons interested in such lands, or in case of his disability for any cause, then one of the Justices of the Sessions shall, after the expiration of the said sixty days. appoint in writing three disinterested freeholders, who shall not have been named by the parties interested in the appeal, and who shall be residents of the county, but not of the town, in which the road is located, as referees to hear and determine all the appeals that may have been brought within the said sixty days. The Judge, or Justice, must, also, notify the referees of their appointment, and deliver to them all papers pertaining to the matters referred to them.[1]

21. Upon receiving notice of their appointment, the referees are authorized to hear and determine the appeal or appeals referred to them; but before proceeding to hear the same, they must be sworn by some officer authorized to take affidavits to be read in courts of record, faithfully to hear and determine the matters so referred to them. The decision of such referees must be filed in the office of the Town Clerk in which the road is located, and be carried into effect by the Commissioners of Highways. Such decision cannot be altered within four years from the time of filing the same. The fees of the referees are to be paid by the party appealing, where the decision of the Commissioners is confirmed; otherwise, by the county.[2]

22. In all cases of assessments of damages for laying out, or altering a private road, the Commissioners of Highways of the town where the same is situated, must serve a notice on the Town Clerk, and on the person, or persons, interested in the road, specifying a time when a jury of the town will be summoned to assess the damages for laying out or altering such road. The time must not be less than six, nor more than ten days, from the time of service of the notice. At the time mentioned in the notice, the Town Clerk will draw twelve jurors from the last jury list, in the same manner as on applications for re-assessments; and the drawing will be certified to a Justice of the Peace, the jurors summoned, and their proceedings be conducted as on the aforesaid applications for re-assessments. The same jury will assess all damages required to be assessed for the same road. All damages assessed for laying out, or altering any private road, together with the costs of the assessment, are to be paid by the party applying for the road.[3]

23. All damages finally assessed, or agreed upon, by the Com-

<hr>

[1] Laws of 1845, chap. 180; Laws of 1887, chap. 455.

[2] Laws of 1847, chap. 455.
[3] Laws of 1847, chap. 455.

missioners of Highways, for the laying out of any road, except private roads, are to be laid before the Board of Supervisors, by the Supervisor of the town, to be audited with the charges of all persons or officers employed in making such assessment; and such damages are to be levied and collected in the town in which the road is located, in the same manner as other charges for which said town is liable.[1]

24. No private road can be laid out over the lands of any person, without his consent, or the decision of a jury.[2]

25. Where there are three Commissioners in any town, any order signed by two of them will be valid, if it appear in such order, that all the Commissioners met and deliberated on the subject of the order, or were duly notified to attend a meeting of the Commissioners for the purpose of deliberating thereon.[3]

26. Commissioners of Highways cannot maintain an action in their official name or title, but must use their individual names, affixing their official title, as " E. F. Commissioner of Highways of the town of   , in the county of   , plaintiff, &c."[4]

27. A bond taken in the name of a Commissioner of Highways, for the benefit of the town even, is absolutely void—as Commissioners have no authority to take a bond *virtute officii.*[5]

28. For the provisions of the Revised Statutes in relation to Highways, see Title 1, of Chapter 16, of Part I.

29. The Commissioners of Highways of adjoining towns may enter into contracts to build or repair bridges over streams dividing such towns, and may be sued thereon.[6]

30. Where a public highway has been transferred to a plank road company, and the interest of the public in the road is paid for, the corporation succeeds to all the rights of the town Commissioners, in respect of making repairs, &c.[7]

FORMS.

§ 491. *Appointment of a Commissioner to fill a Vacancy.*

County, }
Town of   , } ss:

Whereas, E. F., duly elected [*or,* appointed] a Commissioner of Highways in and for said town, to serve until the   day of

---

1 Laws of 1847, chap. 455.
2 4 Hill, 410; 6 Id., 47; Amended Constitution of New York, Art. 1. § 7.
3 1 R. S. (3d ed.) 641, § 154; 22 Wendell, 134.
4 4 Hill, 135; 5 Id., 215; 1 Denio, 510.
5 4 Barbour's S. C. Rep., 51.
6 Laws of 1841, chap. 225.
7 3 Barbour's S. C. Rep., 459.

18   , has deceased, [*or*, has removed from said town; *or, as the case may be:*] by reason whereof a vacancy exists in the office of such commissioner:

Now, therefore, we, the undersigned, three Justices of the Peace of the said town, [*or*, the Supervisor and two Justices of the Peace of the said town,] do hereby appoint R. F., to serve as such Commissioner, in the stead of the said E. F., until the next annual town meeting, to be held in said town, on the   day of   next.

Given under our hands, this   day of   , 18   .

G. H. } Justices of
S. T. } the Peace.
L. M. }

---

§ 492. *Commissioner's Bond.*

Know all men by these presents: That we, E. F., L. M., and S. T., of the town of   , in the county of   , are held and firmly bound unto A. B., Supervisor of said town of   , in the penal sum of one thousand dollars, to be paid to the said A. B., and his successor in office; to which payment, well and truly to be made, we bind ourselves, and our, and each of our heirs, executors, and administrators, jointly and severally, firmly by these presents. Sealed with our seals, and dated the   day of   A. D. 18   .

Whereas, the above bounden E. F. has been duly elected, [*or*, appointed,] a Commissioner of Highways in and for the said town of   , to serve for the term of three years from the   day of   , 18   , [*or, if appointed to fill a vacancy, say:* to serve until the   day of   , 18   ,] and until a successor shall be duly elected or chosen: Now, therefore, the condition of this obligation is such, that if the said E. F. shall faithfully discharge his duties as such Commissioner, and within ten days after the expiration of his term of office, pay over to his successor what money may be remaining in his hands as such Commissioner, and render to such successor a true account of all moneys received and paid out by him as such Commissioner, then the above obligation to be void; else to remain in force.

Sealed, signed, and delivered, }   E. F. [L. S.]
    in presence of   }   L. M. [L. S.]
          G. H.   }   S. T. [L. S.]

I approve of the sureties named in the above bond. Dated at   , the   day of   , 18   .

A. B., Supervisor of the town of   .

§ 493. *Order for Ascertaining a Road Imperfectly Described, or not Recorded.*

Town of

County, } ss:

Whereas, a road leading from   to   , in said town of   , now used as a highway, was laid out by the Commissioners of the said town, on the   day of   , 18 , but not sufficiently described of record, [*or,* has been used for twenty years for such highway, but has never been recorded:] Now, therefore, I, the undersigned, the Commissioner of Highways of said town, [*or,* we, &c., the Commissioners, &c.; *or,* two of the Commissioners, &c., all of the said Commissioners having been duly notified to attend and deliberate on the subject of this order,] do order that said road be ascertained, described, and entered of record, in the Clerk's office of said town, according to a survey which has been made under my [*or,* our] direction, as follows: [*insert the survey.*] [*If only one line is surveyed, add:* And I do further order, that the line of said survey be the centre [*or,* west line] of said road, and that the said road be of the width of   rods.]

Given under my hand, [*or,* our hands,] this   day of   , A. D. 18 .

E. F., Commissioner.

---

§ 494. *Annual Account for the Town Auditors.*

To the Board of Town Auditors of the Town of   , in the County of   :

The annual account of the Commissioner of Highways of the said town of   , for the year ending the   day of   , 18 , showeth as follows, viz.:

1. The labor assessed in said town, during the year ending on the   day of   , 18, , is   days, and the amount of said labor actually performed is   days; as appears by the returns made to me by the several Overseers of Highways in said town.

2. I have received for fines and commutations, under the statutes relative to highways, the sum of   dollars, as follows, viz:

Date.	From whom received.	On what account.	Amount received.
18 .			
July 6,	John Jones,	Balance of money received by him as Overseer,	$7,85
Oct. 9,	James Jackson.	Fine for obstructing highway,	$5,00

3. The improvements which have been made on the roads and bridges in said town of   , during the said year, are [*state the improvements;*] and the condition and situation of the roads and bridges in said town is, &c., [*state the situation.*]

4. The following improvements, in my opinion, are necessary improvements to be made on the roads and bridges in said town, to wit: [*state the improvements deemed necessary;*] and the expense of making such improvements, beyond what the labor to be assessed this year will accomplish, is estimated by me at $.

Given, &c., [*as in* § 493.]

---

§ 495. *Statement and Estimate for the Supervisor.*

To the Supervisor of the town of   , in the County of   :

The Commissioner of Highways of said town reports, that the following improvements, viz: [*follow the 3d and 4th clauses of the Report to the Town Auditors, as near as may be.*]

Given, &c., [*as in* § 493.]

---

§ 496. *Notice of Application for Additional Sum.*

PUBLIC NOTICE.

Notice is hereby given, to the electors of the town of   , in the county of   , that I, the undersigned, the Commissioner of Highways of said town, am of opinion that the sum of two hundred and fifty dollars, as now allowed by law, will be insufficient to pay the expenses actually necessary for the improvement of roads and bridges in said town; and that the additional sum of $ is necessary to make a bridge across the   , near the house of   , in said town, [*or,* to repair the bridge, &c.; *or,* to improve the road at, &c.:] And that I shall apply at the next annual town meeting of said town, in open town meeting, for a vote authorizing the said sum of $, to be raised for the purpose aforesaid.

Dated the   day of   , 18 .

E. F., Commissioner.

---

§ 497. *Order dividing Town into Districts.*

          County, }
Town of   , } ss

I, E. F., the Commissioner of Highways of said town of   do hereby order, that the said town be divided into   road districts, as follows, to wit: Road district number one shall embrace all of the highway commencing at [*description:*] and all the inhabitants liable to work on the highways, residing therein, shall be and are hereby assigned to work on said district number one. [*If any inhabitants residing out of the district, are assigned to the district, add:* And the following inhabitants residing out of the said district, are assigned and required to work on the same, viz: A., B., C., &c.:] District number two, shall, &c. [*Continue as aforesaid, until the whole town is divided.*]

Given, &c., [*as in* § 493.]

---

§ 498. *Appointment of Overseer, in case of Vacancy.*

County, } ss:
Town of   , }

Whereas, a vacancy has occurred in the office of Overseer of Highways, for road district number   , in said town, by reason of the removal [*or*, refusal to serve; *or*, death] of O. P., elected to said office: Now, therefore, I, the undersigned, the Commissioner of Highways of said town, [*or*, We, &c., the Commissioners of, &c.; *or*, two of the Commissioners of, &c., all of said Commissioners having been duly notified to attend and deliberate on the subject of this warrant,] do hereby appoint M. B., Overseer of Highways, of and for the said road district, number   , in said town, to fill the said vacancy.

Given, &c., [*as in* § 493.]

---

§ 499. *Overseer's List of Persons Liable to do Highway Labor.*

Town of   , ss:

I, O. P., Overseer of Highways for road district number   , in the town of   , in the county of   , do certify, that the following is a true and correct list of all the inhabitants who are liable to work on highways, in said road district number   . viz:

John Smith,	James Jackson,
George Johnson,	Richard Roe,
&c., &c.,	&c., &c.

Dated the   day of   , 18 .   O. P. Overseer.

---

§ 500. *List and Statement of Non-Resident Lands.*

A list and statement of the contents of all lots, pieces, or parcels of land, within the town of   · , in the county of   , owned by non-residents therein:

Owners.	No. of District.	Description.	Value.	No. of days.
A. B.	21.	East half of sub-division No. , &c.	$2,000 00	10

Given, &c., [*as in* § 493.]

---

§ 501. *Assessment of Highway Labor.*

County, }
Town of   , } ss:

I, E. F„ the Commissioner of Highways of the said town of   ,
having proceeded to ascertain, estimate and assess, the highway labor to be performed in said town for the ensuing year; [*or*, We, &c.,
the Commissioners, &c.; *or*, two of the Commissioners of Highways
of the said town of   , having met in said town on the
day of   , 18   , and proceeded to ascertain, estimate and assess,
the highway labor to be performed in the said town for the ensuing
year; all the Commissioners of Highways of said town having been
duly notified to attend the said meeting of the Commissioners for the
purpose of deliberating thereon;] have made out the estimate and
assessment for road district number   , in said town, to wit:

1. The inhabitants of said town assigned to said road district, are
assessed as follows, viz:

Names.	No. of Days.
John Doe,	1
John Stiles,	10
Richard Roe,	8

[*If there are any non-resident lands in the town, then add:*

2. The lands owned by non-residents of said town, and situate
therein, are assessed as follows, viz:

Owner's name.	Description of lands.	Value.	Assessment:
James Jackson.	Lot No. , &c:	$1,000 00	Four days.]

Given, &c., [*as in* § 493.]

---

§ 502. *Appeal to Three Judges, by Non-Resident.*

County, }
Town of   , } ss:

A. B., a non-resident owner of lands in said town, considering, [*or*.
C. D., an agent of A. B., a non-resident owner of lands in said
town, who considers] himself aggrieved in the assessment for high-

way labor made by E. F., the Commissioner of Highways of said town, on the following described lands, to wit: [*insert the description as by the Commissioner,*] doth hereby appeal from the assessment of said Commissioner, to the Hon. G. H., S. T., and L. M., three of the Judges of the Court of Common Pleas, [*or,* the Judge and Justices of the Court of Sessions,] of the said County of   .

Dated   , the   day of   , 18   .

A. P
[*or,* A. B., by C. D., Agent.]

---

§ 503. *Notice to Commissioner of Appeal.*

To E. F., Commissioner of Highways of the Town of   :

You are hereby notified that, considering myself aggrieved by your assessment for highway labor, on the land owned by me, in said town, I have this day appealed to the honorable G. H., S. T., and L. M., three of the Judges, &c., [*as in* § 502,] of the county of   , who will convene at the house of R. F., on the day of   , at   o'clock in the   noon, to decide on said appeal.

Dated the   day of   , 18   .

Yours, &c.,   A. B.

---

§ 504. *Commissioner's Consent to Work in another District.*

Whereas. A. B., a resident of road district number   , in the town of   , in the county of   , is assessed   days' labor, in district number   , in said town, for lands situate in district number   , and, at his request, I hereby approve of his applying the work assessed in respect to such lands, in the district where they are situated.

Given, &c. [*as in* § 493.]

---

§ 505. *Overseer's Warrant.*

To O. P., Overseer of Road District No.   , in the Town of   , the description of which is as follows, viz: [*give description.*]

You are hereby commanded and required, to take charge of the men whose names are hereunto annexed, and cause them faithfully to work the number of days herein specified, (one-half to be done on

M

the   day of   next,) and make return to me on the
second Tuesday next preceeding the annual meeting of said town.
     Given, &c., [*as in* § 493.]

                                        E. F., Commissioner.

Names.	No. of days.	Names.	No. of days.
John Jones.	4	James Jackson.	3 1-2

§ 506. *New Assessment by an Overseer.*

Town of   , ss:

     Whereas, the quantity of labor assessed on the inhabitants of road
district number   , in said town of   , for the year
18 , is deemed insufficient by the subscriber, the Overseer of Highways of said district, to keep the roads in said district in repair:

     I have, therefore, made another assessment on the actual residents
in said road district, in the same proportion, as near as may be, and
not exceeding one-third of the number of days assessed in the same
year by the Commissioner of Highways of the said town of   ,
on the inhabitants of said district; which assessment is as follows, to
wit:

Names.	No. of days.	Names.	No. of days.
A. B.	1	L. M.	4
G. H.	10	S. T.	3

Given under my hand, this   day of   18 .

                                        O. P., Overseer.

§ 507. *Overseer's Notice to Agent of Non-Resident.*[1]

To C. D., agent of A. B., a non-resident owner of lands in the town
     of   , in the county of   :

     Take notice, that A. B., a non-resident, is assessed   days'
labor, in road district number   , in said town, and that said
labor is required to be performed on the   day of   next,
and the   days following, near the house of E. F. and the
river, in said district.

     Dated the   day of   , 18 .

          Yours, &c.,   O. P., Overseer.

---

[1] The notice is to be given at least five days previous to the time appointed.

§ 508. *Notice in case of Non-Residents.*[1]

Notice is hereby given, that the labor assessed on the several tracts of land in the town of   , in the county of   , hereinafter mentioned, which have been assessed as owned by non-residents, is to be performed on the   day of   next, on the highway in said district, between the dwelling houses of E. F. and C. D.; and the owners of said land, or their agents, are hereby required to cause the said labor to be performed accordingly:

Owner's name.	Description of land or tract.	Assessment
John Doe.	South part of lot No. 50, 100 acres.	Ten days.

Dated the   day of   , 18   .

O. P., Overseer.

§ 509. *Assessment for a Scraper.*

Town of   , ss:

Whereas, the Commissioner of Highways in said town of   has directed and empowered the Overseer in district number   , in said town, to procure a good and sufficient iron, or steel shod scraper, [*add*, and plow, *if necessary*,] for the use of said road district; and whereas, the moneys arising from commutations and fines within the said district, are insufficient for that purpose: Now, therefore, I, the undersigned, Overseer of said district, have assessed the deficiency upon the inhabitants of the district, in the proportion they are respectively assessed on the assessment roll of said town, as follows, to wit:

A. B., ... $1 00
C. D., ... 0 50

Given, &c., [*as in* § 506.]

§ 510. *Complaint to Commissioner against Overseer.*

To the Commissioner of Highways of the Town of   , in the County of   :

The complaint of A. B., a resident of the town of   , aforesaid, respectfully showeth: That O. P., the Overseer of Highways

---

[1] This notice is to be posted on the outer door of the building where the last town meeting was held, at least twenty days before the time appointed for performing the labor provided, however, that no agent of the owners can be found in the town.

for road district number _____ , in said town, has neglected and refused to warn T. W. to work on the highways in said district, after having been required by you so to do; [or, has neglected to collect the sum of one dollar, imposed as a fine upon R. F., for neglect to appear and work upon the highways in said district:] and I, the said A. B., hereby require you to prosecute the said O. P., for the said offence. Dated the _____ day of _____ , 18 _____ .

A. B.

---

§ 511. *Security to be Given by the Complainant.*

Know all men by these presents: That we, A. B. and C. D., of the town of _____ , in the county of _____ , are held and firmly bound, unto E. F., the Commissioner of Highways of the town of _____ , in the county of _____ , in the sum of $ _____ , for the payment of which sum we bind ourselves and our legal representatives, jointly and severally. Sealed with our seals. Dated, &c.

The condition of this obligation is such, that if A. B. does well and truly indemnify, and save harmless, the said Commissioner, against the costs which may be incurred in prosecuting O. P., the Overseer of Highways in road district number _____ , in said town, for the penalty incurred by him, for the refusal or neglect set forth in the complaint of A. B., this day made to the said Commissioner, then this obligation to be void; otherwise, in force.

A. B. [L. S.]
C. D. [L. S.]

---

§ 512. *Assessment of Persons left out of the List.*

Town of _____ , ss:

The persons hereinafter named having been left out of the within [or, annexed] list for road district number _____ , in said town, [or, having become inhabitants of said district since the making of the said list:] I do hereby assess the said persons to work on the highways in said district, as follows, to wit:

Names.	*No. of Days.*
John Denn,	4
Richard Fenn,	3

Given, &c., [as in § 506.]

§ 513. *Appeal to Commissioner from Assessment of Overseer.*

To E. F., Commissioner of Highways of the Town of   , in
    the County of   :

The undersigned having been assessed by the Overseer of road district number   , in said town,   days' labor on the highways, on the ground that he is a new inhabitant of said district, [*or,* that his name had been omitted by the Commissioner in said town;] and considering himself aggrieved by said assessment, doth hereby appeal to you from the same.

Dated the   day of   , 18 .   A. B.

---

§ 514. *Complaint against a Person Refusing to Work.*

        County, ⎱
Town of   . ⎰ ss:

I, O. P., Overseer of Highways for road district number   , in said town, hereby make complaint on oath to G. H., a Justice of the Peace of said town, that I gave Richard Roe, who resides in said district, and is assessed to work on highways therein, twenty-four hours' previous notice, to appear with a shovel, on the   day of   instant, at 8 o'clock, A. M., at the dwelling house of E. F., for the purpose of working on the highways in said district, under my direction as such Overseer; and that the said Richard Roe neglected to appear, either in person, or by an able bodied man as a substitute, or pay the commutation money for said work, [*or,* appeared, pursuant to notice, but worked only   hours, and then departed; *or,* appeared, pursuant to notice, but remained idle; *or,* did not work faithfully; *or,* hindered others from working;] nor has he rendered any satisfactory excuse for such neglect, [*or.* conduct.]

Sworn to before me, this ⎱
    day of   , 18 , ⎰   O. P., Overseer.
        G. H., Justice of the Peace.

---

§ 515. *Complaint against a Person for not Furnishing a Team.*

        County, ⎱
Town of   , ⎰ ss:

I, O. P., Overseer of Highways for road district number   , in said town, hereby make complaint to G. H., a Justice of the Peace of said town, that I gave to John Jones, who resides in said district, and is assessed to work   days on the highways therein, and has a cart, [*or,* wagon; *or,* plow;] with a pair of horses, [*or,* oxen,] and a man to manage them, and who has not commuted for his said

assessment, twenty-four hours' previous notice, to furnish, on the
     day of   , 18   , at 8 o'clock, A. M., at the
house of E. F., in said district, a wagon with horses, [or, a cart with
a yoke of oxen,] and a man to manage them, for the purpose of
working one day on the road in said district, under my direction as
such Overseer; and the said Richard Roe has neglected to furnish
said wagon and horses [or, cart and oxen,] and a man to manage
them, or to pay the commutation money for said work; nor has he
rendered any satisfactory excuse therefor.
     Sworn, &c., [as in § 514.]

-----

§ 516. *Summons for Refusing to Work.*[1]

Town of
                     } ss:
          County,

To any Constable of said town, greeting:
     Whereas, complaint on oath has been made before me, G. H., a
Justice of the Peace of said town, by O. P,, Overseer of Highways
in road district number   , in said town, that Richard Roe, who
is assessed for highway labor in said district, and has been duly notified to perform such work, has neglected to appear in pursuance of
such notice, either in person, or by an able bodied substitute, and
perform such labor, [or, as in § 514:] You are therefore hereby
commanded, in the name of the people of the State of New York,
to summon the said Richard Roe forthwith to appear before me, at
my office in said town, to show cause why he should not be fined
according to law, for such refusal or neglect, as in said complaint alleged.
     Given under my hand, at   , this   day of   , 18 .
                              G. H., Justice of the Peace.

-----

§ 517. *Conviction Endorsed on the Complaint.*

Town of   ,
                     } ss:
          County,

     The within named Richard Roe, having been duly summoned to
appear before me, G. H., the Justice within named, to show cause
why a fine should not be imposed upon him for the offence set forth
in the within complaint, and no sufficient cause having been shown
by the said Richard Roe to the contrary, I do impose a fine of
dollars, [or, as the case may be,] upon the said Richard Roe, for the
said offence, together with   dollars and   cents for the
costs of this proceeding against him.
     Given, &c., [as in § 516.]

-----

[1] This summons is to be served personally, or by leaving a copy at the place of abode of
the person named therein

§ 518. *Warrant to Collect a Fine.*[1]

Town of ,
County, } ss :

To any Constable of said town, greeting:

Whereas, complaint was made to me, G. H., a Justice of the Peace of said town, by O. P., Overseer of Highways for road district number , in said town, that Richard Roe, who was assessed, &c.; [*recite as in complaint:*] Whereupon a summons was issued by me, requiring the said Richard Roe to appear before me at my office in , aforesaid, forthwith, to show cause why he should not be fined for such neglect, [*or, refusal; or, as the case may be:*] which summons was duly served and returned to me: and the said Richard Roe not having shown any sufficient cause to the contrary, I have imposed a fine of $ on him for his offence, complained of as aforesaid, and taxed the costs of the proceedings on said complaint at $.

You are therefore hereby commanded to levy the said fine and costs, of the goods and chattels of the said Richard Roe, and bring the said moneys before me without delay.

Witness my hand and seal, this day of , 18 .

G. H., Justice, [L. S.]

---

§ 519. *Overseer's List of Non-Resident Lands, for Supervisor.*[2]

To the Supervisor of the Town of , in the County of :

I, O. P., Overseer of Highways for road district number , in said town, do certify, that the following is a correct list of all the lands of non-residents which were taxed or assessed for highway labor, in the year 18 , on the list delivered to me as such Overseer, and on which the labor assessed by the Commissioner of Highways of said town has not been paid; and a correct account of the amount of labor unpaid:

Owners.	Description.	Value.	Assessment.
John Jones.	Lot No. , east half.	$1,000.	Three days.

Given under my hand, this day of , 18 .

O. P., Overseer.

---

1 The money collected is to be paid to the Overseer, who is required to expend the same in improving the roads and bridges in the district. Every penalty collected for refusal, or neglect to work, is to be set off against the assessment on which it was founded, estimating one dollar for every day's work. 1 R. S. (3d. ed.) 626, § 56.

2 The list is to be made out on or before the first day of October in each year, and verified by affidavit taken before some Justice of the Peace of the town.

§ 520. *Affidavit to Accompany the Overseer's List.*

County, ss:

O. P., Overseer of Highways for road district number   , in the town of   , in said county, being duly sworn, says, that in relation to the lands described in the above list, he has given the notice required by the 33d and 34th sections of the 1st title of the 16th chapter of part first of the Revised Statutes; and that the labor for which the said lands are returned has not been performed.

Sworn, &c., [*as in* § 514.]

---

§ 521. *Annual Account of an Overseer.*[1]

Town of   , ss:

I, O. P., Overseer of Highways for road district number   , in said town, hereby render to the Commissioner of Highways of said town the following account:

1st. The names of all persons assessed to work on the highways in said district, and the number of days assessed to each, are as follows, to wit:

Names.	No. of days.	Names.	No. of days.
James Jackson.	4	John Jones.	2 1-2

2d. The names of all those who have actually worked on the highways, with the number of days they have so worked, are as follows, to wit:

Names.	No. of days.	Names.	No. of days.
James Jackson.	4	John Jones.	2-12.

3d. The names of all those who have been fined, and the sums in which they have been fined, are as follows, to wit:

Names.	Amount of fine.	Names.	Amount of fine.
Richard Roe.	$10	James Brown.	$3.

---

[1] The account is to be rendered on the second Tuesday next preceeding the annual town meeting, and verified by oath, to be administered by the Commissioner.

4th. The names of all those who have commuted, and the manner in which the moneys arising from fines and commutations have been expended by me, are as follows, to wit:

Names.	Amount.	Names.	Amount.
John Smith.	$1 87 1-2	Richard Smith.	$1 25

I have received for fines and commutations, as above set forth, the sum of $, of which amount I have expended the sum of $, in repairing the bridge across the   creek, &c., [*give particulars;*] and no moneys remain in my hands unexpended, [*or*, the sum of $ remains in my hands unexpended.]

5th. The lands which I have returned to the Supervisor of said town of   , for non-payment of taxes, and the amount of tax on each tract of land so returned, are as follows, to wit:

Owners.	Description.	Value.	No. of Days returned.
John Jones.	Lot No. , east half of, &c.	$1000	3

In witness whereof, I have hereunto subscribed my name, the day of   , 18 . O. P., Overseer.

---

§ 522. *Oath to the above Account.*

County ss:

O. P., Overseer of Highways for road district number   , in the town of   , in said county, being sworn, says, that the foregoing account, by him rendered, is in all respects just and true.

Sworn, &c., [*as in* § 514.]

---

§ 523. *Application for the Alteration of a Road.*[1]

To E. F., Commissioner of Highways of the Town of   , in the County of   :

The undersigned, a resident of said town, [*or*, owning lands in said town,] and liable to be assessed for highway labor therein, hereby makes application to you to alter the highway leading from the house of A. B. to the   turnpike in said town, as follows: [*insert a particular description of the proposed alteration.*] The proposed alteration passes through lands which are not improved, enclosed, or cultivated, [*or*, passes through the lands of C. D. and G. H., who give their consent to said alteration.] Dated the   day of   , 18 . L. M.

. The application must be made by some person liable to be assessed. it is also required to be in writing, addressed to the Commissioner, and signed by the person applying.

§ 524. *Consent of Parties Interested, to Accompany the Application.*

To E. F., Commissioner of Highways of the town of   :

We do hereby signify our consent to the proposed alteration, mentioned in the within [*or*, annexed] application.

Dated, &c., [*as in* § 523.]   C. D.
                                              G. H.

---

§ 525. *Application to Lay Out a New Road.*[1]

To E. F., Commissioner of Highways of the Town of   , in the County of   :

The undersigned persons, liable to be assessed for highway labor in said town, do hereby make application to you to lay out a new road, of the width of   rods, through lands not enclosed, improved, or cultivated; except that a part of said proposed road passes over the lands of R. L.,•who has consented to the laying out of said road, and executed a written consent, hereunto annexed, [*or*, has signified his consent by signing this petition;] which said road shall be described as follows, &c., [*give description.*]

Dated, &c., [*as in* § 523.]   L. M.
                                              R. S.

---

§ 526. *Order of Commissioner Altering a Highway.*[2]

          County, }
Town of   , } ss:

It is hereby ordered and determined by E. F., the Commissioner of Highways of said town, [*or*, the Commissioner, &c.; *or*, two of the Commissioners, &c., all of said Commissioners having been duly notified to attend and deliberate on the subject of this order,] that a highway be laid out in the said town, [*if there was an application, say:* upon the application of L. M.,] commencing near the easterly end of the bridge over   creek, and running thence northerly, along the bank of said creek, to the highway near the dwelling house of A. B., and partly through the improved lands of C. D. and G. H., who have consented thereto. The courses and distances of said road, according to a survey thereof, which the said Commissioner has [*or*,

---

[1] This application is to be made in the same manner as the application, § 523.

[2] Every order of the Commissioners laying out, altering, or discontinuing a highway, with the survey made by them, is to be filed and recorded in the office of the Town Clerk, who is required to put a copy of the order on the door of the house where the town meeting is annually held; and the time limited fo appealing from any such order will be computed from the time of recording the same. 1 R. S. (3d. ed.) 628, §§ 67, 68.

Commissioners have] caused to be made, are as follows: Beginning, &c.: [*Insert the survey.*] It is further ordered, that the above described line be the centre of said highway, and that the said highway be of the width of . rods.

In witness whereof, I, the said Commissioner, have hereunto subscribed my name, this day of , 18 .

E. F., Commissioner.

---

§ 527. *Release, by Owner.*

A highway having been laid out, on the day of the date hereof, by E. F., the Commissioner of Highways of the town of , in the county of , on the application of L. M., through certain improved lands belonging to me, commencing at, &c., [*insert the description of the route as in the order:*] Now, therefore, know all men by these presents, that I, the said C. D., for value received, do hereby release all claim to damages, by reason of the laying out and opening the said highway.

Witness my hand and seal, this day of , 18 .

C. D. [L s.]

---

§ 528. *Notice to be Given by Applicants for Laying out a Highway.*[1]

PUBLIC NOTICE.

Notice is hereby given, that the subscriber has made application to the Commissioner of Highways of the town of , in the county of , to lay out a highway in said town, commencing, &c., [*give description as in the application;*] which highway will pass through the improved lands [*or*, enclosed; *or*, cultivated lands; *as the case may be*] of C. D., and that twelve freeholders of the said town will meet at the house of R. P., in said town, on the day of instant, [*or*, next,] at o'clock in the noon, to examine the ground through which the said highway is proposed to be laid.

Dated the day of , 18 .

L. M.

---

§ 529. *Freeholder's Certificate.*[2]

County, } ss:
Town of , }

We, the undersigned, freeholders of the town of , in said county, who are not interested in the lands through which the high-

---

[1] The notice is to be posted up at three of the most public places in the town, at least six days before the time specified for the meeting of the freeholders.

[2] The freeholders are to be sworn by a Justice of the Peace, or any officer authorized to administer oaths, " well and truly to examine and certify in regard to the necessity and propriety of the highway applied for."

way hereinafter described is proposed to be laid, nor of kin to the owner thereof, having met on the day of the date hereof, at the house of R. P., in said town, do hereby certify, that after having been duly sworn, we personally examined the route of the said proposed highway, and heard the reasons offered for and against the laying out of the same; and-that, in our opinion, it is necessary and proper to lay out such highway, pursuant to the application of L. M., commencing, &c., [*insert the description;*] which said highway will pass through the improved [*or,* enclosed; *or,* cultivated] lands of C. D.

In witness whereof, we have hereunto subscribed our names, this day of , 18 .
G. H.
&c., &c.

---

§ 530. *Notice to Occupant, on Application to Lay Out a Highway.*[1]

To Mr. C. D.:

Take notice, that I, the undersigned Commissioner of Highways of the town of , in the county of , will attend at the house of R. P., in said town, on the day of , 18 , at . o'clock in the noon, to decide on an application made by L. M. to me, to lay out a highway, commencing, &c. [*give description:*] which highway will pass through your enclosed [*or,* improved; *or,* cultivated] lands; and twelve freeholders have certified that it is proper and necessary to lay out said highway.

Dated the day of , 18 .
Yours, &c.,
E. F., Commissioner

---

§ 531. *Order Laying Out a Highway through Improved Lands, without the Consent of the Owner.*

County, } ss:
Town of ,

Whereas, upon the application of L. M., a resident in said town, liable to be assessed to work on the highways therein, for the laying out of the highway hereafter described, and on the certificate of twelve reputable freeholders of the town, convened and duly sworn

---

1 The notice is to be served by delivering it to the occupant, or leaving it at his dwell- ing house, at least three days before the time of the meeting.

after due public notice, as required by the statute, certifying that such highway was necessary and proper; notice in writing, of at least three days, was given in due form of law to C. D. and G. H., the occupants of the land through which such highway is to run, that the undersigned, E. F., the Commissioner of Highways of said town of   , would attend at the house of R. P., in said town, on the   day of   , 18   , at o'clock in the   noon, to decide on the application aforesaid: Now, therefore, it is ordered, determined and certified, after hearing all the reasons for and against the same, that a public highway shall be and the same is hereby laid out, pursuant to said application, whereof a survey has been made, and is as follows, to wit: Beginning, &c., [*as in the survey;*] and the line of said survey is to be the centre of the said highway, which is to be   rods in width.

In witness, &c., [*as in § 526.*]

---

§ 532. *Agreement as to Damages on Laying Out Road.*[1]

Whereas, a public highway was laid out, on the   day of   , 18 , by E. F., Commissioner of Highways of the town of   , in the county of   , on the application of L. M., through the enclosed [*or,* improved; *or,* cultivated] lands of C. D., commencing, &c., [*insert the description of the highway as in the order:*] Now, therefore, it is hereby agreed between the said Commissioner and the said C. D., that the damages sustained by the said C. D., by reason of the laying out and opening the said highway, be liquidated and agreed upon, at   dollars.

In witness whereof, the said Commissioner, and the said C. D., have hereunto subscribed their names, the   day of   18 .

E. F.

C. D

---

§ 533. *Application of a Commissioner of Highways, to the County Court, to appoint Commissioners to assess Damages.*

To the County Court of   County:

The undersigned, E. F., Commissioner of Highways in and for the town of   , in said county, hereby makes application to

---

[1] The Commissioner and party interested cannot exceed one hundred dollars in this agreement. When executed, it is to be filed in the office of the Town Clerk

the County Court thereof, in conformity to tne statute, for the appointment of Commissioners to assess the damages for laying out [*or, altering; or, discontinuing*] the highway in said town commencing at the house of L. M. and terminating on the left bank of the river; the said highway having been so laid out [*or, altered; or, discontinued*] by an order made by the undersigned, on the day of   , 18   .

Dated the   day of   , 18   .

                      E. F., Commissioner of Highways in
                        and for the Town of   .

---

§ 534. *Appointment of Commissioners.*

At a County Court held in and for the County of   , at the Court House in said county, on the   day of   , A. D. 18   .

Present, J. P. H., County Judge:

On reading and filing the application of E. F., Commissioner of Highways in and for the town of   , in the said county of   , it is hereby ordered, in accordance with the terms of the said application, that G. H., S. T., and L. M., be appointed Commissioners to assess the damages for laying out [*or, altering; or, discontinuing*] the highway [*describe the highway as in the application*] mentioned in the said application.

                        E. B. C., Clerk.

---

§ 535. *Notice to the Commissioners of their Appointment.*

To G. H., S. T., and L. M.:

You are hereby notified that you have been duly appointed by the County Court of the County of   , Commissioners to assess the damages for laying out [*or, altering; or, discontinuing*] the highway [*describe the highway as in the application;*] and that you are required to meet the undersigned at the house of O. P., in the Town of   , in said county, on the   day of   next, [*or, instant,*] at   o'clock in the   noon, to take a view of the said premises, and to hear and determine the matter aforesaid.

Dated, &c., [*as in § 533.*]

---

§ 536.   *Oath of Commissioners.*

I do solemnly swear [*or, affirm*] that I will support the Constitution of the United States, and the Constitution of the State of New

York; and that I will faithfully discharge the duties of Commissioner to assess the damages for laying out [or, altering; or, discontinuing] the highway in the town of   , in the county of   , commencing at, &c., [*describe the highway as in the application,*] according to the best of my ability.

---

§ 537. *Oath to be Administered by the Commissioners to Witnesses.*

The evidence you shall give touching the assessment of damages for the laying out [or, altering; or, discontinuing] the highway in question, shall be the truth, the whole truth, and nothing but the truth. So help you God.

---

§ 538. *Assessment of the Commissioners.*

County, ss:

We, the undersigned Commissioners, [or, We, the undersigned, being a majority of three Commissioners, all having met together and acted,] appointed by the County Court of   County, to assess the damages for laying out [or, altering; or, discontinuing] the highway, [*describe the highway, as in the application,*] which said highway has been so laid out [or, altered; or, discontinued] by an order of E. F., Commissioner of Highways of the town of   , in said county, dated the   day of   , 18   , having taken the oath prescribed by the Constitution, viewed the premises, and heard the parties, and such witnesses as were offered, do assess the damages for laying out [or, altering; or, discontinuing] the said highway, as follows: To A. B. the sum of   dollars, as and for the damages sustained by him, by reason of the laying out [or, *as aforesaid*] the said highway; to C. D. the sum of, &c., &c., [*specify all the parties to whom damages may be awarded.*]

In witness whereof, we have hereunto set our names, this   day of   , A. D. 18   .

G. H. ⎫
S. T. ⎬ Commissioners.
L. M. ⎭

---

§ 539. *Notice of Re-Assessment.*

Sir: Take notice, that I consider myself aggrieved by [or, *if the notice is given by a Commissioner of Highways, say:* Take notice, that I am dissatisfied with] an assessment of damages made on the   day of   , 18   , by G. H., S. T., and L. M., Com-

missioners for that purpose appointed by the County Court of
County, for laying out [or, altering; or, discontinuing] the highway
[*describe the highway as in the assessment,*] which said assessment is
now on file in your office; and that a jury will be drawn by R. P.,
Town Clerk of the town of   , [*the adjoining town,*] at his
office in the said town of   , on the   day of
next, [or, instant,] at   o'clock in the   noon, to re-assess the
said damages. Dated the   day of   , 18   .

A. B.,

[or, E. F., Commissioner of Highways
in and for the Town of   .]

To C. D., Town Clerk of the Town of   ,
    [or, To Mr. M. B.—*the party claiming damages.*]

---

§ 540. *Notice to the Town Clerk of an Adjoining Town to draw a Jury.*

Sir: You are hereby required, in accordance with the statute in
such case made and provided, to draw a jury of twelve jurors, on the
          day of   next, [or, instant,] at   o'clock in the   noon
of that day, to re-assess the damages for laying out [or, *as the case
may be*] the highway, [*describe the highway as in the assessment;*]
the same having been assessed by G. H., S. T., and L. M., Commissioners for that purpose appointed by the County Court of
County, but I conceiving myself aggrieved by [or, I being dissatisfied
with] the said assessment.

Dated, &c., [*as in* § 539.]
To R. P., Town Clerk of the Town of   .

---

§ 541. *Certificate of the Drawing of the Jury.*

County, } ss:
Town of   , }

I do certify that, upon the application of A. B., [or, E. F., Commissioner of Highways in and for the town of   ,] in pursuance
of the statute in such case made and provided, on the   day of
          , 18   , at   o'clock in the   noon, at my office in the
said town of   , E. B., M. T., O. R., &c., &c., [*name all the
jurors,*] were drawn by me as jurors to re-assess the damages for
laying out, [or, *as the case may be*] the highway, [*describe the highway;*] the said damages having been heretofore assessed by G. H.,
S. T., and L. M., Commissioners for that purpose appointed by the
County Court of   County; but the said A. B., conceiving

himself aggrieved by [*or*, the said E. F. being dissatisfied with] the said assessment.

Given under my hand, this   day of   , 18 .

R. P., Town Clerk of the
Town of   .

---

§ 542. *Summons of the Justice.*

County, } ss:
Town of   , }

To any Constable of the town of   , in said county, greeting:

You are hereby commanded to summon E. B., M. T., O. R., &c., &c., [*name all the jurors drawn,*] jurors regularly drawn by R. P., Town Clerk of the town of   , to re-assess the damages for laying out [*or, as the case may be*] the highway, [*describe the highway, as in the certificate of drawing,*] to meet at the house of O. P., in the town of   , aforesaid, on the   day of   next, [*or, instant,*] at   o'clock in the   noon of that day, for the purpose above specified. And have you then there this precept.

Given under my hand, this   day of   , 18 .

G. H., Justice of the Peace.

---

§ 543. *Oath of the Jurors.*

You will well and truly determine and re-assess such damages as shall be submitted to your consideration. So help you God.

---

§ 544. *Oath to Witnesses.*

The evidence you shall give upon this re-assessment of damages for laying out [*or, as the case may be*] the highway in question, shall be the truth, the whole truth, and nothing but the truth. So help you God.

---

§ 545. *Verdict of the Jury.*

County, } ss:
Town of   , }

We, the subscribers, the jurors drawn, summoned and sworn, to re-assess the damages for laying out [*or, as the case may be,*] the highway, [*describe the highway,*] in pursuance of the order of E. F., Commissioner of Highways in and for the town of   , bearing

20

date the   day of   , 18 , having viewed the premises, and heard the parties. and such witnesses as were offered before us, do hereby re-assess the damages aforesaid, as follows: To A. B., the sum of   dollars, for the damages sustained by him by reason of the laying out [*or, as the case may be*] the said highway; to C. D., the sum of, &c., [*specify all the parties to whom damages may be awarded.*]

In witness whereof, we have hereunto set our hands, this
day of   , 18 ,   E. B.,
                                         M. T.,   ⎫
                                         O. R.,   ⎬ Jurors.
                                         &c. &c., ⎭

§ 546. *Certificate of the Justice.*

County, ⎫
         ⎬ ss:
Town of ⎭

I, G. H., one of the Justices of the Peace of said town, do certify, that the above is the verdict of the jury summoned by my summons, and drawn and sworn by me to determine and re-assess the damages for the laying out [*or, as the case may be*] the highway mentioned in the said verdict.

Given, &c., [*as in* § 542.]

§ 547. *Application to Discontinue an Old Road.*[1]

To E. F., the Commissioner of highways of the town of   , in
    the County of   :

I, the undersigned, A. B., a resident of said town, liable to be assessed for highway labor therein, hereby make application to you, the said Commissioner, to discontinue the old road in said town, commencing near my dwelling house, [*give description of the part sought to be discontinued,*] on the ground that the said road has become useless and unnecessary.

Dated, &c.   A. B.

§ 548. *Oath to Freeholders on Application to Discontinue.*

You, and each of you, do solemnly swear, that you will well and truly examine and certify, in regard to the propriety of discontinuing the road, for which application has been made by A. B.

---

[1] The Commissioner receiving the application, is required to summon twelve disinterested freeholders, to examine the premises and consider such application.

§ 549. *Certificate to Discontinue.*

County, } ss:

Town of , }

We, the undersigned, disinterested freeholders of said town of , having met at the house of R. P., in said town, on this day of , 18 , in pursuance of the summons of E. F., the Commissioner of Highways of the said town, in order to examine and certify in regard to the propriety of discontinuing the road described in the annexed application of A. B., do certify, that we have personally examined the said road, and that in our opinion the same is useless and unnecessary, and ought to be discontinued.

In witness whereof, we have hereunto subscribed our names, this day of , 18 . G. H.,

&c., &c.

---

§ 550. *Order for Discontinuing a Road.*[1]

County, }

Town of , }

Upon the application of A. B., of said town, for the discontinuance of the road hereinafter described; and on the certificate of twelve disinterested freeholders, duly summoned and sworn, who have in due form certified that said road is useless and unnecessary; it is hereby ordered by E. F., the Commissioner of Highways of said town of , [*or,* the Commissioners, &c.; *or,* two of the Commissioners, &c., all of said Commissioners having been duly notified to attend and deliberate on the subject of this order,] that the said road, of which the following is a survey, made by the direction of the said Commissioner, [*or,* Commissioners,] viz: [*insert survey,*] be and the same is hereby discontinued, [*or,* be not discontinued.]

In witness, &c., [*as in* § 526.]

---

§ 551. *Appeal to the County Judge from the Determination of the Commissioner, or Commissioners, of Highways.*

To J. P. H., Esq., County Judge of County:

I, A. B., of the town of , in said county, conceiving myself aggrieved by the determination of E. F., Commissioner of Highways of said town of , made on the day of , 18 , in

---

[1] All applications, certificates and papers, relative to the laying out, altering or discontinuing, any road, are to be filed in the office of the Town Cier, as soon as the subiec matter of the same be decided. (1 R. S 518.)

laying out [*or*, altering; *or*, discontinuing; *or*, in refusing to lay out, *or*, as aforesaid] a highway in said town, upon the application of C. D., do hereby appeal to you from such determination. The said highway [*or*, alteration of the said highway] is described in the order of the said Commissioner, filed and recorded in the office of the Town Clerk of said town of , on the day of , 18 , * as follows: [*insert description.*] The grounds upon which this appeal is made, are [*state the same particularly;*] and said appeal is brought to reverse entirely the determination of the said Commissioner, [*or*, to reverse the determination, &c., *specifying the part sought to be reversed.*]

Dated this day of , 18. A. B.

---

§ 552. *Appointment of Referees by the County Judge.*

County, ss:

Whereas, on the day of , A. D., 18 , A B., of the town of , in said county, appealed to me from the order and determination of E. F., Commissioner of Highways of said town, contained in his order, filed, &c., [*as in* § 551, *to the* *: *if, however, the referees are to hear several appeals, all should be mentioned in the appointment:*] Now, therefore, in accordance with the statute in such case made and provided, I do hereby appoint G. H., S. T., and L. M., residents of the said county, but not of the said town of , referees to hear and determine the said appeal, [*or* appeals.]

Given under my hand, this day of , 18 .

J. P. H., County Judge.

---

§ 553. *Appointment of Referees by one of the Justices of the Sessions, where the County Judge is Interested, or otherwise Disabled.*

County, ss:

Whereas, on the day of , A. D., 18 , A. B., of the town of , in said county, appealed to the Hon. J. P. H., County Judge of said county, from the order and determination of E. F., Commissioner of Highways of said town, contained in his order, filed, &c., [*as in* § 551, *to the* *, *or follow the direction in* § 552:] and whereas the said County Judge is a resident of the said town of , [*or*, is interested in the lands through which the said road is laid out; *or*, is of kin to A. B., one of the persons interested in the lands through which said road is laid out; *or, if the judge be disabled for any other cause, state the fact:*] Now, therefore, in accordance with the statute in such case made and provided, I, the undersigned, one of the Justices of the Sessions of the said county of   , do hereby appoint G. H., S. T., and L. M., residents of the said county, but not of the said town of   , referees to hear and determine the said appeal, [or, appeals.]

    Given under my hand, this   day of   , 18 .

E. W. B., Justice of the Sessions.

---

§ 554. *Notice to the Referees of their Appointment.*

To G. H., S. T., and L. M:

    Take notice, that you have been duly appointed by me, as referees to hear and determine an appeal made from the order and determination of E. F., Commissioner of Highways of the town of   , in the county of   , contained in his order, filed, &c., [*as in* § 551 *to the* *; *or, if there are other appeals, specify them also:*] and that the papers herewith delivered, are all the papers pertaining to the matter [*or,* matters] referred to you as aforesaid.

    Dated the   day of   , 18 .

J. P. H., County Judge of   County;
[*or,* E. W. B., Justice of the Sessions of   County.]

---

§ 555. *Notice to be given by the Referees to the Commissioner.*

To E. F., Commissioner of Highways of the town of   , in the
    County of   ,

    Take notice, that we have been duly appointed referees to hear and determine an appeal made to J. P. H., County Judge of the county of   , by A. B., of said town of   , from your determination contained in your order, made on the   day of   , 18   , and filed and recorded in the office of the Town Clerk of said town, on the   day of   , 18   , refusing to lay out &c., [*as in the appeal;*] and that we shall attend at the house of O. P., in said town, on the   day of   instant, [*or,* next,] at   o'clock in the   noon of that day, to hear and determine such appeal.

    Dated the   day of   , 18 ,   G. H.,
    S. T., } Referees.
    L. M.,

---

§ 556. *Notice to the Appellant, or Applicant.*

To A. B.:

    Take notice, that we shall attend at the house of O. P., in the town of   , in the county of   , on the   day of instant, [or, next,] at   o'clock in the   noon of that day, to hear and determine the appeal made by you [or, made by A. B.] to J. P. H., County Judge of said county, from the order and determination of E. F., Commissioner of Highways of the said town of   , contained in his order made on the   day of   , 18   , and filed and recorded in the office of the Town Clerk of said town, on the   day of   , 18   , refusing to lay out, &c., [as in the appeal.]

Dated, &c., [as in § 555.]

---

§ 557. *Subpœna on an Appeal.*

County, ss:

To M. B., R. F., and P. T., greeting:

You, and each of you, are hereby commanded, in the name of the people of the State of New York, to appear before us, at the house of O. P., in the town of   , in said county, on the   day of   instant, [or, next,] at   o'clock in the   noon of that day, to testify in the matter of an appeal made by A. B., from a determination of E. F., Commissioner of Highways of the said town of   , on the part of the said A. B., appellant, [or the said E. F., Commissioner.]

Given under our hands, this   day of   , 18   .

G. H.,
S. T., } Referees.
L. M.,

---

§ 558. *Oath of the Referees.*

You, and each of you, do solemnly swear, that you will faithfully hear and determine the appeal [or, appeals] referred to you.

---

§ 559. *Oath to be Administered to a Witness by the Referees.*

The evidence you shall give upon this hearing of the appeal of A. B., shall be the truth, the whole truth, and nothing but the truth. So help you God.

---

§ 560. *Decision of the Referees upon an Order in relation to Altering or Discontinuing a Road.*

County, ss:

Whereas, on the   day of   , A. D., 18   , A. B., of the town of   , in said county, appealed to the Hon. J. P. H.,

County Judge of said county, from the order and determination of E. F., Commissioner of Highways of said town, contained in his order, filed, &c., [*as in* § 551, *to the* *, *and then add:*] copies of which said appeal and order are hereto annexed; and whereas we, the undersigned, having been duly appointed by the said County Judge, [*or*, by E. W. B., Esq., one of the Justices of the Sessions of the said county, the said County Judge being disabled from acting in the premises,] referees to hear and determine the said appeal, attended at the house of O. P., in the said town of   , on this   day of   , 18   , at   o'clock in the   noon, in pursuance of notice duly given to the said Commissioner, and to the said A. B., the applicant above named, according to the statute in such case made and provided, to hear the proofs and allegations of the parties: And whereas, such hearing having been had in the premises, we do hereby adjudge, decide, and determine, that the order and determination of the said Commissioner* be, and the same is in all things affirmed; [*or*, reversed; *or*, reversed in part, as follows, to wit: *set forth the decision in full.*]

Given, &c., [*as in* § 557.]

---

§ 561. *Decision of the Referees on an Order Refusing to lay out a Road.*

County, ss:

Whereas, &c., [*as in* § 560, *to the* *, *and then add:*] be, and the same is, in all things reversed; and that a highway be, and the same is, hereby laid out, pursuant to the application of the said A. B., pursuant to a survey thereof, which we have caused to be made, as follows, to wit: Beginning, &c., [*insert the survey.*] And we do further order and declare, that the line above mentioned, shall be the centre of the said highway, which is to be the width of   rods.

Given, &c., [*as in* § 557.]

---

§ 562. *Notice to the Occupant of Land to Remove Fences, after a Final Decision.*

To Mr. C. D.:

Take notice, that I, the undersigned, Commissioner of Highways of the town of   , have, by an order duly made and filed with the Town Clerk, bearing date the   day of   , 18   , a copy of which is hereunto annexed, laid out a public highway through your lands; and you are hereby required to remove your fences from within the bounds of said highway, within sixty days after service of this notice.

Dated the   day of   , 18   .

E. F., Commissioner.

---

§ 563. *Order of the Commissioner to Remove Fences, in case of an Encroachment.*

County } ss:
Town of   ,

I, the undersigned, Commissioner of Highways of said town, having ascertained that the public highway therein, leading from the house of C. D. to the house of G. H., is encroached, upon the side thereof, along the lands in the occupation of C. D., by a rail fence erected by the present, or some former occupant thereof, which forms a part of the enclosure of said land; and having caused the said highway to be surveyed, and having ascertained the easterly bounds and limits thereof to be upon and according to the following line, to wit: Beginning, &c., [*insert the survey:*] and that all that narrow strip or piece of land which lies under the said rail fence [*or*, under said rail fence, and between the said rail fence and the line above described, *as the fact may be:*] is a part of the public highway aforesaid: It is therefore ordered, by the undersigned Commissioner of Highways of said town, that the said rail fence be removed, so that the said highway be open and unobstructed, and of the breadth originally intended, which was   rods.

Given, under my hand, this   day of   , 18   .

E. F., Commissioner.

---

§ 564. *Notice to Occupant to Remove Encroachment.*

To Mr. C. D.:

Take notice, that an order, of which a copy is hereunto annexed, has been made by the undersigned, the Commissioner of Highways of the town of   , in the county of   , and you are hereby required, according to the statute in such case made and provided, to remove the fence therein mentioned, within sixty days after service of this notice.

Dated the   day of   , 18   .

E. F., Commissioner.

§ 565. *Precept to Summon Freeholders, in case of an Encroachment.*[1]

County, ⎱
Town of ⎰ ss:

To any Constable of said town, greeting:

You are hereby commanded to summon twelve freeholders of the said town of　　　, to meet at the house of O. P., in said town, on the　　　day of　　　instant, at　　　o'clock in the　　　noon, to inquire whether any encroachment has been made, and by whom, on the highway running by [*or, through*] the land now occupied by C. D., in said town: and to give at least three days' notice to E. F., the Commissioner of Highways of said town, and to C. D., of the time and place at which the said freeholders are to meet; and have you then there the names of the freeholders summoned by you, and this precept.

Given under my hand, this　　　day of　　　, 18　.

G. H., Justice of the Peace.

---

§ 566. *Oath to Jurors.*

You, and each of you, do solemnly swear, that you will well and truly inquire whether any encroachment has been made, and by whom, on the highway now in question.

---

§ 567. *Oath of Witness.*

You do swear, that the evidence you shall give in relation to the encroachment on the highway now in question, shall be the truth, the whole truth, and nothing but the truth.

---

§ 568. *Certificate of Jury.*

County, ⎱
Town of ⎰ ss:

We, the subscribers, freeholders of said town, having been summoned and assembled, on the day of the date hereof, at the house of R. P., in said town, pursuant to a precept issued by G. H., Esq., a Justice of the Peace of the said town, and having been duly sworn by said Justice, on the application of E. F., the Commissioner of Highways of said town, to inquire whether any such encroachment

---

[1] The time specified in the precept for the meeting of the freeholders must not be less than four days after issuing the same.

on the public highway in said town, as is specified in the order of said Commissioner, dated the   day of   last, [or, instant,] has been made, and by whom; and having heard the proofs and allegations produced and submitted, do certify,* that such encroachment has been made by C. D., the present occupant, [or, R. F., the former occupant.]

And we hereby certify, that the particulars of such encroachment are as follows, to wit: That said encroachment commences on the north line of said road, at [insert a description,] and that the rail fence along the land now in the occupation of the said C. D., is upon the public highway, and is an encroachment thereon.

In witness whereof, we have hereunto subscribed our names, this   day of   , 18 .   G. H.
                                                                    &c:, &c.

---

§ 569. *Certificate where no Encroachment is found.*

County, }
Town of   , } ss:

We, the subscribers, &c., [as in § 568 to the *, and then add:] that no such encroachment has been made on the said highway; and we have ascertained and do certify the damages of C. D., the occupant of the land through [or, by] which the said highway runs, by reason of the said Commissioner's proceedings against him, to be   dollars.

In witness, &c., [as in § 568.]

---

§ 570. *Warrant to Collect Costs of Proceedings upon an Encroachment.*[1]

The People of the State of New York to any Constable of the Town of   , in the County of   :

Whereas, E. F.. the Commissioner of Highways of the said town, did, on the   day of   , 18 , make and subscribe an order or certificate for the removal of a certain fence, as an encroachment upon the highway running through land in the said town, in the occupation of C. D., specifying the breadth of the road, and the extent and place of the encroachment: which said encroachment, having been denied by said occupant, a jury of twelve freeholders was, upon the application of said Commissioner, by a precept issued by me, duly summoned to inquire into the premises; and the said jury being duly

---

[1] The warrant is to be issued in ten days after the finding of the jury, provided the costs are not sooner paid.

assembled and sworn, after due notice to said occupant, as required by law, and having heard the proofs and allegations produced and submitted by the parties respectively, certified in writing, that an encroachment had been made by C. D., the occupant of said land: And whereas, the costs of said inquiry amount to　　　dollars and cents, which remain unpaid: you are, therefore, commanded to levy the said costs of the goods and chattels of the said C. D., and bring the same before me without delay.

Witness my hand and seal, the　　　day of　　　, 18　.

G. H., Justice. [L. s.]

---

§ 571. *Order of Commissioners of Adjoining Towns for Laying out a Highway on the Line between the Towns.*

County, ss:

At a meeting of the Commissioners of Highways of the towns of　　and　　　　, in said county of　　　, held in said town of　　　, on this　　　day of　　　, 18　, for the purpose of laying out a highway upon the line between the said towns: It is ordered and determined by the said Commissioners, that a highway be laid out upon the line between the said towns, according to a survey thereof, which the said Commissioners have caused to be made, as follows: [*insert survey;*] and that the said line above described be the centre of the said highway, and that the said highway be of the width of　　rods: And it is further ordered, that the said highway be divided into two road districts, as follows: that part thereof from　　　to　　, shall be one of the said road districts, and shall be allotted to the town of　　　; and the residue of the said highway shall be the other of the said road districts, and shall be allotted to the town of　　.

In witness, whereof, the said Commissioners have hereunto subscribed their names, the　　　day of　　　, 18　.

E. F., Commissioner of Highways of the Town of　　　,
M. P., Commissioner of Highways of the Town of　　　.

---

§ 572. *Application for a Private Road.*

To E. F., the Commissioner of Highways of the Town of　　　, in the County of　　　:

I, A. B., the undersigned, a resident of said town, and liable to be assessed for highway labor, do hereby make application to you, the said Commissioner, to lay out a private road for my use, commencing

&c., [*insert a description of the road as applied for,*] and passing through the land of C. D., in said town.

Dated the　　　day of　　　, 18　.

A. B.

---

§ 573.　*Notice to the Occupant on an Application for a Private Road.*[1]

To C. D., of the Town of　　　, in the County of　　　:

Take notice, that I have applied to E. F., Commissioner of Highways of said town, to lay out a private road for my use through your land [*or, through land of which you are the occupant;*] and that twelve disinterested freeholders will meet on the　　　day of instant, [*or, next,*] at ten o'clock in the forenoon of that day, at the house of R. F., in said town, to view the lands through which the road is applied for; to determine whether the same be necesssary, according to the statute; and to assess the damages.

Dated, &c., [*as in* § 572.]

A. B.

---

§ 574. *Notice to the Town Clerk requiring a Jury to be drawn, to Re-assess the Damages for Laying Out or Altering a Private Road.*

To C. D., Town Clerk of the town of　　　:

Take notice, that I am dissatisfied with the assessment of damages made by the jury of freeholders called and sworn to certify and determine with regard to the necessity and propriety of laying out [*or, altering*] a private road through the land of M. B., in said town, whose certificate, dated on the　　　day of　　　, 18　, is now on file in your office; and that I require you to draw a jury, in accordance with the statute in such case made and provided, on the　　　day of　　　instant, [*or, next,*] at　　　o'clock in the noon of that day, to re-assess the said damages.

Dated the　　　day of　　　, 18　.

E. F., Commissioner of Highways of said town of　　　.

---

[1] The remaining forms necessary in this proceeding, may be prepared from those given in other cases. The freeholders are to be sworn, &c., in the same manner as upon an application to lay out a public road. 1 R. S. (3d ed.) 632, § 93, at seq. The amount of the damages sustained by the opening of a private road, as fixed by the jury, together with the expenses of the proceeding, must be paid by the person to be benefited. Amended Constitution, Art. i, § 7. The Commissioner should make an order establishing the road, in accordance with the certificate of the freeholders, unless he is dissatisfied with the assessment of the damages, in which case he must give the notice to the Town Clerk requiring a jury to be drawn.

§ 575. *Notice to Persons Interested that a Jury will be drawn to Re-assess the Damages.*[1]

To A. B.:

Take notice, that a jury will be drawn by C. D., Town Clerk of he town of   , at his office in said town, on the   day of   instant, [*or*, next,] at   o'clock in the   noon of that day, to re-assess the damages for laying out [*or*, altering] a private road through the land of M. B., in said town, heretofore assessed by a jury of freeholders, to wit, on the   day of   instant, [*or* last past.]

Dated, &c., [*as in* § 574.]   .

---

1 The other forms necessary in this proceeding, may be prepared from those heretofore given in other cases of re-assessments. The jury is to be drawn by the Town Clerk of the town in which the private road is situated, from the jury list of such town; but, in all other respects, the proceedings are to be conducted in the same manner as if it were a question concerning a public road.

CHAPTER XXIII.

HUSBAND AND WIFE.

PRACTICAL REMARKS.

1. Marriage is regarded in law as a civil contract, to which the consent of parties capable of contracting, is essential. From the nature of this contract, it exists during the lives of the two parties, unless dissolved from causes which defeat the marriage, or from relations imposing duties repugnant to matrimonial rights and obligations.[1]

2. The age of consent to marriage, by the civil, as well as the common law, is fixed at fourteen in males, and twelve in females. In the State of Ohio, the age of consent fixed by statute is eighteen in males, and fourteen in females; and in Massachusetts, it is seventeen in males, and fourteen in females.[2]

3. No peculiar ceremonies are requisite, by the common law, to the valid celebration of marriage; the essence of the contract being the consent of the parties, that alone is required. It is not necessary that a clergyman should be present to give validity to a marriage: the consent of the parties may be declared before a magistrate, or simply before witnesses, — or subsequently confessed or acknowledged; or the marriage may be inferred from continual cohabitation, and reputation as husband and wife, except in cases of civil actions for adultery, and in public prosecutions for bigamy.[3]

4. In Maine, Massachusetts and Connecticut, it is required by statute, that there be a publication of bans previous to the marriage; that it be solemnized by a clergyman, or magistrate; and if the male is under twenty-one, or the female under eighteen, the consent of

---

[1] 2 R. S. (3d ed.) 199, § 1; 2 Kent's Commentaries, (2d ed.) 75, et seq; 4 Johnson, 52; 18 Id., 816; 20 Id., 1; 7 Wendell, 47; 1 Hopkins, 498.

[2] 2 Kent's Commentaries, (2d ed.) 78.
[3] 2 Kent's Commentaries (2d ed.) 86, 87; 4 Johnson, 52; 1 Hill, 270.

the parents or guardians must be given. In the State of New York, if the female be under the age of fourteen, the consent of the father, mother, or guardian, is required. Similar legislative regulations exist in New Hampshire, New Jersey, Kentucky, and other States. The most eminent jurists, however, concur in the opinion, that a marriage made according to the common law, without observing any of the statute regulations, would be valid.[1]

5. For the purpose of being registered and authenticated, according to the provisions of the Revised Statutes of this State, marriages are to be solemnized only by the following persons: ministers of the gospel, and priests of every denomination; Mayors, Recorders and Aldermen, of cities; County Judges, and Justices of the Peace. It is the duty of clergymen, magistrates, and other persons who perform the marriage ceremony, to keep a registry of the marriages celebrated by them; and to ascertain, as far as practicable, and note in such registry, the ages of the persons married, and the time thereof, and their places of birth and their residences. It is also their duty, to allow the clerks of the school districts, within which they respectively reside, to inspect such registries, from time to time, and to furnish them such other information in their power as may be necessary to enable them to make the returns required by law. Clergymen and other persons solemnizing marriages, are also required to ascertain that the parties are of sufficient age to contract marriage, and the names and places of residence of two of the attesting witnesses, if more than one be present, and if not, then the name and place of residence of such witness, which facts are, in like manner, to be recorded in their registry of marriages.[2]

6. Whenever a marriage is solemnized, pursuant to the foregoing provisions, the minister, or magistrate, is required to furnish to either party, on request, a certificate thereof, specifying the names and places of residence of the parties married, and that they were known to such minister or magistrate, or were satisfactorily proved, by the oath of a person known to him, to be the persons described in such certificate, and that he had ascertained they were of sufficient age to contract marriage; the name and place of residence of the attesting witness or witnesses; the time and place of such marriage; and that after due inquiry made, there appeared no lawful impediment to such marriage.[3]

7. Every such certificate, signed by a magistrate, if presented to the Clerk of the city or town where the marriage was solemnized, or to the Clerk of the city or town where either of the parties reside, within six months after such marriage, must be filed by such Clerk,

---

[1] 2 Kent's Commentaries, (2d ed.) 90, 91; Laws of 1841, chap. 257.

[2] 2 R. S. (3d ed.) 199, 200, §§ 7-9; Laws of 1847, chap. 152.

[3] 2 R. S. (3d ed.) 200, § 12.

and entered in a book to be provided by him, in the alphabetical order of the names of both the parties, and in the order of time in which such certificate may be filed. A certificate signed by a minister may also be filed and recorded, in like manner, if there be endorsed thereon, or annexed thereto, a certificate of any magistrate residing in the same county with such Clerk, setting forth that the minister by whom such certificate is signed, is personally known to such magistrate, or has acknowledged the execution of the certificate in his presence; or that the execution thereof was proved to such magistrate, by the oath of a person known to him, and who saw the certificate executed. The entry of every such certificate, made by the Clerk, must specify the names and places of residence of the persons married; the time and place of marriage; the name and official station of the person signing the certificate; and the time of filing of the same.[1]

8. Every such original certificate, the original entry thereof, made as above directed, and a copy of such certificate, or of such entry, duly certified, will be received in all courts and places, as presumptive evidence of the fact of the marriage.[2]

9. It is the duty of Clerks of school districts, or, in case of their incapacity or a vacancy in the office, of the Trustees, or one of them, to ascertain, as far as practicable, and report in writing to the Town Clerk, of their town, or Alderman of their ward, on or before the fifteenth day of January in each year, the number of marriages which have occurred in their respective districts during the year preceding the first day of January; the month and day of their occurrence; the names, ages, and residences of the parties; and the names and residences of the officers and clergymen by whom the same were solemnized. The Town Clerks and Aldermen are required, within fifteen days after receiving such reports, to record the same in a book, and transmit a copy thereof, or an abstract, as the Secretary of State may prescribe, to the County Clerks or City Inspectors of their respective counties or cities. In the city of New York, the reports are to be made direct to the City Inspector, instead of through the Aldermen. County Clerks and City Inspectors are to forward an abstract of the reports, within fifteen days after receiving the same, to the Secretary of State, who is required to make a complete abstract, and transmit it to the Legislature, as soon as practicable.[3]

10. The recording of marriage certificates is discretionary with the parties; the registry, however, is obligatory upon all persons performing the ceremony.

---

[1] 2 R. S. (3d ed.) 200, 201, §§ 13–15.
[2] 2 R. S. (3d ed.) 201, § 16.
[3] Laws of 1847, chap. 152.

11. Marriage is not only a *bona fide* and valuable consideration, but the very highest known in law; and marriage settlements and agreements, entered into before marriage, are greatly favored, and will be enforced even as against creditors.[1]

12. By the statute law of New York, all contracts made between persons in contemplation of marriage, remain in full force after the marriage takes place.[2]

13. A settlement after marriage, in pursuance of a prior written agreement, is good against creditors; otherwise, if made in pursuance of a parol agreement.[3]

14. A wife may contract with her husband after marriage, for a transfer of property from him to her, or to trustees for her, provided it be for a *bona fide* or valuable consideration. A voluntary separation by husband and wife, and an agreement by deed, executed by them and a trustee, for the payment of an allowance for her separate maintenance, and containing a covenant of indemnity against debts contracted by her, is valid; although it is well settled by the decisions of our own, and of the English courts, that the rights of the husband cannot be destroyed, nor the disabilities of the wife removed, by such agreement.[4]

15. A wife may make a conveyance to her husband, through a third person.[5]

16. Where a wife leaves her husband without just cause, he is not answerable for her support; but if she offer to return, and he refuse to receive her, his liability is revived.[6]

17. The real and personal property of a married woman, in the State of New York, and the rents, issues, and profits thereof, are not subject to the disposal of her husband, but are her sole and separate property,—except the same be liable for debts contracted by her husband prior to the seventh day of April, 1848, where the marriage was solemnized previous to that day.[7]

18. A married woman, in the State of New York, may receive real or personal property, by gift, grant, devise, or bequest, from any person other than her husband, and hold the same, and the rents, issues, and profits thereof, to her sole and separate use, and convey and devise the same, in the same manner, and with the like effect, as if she were unmarried; the same being neither subject to the disposal of her husband, nor liable for his debts.[8]

---

[1] Laws of 1848, chap. 200; 2 Kents' Commentaries, (2d. ed.) 162, et seq.; 1 Johnson's Ch. Rep., 108, 450; 3 Id., 77, 550; 7 Id., 229; 17 Johnson, 548; 6 Paige, 111, 513.
[2] Laws of 1849, chap. 375.
[3] 3 Johnson's Ch. Rep., 481; 3 Paige, 240, 440.
[4] 2 Kent's Commentaries, (2d. ed.) 166, et seq., 2 Johnson's Ch. Rep., 537; 8 Paige, 67;
2 Wendell, 422; 25 Id., 64; 2 Hill, 260; 3 Id., 399, and authorities there cited.
[5] 2 Barbour's Ch. Rep., 232.
[6] 4 Denio, 46.
[7] Laws of 1848, chap. 200; Laws of 1849, chap. 375.
[8] Laws of 1848, chap. 200; Laws of 1849, chap. 375.

21

19. Where deposits are made by a married woman, or by a single female, afterwards becoming a married woman, in her own name, in any savings' bank or institution, in the State of New York, the same may be paid to her, and her receipt or acquittance, will be a sufficient legal discharge to the corporation.[1]

FORMS.

§ 576. *Short Form of Marriage, for Magistrates.*

The officer performing the ceremony will direct the parties to join hands, and then say: " By this act of joining hands, you do take upon yourselves the relation of husband and wife, and solemnly promise and engage, in the presence of these witnesses, to love and honor, comfort and cherish each other, as such, so long as you both shall live: Therefore, in accordance with the laws of the State of New York, I do hereby pronounce you husband and wife."

§ 577. *Marriage Certificate.*

County, } ss:
Town of , }

I do hereby certify, that on the   day of   instant, [*or*, last past,] at the house of R. F. [*or*,   church,] in said town of   , A. B., of, &c., and E. D., of, &c., were, with their mutual consent, lawfully joined together in holy matrimony, which was solemnized by me, in the presence of M. P., of, &c., and R. F., of, &c., attesting witnesses: And I do further certify, that the said A. B. and E. D. are known to me, [*or*, were satisfactorily proved, by the oath of R. F., known to me,] to be the persons described in this certificate; that I ascertained, previous to the solemnization of the said marriage, that the said parties were of sufficient age to contract the same; and that, after due inquiry by me made, there appeared no lawful impediment to such marriage.

Given under my hand, this   day of   , 18 .
        G. H., Rector of, &c., [*or*, Justice, &c.]

_____

[1] Laws of 1850, chap. 91.

§ 578. *Magistrate's Certificate.*

County, $\big\}$ ss
Town of : $\big\}$

I do hereby certify, that G. H., Rector of, &c., by whom the foregoing [*or*, annexed; *or*, within,] certificate is signed, is personally known to me, and has acknowledged the execution of said certificate in my presence, this   day of   , 18   : [*or*, that on the   day of   , 18   , personally came before me, M. P., to me known, who being by me duly sworn, did depose and say, that he was well acquainted with G. H., Rector of, &c., and knew him to be the same person who executed the foregoing [*or*, annexed; *or*, within] certificate; and that he was present and saw the said G. H., execute the same.]

S. T., Justice, &c.

§ 579. *Oath to Witness Proving Identity of Parties.*

You do solemnly swear, that you will true answers make to all such questions as shall be put to you, touching the identity of A. B. and E. D., here present.

§ 580. *Oath to Witness Proving Certificate.*

You do solemnly swear, that you will true answers make to all such questions as shall be put to you, touching the execution of this certificate.

§ 581. *Marriage Articles.*

This indenture of three parts, made, &c., between A. B., of, &c., of the first part, E. D., of, &c., daughter of, &c., of the second part, and C. D., of, &c., and E. F., of, &c., of the third part, witnesseth: That whereas, the said E. D. is seized in fee, of and in, certain lands and tenements, with their appurtenances, situate, lying and being, [*give the town, county, or state;*] And whereas, a marriage is shortly intended to be solemnized between the said A. B. and E. D., with whom the said A. B. is to have and receive   dollars in money, over and besides the lands, &c., above mentioned, as and for her marriage portion: Now, therefore, it is covenanted and agreed, by and between the said parties to these presents, as follows: *First*, the said A. B., for himself, his heirs, executors and administrators, doth covenant and agree, to and with the said C. D. and E. F., their heirs and assigns, that they, the said A. B., and E. D., his intended wifin case the said intended marriage shall be solemnized, by some good and sufficient conveyance, or conveyances, will settle and assure the aforesaid lands and tenements, with the appurtenances, whereof she, the said E. D., is seized as aforesaid, on and to the said C. D. and E. F., to the use and behoof of the said A. B., during the term of his natural life; and from and after the decease of the said A. B., then to the use and behoof of the said E. D., his intended wife, for and during the term of her natural life; and from and after her decease, then to the use and behoof of the heirs of the body of the said E. D., by the said A. B. lawfully to be begotten; and on the default of such issue, then to the use and behoof of the said E. D., her heirs and assigns forever, and to and for no other use, intent or purpose, whatsoever.

And, *secondly*, for as much as the said A. B. is not at present seized, or possessed, of any estate sufficient to make a jointure for the said E. D., equivalent to her fortune, the said A. B., doth for himself, his heirs, executors and administrators, covenant, grant and agree, to and with the said C. D. and E. F., their heirs and assigns, that in case the said intended marriage shall take effect, he, the said A. B., shall and will, by his last will and testament, in writing or otherwise, give and assure unto the said E. D. the sum of dollars, of lawful money of the United States, to be by her received and taken, to her own proper use and benefit, in case she shall survive the said A. B.

In witness whereof, the said parties have hereunto set their hands and seals, the day and year above written.

Sealed, signed and delivered, ⎰   A. B.,   [L. S.]
     in presence of   ⎱   E. D.,   [L. S.]
          G. H.   &c., &c.,

––––––––––

§ 582. *Settlement of an Estate, in Contemplation of Marriage.*

This indenture of three parts, made, &c., between E. D., of, &c., of the first part, C. D., of, &c., of the second part, and A. B., of, &c., of the third part, witnesseth: That whereas, a marriage is intended to be solemnized between the said parties of the first and third parts, and the said E. D. is possessed of certain personal estate, to wit: the sum of   dollars, which is now deposited in the bank, in the city of   , and   shares of the capital stock of the ·   insurance company in   : Now, therefore, in consideration of the premises, and of one dollar paid by the said C. D. to the said E. D., the receipt whereof is hereby acknowledged, the said E. D. doth hereby assign, transfer and set over, to the said C. D., and his executors and administrators, all the moneys, property and effects, above mentioned, to hold the same to him the said C. D., and his executors and administrators, upon the special trusts and for the uses and purposes following, to wit:

First, That until the solemnization of the said marriage, the said C. D. shall pay over to the said E. D., or shall empower her to receive for her own use, all the income, profits and dividends, arising from the said monies and effects, and from any other estate which may be substituted therefor, as is hereinafter provided.

Second, That from and after the solemnization of the said marriage, and during the coverture of the said E., the said C. D. shall receive and collect the income, profits and dividends, of the said trust moneys and effects, or of any other substituted estate, so often and whenever the same shall be payable; and, after deducting all individual expenses, shall pay over the same, or so much thereof as she shall not direct to be added to the principal for the purpose of accumulation, to the said E., upon her sole and separate receipt therefor, and free from the control or interference of her said husband, or any other person whomsoever.

Third, That in case of the decease of the said E., after the solemnization of the said marriage, and during the life of her said husband, the said money and effects shall be transferred and paid over by the said trustee, to such person or persons, as she, the said E., by an instrument or note in writing, subscribed by her in the presence of at least two competent witnesses, shall order and appoint to receive the same; and in default of her making such appointment, the same shall be transferred and paid to the said A. B.; and in case of his decease before the said property shall be actually transferred and paid over to him, then to such person or persons as would be the legal representatives of the said E., by the statute for the distribution of intestate estates.

Fourth, That in the event of the decease of the said A. B., during the lifetime of the said E., all the property then held in trust under this indenture, shall be transferred and conveyed back to the said E.; and until so transferred the trustee shall pay over to her, or empower her to receive, the income, profits and dividends of the same, for her own use.

Fifth, That the said trustee shall have power, with the approbation, or at the request of the said E., expressed in writing, to sell and dispose of the said trust estate, or any part of it, and the proceeds to invest in other personal or real estate, according to the written direction of the said E.; and the estate so purchased shall be had and held by the trustees, upon the same trusts, and for the same uses and purposes as aforesaid.

Sixth, That in case of the decease of the party of the second part, or of his resignation of said trust, he, or his executors or administrators, shall convey, transfer and pay over. the whole of the trust estate then held by him, to such person, or persons, as may be appointed in writing by the party of the first part, to be the trustee, or trustees, under this indenture; and such new trustee, or trustees, shall have all the powers, and shall hold the trust estate subject to all the provisions, herein set forth and expressed; and the receipt of such new trustee, or trustees, for the trust property, shall be a complete acquittance and discharge to the said party of the second part, his executors and administrators; and, in like manner, other new trustees may be appointed from time to time, as occasion may require.

And the said party of the second part doth hereby signify his acceptance of the said moneys and effects, and doth engage to hold and manage the same, upon the trusts, and for the uses herein mentioned.

And the said party of the third part doth hereby signify his assent to the provisions of this indenture, and doth covenant to and with the said party of the second part, and his successors in the said trust, to permit the said party of the first part, after the solemnization of the said intended marriage, to receive the aforesaid income, profits and dividends, to her sole and separate use, and freely to dispose of the trust estate, by her will, or by her testamentary appointment, and not to interfere with the said trust estate, otherwise than in conformity to the provisions of this indenture.

In witness, &c., [*as in* § 581.]

---

§ 583. *Agreement for Settlement before Marriage.*[1]

This agreement, made and entered into this   day of, &c., between A. B., of, &c., of the first part, and E. D., of, &c., of the second part, [*add the third party, if necessary,*] witnesseth: That whereas a marriage is about to be had and solemnized between the said parties; and the said party of the first part is desirous of making provision for a fit and proper settlement, to and for the use and benefit of the said E. D., his intended wife: Now, therefore, the said party of the first part doth hereby agree, that if the said marriage shall be had and solemnized as aforesaid, he shall or will, on or before the   day of   next, assign, transfer, and set over, unto C. D., of, &c., by good and sufficient transfers, assignments and conveyances,   shares of the capital stock of the   railroad company, now owned by and belonging to the said party of the first part; and also the sum of   · dollars in money; to have

---

[1] Special conditions and provisions may be inserted in the ante-nuptial agreement, extending the benefit of the trust to the children of the parties. See § 582.

and to hold the same unto the said C. D., to and for the sole and separate use and benefit of the said E., during the term of her natural life. And it is further agreed between the said parties, that in case the said C. D. shall refuse to accept the said trust, then the said shares of stock and money as aforesaid, shall be transferred, assigned and set over, unto such person as shall be nominated in writing by the said party of the second part, as such trustee, in the place and stead of the said C. D., to be held by him to and for the use and benefit of the said E., as aforesaid; and that the articles of settlement to be executed in pursuance hereof, shall contain a provision for the appointment of a trustee to fill any vacancy which may transpire, except as above provided, by the nomination in writing of the said party of the second part.

In witness, &c., [*as in* § 581.]

---

§ 584. *Jointure in Lieu of Dower.*

This indenture, made and entered into this   day of, &c., between A. B., of, &c., of the first part, E. D., of, &c., of the second part, and C. D., of, &c., of the third part, witnesseth: That the said A. B., in consideration of a marriage about to be had and solemnized between him, the said A. B., and the said E. D., does, for himself, his heirs and assigns, covenant, grant and agree, to and with the said C. D., his heirs and assigns, that he, the said A. B., his heirs and assigns, shall and will, forever hereafter, stand seized of and in a certain tract or parcel of land, with the appurtenances, situate in the town of   in the county of   , and State of New York, aforesaid, and bounded and described as follows, [*description:*] to the uses following, that is to say: to the use of the said A. B., for and during the term of his natural life, without impeachment of waste, and after his marriage with the said E. D., and after his decease, to her use, so long as she shall remain his widow and unmarried, [*or, during her natural life,*] without impeachment of waste, for her jointure, and in lieu and satisfaction of her whole dower in his estate; and after his decease, and the expiration of her estate, to the use of his heirs and assigns forever. And the said E. D., in consideration of the premises, and in consideration of the sum of one dollar, paid to her by the said A. B., does, for herself, her heirs, executors, and administrators, covenant and agree with the said A. B., that the lands so assigned to her shall be in full satisfaction of her dower in his estate, and shall bar her from claiming the same, if she shall survive, after said marriage; and further, if the said marriage shall be had, and she shall survive him, that she will not claim any share in his personal estate, unless some part thereof be given to her by his will, or some act done by him subsequent to the execution of these presents.

In witness, &c., [*as in* § 581.]

---

§ 585. *Articles of Separation.*

This indenture of three parts, made, &c., between A. B., of, &c., of the first part, and E. B., his wife, of the second part, and C. D., of, &c., of the third part, witnesseth: Whereas, divers unhappy disputes and differences have arisen, between the said party of the first part, and his said wife, for which reason they have consented and agreed to live separate and apart from each other during their natural life: Now, therefore, the said party of the first part, in consideration of the premises, and in pursuance thereof, doth hereby covenant, promise and agree, to and with the said C. D., and also to and with his said wife, that he shall and will allow and permit his said wife, E. B., to reside and be in such place and places, and in such family and families, as she may from time to time choose, or think fit to do; and that he shall not, nor will, at any time sue, molest, disturb, or trouble any person whomsoever, for receiving, entertaining or harboring her; and that he will not claim, or demand, any of her money, jewels, plate, clothing, household goods, or furniture, which the said E. B. now hath in her power, custody, or possession, or which she shall or may at any time hereafter have, or which shall be devised or given to her, or that she may otherwise acquire; and further, that the said party of the first part shall and will well and truly pay, or cause to be paid, unto the said C. D., for and towards the support and maintenance of his wife, the said E. B., the yearly sum of   dollars, free and clear of all charges and deductions whatsoever, for and during her natural life, payable quarterly, at or upon the first day of January, April, July, and October, in each and every year during her said natural life; which the said C. D. doth agree to take, in full satisfaction for her support and maintenance, and all alimony whatever. And the said C. D., in consideration of the sum of one dollar, to him duly paid by the said A. B., doth covenant and agree, to and with the said party of the first part, to indemnify and bear him harmless, of and from all debts of his said wife, E. B., now contracted, or that may hereafter be contracted by her, or on her account; and if the said party of the first part shall be compelled to pay any such debt or debts, the said C. D. hereby agrees to repay the same, on demand, to the said party of the first part, with all damages and loss that he may sustain thereby.

In witness, &c., [*as in* § 581.]

CHAPTER XXIV

HOMESTEAD EXEMPTION LAW.

PRACTICAL REMARKS.

1. In the State of New York, the lot and buildings thereon, occupied as a residence and owned by a debtor, being a householder and having a family, to the value of one thousand dollars, will be exempt from sale on execution after the first day of January, 1851, for debts contracted subsequent to the tenth day of April, 1850. This exemption is to continue after the death of the householder, for the benefit of the widow and family,—some, or one of them continuing to occupy such homestead,—until the youngest becomes of age, and until the death of the widow. No release or waiver of such exemption will be valid, unless the same be in writing, subscribed by the householder, and acknowledged in the same manner as conveyances of real estate are required to be acknowledged.

2. To entitle any property to this exemption, the conveyance thereof must show that it is designed to be held as a homestead, or if already purchased, or if the conveyance does not show the design a notice that the same is designed to be so held, and containing a full description thereof, must be executed and acknowledged by the person owning the property, and recorded in the office of the clerk of the county in which the same is situate.

3. This exemption will not extend to sales for the non-payment of taxes or assessments, or for a debt contracted for the purchase money, or prior to the recording of the deed or notice.

4. Where the premises claimed to be exempt as aforesaid, are worth more than one thousand dollars, in the opinion of a Sheriff holding an execution against the householder, it will be the duty of the former to summon six qualified jurors of his county, who shall upon oath, to be administered by him, appraise the said premises. If the jury are of opinion that the property may be divided without injury to the interests of the parties, they must set off so much

thereof, including the dwelling house, as, in their opinion, will be worth one thousand dollars, and the residue may be sold by the Sheriff in the same manner as other real property not so exempt. If the jury are of opinion that the property cannot be divided as aforesaid, and that the same is worth more than one thousand dollars, they must make and sign an appraisal of the value thereof, and deliver the same to the Sheriff, who will deliver a copy thereof to the execution debtor, or to some of his family of suitable age to understand the nature thereof, with a notice thereto attached, as in the form hereinafter given.[1]

FORMS.

§ 586. *Clause to be Inserted in a Deed of the Property designed to be Exempt.*

The premises above described and hereby conveyed, are designed to be held as a homestead, exempt from sale on execution, according to the provisions of the act entitled "An Act to Exempt from Sale on Execution, the Homestead of a Householder having a Family."—passed April 10, 1850.

§ 587. *Notice to the County Clerk of design to hold a Homestead Exempt, and Acknowledgment.*

To E. B. C., Esquire,
       County Clerk of   County:

Sir: You will please take notice, that I design to hold as a homestead exempt from sale on execution, according to the provisions of the act entitled "An Act to Exempt from Sale on Execution the Homestead of a Householder having a Family."—passed April 10, 1850,—

---

[1] Laws of 1850, chap. 260.

the following described property and premises, to wit: [*Describe the premises in full, in the same manner as in a deed.*]

Dated the   day of   , 18   .

Yours, &c.

A. B.

County, ss :[1]

On this   day of   , in the year one thousand eight hundred and fifty-one, before me personally came A. B., to me known to be the individual who executed the above notice, and acknowledged that he executed the same for the purpose therein mentioned.

W. W., Justice of the Peace in and for said county of   .

---

§ 588. *Release or Waiver of the Exemption.*

In consideration of the sum of one dollar to me in hand paid by C. D., of the town of   , in the county of   , and state of New York, the receipt whereof is hereby acknowledged, I do hereby release and waive any and all benefit of the act entitled "An Act to Exempt from Sale on Execution the Homestead of a Householder having a Family,"— passed April 10, 1850 — so that any property held by me as exempt under or by virtue thereof may be levied upon and sold on any execution issued against me for any demand owing to the aforesaid C. D.

Witness my hand, this   day of   , 18   .

A. B.

[*Add Certificate of Acknowledgment, as in § 587.*]

---

§ 589. *Oath to Jurors.*

You, and each of you, do solemnly swear, that you will well and truly perform the duties of a juror, in regard to the matters submitted to your consideration, according to the act entitled "An Act to Exempt from Sale on Execution the Homestead of a Householder having a Family,"— passed April 10, 1850.

---

[1] For other forms of acknowledgment, see Chapter I.

§ 590. *Certificate of Jurors setting off a Portion of the Premises.*

Supreme Court,

A. B.
against } County, County, ss:
C. D.

We, the undersigned jurors, summoned by the sheriff of said county, who holds an execution against C. D., the defendant in the above entitled cause, in pursuance of the act entitled "An Act to Exempt from Sale on Execution the Homestead of a Householder having a Family," — passed April 10, 1850,— do hereby certify, that we have examined the following described premises situate in the town of   , in said county, to wit: [*insert here a description of the premises:*] which said premises are owned by C. D. aforesaid, and are claimed by him to be exempt from sale on execution according to the act aforesaid, and that in our opinion the said premises* are worth   thousand dollars, and may be divided without injury to the interests of the parties concerned therein: And we do hereby set off to the said A. B., the following described portion of the said premises, to wit: [*describe the same :*] which last mentioned piece or parcel of land, including the dwelling house thereon, and the appurtenances belonging thereto, is, in our opinion, worth   thousand dollars.

Dated   , the   day of   18   .

E. F.,
G. H., } Jurors.
&c.,&c.,

---

§ 591. *Certificate that Property cannot be divided.*

Supreme Court,

A. B.
against }   County, ss:
C. D.

We, the undersigned jurors, &c., [*as in* § 590 *to the* *, *and then add:*] are worth more than one thousand dollars, and cannot be divided without injury to the interests of the parties concerned therein And we do hereby appraise the value of the said premises at   thousand dollars.

Dated, &c., [*as in* § 590.]

§ 592. *Notice of Sheriff to be Attached to the Copy of* § 591, *and Served on the Debtor.*

Supreme Court,
    A. B.
    against
    C. D.

Sir: You will please take notice that the foregoing is a copy of the certificate of appraisal this day made by the jurors, by me summoned as in said certificate mentioned; and that, unless the surplus of the value of the premises described in said certificate, as appraised by said jurors, over and above one thousand dollars, be paid to me within sixty days from the date of the service of this notice, the said premises will be sold, by virtue of an execution issued against you in the above entitled cause.[1]

Dated the   day of   , 18   .

                Yours, &c.,
                    R. T., Sheriff of   County.

To Mr. C. D.

---

[1] If the surplus is not paid within sixty days, the sheriff may advertise and sell the premises, as in other cases; and out of the proceeds of the sale, he must pay the execution debtor one thousand dollars, which will be exempt from execution for one year thereafter, and apply the balance on the execution. The costs, and charges of the sheriff, must be deducted from such balance.

CHAPTER XXV.

JUSTICES' COURTS

PRACTICAL REMARKS.

1. There are but two kinds of actions in the Courts of Justice of this State, whether of record or otherwise, viz: *civil* and *criminal* actions.[1]

2. Justices of the Peace have civil jurisdiction in the following actions, and no other:

1. An action arising on contract, for the recovery of money only, if the sum claimed does not exceed one hundred dollars;

2. An action for damages for an injury to the person or to real property, or for taking, detaining, or injuring, personal property, if the damages claimed do not exceed one hundred dollars;

3. An action for a penalty, not exceeding one hundred dollars, given by statute;

4. An action commenced by attachment of property, as hereinafter specified;

5 An action upon a bond, conditioned for the payment of money, not exceeding one hundred dollars, though the penalty exceed that sum; the judgment to be given for the sum actually due. Where the payments are to be made by instalments, an action may be brought for each instalment, as it shall become due;

6. An action upon a surety bond taken by them, though the penalty or amount claimed exceed one hundred dollars;

7. An action on a judgment rendered in a court of a Justice of the Peace, or of a Justice's or other inferior court, in a city; but no action can be brought on a judgment rendered by a Justice of the Peace, in the same county, within five years after its rendition, except in case of his death, resignation, incapacity to act, or removal from the county,— or that the process in the original action was not personally served on the defendant, or on all the defendants,— or in case of the death of some of

---

[1] Laws of 1849, chap. 438, (Code of Procedure,) § 4

the parties,— or where the docket or record of the judgment has been lost or destroyed.[1]

3. Justices may also take and enter judgment, on the confession of a defendant, where the amount confessed does not exceed two hundred and fifty dollars.[2]

4. No Justice of the Peace has cognizance, however, of a civil action in which the People of this State are a party, except for penalties not exceeding one hundred dollars; nor of an action in which the title to real estate comes in question; nor of a civil action for an assault, battery, false imprisonment, libel, slander, malicious prosecution, criminal conversation, or seduction; nor of a matter of account, where the sum total of the accounts of both parties, proved to the satisfaction of the Justice, exceeds four hundred dollars; nor of an action against an Executor or Administrator, as such.[3]

5. Civil actions may be commenced in Justices' Courts, either by the voluntary appearance of the parties, or by process. There are three different forms of process — summons, warrant, and attachment. Where a suit is instituted without process, it will be deemed to have been commenced at the time of joining the issue: if a summons or attachment be issued, the suit will be deemed commenced on the day when the process is delivered to the Constable; if the process be a warrant, the suit will be deemed commenced at the time of the arrest of the defendant.[4]

6. There are two kinds of process by summons, generally distinguished as a *long summons* and a *short summons*. A *long* summons is the usual process against all persons residing in the county where it issues; and it is the only one which can issue, *of course*, in any case, against a freeholder, or an inhabitant of any county having a family. A *short* summons is the proper form of process to be issued in favor of a non-resident plaintiff, suing as such, when the defendant cannot be arrested under the provisions of the non-imprisonment act; and it is the only process, except an attachment, which can be issued, in similar cases, against a non-resident defendant. Any other process would be void. But where there are joint debtors, one or more of whom reside in the county, suit may be commenced against them by *long* summons.[5]

7. Warrants may be issued in actions for injuries to the person, rights, or property of another; or for taking or detaining personal property; or for the recovery of money collected by a public officer, for official misconduct or neglect of duty; or misconduct or neglect

---

[1] Laws of 1849, ch. 438, (Code of Procedure) Part I. title vi., § 53; Id., Part II. title i. § 71.
[2] Laws of 1849, chap. 439, (Code of Procedure,) Part I., title vi., § 53, sub. 8; 2 R. S. (3d ed.) 342, §§ 114-116; 9 Wendell, 569.
[3] Laws of 1849, chap. 438, (Code of Procedure,) Part I., title vi., § 54.

[4] 2 R. S. (3d ed.) 325, § 12, 13.
[5] 2 R. S. (3d ed.) 326, 327, § 14 et seq.; Laws of 1831, chap. 300, §§ 30-33; 15 Wendell, 652; 16 Id., 35; 17 Id., 617; 3 Hill, 323; 5 Id., 186; 6 Id., 631; 1 Denio 175 2 Id., 95.

in any professional employment; subject, however, to the provisions of the statute which restrict the use of this process to the following cases, viz: Where the defendant is a non-resident; where it appears to the satisfaction of the Justice, by the affidavit of the applicant, or of any other witness, that the person against whom the warrant is desired, is about to depart from the county, with intent not to return thereto; where the defendant is an inhabitant of the county, having a family, or a freeholder of the same county, and it shall in like manner appear to the satisfaction of the Justice, that the plaintiff will be in danger of losing his demand, unless such warrant be granted; where the plaintiff is a non-resident, and tenders to the Justice security for the payment of any sum which may be adjudged against him in the suit; and at the option of the Justice, against a resident defendant, not a freeholder, nor an inhabitant having a family; or against a defendant upon whom a summons shall have been served, only by leaving a copy, or in any other way than by reading or delivering a copy to him personally, and who shall not have appeared at the time and place appointed in such summons, nor shown good cause for not appearing.[1]

8. There are two kinds of attachments, *long* and *short*. The latter issues against a non-resident defendant, and may be had when a short summons is also a proper process; and either may be taken, at the option of the party. No affidavit is necessary on an application for a short attachment. A *long* attachment issues, when it is made to appear to the satisfaction of the Justice to whom application is made, that the debtor has departed, or is about to depart, from the county where he last resided, with intent to defraud his creditors, or to avoid the service of civil process; or that such debtor keeps himself concealed, with the like intent; the same process issues, under the non-imprisonment act, when the Justice is satisfied that the defendant is about to remove from the county some of his property, with intent to defraud his creditors, or that he has assigned, disposed of, secreted, or is about to assign, dispose of, or secrete, any of his property, with the like intent. The Revised Statutes limit the nature of demands, for which attachments may be sued out, to those existing against the debtor *personally*, whether liquidated or not, arising upon contract, or upon judgments rendered *within this State*. The non-imprisonment act extends the process to suits for the recovery of any debt or damages arising upon contract, express or implied, or upon any judgment, whether rendered in this State or not. The demand, however, must be against the debtor *personally*. In all cases, the facts and circumstances relied on as the foundation for the issuing of an attachment must be set forth distinctly in the affidavit accom-

---

[1] 2 R. S. (3d ed.) 327, 328, §§ 18–23; Laws of 1831, chap. 300; Laws of 1840, chap. 165; Id., chap. 377; 2 Cowen, 429; 3 Wendell, 389; 7 Id., 434; 13 Id., 48; 15 Id., 654; 16 Id., 35; 17 Id., 51; 2 Hill, 296; 1 Denio, 176

panying the application. The only material difference between the proceedings on attachments issued under the statute, and those issued under the non-imprisonment act, subsequent to the issuing of the process, is, that in the latter case, where property is attached, and a copy of the inventory and attachment is not personally served, and the defendant does not appear, the plaintiff may take a short summons; and if the defendant be personally served therewith, or cannot be found after diligent inquiry, the Justice may proceed to hear and determine the cause in the same manner as upon a summons personally served.[1]

9. An affidavit for an attachment, stating facts and circumstances, on belief only, is fatally defective; but if the party swears he has been informed of the facts set forth, the affidavit will be sufficient.[2]

10. On an attachment against joint debtors, a Justice cannot render judgment, where one only of the defendants has been served with the process. The proceeding must be dismissed, or a summons issued.[3]

11. When the name of any defendant sued in a Justices' Court, is not known to the plaintiff, he may be described in a summons, or warrant, by a fictitious name; and if a plea in abatement be interposed by such defendant, the Justice before whom the suit is pending may amend the proceedings, according to the truth of the matter, and proceed in the cause, in like manner as if the defendant had been sued by his right name.[4]

12. It is no part of the official duty of a Justice to deliver a summons to a constable.[5]

13. Where a summons is returned served by copy, and another summons is issued, the suit will be legally continued, even in cases affected by the statute of limitations.[6]

14. The pleadings in courts of Justices of the Peace are—1, the complaint by the plaintiff; 2, the answer by the defendant. The pleadings may be oral, or in writing; if oral, the substance of them must be entered by the Justice in his docket; if in writing, they must be filed by him, and a reference made to them in the docket. The *complaint* must state, in a plain and direct manner, the facts constituting the cause of action. The *answer* may contain a denial of the complaint, or any part thereof, and notice, also, in a plain and direct manner, of any facts constituting a defence. Pleadings are not required to be in any particular form, but must be such as to enable

---

1 2 R. S. (3d ed.) 328, § 27 et seq.; Laws of 1831, chap. 300, § 34; Laws of 1842, chap. 107; 15 Johnson, 196; 3 Cowen, 206; 6 Id., 234; 10 Wendell, 420; 12 Id., 359; 13 Id., 46, 404; 14 Id., 237; 15 Id., 466, 479; 20 Id., 77, 146, 184; 23 Id., 336; 24 Id., 485,; 5 Hill, 264; 6 Id., 311; 1 Denio, 185.

2 4 Denio, 93.
3 2 Comstock, 112.
4 Laws of 1830, chap. 320.
5 3 Denio, 12.
6 3 Denio, 12.

a person of common understanding to know what is meant. Either party may demur to a pleading of his adversary, or any part thereof, when it is not sufficiently explicit to enable him to understand it, or it contains no cause of action or defence, although it be taken as true; if the court deem the objection well founded, it must order the pleading to be amended, and, if the party refuse to amend, the defective pleading must be disregarded. In an action or defence, founded upon an account, or an instrument for the payment of money only, it will be sufficient for a party to deliver the account or instrument to the court, and to state, that there is due to him thereon from the adverse party a specified sum, which he claims to recover or set off.[1]

15. A variance between the proof on the trial, and the allegations in a pleading, will be disregarded as immaterial, unless the court shall be satisfied that the adverse party has been misled to his prejudice thereby. The pleadings in a Justices' Court may be amended, at any time before the trial, or during the trial, or upon appeal, when, by such amendment, substantial justice will be promoted. If the amendment be made after the joining of the issue, and it be made to appear to the satisfaction of the court, by oath, that an adjournment is necessary to the adverse party in consequence of such amendment, an adjournment must be granted. The court may also, in its discretion, require as a condition of an amendment, the payment of costs to the adverse party, to be fixed by the court; but no amendment can be allowed after a witness is sworn on a trial, when no adjournment will be thereby made necessary.[2]

16. In case a defendant does not appear and answer, in an action before a Justice of the Peace, the plaintiff cannot recover without proving his case.[3]

17. At the joining of the issue, the court may require of either party, at the request of the other, to exhibit his account or demand, or state the nature thereof as definitely as may be in his power, at that or some other specified time; and in case of the default of the party, he will be precluded from giving evidence of such parts thereof as shall not have been so exhibited or stated.[4]

18. If the defendant do not appear on the return of a summons or attachment, the Justice before whom the suit is brought may adjourn the cause to a time certain, not exceeding eight days, on the simple motion of the plaintiff, without oath,—and so if the defendant appear and do not object; but the defendant may object, and require as a condition of the adjournment, that the plaintiff, or his attorney, make oath that he cannot, for want of some material testimony, or witness, safely proceed to trial. An adjournment on the application of the

---

[1] Laws of 1849, chap. 438, (Code of Procedure.) Part I., title vi., § 64.

[2] Ibid., loc. cit.
[3] Ibid., loc. cit.
[4] Ibid., loc. cit,

plaintiff cannot be granted at any other time than on the return of a summons or attachment, or the joining of issue without process, except upon an application for a commission, when the plaintiff is entitled to the same time and privileges as a defendant. A defendant may make application for an adjournment, at the time of joining issue, in all cases, except where the suit is commenced by warrant on behalf of a non-resident plaintiff. The defendant, or his attorney, may be required, on such application, to make oath that he cannot safely proceed to trial, for the want of some material testimony, or witness, to be specified by him. In addition to such oath, the defendant must, if required, execute the bond, a form of which is hereinafter given. A defendant may have a second or further adjournment, on giving security, if required, and proving, by his own oath, or otherwise, that he cannot safely proceed to trial, for want of some material testimony, or witness; and that he has used due diligence to obtain such testimony, or witness. Where a suit is commenced by a non-resident plaintiff, the first adjournment is to be not less than three nor more than twelve days, unless the parties and Justice otherwise agree. In no case can the time of adjourning a cause exceed ninety days from the time of joining the issue, except with the consent of parties. A Justice may adjourn a cause, with or without the consent of parties, on his own motion, at the time of the return of a summons or attachment, or of joining issue without process, not exceeding eight days; and he may hold a cause open, or adjourn it, on issuing an attachment for a witness, or a new venire. Justices have a discretion to exercise in refusing or granting an adjournment, which will not be interfered with on appeal, except there be a clear abuse of that discretion.[1]

19. Consent will give a Justice jurisdiction in respect to parties, but not as to the subject matter of a suit.[2]

20. A Justice of the Peace may, when an issue of fact shall have been joined before him, upon the application of a party showing the materiality of the testimony of a witness beyond the reach of a subpœna, issue a commission to one or more persons to examine such witness on oath, upon interrogatories to be settled by the Justice; and whenever the defendant neglects to appear, or to plead in such action or suit, and the plaintiff makes application for a commission to take the deposition of a material witness, the Justice may issue a commission without notice,—the interrogatories accompanying the same being proposed by the plaintiff, and settled by the Justice.[3]

---

[1] 2 R. S. (3d. ed.) 335, 336, § 69, et seq.; 8 Johnson, 426; 11 Id., 407 · 13 Id., 228; 15 Id., 492; 1 Cowen, 112, 234, 253; 2 Id., 425; 7 Id., 869; 1 Wendell, 464; 3 Id., 420; 10 Id., 497; 11 Id., 461, 554; 3 Hill, 323; 7 Id., 77.

[2] 12 Johnson, 285; 17 Id., 63; 3 Hill, 323.
[3] Laws of 1838, chap. 243; Laws of 1841, chap. 138 Laws of 1847, chap. 329.

21. It must be made distinctly to appear, on an application for a commission, that the witness is material, and that he does not reside in the county where the suit is pending, nor in an adjoining county. An affidavit, stating that the witness is in "another county," and that he "is, or may be, material," is not sufficient.[1]

22. Witnesses may be required to attend before any Justice of the Peace, in the same, or in an adjoining county, in pursuance of a subpœna duly served.[2]

23. A Justice of the Peace must enter judgment forthwith, on the verdict of a jury; he cannot wait until the next day.[3]

24. When there is no jury, a Justice must render his judgment within four days after the trial. It need not be entered on his docket within that time, but a memorandum thereof must be made on the papers in the action.[4]

25. The plaintiff must be present, either in person or by attorney, when a verdict is rendered.[5]

26. A Justice of the Peace, on the demand of a party in whose favor he shall have rendered a judgment, must give a transcript thereof, which may be filed and docketed in the office of the Clerk of the County where the judgment was rendered. The time of the receipt of the transcript by the Clerk must be noted and entered in the docket; and from that time the judgment will be a judgment of the County Court. A certified transcript of such judgment may be filed and docketed in the Clerk's office of any other county, and with the like effect, in every respect, as in the county where the judgment was rendered, except, that it shall be a lien, only from the time of filing and docketing the transcript. But no such judgment for a less sum than twenty-five dollars, exclusive of costs, will be a lien upon real property.[6]

27. Where a transcript of a judgment is docketed in the office of the Clerk of the city and county of New York, such judgment will have the same effect as a lien, and be enforced in the same manner as a judgment of the Court of Common Pleas of such city and county.[7]

28. Executions may be issued on a judgment in a Justice's Court, whether rendered before or after the passage of the act of 1849, at any time within five years after the rendition thereof, and must be made returnable sixty days from the date thereof. Where a judgment is docketed with the County Clerk, the execution must be issued by him to the Sheriff of the County, and be executed in the same manner as other executions and judgments of the County Court, or, in the city and county of New York, of the Court of Common Pleas.[8]

1 7 Hill, 77.
2 2 R. S. (3d. ed.) 337, § 81, et seq:
3 3 Denio, 12.
4 2 Comstock, 134.
5 3 Denio, 12.
6 Laws of 1849, chap. 438, (Code of Procedure, Part I., title vi., § 63.
7 Ibid., Part I., title vii., § 68.
8 Ibid., Part I., title vi., § 64.

29. A Justice of the Peace may renew an execution issued by him from time to time, by an endorsement specifying the amount due, if any thing has been paid or collected thereon, and the date of the renewal; the endorsement must be signed by the Justice.[1]

30. An execution issued by a Justice may be renewed while yet unsatisfied, though levy has been made; provided there be not sufficient time to advertise and sell under it.[2]

31. The docket of a Justice is good evidence before himself, without proving its identity, or showing his official character.[3]

32. Where the statute requires a "bond" to be executed, in any proceeding had before a Justice, a mere covenant, or agreement in writing, to become holden, on certain conditions, is not sufficient.

33. Courts of Justices of the Peace, are not courts of record, and judgments rendered before them will be barred by the statute of limitations, even though docketed in the office of the County Clerk, at the expiration of six years from the vendition thereof.[4]

34. The Justices' Courts in the city of New York, and Justices' Courts in other cities, have jurisdiction in all civil actions similar to those in which Justices of the Peace have jurisdiction; and, also, in actions upon the charters or by-laws of the corporations of their respective cities, where the penalty or forfeiture does not exceed one hundred dollars.[5]

35. Justices of the Peace have power to issue process for crimes committed in the county where they reside, but not for those committed in another county, even if the offender be in the county where the Justice resides.[7]

36. Courts of Special Sessions are to be held by a single magistrate, and all offences triable before such courts are to be tried with or without a jury, at the election of the prisoner. Any criminal warrant or process issued for an offence triable before a Court of Special Sessions, must authorize the officer executing it, to take the offender before some magistrate in the town or city where the offence was committed, provided the magistrate issuing the same reside in some other town or city. The city of New York is excepted from the operation of this provision.[8]

---

[1] 2 R. S. (3d. ed.) 347, § 144.
[2] 1 Denio, 574.
[3] 1 Denio, 432.
[4] 1 Denio, 184.
[5] 4 Barbour's S. C. Rep., 442.
[6] Laws of 1849, chap. 438, (Code of Procedure,) Part I., title vii., §§ 66, 67.
[7] 6 Hill, 164.
[8] Laws of 1845, chap. 180, §§ 15, 26.

FORMS.

§ 593. *Summons.*[1]

Town of   ,
         County, } ss:

To any Constable of the said County, greeting:

The people of the State of New York command you to summon A. B. to appear before me, the undersigned, one of the Justices of the Peace of the town aforesaid, at my office, [*or, as the case may be,*] in the said county, on the   day of   , at   o'clock, in the   noon, to answer C. D., in an action arising on contract, [*or,* in an action for damages for an injury to the person of the said C. D.; *or, as the cause of action may be,*] to his damage one hundred dollars or under. And have you then there this precept.

Witness my hand, the   day of   , 18 .

               J. H. B., Justice of the Peace.

---

§ 594. *Affidavit for Short Summons by Non-Resident Plaintiff.*

       County, ss:

C. D., being duly sworn, says that he has, as he verily believes, a good cause of action, arising on contract, [*or,* on a judgment founded on contract,] against A. B., upon which, according to the provisions of the 31st section of the act to abolish imprisonment for debt, and to punish fraudulent debtors, no warrant can issue against the said A. B;* and that this deponent resides in the town of   , in the county of   , and not within the said county of   ; and this deponent prays a short summons against the said A. B., on giving security, according to the statute.

Sworn to, this   day }
of   , 18   , before me, }   C. D.

       C. C., Justice of the Peace.

---

§ 595. *Affidavit for Short Summons against Non-Resident Defendant.*

       County, ss:

C. D., being duly sworn, &c., [*as in § 594 to the *, and then*

---

[1] A *long* summons must be made returnable in not less than six, nor more than twelve days from the date thereof; and a *short* summons in not less than two, nor more than four days. In computing the time, the day of the date is to be excluded, and the return day included.

add:] and that the said A. B. resides in the county of and out of the said county of   ; and this deponent prays a short summons against the said A. B.   C. D

Sworn, &c., [*as in* § 594.]

---

§ 596. *Description of Parties suing in a Particular Character.*

Of Administrators.—A. B. and C. D., administrators of all and singular the goods and chattels, rights and credits, which were of E. F. deceased.

Executors.—A. B. and C.D., executors of the last will and testament of E. F., deceased.

Surviving Executor.—A. B., surviving executor of the last will, &c.

Surviving Partner, or Joint Creditor.—A. B., survivor of A. B. and C. D.

Husband and Wife.—A. B., and C. B. his wife.

Assignee of Bail Bond.—A. B., assignee of A. P., Esq., Sheriff of the county of   .

Assignee of Insolvent Debtor.—A. B., assignee of E. F., an insolvent debtor.

Overseers of the Poor.—A. B. and C. D., Overseers of the Poor of the town of   , in the county of   .

Plaintiff in an Action for a Penalty.—A. B., who sues as well for himself, as for the Overseers of the Poor of the town of   , in the county of   .

---

§ 597. *Affidavit for Warrant, in an Action for a Wrong.*

County, ss:

C. D., being duly sworn, says that he has, as he verily believes, a good cause of action against A. B., for breaking and entering the close of the said C. D., in the town of   , in said county, and taking and carrying away therefrom, &c., [*set forth the cause of action.*] And this deponent further says, that the said A. B., who resides in said county of   , is not a freeholder therein, nor an inhabitant thereof having a family, [*or,* that the said A. B. is not a resident of the said county of   , but a resident of the county of   ; *or,* that he, the said C. D., is a non-resident of said county, and a resident of the county of   , and is willing to give security for the payment of any sum which may be adjudged against him in any suit to be commenced hereupon; *or,* that the said

A. B. lately informed E. F., in the presence of this deponent, that he was about to depart from said county of   , with intent not to return thereto, [*or state other facts and circumstances showing such intention;*] *or*, that this deponent will, as he verily believes, be in danger of losing his said demand, unless such warrant be granted, and that the following are the facts and circumstances on which that belief is founded, viz: [*state the facts;*] and this deponent makes application for a warrant against the said A. B., according to the statute.

Sworn, &c., [*as in* § 594.]   C. D.

---

§ 598. *Affidavit for Warrant, in an Action on Contract.*

County, ss:

C. D., being duly sworn, says that he has, as he verily believes, a good cause of action against A. B., for money collected by the said A. B. in his official character as Constable, [*or*, for the official misconduct, [*or*, neglect of duty,] of the said A. B. as Constable; *or*, for damages arising from the misconduct or neglect of the said A. B., in his professional employment as an attorney:] And this deponent further says, that the said A. B. is a non-resident of said county of, &c., [*or, as in* § 597.] and, therefore, he makes application for a warrant against the said A. B., according to the statute.

Sworn, &c., [*as in* § 594.]   C. D.

---

§ 599. *Recognizance on Issuing Warrant, or Short Summons.*

County, ss:

Be it remembered, that on the   day of   , 18 , application having been made to the undersigned, one of the Justices of the Peace of said county, by C. D., a non-resident of said county, for a warrant, [*or*, short summons,] in his favor against A. B., in an action arising on contract, [*or, as the cause of action may be:*] E. F. thereupon personally came before me, and acknowledged that he owed to the said A. B. one hundred dollars, to be paid if default should be made in the following condition, viz: that the said C. D. shall pay to the said A. B. any sum which may be adjudged against him the said C. D., in the suit to be commenced by the said warrant, [*or*, short summons.]   H. T. C., Justice, &c.

---

§ 600. *Written Security on Issuing Warrant, or Short Summons.*

County, ss:

Application having been made to L. P., Esq., one of the Justices of the Peace of said county, by C. D., a non-resident of the said county, for a warrant in his favor, against A. B., in an action arising on contract, [*or, as the cause of action may be:*] Now, therefore, for value received, and according to the statute in such case made and provided, I do hereby agree with, and become bound to, the said A. B., that the said C. D. shall pay to him any sum which may be adjudged against the said C. D. in the suit to be commenced by the said warrant, [*or,* short summons.]

Dated the   day of   , 18 .   E. F.

Signed, taken, and acknowledged, the }
     day of   , 18   , before me, }
         C. C., Justice, &c.

---

§ 601. *Warrant in a Civil Action.*

County, } ss :
Town of   , }

To any Constable of the said County, greeting:

The people of the State of New York command you to take A. B., and bring him forthwith before me, one of the Justices of the Peace of the said town, to answer C. D. in an action arising on contract, [*or, as the cause of action may be,*] to his damage one hundred dollars, or under; and you are further required, after you have arrested the defendant, to notify the plaintiff of such arrest, and make return hereupon to me, of the manner in which you shall have executed this precept.

Witness my hand, the   day of   , 18 .
       R. H. F., Justice, &c.

---

§ 602. *Application for an Attachment.*

To J. B., Esq., Justice of the Peace of the Town of   , in the County of   :

The subscriber applies to you for an attachment against the property of A. B., on the grounds set forth in the affidavit hereunto annexed. Dated the   day of   , 18 .
         C. D.

---

§ 603. *Affidavit for an Attachment under the Revised Statutes.*

County, ss :

C. D., being duly sworn, says, that A. B. is justly indebted to this deponent [*or, to* E. F.] in the sum of   dollars, over and above all discounts which the said A. B. has against him, as near as he can ascertain the same; which debt arose upon contract, [*or, as the case may be;*]* and that the said A. B. has departed from the said county of   , where he last resided, with intent to defraud his creditors, or with intent to avoid the service of any civil process; [*or,* that the said A. B. is about to depart from the said county of   , &c., *as above; or,* that the said A. B. keeps himself concealed within the said county of   , where he last resided, with intent, &c., [*as above:*] and this deponent further says, &c., [*here state distinctly the facts and circumstances necessary to satisfy the Justice that there are sufficient grounds for the attachment.*]

Sworn, &c., [*as in* § 594.]   C. D.

---

§ 604. *Affidavit for Attachment, under the Non-Imprisonment Act.*

County, ss:

C. D., being duly sworn, says, &c., [*as in* § 603 *to the* *, *and then add:*] and that the said A. B. is about to remove his property from the said county of   , with intent to defraud his creditors, [*or, that the said A. B., has assigned, disposed of, or secreted, his property, with intent to defraud his creditors; or, that the said A. B. is about to assign, dispose of, or secrete, his property, with intent to defraud his creditors;*] and this deponent further says, that, &c.: [*set forth the facts and circumstances, as directed in* § 603.]

Sworn, &c., [*as in* § 594.]   .   C. D.

---

§ 605. *Affidavit for an Attachment against a Non-Resident.*

County, ss:

C. D., being duly sworn, says, &c., [*as in* § 603 *to the* *, *and then add;*] and that the said A. B. is a resident of the town of ·   , in the county of   , and out of the said county of   ; and that no warrant can issue against him, on the demand of the said C. D., according to the act to abolish imprisonment for debt, and to punish fraudulent debtors

Sworn, &c., [*as in* § 594.]   C. D.

---

§ 606. *Bond on Attachment.*[1]

Know all men by these presents: That we, C. D., and E. F., are held and firmly bound unto A. B., in the sum of two hundred dol-

---

[1] No bond is necessary on an attachment against a non-resident. (23 Wendell, 336.) But a non-resident plaintiff must give security, as in other cases.

lars, [*if under the non-imprisonment act, say*, one hundred dollars,] to be paid to the said A. B., his heirs,' executors, administrators, or assigns; for which payment, well and truly to be made, we bind ourselves, our heirs, executors and administrators, jointly and severally, firmly by these presents. Sealed with our seals, and dated the day of   , A. D. 18 .*

Whereas the above bounden C. D. has made application to C. C., Esq., a Justice of the Peace of the town of   , in the county of   , for an attachment in his favor, [*or*, in favor of L. M.,] against the property of the said A. B., in pursuance of the provisions of the Revised Statutes, [*or*, of the act to abolish imprisonment for debt, and to punish fraudulent debtors:] Now, therefore, the condition of this obligation is such, that if the said C. D. [*or*, L. M.] shall pay the said A. B. all damages and costs which he may sustain by reason of the issuing of said attachment, if the said C. D. [*or* L. M.] shall fail to recover judgment thereon; and if such judgment be recovered, and the said C. D. [*or*, L. M.] shall pay the said A. B. all moneys which shall be received by him from any property levied upon by virtue of such attachment, over and above the amount of such judgment, and interest and costs thereon, then this obligation to be void; else of force.

Sealed and delivered }
  in the presence of }
    G. H.

C. D. [L S.]
E. F. [L s.]

---

§ 607. *Attachment.*

       County, } ss:
Town of   , }

To any Constable of the said County, greeting:

Whereas, C. D. has applied for an attachment against the property of A. B., against whom he has a claim for a debt of   dollars, and produced satisfactory proof that the said A. B. is about to depart from the said county of   , where he last resided, [*or, as the case may be*,] with intent to defraud his creditors: Therefore, the People of the State of New York command you, to attach so much of the goods and chattels of the said A. B., as will be sufficient to satisfy the said claim, and safely to keep the same, to satisfy any judgment that may be recovered on this attachment; and that you make return of your proceedings thereon to me, on the   day of   , at   o'clock in the   noon, at my office in the said town. Dated the   day of   , 18 .

            G. H., Justice, &c.

§ 608. *Bond on Adjournment, in Action arising on Contract.*

Know all men by these presents, that we, A. B. and E. F., &c. [*as in* § 606 *to the* *, *inserting such penalty as the Justice may direct, and then add:*]

Whereas, a suit has been commenced before G. H., Esq., Justice of the Peace, by C. D., plaintiff, against A. B., defendant, the trial of which is adjourned until the . day of , 18 , on the application of said defendant: Now, therefore, the condition of this obligation is such, that if the above bounden A. B., and E. F., or either of them, shall pay such judgment as may be rendered against the defendant in said cause, with interest,* if any part of his property, liable to execution, be removed, secreted, assigned, or in any way disposed of, except for the necessary support of himself and family, until the plaintiff's demand shall be satisfied, or until the expiration of ten days after he shall be entitled to have an execution issued on such judgment, then this obligation to be void; otherwise of force.

Sealed, &c., [*as in* § 606.]

———

§ 609. *Bond on Adjournment, in Action for a Wrong.*

Know all men by these presents, that we, A. B., and E. F., &c., [*as in* § 606 *to the* *, *inserting such penalty as the Justice may direct, and then add:*]

Whereas, &c., [*as in* § 608 *to the* *, *and then add:*] if the said defendant shall not render himself upon the execution which may be issued on such judgment, before the return thereof, then this obligation to be void; otherwise of force.

Sealed, &c., [*as in* § 606.]

———

§ 610. *Affidavit of Justification of Bail.*

C. D.
against } Before G. H., Esq., one of the Justices of the Peace
A. B. } of the county of :

County, ss:

E. F., being duly sworn, says that he is a housekeeper, [*or*, freeholder,] now actually residing in the town of , in said county; and that he is worth two hundred dollars over and above what will pay all his debts.   E. F.

Sworn, &c., [*as in* § 594.]

§ 611. *Complaint in an Action arising on Contract.*

In Justice's Court,

A. B.	Before C. C., Esq.
against	Complaint.
C. D.	

A. B., plaintiff, complains that C. D., defendant, owes and is indebted to him in the sum of one hundred dollars, for goods, wares and merchandise, sold and delivered to [*or*, for work and labor performed for] the defendant, on the   day of   , 18   , [*or*, at various times between the   day of   , 18   , and the   day of   , 18   ,] whereupon the plaintiff demands judgment against the defendant for the one hundred dollars, [*add here*, with interest   from the day of   , 18   , *if necessary.*]

A. B., Plaintiff.

---

§ 612. *Complaint for Injuring Personal Property.*

In Justice's Court,

A. B.	Before C. C., Esq.,
against	Complaint.
C. D.	

A. B., plaintiff, complains that C. D., defendant, carelessly and violently ran against the carriage of the plaintiff, with the team and wagon of the defendant, on the   day of   , 18   , and broke and damaged the said carriage to the amount of twenty-five dollars; whereupon, the plaintiff demands judgment against the defendant for the twenty-five dollars.

A. B., Plaintiff.

---

§ 613. *Complaint for Breach of Warranty.*

In Justice's Court,

A. B.	Before C. C., Esq.
against	Complaint.
C. D.	

A. B., plaintiff, complains that C. D., defendant, sold a horse to the plaintiff, on the   day of   , 18   , for the sum of   dollars, and warranted the same to be perfectly sound, kind, and true, but the said horse is blind of the right eye, is vicious and unruly, and not true in the harness, whereby he is injured to the amount of fifty dollars; whereupon the plaintiff demands judgment against the defendant for the fifty dollars.

A. B., Plaintiff.

§ 614. *Complaint for Fraud or Deceit.*

In Justice's Court,

A. B.	Before C. C., Esq.
against	Complaint.
C. D.	

A. B., plaintiff, complains that C. D., defendant, sold a horse to the plaintiff, on the   day of   , 18   , for the sum of   dollars, which said horse, to the knowledge of the defendant, was diseased of the heaves at the time of the sale, but the defendant did not inform the plaintiff thereof; whereby the said horse is injured to the amount of fifty dollars, and the plaintiff demands judgment against the defendant for the same.

A. B., Plaintiff.

---

§ 615. *Complaint for Conversion of Personal Property.*

In Justice's Court,

A. B.	Before C. C., Esq.
against	Complaint.
C. D.	

A. B., plaintiff, complains that on or about the   day of   , 18   , he was possessed, as of his own property, of a certain gold watch, of the value of one hundred dollars, which afterwards, and on or about the   day of   , 18   , came into the hands and possession of C. D., the defendant, who sold the same and converted the proceeds to his own use; whereupon the plaintiff demands judgment against the defendant for the one hundred dollars.

A. B., Plaintiff.

---

§ 616. *Complaint for Injury to Real Property.*

In Justice's Court,

A. B.	Before C. C., Esq.
against	Complaint.
C. D.	

A. B., plaintiff, complains that on or about the   day of   , 18   , C. D., the defendant, [*or,* the horses and cattle of C. D., the defendant,] broke and entered the close of the plaintiff, at   , in the county of   , and trod down and destroyed the grass and products of the soil there growing; whereby the plaintiff has sustained damage to the amount of fifty dollars, and he demands judgment against the defendant for the same.

A. B., Plaintiff.

§ 617. *Complaint by an Assignee.*

In Justice's Court,

A. B.	Before C. C., Esq.
against	Complaint.
C. D.	

A. B., plaintiff, complains that C. D., defendant, was indebted to G. H., on the   day of   , 18   , in the sum of one hundred dollars, for medical services rendered to the said defendant previous to that day, which said indebtedness has been duly assigned to the plaintiff; whereupon the plaintiff demands judgment against the defendant for the one hundred dollars.

A. B., Plaintiff.

---

§ 618. *Answer of Defendant.*

In Justice's Court,

A. B.	Before C. C., Esq.
against	Answer.
C. D.	

C. D., the defendant, answers to the complaint, that on the   day of   18   , he paid the indebtedness mentioned in the complaint, [*or*, that the plaintiff did not perform the work and labor for the defendant, mentioned in the complaint; *or*, that he did not warrant the horse mentioned in the complaint to be perfectly sound, kind, and true.]

C. D., Defendant.

---

§ 619. *Answer, with Notice.*

In Justice's Court,

A. B.	Before C. C., Esq.
against	Answer.
C. D.	

C. D., the defendant, answers to the complaint, that he did not take, and does not detain the property, [*or*, did not break and enter the close,] mentioned in the complaint, as is therein stated; and he gives notice that he will prove on the trial of this action that the property mentioned in the complaint was taken, and is detained by him, with the consent and permission of the plaintiff, [*or*, that he broke and entered the close mentioned in the complaint, in order to remove a quantity of wheat levied on by him as a constable of the county of   , by virtue of an execution against the plaintiff, issued by C. C., Esquire, Justice of the Peace of said county, in favor of G. H., and dated on the   day of   , 18 .]

C. D., Defendant.

§ 620. *Oath on Application for an Adjournment.*[1]

You do swear, that you will true answers make to such questions as shall be put to you, touching the necessity of an adjournment in this cause.

---

§ 621. *Oath of Surety on Adjournment.*

You do swear that you will true answers make to such questions as shall be put to you, touching your competency as surety for A. B., on his application to adjourn this cause.

---

§ 622. *Examination of Witness, on the Application of the Defendant for an Adjournment, in a Cause commenced by Warrant at the Suit of a Non-Resident Plaintiff.*

In Justice's Court,

C. D.
against
A. B.
} Before G. H., Esq., one of the Justices of the Peace of the County of   .

County, ss:

L. M., a witness attending, produced and sworn, by and on behalf of the plaintiff in this cause, being duly sworn, on his direct examination by the plaintiff, says: [*set forth the testimony.*]

Sworn, &c., [*as in* § 594.]

L. M.

---

§ 623. *Subpœna.*

Town of   ,
County,   } ss:

The People of the State of New York, to E. F., L. M., &c., &c., Greeting:

We command you, and each of you, that all business and excuses being laid aside, you and each of you be and appear, in your proper persons, before the undersigned, one of the Justices of the Peace of the said town, at his office in   , in the said county, on the   day of   , at   o'clock in the   noon, then and there* to testify those things which you or either of you know,

---

For other forms of oaths, see those given in Chapter XI.

in a certain† action now depending before the said Justice, between C. D., plaintiff, and A. B., defendant, on the part of the defendant [*or*, plaintiff.] [*If a witness is required to produce some paper or other evidence, insert here:* And you, L. M., are further commanded to bring with you, and then and there produce in evidence, a certain agreement in writing, &c., *or, as the case may be, describing the paper.*] Hereof fail not at your peril.

Witness my hand, this   day of   , 18   .

G. H., Justice of the Peace.

---

§ 624. *Subpœna for Witness to make Affidavit for Attachment.*

Town of   ,
          County, } ss:

The people, &c., [*as in* § 623 *to the* *, *inserting the word* "forthwith" *after* "appear," *and then add,*] to make affidavit of all and singular those things which you, or either of you, know, touching an application made to me by C. D., for an attachment against the property of A. B., and of any facts and circumstances tending to establish the grounds of said application. Hereof, &c., [*as in* § 623 *to the end.*]

---

§ 625. *Subpœna for Special Sessions.*

Town of   ,
          County, } ss:

The People, &c., [*as in* § 623, *to the* †, *and then add:*] matter then and there to be tried between the people of the State of New York, and A. B., on the part of the said people, [*or*, A. B.] Hereof, &c., [*as in* § 623, *to the end.*]

---

§ 626. *Affidavit of Service of Subpœna.*

County, ss:

C. D., the plaintiff named in the annexed subpœna, being duly sworn, says, that on the   day of   , 18   . at the town of   , in said county, he personally served the said subpœna on L. M., a witness therein named, by reading the same [*or*, stating the contents thereof,] to him, at the same time paying [*or*, tendering] to him the sum of twelve and a half cents; that the said L. M., is a

material witness for this deponent on the trial of the cause mention
ed in said subpœna; and that he, the said L. M., has neglected [*or,
refuses*] to attend the trial of said cause.

Sworn, &c., [*as in* § 594.]

C. D.

§ 627. *Oath to Party, Proving Service of Subpœna.*

You do swear, that you will true answers make to such questions
as shall be put to you, touching the service of the subpœna in this
cause.

§ 628. *Attachment for Witness.*

County, ss:

The People of the State of New York, to any Constable of said
County, greeting:

We command you to attach L. M., and bring him before the undersigned, a Justice of the Peace of said county, at his office in the
town of   , forthwith, [*or, as the case may be,*] to testify those
things which he may know, in a certain cause now depending before
the said Justice, between C. D., plaintiff, and A. B., defendant, on
the part of the plaintiff, [*or, defendant;*] and also to answer all such
matters as shall be objected against him, for that he, having been
duly subpœnaed to attend the trial of said cause, has refused [*or,*
neglected] to attend in conformity to such subpœna; and have you
then there this precept.

Witness, &c., [*as in* § 623.]

§ 629. *Notice of Application for a Commission.*

C. D. ⎫
against ⎬ Before G. H., Esq., one of the Justices of the Peace of
A. B. ⎭   the County of   :

Sir: Take notice that an application for a commission to be directed
to S. T., of the   of   , to examine R. P., of the same
place, a witness in the above entitled cause, upon interrogatories to be
annexed to such commission, will be made to G. H., Esq., at his office
in the town of   , on the   day of   , 18   , at
o'clock in the   noon.

Dated   , the   day of   , 18   .

C. D., Plaintiff.

To A. B., Defendant.

§ 630. *Oath of Service of Notice.*

. . . . . . that you will true answers make to such questions as shall be put to you, touching the service of notice of an application for a commission in this cause.

---

§ 631. *Oath on applying for Commission.*

You do swear, that you will true answers make to such questions as shall be put to you, touching the necessity of issuing a commission in this cause.

---

§ 632. *Commission.*[1]

County, ss:

To S. T., of the of : Whereas it appears to me, the undersigned, a Justice of the Peace of the town of , in said county, that R. P., of the of , aforesaid, is a material witness in a certain action now depending before me, between C. D., plaintiff, and A. B., defendant: Now, therefore, confiding in your prudence and fidelity, and in pursuance of the statute, I have appointed, and by these presents do appoint you, Commissioner to examine the said witness; and for that purpose, do authorize you, at certain days and places, to be by you appointed, diligently to examine the said witness, on the interrogatories hereto annexed, on oath to be taken before you; and to cause such examination to be reduced to writing, and signed by such witness and yourself, and return the same, annexed hereto, to me, enclosed under your seal. Given under my hand, at the town aforesaid, the day of , 18 .

G. H., Justice of the Peace.

---

§ 633. *Commissioner's Summons to Witness.*

County, ss:

Whereas, the undersigned has received a commission, issued by G. H., Esq., a Justice of the Peace of the county of , directed for the examination of R. P., a witness in a cause depending before the said Justice, between C. D., Plaintiff, and A. B., defendant: You, the

---

[1] Where a commission is issued to a person not familiar with our laws, it would be well to annex to the commission a copy of § 15, of Art. 2 of title 3, of Chap. 7, of part 3 of the Revised Statutes, in the same manner as in the case of commissions issued out of courts of record.

said R. P., are therefore required to be and appear before me, the said Commissioner, at my dwelling house, in the town of   , on, &c., then and there to be examined, and to testify the truth, according to the best of your knowledge, for and on behalf of the said plaintiff, [or, defendant,] and herein you are not to fail.

Dated the   day of   , 18   .

S. T.

---

§ 634. *Oath to Witness Examined on a Commission.*

You do swear, that the answers to be given by you to the interrogatories proposed to you by the Commissioner here present, to execute a commission directed to him, issued by G. H., Esq., a Justice of the Peace of the county of   , in a certain action there depending before him, between C. D., plaintiff, and A. B., defendant, shall be the truth, the whole truth, and nothing but the truth.

---

§ 635. *Deposition of Witness before Commissioner.*

Deposition of R. P., a witness produced, sworn and examined, on oath, on the   day of   , 18   , at &c., by virtue of a commission issued to S. T., by G. H., Esq., a Justice of the Peace of the county of   , in a certain cause depending before the said Justice, between C. D., plaintiff, and A. B., defendant.

The said R. P. deposes as follows: To the first interrogatory, he saith, [*give answer of witness.*]

To the second interrogatory, he saith, &c.   R. P.

Subscribed and sworn before me, }
this   day of   , 18   . }

S. T., Commissioner.

---

§ 636. *Endorsement of an Exhibit produced before the Commissioner.*

On the   day of   , 18   , at the execution of a commission issued by G. H., Esq., a Justice of the Peace of the county of   , for the examination of R. P., a witness in a certain action depending before the said Justice, between C. D., plaintiff, and A. B., defendant, the within paper writing marked "A," was produced and shown to the said R. P., a witness sworn and examined, and by him deposed unto at the time of his examination as a witness under such commission.   S. T., Commissioner.

§ 637. *Venire.*

Town of   , }
County, } ss:

To any Constable of the said County, greeting:

The People of the State of New York command you to summon twelve good and lawful men, in the town of   , qualified to serve as jurors, and not exempt from serving on juries, in courts of record, and who are in no wise of kin to either party, or interested in the suit hereinafter mentioned, to appear before me, one of the Justices of the Peace of said town, at my office in said town, on the   day of   , 18 , at   o'clock in the   noon, to make a jury for the trial of an action arising on contract, [*or, as the cause of action may be,*] between C. D., plaintiff, and A. B., defendant: And you are also required to make a list of the persons summoned, which you will certify and annex to this venire, and make return thereof to me.

Witness, &c., [*as in* § 623.]

----

§ 638. *Oath on Objection to Constable's Serving the Venire.*

You do swear, that you will true answers make to such questions as shall be put to you, touching the reasons why H. C. should not execute the venire in this cause.

----

§ 639. *Juror's Oath.*[1]

You do swear, well and truly to try the matter in difference between C. D., plaintiff, and A. B., defendant, and, unless discharged by the Justice, a true verdict give, according to the evidence.

----

§ 640. *Oath of Witness.*

You do swear, that the evidence you shall give, relating to this matter in difference between C. D., plaintiff, and A. B., defendant, shall be the truth, the whole truth, and nothing but the truth.

----

1 for other forms of oaths, see those previously given, in Chapter XI.

§ 641. *Constable's Oath on Retiring with Jury.*

You do swear, in the presence of Almighty God, that you will, to the utmost of your ability, keep the persons sworn as jurors on this trial, together, in some private and convenient place, without any meat or drink, except such as shall be ordered by me; that you will not suffer any communication, orally or otherwise, to be made to them; that you will not communicate with them yourself, orally or otherwise, unless by my order, or to ask them whether they have agreed on their verdict, until they shall be discharged: and that you will not, before they render their verdict, communicate to any person the state of their deliberations, or the verdict they have agreed on.

---

§ 642. *Confession of Judgment.*

In Justice's Court,

     C. D.   ⎫
     against   ⎬ Confession for $.
     A. B.   ⎭

In the presence of G. H., Justice of the Peace, I do hereby confess judgment, on a demand arising on contract, [*or as the nature of the demand may be*] to the plaintiff in the above entitled action, for dollars, and consent that the said Justice enter the same against me accordingly.

Dated the   day of   , 18 .   A. B.

---

§ 643. *Affidavit where the Confession is for a Sum exceeding Fifty Dollars.*

         County, ss:

We, C. D. and A. B., the parties named in the foregoing [*or,* annexed] confession of judgment, being duly sworn, severally say, that the said A. B. is justly indebted to the said C. D., in the sum of dollars, over and above all just demands which the said A. B. has against the said C. D.; and that the above [*or,* annexed]confession is not made, or taken, with a view to defraud any creditor.

Subscribed and sworn, before me, ⎫   C. D.
   this   day of   , 18 . ⎭   A. B
         G. H., Justice, &c.

§ 644. *Transcript of Judgment.*

In Justice's Court,

C. D.
against
A. B.

Judgment rendered for the plaintiff, against the defendant, May 6,
   1846, for $28 02

Costs,   1 90

                                     $29 92

Fee for transcript, to be added,   25

County, ss:

I certify that the above is a true copy of a judgment rendered by and before me, and now remaining unsatisfied upon my docket; that the said judgment was rendered in the absence of the defendant, upon contract; [*or, as the case may be:*] and that E. F. and O. P were the witnesses sworn on the part of the plaintiff therein.

Dated the   day of   , 18 .

                                    G. H., Justice, &c.

---

§ 645. *Execution.*

Town of   ,
County,   ss:

To any Constable of said town, greeting:

Whereas, judgment has been rendered before me, one of the Justice of the Peace of the said county, against A. B., defendant, in favor of C. D., plaintiff, for   dollars and.   cents: Therefore, the People of the State of New York command you, to levy the amount of the said judgment, with interest from the   day of   , 18 , on which day judgment was rendered, until received, of the goods and chattels of the said defendant, (except such goods and chattels as are by law exempted from execution,) and bring the money before me sixty days from the date hereof, to render to the said plaintiff: and have you then there this precept. [*If the defendant may be arrested on the execution, add here:* And if no goods or chattels can be found, or not sufficient to satisfy this execution, you are further commanded to take the body of the said A. B., and convey him to the common jail of the said county, there to remain until this execution shall be satisfied and paid.]

Witness my hand, the   day of   , 18 .

                              G. H., Justice of the Peace.

Damages, $

Costs,

Judgment,

Poundage,

    Amount, $

§ 646. *Renewal of Execution.*

The within execution is hereby renewed, [*If necessary, add:* for the sum of   dollars, with interest from this date.]

Dated the   day of   , 18   .

G. H., Justice.

---

§ 647. *Complaint to obtain Surety of the Peace.*

County, ss:

A. B., of said county, being duly sworn, says, that on the day of   , 18   , one C. D., of the town of   , in said county, did threaten to beat and wound [*or, kill, or as the case may be,*] him, the said A. B.; and that he hath just cause to fear that the said C. D. will beat and wound [*or, kill, as the case may be*] him, the said A. B.;* wherefore this deponent prays that the said offender may be bound by recognizance, to answer the said offence at the next Court of Sessions to be held in the said county, and in the meanwhile to keep the peace.   A. B.

Sworn, &c., [*as in* § 594.]

---

§ 648. *Peace Warrant.*

Town of   , } ss:
          County, }

To any Constable of the said County, greeting:

Whereas, A. B. hath this day made complaint, upon oath, before me, G. H., one of the Justices of the Peace of the said town, that on the   day of   , 18   , one C. D., of, &c., [*as in* § 647 *to the* *, *and then add:*] and the said A. B. hath thereupon prayed surety of the Peace: Therefore, the people of the State of New York command you forthwith to apprehend the said C. D., and bring him before me, at my office in said town of   , to be dealt with according to law.

Witness my hand, this   day of   , 18   .

G. H., Justice of the Peace.

---

§ 649. *Commitment on Foregoing Complaint.*[1]

County, ss:

To any Constable of the said County, greeting:

Whereas, A. B. this day made complaint to me in writing, on oath, that C. D., on the   day of   instant, [*or, last past,*]

---

[1] For form of recognizance, see § 708.

threatened to, &c., [*as in the complaint:*] And whereas, it appearing to me, upon the examination of the said complainant, and E. F., and O. P., witnesses, duly made on oath, reduced to writing, and subscribed by them, that there was just reason to fear the commission of the said offence by the said C. D.; and he being brought before me on my warrant, was required to enter into recognizance in the sum of   dollars, with sufficient surety, to appear at the next Court of Sessions to be held in the said county, and not to depart the same without leave, and in the meantime to keep the Peace towards the people of this State, and particularly towards the said complainant. And the said C. D. having refused [*or,* neglected,] to find such security, you are therefore commanded, in the name of the People of the State of New York, forthwith to convey him to the common jail of the said county, and to deliver him to the keeper thereof, who is hereby required to receive the said C. D. into his custody, and him safely keep in the said jail, until he shall find such security, or be discharged by due course of law.

Witness, &c., [*as in* § 648.]

---

§ 650. *Warrant to discharge Prisoner on Finding Security.*

County, ss:

G. H. and S. T., Esqrs., two of the Justices of the Peace of the said County, to the Keeper of the Common Jail of the said County, greeting:

These are to command you forthwith to discharge out of your custody C. D., if detained by you in said common jail, for no other cause than what is specified in his warrant of commitment, made by the said G. H. dated the   day of   , 18   , for not finding sureties of the Peace; he having, since his said commitment, found such sureties before us.

Given under our our hands and seals, this   day of   , 18

                    G. H., Justice, [L. S.]

                    S. T., Justice, [L. S.]

---

§ 651. *Complaint for Assault and Battery.*

County, ss:

A. B., of said county, being duly sworn, says, that on the   day of   , 18   , one C. D. did violently assault and beat him, the said A. B., at the town of   , in said county; wherefore this deponent prays that the said offender may be dealt with according to law.

                    A. B.

Sworn, &c., [*as in* § 594.]

§ 652. *Assault and Battery Warrant.*

Town of   ,
   County, } ss:

To any Constable of the said County, greeting:

Whereas A. B. hath this day made complaint, upon oath, before me, G. H., one of the Justices of the Peace of the said town, that on the   day of   , 18 , at the town of   , in said county, one C. D. did violently assault and beat him, the said A. B.: Therefore, the People of the State of New York command you forth- with to apprehend the said C. D., and bring him before me, at my office in the said town of   , [*or, if the offence be committed in another town, say:* take him before S. T., Esq., or any other magi- strate resident and being in the town of   , aforesaid,] to be dealt with according to law.

Witness, &c., [*as in* § 648.]

---

§ 653. *General Form of Warrant.*

County, ss:

To any Constable of the said county, greeting:

Whereas, A. B. has made complaint, upon oath, before me, G. H., one of the Justices of the Peace of the said county, on this   day of   , 18 , that, &c., [*state the offence, as in the complaint:*] Therefore, the People of the State of New York command you forth- with to apprehend the said C. D., and bring him before me, at my office, in the town of   , in said county, [*or, change the form as in* § 652, *if the offence was committed in another town, and is triable before a Court of Special Sessions,*] to be dealt with accord- ing to law.

Witness, &c., [*as in* § 648.]

---

§ 654. *Complaint for Grand or Petit Larceny.*

County, ss:

A. B., of said county, being duly sworn, says, that certain personal property of the said A. B., [*or, as the case may be,*] to wit: [*de- scribe property,*] of the value of   dollars, or upwards, was stolen and feloniously taken from his dwelling house in the town of   , in said county, on the   day of   , 18 ; and that this deponent suspects that C. D. has stolen and taken the same, as aforesaid ;* wherefore he pays process to apprehend the said offender.   A. B.

Sworn, &c., [*as in* § 594.]

§ 655. *Warrant for Larceny.*

County, ss:

To any Constable of the said County, greeting:

Whereas, A. D. has made complaint, upon oath, before me, G. H., one of the Justices of the Peace of the said county, that on the   day of   , 18   , certain personal property of the said A. B., to wit: [*describe property as in the complaint,*] of the value of   dollars, or upwards, was stolen and feloniously taken from his dwelling house in the town of   , in said county; and that he suspects that C. D. did steal and take the same as aforesaid:* Therefore, &c., [*as in* § 652, *to the end.*]

---

§ 656. *Complaint for Murder.*[1]

County, ss:

A. B., of said county, being duly sworn, says,* that on the day of   instant, [*or, last past,*] at the town of   , in said county, one M. P. was feloniously, wilfully, and of malice aforethought, killed and murdered: and that this deponent has just cause to suspect, and does suspect, that the said murder was committed by R. D., [*or, by a man* [*describe his person,*] but whose name is unknown to the deponent.]

Sworn, &c., [*as in* § 594.]

---

§ 657. *Complaint for Murder by Poisoning.*

County, ss:

A. B., of said county, being duly sworn, says,* that on the day of   instant, [*or, last past,*] at the town of   , in said county, one M. P. died; and that this deponent has just cause to suspect, and does suspect, that on the   day of   , aforesaid, one R. D. did feloniously, wilfully, and of malice aforethought, administer to the said M. P. a certain deadly poison, called arsenic, by reason whereof the said M. P. languished a short time and then died.

Sworn, &c., [*as in* § 594.]

---

[1] The forms of warrants to accompany the complaints for murder, and the subsequent forms to § 705: are not given, for the reason that no difficulty can be experienced in preparing them from §§ 648, 652, 653, and 655. It is only necessary to insert in the general form (§ 653) the precise language of the complaint, commencing at the word "that," after the * in each form, and concluding with the command to arrest, as in 648. Where the word "deponent" occurs, the name of the individual should be inserted in full.

§ 658. *Complaint for Murder by Stabbing.*

County, ss:

A. B., of said county, being duly sworn, says,* that on the
day of   instant, [*or*, last past,] at the town of   , in said
county, one R. D. did, in the presence of this deponent and other
witnesses, feloniously, wilfully, and of malice aforethought, stab one
M. P., with a butcher's knife, and give him several mortal wounds, of
which the said M. P., died immediately, [*or*, languished a short time
and then died.]

Sworn, &c., [*as in* § 594.]

---

§ 659. *Complaint for Murder by Shooting.*

County, ss:

A. B., of said county, being duly sworn, says,* that on the
day of   instant, [*or*, last past,] at the town of   , in
said county, one R. D. did feloniously, wilfully, and of malice aforethought, fire and discharge a gun, [*or*, pistol,] loaded with powder
and ball, at one M. P., and give him one [*or*, several] mortal wound,
[*or*, wounds,] of which the said M. P., &c., [*as in* § 658, *to the end.*]

---

§ 660. *Complaint for Murder by Cutting Throat.*

County, ss:

A. B., of said county, being duly sworn, says,* that on the
day of   instant, [*or*, last past,] at the town of   , in
said county, one R. D., feloniously, wilfully, and of malice aforethought, with a bowie knife, made an assault upon, and did strike and
cut the throat of M. P. therewith, and did give him one mortal wound
thereon, of which the said M. P., &c., [*as in* § 658, *to the end.*]

---

§ 661. *Complaint against Accessory After the Fact.*

County, ss:

A. B., of said county, &c., [*as in either of the preceding complaints for murder, to the end, and then add:*] And that afterwards,
to wit, on the   day of   instant, [*or*, last past,] at the
town of   , in said county, one R. S., well knowing the said
R. D. to have done and committed the said felony and murder, did
feloniously and wilfully conceal [*or*, aid, comfort and assist] the said

R. D., with the intent and in order that the said R. D. might avoid, or escape from, arrest, [or, trial; or, conviction and punishment,] for the said felony and murder.

Sworn, &c., [*as in* § 594.]

---

§ 662. *Complaint for Arson, in the First Degree.*

County, ss:

A. B., of said county, being duly sworn, says,* that on the   day of   instant, [*or, last past,*] in the night time, at the town of   , in said county, one R. D. did unlawfully, wilfully, maliciously and feloniously, set fire to and burn the dwelling house of one M. P., situate in said town; there being at the same time some human being, to wit, [*mention who,*] in the said dwelling house.

Sworn, &c., [*as in* § 594.]

---

§ 663. *Complaint for Arson, in the Second Degree.*

County, ss:

A. B., of said county, being duly sworn, says,* that on the   day of   instant, &c., [*as in* § 662, *to the end, substituting* "in the day time" *for* "in the night time;" *or, say,* at the town of   , in said county, in the night time, one R. D. did unlawfully, wilfully, maliciously and feloniously, set fire to and burn the warehouse of one M. P., situate in said town; which said warehouse was adjoining to, [*or, within the curtilage of,*] the inhabited dwelling house of the said M. P., whereby the said dwelling house was endangered.]

Sworn, &c., [*as in* § 594.]

---

§ 664. *Complaint for Arson, in the Third Degree.*

County, ss:

A. B., of said county, being duly sworn, says,* that on the   day of   instant, at the town of   , in said county, in the day time, one R. D. did wilfully, maliciously and feloniously, set fire to and burn the warehouse, &c., [*as in* § 663, *to the end; or,* in the night time, one R. D. did unlawfully, wilfully, maliciously and feloniously, set fire to and burn a certain school house, situate in school district number   , in said town.]

Sworn, &c., [*as in* § 594.]

§ 665. *Complaint for Setting Fire to a Crop of Grain Growing.*

County, ss:

A. B., of said county, being duly sworn, says,* that on the
day of   instant, [*or,* last past,] at the town of   , in
said county, one R. D. did unlawfully, wilfully, maliciously and feloniously, set fire to and burn a certain crop of barley then growing
in the field of the said A. B., situate in said town.

Sworn, &c., [*as in* § 594.]

---

§ 666. *Complaint for Manslaughter, in Killing Another with an Axe.*

County, ss:

A. B., of said county, being duly sworn, says,* that on the
day of   instant, [*or,* last past,] at the town of   , in
said county, one R. D. did wilfully and feloniously strike one M. P.,
with an axe, then in the hands of the said R. D., and thereby gave
him, the said M. P., one mortal wound, whereof the said M. P. died
immediately, [*or,* languished a short time and then died.]

Sworn, &c., [*as in* § 594.]

---

§ 667. *Complaint for Manslaughter, in Killing an Unborn Child, by Kicking its Mother.*

County, ss:

A. B., of said county, being duly sworn, says,* that on the
day of   instant, [*or,* last past,] at the town of ·   , in
said county, one R. D. did wilfully and feloniously kill an unborn
quick child, of which one E. P. was then and there pregnant, by
kicking the said E. P., with intent to kill her, the said E. P., or the
said unborn quick child.

Sworn, &c., [*as in* § 594.]

---

§ 668. *Complaint for Manslaughter, in Killing an Unborn Child, by Administering Drugs, etc., to the Mother.*

County, ss:

A. B., of said county, being duly sworn says,* that on the
day of   instant, [*or,* last past,] at the town of   , in
said county, one R. D. did wilfully and feloniously administer to one
E. P., who was then and there pregnant with a quick child, a certain
medicine, drug, or substance, called "savin," [*or,* use or employ a

certain instrument, called a "forceps,"] with intent thereby to destroy such unborn quick child: whereof the said unborn quick child died immediately, [or, languished a short time, and then died.]

Sworn, &c., [as in § 594.]

---

§ 669. Complaint for Rape.

County, ss:

A. B., of said county, being duly sworn, says,* that on the day of instant, [or, last past,] at the town of , in said county, one R. D. did violently and feloniously make an assault upon the body of the said A. B. [or, of one E. P.] and her, the said A. B., [or, E. P.,] against her will did then and there ravish and carnally know.

Sworn, &c., [as in § 594.]

---

§ 670. Complaint for Rape, on Female under Ten Years.

County, ss:

A. B., of said county, being duly sworn, says,* that on the day of instant, [or, last past,] at the town of , in said county, one R. D. did feloniously make an assault on C. P., a female child under the age of ten years, and her, the said C. P., then and there wickedly, unlawfully and feloniously, did carnally know.

Sworn, &c., [as in § 594.]

---

§ 671. Complaint for Assault, with Intent to Commit a Rape.

County, ss:

A. B., of said county, being duly sworn, says,* that on the day of instant, [or, last past,] at the town of , in said county, one R. D. did feloniously make an assault on one E. P., with intent her, the said E. P., against her will, then and there feloniously to ravish and carnally know.

Sworn, &c., [as in § 594.]

---

§ 672. Complaint for Forcible Abduction of a Woman, with intent to Compel her to Marry, or Prostitute Herself.

County, ss:

A. B., of said county, being duly sworn, says,* that on the day of instant, [or, last past,] at the town of , in said county, one R. D. did make an assault upon her, the said A. B., [*or,* one E. P.,] and did then and there unlawfully, feloniously, and against her will, take her, the said A. B., [*or,* take the said E. P.,] with the intent to compel her by force [*or,* menaces; *or,* duress] to marry him, the said R. D., [*or,* one L. M.; *or,* with the intent that she should be defiled.]

Sworn, &c., [*as in* § 594.]

---

§ 673. *Complaint for taking Female under Fourteen Years of Age from Her Parent, or Guardian.*

County, ss:

A. B., of said county, being duly sworn, says,* that on the day of   instant, [*or,* last past,] at the town of   , in said county, one R. D. did unlawfully and feloniously take away one M. B., a female infant under the age of fourteen years, from the said A. B., her father, [*or,* guardian, duly appointed, and having the legal charge of her person,] without his consent, for the purpose of prostitution, [*or,* concubinage; *or,* marriage.]

Sworn, &c., [*as in* § 594.]

---

§ 674. *Complaint for Mayhem, or Maiming.*

County, ss:

A. B., of said County being duly sworn, says,* that on the day of   instant, [*or,* last past,] at the town of   , in said county, one R. D., from premeditated design, and by lying in wait for the purpose, did unlawfully and feloniously assault the said A. B., and did then and there put out one of the said A. B.'s eyes, [*or,* one R. D. did unlawfully, violently, maliciously and feloniously, assault the said A. B., with intent to kill [*or,* rob] him, and did then and there slit the nose of the said A. B.]

Sworn, &c., [*as in* § 594.]

---

§ 675. *Complaint for Child Stealing.*

County, ss:

A. B., of said county, being duly sworn, says,* that on the day of   instant, [*or,* last past, at the town of   , in said county, one R. D., did feloniously, maliciously and forcibly, [*or,* fraudu lently, *if no force was used,*] take, [*or,* lead,] and carry away; [*or,* decoy; *or,* entice away;] one R. B., the child of the said A. B., and under the age of twelve years, with intent to detain and conceal the said child from the said A. B.

Sworn, &c., [*as in* § 594.]

---

§ 676. *Complaint for Abandoning Child.*

County, ss

A. B., of said county, being duly sworn, says,* that on the day of   instant, [*or,* last past.] at the town of   , in said county, one R. D. did feloniously expose and leave a certain child named E. D., under the age of   years, of which child said R. D. was the father, [*or,* which child had been confided to the care of the said R. D.,] with intent wholly to abandon the said child.

Sworn, &c., [*as in* § 594.]

---

§ 677. *Complaint for Shooting at, or Attempting to Shoot at, with Intent to Kill, Rob, or Maim.*

County, ss:

A. B., of said county, being duly sworn, says,* that on the day of   instant, [*or,* last past,] at the town of   , in said county, one R. D. did feloniously shoot at him, the said A. B., with a certain gun, loaded with gunpowder and lead, with intent to kill him, the said A. B., [*or,* did feloniously present and level at the said A. B., a pistol, loaded with gunpowder and lead, and attempt, by drawing the trigger thereof, to discharge the same at the said A. B., with intent to kill [*or,* rob; *or,* maim] him, the said A. B.]

Sworn, &c., [*as in* § 594.]

---

§ 678. *Complaint for Assault with Deadly Weapon, with Attempt to Kill.*

County, ss:

A. B., of said county, being duly sworn, says,* that on the day of   instant, [*or,* last past,] at the town of   , in said county, one R. D. did feloniously, with and by means of a certain deadly weapon, to wit, an axe, then in his hands, make an assault upon the said A. B., and him, the said A. B., did then and there, with the said deadly weapon, beat and ill-treat, with intent to kill him, the said A. B.; [or, did, with and by means of his hands, feet and fists, and by such force as was likely to produce death, feloniously assault and beat the said A. B., with intent, &c., *as above.*]

Sworn, &c., [*as in* § 594.]

---

§ 679. *Complaint for Poisoning Food.*

County, ss:

A. B., of said county, being duly sworn, says,* that on the day of   instant, [*or,* last past] at the town of   , in said county, one R. D., with intent to injure and kill one M. B., and divers other persons, did maliciously and feloniously mingle a certain poison called arsenic, with certain food, [*or,* drink; *or,* medicine,] in order that the same might be taken by the said M. B., and other persons.

Sworn, &c., [*as in* § 594,]

---

§ 680. *Complaint for Poisoning Well.*

County, ss:

A. B., of said county, being duly sworn, says,* that on the day of   instant, [*or,* last past,] at the town of   , in said county, one R. D., with intent to injure and kill one M. B., and one or more of the members of his family, and divers other persons, did maliciously and feloniously mingle a certain poison, called arsenic, with the waters of the well belonging to the said M. B., and situate near his dwelling house, to which the said M. B., and the members of his family, and divers other persons of the said town, were used to resort for the purpose of obtaining water for drinking and culinary purposes, in order that the said poison, so mingled with the waters aforesaid, might be taken by the said M. B., and one or more of the members of his family, and divers other persons.

Sworn, &c., [*as in* § 594.]

---

§ 681. *Complaint for Assault, with Intent to Rob, or Commit Burglary.*

County, ss:

A. B., of said county, being duly sworn, says,* that on the day of   instant, [*or,* last past,] at the town of   , in said county, one R. D. did feloniously make an assault upon the said A. B., with intent to commit robbery upon the said A. B., by feloniously taking the money of the said A. B. from his person, by violence thereto, and against his will; [*or*, with intent to commit burglary in the dwelling house of the said A. B., situate in the town of   .]

Sworn, &c., [*as in* § 594.]

---

§ 682. *Complaint for Burglary.*

County, ss:

A. B., of said county, being duly sworn, says,* that on the   day of   instant, [*or*, last past,] at the town of   , in said county, one R. D. did feloniously and burglariously break and enter the dwelling house of the said A. B., situate in the said town, by picking the lock of the outer door thereof; [*or*, by breaking the fastening of one of the window shutters thereof; *or*, by unlocking the outer door thereof, by means of false keys,] with intent to steal, take and carry away, from said dwelling house, divers goods and chattels therein, belonging to the said A. B.; the wife and family of the said A. B. being at the time in said dwelling house; [*or*, with intent to rob the said A. B. of his goods and chattels, in his presence and against his will, by force and violence to his person, he, the said R. D., being at the time armed with a dangerous weapon, to wit, with a pistol; and the said A. B., and his family, being in the said dwelling house.]

Sworn, &c., [*as in* § 594.]

---

§ 683. *Complaint for Felony and Burglary in Shop.*

County, ss:

A. B. of said county, being duly sworn, says,* that on the   day of   instant, [*or*, last past,] at the town of   , in said county, one R. D. did feloniously and burglariously break and enter the shop of the said A. B. by [*describe the manner*,] being within the curtilage of the dwelling house of the said A. B., there situate, but not forming part thereof, &c., [*as in* § 682 *to the end, omitting the allegation in regard to the family being present.*]

Sworn, &c., [*as in* § 594.]

---

§ 684. *Complaint for Burglary in entering Store.*

County, ss:

A. B., of said county, being duly sworn, says,* that on the   **day** of   instant, [*or*, last past,] at the town of   , in said County, one R. D. did feloniously and burglariously break and entr r the store of the said A. B., there situate, by [*describe the manner*,] in which goods and merchandise were then kept for sale, with intent feloniously to steal, take and carry away, the goods and chattels of the said A. B. therein, to wit, the goods and merchandise aforesaid, or some part or portion thereof.

Sworn, &c., [*as in* § 594.]

---

§ 685. *Complaint for Constructive Burglary.*

County, ss:

A. B., of said county, being duly sworn, says,* that on the day of instant, [*or*, last past,] at the town of , in said county, one R. D. did feloniously and burglariously break and enter the dwelling house of the said A. B., situate in said town, by knocking at the outer door thereof, and demanding to speak with the said A. B., and, upon the said A. B. opening the door for that purpose, rushing and entering into the said dwelling house, with intent to rob the said A. B. of his goods and chattels, in his presence and against his will, by force and violence to his person; the said A. B. and his family being at the time in said dwelling house.

Sworn, &c., [*as in* § 594.]

---

§ 686. *Complaint for Forgery.*

County, ss:

A. B., of said county, being duly sworn, says,* that on the day of instant, [*or*, last past,] at the town of , in said county, one R. D. did falsely and feloniously forge and counterfeit [*or*, alter,] a certain paper writing, being, or purporting to be, a will [*or*, deed,] by which a right or interest in real or personal property was, or purported to be, transferred, with intent to defraud the said A. B., [*or*, a certain paper writing, purporting to be a certificate of the acknowledgment of the execution of a certain deed or conveyance from the said A. B. to S. T., of certain lands situate in said county, before one G. H., a Justice of the Peace; which said deed or conveyance was of a nature, or proper, to be recorded according to law, with intent to defraud the said A. B.; or, did falsely and feloniously make, forge and counterfeit, a certain promissory note, purporting to be the promissory note of the said A. B., for the payment of dollars to C. D., thirty days after date, with intent to defraud the said A. B.]

Sworn, &c., [*as in* § 594.]

§ 687. *Complaint for Passing, or Offering to Pass, Counterfeit Bank Notes.*

County, ss:

A. B., of said County, being duly sworn, says,* that on the day of instant, [*or*, last past,] at the town of , in said county, one R. D. did feloniously sell and exchange, [*or*, offer to sell and exchange,] to and with the said A. B., for a valuable consideration, to wit, the sum of ten dollars in silver coin, [*or*, goods and merchandise of the value of ten dollars,] two forged and counterfeit negotiable notes, commonly called bank notes, purporting to be the promissory notes of, and to have been issued by, the Bank, for the payment of the sum of five dollars each; he, the said R. D., well knowing the said bank notes to be forged and counterfeited, and with the intent to deceive and defraud the said A. B.

Sworn, &c., [*as in* § 594.]

---

§ 688. *Complaint for Altering or Counterfeiting Bank Notes.*

County, ss:

A. B., of said county, being duly sworn says,* that on the day of instant, [*or*, last past,] at the town of , in said county, one R. D. did feloniously counterfeit, [*or*, counterfeit and alter,] a certain bank or promissory note, purporting to be the promissory note of, and to be issued by the Bank, for the payment of the sum of ten dollars, [*if the charge is for altering a note, insert here:* in such a manner as to make the same resemble and purport to be a bank or promissory note for the payment of the sum of one hundred dollars,] with intent to defraud the said bank, or some person or persons, or body politic or corporate, to this deponent unknown.

Sworn, &c., [*as in* § 594.]

---

§ 689. *Complaint for Obtaining Property by a False Token, or by Falsely Personating Another.*

County, ss:

A. B., of said county, being duly sworn, says,* that on the day of instant, [*or*, last past,] at the town of , in said county, one R. D. did designedly, falsely, and feloniously, by color of a certain false token or writing, [*or*, counterfeit letter,] obtain from the said A. B., certain goods and chattels, of the value of dollars, to wit: [*describe the property;*] [*or*, did falsely and feloniously personate and represent himself to be one C. D., and did then and there, and in such assumed name and character, obtain a certain horse of the value of   dollars, intended to be delivered to the said C. D.]

Sworn, &c., [*as in* § 594.]

---

§ 690. *Complaint for Obtaining Money, or Property, by False Pretences.*

County, ss:

A. B., of said county, being duly sworn, says,* that on the day of   instant, [*or,* last past,] at the town of   , in said county, one R. D. did designedly and feloniously, and by the false pretence that he, the said R. D., was sent and authorized by one C. D., [*or,* that he owned a farm, containing one hundred acres, or thereabouts, situate in the town of   , in said county, free of all incumbrances; *or,* that he was worth   dollars, after the payment of all his debts and liabilities; *or,* that he owned and was possessed of personal property to the value of   dollars, and was not a householder, or man of family, whereby the same would be exempt from execution against him; *or,* that he was entirely free and clear from all debts and liabilities, of every name and description,] demand and receive [*or,* obtain on credit,] from the said A. B., a large sum of money, to wit, the sum of   dollars, [*or,* goods and merchandise of the value of   dollars,] with the intent to cheat and defraud the said A. B.

Sworn, &c., [*as in* § 594.]

---

§ 691. *Complaint for Robbery.*

County, ss:

A. B., of said county, being duly sworn, says,* that on the day of   instant, [*or,* last past,] at the town of   , in said county, one R. D. did violently and feloniously make an assault upon him, the said A. B.; and, by putting him, the said A. B., in bodily fear and danger of his life, did then and there steal, take and carry away, &c., [*describe property taken.*]

Sworn, &c., [*as in* § 594.]

---

§ 692. *Complaint for Embezzlement.*

County, ss:

A. B., of said county, being duly sworn, says,* that on the day of   instant, [*or,* last past,] at the town of   , in said county, one R. D., being a servant [or, clerk] of the said A. B., and not being an apprentice, nor within the age of eighteen years, did feloniously embezzle, and convert to his own use, without the consent of the said A. B., [describe property,] belonging to the said A. B.

Sworn, &c., [as in § 594.]

---

§ 693. Complaint for Receiving Stolen Goods.

County, ss:

A. B., of said county, being duly sworn, says,* that on the day of   instant, [or, last past,] at the town of   , in said county, one R. D. did feloniously receive or buy, of one O. P., certain goods and chattels, to wit: [describe the property,] he the said R. D., well knowing the said goods and chattels to have been feloniously stolen and taken from him, the said A. B.

Sworn, &c., [as in § 594.]

---

§ 694. Complaint for Perjury.

County, ss:

A. B., of said county, being duly sworn, says,* that in a certain action at law, tried on the   day of   instant, [or, last past,] at the town of   , in said county, before H. R. F., Esq., one of the Justices of the Peace of the said county, in which the said A. B. was plaintiff and one C. D. defendant, the said Justice having jurisdiction over the said action, and full power and authority to try the same, and to administer oaths to all witnesses sworn upon such trial, one R. D. was produced as a witness on the part of C. D., the defendant aforesaid, and was duly sworn to speak the truth, &c., [follow the language of the oath administered:] and that the said R. D., being interrogated as such witness, whether the said A. B. was at the dwelling house of the said C. D., on the   day of   , 18   , which inquiry was material and pertinent to the issue joined in the action aforesaid, did then and there, to wit, at the time and place aforesaid, falsely, wilfully and corruptly, depose and swear, that the said A. B. was at the dwelling house of the said C. D., on the said   day of   , 18   , whereas, in truth and in fact, the said A. B. was not at the dwelling house of the said C. D., on the said   day of   , 18   ; whereby the said R. D. did then and there, to wit, at the time and place aforesaid, wilfully and corruptly swear falsely, and commit wilful and corrupt perjury.

Sworn, &c., [as in § 594.]

§ 695. *Complaint for Bigamy.*

County, ss:

A. B., of said county, being duly sworn, says,* that on the day of   instant, [*or*, last past,] at the town of   , in said county, one R. D., being then married to M. D., did wilfully and feloniously marry and take to wife, one E. B.; the said R. D. well knowing that his said former wife, M. D., was then living and in full life.

Sworn, &c., [*as in* § 594.]

---

§ 696. *Complaint for Marrying the Wife of Another.*

County, ss:

A. B., of said county, being duly sworn, says,* that on the day of   instant, [*or*, last past,] at the town of   , in said county, one R. D. did knowingly, unlawfully and feloniously, marry, and take to wife, one M. R., she being then married, and the wife of R. R.

Sworn, &c., [*as in* § 594.]

---

§ 697. *Complaint for Malicious Mischief.*

County, ss:

A. B., of said county, being duly sworn, says,* that on the day of   instant, [*or*, last past,] at the town of   , in said county, one R. D. did wilfully and maliciously administer to a certain horse, the property of the said A. B., a certain deadly poison, called arsenic, by mixing the same with the food of the said horse.

Sworn, &c., [*as in* § 594.]

---

§ 698. *Complaint for Malicious Trespass, or for Girdling Trees.*

County, ss:

A. B., of said county, being duly sworn, says,* that on the day of   instant, [*or*, last past,] at the town of   , in said county, one R. D. did wilfully, maliciously and unlawfully, cut down and destroy [*or*, wilfully and maliciously girdle,] certain growing trees, situate on the land of the said A. B., in said town

Sworn, &c., [*as in* § 594.]

§ 699. *Complaint for Procuring Abortion.*

County, ss:

A. B., of said county, being duly sworn, says,* that on the day of   instant, [*or,* last past,] at the town of   , in said county, one R. D. did wilfully and unlawfully administer a certain drug called "savin," [*or,* did use and employ a certain instrument called a "forceps,"] on the body of E. M., she being then pregnant, with intent thereby to procure the miscarriage of the said E. M.

Sworn, &c., [*as in* § 594.]

---

§ 700. *Complaint for Making an Affray.*

County, ss:

A. B. of said county, being duly sworn, says,* that on the day of   instant, [*or,* last past,] at the town of   , in said county, one R. D. did, in a tumultuous manner, make an affray, wherein one R. B. was assaulted, beat and abused, by the said R. D., without any just and reasonable cause.

Sworn, &c., [*as in* § 594.]

---

§ 701. *Complaint for Cruelty to Animals.*

County, ss:

A. B., of said county, being duly sworn, says,* that on the day of   instant, [*or,* last past,] at the town of   , in said county, one R. D. did cruelly and maliciously kill [*or,* maim; *or,* beat and torture] a certain bay gelding horse belonging to him, the said R. D., [*or,* to one O. D.]

Sworn, &c., [*as in* § 594.]

---

§ 702. *Complaint for a Rout, or Riot.*

County, ss:

A. B., of said county, being duly sworn, says,* that on the day of   instant, [*or,* last past,] at the town of   , in said county, R. D., D. D., A. D., &c., &c., did unlawfully, tumultuously and routously, assemble together, to the manifest terror and disturbance of the citizens then and there being, with an intent mutually to assist each other, against all who should oppose them, in the execution of a certain enterprise, to wit, the assault and beating of one T. M., with force and violence, and against the peace: and being so assembled, together with divers other persons unknown, they did, afterwards, to wit, on the day and at the place aforesaid, proceed in a noisy, riotous and tumultuous manner, towards the house of the said T. M., in order to assault and beat him, the said T. M.; [*if the assault was committed, add:* and did then and there violently and maliciously assault and beat the said T. M.]

Sworn, &c., [*as in* § 594.]

---

§ 703. *Complaint for Selling Unwholesome Food.*

County, ss:

A. B., of said county, being duly sworn, says,* that on the day of   instant, [*or, last past,*] at the town of   , in said county, one R. D. did knowingly, unlawfully and wickedly, sell to one M. B., a quarter of lamb, which had become tainted and unwholesome.

Sworn, &c., [*as in* § 594.]

---

§ 704. *Complaint for Disturbing a Religious Meeting.*

County, ss:

A. B., of said county, being duly sworn, says,* that on the day of   instant, [*or, last past,*] at the town of   , in said county, one R. D. did wilfully and unlawfully disturb, interrupt and disquiet, an assemblage of people, collected for the purpose of religious worship, by loud and profane discourse, [*or,* by rude and riotous noises; *or,* by rude and indecent behavior.]

Sworn, &c., [*as in* § 594.]

---

§ 705. *Complaint to Obtain a Search Warrant.*

County, ss:

A. B., of said county, being duly sworn, says, that certain personal property of the said A. B., [*or,* of one C. D.,] to wit: [*describe the property;*] of the value of   dollars, or upwards, was stolen and feloniously taken from his dwelling house in the town of   , in said county, on the   day of   instant, [*or,* last past:]* and that this deponent suspects that R. D. has stolen and taken the same as aforesaid; and that the said property, or a part thereof, is now concealed in the dwelling house of the said C. D., in the said county; wherefore process is applied for to search the same.

Sworn, &c., [*as in* § 594.]

A R

§ 706. *Search Warrant.*

County, ss:

To the Sheriff of said County, or to any Constable of the Town [*or,*
    City*]* of   , in said County, greeting:

Whereas, A. B. has made complaint, upon oath, before me, J. H.
B., one of the Justices of the Peace of the said county, that, &c.,
[*as in* § 705, *to the* *, *and then add*:] and that he suspects that R.
D. did steal and take the same, as aforesaid; and that the said property, or a part thereof, is now concealed in the dwelling house of
the said R. D., in said county: Therefore, the people of the State of
New York command you to search the place where the said property
is suspected to be concealed, in the day time, [*or,* as well in the night
time, as in the day time,] and that you bring the same before me.

Witness, &c., [*as in* § 648.]

---

§ 707. *Oath of Complainant, or Witness on Complaint.*

You do swear in the presence of Almighty God, that you will true
answers make to such questions as shall be put to you, touching this
complaint against C. D.

---

§ 708. *Recognizance in Justices' Courts.*

State of New York, }
    County, } ss:

We, C. D. and E. F., of   , in said county, acknowledge
ourselves to be severally indebted to the people of the State of New
York; that is to say: the said C. D. in the sum of   dollars,
and the said E. F. in the sum of   dollars, to be well and
truly paid, if default shall be made in the condition following:

The condition of this recognizance is such, that if the said C. D.
shall personally appear at the next Court of Oyer and Terminer, [*or,*
Court of Sessions,] to be held in and for said county,* then and
there to answer to a complaint against him for, &c., [*state the complaint,*] and to do and receive what shall, by the court, be then and
there enjoined upon him: [*if the recognizance is entered into by a
witness and surety, say:* then and there to give evidence on the
part of the said people against C. D., charged with, &c., [*as the offence may be,*] as well to the grand jury as to the petit jury,]* and
shall not depart the court without leave;] [*in a recognizance on a
peace warrant: insert here:* and in the meanwhile shall keep the
peace towards the people of this State, and particularly towards A

B., *and omit all that part of the form between the two *s,*] then this recognizance to be void; otherwise of force.

Taken, subscribed, and acknowledged, ⎫　　C. D.　[L. s.]
the　　　day of　　, 18　, before me, ⎭　　E. F.　[L. s.]

　　　　　　　　　　　　　　G. H., Justice, &c.

---

§ 709. *Record of Conviction at Special Sessions.*

State of New York, ⎫ ss:
　　County, ⎭

Be it remembered, that at a Court of Special Sessions, held by the undersigned, a Justice of the Peace of the said county, this day of　　　, 18　, at his office in the town of　　　, in said county, C. D. was brought before the said court, charged on the oath of A. B., with having, on the　　　day of　　, 18　, at the town of　　　, in said county, &c., [*state the offence:*] which charge, [*or, charges,*] being stated in the warrant by me issued, [*or, issued by S. T., Esq.,* one of the Justices of the Peace of the said county,] was [*or, were*] distinctly read to the defendant in open court, to which he plead not guilty, [*or, guilty:*] whereupon such proceedings were had in the said court, that the defendant was convicted of the charge [*or, charges*] above specified,* and the court rendered judgment thereon, that the said C. D., &c., [*as the judgment may be.*]

In witness whereof, I have hereunto subscribed these presents, the　　　day of　　　, 18　.

　　　　　　　　　　　　　　G. H., Justice of the Peace.

---

§ 710. *Commitment from Special Sessions.*

State of New York, ⎫ ss:
　　County, ⎭

To any Constable of the said County, greeting:

At a Court of Special Sessions, duly held by the undersigned, &c., [*as in* § 709, *to the* *, *and then add:*] and the court having rendered judgment thereon, that the said C. D., &c., [*as the judgment may be;*] Therefore the people of the State of New York command you to convey the said C. D. to the common jail of the said county, the keeper whereof is hereby required to keep him in safe custody in the said jail, until the judgment so rendered be satisfied, or he be discharged by due course of law.

Witness, &c., [*as in* § 648.]

CHAPTER XXVI.

LANDLORD AND TENANT.

PRACTICAL MARKS.

1. The relation of landlord and tenant exists, wherever there is a contract for the possession and profits of lands or tenements, on one side; and a recompense, by payment of rent, or some reciprocal consideration, on the other. The contract is called a lease, or demise, and may be for life, for a term of years, or at the will of one of the parties. If the lessee, or tenant, parts with any portion of the term, the contract assigning such portion is called an underlease.[1]

2. The law will imply a tenancy, from the mere occupation of premises, pending the execution of a lease; or an occupation and payment of rent under an invalid agreement; or where a tenant for years holds over after the expiration of his term, with the landlord's consent; or from the mere payment of rent, where it bears any reasonable proportion to the value of the premises. And where the tenant continues in possession for two weeks after the expiration of his term, though alledging that he does not intend to remain, the landlord may regard him as a tenant for another year, if he thinks proper to do so.[2]

3. A bargain for rooms in a boarding-house is not a lease.[3]

4. Leases for a year, or any less time, may be made by a verbal agreement; in all other cases, they must be in writing, and if for life, executed under seal, and in the presence of a witness.[4]

5. A covenant to pay rent, founded upon a lease for five years, not reduced to writing, is void for want of consideration.[5]

6. A lease of three years, or for any longer period, must be recorded in the county where the premises are situated, in the same manner as conveyances of real estate; otherwise it is void as against

---

[1] 7 Cowen, 326.
[2] 4 Cowen, 350, 473, 1 Denio, 113.
[3] 1 Denio, 602.

[4] 2 R. S. (3 d ed.) 22, § 137; 1d 194, § 8; 16 Wendell, 465; 21 Id., 492; 10 Paige, 393, 537.
[5] 7 Hill, 83.

a subsequent purchaser in good faith, and for a valuable consideration. Leases for life or lives, or for years, in the counties of Albany, Ulster, Sullivan, Herkimer, Dutchess, Columbia, Delaware and Schenectady, in the State of New York, need not be recorded.[1]

7. In South Carolina, a conveyance of an estate in land for life, or lives, must be in writing, signed, sealed and delivered. In Virginia and Kentucky, the same rule prevails as to all estates or interests in land exceeding a term of five years; and in Rhode Island and Vermont, as to all estates exceeding a term of one year. In Louisiana, all conveyances of land must be in writing, and registered in the office of a notary.[2]

8. A lease for years, without saying how many, is good for two years. In the city of New York, if no time is agreed on as to the duration of an agreement for the occupation of lands or tenements, it will be deemed valid until the first day of May next after possession is given.[3]

9. Where a lessor consents to a change of tenancy, and accepts a substituted tenant, the first tenant is discharged.[4]

10. A new lease, if valid, whether by parol or not, will operate as a surrender of a former lease.[5]

11. The interest of a tenant under a lease executed by a mortgagor, subsequent to the execution of a mortgage, is extinguished by a foreclosure and sale under such mortgage.[6]

12. Where a fraudulent representation is made by a landlord, as to the property demised, or the extent of his rights, the lessee is entitled to a deduction from the rent for the fraud.[7]

13. Interest is recoverable on a covenant for the payment of rent, from the time the rent is due, even where the rent is payable in grain or services, the value of which is not liquidated by the lease.[8]

14. A covenant by the lessee to pay assessments runs with the lease, and the assignee of the term is bound by it.[9]

15. There are four kinds of leases—*for life or lives, for years, at will,* and *by sufferance.* A tenant at will is one who occupies under an agreement to be determined at the pleasure of either of the parties. One who enters under an agreement to purchase, or for a lease, but has not paid rent, is a tenant at will; a parol gift of lands has also been held to create this species of tenancy. If the agreement be to let premises so long as the parties choose, reserving a compensation to be paid daily, it creates a tenancy at will. A notice to quit terminates a tenancy at will, and turns it into a tenancy from year to year. Where a tenant holds over after the expiration of his

---

[1] 2 R. S. (3d ed.) 40, §1 ; Id., 47, §§ 44, 49 ; Wendell, 485; 6 Id., 213; 8 Id., 260.
[2] 4 Kent's Commentaries, (2d ed.) 451.
[3] 2 R. S. (3d ed.) 29, § 1.
[4] 2 Barbour's S. C. Rep., 180.

[5] 2 Barbour's S. C. Rep., 180.
[6] 3 Denio, 214.
[7] 1 Comstock, 305.
[8] 2 Comstock, 135
[9] 2 Comstock, 394.

term, or where a person selling lands refuses to deliver them up, and continues in possession, a tenancy by sufferance is created.[1]

16. No lease or grant of agricultural land, for a longer period than twelve years, made subsequent to the first day of January, one thousand eight hundred and forty-seven, in which any rent, or service of any kind, is reserved, will be valid ; and all fines, quarter sales, and other like restraints upon alienation, reserved in any grant of land subsequent to that day, will likewise be void.[2]

17. A tenancy at will, or by sufferance, may be terminated by the landlord's giving one month's notice in writing to the tenant. In the Eastern States, three months, and in the Middle and Southern States, six months' notice is required. A tenant may also give notice of his intention to quit the premises, and if he does not yield possession at the time specified in his notice, he is liable to pay double rent.[3]

18. A tenancy from year to year may be determined, in New York and Vermont, by a notice of at least half a year, (182 days, or six calendar months,) ending with the period of the year at which the tenancy commenced. In Massachusetts, reasonable notice is required, and a notice of sixty days has been held sufficient. In Pennsylvania, the notice is one of three months, in all cases.[4]

19. Where a tenancy is for a short period—as for a quarter, a month, or a week—the length of the notice must be regulated by the letting ; as a month's notice for a month's letting, and a week's notice for a week's letting.[5]

20. Distress for rent has been abolished in the State of New York. In all cases where the right of re-entry is reserved and given to a grantor, or lessor, in any grant or lease, in default of a sufficiency of goods and chattels whereon to distrain, such re-entry may now be made at any time after default in the payment of the rent, provided fifteen days' notice in writing, of the intention to re-enter, be given by the grantor or lessor, his heirs or assigns, to the grantee or lessee, _is heirs, executors, administrators, or assigns ; and this, notwithstanding there be a sufficiency of goods and chattels to satisfy the rent, provided the same were taken in distress.[6]

21. The mode of re-entry above provided, by giving a notice of fifteen days, does not repeal that under the Revised Statutes ; the former is merely an additional mode.[7]

22. A tenant or under tenant, or his assigns or legal representatives, may be removed from any premises occupied by him, by any

[1] 4 Johnson, 150; 4 Cowen, 349; 11 Wendell, 619; 23 Id., 516.
[2] Amended Constitution of New York, Article 1., §§ 14, 15.
[3] 2 R. S. (3d ed.) 30, §§ 7-9; 11 Wendell, 616.
[4] 4 Kent's Commentaries, (2d ed.) 111-113; 1 Johnson, 322; 8 Cowen, 13.
[5] 4 Kent's Commentaries, (2d ed.) 113.
[6] Laws of 1846. chap. 274.
[7] 2 Barbour's S. C. Rep., 316.

Judge of the County Courts of the county, or by any Justice of the Peace of the city or town where such premises are situated ; or by any Mayor or Recorder of the city where such premises are situated; or in the city of New York, by the Mayor, Recorder, any Justice of the Marine Court, or any one of the Justices of the Justices' Court of the city of New York; where such tenant holds over and continues in possession of the premises, or any part thereof, after the expiration of his term, without permission of the landlord ; or where the tenant holds over without permission after default in the payment of rent, and a demand has been made of the rent, or three days' notice in writing served on the tenant, requiring payment of the rent or possession of the premises ; or where the tenant or lessee of a term of three years, or less, has taken the benefit of any insolvent act, or been discharged from liability to imprisonment ; or where one holds over and continues in possession of any real estate which has been sold under an execution against him, after a title under such sale has been perfected.[1]

23. Rent previously due may be collected by action, after the summary removal of the tenant for non-payment of rent.[2]

 any tenant, being in arrear for rent, desert the demised premises, and leave the same unoccupied and uncultivated, any Justice of the Peace of the county may, at the request of the landlord, and upon due proof that the premises have been so deserted, go upon and view the premises ; and upon being satisfied, upon such view, that the premises have been so deserted, he shall affix a notice in writing upon a conspicuous part of the premises, requiring the tenant to appear, &c., as in the form hereinafter given, at some time to be specified in the notice, not less than five nor more than twenty days after the date thereof.[3]

25. Where any forcible entry is made into any lands or possessions: or where the entry is made in a peaceable manner, and the possession held by force, the person so forcibly put out, or so forcibly holden out, of possession, and the guardian of any such person being a minor, may be restored to such possession, by making complaint to a Justice of the Supreme Court, or County Judge; any Mayor, Recorder, or Alderman, of any city ; or, in the city of New York, in addition to the officers already named, to any Justice of the Superior, or Marine Court, or any Justice.[4]

26. An affidavit made by an agent, under the statute authorizing summary proceedings to recover possession of land, must state the

---

[1] 2 R. S. (3d ed.) 503, § 28 ; Laws of 1849, chap. 193 ; 6 Cowen, 448 ; 8 Id., 68 ; 6 Wendell, 281 ; 9 Id., 227 ; 11 Id., 616 ; 15 Id., 226 ; 17 Id., 464 ; 19 Id., 103 ; 21 Id., 587 ; 1 Hill, 512 ; 5 Id., 314, 507 ; 1 Denio, 190.
[2] 3 Denio, 452.

[3] 2 R. S. (3d ed.) 503, §§ 24, 25.
[4] 2 R. S. (3d ed.) 599, § 1, et seq. ; 8 Johnson, 464 ; 11 Id., 504 ; 13 Id., 40 ; 8 Cowen, 226 ; 4 Wendell, 213 ; 9 Id., 50 ; 11 Id., 157 1 Hall's Superior Court Rep , 240.

fact of the agency in positive terms; it will not answer merely to describe the person as agent.[1]

FORMS.

§ 711. *Landlord's Certificate of Renting.*

This is to certify, that I have, this   day of   , 18 , let and rented unto C. D. my house and lot, known as number   , in   street, in the   of   , with the appurtenances, and the sole and uninterrupted use and occupation thereof, for one year, to commence the   day of   next, at the yearly rent of   dollars, payable quarterly: [*add*, with all taxes and assessments, *where the same are to be paid by the tenant.*]

A. B.

§ 712. *Tenant's Agreement.*

This is to certify, that I have hired and taken from A. B. his house and lot, known as number   , in   street, in the of   , with the appurtenances, for the term of one year, to commence the   day of   next, at the yearly rent of dollars, payable quarterly. [*Insert the clause in relation to taxes, if necessary.*]   And I do hereby promise to make punctual payment of the rent in manner aforesaid, except in case the premises become untenantable from fire or any other cause, when the rent is to cease: And I do further promise to quit and surrender the premises, at the expiration of the term, in as good state and condition as reasonable use and wear thereof will permit, damages by the elements excepted.*

Given under my hand and seal, the   day of   , 18 .

In presence of }
   G. H.   }

C. D. [L. s.]

§ 713. *Security for Rent.*

In consideration of the letting of the premises above described, and for the sum of one dollar, I do hereby become surety for the punctual payment of the rent, and performance of the covenants, in the above

---

[1] 4 Denio, 71.

written agreement mentioned, to be paid and performed by C. D., as therein specified ; and if any default shall at any time be made therein, I do hereby promise and agree to pay unto the landlord in said agreement named, the said rent, or any arrears thereof that may be due, and fully satisfy the conditions of the said agreement, and all damages that may accrue by reason of the non-fulfilment thereof, without requiring notice or proof of demand being made.

Given under my hand and seal, the　　　day of　　　, 18 .

E. F. [L. s.]

---

§ 714. *Landlord's Certificate, where Tenant is Not to Underlet, or Occupy for any Business deemed Extra Hazardous.*

This is to certify, that I, C. D., have let and rented unto A. B., the premises known as number　　　, in　　　street, in the　　　of　　　, for the term of one year from the first day of　　　next, at the yearly rent of　　　dollars, payable quarterly.* The premises are not to be used or occupied for any business deemed extra-hazardous on account of fire; nor shall the same, or any part thereof, be let or underlet, except with the consent of the landlord, in writing, under the penalty of forfeiture and damages.

Given under my hand, this　　　day of　　　, 18 .

C. D.

---

§ 715. *Tenant's Agreement in Foregoing Case.*

This is to certify, &c., [*as in* § 712 *to the* *, *and then add:*] And I do hereby engage not to let or underlet, the whole or any part of the said premises, or to occupy the same in any business deemed extra-hazardous on account of fire, without the written consent of the landlord, under the penalty of forfeiture and damages.

Given, &c., [*as in* § 712.]

---

§ 716. *Tenant's Agreement, Embracing a Pledge of his Property, as Security.*

This is to certify, that I, A. B., have hired and taken from C. D., the premises known as number　　　, in　　　street, &c., [*as in* § 712 *to the* *, *and then add:*] And I do hereby mortgage and pledge all the personal property, of what kind soever, which I shall at any time have on said premises, and whether the same be exempt by law from sale under execution or not, to the faithful performance of these covenants ; hereby authorizing the said C. D., or his assigns, without legal process, to seize upon and sell the same, in case of any failure on my part to perform the said covenants,·or any or either of them,—and out of the proceeds of such sale to pay and discharge all arrearages of rent and expenses, and to return the surplus moneys, if any there be, to me or my representatives.

Given under my hand and seal, this　　day of　　, 18　.

A. B. [L. S.]

§ 717. *Landlord's Certificate, under the Exemption Act of* 1842.

This is to certify, &c., [*as in* § 714, *to the* *, *and then add:*] The above lease is upon the further condition, that the said tenant shall make punctual payment of the rent, in manner aforesaid, and shall quit and surrender the premises, at the expiration of the said term, in as good state and condition as reasonable use and wear thereof will permit, damages by the elements excepted, and shall not assign, let or underlet, the whole or any part of the said premises, or occupy the same for any business deemed extra-hazardous on account of fire, without the written consent of the landlord, under the penalty of forfeiture and damages.

And the said tenant, for the consideration aforesaid, has waived the benefit of the exemption specified in the first section of the act entitled " An Act to extend the exemption of household furniture and working tools from distress for rent and sale under execution," passed April 11th, 1842, and has agreed that the property thereby exempted shall be liable, and also that all property liable to distress for rent shall be so liable, whether on or off the said premises, wheresoever and whensoever the same may be found.

Given, &c., [*as in* § 714.]

§ 718. *Tenant's Agreement, Waiving the Benefit of the Exemption Act of* 1842.

This is to certify, &c., [*as in* § 712 *to the* *, *and then add :*] And I do hereby promise, in consideration thereof, to make punctual payment of the rent, in manner aforesaid, and quit and surrender the premises at the expiration of the said term, in as good state and condition as reasonable use and wear thereof will permit, damages by the elements excepted, and not to assign, let or underlet, the whole or any part of the said premises, or occupy the same for any business deemed extra-hazardous on account of fire, without the written consent of the landlord, under the penalty of forfeiture and damages.

And I do hereby, for the consideration aforesaid, waive the benefit of the exemption specified in the first section of the act entitled "An Act to extend the-exemption of household furniture and working tools from distress for rent and sale under execution," passed April 11th, 1842, and agree that the property thereby exempted, shall be liable to distress for said rent; and also, that all property liable to distress for rent shall be so liable, whether on or off the said premises, wheresoever and whensoever the same may be found.

Given, &c., [*as in* § 712.]

---

§ 719. *Agreement for a Lease.*

This agreement, made the   day of, &c., between A. B. of, &c., and C. D., of, &c., witnesseth: That the said A. B. hereby agrees to demise and let to the said C. D., by indenture, to be executed on the   day of   next, the dwelling-house and lot now occupied by the said A. B., in the village of   , to have and to hold the same unto the said C. D., his executors, administrators and assigns, from the first day of   next, for and during the term of five years, at or under the yearly rent of one hundred dollars, payable quarterly, clear of all taxes and assessments: in which lease there shall be contained covenants on the part of the said C. D., his executors, &c., to pay rent, (except in case the premises are destroyed by fire, the rent is to cease until they are re-built,) and all taxes and assessments; to keep the premises in good repair, (damages by fire excepted;) not to carry on any offensive business upon the same; and to deliver up peaceable possession of the said premises at the expiration of the term aforesaid: and the said lease shall also contain covenants on the part of the said A. B., his heirs and assigns, for quiet enjoyment; to renew said lease at the expiration of the term aforesaid, at the request of the said C. D., to be made fifteen days prior to the time of such expiration, for a further term of five years; and that, in case the said premises shall be destroyed by fire, the said A. B. will forthwith proceed to re-build the same.

And it is agreed between the aforesaid parties, that the costs and charges of making, executing and recording, the said lease, and duplicate thereof, shall be equally borne and divided between them.

In witness whereof, the said parties have hereunto set their hands and seals, the day and year first above written.

Sealed and delivered   }
  in presence of   }   A. B. [L s.]
    G. H.   C. D. [L s.]

§ 720. *Lease and Chattel Mortgage.*

This agreement, made the   day of   , 18 , between A. B., of, &c., of the first part, and C. D., of, &c., of the second part, witnesseth: That the said A. B. has agreed to let, and hereby does let, and the said C. D. has agreed to take, and hereby does take, all the premises known as number 347,   street, in the city of   , for one year commencing the   day of   , 18 , and ending the   day of   , 18 , at twelve o'clock, noon, of that day, at the annual rent of   dollars, payable in equal quarterly payments.

And the said C. D. hereby covenants and agrees to pay the rent in manner aforesaid; to permit the said A. B., or his agent, to enter the said premises at all reasonable hours in the day time, to make such repairs and alterations as may be necessary for the preservation thereof, and to exhibit the same to persons wishing to rent, after the   day of   , 18 , and put notices "To Let," on the walls thereof; to quit and surrender the said premises, at the expiration of the said term, in as good state and condition as reasonable use and wear thereof will permit, damages by the elements excepted; and that he will not assign, let or underlet, the whole or any part of the said premises, or occupy the same for any business deemed extra-hazardous, without the written consent of the said A. B., or his agent.

And the said C. D., in consideration of the premises, and of the sum of one dollar to him paid by the said A. B., doth hereby grant, bargain and sell, unto the said A. B., all and singular the following goods and chattels, [*or*, the goods and chattels, mentioned in the schedule hereto annexed:] viz: [*describe property if there be no schedule:*] To have and to hold the said goods and chattels to the said A. B., forever; upon the condition, however, that if the said C. D. shall well and truly pay, or cause to be paid, unto the said A. B., the rent above reserved, punctually, at the several times when the same shall become due, as aforesaid, then the said bargain and sale shall be null and void. But in case default shall be made in the payment of the said rent, or any part thereof, at the several times mentioned as aforesaid, and the same remain unpaid five days after the same becomes due and payable, then it shall be lawful for the said A. B. to take possession of the said goods and chattels, wherever the same may be found, and to sell the same at public sale, (first giving three days' notice of the time and place of such sale,) or so much thereof as may be necessary to pay the rent due, and the balance of rent for the whole unexpired term, whether due or not due, and all costs and expenses that may have accrued on account thereof, rendering the remaining goods and chattels, and the surplus money from said sale, if any there shall be, unto the said C. D., or his representative.

And it is further agreed between the said parties to these presents, that if at any time default shall be made in the payment of the said rent, or any part thereof, at the times above specified, the said A. B. shall and may re-enter the said premises, and remove all persons therefrom; and the said C. D. hereby expressly waives the service of any notice in writing of the intention to re-enter, or any legal process or proceeding to put the said A. B. in possession; and, also, that in case the said C. D. shall sell, assign or dispose of, or attempt to sell, assign, or otherwise dispose of, the goods and chattels aforesaid, or shall attempt to remove the same from the   of   , it shall and may be lawful for the said A. B. to take possession of the same, and retain them in his possession until the said rent shall be paid, or until default in the payment thereof. But until default be made in the payment of the said rent, the said goods and chattels (unless the said C. D. shall sell, or attempt to sell, or remove the same, as aforesaid,) shall remain in the possession of the said C. D.[1]

In witness, &c., [*as in* § 719.]

---

§ 721. *Agreement between a House-Keeper and Lodger.*

This agreement, by and between A. B., of, &c., and C. D., of, &c., made the   day of, &c., witnesseth: That the said C. D., in consideration of the agreement hereinafter contained, to be performed by A. B., has let to the said A. B. the entire first floor, and one room in the attic story, or garret, with the use of the offices, and of the yard for drying linen, or beating carpets or clothes, being part of the dwelling-house now occupied by the said C. D., situate in the village of   ', [*or,* known as number   in   street, in the city of Albany,] for and during the term of two years from the day of the date hereof; to hold to the said A. B., for the said term of two years, at the yearly rent of   dollars, payable quarterly to the said C. D. In consideration of the premises, A. B. agrees to pay to the said C. D., the aforesaid yearly rent of   dollars, at the times above limited for the payment thereof; and at the end of the said term, or in case of any default in the payment, to yield and deliver up to the said C. D., or his assigns, on request, the quiet and peaceable possession of the premises above described, and leave them in as good condition and repair as they shall be on his taking possession thereof, reasonable wear excepted.

In witness, &c., [*as in* § 719.]

---

[1] A lease, containing a mortgage of personal property, or a copy thereof, should be filed in the same manner as chattel mortgages, in order to have the lien valid against third persons.

§ 722. *Indenture of Lease.*

This indenture, made the   day of   , in the year of our Lord one thousand eight hundred and   , between A. B., of, &c., of the first part, and C. D., of, &c., of the second part, witnesseth: That the said party of the first part, for and in consideration of the rents, covenants and agreements, hereinafter mentioned, reserved and contained, on the part and behalf of the party of the second part, his executors, administrators and assigns, to be paid, kept and performed, hath granted, demised, and to farm letten, and by these presents doth grant, demise, and to farm let, unto the said party of the second part, his executors, administrators and assigns, all [*give description of premises:*] To have and to hold the said above mentioned and described premises, with the appurtenances, unto the said party of the second part, his executors, administrators and assigns, from the   day of   , one thousand eight hundred and   , * for and during, and until the full end and term of, ten years thence next ensuing, and fully to be complete and ended, [*or, for and during the natural life of E. F.;*] yielding and paying therefor, unto the said party of the first part, his heirs or assigns, yearly, and every year, during the said term hereby granted, the yearly rent or sum of   dollars, lawful money of the United States of America, in equal quarter [*or, half*] yearly payments, to wit: on the first day of May, August, November, and February, in each and every year during the said term: Provided always, nevertheless, that if the yearly rent above reserved, or any part thereof, shall be behind or unpaid, on any day of payment whereon the same ought to be paid, as aforesaid; or if default shall be made in any of the covenants herein contained, on the part and behalf of the said party of the second part, his executors, administrators and assigns, to be paid, kept and performed, then and from thenceforth it shall and may be lawful for the said party of the first part, his heirs or assigns, into and upon the said demised premises, and every part thereof, wholly to re-enter, and the same to have again, re-possess and enjoy, as in his or their first and former estate, any thing hereinbefore contained to the contrary thereof in any wise notwithstanding. And the said party of the second part, for himself and his heirs, executors and administrators, doth covenant and agree, to and with the said party of the first part, his heirs and assigns, by these presents, that the said party of the second part, his executors, administrators or assigns, shall and will, yearly, and every year, during the term hereby granted, well and truly pay, or cause to be paid, unto the said party of the first part, his heirs or assigns, the said yearly rent above reserved, on the days, and in the manner, limited and prescribed, as aforesaid, for the payment thereof, without any deduction, fraud, or delay, according to the true intent and meaning of these presents: [*if necessary, insert:* and that the said party of the second part, his executors, administrators, or assigns, shall and will, at their own proper costs and charges, bear, pay and discharge, all such taxes, duties and assessments whatsoever, as shall or may, during the said term hereby granted, be charged, assessed, or imposed upon the said described premises:] and that on the last day of the said term, or other sooner determination of the estate hereby granted, the said party of the second part, his executors, administrators, or assigns, shall and will peaceably and quietly leave, surrender and yield up, unto the said party of the first part, his heirs or assigns, all and singular the said demised premises. And the said party of the first part, for himself, his heirs and assigns, doth covenant and agree, by these presents, that the said party of the second part, his executors, administrators, or assigns, paying the said yearly rent above reserved, and performing the covenants and agreements aforesaid, on his and their part, the said party of the second part, his executors, administrators and assigns, shall and may at all times during the said term hereby granted, peaceably and quietly have, hold and enjoy, the said demised premises, without any manner of let, suit, trouble or hindrance, of or from the said party of the first part, his heirs or assigns, or any other person or persons whomsoever.

In witness, &c., [*as in* § 719.]

---

§ 723. *Farming Lease on Shares, with Agreement to Renew.*

This indenture made, &c., [*as in* § 722 *to the* *, *and then add:*] for and during the term of three years next ensuing, to be fully complete and ended: To have and to hold the said demised premises, unto the party of the second part, his heirs, executors and administrators, for his and their sole and proper use and benefit, for and during the term aforesaid, together with all the tenements and hereditaments thereunto appertaining, and all the stock and farming utensils, of every name and nature, now being in or upon the same, belonging to the said party of the first part.

In consideration whereof, the said party of the second part hereby covenants and agrees, to and with the party of the first part, that he will occupy, till, and in all respects cultivate the premises above mentioned, during the term aforesaid, in a husbandlike manner, and according to the usual course of husbandry practiced in the neighborhood; that he will not commit any waste or damage, or suffer any to be done; that he will keep the fences and buildings on the said premises in good repair, reasonable wear thereof and damages by the elements excepted; and that he will deliver to the said party of the first part, his heirs, executors or administrators, or to his or their order, one equal half of all the proceeds and crops produced on the said farm and premises aforesaid, of every name, kind and description,—to be divided on the said premises, in the mow, stack, or half bushel, according to the usual course and custom of making such divisions in the neighborhood, and in a seasonable time after such crops shall have been gathered and harvested.

It is further understood and agreed between the aforesaid parties, that the party of the first part shall find one equal half of all seed or seeds, necessary to be sown on said premises, and pay all taxes and assessments upon the same; that the party of the second part is to do, or cause to be done, all necessary work and labor in and about the cultivation of the said premises; that he is to have full permission to inclose, pasture, or till and cultivate, the said premises, so far as the same may be done without injury to the reversion, and to cut all necessary timber for firewood, farming purposes, and repairing fences; and that he is to give up and yield peaceable possession of the said premises, at the expiration of his said term; [*if the lease is executed by a person having only a life estate, insert:* and that the said term shall be determined and ended by the death of the party of the first part, at any time within the said period of three years.]

And the said party of the first part, in consideration of the premises, and of the sum of one dollar to him in hand paid by the party of the second part, hereby promises and agrees, to and with the party of the second part, to make and execute unto him a new lease, similar in all respects to this, and to run for the same period of three years, of the premises aforesaid, upon the due request and application of the said party of the second part, made within twenty days prior to the expiration of the aforesaid term granted by these presents.

In witness, &c., [*as in* § 719.]

---

§ 724. *Surrender of a Term of Years to the Person having the Reversion.*

This indenture, made the   day of   , between A. B., of, &c., of the one part, and C. D., of, &c., of the other part: Whereas, the said C. D., by his indenture of lease, bearing date, &c., did demise and to farm let, &c., [*recite the property and term as in the lease:*] Now these presents witness, that for and in consideration of   dollars, to the said A. B. in hand paid, at the sealing and delivery of these presents, by the said C. D., and to the intent and purpose that the said term in the said lands and premises may be wholly merged and extinguished, he, the said A. B., hath given, granted and surrendered, and by these presents doth give, grant and surrender, unto the said C. D., and his heirs, all the said lands and premises in the said indenture of lease contained and demised, as aforesaid, and all the estate, right, title, interest, term of years property, claim and demand, whatsoever, of him, the said A. B., of, in, to, or out of, the same, or any part or parcel thereof: to have and to hold the said lands and premises to the said C. D., his heirs and assigns, and to their own proper use and behoof.

And the said A. B. doth hereby, for himself, his heirs, executors and administrators, covenant and agree, to and with the said C. D., his heirs and assigns, that he, the said A. B., hath not, at any time heretofore, made, done, committed, executed, permitted, or suffered, any act, deed, matter, or thing, whatsoever, whereby, or wherewith, or by reason or means whereof, the said lands and premises hereby assigned or surrendered, or any part or parcel thereof, are, or is, or may, can, or shall be, in any wise impeached, charged, affected, or incumbered.

In witness, &c., [*as in* § 719.]

---

§ 725. *Surrender of a Lease to the Lessor, by Endorsement.*

Know all men by these presents: That I, the within named A. B. in consideration of   dollars, to me in hand paid at or before the ensealing and delivery of these presents, do for myself, my executors and administrators, bargain, sell, surrender, and yield up, from the day of the date hereof, unto the within named C. D., and his heirs, [*or*, his executors and administrators,] as well the within indenture of lease, as the lands and premises therein mentioned, and the term of years therein yet to come, with all my right, title and interest thereto; and I do hereby covenant, that the same are free and clear of all incumbrances of what kind soever, at any time by me, or by my privity, consent, or procurement, done, committed, or suffered.

Given, &c., [*as in* § 716.]

---

§ 726. *Notice to Quit, by the Landlord*[1]

Please to take notice, that you are hereby required to surrender, and deliver up possession of the house and lot known as lot number   , in   street, in the   of   , which you now hold of me; and to remove therefrom on the   day of

---

[1] The notice must be delivered to the tenant personally, or to some person of proper age residing on the premises; and if neither the tenant, nor any such person, can be found, the notice may be posted on some conspicuous place on the premises.

next, pursuant to the provisions of the statute relating to the rights and duties of landlord and tenant.

Dated this day of , 18 .

      Yours, &c.,   A. B., Landlord.

To C. D.

---

§ 727. *Notice to Quit, by the Tenant.*

Please to take notice, that on the day of next, I shall quit possession and remove from the premises I now occupy, known as house and lot number , in street, in the of .

Dated this day of , 18 .

      Yours, &c.,   C. D.

To A. B., Landlord.

---

§ 728. *Notice by Landlord, where the Commencement of the Tenancy is Uncertain.*

To C. D.:

I hereby give you notice to quit, and deliver up, on the day of next, the possession of the messuage or dwelling-house, [*or*, rooms and apartments; *or*, farm lands and premises,] with the appurtenances, which you now hold of me, situate in the of , in the county of , provided your tenancy originally commenced at that time of the year: or otherwise, to quit and deliver up the possession of the said messuage, &c., at the end of the year of your tenancy, which shall expire next after the end of one-half year from the time of your being served with this notice.

Dated, &c., [*as in* § 726.]

---

§ 729. *Notice to Tenant to Quit the Premises, or Pay Double Value.*

Sir: I hereby give you notice to quit, and yield up, on the day of next, possession of the messuage, lands, tenements and hereditaments, which you now hold of me, situate at , in the town of , and county of ; in failure whereof, I shall require and insist upon double the value of the said premises, according to the statute in such case made and provided.

Dated, &c., [*as in* § 726.]

§ 730. *Notice of Intention to Re-enter, under the Law of* 1846.

To C. D.:

You are hereby notified, that I shall re-enter the premises known as number 347,　　　　street, in the city of　　　, now occupied by you under a demise from me, on the　　　day of　　　next, you having made default in the payment of the rent for the same.

Dated, &c., [*as in* § 726.]

---

§ 731. *Oath of Holding Over—to be Made by the Landlord, or Lessor, or his Legal Representatives, Agents, or Assigns.*

　　　　County, ss:

A. B., of said county, merchant, being duly sworn, doth depose and say, that on or about the　　　day of　　　, A. D. 18　, he let and rented unto C. D., of　　　, in said county, the house and lot known as number　　　, in　　　street, in　　　, aforesaid, for the term of one year from the first of May then next which said term has expired; and that the said C. D., or his assigns, hold over and continue in possession of the said premises * without the permission of this deponent.

　　Sworn to, this　　day of　　,
　　　　18　, before me,
　　　　　　　A. M., Justice of the Peace.

---

§ 732. *Summons to Remove Tenant Holding Over.*

To C. D., of　　　, or any other person claiming possession of the premises hereinafter mentioned:

Whereas, A. B., of said　　　of　　　, has made oath, and presented the same to me, that on or about the　　　day of　　　,

---

¹ The section of the statute, (Laws of 1846, chap. 274, § 3,) under which this notice may be given, was designed to protect parties to leases then in existence, after the abolition of distress for rent. The notice, therefore, is necessary only in cases where the right to re-enter was reserved, provided there was not a "sufficiency of goods and chattels whereon to distrain." Service of the notice must be made personally, on the grantee or lessee, or by leaving the same at his dwelling-house on the premises.

² Previous to issuing this summons, in the case of a tenancy at will, or by sufferance, the magistrate must be satisfied by affidavit, that the tenancy has been terminated by giving the requisite notice. Where a person holds over when real estate has been sold on an execution, the magistrate must be satisfied in like manner, that a demand of possession of the premises has been made. The time specified in the summons to appear and show cause, should be either on the same day, if reasonable, or not less than three, nor more than five days, from the time of serving such summons. The service may be made, by delivering to the tenant to whom it shall be directed, a true copy of the summons, and at the same time showing him the original; or, if the tenant be absent from his last or usual place of residence, by leaving a copy thereof at such place, with some person of mature age residing on the premises. (2 R. S., (3d ed.,) 604, §§ 30, 31, et seq.)

he rented unto you, the said C. D., the house and lot known as number   , in   street, in said   , for the term of   , from the   day of   , then next ensuing; and that you, or your assigns, hold over and continue in possession of the said premises after the expiration of the aforesaid term therein, without the permission of the landlord: Therefore, in the name of the people of the State of New York, you are hereby summoned and required, forthwith to remove from the said premises, or show cause before me, at my office in   , on the   day of   , at   o'clock in the   noon, why possession of the said premises should not be delivered to the landlord.

Witness my hand, the   day of   18   .

G. H., County Judge.

---

§ 733. *Affidavit of Service of Summons.*

County, ss:

R. F., of said county, being duly sworn, says, that on the   day of   instant, he personally served the within summons upon C. D., the tenant therein named, by delivering a true copy thereof to him in person, and at the same time showing him the said original summons.

Sworn, &c., [*as in* § 731.]   R. F.

---

§ 734. *Warrant to Put in Possession, where Tenant Holds Over, and does not Appear to the Summons.*

To the Sheriff of the County of   [*or*, to any one of the
     Constables, or Marshals, of the City of   *or*, of the
     Town of   , in the County of   ,] greeting:

Whereas, A. B., of the   of   , in said county, has made oath, and presented the same to me, that on or about the day of, &c., [*as in* § 731 *to the*, and then add:*] without the permission of the landlord; Whereupon I issued a summons requiring the said tenant forthwith to remove from the said premises, or show cause before me at a certain time now past, why the possession of the said premises should not be delivered to the landlord; and no sufficient cause having been shown to the contrary, and I being satisfied, by due proof, of the service of the said summons, do therefore, in the name of the people of the State of New York, command you to remove all persons from the said premises, and to put the landlord in full possession thereof.

Witness, &c., [*as in* § 732.]

§ 735. *Affidavit of Default in Paying Rent.*

County, ss:

A. B., of   , in said county, being duly sworn, says, that C
D. is justly indebted unto him in the sum of one hundred dollars,
due the   day of   , 18   , for the rent of a house and lot
known as number   , in   street, in   , aforesaid;
that he has demanded the said rent from the said C, D., who has
made default in the payment thereof, pursuant to the agreement
under which the premises were let, and that he holds over and continues in possession of the same, without the permission of the landlord, after default in the payment, as aforesaid.

Sworn, &c., [*as in* § 731.]   A. B.

---

§ 736. *Summons on Foregoing Affidavit—to be Served, &c.,*
as § 732.

To C. D., and each and every person in possession of the demised
    premises hereinafter mentioned, or claiming possession thereof:

Whereas, A. B., of the   of   , in the county of
       , has made oath that you are justly indebted to him in the
sum of one hundred dollars, due the   day of   , 18   ,
for rent of the house and lot known as number   , in
street, in   , aforesaid; that he has demanded from you the said
rent, and that default has been made in the payment thereof, pursuant to the agreement under which the premises were let; and that
you hold over and continue in possession of the same, without the
permission of the landlord, after default in the payment of the rent,
as aforesaid. Therefore, you, and each of you, are hereby summoned and required, forthwith to remove from the said premises, or show
cause before me, at, &c., on the   day of   18   , at
o'clock in the   noon of that day.

Witness, &c., [*as in* § 732.]

---

§ 737. *Warrant to Put in Possession.*

To the Sheriff, &c., [*or, as in* § 734,] greeting:

Whereas, A. B., of   , in said county, made oath that C.
D. was justly indebted to him in the sum of one hundred dollars, for
rent of the house and lot known as number   , in
street, in   , aforesaid; that he demanded the said rent from
the said C. D., who had made default in the payment thereof, pursuant to the agreement under which the premises were let, and that
he held over and continued in possession of the same without the

permission of the landlord, after such default; whereupon I issued a summons requiring the tenant, and every person in possession of the said premises, or claiming the possession thereof, forthwith to remove therefrom, or show cause before me, at a certain time now past, why the possession of the premises should not be delivered to the said landlord;* and no good cause having been shown or any way appearing to the contrary, and due proof of the service of such summons having been made to me, you are commanded to remove all persons from the said premises, and put the said A. B. into the possession thereof.

Witness, &c., [*as in* §732.]

---

§ 738. *Return of Officer to Warrant.*

Pursuant to the command of the above warrant, I have this day put the landlord into full possession of the premises therein mentioned.

Dated this   day of   , 18   .

H. C., Constable, [or, Marshal,] of, &c.

---

§ 739. *Affidavit to Oppose Issuing Warrant of Removal.*[1]

County, ss:

C. D., of   , being duly sworn, says, that he denies the following allegations stated in the oath of C. D., made on the   day of   , 18   , in order to obtain the removal of this deponent from the following premises: [*describe them:*] that is to say: he denies that [*state the facts denied.*]

Sworn, &c., [*as in* § 731.]

---

§ 740. *Precept for a Jury where the Removal is Opposed.*

To the Sheriff, &c., [*or, as in* § 734,] greeting:

Whereas, on the   day of   , 18   , A. B., of   made oath, and presented the same to me, stating that, &c.; [*as in* § 737, *to the* *, *and then add:*] and whereas, the said C. D. hath

---

[1] Where the person in possession of the demised premises, or claiming the possession, makes an affidavit to oppose the warrant of removal, the matter controverted must be tried by a jury, provided either party demand the same, at the time of showing cause, before the adjournment, and pay the necessary costs and expenses of obtaining the jury, otherwise the magistrate before whom the proceedings are had will decide the controversy. (Laws of 1849, chap. 193.)

upon his oath denied the aforesaid allegations of the said A. B.: You are therefore hereby commanded, in the name of the people of the State of New York, to summon, [*insert the names of twelve persons,*] being twelve reputable persons, qualified to serve as jurors in courts of record, and nominated by me for the purpose, to appear before me, at, &c., on, &c., [*not more than three days after the date of the precept,*] for the purpose of trying the matter in difference between the said A. B. and C. D.

Witness, &c., [*as in § 732.*]

---

§ 741. *Juror's Oath.*[1]

You, and each of you, do swear, that you will well and truly try, hear and determine the matters in difference now depending before me, between A. B. and C. D., the parties to this proceeding, and a true verdict give therein according to evidence. So help you God.

---

§ 742. *Officer's Oath to Keep Jury, after Evidence Given.*

You do swear, that you will well and faithfully keep, in some private and convenient place, this jury committed to your charge, without meat or drink, water excepted. You shall not suffer any person to speak to them, nor speak to them yourself, unless to ask them if they have agreed upon their verdict, until they have agreed on their verdict, or are sooner discharged by me. So help you God.

---

§ 743. *Security for Rent on Proceeding for Non-Payment.*[2]

We hereby jointly and severally engage to pay A. B. the sum of   dollars, for rent due him for the occupation of, [*describe the premises,*] and for the costs and charges of a certain application to remove the undersigned C. D. from the said premises, under the provisions of the statute authorizing summary proceedings to recover

---

[1] Six of the jurors summoned are to be drawn by the magistrate, in the same manner as in justices' courts. The finding of the jury before a justice of the peace, or his decision, where no jury is called, must be entered in his docket, and judgment rendered therefor. The judgment must also include the costs of the prevailing party, according to the rates prescribed for similar services in civil actions in justices' courts, and the warrant for delivery must direct the collection of such costs, or an execution may be issued for that purpose. (Laws of 1849, chap. 193.)   Where proceedings are had before a justice of the peace, they may be removed to the County Court by appeal. (See the note to § 748, p.403.)
[2] Upon giving security satisfactory to the magistrate, the issuing of the warrant of removal will be stayed.

the possession of land in certain cases, within ten days from the date hereof.

   Dated and sealed, this   day of   , 18 .

C. D. [L. S.]
E. F. [L. S.]
L. M. [L. S.]

---

§ 744. *Notice to Remove, in a case of Tenancy at Will, to be Served as in § 732.*

To C. D., of   :

   You are hereby required to remove from, and quit the premises which you now hold of me, situate in the village of   , in the county of   , within one month after service of this notice.

   Dated the   day of   , 18 .

Yours, &c.,   A. B.

---

§ 745. *Affidavit to be Made by the Landlord to obtain Summons, in a Case of Tenancy at Will.*

     County, ss:

   A. B., of   , in said county, being duly sworn, says, that since the   day of   , in the year   , C. D., of the same place, has held and occupied the house and lot in the of   , on   street, where the said C. D. now resides, as the tenant of this deponent, and at his will, and without any certain time agreed on for the termination of said tenancy; and that this deponent caused a notice in writing to be served on the said C. D., in due form of law, on the   day of   last past, requiring him to remove from the said premises within one month from the day of service thereof; And this deponent further says, that the said time has expired, and that the said C. D., or his assigns, hold over and continue in possession of the said premises after the expiration of the said time, without the permission of this deponent.

   Sworn, &c., [*as in* § 731.]   A. B.

---

§ 746. *Summons thereon to the Tenant, to Remove or Show Cause.*

To C. D., of   :

   Whereas, A. B. has made oath in writing, and presented the same to me, that since the   day of   , in the year you have held and occupied the house and lot in the   . of

in   street, where you now reside, as his tenant, and at his
will, without any certain time agreed on for the termination of said
tenancy; and that he caused a notice in writing to be served on
you in due form of law, on the   day of   last past, requiring
you to remove from said premises within one month from the day
of the service thereof; and that the said time hath expired, but that
you, or your assigns, hold over and continue in possession of said
premises after the expiration of said time, without the permission of
the said landlord:

Therefore, in the name of the people of the State of New York,
you are hereby summoned and required, forthwith to remove from
the said premises, or show cause before me, at my office, in the town
of   , in said county, on the   day of   * instant, why
possession of the said premises should not be delivered to the said
landlord.

Witness, &c., [*as in* § 732.]

----

§ 747. *Warrant to Remove the Tenant.*

To any Constable of the Town of   , in the County of   ,
    greeting:

Whereas, A. B. made oath in writing, and presented the same to
me, that since the   day of   , in the year   . C.
D., of   , has held and occupied the house and lot in the
of   , in   street, where he now resides, as his tenant
and at his will, without any certain time agreed on for the termination of said tenancy; and that he caused a notice in writing to be
served on him, the said tenant, in due form of law, on the   day
of   last, requiring him to remove from said premises within
one month from the day of the service thereof: and that the said
time has expired, but that the said tenant, or his assigns, held over
and continued in possession of said premises after the expiration of
said time, without the permission of said landlord; whereupon I issued
a summons, requiring the tenant to remove from said premises, or
show cause before me, at a certain time now past, why the landlord
should not be put in possession of said premises; and due proof of
the service of said summons having been made to me, and no good
cause against the landlord's application having been shown, or any
way appearing: Therefore, the people of the State of New York
command you to remove all persons from the said premises, and put
the said A. B. into the full possession thereof.

Witness, &c., [*as in* § 732.]

§ 748. *Affidavit for Appeal to County Court.*[1]

County, ss:

C. D. of said county, being duly sworn, deposes and says, that on the   day of   18 , A. B., of   , in said county, made and presented to G. H., Esquire, a Justice of the Peace, in and for said county, his affidavit, of which the following is a copy, to wit:

[*Insert here the affidavit.*]

Whereupon the said Justice issued his summons, dated on the   day of   , 18 , requiring this deponent forthwith to remove from the premises, in the said affidavit of the said A. B. mentioned, or to show cause before the said Justice, at his office in   , on the   day of   , 18 , at   o'clock in the   noon, why possession of the said premises should not be delivered to the landlord ; [*If the summons is informal, insert a copy of it;*] on which said day, to wit, the   day of   , 18 , the said A. B. and the said C. D. appeared before the said Justice, whereupon the following proceedings were had: [*Here state the proceedings, with the evidence of the witnesses, if any were sworn.*]

Deponent further says, that upon such hearing, the Justice gave judgment for the said A. B., that the said premises in his said affidavit mentioned, should be delivered to him as the landlord ; [*or, against the said A. B., and that the said premises in his said affidavit mentioned, should not be delivered to him as the landlord.*]

And deponent assigns the following grounds of error, upon which he appeals to the County Court of the said county of   , to wit:

[*State the grounds of error distinctly and concisely.*]

Sworn, &c., [*as in* § 731.]   C. D.

I hereby allow the within appeal, this   day of   , 18 .

J. P. H., County Judge,

---

1 The proceedings before a Justice of the Peace, under the act authorizing the removal of tenants, &c., may be removed by appeal to the County Court of the county, in the same manner, and with the like effect, and upon like security, as appeals from the judgment of Justices of the Peace in civil actions; but the decision of the County Judge must be a reversal or affirmance of the justice's judgment, and will be final. But where the tenant appeals, and desires the issuing of the warrant or execution to be stayed, security must also be given for the payment of all rent, accruing or to accrue subsequent to the application to the Justice. The security must in all cases be approved by the County Judge at the time of allowing the appeal, and served on the justice with the affidavit for appeal. (Laws of 1849, chap. 193.)

§ 749. *Notice of Appeal.*[1]

In the matter of }
A. B., landlord, { Summary proceeding to recover possession of
   against { land, before G. H., Esq., Justice of the Peace.
C. D., tenant. }

Sir: Please take notice, that C. D., above named, appeals from the judgment rendered against him by G. H., Esquire, Justice of the Peace aforesaid, on the   day of   last, which judgment is mentioned and referred to in the within [*or, annexed*] affidavit, and herewith served on you, to the County Court of the county of   ; and that the said appeal will be heard by the Hon. J. P. H., County Judge, at his office in the city of   , on the   day of   next, at ten o'clock in the forenoon.

Dated   , July 30th, 18 .   C. D.
To A. B.

---

§ 750. *Undertaking on Appeal.*

In the matter of }
A. B., landlord, { Summary proceeding to recover possession of land,
   against { before G. H. Esq., Justice of the Peace.
C. D., tenant. }

C. D., above named, having appealed to the County Court of   county, from the judgment rendered against him in this proceeding, [*describe the judgment:*] Now, therefore, in order to stay the execution of the said judgment, and in consideration thereof, we, L. M. and S. T., undertake and promise to, and with the said A. B., that if judgment be rendered against the said C. D., on the said appeal, and execution thereon be returned unsatisfied in whole or in part, we will pay the amount unsatisfied: [*If the appeal is made by a tenant, add:* And we do further promise and undertake, to and with the said A. B., that the said C. D. shall punctually pay all rent accruing or to accrue upon said premises subsequent to the applica-

---

[1] A copy of the affidavit for appeal, and a notice of the appeal, must be served on the opposite party, within twenty days after the rendition of the judgment, and also on the justice. If the party be a resident of the county, the service may be personal, or by leaving the copy of the affidavit and notice at his residence, with some person of suitable age and discretion; if not a resident, the service may be on the attorney or agent, if any, who is a resident of the city or county, who appeared for him on the trial.

tion to the Justice, at the time or times when the same becomes due and payable, and that in default thereof, we will pay the same.]

Witness our hands and seals, this   day   of 18   .

L. M.   [L. s.]
S. T.   [L. s.]

I approve of the above undertaking and the surety [or, sureties,] therein mentioned.

J. P. H., County Judge.

---

§ 751.   *Petition and Affidavit, where Premises are Vacated.*

To S. T., one of the Justices of the Peace of the county of   :

The petition of A. B., of   in said county, respectfully showeth: That he demised to C. D., of, &c., the premises lately occupied by the said C. D., on   street, in the village of   . in said county, for the term of one year from the   day of   , one thousand eight hundred and   , at the yearly rent of   dollars, payable quarter yearly;   that the said C. D. entered into the possession of the said premises as tenant thereof, by virtue of the said demise, and is now indebted to your petitioner in the sum of   dollars, for one quarter's rent of the said premises, due the   day of   , 18   ; and that he has deserted the same, leaving the said rent in arrear, and the premises unoccupied and uncultivated.

Your petitioner, therefore, requests that you go upon and view the premises, and if satisfied, upon such view, that the premises are so deserted, that you affix a notice in writing upon a conspicuous part thereof, requiring the tenant to appear and pay the said rent.

Dated the   day of   , 18   .   A. B.

County, ss:

A. B., of said county, being duly sworn, says, that the facts set forth in the above petition subscribed by him, are true.

Sworn, &c., [*as in* § 731.]

---

§ 752.   *Notice of Justice on Foregoing Petition.*

NOTICE.

To C. D., of   :

You are hereby notified, that at the request of A. B., your landlord, and upon due proof made to me that he had demised to you the premises upon which this notice is affixed, and that you were in arrear for one quarter's rent, amounting to   dollars; and that you had deserted the premises, leaving such rent in arrear, and left them unoccupied and uncultivated, I have viewed the said premises, and am satisfied, upon such view, that the same have been so deserted; Therefore, you are hereby required to appear, on the   day of   , at   o'clock in the   noon, at the place where this notice is affixed, and pay the rent due, or the landlord will be put in possession of the premises.

Dated the   day of   , 18   .

           S. T., Justice of the Peace.

---

§ 753.   *Record of Justice, where Premises are Deserted.*[1]

State of New York, } ss:
       County, }

Be it remembered, that on the   day of   , one thousand eight hundred and   , A. B., by petition presented to me, set forth that he had demised to C. D., &c., [*as in petition;*] and for which there is now due to the said A. B., for arrears of rent for the same, the sum of   dollars; that C. D. deserted the premises, leaving the said rent in arrear, and left the premises unoccupied and uncultivated; whereupon, at the request of the said A. B., and upon due proof of the facts set forth as above, I did go upon and view the premises, and was satisfied, upon such view, that the premises were so deserted: Therefore, a notice in writing was affixed by me upon the front door of the dwelling-house thereupon, requiring the said C. D. to appear on the   day of   , at   o'clock in the   noon, at the place where the said notice was so affixed, and pay the rent due; at which time and place I again viewed the premises, and the tenant not appearing and denying that any rent was due to the landlord; nor he, nor any person for him appearing to pay the rent in arrear, I did put the said A. B., the landlord, in possession of the premises above mentioned, free and clear of any demise to the said C. D., the same being by law from thenceforth declared void.

Witness my hand, this   day of   , 18   .

           S. T., Justice, &c.

---

[1] If the tenant appear at the time specified in the notice, and deny that any rent is due to the landlord, all proceedings will cease; but if, upon the second view, the tenant or some one for him, does not appear and pay the rent in arrear, then the Justice may put the landlord into possession, and any demise of the premises to the tenant will, from thenceforth, become void. An appeal from the Justice's proceedings may be made by the tenant, at any time within three months after such possession is delivered, to the County Court of the county. Security is to be given satisfactory to the Justice, as in § 754, and he is also to be served with notice of the appeal. The Justice must serve the landlord with the like notice of the appeal, and return the proceedings had before him to the court, within ten days after the notice and security shall be given by the tenant. The court is required to examine the proceedings, and hear the proofs and allegations of the parties, in some summary way, and such court may order restitution of the premises to be made to the tenant, with costs to be paid by the landlord; in case of affirmation, cost may be awarded against the tenant.

§ 754. *Bond on Appeal from Justice's Proceedings.*

Know all men, &c.; [*as in the usual form, to the condition, and then add:*] Whereas, certain proceedings have been had, at the instance of A. B., against C. D., before S. T., one of the Justices of the Peace of the county of   , under color of the provisions of the statute authorizing summary proceedings to obtain possession of demised premises when deserted by the tenant; whereby the said A. B. was, on the   day of   last, put into the possession of certain premises by him demised to the said C. D., from which proceedings the said C. D. hath appealed to the County Court of said county.

Now, therefore, the condition of this obligation is such, that if the said C. D. shall well and truly pay to the said A. B. all costs of such appeal which may be adjudged against such tenant, then this obligation shall be void; otherwise of full force.

Sealed and delivered)
  in presence of   }
     A. M.   )

C. D. [L. S.]
E. F. [L. S.]

I approve of this bond as the security for the appeal therein mentioned.

                       S. T., Justice.

---

§ 755. *Notice to the Justice of the Appeal.*

To S. T., Esq., Justice of the Peace:

Sir: I have appealed, and do hereby appeal, to the County Court of the county of   , from your proceedings at the instance of A. B., by which he has been put in possession of the premises lately occupied by me, in the town of   , in the county of   , under color of the provisions of the statute authorizing summary proceedings to recover possession of lands in certain cases: And of this you will take notice, and return the proceedings had before you to the said court, within ten days. Dated the   day of   , 18 .

             Yours, &c.,   C. D.

---

§ 756. *Notice to the Landlord of the Appeal.*

To A. B.:

Sir: You will take notice, that C. D., upon giving the required security, has this day appealed to the County Court of the county of   , from my proceedings at your instance, and by which you have been put in possession of the premises situate in   , in said county, and demised by you to the said C. D., for the term of   years.

Dated   this   day of   , 18

             Yours, &c.,   S. T., Justice.

§ 757. *Complaint for Forcible Entry, and Affidavit.*[1]

County, ss:

The complaint of A. B., of   , in said county, to G. H., Esq.,
County Judge of said county, showeth: That C. D., of   , aforesaid, on the   day of   , in the year   , at the town
of   , in the county of   , aforesaid, did unlawfully make a
forcible entry into the lands and possessions of this complainant, to
wit: the dwelling-house and appurtenances of this complainant there
situate, bounded, &c., [*insert boundaries;*] and then and there did
violently, forcibly, and unlawfully, and with strong hand, eject and
expel the complainant from his said lands and possessions, wherein
this complainant had, at the time aforesaid, an estate of freehold, [*or,
such other estate, as the case may be,*] then and still subsisting; and
that the said C. D. still doth hold and detain the said lands and possessions from the said A. B., unlawfully, forcibly, and with strong
hand, and against the form of the statute in such case made and provided.

Dated this   day of   , in the year   .

                                                        A. B.

County, ss:

A. B., of   , in said county, being duly sworn, says, that the
facts and circumstances stated and set forth in the foregoing complaint, by him signed, are true.

Sworn, &c., [*as in* § 731.]   A. B.

---

§ 758. *Precept to Summon the Jury of Inquiry.*

County, ss:

To the Sheriff, or any Constable, of the County of   :

In the name of the People of the State of New York, you are hereby commanded to cause to come before me, at the house of   ,
in the town of   , in said county, on the   day of   instant, at   o'clock in the   noon, twenty-four good and lawful
inhabitants of the said county, duly qualified by law to serve as jurors,

---

[1] The complaint may be made by any party in the actual and peaceful possession of lands
at the time a forcible entry is made, or in the constructive possession where there is a forcible holding out. Upon receiving the complaint, the Judge issues the precept to summon a
jury, to the Sheriff or a Constable of the county, and at the same time notifies the party
against whom the complaint is made, of the time and place of trial: which notice is to be
served in the same manner as directed in the note to § 732. At the time appointed for the
return of the precept, the Judge administers an oath to the persons returned summoned,
who appear, not being less than thirteen, nor more than twenty-three, well and truly to inquire into the matters complained of, and a true inquisition thereon to make. The jury then
proceed to inquire into the matter, and hear the testimony; the inquisition is to be made and
signed before the Judge, and delivered to him.

to inquire upon their oaths for the said people, of a certain forcible entry and detainer unlawfully made by C. D., as is said, into the dwelling-house of one A. B., in the town of   , in said county, against the form of the statute in such case made and provided. And have you then there this precept.

Given under my hand, the   day of   , in the year

G. H., County Judge.

---

§ 759. *Notice to the Person Complained of.*

To C. D.:

On the complaint of A. B., of the town of   , in the county of   , made to me, the undersigned, G. H., County Judge of said county, that you did unlawfully make a forcible entry into the dwelling-house of the said A. B., situate in said town, and bounded, [*insert description,*] and then and there did violently, forcibly, unlawfully, and with strong hand, eject and expel the said A. B. from his said dwelling-house, and do still unlawfully and forcibly, and with strong hand, detain and hold the said dwelling-house, and the possession thereof, from the said A. B.: I have this day issued my precept, directed to the Sheriff, or any Constable, of said county, commanding him to cause to come before me, at the house of   , in the town of   , in said county, on the   day of   instant, at   o'clock in the   noon, twenty-four good and lawful inhabitants of the said county, duly qualified by law to serve as jurors, to inquire upon their oaths of the said forcible entry and detainer; of all which you are notified.

Dated this   day of   , 18 .

G. H., County Judge.

---

§ 760. *Affidavit of Service of Preceding Notice.*

County, ss:

R. F., of said county, being duly sworn, says, that on the   day of   instant, he served a notice, of which the annexed is a copy, on C. D., by delivering the same to him personally, [*or,* by delivering the same on the premises in question, to A. D., the son of the said C. D., of the age of twenty years and upwards, because the said C. D. could not be found; *or,* by affixing the same on the front door of the house in question, there being no person on the premises· *or,* by affixing the same on the post at the principal entrance of said

R

premises, being a public and suitable place, and there being no house
or person on said premises.]

Sworn, &c., [*as in* § 731.]   R. F.

---

§ 761. *Inquisition of the Jury.*

State of New-York, ⎱ ss:
      County, ⎰

An inquisition taken at the house of   , in the town of
      , in the county of   , on the   day of
      , in the year   , by the oaths and affirmations of E.
F., &c., [*insert the names of the jurors sworn, or by whom the inquisition is signed.*] inhabitants of said county, duly qualified to
serve as jurors, before G. H., Esq., County Judge of said county,
who say upon their oaths and affirmations aforesaid, that A. B., of
the town of   , aforesaid, long since had an estate of freehold, [*or, as the estate may be;*] in the dwelling-house, with the appurtenances, situated in the town of   , aforesaid, and
bounded, &c., [*as in complaint;*] and that the said A. B. was long
since lawfully and peaceably possessed thereof; and that his said estate and possession so subsisted and continued, until C. D., of the
same place, on the   day of   , &c., did forcibly
and unlawfully, and with strong hand, enter into the said land and
premises, and expel him, the said A. B., therefrom; and the said A.
B., so expelled from the said dwelling-house, with the appurtenances
aforesaid, from the said   day of, &c., until the day of the
taking of this inquisition, unlawfully and forcibly, and with strong
hand, did keep out, and doth yet keep out, to the great disturbance
of the people of the State of New York, and contrary to the form
of the statute in such case made; and that the said estate of the
said A. B. still subsists therein..

And we, the jurors aforesaid, whose names are hereto set, do, on
the evidence produced before us, find the inquisition, aforesaid, true.
                                              E. F., &c., &c.

---

§ 762. *Venire for Petit Jury.*

County, ss:

To the Sheriff, or any Constable, of said County, greeting:

The People of the State of New York command you to summon,
personally, twelve good and lawful men of the town of   ,

---

¹ If the inquisition is not traversed within twenty-four hours, the Judge issues his warrant
to make restitution immediately. The party complained against may, however, traverse
the inquisition, in writing, (§ 739,) denying the forcible entry or forcible holding out, or al-

in said county, duly qualified to serve as jurors, and not exempt from serving on juries in Courts of Record, and in no wise of kin to A. B., or to C. D., to come before G. H., Esq., County Judge of said county, at the house of   , in the town of   , aforesaid, on the   day of   instant, to make a jury of the county, upon their oaths to try a certain traverse of an inquisition found upon the complaint of A. B., and now pending before the said Judge, against C. D., of   county, for a certain forcible and unlawful entry made by the said C. D., into the dwelling-house of the said A. B., in the town of   , in said county, and for the forcible and unlawful detainer thereof, against the form of the statute in such case made and provided; and that you make a list of the persons summoned, certify and annex the same to this precept, and make return hereof to me.

Given, &c., [*as in* § 758.]

---

§ 763. *Warrant to the Sheriff, or Constable, to make Restitution.*[1]

County, ss:

The People of the State of New York, to the Sheriff, or any Constable, of said County, greeting:

Whereas, A. B., of   , in said county, did, on the   day of   last, make complaint, duly verified by oath, to the undersigned, G. H., County Judge of said county, that C. D., of   , aforesaid, on the   day of, &c., [*recite the complaint, and the subsequent proceedings, and then add:*]

You are, therefore, hereby commanded to go to the said premises, taking with you the power of the county, if necessary, and cause the

---

leging that he or his ancestors, or those whose interest he claims, have been in quiet possession of the premises, for three whole years next before such inquisition found, and that his interest therein is not ended or determined ; and if the traverser pay to the Judge the fees of summoning a jury to try such traverse, and the jurors' and Judge's fees on such trial, all further proceedings on the complaint will be stayed until the traverse be tried. Any person may make affidavit before the Judge, that the party complained of is his tenant, under a valid subsisting demise, and traverse the inquisition in like manner. Upon such traverse being made, the Judge issues his precept to summon twelve jurors to try the same, at a time not less than four, nor more than eight days thereafter. Twenty-four hours' notice to a juror is sufficient. The jurors are to be impanneled and sworn, as in civil actions. On the trial, the title is not to be investigated ; except so far as the complainant is required to show the actual or constructive possession required by the statute ; and the tenant may show three years' possession, as above mentioned, which showing will be a complete bar to the prosecution. If the jury find for the complainant, the Judge issues a warrant to make restitution, unless the proceedings be removed to the Supreme Court, by certiorari, which may be allowed by a Justice of the Supreme Court, or other officer authorized to perform the duties of such Justice at chambers.

[1] All the proceedings are to be recited in the warrant of restitution, and the Judge is required, in the same or in a separate precept, to direct the costs and expenses to be levied and collected, in the same manner as on judgments in Justices' Courts, in personal actions. This form of warrant may be adapted to either case, whether the original inquisition be traversed, or otherwise.

said A. B. to be restored and put in full possession of the said dwelling-house and premises, according to his estate and right therein before the said entry, in pursuance of the statute in such case made and provided.

And you are also commanded to levy the sum of $, of the goods and chattels of the said C. D., (excepting such goods and chattels as are by law exempt from execution,) and to bring the money before me within thirty days from the date hereof, to render to the said A. B.; and if no goods or chattels can be found, or not sufficient to satisfy the said sum of money, you are commanded to take the body of the said C. D., and convey him to the common jail of the said county, there to remain until the said sum of money, and your fees for collecting the same, shall be satisfied and paid.

Given, &c., [*as in* § 758.]

————

§ 764.   *Complaint for a Forcible Detainer, or Holding Out after a Peaceable Entry, and Affidavit.*

          County, ss:

The complaint of A. B., of   , in said county, to G. H., Esq., County Judge of said county, showeth;

That the said A. B., on the   day of   , in the year   , and long before that day, had an estate of freehold, [*or*, a term of years, *as the case may be*,] in all that certain lot of land, with the house and other buildings thereon, and the appurtenances, situate in the town of   , in said county, bounded as follows: [*insert description*,]; and which said estate of freehold [*or*, which said term of years] is still subsisting; And that C. D., of the town of   , aforesaid, on the   day of   , aforesaid, while the said A. B. was in the possession of the said premises, entered thereon in a peaceable manner, and thenceforth by force, and with strong hand, hath held and kept, and still holds and keeps, the said A. B., out of the possession thereof, contrary to the form of the statute in such case made and provided.

          County, ss:

A. B., of   , in said county, being duly sworn, says, &c., [*as in the affidavit to* § 757, *to the end.*]

CHAPTER XXVII.

LUNATICS.

PRACTICAL REMARKS.

1. No patient can be admitted into the State Lunatic Asylum, at Utica, except upon an order of some Court, Justice, or Judge, without lodging with the Superintendent,—first, a request under the hand of the person by whose direction he is sent, stating his age and place of nativity, if known; his christian and surname, place of residence, occupation, and degree of relationship, or other circumstances of connection between him and the person making the request,—and second, a certificate, dated within two months, under oath, signed by two respectable physicians, of the fact of his being insane. Each person signing such request or certificate, must annex to his name his profession or occupation, and the town, county, and state, of his residence, unless these facts appear upon the face of the document.[1]

2. When a person in indigent circumstances, not a pauper, becomes insane, application may be made in his behalf to the County Judge of the county in which he resides; and said Judge is required to give reasonable notice to one of the superintendents of the poor of the county, or overseer of the town, to be charged with the support of the lunatic, and to call two respectable physicians, and other credible witnesses, and investigate the facts of the case, either with or without a jury, at his discretion. If the Judge is satisfied of the insanity and indigence of the person, and that he became so within one year previous, he will give his certificate, which, if authenticated by the County Clerk and seal of the County Court, will admit such person into the Asylum, to be supported there at the expense of his county, until he be restored to soundness of mind, if effected in two

---

[1] Laws of 1842, chap. 135, § 19.

years. On granting the certificate the Judge may, in his discretion, require the friends of the patient to give security to the Superintendent of the Poor of the county to remove the patient from the Asylum at the end of two years, in case he does not recover.[1]

3. The expenses of a lunatic sent to the Asylum in indigent circumstances, but not a "pauper," or "furiously mad," cannot be charged to his town by the county.[2]

FORMS.

§ 765. *Request to Superintendent for the Admission of a Patient.*
To C. R., Esq., Superintendent of the State Lunatic Asylum at
    Utica:

I hereby request that C. D., [*give the name of the patient in full,*] my son, [*or, lately in my employ: or, as the case may be,*] who resides in the town of   , in the county of   , and State of   , may be admitted as a patient into the said asylum. Said C. D. was born in the town [*or,* parish] of   , in the county of   , and State [*or,* kingdom; *or,* province,] of   : his age is   years, and his occupation a clerk, [*or, as the case may be.*]

              A. B., Merchant, of the town of   , in
              the county of   , and State of   .

---

§ 766. *Certificate of Physicians to Accompany the Request.*
    In the matter of }
C. D., a lunatic: }

We, the undersigned physicians, residing in the town of   , in the county of   , and State of New York, do hereby certify, that we have carefully examined into the mental state and condition of C. D., above named; and that, in our opinion, formed upon such examination, the said C. D. is insane.

    Given under our hands, this   day of   , 18 .

                            L. B.
                            S. W.

---

[1] Laws of 1842, chap. 135, § 26; Laws of 1850, chap. 282. [2] 7 Hill, 171.

County, ss:

L. B. and S. W., of said county, being by me severally sworn, depose and say, and each for himself deposes and says, that the facts stated and set forth in the above certificate, by him signed, are true.

Sworn to, this   day of   ,   L. B.

18   , before me,   S. W.

H. T. C., Justice of the Peace.

---

§ 767. *Application to County Judge, and Affidavit.*

To the Hon. J. P. H., County Judge of the County of   :

The petition of A. B., of the town of   , in said county, respectfully showeth: That C. D., now a resident of the said town, is, and for the term of   years last past, has been, a lunatic; that he is now in the care and custody of E. F., at the town aforesaid; that he is in indigent circumstances, and has no property in his own possession, or held by any person in trust for him, sufficient for his support, [*or*, for the support of himself and family,] under the visitation of insanity aforesaid: Your petitioner therefore prays, that an examination and investigation may be had in the premises, pursuant to the provisions of the act entitled "An Act to organize the State Lunatic Asylum, and more effectually to provide for the care, maintenance, and recovery of the insane," passed April 7, 1842, and the act entitled "An Act in relation to the State Lunatic Asylum," passed April 10, 1850.

A. B.

County, ss:

A. B., of said county, being duly sworn, says, that the facts and circumstances stated and set forth in the foregoing petition, by him signed, are true.

Sworn, &c., [*as in* § 766.]   A. B.

---

§ 768. *Order of Judge on the Foregoing Petition.*

In the matter of C. D.,
an alledged indigent lunatic:

Upon the petition of A. B., of the town of   , in the county of   , herein presented to me, and duly verified, it is ordered: That J. T. P. and D. D., two respectable physicians of the said county, be hereby designated and appointed, pursuant to the provisions of the act entitled, &c., [*as in* § 767,] to examine the said C. D. in respect to his alledged insanity, within   days after they shall be respectively served with a copy of this order, certified by me; and that they appear before me at my office in   , on the

day of   instant, [or, next,] at   o'clock in the
noon, and certify their respective opinions in relation thereto;
and that, at the time and place aforesaid, other witnesses be examined touching the mental condition and pecuniary circumstances of
the said C. D.

J. P. H., County Judge of the county of   .

---

§ 769. *Subpœna to Witness.*

County, ss:

To E. F., O. P., &c., &c., of said County, greeting:

You, and each of you, are hereby commanded, in the name of the
people of the State of New York, to appear before me, at my office
in   , on the   day of   instant, [or, next,] at
          o'clock in the   noon, to testify what you, or either
of you, may know, touching the mental condition and pecuniary circumstances of C. D., now of the town of   , in said county.

Given under my hand, at   , this   day of   , 18   .

J. P. H., County Judge, &c.

---

§ 770. *Notice to Superintendent or Overseer.*

To E. F., one of the Superintendents of the Poor of the County of
          [or, an overseer of the poor of the town of   in the
County of   .]

SIR: You will please take notice that an application has been
made to me in behalf of C. D., of ·   in said county, an alledged
indigent lunatic, praying for an examination and investigation under
the act entitled "An Act to organize the State Lunatic Asylum, &c.,"
passed April 7, 1842, and the act entitled "An Act in relation to
the State Lunatic Asylum," passed April 10, 1850; and that a hearing upon the said application will be had at my office in the   of
          , on the   day of   , instant, [or, next,] at
ten o'clock in the forenoon of that day.

Yours, &c.,
J. P. H., County Judge of said
County of   .

---

§ 771. *Certificate of Physicians, and Affidavit.*

In the matter of C. D.,   }
an alledged indigent lunatic: }

We do hereby certify, that in pursuance of the order of J. P. H,
County Judge of the county of   , made in the above entitled

matter, and bearing date the   day of   , 18   , we have carefully examined into the mental state and condition of C. D., above named, and particularly in reference to his alledged insanity; and that, in our opinion, derived from such examination, the said C D. is a confirmed lunatic.

Given under our hands, this   day of   , 18   .

J. T. P.

D. D.

County, ss:

J. T. P. and D. D., of said county, being by me severally sworn, depose and say, and each for himself deposes and says, that the facts stated and set forth in the foregoing certificate, by them signed, are true.

J. T. P.

Sworn, &c., [*as in* § 766.] **D. D.**

---

§ 772. *Certificate of Judge.*[1]

In the matter of C. D., }
an alledged indigent lunatic: }

Application having been made to me, by A. B., of the town of   , in the county of   , for an examination into the mental state and condition, and alledged indigence, of C. D., of the said town of   , under the provisions of the act entitled, &c., [*as in* § 767:] I thereupon appointed J. T. P. and D. D., two respectable physicians of the said county, to examine said C. D., who have appeared before me, and certified that the said C. D. is a confirmed lunatic; and I have also taken the depositions of witnesses touching the indigence and lunacy of the said C. D.: Now, therefore, I do hereby adjudge and certify, that it satisfactorily appears to me, from said certificate and depositions, that the said C. D. is a lunatic, that he became such lunatic within one year prior to the date hereof, that he has no estate of any kind, either in possession, or held by any person in trust for him, sufficient for his support, [*or,* for the support of himself and his family,] under the visitation of insanity as aforesaid.

Given, &c., [*as in* § 769.]

J. P. H., County Judge, &c.

---

[1] The depositions taken before the Judges should be reduced to writing, and entitled as in § 772. The certificate of the physicians, and other papers, together with a report of the proceedings and the decision, are to be filed by the Judge in the office of the County Clerk. He is also required to report the facts to the Board of Supervisors.

27

CHAPTER XXVIII.

MECHANICS' AND LABORERS' LIEN.

1. Any person who, by virtue of any contract with the owner or his agent, or any person who, in pursuance of any agreement with any such contractor, and in conformity with the terms of the contract with such owner or agent, performs any labor, or furnishes materials, in building, altering or repairing, any house or other building, or appurtenances, in the several cities of the State, and in the villages of Williamsburgh, Geneva, and Canandaigua, has a lien upon such house or building, and appurtenances, and upon the lot on which the same may stand, to the extent of the owner's interest therein; but the aggregate of all the liens for labor and materials, in any case, is not to exceed the price stipulated to be paid therefor by the owner or his agent. In order to perfect this lien, specifications of the work to be performed, or materials to be furnished, stating the prices to be paid therefor, or a true copy of the contract, if there be any in writing, must be filed in the office of the Clerk of the county, and a notice thereof served on the owner, or his agent, within twenty days after making such contract, or commencing such labor, or furnishing such materials. The County Clerk enters in a book alphabetically, the names of the owners, and opposite to them the names of the contractors, or laborers, or other persons claiming a lien, and the lot of land on which the work is to be done, or materials furnished, and the time of filing the specification, or copy of the contract. The book in which these entries are made, is called "The Mechanics' and Laborors' Docket." The lien thus created, takes effect from the time of the filing of the specification, or copy of the contract, and continues in force for the space of one year thereafter.

2. In order to enforce this lien, the owner, contractor, laborer, or

person furnishing materials, must serve a notice on the other party, personally, to appear and submit to an accounting and settlement, in the Court of Common Pleas of the city and county of New York, or in the County Court, or any Justice's Court of such county, (except in New York,) or in the Marine Court in the city of New York, as in the form hereinafter given. Within ten days after service of such notice, the owner, or his agent, is to be personally served with a bill of the particulars of the amount claimed to be due, and with a notice to produce a bill of particulars of any offset which may be claimed, within ten days thereafter. If the contractor, laborer, or person furnishing materials, does not appear and produce his claim, in pursuance of the notice to be served, as aforesaid, he loses his lien. If the owner does not appear, his default may be entered, and a writ of inquiry issued to the Sheriff ; or, if in the Marine Court of the city of New York, or in a Justice's Court in any other city or county, the damages may be assessed, and judgment rendered, and execution issued thereupon, as in actions on contract. Where the parties appear, issue must be joined on the claims made; notices of set-off and of trial, if necessary, be served ; and the same proceedings had as in actions on contract.

3. Within thirty days after labor has been performed, or materials furnished, the person claiming payment therefor must either deliver to the owner, or his agent, a statement in writing, signed by himself and the contractor, specifying how much is due, or take the necessary proceedings against the contractor, as above directed ; otherwise the lien will be lost.

4. The owner is required to pay the amount agreed to be due by the statement of the laborer and contractor, or the judgment, if any be recovered ; which will be deemed a payment on the contract. If the owner neglect to pay the sum due, for ten days after service of the statement, or of a transcript of the judgment, the Clerk of the county, on having filed with him a duplicate copy of the statement signed by the laborer, or person furnishing materials, and the contractor, as aforesaid, with an affidavit that the same is a true copy, or a transcript of the judgment, with an affidavit of demand of the amount due, of the owner or agent, and of the refusal or neglect to pay, may issue an execution against such owner, in the same form as upon a judgment recovered on contract, on the day of the attaching of such lien, reciting that such execution is issued pursuant to the tenth section of the act of 1844 ; which execution will be subject to the jurisdiction and control of the court, as are also the liens and judgments docketed by virtue of the foregoing provisions.

5. Any person who shall furnish materials, or perform any labor, as above specified, may certify to the owner, or his agent, at any time previous to, or during the progress of the work, that he will discharge such owner, or his agent, from any liability on the lien ; and such

certificate, executed by the person in presence of a subscribing witness, will be conclusive in barring such person from any lien.[1]

6. There is a special lien law applicable to the county of Richmond only, which may be found in Volume III, of the Revised Statutes, (3d ed.) p. 717.

FORMS.

§ 773. *Notice to Owner or Agent, of Filing Specification.*

Sir: You will please to take notice, that I have this day filed in the office of the Clerk of the county of   , a specification of work, [*or*, materials,] contracted to be performed [*or*, furnished] by me, and the prices agreed to be paid for the same, by E. F., of the city [*or*, village] of   : and that the said work is [*or*, materials are] to be done [*or*, furnished] upon and for the dwelling-house known as number   , in   street, in said city, [*or*, village.]

Dated   , the   day of   , 18 .

C. D.

To Mr. A. B., of   .

---

§ 774. *Notice of Filing Contract.*

Sir: You will please to take notice, that I have this day filed in the office of the County Clerk of the county of   , a true copy of a contract, made and executed between E. F., of the city [*or*, village] of   , and the undersigned C. D., dated the   day of   , 18 : and that the said contract relates to work or labor to be done [*or*, materials to be furnished] on or about the dwelling-house known as number   , in   street, in said city, [*or* village.]

Dated, &c., [*as in* § 773.]

C. D.

---

§ 775. *Notice to Appear and Submit to Account, &c.*[2]

Sir: You will please to take notice, that you are required to appear in the Court of Common Pleas of the city and county of New York, [*or*, the County Court of the county of   ; *or*, before G.

---

[1] Laws of 1844, chap. 220; Id., chap. 305; Laws of 1845, chap. 235; 4 Hill, 193; 7 Id., 525.
[2] The notice must be served twenty (ten, in the city of New York,) days before the time for appearance.

H., Esq., a Justice of the Peace of the county of   ,] either in person or by attorney, on the   day of   next, and submit to an accounting and settlement in said court, of the amount due, or claimed to be due, for work and labor done [*or*, materials furnished] by the undersigned, under a contract made between E. F., of said city of   , [*or*, village of   ,] and myself, bearing date the   day of   , 18   , on or about the dwelling-house known as number   , in   street, in said city, [*or*, village,] and a copy whereof is on file in the office of the Clerk of the county of   .

Dated, &c., [*as in* § 773.]

---

§ 776. *Notice to Produce Bill of Particulars of Offset.*

Sir : You will please to take notice, that you are required to produce and serve on the undersigned, at his dwelling-house, in the city [*or*, village] of   , within ten days after service hereof, a bill of particulars of any offset which may be claimed to the account herewith presented ; and you will also take notice, that the following is a bill of particulars of the amount claimed to be due by the undersigned, viz: [*set forth the particulars, as in an ordinary account.*]

Dated, &c., [*as in* § 773.]

---

§ 777.   *Statement of Labor Done, or Materials Furnished, to be Signed by the Person Doing the Work, or Furnishing the Materials, and the Contractor, and Delivered to the Owner or his Agent.*

We do hereby certify and agree, that the undersigned C. D., has performed labor [*or*, furnished materials] on or about the dwelling-house known as number   , in   street, in the city [*or*, village] of   , to the value of   dollars; of which you will please take notice.

Dated, &c., [*as in* § 773.]   C. D.
To Mr. A. B.   E. F.

---

§ 778.   *Writ of Inquiry from the Court.*

The People of the State of New York, to the Sheriff of the County of   , greeting;

[L. S.]   Whereas, C. D., lately in our Court of Common Pleas of our city and county of New York, [*or*, our County Court of our said county of   ,] before the Judges [*or,* Judge] thereof, at the court-house in the city [*or,* town] of produced and showed to the said court, that on the   day of   , 18   , in pursuance of an act entitled " An Act for the better security of mechanics and others erecting buildings and furnishing materials therefor, in the city and county of New York," passed April 29, 1844, [*or,* in the several cities in this State, (except the city of New York,) and in the villages of Syracuse, Williamsburgh, Geneva, Canandaigua, Oswego and Auburn, " passed May 7, 1844,]* he personally served A. B. with a notice to appear and submit to an accounting and settlement in the said court, of which the following is a copy, viz: [*copy notice:*] And whereas, on the   day of   , 18   , that being the day on which the said A. B. was required to appear in and by the said notice, he, the said A. B., did not appear, but made default; whereupon such proceedings were had in our said court, before our said Judges [*or,* Judge] thereof, that the said C. D. ought to recover against the said A. B. his damages on occasion of the premises; but because it is unknown to our said Judges, [*or,* Judge,] what damages the said C. D. has sustained; Therefore, we command you, that by the oaths of twelve good and lawful men of your county, you dilligently inquire what damages the said C. D. hath sustained, as well by means of the premises aforesaid, as for his costs and charges in this behalf expended; and that you send to our said court, before our Judges [*or,* Judge] thereof, at the court-house, [*or,* city hall,] in the town [*or,* city] of   , on the   day of   next, the inquisition which you shall thereupon take, under your seal, and the seals of those by whose oaths you shall take that inquisition, together with this writ.

Witness, G. H., Esq. First Judge, [*or,* County Judge,] at the City Hall of the city of New York, [*or,* court-house in the town [*or,* city] of   ,] on the   day of   18   .

                                        P. V., Clerk.

---

§ 779. *Affidavit for Execution.*

County, ss :

C. D., of said county, being duly sworn, says, that the annexed statement is a true copy of an original statement delivered by him, personally, to A. B., on the   day of   , 18   , and that the amount specified to be due in said statement now remains unpaid, [*or,* that on the   day of   , 18   , and more than ten days prior to this day, he demanded of A. B., the payment of the judgment of which the within is a correct transcript, and that the said A. B. refused to pay the same.]

Sworn to, this   day of   ,
    18   , before me,   A. R.
            G. H., Justice of the Peace.

§ 780. *Execution by County Clerk.*

The People of the State of New York, to the Sheriff of the city and county of New York, [*or*, of the county of   ,] greeting:

[L. S.]   We command you, that of the goods and chattels of A. B., in your bailiwick, you cause to be made dollars, which C. D., lately, in our Court of Common Pleas of the said city and county, [*or*, in our County Court of said county of   ,] recovered against the said A. B., in pursuance of the tenth section of an act, &c., [*as in* § 778, *to the* * *and then add:*] whereof the said A. B. is convicted, as appears of record; and if sufficient goods and chattels of the said A. B. cannot be found in your county, that then you cause the amount of   dollars, aforesaid, to be made of the real estate whereof the said A. B. was seized, on the   day of   , 18   , or at any time thereafter, in whose hands soever the same may be, and have you those moneys before our Judges of our said Court of Common Pleas, [*or*, our Judge of our said County Court,] at the City Hall in the city and county of New York, [*or*, court-house in the city [*or*, town] of   ,] at the expiration of sixty days from the receipt hereof by you, together with this writ.

Witness, &c., [*as in* § 778.]

CHAPTER XXIX.

NATURALIZATION.

PRACTICAL REMARKS.

1. Congress has the exclusive power of establishing uniform rules of naturalization.[1]

2. The terms upon which any alien, being a free white person, can be naturalized, are as follows, viz: It is required that he declare on oath, before a State court, being a court of record with a seal and clerk, and having common law jurisdiction; or before a Circuit or District Court of the United States; or before a clerk of either of said courts; two years, at least, before his admission, his intention to become a citizen, and to renounce his allegiance to his own sovereign. This declaration need not be previously made, if the alien resided here previous to the 18th June, 1812, and has since continued to reside here; nor if he be a minor under twenty-one years of age, and shall have resided in the United States three years next preceding his arrival to majority. It is sufficient to be made at the time of his admission, and that he then declare on oath, and prove to the satisfaction of the court, that for three years' next preceding, it was his *bona fide* intention to become a citizen; and then the five years' residence, including the three years of his minority, will entitle him to admission as a citizen, on complying with the other requisites of the law. At the time of his admission, his country must be at peace with the United States, and he must take an oath, before one of the courts above mentioned, to support the Constitution of the United States, and likewise, on oath, renounce and abjure his native allegiance. He must, at the time of his admission, satisfy the court, by other proof

---

[1] 1 Kent's Commentaries, (2d ed.) 424 ; 2 Wheaton, 269 ; 5 Id , 49.

than his own oath, that he has resided five years, at least, within the United States, and one year, at least, within the State where the court is held; and if he shall have arrived after the peace of 1815, his residence must have been continued for five years next preceding his admission, without being at any time, during the said five years, out of the territory of the United States. He must satisfy the court that, during that time, he has behaved as a man of good moral character, attached to the principles of the Constitution of the United States, and well disposed to the good order and happiness of the same. He must, at the same time, renounce any title, or order of nobility, if any he has.[1]

3. The children of persons duly naturalized, being minors at that time, will, if dwelling in the United States, be deemed citizens. If, any alien shall die after his declaration, and before actual admission as a citizen, his widow and children will be deemed citizens.[2]

4. Any alien who may purchase and take a conveyance of lands or real estate in the State of New York, or to whom the same may be devised, or would descend if he were a citizen, and who shall have filed the deposition or affirmation, a form of which is hereinafter given, or who may file the same within one year from the time of such purchase, devise, or descent cast, may hold or convey such land or real estate, during the term of five years from the 10th day of April, 1843, in the same manner as if he were a citizen.[3]

5. A married woman, who is an alien, may be naturalized.[4]

FORMS.

§ 781. *Declaration of Intention, and Certificate of Clerk.*

I, A. B., do declare on oath, that it is *bona fide* my intention to become a citizen of the United States, and to renounce forever all allegiance and fidelity to all and any foreign prince, potentate, state, and sovereignty, whatever; and particularly to Victoria, Queen of the United Kingdom of Great Britain and Ireland, [*or, as the name and title of the sovereign may be.*]

Sworn in open court, this day of , 18 , before me, W. B., Clerk of the Court of .

A. B.

---

[1] Laws of U. S., 1802, chap. 28; Id., 1813, chap. 184; Id., 1866, chap. 22; Id., 1824, chap. 186; Id., 1828, chap. 106; 7 Hill, 56, 137.

[2] 2 Kent's Commentaries, (2d ed.) 64, 65; Laws of U. S. 1804, chap. 47.

[3] 2 R. S. (3d ed.) 4, 6, §§ 16–21; Laws of 1830, chap. 171; Laws of 1836, chap. 339; Laws of 1838, chap. 32; Laws of 1843, chap. 87; Laws of 1845, chap. 115; 6 Paige, 114; 6 id., 446; 20 Wendell, 338; 21 id., 59; 2 Hill, 67.

[4] 20 Wendell, 338

I, W. B., Clerk of the   Court of.   , being a court of record, having common law jurisdiction, and a clerk and seal, do certify that the above is a true copy of the original declaration of intention of A. B. to become a citizen of the United States, remaining of record in my office.

In testimony whereof, I have hereunto subscribed my name, and affixed the seal of the said court, the   day of   , one thousand eight hundred and   .

[L. S.]   W. B., Clerk.

---

§ 782. *Oath of Alien.*

United States of America ; State }
     of New York,   County, } ss:

A. B., being duly sworn, doth depose and say, that he is a resident in the State of New York, and intends always to reside in the United States, and to become a citizen thereof, as soon as he can be naturalized ; and that he has taken such incipient measures as the laws of the United States require, to enable him to obtain naturalization

Sworn before me, the   }
    day of   , 18   .   }

       W. B., Clerk of   Court.

---

§ 783. *Affidavit of Alien under Eighteen Years of Age at the time of his Arrival.*

In the matter of C. D., } State of New York,   County, ss:
   on his naturalization, }

C. D., being duly sworn, says, that, for the continued term of five years last past, he has resided within the United States, without being at any time, during the said five years, out of the territory of the United States, and that for one year last past, he has resided within the State of New York ; and that, at the time he so arrived in the United States, he had not attained his eighteenth year.

Sworn in open court, this   day }
    of   , 18   , before me,   }

       W. B., Clerk of the   Court of   .

---

§ 784. *Oath to Support the Constitution in preceding case.*

I, C. D., do solemnly swear, that I will support the Constitution of the United States, and that I do absolutely and entirely renounce and abjure all allegiance and fidelity to any foreign prince, potentate, state, or sovereignty, whatever, and particularly to Ernest Augustus, King of Hanover, of whom I was a subject.

Sworn, &c., [*as in* § 783.]   C. D.

---

§ 785 *Proof of Good Behavior, &c., to Accompany the foregoing Oath.*

State of New York, } ss:
  County,

E. F., of said county, being duly sworn, doth depose and say, that he is a citizen of the United States; that he is well acquainted with the above named C. D.; and that the said C. D. has resided within the limits, and under the jurisdiction of the United States, for five years last past, and, for one year last past, within the State of New York; and that during the same period he has behaved himself as a man of good moral character, attached to the principles of the Constitution of the United States, and well disposed to the good order and happiness of the same. And he further saith, that, at the time the said C. D. arrived in the United States, he had not attained his eighteenth year.

Sworn, &c., [*as in* § 783.]   E. F .

---

§ 786. *Declaration of Intention to become a Citizen for Three Years past.*

I, C. D., do declare, on oath, that it is *bona fide* my intention, and has been for the last three years, to become a citizen of the United States, and to renounce forever all allegiance to all and every foreign prince, potentate, state, and sovereignty, whatever, and particularly to Ferdinand, Emperor of Austria.   C. D.

Sworn, &c., [*as in* § 783.]

---

§ 787. *Certificate of Citizenship.*

United States of America; State } ss:
  of New York,   County,

Be it remembered, that on the   day of   , in the year of our Lord one thousand eight hundred and   , A. B., late of   , in the kingdom of France, at present of   , in the State of   , aforesaid, appeared in the   Court of (the said court being a court of record, having common law juris-diction, and a clerk and seal,) and applied to the said court to be admitted to become a citizen of the United States of America, pur-suant to the directions and requisitions of the several acts of Con-gress in relation thereto: And the said A. B. having thereupon produced to the court such evidence, made such declaration and renunciation, and taken such oath as are by the said acts required; thereupon it was ordered by the said court, that the said A. B. be admitted, and he was accordingly admitted by the said court, to be a citizen of the United States of America.

In testimony whereof, the seal of the said court is hereunto affixed, this   day of   , in the year one thousand eight hundred and   , and in the year of our independence the   .

[L. S.] By the Court.   W. B., Clerk.

[*For the form of the oath, see* § 784.]

---

§ 788. *Deposition of Alien to enable him to hold Real Estate.*[1]

United States of America; State } ss:
   of New York,   County, }

A. B., being duly sworn, doth depose and say, that he is a resident of the State of New York, and intends always to reside in the United States, and to become a citizen thereof, as soon as he can be naturalized; and that he has taken such incipient measures as the laws of the United States require, to enable him to obtain naturali-zation.

Sworn to before me, this   }
   day of   , 18   .   }
                     G. H., County Judge.

---

[1] The deposition, or affirmation, is to be made, or taken, before any officer authorized to take the proof of deeds, and is to be filed and recorded in the office of the Secretary of State.

CHAPTER XXX.

OFFICIAL OATH AND BOND.

PRACTICAL REMARKS.

1. All persons elected or appointed to any civil office in this State, and in the several counties and cities thereof, are required to take the official oath of office. Supervisors, Town Clerks, Assessors, Overseers of the Poor, Commissioners of Highways, and Town Sealers, are also required to take such oath, within ten days after receiving notice of their election or appointment.

2. Official bonds are to be executed within the time prescribed for taking the oath of office, unless otherwise directed by law.

3. Overseers of Highways, and Poundmasters, are required to give notice to the Town Clerk, in writing, signifying their acceptance of their respective offices, within ten days after receiving notice of their election or appointment.

4. The official oaths and bonds of town officers are to be filed with the Town Clerk, except that the bond of a Collector is to be filed with the County Clerk, and that Justices of the Peace are required to file their oaths of office, within fifteen days after the first day of January next after their election, in the offices of the County Clerks of their respective counties.[1]

5. A person elected to the office of Justice of the Peace, and not taking the oath, but entering upon the duties of the office, is Justice *de facto*, although he is guilty of a misdemeanor.[2]

---

[1] Amneded Constitution of New York, Art. xii; 1 R. S. (3d ed.) 123, § 22, et seq.; Id., 395 § 29, et seq.

[2] 2 Barbour's S. C. Rep., 320.

FORMS.

§ 789. *Official Oath.*

I do solemnly swear, [*or,* affirm,] that I will support the Constitution of the United States, and the Constitution of the State of New York, and that I will faithfully discharge the duties of [*give the title of the office*] according to the best of my ability.

A. B.

Sworn and subscribed, this day }
  of , 18 , before me, }
    P. V., Clerk of the County of   .

---

§ 790. *Notice of the Acceptance of a Town Office.*

To C. D., Clerk of the Town of , in the County of :
 Take notice, that I hereby accept the office of Overseer of Highways of district No. , in said town of .
 Dated the day of , 18 .

O. P.

---

§ 791. *Instrument to be given by a Constable and his Sureties.*

H. C. B., chosen [*or,* appointed] Constable of the town of , in the county of ; and L. M. and S. T., as sureties of the said H. C. B., do hereby jointly and severally agree to pay to each and every person who may be entitled thereto, all such sums of money as the said Constable may become liable to pay, on account of any execution which shall be delivered to him for collection.

 Dated the day of , 18 .
Executed in the presence of, and } H. C. B. [L. s.]
 the sureties approved by, } L. M. [L. s.]
E. F., Supervisor, [*or,* C. D., Town S. T., [L. s.]
   Clerk] of the Town of   .

---

§ 792. *Sheriff's Bond.*[1]

Know all men by these presents: That we, A. P., L. M., and S. T., of the town of , in the county of , are held and

---

[1] The penal sum of the Sheriff's bond in the city of New York, is twenty thousand dollars: and there must be two sureties. In other counties, the bond must be in the penal sum of ten thousand dollars, with two or more sureties.

firmly bound unto the people of the State of New York, in the penal sum of   thousand dollars, to be paid to the said people; for which payment, well and truly to be made, we bind ourselves, our and each of our heirs, executors and administrators, jointly and severally, firmly by these presents.

Sealed with our seals, and dated the   day of   , A. D. 18 .*

Whereas, the above bounden A. P. hath been elected to the office of Sheriff of the county of   , aforesaid, at the general election [or, at a special election] held therein, on the   day of   : Now, therefore, the condition of the above obligation is such, that if the said A. P. shall well and faithfully, in all things, perform the duties and execute the office of Sheriff of the said county of   , during his continuance in the said office, by virtue of the said election, without fraud, deceit, or oppression, then the above obligation to be void; else to remain in full force.

A. P. [L. S.]

Executed in the presence of, and }
the sureties approved by, }

L. M. [L. S.]
S. T. [L. S.]

P. V., Clerk of the County of   .

---

§ 793. *Oath of Sheriff's Sureties, to be Indorsed on the Bond.*

I, L. M, one of the sureties named in the within bond, do solemnly swear, that I am a freeholder within the State of New York, and worth the sum of   thousand dollars, over and above all debts whatsoever owing by me.

L. M.

Sworn and subscribed, this   day }
of   , 18   , before me, }

P. V., Clerk of the County of   .

---

§ 794. *Bond of a Deputy Sheriff.*

Know all men by these presents: That we, G. H., S. T., and O. P., of the town of   , in the county of   , are held and firmly bound unto A. P., Esquire, Sheriff of the said county of   , in the penal sum of   thousand dollars, to be paid to the said A. P.; for which payment, &c. [as in § 792 to the *, and then add:]

Whereas the above bounden G. H. has been appointed to the office of Deputy Sheriff in and for the said county of   , by the above named A. P., Sheriff, as aforesaid; Now, therefore, the condition of this obligation is such, that if the said G. H. shall save and keep the said A. P. harmless of and from any liability incurred by and through any act of the said G. H., as such deputy, as aforesaid, then this obligation to be void, otherwise of force.

Signed and sealed in   )   G. H. [L. s.]
   presence of   }   S. T. [L s.]
       C. D.   )   O. P. [L s.]

---

§ 795. *General Form of an Official Bond.*

Know all men by these presents: That we, A. B., C. D., and E. F., of, &c., are held and firmly bound unto the people of the State of New York, [*or, the officer, or officers, to whom the bond is to be given,*] in the penal sum of   dollars, to be paid to the said people, [*or officer, or officers, as aforesaid;*] for which payment, &c., [*as in § 792, to the *, and then add:*]

Whereas, the above bounden A. B. has been appointed [*or,* elected] to the office of   , [*give the title of the office:*] Now, therefore, the condition of the above obligation is such, that if the said A. B. shall, &c., [*follow the language of the statute prescribing the form of the condition,*] then the above obligation to be void; else to remain in full force.

Signed and sealed in   )   A. B. [L. s.]
   presence of   }   C. D. [L. s.]
      G. H.   )   E. F. [L s.]

CHAPTER XXXI.

PARTNERSHIP.

PRACTICAL REMARKS

1. Partnership is a contract between two or more persons, to place their money, effects, labor and skill, or some or all of them, in any lawful commerce or business, and to divide the profit, and bear the loss, in certain proportions. *Universal* partnership is a contract by which the parties agree to make a common stock of all the property they respectively possess. *Particular* partnerships are such as are 'formed for any business not of a commercial nature. *Commercial* partnerships are formed for the purchase of personal property, and the sale thereof, either in the same state, or changed by manufacture; or for carrying persons or personal property, for hire, in ships or other vessels, or conveyances.[1]

2. The leading principles of a contract of partnership are, a common interest in the stock of the company, and a personal responsibility for the partnership engagements.[2]

3. In order to constitute partners, between the parties, there must be a voluntary contract, and each party must engage to bring into the common stock something that is valuable, whether it be money, property, or services; and there must also be a communion of profits. The shares must be joint, though it is not necessary that they should be equal.[3]

4. A parol agreement to enter into partnership immediately, is valid,—so, also, is an agreement to enter into partnership in future, if the parties really go into partnership.[4]

---

[1] 3 Kent's Commentaries, (2d ed.,) 23, et seq.; Story on Partnership, 2, et seq.
[2] 3 Kent's Commentaries, (2d ed.,) 24.
[3] 3 Kent's Commentaries, (2d ed.) 25; 9 Johnson, 307; 10 Id., 226; 15 Id., 409; 16 Id., 34, 489; 1 Wendell, 457; 18 Id., 175; 1 Hill, 572; 3 Id., 162; 4 Paige, 148.
[4] 2 Barbour's Ch. Rep., 336.

5. Persons are answerable to the world as partners, if they permit their names to be used in a firm, or participate in the profits of a trade: and each individual is liable to the whole amount of the debts, without reference to the proportion of his interest.[1]

6. Where two or more persons agree to have any business in which they are jointly concerned, carried on in the name of one, his name is the co-partnership name or title.[2]

7. A partner cannot bind his co-partner by a contract under seal, (except it be a release or an assignment of a chose in action due to the firm,) without his previous assent, or subsequent indorsement.[3]

8. Part owners of ships are generally regarded as tenants in common, and not as partners, or joint tenants.[4]

9. A co-partnership cannot be proved by general reputation ; but other facts and circumstances must be adduced in order to establish it.[5]

10. On an execution against one of several co-partners, the property of the firm may be seized, removed and sold, by the officer, and the purchaser at the sale will become a tenant in common with the other partner or partners ; but the right which such purchaser may acquire will be subject to the adjustment of the partnership concerns, and the debts of the firm must be first satisfied out of the partnership effects.[6]

11. After the dissolution of a partnership, neither party can make any disposition of the partnership effects, inconsistent with the primary duty of paying the partnership debts ; though either party may receive payment of debts due the firm, and apply the amount received on the partnership liabilities.[7]

12. After the dissolution of a partnership, the promise of one partner will not revive a debt barred by the statute of limitations ; for the dissolution revokes the presumed agency, except so far as relates to winding up the business of the firm.[8]

13. A species of partnership, similar to the French system of *commandite*, may be formed in this State, by two or more persons, for the transaction of any mercantile, mechanical or manufacturing business. Such partnerships may consist of one or more persons, who shall be called general partners, and shall be jointly and severally responsible as general partners in other cases; and of one or more persons who shall contribute, in actual cash payments, a specific sum, as capital, to the common stock, who shall be called special partners, and who

---

[1] 9 Johnson, 470; 14 Id., 315; 19 Id., 226; 1 Wendell, 457; 5 Id., 274; 6 Id., 263; 18 Id., 175.
[2] 1 Denio, 402.
[3] 9 Johnson, 285; 19 Id., 513; 1 Wendell, 326; 9 Id., 437; 12 Id., 53; 20 id., 251; 2 Hill, 595; 5 Id., 163.

[4] 1 Johnson, 106; 20 Id., 611.
[5] 20 Johnson, 176; 11 Wendell, 96; 20 Id., 81; 3 Hill, 333.
[6] 3 Denio, 123, 2 Barbour's Ch. Rep. 167.
[7] 2 Barbour's S. C. Rep., 625.
[8] 2 Comstock, 622.

shall not be liable beyond the fund so contributed by him, or them, to the capital.[1]

14. In order to form a limited partnership, a certificate must be made and signed by the parties, as in the form hereinafter given. An affidavit of one or more of the general partners must also be made, stating that the sums specified in the certificate as having been contributed by the special partners, have been actually and in good faith paid in cash. The certificate must be acknowledged and filed, with the affidavit, in the office of the Clerk of the county in which the business is to be carried on; and, if such business is to be conducted in more than one county, transcripts of the certificate and acknowledgment must be filed in such other counties. The terms of the partnership, when registered, are to be published for at least six weeks immediately after such registry, in two newspapers, to be designated by the Clerk of the county, and to be published in the senate district in which the business shall be carried on.[2]

15. In publishing the terms of a limited partnership, they must be in all respects truly stated, in each newspaper, or the special partners will become liable as general partners.[3]

16. The general partners only may transact the business of a limited partnership. A special partner may examine into the state of the partnership concerns, and advise as to their management; but his name cannot be used in the transactions of the firm; nor can he interfere in the management thereof, either as agent, attorney, or otherwise, without rendering himself liable as a general partner. The business is to be conducted under a firm, in which the names of the general partners only can be inserted, without the addition of the word "company," or any other general term.[4]

17. Every association, or company, formed for the purpose of the transportation of passengers or property, either by boats, vessels or stages, is required to make a statement of the names of the persons composing such association, or company, and to file a copy thereof in the office of the Clerk of each county through which its business is transacted. Until such statement be filed, no suit will be abated, on account of the non-joinder of any of the members of the association, or company, against which the action may be brought.[5]

---

[1] 2 R. S. (3d ed.,) 49, §§ 1, 2; 7 Paige, 585.
[2] 2 R. S. (3d ed.,) 49, 50, § 4, et seq.; 24 Wendell, 496; 5 Hill, 309; 6 Id., 479.
[3] 3 Denio, 435.
[4] 2 R. S. (3d ed.,) 50, § 13; Id., 51, § 1 24 Wendell, 496; 5 Hill, 309; 6 Id. 479.
[5] Laws of 1836, Chap. 385.

FORMS.

§ 796. *Articles of Co-partnership.—General Form.*

Articles of agreement, made the   day of   , one thousand eight hundred and   , between A. B., of, &c., of the one part, and C. D., of, &c., of the other part, witnesseth, as follows: The said parties above named have agreed to become co-partners in business, and by these presents do agree to be co-partners together, under and by the name, or firm of B. and D., in the business of wholesale dry goods merchants, and in the buying, selling and vending all sorts of goods, wares and merchandise, to the said business belonging, and to occupy the store No.   , in   street, in the city of   ; their co-partnership to commence on the   day of   18   , and to continue for the term of five years from thence next ensuing, fully to be complete and ended; and to that end and purpose, the said A. B. and C. D. have delivered in as capital stock, the sum of twenty thousand dollars, share and share alike, to be used and employed in common between them, for the support and management of the said business, to their mutual benefit and advantage.

And it is agreed, by and between the parties to these presents, that at all times during the continuance of their co-partnership, they, and each of them, will give their attendance, and do their and each of their best endeavors, and, to the utmost of their skill and power, exert themselves, for their joint interest, profit, benefit and advantage, and truly employ, buy, sell and merchandise, with their joint stock, and the increase thereof, in the business aforesaid: And also, that they shall, and will, at all times during the co-partnership, bear, pay and discharge, equally between them, all rents and other expenses that may be required for the support and management of the said business; and that all gains, profits and increase, that shall come, grow, or arise, from or by means of their said business, shall be divided between them, the said co-partners, share and share alike; and all loss that shall happen to their said joint business, by ill commodities, bad debts, or otherwise, shall be borne and paid equally between them: And it is agreed, by and between the said parties, that there shall be had and kept, at all times during the continuance of their co-partnership, perfect, just and true books of account, wherein each of the said co-partners shall enter and set down, as well all money by them, or either of them, received, paid, laid out and expended, in and about the said business, as also all goods, wares, commodities and merchandise, by them, or either of them, bought or sold, by reason or on account of the said business, and all other matters and things whatsoever, to the said business and management thereof in any wise belonging; which said books shall be used in common between the said co-partners, so that either of them may have access thereto, without any interruption or hindrance of the other: And also, the said co-partners, once in each year, during the continuance of the said co-partnership, as aforesaid (to wit: on the   day of   , in each year,) or oftener if necessary, shall make, yield and render, each to the other, a true, just and perfect, inventory and account, of all the profits and increase by them, or either of them made, and of all loss by them, or either of them, sustained; and also, of all payments, receipts and disbursements, and of all other things by them made, received, disbursed, acted, or suffered, in their said co-partnership and business; and the same account being so made, they shall, and will, clear, adjust, pay and deliver, each to the other, at the time, their just share of the profits so made as aforesaid. And the said parties hereby mutually covenant and agree, to and with each other, that during the continuance of the said co-partnership, neither of them shall, nor will, indorse any note, or otherwise become surety for, any person or persons whomsoever, without the consent of the other of the said co-partners: And at the end, or other sooner determination of their co-partnership, the said co-partners, each to the other, shall and will make a true, just, and final account, of all things relating to their said business; and in all things truly adjust the same, and all and every stock and stocks, as well as the gains and increase thereof, which shall appear to be remaining, either in money, goods, wares, fixtures, debts, or otherwise, shall be divided between them, share and share alike.

In witness whereof, the said parties to these presents have hereunto set their hands and seals, the day and year above written.

Signed and sealed in ⎱
   presence of   ⎰
     G. H.

A. B. · [L. S.]
C. D. [L. S.]

---

§ 797. *Articles of Co-partnership between Country Merchants.*

Articles of agreement made and entered into, this   day of   , A. D. 18   , between A. B., of, &c., of the one part, and C. D., of, &c., of the other part, witnesseth, as follows: The said A. B. and C. D. have joined, and by these presents, do join themselves, to be co-partners together, in the business of general country merchants, and all things thereto belonging: and also, in buying, selling and retailing, all sorts of wares, goods, merchandise and commodities, and all kinds of produce usually kept and sold in a country store, and in such commission business as may appertain to the same;

which said co-partnership is to be conducted under the name, style and firm, of B. and D., at the village of   , in the town of   , aforesaid, and shall continue from the   day of   , 18   , for and during, and unto the end and term of   years, from thence next ensuing, fully to be complete and ended:

And to that end and purpose the said parties to these presents have, the day of the date hereof, delivered in as stock, the sum of   dollars, share and share alike, to be used, laid out and employed, in common between them, for the management of the said business of merchandising, as aforesaid, to their mutual benefit and advantage: And it is agreed between the said parties to these presents, that the capital stock of the firm hereby constituted, shall be made and kept up to the sum of   dollars, share and share alike; that the same may at any time be reduced, or extended, by agreement between the parties hereto; and that the said capital stock, together with all credits, goods, wares, or commodities, bought or obtained by the said firm, by barter or otherwise, shall be kept, used and employed, in and about the business aforesaid; and for that purpose, each partner shall have power to use the name of the firm, and to bind the same, in making contracts and purchasing goods, at the city of New York, or elsewhere, and in otherwise trading, buying and selling, on account of the said firm, and for the benefit and behoof thereof, and not otherwise; provided, however, that neither partner shall contract liabilities in the name, and on the credit of the firm, in purchasing and replenishing their stock of goods and merchandise, to exceed the sum of   dollars, without the consent of the other partner: And also, that neither of the said co-partners shall, or will, during the said term, exercise, or follow, the trade, or business, of merchandising, as aforesaid, in the county of   , aforesaid, for his private benefit or advantage; but shall, at all times, do his best endeavor, in and by all lawful means, to the utmost of his skill, power and cunning, for the joint interest, profit, benefit and advantage, of the firm aforesaid; and truly employ, buy, sell and merchandise with the stock aforesaid, and the increase and profit thereof, in the business of merchants aforesaid, without fraud or covin; and also, that the said parties shall and will, at all times during the said copartnership, bear, pay and discharge, equally between them, all rents and other expenses, &c., [*as in the preceding form to the end; or, insert such other special covenants as the parties may require.*]

In witness, &c., [*as in* § 796.]

§ 798. *Agreement to Renew Partnership, to be Indorsed on the Original Article.*

Whereas, the partnership formed by, and mentioned in, the within article of agreement, has this day expired, [*or,* will expire on the   day of   next,] by the limitations contained herein: It is therefore hereby agreed, that the same shall be continued, on the same terms, and with all the provisions and restrictions in said agreement mentioned, for the further term of   years from this date, [*or,* from the   day of   next.]

    Witness our hands and seals, this   day of   , 18 .

In presence of }   A. B. [L. s.]
    G. H.   }   C. D. [L. s.]

---

§ 799. *Agreement of Dissolution, to be Indorsed on the Original Article.*

By mutual consent of the undersigned, the parties to the within agreement, the partnership thereby formed is wholly dissolved, except so far as it may be necessary to continue the same for the final liquidation and settlement of the business thereof ; and said agreement is to continue in force until such final liquidation and settlement be made, and no longer.

    Witness, &c., [*as in* § 798.]

---

§ 800. *Certificate of Limited Partnership.*

State of New York, } ss :
    County, }

    This is to certify, that the undersigned have formed a limited partnership, pursuant to the provisions of the Revised Statutes of the State of New York, under the name or firm of B. & D. ; that the general nature of the business to be transacted is the buying and selling groceries, and such other articles as are usually dealt in by wholesale and retail grocers : that A. B. and C. D., who respectively reside in the city of New York, are the general partners ; that E. F., who resides at   , in the county of   , in the State of New York, and L. M., who resides at   , in the county of   , in the State of New Jersey, are the special partners ; that the said E. F. has contributed the sum of ten thousand dollars, as capital towards the common stock, and the said L. M. has contributed the sum of five thousand dollars, as capital towards the common stock ; and that the said partnership is to commence on the   day of   , 18   , and is to terminate on the   day of   , 18   .*

   Dated this   **day of**   , one thousand eight hundred and   .

A. B.
C. D.
E. F.
L. M.

---

§ 801. *Certificate of Acknowledgment.*

      County, ss:

On this   day of   , 18   , A. B., C. D., E. F., and L. M., known to me to be the persons described in, and who made and signed the preceding certificate, came before me, and severally acknowledged that they had made and signed the same.

M. U. Judge of New York Common Pleas.

---

§ 802. *Affidavit to be Filed with the Certificate.*

      County, ss:

A. B., of said county, being duly sworn, says, that he is one of the general partners named in the above certificate, and that the sums specified in the said certificate to have been contributed by the special partners to the common stock, have been actually and in good faith paid in cash.

   Subscribed and sworn before me,   }
     this   day of   , 18 .}
     M. U., &c.

A. B.

---

§ 803. *Designation of the Newspapers in which the Publication is to be made.*

   Let the terms of the limited partnership between A. B., C. D., E. F., and L. M., be published in the   .   , and the   , which papers are published in   , in   county.

J. C., Clerk of the City and County of New York.

' The certificate must be acknowledged, (not proved,) before a Justice of the Supreme Court, or a Judge of the County Courts, in the same manner as conveyances of real estate. The affidavit may be made before a Judge, or a Commissioner of Deeds, or the County Clerk.

§ 804. *Notice to be Published.*

NOTICE OF LIMITED PARTNERSHIP.

Notice is hereby given, that A. B., and C. D., who respectively reside in the city of New York; E. F., who resides at   , in the county of   , in the State of New York, and L. M., who resides at   , in the county of   , in the State of New Jersey, have formed a limited partnership, pursuant to the provisions of the Revised Statutes of the State of New York, for the buying and selling groceries, and such other articles as are usually dealt in by wholesale and retail grocers[1], in which all the parties interested are the said A. B. and C. D., who are the general partners, and the said E. F. and L. M., who are the special partners; that the said E. F. has contributed, &c., [*as in* § 800 *to the* *.] Dated New York, July 1st, 1847.

A. B.
C. D.
&c., &c.,

---

[1] The place where the business is to be carried on may be inserted here, although the statute does not seem to require it.

CHAPTER XXXII.

PATENTS.

PRACTICAL REMARKS.

1. Patents are granted to any person, or persons, for the term of fourteen years, for any new and useful art, machine, manufacture, or composition of matter, or any new and. useful improvement on any art, machine, manufacture, or composition of matter, not known or used by others, before his or their discovery or invention thereof, and not, at the time of the application for a patent, in public use, or on sale, with his or their consent, or allowance, as the inventor or discoverer.[1]

2. A patent may also be granted, for the term of seven years, for a design for a manufacturer; or for a design for the printing of woolen, silk, cotton, or other fabrics; or a design for a bust statute, or *bas-relief*, or composition in *alto* or *basso-relievo*; or an impression or ornament to be placed on any article of manufacture; or a pattern, or print, or picture, to be either worked into, or worked on, or printed, or painted, or cast, or otherwise fixed on any article of manufacture; or a shape or configuration of any article of manufacture not before known or used by others. Such design, impression, or configuration, must be entirely new and original. A patent for a design, impression, or configuration, can issue only to a citizen, or to citizens, of the United States; or to an alien, or aliens, who shall have resided one year in the United States, and taken the oath of his or their intention to become a citizen, or citizens.[2]

3. Where the term for which a patent is granted is fourteen years, it may be renewed for seven years, on application, in writing, to the Commissioner of Patents, notice of which application must be published in one or more of the principal newspapers in Washington, and in such other papers published in the section of the country

---

[1] Laws of U. S., 1836. | [2] Laws of U. S., 1842.

most interested, adversely to the extension, as the Commissioner may direct; and any person may appear and show cause against such extension, to the Board, composed of the Secretary of State, Commissioner of Patents, and Solicitor of the Treasury, who are authorized to decide the question.

4. The assignment of a patent may be to the whole, or to an undivided part, by any instrument in writing. All assignments of patents, or conveyances of the right to use the same, in any specified district, must be recorded in the patent office, within three months from the date of the same.

5. Before any inventor can receive a patent for any new invention or discovery, he must deliver a written description of his invention or discovery, specifying the manner in which the same is made, or compounded ; the improvement therein which he claims as his own invention or discovery; and the application of the principle or character which distinguishes it from other inventions. The application must also be accompanied by duplicate drawings and written references, when the nature of the case will admit, which are to be signed by the patentee, and attested by two witnesses, except when the specification refers to them by letters or figures. A model, or a specimen of the ingredients and of the composition of matter, must also be delivered at the patent office, or to one of the agents appointed to receive models, &c.

6. A caveat, setting forth the design and purposes of any invention, may be filed in the patent office by any citizen; or by an alien who shall have been a resident in the United States one year next preceding, and shall have made oath of his intention to become a citizen; who shall have made any new invention, on paying the sum of twenty dollars, which will be deemed part of the regular fee, if the patent is afterwards issued. If an application be made, within one year after filing the caveat, for a patent for any invention which may interfere with that specified in the caveat, the Commissioner is required to give notice by mail to the person filing the same, who will be required to file his specifications, &c., within three months.

7. The following are the fees payable at the patent office: If a citizen of the United States, or an alien resident in the United States one year next preceding the application, and who shall have made oath of his intention to become a citizen, thirty dollars, as a patent fee; if a subject of the King of Great Britain, five hundred dollars; if a citizen of any other country, three hundred dollars. On extending a caveat, the fee is twenty dollars; on entering an application for the decision of arbitrators, twenty-five dollars; on entering a patent beyond the fourteen years, forty dollars; for recording each assignment, or transfer, if not over three hundred words, one dollar— if more than three hundred words, and less than one thousand, two dollars—if more than one thousand words, three dollars; for adding

the specification of a subsequent improvement, fifteen dollars; on surrendering an old patent for a re-issue, to correct a mistake of the patentee, fifteen dollars; for every additional patent in case of re-issue, thirty dollars; for a disclaimer, ten dollars; for copies of papers, ten cents per folio. The fee on an application for a patent for a design, impression, or configuration, is one-half the sum required in other cases. All fees are payable in advance in specie.

8. Every married woman, who is a resident of the State of New York, and who may receive a patent for her own invention, may hold and enjoy the same, and all the proceeds and benefits thereof, and of such invention, to her own separate use, free and independent of her husband and his creditors; and may transfer and dispose of the same, in the same manner as if she were unmarried; but she cannot contract any pecuniary obligations to be discharged at any future time.[1]

FORMS.

§ 805. *Petition.*

To the Commissioner of Patents:

The petition of A. B., of   , in the county of   , and State of   , respectfully represents: That your petitioner has invented a new and improved mode of preventing steam boilers from bursting, which he verily believes has not been known or used prior to the invention thereof by your petitioner. He therefore prays that letters patent of the United States may be granted to him therefor, vesting in him, and his legal representatives, the exclusive right to the same, upon the terms and conditions expressed in the act of Congress in that case made and provided; he having paid thirty dollars into the treasury, and complied with the other provisions of the said act.   A. B.

---

§ 806. *Specification.*

To all whom it may concern:

Be it known, that I, A. B., of   , in the county of   , and State of New York, have invented a new and improved mode of

---

[1] Laws of New York, 1845, chap. 11.

preventing steam boilers from bursting; and I do hereby declare, that the following is a full and exact description of the said invention:

The nature of my invention consists in providing the upper part of a steam boiler with an aperture, in addition to that for the safety valve; which aperture is to be closed by a plug, or disk, of alloy, which will fuse at any given degree of heat, and permit the steam to escape, should the safety-valve fail to perform its functions. To enable others skilled in the art to make and use my invention, I will proceed to describe its construction and operation: I construct my steam boiler in any of the known forms, and apply thereto guage-cocks, a safety-valve, and the other appendages of such boilers; but in order to obviate the danger arising from the adhesion of the safety-valve, and from other causes, I make a second opening in the top of the boiler, similar to that made for the safety-valve, as shown at A, in the accompanying drawing; and in this opening I insert a plug, or disk, of fusible alloy, securing it in its place by a metal ring and screws, or otherwise. This fusible alloy, I, in general, compose of a mixture of lead, tin and bismuth, in such proportions as will insure its melting at a given temperature, which must be that to which it is intended to limit the steam, and will, of course, vary with the pressure the boiler is intended to sustain. I surround the opening containing the fusible alloy, by a tube, B, intended to conduct off any steam which may be discharged therefrom. When the temperature of the steam in such a boiler rises to its assigned limit, the fusible alloy will melt, and allow the steam to escape freely, thereby securing it from all danger of explosion. What I claim as my invention, and desire to secure by letters patent, is the application to steam boilers of a fusible alloy, which will melt at a given temperature, and allow the steam to escape, as herein described, using any metallic compound which will produce the intended effect.

Witness, G. H.   A. B.
      E. F.

---

§ 807. *Specification of a Machine.*[1]

To all whom it may concern:

Be it known, That I, A. B., of   , in the county of   , and State of   , have invented a new and useful machine for   , [*state the use and title of the machine; and if the application is for an improvement, it should read thus:* a new and useful Improvement on a [*or,* on the] machine, &c.]: and I do hereby

---

[1] Where the specification is of an improvement, the original invention should be disclaimed, and the claim confined entirely to the improvement.

declare that the following is a full, clear, and exact description, of the construction and operation of the same, reference being had to the annexed drawings, making a part of this specification, in which figure 1, is a perspective view; figure 2, a longitudinal elevation; figure 3, a transverse section, &c., [*describe all the sections of the drawings, and refer to the parts by letters. Then give a description of the construction and operation of the machine, and conclude with the claim, which should express the nature and character of the invention, and identify the part or parts claimed, separately, or in combi nation.*]

Witness, G. H.   A. B.
       E. F.

---

§ 808. *Oath to Accompany Specification.*

County of   , State of   , ss:

On this   day of   , 18 , before the subscriber, a Justice of the Peace in and for the said county, personally appeared the within named A. B., and made solemn oath, [*or,* affirmation,] that he verily believed himself to be the original and first inventor of the mode herein described for preventing steam boilers from bursting: and that he did not know, or believe, that the same was ever before known or used; and that he was a citizen of the United States.

                            G. H., Justice of the Peace.

---

§ 809. *Application for a Patent on a Design.*

To the Commissioner of Patents:

The petition of A. B., of the town of   , and county of   , in the State of   , respectfully represents: That your petitioner has invented or produced a new and original design or figure to be stamped or printed on fabrics, which, when thus printed, are termed calicoes, which he verily believes has not been known prior to the invention or production thereof by your petitioner. He therefore prays that letters patent of the United States may be granted to him therefor, vesting in him and his legal representatives the exclusive right to the same, upon the terms and conditions expressed in the act of Congress in that case made and provided; he having paid fifteen dollars into the treasury, and complied with the other provisions of the said act.   A. B.

§ 810. *Certificate of Deposit of the Patent Fee.*

The Bank of   :

The Treasurer of the United States has credit at this office, for   dollars in specie, deposited by A. B., of the town of   , in the county of   , and State of   , the same being for a patent for a steam boiler, [*or, as the case may be.*]

---

§ 811. *Withdrawal, with Accompanying Receipt.*

Sir: I hereby withdraw my application for a patent for improvements in the steam boiler, now in your office, and request that twenty dollars may be returned to me, agreeably to the act of Congress authorizing such withdrawal.   A. B.

Washington, March 15, 1847.

Received of the Treasurer of the United States, per Hon. E. B., Commissioner of Patents, twenty dollars, being the amount refunded on withdrawing my application for a patent for improvements, &c.

---

§ 812. *Surrender of a Patent for Re-issue.*

To the Commissioner of Patents:

The petition of A. B., of   , in the county of   , and State of   , respectfully represents: That he did obtain letters patent of the United States, for an improvement in the boilers of steam engines, which letters patent are dated on the first day of March, 18 ; that he now believes that the same is inoperative and invalid, by reason of a defective specification, which defect has arisen from inadvertence and mistake. He therefore prays that he may be allowed to surrender the same, and requests that new letters patent may issue to him for the same invention, for the residue of the period for which the original patent was granted, under the amended specification herewith presented; he having paid fifteen dollars into the treasury of the United States, agreeably to the requirements of the act of Congress in that case made and provided.

---

§ 813. *Assignment of a Patent Right.*

Whereas, letters patent, bearing date the   day of   , A. D. 18 , were granted and issued by the government of the United States, under the seal thereof, to A. B., of, &c., for an improvement in machinery, for sawing and jointing building staves, of all sorts and sizes, [*a general description of the invention should be given,*] a more full and particular description whereof is annexed to the said letters patent, in a schedule; by which letters patent, the full and exclusive right and liberty of making and using the said invention, and of vending the same to others to be used, was granted to the said A. B., his heirs, executors, administrators and assigns, for the term of fourteen years from the date thereof :* Now, therefore, this indenture witnesseth: That I, the said A. B., for and in consideration of the sum of   dollars, to me in hand paid, by C. D., of, &c., the receipt whereof is hereby acknowledged, have granted, assigned and set over, and by these presents do grant, assign and set over, unto the said C. D., his executors, administrators and assigns, the said letters patent, and all my right, title and interest, in and to the said invention, so granted unto me; to have and to hold the said letters patent and invention, unto the said C. D., his executors, administrators and assigns, in as full and ample a manner, to all intents and purposes, as I might have or hold the same, were these presents not executed, for and during the rest and residue of the said term of fourteen years.

In witness whereof, I have hereunto set my hand and seal, this day of   , 18 .

In presence of)
  G. H.   }   .   A. B. [L. S.]
  E. F.

---

§ 814. *The same, where the Patentee has Sold a Moiety, and he and the Assignee Sell the Right for a single State.*

Whereas, &c., [*as in § 813, to the* *, *and then add:*] and whereas the said A. B. has duly sold and assigned the undivided half or moiety, of the said letters patent and invention, and his right, title and interest, in and to the same, to E. F., of, &c., his executors, administrators and assigns, by indenture, dated the   day of   , A. D. 18   : Now, therefore, this indenture witnesseth: That we, the said A. B. and E. F., for and in consideration of the sum of   dollars, to us in hand paid, by C. D., of, &c., the receipt whereof is hereby acknowledged, have granted, bargained and set over, and by these presents do grant, bargain and set over, unto the said C. D., his executors, administrators and assigns, the full and exclusive right of making, constructing, using, and vending to others to be used, the said invention and improvement, as above mentioned, in and for the State of New York; to have and to hold the same unto the said C. D., his executors, administrators and assigns, in and for the State aforesaid, in as full and ample a manner, to all intents and purposes, as we might have or hold the same, were these presents not executed, for and during the rest and residue of the said term of fourteen years.

In witness, &c., [*as in* § 813.]

---

§ 815. *Assignment of the Right in a Patent for One or More States.*

Whereas, I, A. B., of   , in the county of   , and State of   , did obtain letters patent of the United States, for certain improvements in steam engines, which letters patent bear date the first day of March, 1835; and whereas, C. D., of   , aforesaid, is desirous of acquiring an interest therein: Now this indenture witnesseth, that for and in consideration of the sum of two thousand dollars, to me in hand paid, the receipt whereof is hereby acknowledged, I have assigned, sold and set over, and do hereby assign, sell and set over, all the right, title and interest, which I have in the said invention, as secured to me by said letters patent, for, to, and in, the several States of New York, New Jersey and Pennsylvania, and in no other place or places: the same to be held and enjoyed by the said C. D., for his own use and behoof, and for the use and behoof of his legal representatives, to the full end and term for which the said letters patent are or may be granted, as fully and entirely as the same would have been held and enjoyed by me, had this assignment and sale not have been made.

In witness, &c., [*as in* § 813.]

---

§ 816. *Assignment before Obtaining Letters Patent, which must be Recorded preparatory thereto.*

Whereas, I, A. B., of   , in the county of   , and State of   , have invented certain new and useful improvements in the boilers of steam engines, for which I am about to make application for letters patent of the United States; and whereas, C. D., of   , aforesaid, has agreed to purchase from me, all the right, title and interest, which I have, or may have, in and to the said invention, in consequence of the grant of letters patent therefor, and has paid to me, the said A. B., the sum of five thousand dollars, the receipt of which is hereby acknowledged. Now this indenture witnesseth: That for and in consideration of the said sum to me paid, I have assigned and transferred, and do hereby assign and transfer, to the said C. D., the full and exclusive right to all the improvements made by me, as fully set forth and described in the specification which I have prepared and executed, preparatory to the obtaining of

29

letters patent therefor. And I do hereby authorize and request the Commissioner of Patents to issue the said letters patent to the said C. D., as the assignee of my whole right and title thereto, for the sole use and behoof of the said C. D., and his legal representatives.

In witness, &c., [*as in* § 813.]

---

§ 817. *Disclaimer.*[1]

To the Commissioner of Patents:

The petition of A. B., of　　　, in the county of　　　, and State of　　　, respectfully represents: That he has, by assignment, duly recorded in the patent office, become the owner of a right for the several States of Massachusetts, Connecticut and Rhode Island, to certain improvements in the steam engine, for which letters patent of the United States were granted to C. D., of Boston, in the State of Massachusetts, dated on the first day of March, 1835; that he has reason to believe, that, through inadvertence and mistake, the claim made in the specification of said letters patent is too broad, including that of which the said patentee was not the first inventor. Your petitioner, therefore, hereby enters his disclaimer to that part of the claim in the aforenamed specification, which is in the following words, to wit: "I also claim the particular manner in which the piston of the above described engine is constructed, so as to insure the close fitting of the packing thereof to the cylinder, as set forth;" which disclaimer is to operate to the extent of the interest in said letters patent vested in your petitioner, who has paid ten dollars into the treasury of the United States, agreeably to the requirements of the act of Congress in that case made and provided.

A. B.

---

§ 818. *Caveat.*

To the Commissioner of Patents:

The petition of A. B., of　　　, in the county of　　　, and State of　　　, respectfully represents: That he has made certain improvements in the mode of constructing the boilers of steam engines, and that he is now engaged in making experiments for the purpose of perfecting the same, preparatory to his applying for letters patent therefor. He therefore prays, that the subjoined description of his invention may be filed as a caveat, in the confidential

---

[1] When the disclaimer is made by the original patentee, it must be so worded as to express that fact.

archives of the patent office, agreeably to the provisions of the act of Congress in that case made and provided; he having paid twenty dollars into the treasury of the United States. and otherwise complied with the requirements of the said act.

March 1, 1838.   A. B.

---

§ 819. *Addition of New Improvements.*

To the Commissioner of Patents:

The petition of A. B., of   , in the county of   , and State of   , respectfully represents: That your petitioner did obtain letters patent of the United States, for an improvement in the boilers of steam engines, which letters patent are dated on the day of   , 18 ; that he has since that date, made certain improvements on his said invention, and that he is desirous of add-ing the subjoined description of his said improvement to his original letters patent, agreeably to the act of Congress in that case made and provided; he having paid fifteen dollars into the treasury of the United States, and otherwise complied with the requirements of the said act.   A. B.

---

§ 820. *Oath on Restoring Drawings, to Replace the Originals Destroyed in the Patent Office.*

County of   ⎱ ss:
State of   ⎰

On this   day of   , 18. , before the subscriber, a Justice of the Peace in and for said county, personally appeared A. B., of   , in the State of   , and made solemn oath, that he is the inventor [*or*, is interested in the invention, as adminis-trator, &c.,] of an improved mode of preventing the explosion of steam boilers, for which letters patent of the United States were granted to him, [*or*, to C. D.,] dated the   day of   , 18 , and that the annexed drawing [*or*, sketch] is, as he verily believes, a true delineation of the invention described in the said letters patent.

G. H., Justice, &c.

CHAPTER XXXIII.

PENSION VOUCHERS.

PRACTICAL REMARKS.

1. When application is made for the payment of a pension, the identity of the person must be established by affidavit, setting forth a copy of the original certificate, &c., as in the following forms. The deposition must be signed by the deponent, and where the pension has been increased since the certificate was given, the magistrate will note the fact. The requisite depositions may be taken before any officer authorized to administer oaths.

2. Where a pension has remained unclaimed, by any pensioner, for the term of fourteen months after the same became due and payable application must be made to the Department of the Interior, at Washington ; and in such case, additional proof of the identity of the applicant will be required.

3. All interlineations in pension-vouchers should be carefully noted by the magistrate, before the execution.

4. When application for the payment of a pension is made by an attorney, he must deposit with the agent the power of attorney, duly acknowledged, and dated on or subsequent to the day on which the pension claimed became due, together with an affidavit made by himself.

5. In all cases of payments upon a power of attorney, the Justice of the Peace, or Magistrate, before whom the power is executed, must have lodged with the agent, the certificate of the clerk of some court of record, under the seal of the court, that he is legally authorized to act as such, and, also, a paper bearing his proper signature, certified of be such, by the clerk of some court of record.

6. In case of the death of any pensioner, the arrears due to him at the time of his death, must be paid as follows :

1. To the widow of the deceased, or to her attorney, proving herself to be such before a court of record; or,

II. If there be no widow, then to the executor or administrator on the estate of such pensioner, for the sole and exclusive benefit of the children, to be by him distributed among them in equal shares; but the arrears of pension are not to be considered a part of the assets of the estate, nor as liable to be applied to the payment of the debts of such estate, in any case whatever.

7. In case of the death of a pensioner who is a widow, leaving children, the amount of pension due at the time of her death, must be paid to the executor or administrator, for the benefit of her children, as directed in the foregoing paragraph.

8. In case of the death of a pensioner, whether male or female, leaving children, the amount of pension in arrear may be paid to any one, or each of them, as they may prefer, without the intervention of the administrator. If one of the children is selected to receive the amount due, he, or she, must produce a power of attorney from the others for that purpose, duly authenticated.

9. If there be no widow, child, or children, then the amount due a pensioner, at the time of his death, must be paid to the legal representatives of the deceased.

10. Where an executor or administrator applies for the pension, due to a deceased person, he must deposit with the agent for paying pensions, a certificate of the Clerk of the Court, Judge of Probate, Register of Wills, Ordinary, or Surrogate, as the case may be, stating that he is duly authorized to act in that capacity, on the estate of the deceased pensioner, and, if a male, that it has been proved to his satisfaction that there is no widow of the said pensioner living.

11. The original certificate of pension must be surrendered at the time the moneys due a deceased pensioner are paid; or, if such certificate cannot be obtained for surrendry, substantial evidence of the identity, and that due search and inquiry have been made for the certificate, and that it cannot be found, must be produced. The date of the pensioner's death must be proved before a court of record.

12. Where facts are proved before the clerk of a court, his certificate, stating the same, under his seal of office, must be obtained.

13. When the guardian of a pensioner applies for a pension, he must, in addition to the evidence of the pensioner's identity, deposit with the pension-agent a certificate from the proper authority, stating that he is, at that time, acting in that capacity, and also, satisfactory evidence that his ward was living at the date the pension claimed became due.

14 Pension agents are authorized to administer all oaths required to be administered to pensioners or their attorneys, and to charge the same fees as magistrates are authorized to do by the laws of their respective States.[1]

---

[1] Laws of U. S. 1840.

FORMS.

§ 821. *Oath of Pensioner.*

State of
    County, } ss:

Be it known, that before me, G. H., a Justice of the Peace, in and for the county aforesaid, duly authorized by law to administer oaths, personally appeared A. B., and made oath, in due form of law, that he is the identical person named in an original certificate in his possession, of which (I certify) the following is a true copy; [*insert here a copy of the certificate of pension, including name*s *and dates;*] that he now resides in , and has resided there for the space of years last past, and that previous thereto he resided in ;* and that he has not been employed, or paid, in the army, navy, or marine service of the United States, from the day of , to .*

 Sworn and subscribed, this }   A. B.
day of , 18 , before me, }
   G, H., Justice of the Peace.[1]

---

§ 822. *Certificate, where Pension has not been Drawn for Fourteen Months—to be Annexed to the Foregoing Deposition.*

State of
    County, } ss:
May 1st, 1849.

 I, G. H., a magistrate in the county above named, do hereby certify, that I have the most satisfactory evidence, viz: [*state what the evidence is, whether personal knowledge, or the affidavits of respectable persons, giving their names:*] that A. B., who has this day appeared before me to take the oath of identity, is the identical person named in the pension certificate, which he has exhibited before me, numbered , and bearing date at the War Office, the day of , 18 , and signed by W. L. M., Secretary of War.

 Given under my hand, at , on the day and year above written.

       G. H., Justice of the Peace.

---

[1] Where the pension has been increased since the certificate was given, the magistrate must note that fact. In the case of a revolutionary pensioner, that part of § 821 between the two *'s may be omitted.

§ 823. *Certificate of the Clerk, to Accompany § 822.*

State of New York, } ss:
      County, }

I, W. B. , Clerk of the   Court, of the county and State aforesaid, do hereby certify, that G. H. is a Justice of the Peace, in and for said county, duly commissioned and qualified; that his commission was dated on the   day of   , 18   , and will expire on the   day of   , 18 ; and that his signature above written is genuine.

[L. s.]   Given under my hand, and the seal of said county, this
         day of   , 18   .   W. B., Clerk.

§ 824. *Power of Attorney, and Acknowledgment.*

Know all men by these presents: That I, A. B., of   , a revolutionary [*or*, an invalid, *as the case may be*,] pensioner of the United States, do hereby constitute and appoint E. F. my true and lawful attorney, for me, and in my name, to receive from the agent of the United States for paying pensions in Albany, State of New York, my pension from the   day of   , 18   , to the day of   , 18   .

Witness my hand and seal, this   day of   , 18   .
Sealed and delivered in }
     presence of   }   A. B. [L. s.]
       C. D.

State of   , } ss:
        County, }

Be it known, that on the   day of   , 18   , before the subscriber, a Justice of the Peace in and for said county, duly authorized by law to administer oaths, personally appeared A. B., above named, and acknowledged the foregoing power of attorney to be his act and deed.

In testimony whereof, I have hereunto set my hand, the day and year last above mentioned.

                 G. H., Justice of the Peace.

§ 825. *Oath of the Attorney.*

State of   , } ss:
       County, }

Be it known, that on the   day of   , 18   , before the subscriber, a Justice of the Peace in and for said county, duly authorized by law to administer oaths, personally appeared E. F., the attorney named in the foregoing power of attorney, and made oath that he has no interest whatever in the money he is authorized to receive, by virtue of the foregoing power of attorney, either by any pledge, mortgage, sale, assignment, or transfer; and that he does not know or believe that the same has been so disposed of to any person whatever.

Sworn and subscribed, the day and year }   E. F.
last above mentioned, before me,   }
         G. H., Justice of the Peace.

---

§ 826. *Oath of Guardian for Pensioner.*

State of   , } ss:
      County, }

Be it known, that before me, H. T. C., a Justice of the Peace in and for said county, duly authorized by law to administer oaths, personally appeared G. H., guardian of A. B., and made oath, in due form of law, that the said A. B. is still living, and is the identical person named in the original certificate in his possession, of which (I certify) the following is a true copy: [*insert here a copy of the certificate of pension, including names and dates:*] That he resides in   , and has resided there for the space of   years past, and that previous thereto he resided in   .

Sworn and subscribed, this   }   G. H., Guardian.
day of   , 18 , before me, }
     H. T. C., Justice of the Peace.

---

§ 827. *Oath of a Widow, a Pensioner.*

State [*or,* Territory] of   , } ss:
     County of   , }

Be it known, that before me, G. H., a Justice of the Peace, duly authorized by law to administer oaths, in and for the county aforesaid, personally appeared M. B.; and made oath, in due form of law, that she is the identical person named in an original certificate in her possession, of which (I certify) the following is a true copy: [*Insert here a copy of her certificate of pension, including names and dates:*] That she has not intermarried, but continues the widow of the above mentioned A. B. ; and that she now resides in   , and has resided there for the space of   years past; and that previous thereto she resided in   ; of the truth of which statements I am fully satisfied.

Sworn to and subscribed, this   }   M. B.
day of   , 18 , before me, }
     G. H., Justice of the Peace.

§ 828. *Oath of a Widow, who drew a Pension under the Act of March 3d, 1843.*

$ _____

United States of America, }
    State of   , } ss:
         County, }

Be it known, that before me, G. H., a Justice of the Peace, in and for the county aforesaid, duly authorized by law to administer oaths, personally appeared M. B., and made oath, in due form of law, that she is the identical person who drew a pension under the act of the 3d of March, 1843, on account of the revolutionary service of her husband, the late, [*insert here the name and rank of the husband,*] at the rate of $ per annum; that she now makes this affidavit for the purpose of drawing a pension under the act of Congress, passed on the 17th of June, 1844, entitled "An Act to continue the pensions of certain widows;" that she has not intermarried, but continues to be a widow; that she now resides in   , in the county of   , and State of   , and has resided there for the space of   years past; and that previous thereto she resided in   .

Sworn to and subscribed, this   day ⎫
    of   , 18 , in presence of   ⎬   M. B.
    R. P. before me,   ⎭
         G. H., Justice of the Peace.

---

§ 829. *Oath of Identity for the Widow, or Child, of a Deceased Pensioner.*

State of   , } ss:
         County, }

Be it known, that before me. G. H., a Justice of the Peace in and for the county aforesaid, duly authorized by law to administer oaths, personally appeared M. B., and made oath. in due form of law, that she [*or, he*] is the widow [*or, son; or, daughter*] of A. B., the identical person who was a pensioner. and is now dead, and to whom a certificate of pension was issued, which is herewith surrendered:

That the deceased pensioner resided in   , in the State of   , for the space of   years before his death; and that previous thereto he resided in   .[1]

Sworn and subscribed, this   ⎫
day of   , 18 , before me, ⎬   M B.
         G. H., Justice of the Peace.

---

[1] Where the pension has been increased, the magistrate should ???? ??? The above form may be used for an executor or administrator, by substituting the word "executor" or "administrator" for "widow."

T

§ 830. *Power of Attorney for the Widow, or Child, of a Deceased Pensioner.*[1]

Know all men by these presents: That I, M. B., of   , in the county of   , State of   , widow [*or*, child,] of A. B., who was a revolutionary [*or*, an invalid] pensioner of the United States, do hereby constitute and appoint E. F., my true and lawful attorney, for me, and in my name, to receive from the agent of the United States for paying pensions in   , State of   , the balance of said pension from the   day of   , 18   , to the   day of   , 18   , being the day of his death.

Witness my hand and seal, this   day of   , 18   .

Sealed and delivered ⎱
    in presence of   ⎰
.C. D.

M. B. [L. S.]

---

§ 831. *Certificate of the Court as to the Death of a Pensioner.*

State of   , ⎱
County of   . ⎰ ss:

I, W. B., Clerk of the Court of   , holden at   , in and for   , do hereby certify, that satisfactory evidence has been exhibited to said court, that A. B. was a pensioner of the United States at the rate of   dollars per   ; was a resident of the county of   , in the State of   , and died in the   , in the State of   , in the year 18   , on the   day of   ; that he left a widow, [*or*, left no widow; *or*, left a child, *or*, left children,] whose name is [*or*, whose names are] M. B., [*or*, R. B., C. B., &c., &c.] [*If the certificate has been lost, insert here, in addition:* And that the pension certificate of said pensioner has been lost, and, after due search and inquiry therefor, it cannot be found.]

In testimony whereof, I have hereunto set my hand and affixed

[L. S.]   my seal of office, at   , this   day of   , in the year of our Lord 18   .

W. B., Clerk of the   .

---

§ 832. *Oath where Pension Certificate is Illegally Withheld.*

State of   , ⎱
    County, ⎰ ss:

Be it known, that before me, G. H., a Justice of the Peace, in and for the county aforesaid, duly authorized by law to administer oaths,

---

[1] For forms of acknowledgment, and attorney's oath, see §§ 824 and 825. Where one of the children is appointed by the others to receive the balance, the attorney's oath is not required.

personally appeared A. B., and made oath, in due form of law, that he [*or*, she] is the identical A. B. named in an original pension certificate now illegally withheld by, [*here state the facts respecting the detention of the pension certificate;*] that he [*or*, she] is entitled to a pension of [*insert the amount to which the pensioner is entitled at the time of making the oath,*] dollars per month; that he [*or*, she] now resides in   , and has resided there for the space of   , years past; and that previous thereto, he [*or*, she] resided in   .

    Sworn and subscribed, this   A. B.
day of   , 18 , before me,
          G. H., Justice of the Peace.

---

§ 833. *Certificate of Magistrate and Clerk, to Accompany* § 832.

State of   ,
      County, ss:
May 1st, 1849.

    Conformably to the regulations of the War Department of the 27th of October, 1832, I, G. H., a magistrate in the county above named, do hereby certify that I have the most satisfactory evidence, viz: [*state what the evidence is; whether personal knowledge, or the affidavits of respectable persons, giving their names,*] that A. B., who this day appeared before me to take the oath of identity, is the identical pensioner he [*or*, she] declares himself [*or*, herself] to be, in the annexed affidavit; and I am also satisfied that the statement made by him [*or*, her] in relation to the pension certificate, is true.

    Given under my hand, at   , the day and year above written.
          G. H.

    I, W. B., Clerk of the   Court of   county, certify that G. H. is a magistrate, as above, and that the foregoing certificate, purporting to be his, is genuine.

    In testimony whereof, I have hereunto affixed my seal of office,
[L. s.]   and subscribed my name, this   day of   .
      in the year   .
      W. B., Clerk of the   Court of   county.

CHAPTER XXXIV.

PLANK AND TURNPIKE ROADS.

PRACTICAL REMARKS.

1. Any number of persons, not less than five, may form themselves into a corporation for the purpose of constructing and owning a plank or turnpike road, under the Laws of the State of New York. In order to form such a corporation, notice of the time and place or places, where books for subscribing to the stock of such road will be opened, must be given in at least one newspaper, printed in each county through which the road is to be constructed. When stock to the amount of five hundred dollars for each mile of the proposed road has been subscribed in good faith, the subscribers may choose directors and make and sign articles of association, which articles are to be filed in the office of the Secretary of State; and thereupon the subscribers will become a body corporate, clothed with the powers and privileges, and subject to the liabilities of corporations generally, as contained in titles three and four of chapter eighteen of the first part of the Revised Statutes, (volume I, 3d edition, pp. 713–736.)[1]

2. The articles of association are not to be filed till five per cent. on the amount of stock subscribed shall have been, in good faith, paid in to the directors in cash, to be verified by the affidavit of at least three of the directors. Copies of the articles, and of the affidavit indorsed, certified to be correct by the Secretary of State, may be read in any state court as presumptive evidence of the incorporation of the Company, and of the facts therein stated.

---

[1] Laws of 1847, chap. 210; Id., chap. 287; | Laws of 1849, chap. 250; Laws of 1850, Id., chap. 398; Laws of 1848, chap. 360; | chap. 71.

3. Whenever a plank or turnpike road company desires to construct a road through any part of any county, application must be made to the Board of Supervisors, notice of which must be published for six successive weeks, in all the newspapers printed in the county, or in three, if there be more than three. Special meetings of the Board of Supervisors may be called to hear the application, any three of the members thereof fixing the time of the meeting. The expenses of a special meeting are to be paid by the Company, for whose benefit the same is called. Upon the hearing of the application, owners of land on the line of the proposed road, and all persons residing in the county, may appear and be heard; and testimony may be taken by the Board, or by any judicial officer authorized by it. If the Board are of opinion that the public interests will be promoted by the construction of the proposed road, they may, by a majority vote, authorize the same to be laid out and constructed.

4. Where a road is authorized to be constructed by a Board of Supervisors, they must appoint three disinterested persons, not the owners of real estate in any town through which the proposed road is to be constructed, or in any town adjoining such town, as Commissioners to lay out the same. The Commissioners are required to hear all persons interested, at such time or times as they may appoint, to take testimony, to determine the width of the road, and to make an actual survey and description thereof, as laid out by them. The survey is to be signed and acknowledged in the same manner as conveyances of real estate, and recorded in the Clerk's office of the county. Where a road is proposed to be constructed in more than one county, Commissioners are to be appointed in each county. Each Commissioner is entitled to receive two dollars per day for his fees, to be paid by the Company.

5. No plank or turnpike road can be laid out through an orchard of the growth of four years or more, to the injury of fruit trees, or through a garden cultivated four years or more, unless with the consent of the owner of such orchard or garden; nor can any such road be laid out through any dwelling-house, or building connected therewith, or any yard, or inclosure properly appurtenant thereto, without the consent of the owner; neither can a plank or turnpike road company, bridge any stream navigable by vessels or steamboats, or in any manner so as to obstruct the passage of rafts twenty-five feet in width.

6. Where the route of a plank or turnpike road has been laid out and surveyed by Commissioners, the Company may enter upon and take possession of the lands described in the survey, provided the same be purchased of the owners thereof. But if, on account of the inability or unwillingness of the owners to sell or convey, the right to such lands cannot be acquired, application must be made to the County Judge, by whom a jury will be drawn to hear the parties

interested, take testimony, and ascertain and assess the damages. The verdict of the jury will be final, unless application be made within twenty days to the Supreme Court for a new trial, and unless such application be granted.

7. Lands may be obtained by a plank or turnpike road company, for the construction of a road, by purchase of the owner or owners, and in such case no application to the Board of Supervisors will be necessary. An accurate survey must be made by a practical surveyor, signed by the President and Secretary of the Company, acknowledged by them, and recorded in the County Clerk's office.

8. Where it is desired to construct a plank or turnpike road on the line of a public highway, the Supervisor and Commissioners of Highways of any town, or a majority of them, if there be more than one Commissioner, may, with the consent in writing of at least two-thirds of all the owners of land along such highway, actually residing on the line of the proposed road and on such highway, agree with the Company upon the compensation and damages. This agreement must be in writing, and must be filed in the office of the Town Clerk. In case such agreement be entered into, and an accurate survey be made, signed, acknowledged, and recorded, no application to the Board of Supervisors will be necessary ; otherwise, the damages must be ascertained by a jury to be called by the County Judge; and if the Supervisor and Commissioners refuse to give their consent to the construction of the proposed road, application must be made to the Board of Supervisors for their assent. Moneys received by Commissioners of Highways for compensation and damages, must be expended in improving the highways in their respective towns.

9. Three inspectors of plank and turnpike roads are to be appointed by the Board of Supervisors in each county in which any such roads may be constructed. They hold their offices during the pleasure of the Board, and are allowed two dollars per day for their services, to be paid by the Company whose road they may inspect.

10. Plank and turnpike roads are not to exceed four rods in width, except with the consent of the owners of adjoining lands; and the Commissioners, or Inspectors, may fix the width at four rods, or less than that, if they choose so to do.

11. Whenever a plank or turnpike road Company has constructed three consecutive miles of their proposed road, they may apply to the Inspectors, or a majority of them, to inspect the road; and if such inspectors, or a majority of them, certify that a sufficient number of miles of road have been constructed according to law, upon filing their certificate, the Company will be authorized to take toll. Toll gates, however, are not to be erected within three miles of each other, on the same road.

12. The rates of toll on plank roads are not to exceed one and a half cents per mile, for vehicles drawn by two animals—one-half cent

per mile to be added for each additional animal more than two; three-quarters of a cent per mile, for every vehicle drawn by one animal; or half a cent per mile, for every score of sheep or swine, and for every horse and rider, or led horse. Turnpike companies may collect three-quarters of a cent per mile, for every vehicle drawn by one animal; one and one-quarter cent per mile, for every vehicle drawn by two animals—one-quarter cent per mile to be added for every animal more than two; one cent per mile, for every score of neat cattle; and one-half cent per mile, for every score of sheep or swine. Rates of tolls may be determined by the distance between toll gates, instead of the distance actually traveled, except that where persons reside within one mile of a gate, only half tolls are to be exacted from them at such gate.[1]

13. Persons going to or from any court to which they have been summoned as jurors, or subpœnæd as witnesses; going to or from any training at which they are by law required to attend; going to or from religious meetings; going to or from any funeral, or belonging to a funeral procession; or going to any town meeting or election at which they are entitled to vote, for the purpose of voting, and returning therefrom; are exempt from the payment of tolls at the gates of plank road companies. Farmers going to or returning from their work on their farms, when not employed in the transportation of other persons or their property, and troops in the actual service of the State, or of the United States, are also exempt from tolls on plank roads. Persons going to or returning from any grist mill or blacksmith's shop, where they ordinarily get their grinding or blacksmith's work done, for the express purpose of getting grinding or blacksmith's work done, are exempt from the payment of toll at one gate only, within five miles of their residence, provided the plank road be constructed on a public traveled highway.

14. The business and property of a plank or turnpike road company must be managed and conducted by a Board of Directors, consisting of not less than five, nor more than nine, who are to be elected annually, after the first year, at such time and place as may be designated in the by-laws of the corporation. Vacancies are to be filled by the remaining directors, for the remainder of the year.

15. It is the duty of the directors of every plank or turnpike road company, to make an annual report to the Secretary of State, under the oath of at least two of the directors, stating the cost of their road; the amount of their capital stock; the amount expended; the amount paid in; the whole amount and the annual amount of tolls and earnings, in separate items; the amount set apart for a reparation fund; and the amount of indebtedness of the company, with the object for which it accrued.

---

[1] 1 Caines' 182; 23 Wendell, 193.

16. Branches may be constructed by plank road companies, with the written consent of a majority of the inspectors; and the capital stock may be increased, for that purpose, not exceeding two thousand dollars for each mile of additional road.

17. The inhabitants of any road district in the State may grade, gravel, or plank, the road or roads in such district, by anticipating the highway labor of such road district, for one or more years, and applying it to the immediate construction of such plank or gravel road; and they will thereupon be exempt from the labor so anticipated, except so far as their labor may be required to keep such road or roads in repair. Any road so constructed will be a free road.

FORMS.

§ 834. *Notice of Subscription.*

PLANK ROAD NOTICE.

Notice is hereby given, that books of Subscription to the capital stock of a company proposed to be incorporated for the construction of a plank [or, turnpike] road from   to   , to be called "The   Road Company," will be opened at the house of O. P., in the city of   , on the   day of   , 18   , and that such books will remain open at the said place until the whole amount of the capital stock shall be subscribed.

Dated   , 18 .

---

§ 835. *Articles of Association for the Formation of a Plank Road Company.*

Articles of Association made and entered into this   day of   , by and between the persons whose names are hereunto subscribed, Witnesseth:

First—That we, the undersigned, do hereby form ourselves into a Corporation, for the purpose of constructing and owning a Plank Road from   to   , wholly within the county of   , [or, counties of   , and   ] and State of New York.

Second—The name of such Corporation shall be   , and the same shall continue   years from the day of the date of these articles.

Third—The capital stock of said Corporation shall be   dollars, and shall be divided into   shares, of   dollars each.

Fourth—There shall be   Directors of said Company, and A. B., C. D., &c., of the town of   , &c., shall be the first Directors thereof.

Fifth—Said Road shall commence at   , in the town of   , in said county of   , and run thence, through a part of said town of   , to the town of   ; thence through said town of   , to the village of   ; thence through said village, &c., [*describe the route to the place of termination, giving each town, village and city through which it is proposed to construct the road.*]

Sixth—It shall be the duty of the Directors, to issue Scrip to those who shall be entitled to stock in said Company; when five per cent. on the amount of such stock shall have been paid in thereon, which Scrip shall be signed by the President and countersigned by the Secretary of said Company.

Seventh—It shall be the duty of the Treasurer, to indorse upon the Scrip, which shall be held by any Stockholder, every sum which shall be received by such Treasurer thereon, and the time when any such sum shall be so received.

Names of Stockholders.	Residence, (Town or Village.)	County	No. Shares

§ 836. *Scrip Certificate.*

The   Plank Road Company.

This certifies that A. B., of   is entitled to   shares of the capital Stock of the   Plank Road Company, each share being   dollars, upon each share of which there has been paid the sum of   , subject to such future payments as may from time to time he required by the Directors and the conditions of the Articles of Incorporation; said Stock is transferable only on the books of the Corporation, by the Stockholder in person. or by his attorney, and on surrender of this certificate. In testimony whereof, the President and Secretary have hereunto set their hands at   , this   day of   , 185   .

S. G., Secretary.   30   I. B., President.

§ 837. *Affidavit of Amount of Stock paid in*

State of New York, }
    County, ss: }

A. B., C. D., and E. F., being duly sworn, depose and say, and each for himself deposeth and saith, that they are Directors of "The   Road Company," and that five per cent. of the capital stock of said Company, described in the within articles of association, has been actually and in good faith paid in to the Directors thereof, is cash.

Sworn to before me   ,)   A. B.
this   day of   , 18 .   )   C. D.
            G. H., County Judge.   )   E. F.

[*Or any officer authorized to administer oaths.*]

---

§ 838. *Notice of Application to Board of Supervisors.*[1]

PLANK ROAD NOTICE.

                            by "The   Road Company."

Notice is hereby given that application will be made to the Board of Supervisors of the county of   , at their annual meeting to be held at the Court House in the   of   , on the   day of   18 , for their assent to the construction of a plank [*or*, turnpike] road, from the   of   to the   of   , in said county.

Dated   , 18 .

---

§ 839. *Conveyance of Right of Way by Owner.*

This Indenture, made this   day of   , 18 , between A. B., of the town of   , in the county of   , and State of New York, of the first part, and " The   Road Company," of the second part, Witnesseth: That the said party of the first part, for and in consideration of   dollars to him in hand paid, and also in consideration that the said   Road Company shall commence and complete a plank road from the   of   to   , has bargained and sold, and by these presents does bargain, sell and convey unto the said party of the second part, and its successors, the right of way over and through the lands

---

[1] Where a special meeting is called to hear an application, each member of the Board must be notified of the time and place of such meeting, at the expense of the Company.

of the said party of the first part, for the purpose of laying, constructing, and using such plank road. Said road is to be laid out,
constructed and used on the line of the highway, [*or, as the case
may be,*] leading from   to   , and to be not exceeding
four rods in width, including the line and width of the present highway.

The route hereby intended to be conveyed, begins at the north
line of lands now owned by   and occupied by   , and
runs thence northerly to the south line of land owned by
and occupied by   , in said county of Cayuga.

Witness the hand and seal of the said party of the first part the
day and year first above written.

Sealed and delivered   }
    in presence of   }   A. B. [L. s.]
        R. P.   }

---

§ 840. *Consent of Inhabitants.*

We, the undersigned, owners of land along the highway leading
from   to   , and residing on said highway, do hereby
give our consent to the construction of a plank [*or,* turnpike] road
on the line of said highway from   to   aforesaid.

Witness our hands this   day of   , 18 .

A. B.
&c., &c.

---

§ 841. *Release of Right of Way, by Supervisor and Commissioners.*

This Agreement, made this   day of   , between G.
H., Supervisor of the town of   , in the county of   ,
and A. B., C. D., and E. F., Commissioners of Highways of said
town, of the first part, and the   Plank Road Company of
the second part, Witnesseth: That the said parties of the first part
do hereby sell and convey unto the said party of the second part,
in consideration of   dollars to them in hand paid, by the said
party of the second part, the receipt whereof is hereby acknowledged, the right to use and occupy the highway, &c., [*describe the
route,*] for the purpose of constructing, owning and using a Plank
Road thereon, during the time it shall be needed, or required, therefor by the said Company.

Witness our hands, as such Supervisor and Commissioners of the
town aforesaid, the day and year first above written.

Signed in presence of }   G. H., Supervisor.
      R. F.   }   A. B., } Commissioners of
                              C. D., } Highways of the
                              E. F., } Town of

§ 842. *Acknowledgment of a Survey.*

State of New York, ⎫
⠀⠀⠀⠀County, ⎬ ss.

⠀⠀On this⠀⠀⠀⠀day of⠀⠀⠀⠀, 18⠀⠀, before me, personally appeared A. B., C. D., and E. F., Commissioners appointed by the Board of Supervisors of the county of⠀⠀⠀⠀, to lay out a road, to be constructed by the⠀⠀⠀⠀Company, from⠀⠀⠀⠀to⠀⠀⠀⠀, [*or, A. B. and C. D., the President and Secretary, respectively, of the⠀⠀⠀⠀Company,*] and severally acknowledged that their signatures to the foregoing [*or, within*] survey of the said⠀⠀⠀⠀road, were true and genuine.

⠀⠀⠀⠀⠀⠀⠀⠀⠀⠀⠀⠀⠀⠀⠀⠀G. H., County Judge.

⠀⠀⠀⠀[*Or any officer authorized to take acknowledgments.*[1]]

---

§ 843. *Notice to Pay in Installment.*

⠀⠀⠀⠀⠀⠀⠀⠀Office of the⠀⠀⠀⠀Road Company, ⎫
⠀⠀⠀⠀⠀⠀⠀⠀⠀⠀⠀⠀July⠀⠀⠀⠀, 18⠀⠀. ⎬

Sir:

⠀⠀By order of the Board of Directors of the⠀⠀⠀⠀Road Company, you are required to pay in to the Treasurer, at his office in⠀⠀⠀⠀, a second installment of⠀⠀⠀⠀per cent. on your stock, on or before the⠀⠀⠀⠀day of⠀⠀⠀⠀, 18⠀⠀.

⠀⠀⠀⠀⠀⠀⠀⠀⠀⠀⠀⠀⠀⠀Yours, &c.,

⠀⠀⠀⠀⠀⠀⠀⠀⠀⠀⠀⠀⠀⠀⠀⠀S. G., Secretary.

To Mr. A. B.

---

§ 844. *Proxy.*

[*For Proxy, Oaths, and Affidavits, Power to receive Dividends, and other forms used by Corporations or Stockholders, see Chapter VII.*]

---

§ 845. *Notice of Drawing Jury to Assess Damages.*

⠀⠀⠀⠀⠀⠀⠀⠀⠀⠀Office of the⠀⠀⠀⠀Company, ⎫
⠀⠀⠀⠀⠀⠀⠀⠀⠀⠀⠀⠀July⠀⠀⠀⠀, 18⠀⠀. ⎬

To Mr. A. B. :

⠀⠀Please take notice, That on the⠀⠀⠀⠀day of⠀⠀⠀⠀, 18⠀⠀, at 10 o'clock A. M., Hon. J. P. H., County Judge of⠀⠀⠀⠀county, will

---

[1] For other forms, where the signatures are proved by a subscribing witness, or the parties are not known to the officer, see Chap. I.

attend a drawing from the grand jury-box of   county, at the office of the County Clerk, in the city of Auburn, said drawing to be made by E. B. C., County Clerk of Cayuga county, pursuant to an order of said Judge, of twenty-four competent and disinterested Jurors, and as many more as said Judge shall direct, to ascertain the compensation and damages of each person owning land on or adjoining the line of the   road, running through the town of   , in said county, on the straight road (so called) from   to   , between the north line of said town and the house of C. D,; said road being of the width of four rods, as surveyed by G. H., and located by L. M., S. T., and V. W., Commisioners duly appointed by the Board of Supervisors of   county for such purpose; and also to ascertain the compensation and damages of the town of ·   , for taking said road to construct a plank road thereon, [*or*, of the persons owning land on the line of the said proposed road.[1]]

By order of the Board of Directors.

S. G., Secretary

---

§ 846. *Notice of Meeting of Jury.*

Office of the   Company, ⎫
July   , 18   . ⎬

To Mr. A. B. :

Please take notice, That a jury drawn in pursuance of the Statute in such case made and provided, to ascertain the compensation and damages of the several owners of land on the line of the   road, between the north line of the town of   , and the house of C. D., on the line of the present highway, called the straight road, and being of the width of four rods, and also to ascertain the compensation and damages of the town of   for the same, will meet, pursuant to an order made by Hon. J. P. H., County Judge of   county, at   on the   day of   , 18   , at   o'clock in the   noon, to ascertain such damages and compensation.

By order of the Board of Directors.

S. G., Secretary

---

[1] If the jury are to assess the damages both of the town and private individuals, it should be mentioned in the notice.

CHAPTER XXXV.

POOR LAWS.

PRACTICAL REMARKS.

1. The father, mother, and children, who are of sufficient ability, of any poor person who is blind, old, lame, impotent, or decrepit, so as to be unable to maintain himself, must, at their own charge, relieve and maintain such poor person, in such manner as shall be approved by the Overseers of the Poor of the town; and upon the failure so to do, such Overseers may apply to the Court of Sessions of the county, to compel such relief.[1]

2. Whenever the father, or mother, being a widow, or living separate from her husband, shall abscond from their children, or a husband from his wife, leaving any of them chargeable, or likely to become chargeable, upon the public, for support, the Overseers of the Poor may apply to any two Justices of the Peace of any county in which any estate, real or personal, of the said father, mother, or husband, may be situated, for a warrant to seize the same. In those counties where all the Poor are a charge upon the county, the Superintendents of the Poor have the same powers as Overseers of the Poor in respect to compelling relatives to maintain paupers, and the seizure of the property of any parent absconding and abandoning his family.[2]

3. Every person who is blind, lame, old, sick, impotent, or decrepit, or, in any other way disabled, or enfeebled, so as to be unable by his work to maintain himself, must be maintained by the county or town in which he may be.[3]

---

[1] 1 R. S. (3d ed.,) 782, § 1. et seq.; 7 Cowen, 235.

[2] 1 R. S. (3d ed.,) 783, § 8, et seq. ; Id., 784 § 13; 21 Wendell, 181.

[3] 1 R. S. (3d ed.,) 784, § 14.

4. Three County Superintendents of the Poor are chosen at the annual November election, in each county in this State, except the city and county of New York,—one Superintendent being annually elected,—to serve for three years from the first day of January next after such election. The Board of Supervisors of any county may, however, at any annual meeting, direct only one Superintendent to be elected, who will hold his office for three years.[1]

5. Every person elected to the office of County Superintendent of the Poor, must, before the first day of January succeeding his election, take the oath of office, and execute a bond, conditioned as in § 847, to the Supervisors of the county, in such penalty, and with two or more sufficient sureties, as the board may direct and approve. The bond, with the approbation of the board indorsed by their clerk, is to be filed in the office of the County Clerk. In the recess of the board, the sureties may be approved by the County Clerk.[2]

6. The County Superintendents constitute a corporation, by the name of the Superintendents of the Poor of the county in and for which they are so elected, and have the general supervision and control of the relief and support of the poor in such county. They are authorized to audit and settle all accounts, and to draw from time to time on the County Treasurer for all necessary expenses incurred in the discharge of their duties, and are required to account therefor, to the Board of Supervisors at their annual meeting.[3]

7. It is the duty of the Superintendents of the Poor of each county, during the month of December in each year, to report to the Secretary of State, the number of paupers relieved, or supported, in such county, the preceding year, with the sex, and native country, of each pauper, and the expense of their support or maintenance.[4]

8. In those counties where all the poor are not a county charge, the Supervisors of the respective towns are required to report to the Clerk of the Board of Supervisors, within fifteen days after the accounts of the Overseers have been settled by the Board of Town Auditors, an abstract of all such accounts. These abstracts are to be delivered by the Clerk of the Board of Supervisors to the County Superintendents, to be included by them in their report to the Secretary of State.[5]

9. Every person of full age, who has been a resident and inhabitant of any town, for one year, and the members of his family who have not gained a separate settlement, will be deemed settled in such town, so far as the provisions of law relative to the support of the poor are concerned.[6]

[1] Laws of 1847, chap. 498; Laws of 1849, chap. 116.
[2] Laws of 1848, chap. 327; Laws of 1850, chap. 12.
[3] 1 R. S. (3d ed.,) 785, § 18, et seq; Laws of 1831, chap. 277; Laws of 1832, chap. 26, 292; 10 Wend., 612; 4 Hill,553; 8 Paige,409.
[4] 1 R. S. (3d ed.,) 798, § 81; Laws of 1842, chap. 214; Laws of 1849, chap. 100.
[5] 1 R. S. (3d ed.,) 799, § § 85, 66.
[6] 1 R. S. (3d ed.,) 788, § 33; Laws o' 1830 chap. 320.

10. The electors of each town in this State, except in the counties of Montgomery, Kings and New York, have the power at their annual town meeting, to determine whether they will choose one or two Overseers of the Poor, and the number determined upon will be the number to be elected. Such overseers have the discretionary right to expend a sum not exceeding ten dollars, for the relief of one poor person or family, without any order from a Justice of the Peace therefor.[1]

11. The Overseers of the Poor in the several towns in the county of Livingston, may relieve poor persons within their respective towns, previous to their removal to the county house, but at the expense of such towns. The names of the persons so relieved must be entered in a book, which is to be laid before the Town Auditors at the time of auditing the accounts of such Overseers. The foregoing provisions may be extended to any county in the State, provided the Board of Supervisors, by resolution, declare their intention to adopt them.[2]

12. It is not lawful for any officer whose duty it is to provide for the maintenance, care, or support, of indigent persons, at public expense, to put up at auction the keeping, care, and maintenance, of such person, to the lowest bidder; and any contract so made with a bidder will be absolutely void.[3]

13. All idle persons, who, not having any visible means to maintain themselves, live without employment; all persons wandering abroad, and lodging in taverns, groceries, beer-houses, out-houses, market places, sheds, or barns, and not giving a good account of themselves; all persons wandering abroad and begging, or who go about from door to door, or place themselves in the streets, highways, passages, or other public places, to beg or receive alms, are to be deemed vagrants, and may be taken before a magistrate, to be committed to the county poor house, if proper objects for relief; or, if otherwise, to the county jail. Children found begging are to be sent to the poor house, and may be bound out by the Superintendents, or Overseers of the poor, or Commissioners of the Alms house.[4]

14. If the committee, or the relatives of a lunatic or mad person, refuse or neglect to confine and maintain such person, the Overseers of the Poor may apply to any two Justices of the Peace of the city, or town, where such lunatic shall be found, for a warrant to apprehend and confine such person.[5]

15. Overseers of the Poor may designate and describe any person whom they discover to be a habitual drunkard, in writing, and by written notice require every person dealing in spirituous liquors or

---

[1] Laws of 1845, chap. 180.
[2] Laws of 1845, chap. 334; Laws of 1846, chap. 245.
[3] Laws of 1848. chap. 176.
[4] 1 R. S. (3d ed.,) 802, § 1, et seq.
[5] 1 R. S. (3d ed.,) 805, § 1, et seq.

any other person, not to give or sell spirituous liquors to such drunkard.[1]

16. If any woman be delivered of a bastard child, which shall be chargeable, or likely to become chargeable, to any county, city, or town; or be pregnant of a child likely to be born a bastard, and to become so chargeable, the Superintendents of the Poor of the county, or any of them, or the Overseers of the Poor of the town, or any of them, are required to apply to some Justice of the Peace, to inquire into the facts and circumstances of the case. Superintendents of the Poor may compromise with, and discharge, putative fathers of bastards, upon such terms as they may think to be just. When any such compromise is made, the mother may receive the money, on giving security for the maintenance of the child.[2]

FORMS

§ 847. *Bond of County Superintendent.*

Know all men by these presents: That we, G. H., C. D., and E. F., of, &c., are held and firmly bound unto the Supervisors of the county of   , State of   , in the penal sum of   dollars, to be paid to the said Supervisors, for which payment well and truly to be made, we bind ourselves, our, and each of our heirs, executors and administrators, jointly and severally, firmly by these presents.

Sealed with our seals, and dated the   day of   , A. D. 18   .

Whereas, the above bounden G. H. has been duly elected to the office of County Superintendent of the Poor for the county of   , aforesaid, to serve for the term of three years from the first day of January, A. D. 18   : Now, therefore, if the said G. H. shall faithfully execute the duties of his office, and shall pay, according to law, all moneys which shall come to his hands, as Superintendent of the Poor, and render a just and true account thereof to the Board of Supervisors, then the above obligation to be void; else to remain in full force.

Signed and sealed in }
   presence of   }
      A. M.   }

G. H. [L. S.]
C. D. [L. S.]
E. F. [L. S.]

The sureties in the above bond were duly approved by the Board of Supervisors, this   day of   , 18   .

D. M., Clerk of the Board.

-----

[1] 1 R. S. (3d ed.,) 817, § 1, et seq.
[2] 1 R. S. (3d ed.,) 823, § 5; Laws of 1832, chap. 26; Laws of 1838, chap. 202 10 Johnson, 93; 3 Hill, 116.

§ 848. *Application to Compel a Person to support a Poor Relative.*

To the Court of Sessions of the County of :

The application of the undersigned, E. F., Overseer of the Poor o. the town of , in said county, respectfully represents: That A. B., a poor person, who is blind, [*or*, lame, old, impotent, or decrepit, *as the case may be*,] so as to be unable by work to maintain himself, [*or*, herself,] is in the said town; that C. B., who resides at , in the said county, is the father of the said A. B., and has failed, at his own charge, to relieve and maintain the said A. B. in such manner as has been approved by the undersigned: Wherefore, pursuant to the provisions of section 2, title 1, chapter 20, part 1, of the Revised Statutes of the State of New York, the undersigned hereby applies for an order to compel the said C. B., who is of sufficient ability, to relieve and maintain the said A. B., in the manner to be in such order specified.

Dated at the town of , this day of , 18 .

E. F., Overseer of the Poor.

---

§ 849. *Notice to Accompany the Foregoing Application.*[1]

To C. B.:

You will take notice, that on the day of , at ten o'clock in the forenoon, or as soon thereafter as a hearing can be had, the undersigned, Overseer of the Poor of the town of , will apply to the Court of Sessions of the county of , at the court house in the town of , in said county, for an order to compel the relief applied for by the application, which will, at the time and place above mentioned, be presented to the said court, and of which the annexed is a copy.

Dated at , this day of , 18 .

E. F., Overseer of the Poor.

---

§ 850. *Affidavit of Service.*

County, ss:

E. F., of the town of , in said county, being duly sworn, says, that on the day of , he served a copy of the annexed notice and application, on C. B., therein named, by delivering the same to him, [*or*, by leaving the same at his last place of residence, with O. P., a person of mature age.]

Sworn to, before me, this }
day of , 18 . }

E. F.

G. H., Justice, &c.

---

[1] A copy of the application with the above notice, should be personally served on the person to whom it is directed, or be left at his last place of residence with some person of mature age. It will be borne in mind, that in those counties where all the poor are a county charge, the application, (§ 848,) should be made by a County Superintendent and the forms from § 848 to § 854, may be varied for the purpose.

§ 851. *Warrant to Seize the Goods of an Absconding Father,*
Husband, or Mother.

County, ss:

To E. F., Overseer of the Poor of the Town of   , in said
county:

It appearing to us, two of the Justices of the Peace of said county, as well by the application and representation to us made by you,
the said Overseer, as upon due proof of the facts before us made,
that A. B., late of said town, has absconded from his wife and children, leaving the said wife and children chargeable [*or*, likely to become chargeable] to the public for support; and that the said A. B.
has some estate, real or personal, in said county, whereby the public
may be wholly or in part indemnified against said charge: We therefore authorize you, the said Overseer of the Poor, to take and seize
the goods, chattels, effects, things in action, and the lands and tenements of the said A. B., wherever the same may be found in said
county: And you will, immediately upon such seizure, make an inven
tory of the property by you taken, and return the same, together
with your proceedings, to the next Court of Sessions of said county.

Given under our hands, in the town of   , this   day
of   , 18   .
G. H. ⎫
S. T. ⎬ Justices.

---

§ 852. *Return of Overseer to the Foregoing Warrant.*

County, ss.:

To the Court of Sessions of said County:

The undersigned, to whom the annexed warrant is addressed, on
the   day of   , 18   , in the county of   ,
therein mentioned, seized, by virtue of the said warrant, the property
of which an inventory is hereunto annexed; and the proceedings of
the undersigned, subsequent to the said seizure, are as follows: [*state*
the proceedings particularly.] All which is herewith respectfully returned.

Dated, &c., [*as in* § 848.]

---

§ 853. *Bond to be Given by Party where Property has veen Seized.*[1]

Know all men by these presents: That we, A. B. and L. M., both
of the town of   , in the county of   , are held and

---

[1] Upon the execution of the bond and approval of the security, by any two Justices of the
town the warrant must be discharged, and the property restored.

firmly bound unto E. F., Overseer of the Poor of the town of   ,
in the sum of   dollars, for the payment whereof to the said
Overseer, or his successor in office, we bind ourselves, our heirs, executors and administrators, jointly and severally, firmly by these
presents.

   Sealed with our seals, and dated at   , this   day
of   , 18 .

   The condition of this obligation is such, that whereas the said Overseer of the Poor lately seized the property of the said A. B., under
a warrant issued by G. H. and S. T., two Justices of the Peace of
the county of   , upon due proof to them given, that the said A.
B. had absconded from his wife and children, leaving them chargeable
[or, likely to become chargeable] upon the public for support ; and
the said A. B. having returned, and being desirous of having his
property so taken restored to him : Now, therefore, if the said wife
and children so abandoned shall not become chargeable either to said
town or county, then this obligation is to be void ; otherwise of force.

Sealed and delivered, and the security ⎫	A. B. [L. S.]
approved, by and before us, two of ⎬	C. D. [L. S.]
the Justices of the town of . ⎭	

                         G. H., ⎫ Justices.   .
                         S. T., ⎬

------

§ 854. *Order to Discharge the Warrant, and to Restore Property.*

        County, ss :

To E. F., Overseer of the Poor of the Town of   , in said
     county :

   Whereas, by a warrant to you directed, bearing date the   day
of   , 18 , you were authorized to seize the goods, chattels,
effects, things in action, and the lands and tenements, of A. B., upon
proof that he had absconded from his wife and children, leaving them
chargeable to the public for support : And whereas, the said A. B.
has returned, and now supports his wife and children so adandoned,
[or, has given security to the Overseer of the Poor, satisfactory to
us, that his said wife and children shall not become chargeable either
to said town or county :] We do, therefore, hereby discharge the said
warrant issued against the said A. B., and direct the property taken
by virtue thereof to be restored to him.

   Given, &c., [as in § 851.]

§ 855. *Notice from one Town to another, in a County where the Towns are Liable to Support their own Poor, requiring the Overseer of the Town in which the Pauper has a Residence, to Provide for his Support.*[1]

County, ss:

To E. F., Overseer of the Poor of the Town of   , in said county:

You are hereby notified, that A. B., a pauper, who has gained a settlement in your town, to which he belongs, is in the town of   , in said county, and is supported at the expense of the said town of   , for which the undersigned is Overseer: You are therefore required to provide for the relief and support of the said pauper.

Dated at   , this   day of   , 18 .

R. F., Overseer of the Poor of the Town of   .

---

§ 856. *Notice that the Allegation of Settlement will be Contested.*

County, ss:

To R. F., Overseer of the Poor of the town of   , in said county:

You will take notice, that the undersigned, Overseer of the Poor of the town of   , in said county, will appear before the Superintendents of the Poor of the said county, at the poor house, [*or, as the case may be,*] on the   day of   , at ten o'clock in the forenoon, to contest the alledged settlement of A. B., a pauper, as set forth in your notice of the   instant.

Dated, &c., [*as in* § 849.]

---

§ 857. *Subpœna of the Superintendents.*

County, ss:

The People of the State of New York, to C. D.:

You are hereby required personally to appear before the undersigned, Superintendents of the Poor of the said county, at the poor house, [*or, such place as is designated in the notice,*] on the day of   , 18 , at ten o'clock in the forenoon, to testify in behalf of the Overseer of the Poor of the town of   , in said county, concerning the alledged settlement of A. B., a pauper.

Given under our hands, this   day of   , 18

G. H.,
L. M.,
&c., &c. } Superintendents of the Poor.

---

[1] This notice should be served on the Overseer by some person who can make oath to such service, if the same should become necessary. If the Overseer on whom the notice is served desires to contest the settlement, he must, within ten days after such service, give notice to the other Overseer to appear before the Superintendents, in not less than ten and not more than thirty days from the service of such notice, and contest the settlement. The Superintendents are authorized to issue subpœnas, and to compel the attendance of witnesses on the hearing.

§ 858. *Superintendents' Decision.*[1]

County, ss:

We, the undersigned, Superintendents of the Poor of said county, having convened, as required by the Overseer of the Poor of the town of   , in said county, pursuant to notice, to hear and determine a controversy which had arisen between the said Overseer, and the Overseer of the town of   , in said county, concerning the settlement of A. B., a pauper, do hereby decide, upon such hearing, as aforesaid, that the legal settlement of the said A. B., as such pauper, is [*or, is not*] in the said town of   . And the undersigned hereby award to the Overseer of the Poor of the town of   , the prevailing party, the sum of   dollars, costs of said proceeding, by him expended.

Given, &c., [*as in* § 857.]

---

§ 859. *Superintendents' Notice that Pauper will be supported at the Expense of a Town, in a County where the Towns Support their own Poor.*[2]

County, ss:

To E. F., Overseer of the Poor of the town of   , in said county:

A. B. a pauper, having been sent to the poor house as a county pauper, and the undersigned, Superintendents of the Poor of said county, having inquired into the fact, and being of opinion that the said pauper has a legal settlement in the town of   , in said county, pursuant to the provisions of Section 35, of title 1, of Chapter 20, of Part 1, of the Revised Statutes of New York, you are hereby notified, that the expenses of the support of said pauper will be charged to the town of   , unless you, the Overseer of said town, within [*insert the time, to be not less than twenty days*] after the service of this notice, show that the said town of   ought not to be so charged.

Given, &c., [*as in* § 857.]

---

[1] The decision is to be entered in the book of the Superintendents, and a duplicate thereof filed in the office of the County Clerk, within thirty days; each decision will be final and conclusive in the premises. The costs awarded cannot exceed ten dollars.

[2] This notice is to be given within thirty days after the pauper shall have been received. On the application of the Overseer, the Superintendents may re-examine the matter and take testimony, and make a final decision therein.

§ 860. *Decision of Superintendents, after Re-examining Settlement of Pauper, on Application of the Overseer—to be entered and filed in the same manner as* § 858.

County, ss:

We, the undersigned, Superintendents of the Poor of the said county, having, on the application of the Overseer of the Poor of the town of   , re-examined the subject matter of a notice duly served on him, of which the annexed is a copy, and taken testimony in relation thereto, do hereby decide that A. B., the pauper therein mentioned, has a legal settlement in the said town of   , to which, as such pauper, he belongs, [*or*, has not a legal settlement in said town of   .]

Given, &c., [*as in* § 857.]

———

§ 861. *Certificate of a Superintendent that a Person is a County Pauper, on the Application of the Overseer of a Town.*

County, ss:

The Overseer of the Poor of the Town of   , having given notice to the undersigned, that A. B., a poor person, being in said town, should be supported as a county pauper; I do hereby certify, that I have inquired into the circumstances, and am satisfied that the said pauper has not gained a legal settlement in any town in said county, and that the said A. B. is chargeable to the said county.

Dated at   , this   day of   , 18 .

G. H., Superintendent of the Poor.

———

§ 862. *Notice of Hearing on the Foregoing Certificate, before the Board.*[1]

County, ss:

To E. F., Overseer of the Poor of the Town of   , in said county:

You are hereby notified, that on the   day of   , at ten o'clock in the forenoon of that day, the board of Superintendents of the Poor of said county will proceed to a hearing of the allegations and proofs which may be then presented in relation to the legal settlement of A. B., in the town of   ; and after such hearing,

---

[1] Every case in which a certificate is granted must be reported to the board, who may, at their next meeting, affirm or annul it. Notice of the hearing should be served on the Overseer not less than twenty days previous thereto; and the final decision of the Superintendents is to be entered and filed as specified in the note to § 858.

will affirm or annul the certificate given by G. H., one of the undersigned, on the   day of   , 18   , declaring that the said A. B. was chargeable upon the county.

Given, &c., [*as in* § 857.]

---

§ 863. *Decision of the Board of County Superintendents.*

County, ss:

G. H., one of the Superintendents of the Poor of said county, having reported to the Board of County Superintendents of the Poor for said county, the case mentioned in the certificate, a duplicate [*or,* copy] whereof is hereunto annexed, the said board, after due notice given to the Overseer of the Poor of the town of   , in said county, and after hearing the allegations and proofs in the premises, do hereby annul [*or,* affirm] the said certificate, and decide that the legal settlement of A. B., named therein, is in the town of
in said county.

Given, &c., [*as in* § 857.]

---

§ 864. *Decision by the Board of Superintendents, upon the Refusal of the Superintendent to give the Certificate.*

County, ss:

Notice having been given by the Overseer of the Poor of the town of   , in said county, to G. H., one of the Superintendents of the Poor of the said county, that A. B., a poor person, being in said town, should be supported as a county pauper, and the said Superintendent having refused [*or,* neglected] to give the certificate prescribed by Section 36, Title 1, Chapter 20, Part 1, of the Revised Statutes of the State of New York, and the undersigned, constituting the Board of County Superintendents of the poor for said county, having, on the application of the said Overseer, summarily heard the matter, do hereby determine and decide that the said pauper has not gained a legal settlement in any town of the said county, and should be supported as a county pauper, [*or,* has gained a legal settlement in the town of   , in said county:] And we do hereby award to the Overseer of the town of   , the sum of
        , [*not exceeding ten dollars,*] costs of said proceeding, by him in this behalf expended.

Given, &c., [*as in* § 857.]

§ 865. *Order of the Overseer of a Town to Remove a Poor Person to the County Poor House.*

County, ss:

A. B. having applied for relief to me, the undersigned, Overseer of the Poor of the town of   , in said county, I have inquired into his [*or,* her] state and circumstances, and it appearing that he [*or,* she] is in such indigent circumstances as to require permanent relief and support, and can be safely removed, I hereby order him [*or,* her] to be removed to the county house, to be relieved and provided for, as his [*or,* her] necessities may require, at the expense of said county, [*or,* town.]

Dated, &c., [*as in* § 849.]

---

§ 866. *Certificate of the Keeper of the Poor House, for the Expense of Removing a Pauper.*

| $2. Treasurer of County :
Pay G. D. two dollars and cents for transporting A. B., from to the county poor house.
, May , 18 .
No. . | Treasurer of County :
This certifies that G. D. is entitled to two dollars, and cents, at the rate prescribed by the Superintendents, for transporting A. B. from the town of to county poor house, being miles.
, May . , 18 .
Countersigned, C. D., Keeper,
G. H. } Sup'ts.
No. . L. M. } |

---

§ 867. *Superintendent's Order to Expend over Ten Dollars.*

E. F., Overseer of the Poor of the town of   , in said county, having applied to me for an order authorizing the expenditure of a greater sum than ten dollars for the relief of A. B., I have inquired into the facts of the case; and being satisfied that the said A. B. cannot properly be removed to the county poor house, and that he is in need of further relief, I do hereby direct the continuance of the weekly allowance of   dollars, until the expenditure amount to   dollars over and above the sum of ten dollars.

Dated, &c., [*as in* § 861.]

---

§ 868. *Notice of the Improper Removal of a Pauper from another County.*[1]

County, ss:

To the Superintendents of the Poor of the county of   :

You are hereby notified, that A. B., a poor and indigent person, has been improperly sent, [*or,* carried; *or,* brought; *or,* removed,

---

[1] The notice is to be served on any one of the Superintendents, who must deny the allegations contained therein, within thirty days, unless they acquiesce in the same.

or, enticed to remove, *as the case may be*,] from the said county of ——, to the county of ——, without legal authority, and there left, with intent to make the said county of ——, to which the said removal was made, chargeable with the support of the said pauper. You are therefore required, pursuant to the provisions of Section 59, Title 1, Chapter 20, Part 1, of the Revised Statutes of the State of New York, forthwith to take charge of such pauper.

Given, &c., [*as in* § 857.]

---

§ 869. *Annual Report of the Superintendents of the Poor, to the Secretary of State.*

The Superintendents of the Poor of the county of ——, in pursuance of the provisions of the Revised Statutes for "the relief and support of indigent persons," present to the Secretary of State their annual report, as follows:

The number of paupers relieved or supported during the year preceding the 1st of December instant, was ——: of the persons thus relieved, the number of county paupers was ——; and the number of town paupers ——.

The whole expense of such support was..$——
Of this sum, there was paid for transportation of paupers,....................——
Allowance made to Superintendents for their services,.........................——
   do   do   Overseers,   do   do ....——
   do   do   Justices,   do   do ....——
   do   do   Keepers and officers, do ....——
   do   do   Physicians, for services and medicines,.............——
The actual value of the labor of the paupers maintained, was..................——
The estimated amount saved in the expense of their support, in consequence of their labor, was..——

The sum actually expended, over and above the labor and earnings of the paupers, divided by the average number kept during the year, gives —— dollars and —— cents per week, as the actual expense of keeping each person.

The county poor house has —— acres of land attached to it, and the whole establishment is valued at......................................$——
The number of persons in the poor house on the 1st of December instant, was....——
Of this number, there were of males,..——
   do   do   females,...——
Of the males, there were of 16 years of age and under,........................——
Of the females of the same age,...——

Of the persons relieved or supported during the year, there were —— foreigners; —— lunatics; —— idiots; and —— mutes: of the mutes, —— were between the ages of 10 and 25 years.

The number of paupers received into the poor house during the year, was.......——
Born in the poor house,...——
Died during the year,...——
Bound out,..——
Discharged,...——
Absconded,..——

The children in the poor house, over six and under sixteen years of age, have been instructed —— months, by a teacher at the poor house: [*or*, sent to the district school house —— months,] and the

whole number of children taught during the year, was   .
[*This number is to embrace all the children who have been taught in the course of the year.*]

Given, &c., [*as in* § 857.]

---

§ 870. *Supervisor's Report for a Town, where all the Poor are not a County Charge, to be made to the Clerk of the Board of Supervisors.*

The Supervisor of the town of   , in the county of   , respectfully reports to the Clerk of the Board of Supervisors, as follows:

The number of paupers relieved, or supported, in said town, during the year preceding the   day of   , 18   , as appears from the accounts of the Overseers of the Poor, was, &c., [*as in the preceding form to the *, omitting the allowance to the Superintendents, and inserting such other charges as there may be, and then add:*]

Of the whole number of paupers relieved by the Overseers during the year, they report there were   foreigners;   lunatics;   idiots; and   mutes. The number of paupers under their charge at the time of auditing their accounts, is stated at   ; of which   were males, and   , females.

I hereby certify, that the foregoing is a correct abstract of the accounts of the Overseers of the Poor of the town of   , for the year ending on the   day of   , 18   , as the same have been settled by the Board of Town Auditors.

Dated this   day of   , 18   .

         S. T., Supervisor.

---

§ 871. *Complaint against a Beggar or Vagrant.*

     County, ss:

A. B., of the town of   , in said county, being sworn, says, that E. F., now in said town, is an idle person, not having visible means to maintain himself, and living without employment; and is, as the said deponent believes, a vagrant, within the meaning and intent of the statute, and this deponent therefore complains of the said E. F.

Sworn, &c., [*as in* § 850.]

---

§ 872. *Warrant on Foregoing Complaint.*

Town of   } ss:
     County, }

A. B., of the town of   , in said county, has this day made complaint, on oath, before me, the undersigned Justice of the Peace, of the said town, that E. F., &c., [*as in the complaint:*] You are therefore hereby commanded, in the name of the people of the State of New York, forthwith to arrest the said E. F., and bring him before me, the said Justice, at my office, in   , aforesaid, to answer to the said complaint, and to be dealt with in the premises, according to law.

Witness my hand, this   day of   18 .

         G. H., Justice of the Peace.

---

§ 873. *Record of Conviction of a Vagrant.*[1]

County, ss:

Be it remembered, that E. F. was this day brought before me, the undersigned, a Justice of the Peace of the town of   , in said county, at my office in said town, upon the charge and accusation that he was found in the said town, an idle person, not having visible means to maintain himself, and living without employment, [*or, as the case may be,*] and a vagrant within the intent and meaning of the statute in such case made and provided ; and I, the said Justice, being satisfied, upon due and personal examination of said E. F., and by his confession now before me had and made, [*or,* upon competent testimony now before me had and given,] that said charge and accusation are in all respects true, the said E. F. is therefore duly convicted before me of being a vagrant, within the true intent and meaning of said statute ; and it appearing to me that the said E. F. is not a notorious offender, and that he is a proper object for relief, I adjudge and determine that said E. F. be committed to the county poor house of said county, [*or,* the alms house; *or,* poor house of the said town,] for the term of forty days, there to be kept at hard labor ; [*or,* it appearing to me that said E. F. is an improper person to be sent to the poor house, I do therefore adjudge and determine, that the said E. F. be committed to the common jail of said county for the term of thirty days.]

Given under my hand and seal, this   day of   , 18 .

       G. H., Justice, &c.   [L. s.]

---

§ 874. *Commitment.*

County ss :

To any Constable of said County, greeting

Whereas E. F. has been this day duly convicted before me, the undersigned Justice of the Peace of the town of   , in said county, of being a vagrant ; and inasmuch as it appears to me that

---

[1] It is the duty of every peace officer to take any person whom he may discover to be a vagrant, before a magistrate for examination. In such cases, no complaint or warrant will be necessary. The Justice has the power to commit a vagrant to the poor house for a term not exceeding six months, and to the county jail not exceeding sixty days ; in the latter case, the

said E. F. is not a notorious offender, and is a proper subject for relief, [or, is an improper person to be sent to the poor house,] I have adjudged that the said E. F. be committed as hereinafter expressed : You are therefore hereby commanded, in the name of the people of the State of New York, to convey the said E. F. to the county poor house, [or, alms house ; or, town poor house,] the keeper whereof is required to keep him therein, at hard labor, for the term of forty days; [or, to convey the said E. F. to the common jail of said county, the keeper whereof is required to detain him in safe custody therein, for the term of thirty days.]

Given, &c., [as in § 873.]

---

§ 875. *Warrant to Commit a Child to the County Poor House.*[1]

County, ss :

To any Constable of said County, greeting :

Whereas, complaint on oath, and due proof, have this day been made to me, one of the Justices of the Peace of said county, that a male [or, female] child of the name of A. B., has been found in the town [or, city] of   , in said county, begging for alms : You are therefore hereby commanded, in the name of the people of the State of New York, to convey the said child to the poor house in said county, [or, town ; or, the alms house of said city,] the keeper whereof is required to detain, keep, employ and instruct, said child, in such useful labor as he [or, she] may be able to perform, until discharged therefrom by the County Superintendents of the Poor, [or, by the Commissioners of such alms house; or, by the Overseers of the Poor,] or bound out as an apprentice by them.

Witness, &c., [as in §872.]

---

§ 876. *Warrant to Confine a Lunatic.*[2]

County, ss :

To the Overseer of the Poor, and Constables, of the Town of   ,
in said County, greeting :

A. B., a lunatic, having been found in said town, so far disordered in his senses as to endanger his own person, [or, the persons and

---

person may be kept on bread and water only, for one-half the time, if the Justice so direct. The record of conviction must be filed in the County Clerk's office. The Justice may also cause the person complained of to be searched previous to his commitment, and if any property is found, it may be applied for his support while in confinement.

[1] When a child is found begging in any public place, any Justice of the Peace, on complaint and proof thereof, is required to commit such child to the poor house. For the forms of indentures which Superintendents or Overseers may desire to use, see those hereinbefore given in Chapter III.

[2] The Overseer must provide a suitable place for the confinement of a lunatic. If the application for the arrest is made by a Superintendent, he is required to do the same.

property of others,] if permitted to go at large ; and no provision having been made, either by the relatives, or any committee, for confining and maintaining such lunatic, the undersigned, two of the Justices of the Peace of said town, on the application of the Overseer of the Poor of said town, [or, upon our own view,] being satisfied, upon examination, [or, upon information on oath to us given,] that the said A. B. should be forthwith confined : You are therefore hereby commanded, to cause the said lunatic to be safely locked up in such secure place as said Overseer may provide, in conformity to law.

Given, &c., [as in § 851.]

---

§ 877. *Notice to Tavern Keeper—Designation of Habitual Drunkard, &c.*[1]

Town of

County, } ss :

I, the undersigned, Overseer of the Poor of said town, having discovered A. B., of said town, to be a habitual drunkard, do hereby designate him as such habitual drunkard, and describe him as follows: [*description :*] And every merchant, distiller, shop-keeper, tavern-keeper, or other dealer in spirituous liquors, is required not to give or sell, under any pretence, any spirituous liquors to the said A. B.

Dated, &c., [as in § 849.]

---

§ 878. *Notice to Overseer by Justice.*

To E. F., Overseer of the Poor of the Town of :

You are hereby notified, that A. B., who has been designated by you as a habitual drunkard, has applied to me for a process to summon a jury to try and determine the fact of such drunkenness: And that I have fixed upon the day of instant, at o'clock in the noon, at my office in said town, as the time and place for such trial.

Dated , this day of , 18 .

G. H., Justice of the Peace.

---

[1] Copies of the notice should be personally served on all persons required to obey it. The person designated as a drunkard may contest the fact before a jury. For that purpose, he must apply to a Justice of the Peace for a venire ; immediate notice of which, and of the time and place of the hearing, is to be given to the Overseer by the Justice. The jury are to be summoned, returned, &c., and witnesses subpœnaed, &c., in the same manner as in ordinary suits before Justices of the Peace. The verdict of the jury is to be entered by the Justice in his docket. If the jury find that the person is a habitual drunkard, judgment must be entered against him, and an execution issued for the costs ; if the jury find the contrary, judgment must be rendered accordingly, but no execution can be issued against the Overseer, unless he acted in bad faith, and did not have reasonable cause for making the designation.

§ 879. *Venire.*

County, ss :

To any Constable of the Town of   , in said County, greeting :

You are hereby commanded, in the name of the people of the State of New York, to summon a jury of twelve persons, competent to serve on juries, to appear at my office, in   , aforesaid, on the   day of   instant, at   o'clock in the   noon, to try the fact, whether A. B., of said town, is a habitual drunkard ; he having been designated as such by the Overseer of the Poor of said town ; and you will have then there a panel of the names of the jurors you shall so summon, and this precept.

Witness, &c., [*as in* § 872.]

---

§ 880. *Jurors' Oath.*

You do swear, that you will well and truly try the fact of the alledged habitual drunkenness of A. B., and a true verdict give, according to evidence.

---

§ 881. *Oath of Witness.*

You do swear, that the evidence you shall give, touching the fact of the habitual drunkenness of A. B., shall be the truth, the whole truth, and nothing but the truth.

---

§ 882. *Execution Against the Drunkard.*

County, ss :

To any Constable of said County, greeting :

Whereas, A. B.,   , in said county, was designated and described by E. F., Overseer of the Poor of said town, as a habitual drunkard ; and by the verdict of a jury duly impanneled, drawn and sworn, before me, the undersigned Justice, upon the application of the said A. B.,* it is found that he is a habitual drunkard ; whereupon, I have rendered judgment against the said A. B., for the costs of the said Overseer in attending the trial, amounting to the sum of   dollars : You are therefore hereby commanded, in the name of the people of the State of New York, to levy the said costs of the goods and chattels of the said A. B., (excepting such goods as are exempt by law from execution,) and bring the money which you shall collect, within thirty days from the date hereof, before me, at my office in   , to render to said Overseer ; and if no such goods and chattels, or not sufficient to satisfy this execution, can be found, you are further required to take the body of the said A. B., and convey him to the common jail of said county, there to remain until this execution be paid, or he be thence discharged according to law.

Witness, &c., [*as in* § 872.]

---

§ 883. *Execution Against the Overseer.*

County, ss :

To any Constable of said County, greeting :

Whereas, A. B., &c., [*as in* § 882, *to the*, and then add :*] it is found that he is not a habitual drunkard ; and inasmuch as it appeared to me that the said Overseer of the Poor did not act in good faith, and that he had not reasonable cause to believe the said A. B. to be a habitual drunkard, I have entered judgment against the said E. F., Overseer, for the costs of the said A. B., amounting to the sum of   dollars : You are therefore hereby commanded, in the name of the people of the State of New York, to levy the said costs, &c., [*as in an ordinary execution.*]

---

§ 884. *Revocation by the Overseer, where a Drunkard Reforms.*

Town of   ,
    County,   } ss :

Being satisfied that A. B., respecting, whose drunkenness a notice has heretofore been given by me, [*or, by O. P., Overseer of the Poor of said town,*] has reformed and become temperate, I do hereby revoke and annul the said notice.

Dated, &c., [*as in* § 849.]

---

§ 885. *Complaint against a Disorderly Person.*[1]

County, ss.

A. B., of said town, being duly sworn, says, that C. D. is, as the said deponent believes, a disorderly person, within the meaning of

---

[1] The Justice issues his warrant on the complaint, in the same form as in § 872, except that it is drawn in accordance with the charge in the complaint. Upon the examination of the offender, if the charge is sustained by his own confession, or by competent testimony, the Justice may require him to find sureties for his good behavior for one year. If the offender do not find sureties, the record of conviction must be signed, and he be committed to jail until such sureties be found, or he be discharged according to law. The forms, § 873 and § 874, may be varied so as to be applicable to this proceeding. (1 R. S., 3d ed., 819, § 2. et seq. ; Laws of 1833, chap. 11 ; 1 Hill, 355 ; 6 Id., 75.)

the statute in such case made and provided; in this, to wit: that the said C. D., [*insert the facts on which the charge is founded, and conclude as in* § 871.]

---

§ 886. *Recognizance of a Disorderly Person.*
County, ss:

We, C. D., E. F., and L. M., of   , in said county, acknowledge ourselves indebted to the people of the State of New York; that is to say, the said C. D., in the sum of   dollars, and the said E. F., and L. M., each in the sum of   dollars. to be respectively made and levied of our several goods and chattels, lands and tenements, to the use of the said people, if default shall be made in the condition following:

The condition of the above recognizance is such, that if the said C. D. shall be and continue of good behavior towards the people of the State of New York, for the space of one year from and after this day, then such recognizance to be void; otherwise of force.

Taken, subscribed, and acknowledged, }   C. D. [L. s.]
before me, this   day of   , 18 . }   E. F. [L. s.]
          G. H., Justice, &c.   L. M. [L. s.]

---

§ 887. *Discharge of Disorderly Persons, to be Granted by any Two Justices.*

County, ss:

To the Keeper of the Common Jail of said County, greeting:

Whereas, C. D. was lately committed to your custody in said jail, by the warrant of L. M., a Justice of the Peace of the said county upon the conviction of the said C. D., before the said Justice, of being a disorderly person, and upon the failure of the said C. D. to procure sureties for his good behavior, according to law; and whereas, the said C. D. has given such sureties as were originally required by the said Justice, from him: Now, therefore, we, being two of the Justices of the Peace of said county, do hereby require you to discharge the said C. D. out of your custody, under his commitment, as aforesaid.

Given, &c., [*as in* § 851.]

---

§ 888. *Jailer's Report Relative to Disorderly Persons.*
County, ss:

To the Court of Sessions of said County:

The following is a list of the persons committed as disorderly per-

---

[1] The jailer is required to make his report of the disorderly persons confined, on the first day of each term of the court.

sons to the common jail of said county, since the last session of the said court, and now in custody of the undersigned, with the nature of their offences, the names of the Justices committing them, respectively, and the time of imprisonment, viz:

List of persons committed, and now in custody.	Nature of their offences, respectively.	Names of the Justices committing them.	The time of imprisonment.

Dated at　　　　, in said county, the　　　day of　　　, 18　.

J. C., Keeper of the Jail of said County.

§ 889. *Application of a Superintendent, or Overseer, of the Poor, in a case of Bastardy.*

County, ss:

To G. H., Esq., a Justice of the Peace of said county:

E. B. having been delivered of a bastard, which is chargeable [*or*, likely to become chargeable] to the said county, [*or*, to the town of , in said county;] [*or*, E. B., being pregnant of a child likely to be born a bastard, and to become chargeable, &c.,] the undersigned, a Superintendent of the Poor of the said county, [*or*, the Overseer of the Poor of said town,] pursuant to the statute in such case made and provided, makes application to you to inquire into the facts and circumstances of the case.

Dated. &c., [*as in* § 849, *or* § 861.]

§ 890. *Examination Before Birth.*

County, ss :

E. B., of the town of　　　, in said county, being duly sworn, says, that she is now with child, and that the child of which she is pregnant is likely to be born a bastard, and to become chargeable to said county ; [*or*, to the town of　　　, in said county ;] and that C. D., of　　　, is the father of said child.

Subscribed and sworn, this　　　　　　　　　E. B.
day of　　　, 18　, before me,

G. H., Justice.

§ 891. *Examination After Birth.*

County, ss :

E. B., of the town of　　　, in said county, being duly sworn, says, that on the　　　day of　　　last, she was delivered of a hastard child, which ls chargeable [or, likely to become chargeable] to said county ; [or, to the town of   , in said county ;] arfd that C. D., of, &c., [as in § 890, to the end.]

---

§ 892. Warrant to Apprehend Reputed Father.[1]

County, ss:

To any Constable of said County, greeting :

Whereas, E. B., of   , in said county, upon her examination, on oath, before me, the undersigned, a Justice of the Peace of said county, this day had, did declare that, &c., [as in the examination:] And whereas, E. F., Overseer of the Poor of said town, [or, one of the Superintendents of, &c., as the case may be,] in order to indemnify the said town, [or, county,] in the premises, has applied to me to inquire into the facts and circumstances of the case, and to issue my warrant to apprehend the said C. D., &c.: You are therefore hereby commanded, in the name of the people of the State of New York, forthwith to apprehend the said C. D., and bring him before me, at my office in   , aforesaid, for the purpose of having an adjudication respecting the filiation of such bastard child, [or, of such child likely to be born a bastard.]

Witness, &c., [as in § 872.]

---

§ 893. Subpœna in a Case of Bastardy.

County, ss:

To R. F., O. P., &c., greeting;

You are hereby commanded, in the name of the people of the State of New York, personally to appear before G. H., and the undersigned S, T., two of the Justices of the Peace of said county, forthwith, [or, as the case may be,] at the office of the said S. T., in   , in said county, to testify what you do know touching the father of a bastard child, wherewith E. B. alledges she is now pregnant, [or, which was lately born of E. B.]

Witness, &c., [as in § 872.]

---

[1] The warrant in a case of bastardy can only be issued on the application of a Superintendent, or an Overseer. Where other testimony is offered beside that of the mother, previous to issuing the warrant, the examination should be varied accordingly. Where the Justice issuing the warrant has died, or vacated his office, or is absent on the return of the warrant, the putative father must be taken before some other Justice of the same town, who will thereupon proceed in the matter. When the reputed father is brought before the Justice, the latter is required to notify some other Justice to attend and assist in the examination, &c. Either of the Justices may issue subpœnas, and the attendance of witnesses may be compelled, as in ordinary cases. If the Justices are not prepared to proceed, or the reputed father desires an adjournment, for sufficient reasons, the examination may be adjourned not exceeding six weeks, on executing the bond, (§ 894,) the penalty of which must be a sufficient sum fully to indemnify the town or county. (1 R. S., 3d ed, 825. § 4, et seq.; 10 Johnson, 93.)

§ 894. *Bond on Adjournment.*

Know all men by these presents : That we, C. D. and R. F., of   , in the county of   , are held and firmly bound unto the people of the State of New York, in the sum of   dollars, for the payment whereof to the said people,.we bind ourselves, our heirs, executors and administrators, jointly and severally, firmly by these presents. Sealed with our seals, and dated this   day of   , 18 .*

The condition of this obligation is such, that .whereas the above named C. D. has been this day brought before G. H. and S. T., two of the Justices of the Peace of said county, charged upon the oath of E. B., of   , aforesaid, with being the father of a bastard child, with which the said E. B. alledges she is pregnant, [*or*, of a bastard child lately born of the said E. B.:] And whereas, at the request of the said C. D., and for sufficient reasons given, the said Justices have determined to adjourn the said examination and adjudication, upon the execution of this bond, until the   day of   instant, at   o'clock in the   noon, at the office of the said G. H., in   : Now, therefore, if the said C. D. shall personally appear before the said Justices, at the time and place last aforesaid, and not depart therefrom without leave, then this obligation is to be void ; otherwise of force.   C. D. [L. S.]

Sealed, &c., [*as in* § 853.]   R. F. [L. S.]

---

§ 895. *Order of Filiation.*[1]

County, ss:

Whereas, we, the undersigned, being two of the Justices of .the Peace of said county, have this day associated, at   , in said county, upon the application of E. F., Overseer of the Poor of the

---

[1] Upon the examination and hearing before the Justices, the mother must be again examined on oath, in the presence of the reputed father; and such other testimony must be heard as may be offered in relation to the matter. If the Justices determine that the person under arrest is not the father, he must be forthwith discharged; if they determine that he is such father, they are required to make the order of filiation. If the mother be in indigent circumstances, the sum to be paid for her sustenance must be specified in the order. The statute requires all the proceedings in a case of bastardy to be reduced to writing, and signed by the Justices. If the order is made sufficiently comprehensive, there will be no necessity for a further statement. (1 R. S., 3d ed., 824, § 11, et seq.) The adjudication of the two Justices in a case of this kind is final, if it be in favor of the reputed father, unless appealed from. (19 Wendell, 154; 5 Hill, 443.) Upon receiving notice of the order of filiation, the reputed father must immediately pay the costs, and execute the bond conditioned for the due performance of the order, or to appear at the next term of the Court of Sessions. If he neglect or refuse to execute the bond, the Justices are required to commit him to the county jail until such bond be executed, or he be discharged by the Court of Sessions. (1 R. S., 3d ed., 823, §§ 7, 8; Id., 825, § 14, et seq.) A bond given to appear at the next term of the court as above specified, is not a recognizance, but matter *in pais*, like any other deed. (5 Hill, 647.) If the reputed father refuses to pay the costs, he may be committed, notwithstanding he may have given the bond. (2 Denio, 127.)

town of   , [*or*, Superintendent of the Poor of said county,] for the purpose of making an examination and determination touching a certain bastard child, lately born in said town, of the body of E. B., [*or*, of a certain child wherewith E. B. is said to be pregnant, and which when born will be a bastard,] and chargeable [*or*, likely to become chargeable] to said town, [*or*, county,] and of which child C. D. was alledged to be the father; And, whereas, we have duly examined the said E. B. on oath, in the presence of the said C. D., touching the father of said child, and have also heard the proofs and allegations to us offered in relation thereto, as well on the part and behalf of the said Overseer, [*or*, Superintendent,] as of the said C. D.: whereby it appears that the said E. B. was, on the   day of   last, delivered of a bastard child in said town, [*or*, that the said E. B. is now pregnant of a child, which, when born, will be a bastard,] and which is chargeable [*or*, likely to become chargeable] to said town, [*or*, county,] and that the said C. D. is the father of said child: We do, therefore, adjudge him, the said C. D., to be the father of said bastard child: And further, we do hereby order that the said C. D. pay to the Overseer of the Poor of said town of   , [*or*, to the Superintendents of the Poor of said county,] for the support of said child, the weekly sum of one dollar, so long as the said child shall continue chargeable to said town, [*or*, county:] And inasmuch as it appeared to us, and we find, that the said E. B. is in indigent circumstances, we determine and order that said C. D. pay to the said Overseer of the Poor, [*or*, Superintendents,] for the sustenance of the said E. B., during her confinement and recovery therefrom, the sum of twenty dollars. And we do hereby certify the reasonable costs of apprehending and securing the said father, and of the order of filiation, at the sum of   dollars.

Given, &c., [*as in* § 851.]

---

§ 896. *Bond upon Order of Filiation.*

Know all men, &c.: [*as in* § 894, *to the* *, *and then add:*] The condition of this obligation is such, that whereas, by an order this day duly made and subscribed by the undersigned, Justices of the Peace of said county, it is adjudged that the said C. D. is the father of a bastard child of which E. B. is pregnant, and which is likely to become chargeable [*or*, of a bastard child lately born in said town, of E. B., and which is chargeable] to said town, [*or*, county:] And it was thereupon ordered by the said Justices that, &c., [*recite the order for the support of the bastard and sustenance of the mother, as in* § 895:] Now, therefore, if the said C. D. shall pay the sums for the support of the bastard child, and the sustenance of its mother, as the same are ordered by the said Justices, as aforesaid, or as shall at any time hereafter be ordered by the Court of Sessions of said county and shall fully. and amply indemnify the said town, [*or, county,*] and every other county, town, or city, which may have incurred any expense, or may be put to any expense, for the support of such child or its mother during her confinement or recovery therefrom, against all such expenses, then this obligation to be void; otherwise of force. [*If the party intends to appeal, instead of the foregoing, say:*] Now, therefore, if the said C. D. shall personally appear at the next Court of Sessions of said county, and shall not depart the said court without leave, then this obligation to be void; otherwise of force.]

Sealed, &c., [*as in* § 853.]

---

§ 897. *Warrant to Commit Putative Father.*

County, ss:

To any Constable of said County, greeting:

Whereas, by an order of filiation this day made by us, the undersigned Justices of the Peace of said county, at   , in said county, we did adjudge C. D. to be the father of a bastard child, begotten upon the body of E. B., of said town, and did thereupon order that the said C. D. pay, &c., [*set forth the direction for the support of the child, the sustenance of the mother, and the amount of costs and charges required to be paid, as in the order:*] And whereas, upon the making and subscribing·such order, we did require the said C. D. immediately to pay the costs so certified, and to enter into a bond to the people of this State, in the penal sum of   dollars, with good and sufficient sureties, to be by us approved, with one or other of the conditions, which, by the statute in such case made and provided, is prescribed : And whereas, due notice of our said order has been given to the said C. D., but he has wholly neglected either to pay the said costs and charges, or to execute the bond as aforesaid, [*or, as the case may be :*] You are therefore hereby commanded, in the name of the people of the State of New York, to convey the said C. D. to the common jail of the said county, the keeper whereof is hereby required to receive and detain the said C. D. in custody in said jail, until he shall be discharged by the Court of Sessions of the said county, or shall execute such bond, in the penalty required, as aforesaid.

Given, &c., [*as in* § 851.]

---

§ 898. *Warrant to Release Putative Father from Jail.*

County, ss :

To the Keeper of the Common Jail of said county, greeting :

Whereas, by the warrant of the undersigned, Justices of the Peace of said county, bearing date the   day of   instant, C.,

D. was committed to your custody in said jail, being charged as the reputed father of a bastard, whereof it was testified to us that E. B., of   , in said county, was pregnant, and which was likely to become chargeable to said town, [or, county,] for not paying the costs by us certified, and executing the bond consequent upon our order of filiation, as by the statute required : and whereas, it is now testified and appears to us, upon due proof before us given, that said E. B. hath married before her delivery of said child, [or, has miscarried of such child ; or, was not pregnant.] You are, therefore, hereby commanded, in the name of the people of the State of New York, forthwith to discharge the said C. D. out of your custody, under the commitment upon our warrant, as aforesaid.

Given under our hands and seals, &c., [as in § 851.]

---

§ 899. *Indorsement on a Warrant of Arrest, to be Executed in a Foreign County.*[1]

I, the within named Justice of the Peace, direct that the penal sum in which any bond shall be taken of the within named C. D., shall be   dollars.   G. H., Justice.

---

§ 900. *Indorsement of Justice in a Foreign County.*

County, ss :

The within warrant, with the indorsement made thereon by the Justice by whom it was issued, of the sum required to be put in the bond, having been presented to me, the undersigned, a Justice of the Peace of said county ; and proof having been made of the handwriting of the Justice who issued the said warrant, the arrest of the said C. D. is hereby authorized, if he can be found within the county of

Dated, &c., [as in § 878.]

---

[1] The indorsement of the penal sum in which a bond may be executed, must be made in all cases, where a warrant is to be executed in a foreign county. In order to execute the warrant, the indorsement of a Justice in such county is requisite. The indorsement is to be made upon proof of the handwriting of the Justice issuing the warrant, as in other cases. When the person charged is arrested, he must be taken before the Justice who indorsed the warrant, or some other Justice of the same county, in order that he may be discharged on executing the bond required by statute, (§ 901) if he shall elect to do so. When the bond is executed, the Justice must indorse his certificate of discharge, &c., on the warrant, and deliver the same, together with the bond to the Constable, who is required to return them to the Justice originally issuing the warrant, in fifteen days. If the reputed father refuse or neglect to execute the bond, he must be taken before the Justice who issued the warrant, and the same proceedings are thereupon to be had as if the arrest had been made in the same county. If the bond be given conditioned to indemnify, &c., no other proceedings are necessary, except the return as above mentioned ; but if the condition be to appear at the Court of Sessions, &c., the Justice who issued the warrant must call another Justice to assist him, and proceed to take the examination, &c., as in other cases. (1 R. S., 3d ed , 823, § 7 ; Id., 826, § 18, et seq.; 1 Johnson, 486 ; 13 Wendell, 598.)

§ 901. *Bond on Arrest in Foreign County.*

Know all men, &c. : [*as in* § 894, *to the* *, *and then add :*]
Whereas, the said C. D. has been this day brought before the undersigned, one of the Justices of the Peace of the county of   ;
by virtue of a warrant issued by G. H., one of the Justices of the
Peace of. the county of   , whereon the name of said Justice,
[*or,* of O. M., one of the Justices of the Peace of the said county
of   , is indorsed, with an authority to arrest the said C. D.,
in said county of   ; in which warrant it is recited that E. B.,
of   , in said county of   , upon her examination on oath, before the said G. H., Justice, did declare herself pregnant of a child,
which is likely to be born a bastard, and to become chargeable [*or,*
did declare that she was, on the   day of   last, at   ,
aforesaid, delivered of a bastard child, which is chargeable] to said
town [*or,* county :] And upon the said warrant is indorsed the direction of the said G. H., that the penal sum in which any bond
should be taken of the said C. D., should be $. Now,
therefore, if the said C. D. shall indemnify the said town [*or,* county] of   , and every other county, town, or city, which may
have incurred any expense, or may be put to any expense, for the support of such child, or of its mother during her confinement and recovery therefrom, against all such expenses, and shall pay the costs of apprehending him, the said C. D., and of any order of filiation that
may be made in this matter, [*or,* if the said C. D. shall appear
at the next Court of Sessions of the said county of   , and
not depart the said court without leave,] then the above obligation to
be void ; otherwise of force.

Sealed and delivered, and the)   C. D. [L. S.]
    security approved by me, }   E. F. [L. S.]
        M. B., Justice, &c.

---

§ 902. *Certificate of Discharge, on Executing the Foregoing Bond.*

County, ss :
I certify that the within named C. D., who was brought before me,
one of the Justices of the Peace of the county of   , by virtue
of the within named warrant, was discharged from arrest by me,
upon his executing a bond pursuant to statute.
Dated, &c. [*as in* § 878.]

---

§ 903. *Order of Filiation in the Absence of the Reputed Father,*
Apprehended in a Foreign County.

County, ss :
C. D. having been apprehended in the county of   , in the
State of New York, by virtue of a warrant, and the direction and

authority thereon indorsed, of which the following are copies, to wit: [*insert copies,*] was carried before M. B., Esq., a Justice of the Peace of said county of   , who took from him, the said C. D., a bond to the people of the State of New York, with good and sufficient sureties, in the sum directed in the indorsement on the said warrant, conditioned that the said C. D. shall appear at the next Court of Sessions to be holden in said county of   , and not depart the said court without its leave : and the said bond having been in due form of law returned to the undersigned, G. H., the Justice who issued the said warrant, he thereupon immediately called to his aid the undersigned, S. T., another Justice of the same county, and the said Justices proceeded to make examination of the matter, on the   day of   , 18 , at   , in said town, and then and there heard the proofs that were offered in relation thereto ; by which it was proven, that the said E. B., being in the said town of   , has been delivered of a bastard child, which is chargeable to the said town of   , and that C. D. is the father of such child, [*or, as in* § 895.]

We, the Justices aforesaid, do therefore adjudge, &c., [*as in* § 895.]

---

§ 904. *Warrant to Commit a Mother who Refuses to Disclose the Name of the Father.*[1]

County, ss :

To any Constable of said County, greeting :

Whereas we, the undersigned, Justices of the Peace of said county, being now associated for the purpose of examining into and making order for the indemnity of the town of   , in said county, [*or,* for the indemnity of said county,] against the support of a certain child, said to have been born a bastard of the body of E. B., and chargeable [*or,* likely to become chargeable] to said town, [*or,* county,] upon the application of E. F., Overseer of the Poor of said town, [*or,* a Superintendent of the Poor of said county,] have required the said E. B., who is now before us, to submit to an examination on oath, in the presence of C. D., who has been brought before us charged with being the father of said child, to testify touching such charge, and to disclose the name of such father, but the said E. B. wholly refuses to testify and disclose ; and inasmuch as it now appears

---

[1] The mother of a bastard child is to be regarded as a witness against the father, and may be subpœnæd to appear and testify, and her attendance compelled as in other cases. If, on appearing before the Justice, she refuse to testify and disclose the name of the father, such Justice may, after the expiration of one month from the time of her confinement, if she shall be sufficiently recovered, commit her to the common jail of the county, by a warrant under his hand, or under the hands of the two Justices attending to take the examination. (1 R S., 3d ed., 826, § 20 ; 4 Wendell, 555.)

to us, upon due proof thereof, given on oath before us, that more than a month has elapsed since the said E. B. was delivered of said child and that she is now sufficiently recovered from her confinement: You are therefore hereby commanded, in the name of the people of the State of New York, to take the said E. B., and convey her to the common jail of the said county, the keeper whereof is required to detain the said E. B. in his custody in said jail, until she shall so testify and disclose the name of such father.

Given, &c., [*as in* § 851.]

---

§ 905. *Summons where Mother has property in her own Right.*[1]

County, ss :

To any Constable of said County, greeting :

You are hereby required to summon E. B., of   , in said county, to appear before us, the undersigned, Justices of the Peace of said county, on the   day of   instant, at two o'clock in the afternoon, at the office of the undersigned, G. H. to show cause, if any she may have, why we should not make an order for the keeping of a bastard child, said to have been lately born of the said E. B., and chargeable [*or*, likely to become chargeable] to said county, [*or*, town,] by charging the said E. B. with the payment of money weekly, or other sustentation; E. F., Overseer of the Poor of said town, [*or*, Superintendent of the Poor of said county,] having applied to us for that purpose.

Given, &c., [*as in* § 851.]

---

§ 906. *Order to Compel the Mother to Pay for Support of the Child.*

County, ss :

Whereas, G. H., one of the Superintendents of the Poor of said county, [*or*, E. F., Overseer of the Poor of the town of   , in said county,] has made application to us, two of the Justices of the

---

[1] Where the mother of a bastard child is possessed of property in her own right, two Justices of the Peace of the county, on the application of a Superintendent or Overseer, may inquire into the matter, and make an order charging the mother with the weekly payment of an allowance, or sustenance, for the support of such child. A copy of the order, when made, should be served on the mother, and if she desire to appeal from the same to the Court of Sessions, she must execute a bond, in such penal sum, and with such sureties, as the Justices shall direct to appear at such court, and not depart without leave. The form given in the case of a putative father, (§ 896,) may be varied for this purpose. If, after service of the order, the mother refuse or neglect to comply therewith, she may be summarily committed to jail. (I R. S., 3d ed., 825, § 21, et seq.) If she execute the bond, the Justices must transmit it, together with their order of sustenance, to the Clerk of the county, before the sitting of the court.

Peace of said county, complaining that E. B., of   , in said county, was lately delivered at   , aforesaid, of a bastard child, which is chargeable [*or*, likely to become chargeable] to said county, [*or*, town,] and that said E. B. is possessed of property in her own right, and is of sufficient ability to support said child; and desiring that we should examine into the matter and make order for the indemnity of the said county, [*or*, town.] And whereas, upon examination into the matter of said application, and upon due proof thereof, on oath before us given, and the said E. B., although present at such examination, not showing any sufficient cause to the contrary, [*or*, and the said E. B. neglecting to appear before us and show cause, if any she might have, to the contrary, although duly summoned so to appear,] we do therefore hereby order, that the said E. B. pay weekly to said Superintendent, [*or*, to said Overseer,] the sum of   , for the support of said child; [*If necessary, insert here*, unless the said E. B. shall nurse and take care of said child herself.]

Given, &c., [*as in* § 851.]

---

§ 907. *Warrant to Commit Mother for not Executing Bond.*

County, ss:

To any Constable of said County, greeting:

Whereas, by an order duly made by us, the undersigned Justices of the Peace of said county, bearing date the   day of   instant, in relation to the keeping of a certain bastard child, lately born in said county, of the body of E. B., which is chargeable to the town of   , [*or*, said county,] we directed, &c., [*as in the order*;] which order was so made upon the application of E. F., Overseer of the Poor of said town, [*or*, a Superintendent of the Poor of said county;] and after due notice to the said E. B., to show cause, if any she might have, against the making of such order: And whereas, a copy of said order, subscribed by us, has been served upon the said E. B.; and she has neither executed the bond by law required for her appearance, at the next Court of Sessions, &c., nor complied with the requirements of the said order: You are therefore hereby commanded, in the name of the people of the State of New York, to take the said E. B., and convey her to the common jail of said county, there to remain, without bail, until she shall comply with said order, or execute the bond authorized by statute, as aforesaid.

Given, &c., [*as in* § 851.]

§ 908. *Warrant to Seize the Property of Absconding Father of Bastard.*

County, ss.:

To E. F., Overseer of the Poor of the town of   , in said
    county, [*or*, To the Superintendents of the Poor of said county:]
  It appearing to us, two of the Justices of the Peace of said county,
as well by the representation and application to us made by the said
Overseer, [*or*, the said Superintendents,] as upon due proof of the
facts before us given, that C. D. is the father of a bastard child,
whereof E. B., of said town, is now pregnant, and which, when born,
is likely to become chargeable to said town, [*or*, county,] [*or*, that
C. D. is the father of a bastard child lately born in said town, of E.
B., and which is chargeable, or likely to become chargeable, to said
town [*or*, said county,] and that said C. D. has absconded from said
town, which is the place of his ordinary residence, leaving in said
county some estate, real or personal:] We therefore authorize you,
&c., [*as in* § 851.]

---

§ 909. *Order reducing the sum to be Paid by the Father or Mother of a Bastard Child.*

County, ss:

To E. F., Overseer of the Poor of the town of   , in said
    county; [*or*, the Superintendents of the Poor of said county:]
  Whereas, by an order of filiation by us made, bearing date the
day of   last, we did determine that C. D. was the father of a
certain bastard child, then lately born in   , aforesaid, of one
E. B., and did thereupon direct, among other things, that the said C.
D. should pay to you, the said Overseer, [*or*, Superintendents,] for
the support of said child, the weekly sum of one dollar, so long as
said child should continue chargeable to said town, [*or*, county:] And
whereas, upon the application of the said C. D., we have this day
inquired into the circumstances of the case, and heard the proofs and
allegations to us submitted in relation thereto; and it appearing to
us, upon such inquiry, that the circumstances in relation to said bastard child, render it proper and expedient that the sum required to
be paid by the said C. D., by our former order, should be reduced as
hereinafter expressed; and inasmuch as you, the said Overseer, [*or*,
Superintendents,] have shown before us no sufficient reason against
such reduction, although appearing before us, [*or*, notified to appear
before us and show cause, if any you might have:] We do, therefore
reduce the sum required to be paid by the said C. D., by our former
order as aforesaid, to the weekly sum of   .
  Given, &c. [*as in* § 851.]

§ 910. *Notice, by Superintendent, or Overseer, that Application will be made to the Court of Sessions to increase the Amount Payable in the Order of Filiation.*[1]

To C. D. :

You will take notice, that I shall make application to the next Court of Sessions of the county of   ., to be holden at   , in said county, on the   day of   , at ten o'clock in the forenoon, to increase the sum directed to be paid by the order of filiation, of which the annexed is a copy, for the support of the bastard child named therein; which said application will be founded on the affidavits, copies of which are also hereto annexed.

Dated   , this   day of   , 18 .

L. M., Superintendent of the Poor.

---

§ 911. *Notice, to be given to Superintendent, or Overseer, for Reducing Amount in the Order of Filiation.*

To L. M., Superintendent, [*or*, E. F., Overseer,] of the Poor :

You will take notice, that I shall make application to the next Court of Sessions of the county of   , to be holden at   , in said county, on the   day of   , 18 , at ten o'clock, in the forenoon, to reduce the amount directed to be paid by the order, &c., [*as in* § 910, *except that the notice must be signed by the other party.*]

---

§ 912. *Notice of Appeal from Order of Filiation.*[2]

To G. H., and S. T., Esqrs., Justices of the Peace of the County of   :

You will take notice, that the undersigned, conceiving himself aggrieved by the order made by you, of which a copy is annexed, hereby appeals therefrom to the next Court of Sessions, to be holden in said county.

Dated   , this   day of   , 18 .

C. D.

---

[1] The above notices, (§ 910 and § 911,) with the accompanying papers, must be served on the party to be notified, at least ten days before the application is to be made.

[2] An appeal may be made to the court by the reputed father, or by the Superintendent or Overseer, from any order or determination of the Justices, notice of which, with a copy of the order, must be served on each Justices, and on the opposite party. (1 R. S., 3d ed., 627, § 24.)

CHAPTER XXXVI.

POWERS OF ATTORNEY.

PRACTICAL REMARKS.

1. A letter, or power of attorney, is a written delegation of authority, by which one person enables another to do an act for him.

2. Where a power is special, and the authority limited, the attorney cannot bind his principal by any act in which he exceeds that authority; but the authority of the attorney will be so construed, as to include all necessary means of executing it with effect.[1]

3. An authority to enter up a judgment against two persons, will not warrant a judgment against one alone.[2]

4. The declarations of one holding a letter of attorney, made in the course of his dealings as such, with a third person, will bind the principal equally with the articles to which they relate.[3]

5. Written powers are always to receive a strict interpretation.[4]

6. The adoption of one part of a transaction, done under an assumed agency, is an adoption of the whole.[5]

7. Notice given to an agent, relating to business which he is authorized to transact, and while actually engaged in transacting it, will in general enure as notice to the principal.[6]

8. Where an act of agency is required to be done in the name of the principal, under seal, the authority of the agent must be under seal. An authority to convey lands must be in writing; though it is otherwise of a contract to convey.[7]

---

[1] 13 Johnson, 307; 19 Id., 363; 1 Hill, 155; 3 Id., 262.
[2] 1 Hill, 155.
[3] 3 Hill, 262.
[4] 3 Hill. 262

[5] 24 Wendell, 325; 3 Hill, 552; 6 Id., 107, 137.
[6] 9 Johnson, 163; 6 Hill, 101.
[7] 2 R. S. (3d ed.,) 194, § 6, et seq.; 6 Wendell, 461; 10 Id., 436; 13 Id., 481; 16 Id., 25, 28; 2 Hill, 485; 5 Id., 107.

9. It is not necessary that a letter of attorney to convey land should be recorded; though when duly proved or acknowledged, in the same manner as conveyances of real estate, it may be so recorded. When such letter of attorney has been recorded, the instrument revoking it must also be recorded, in the same office.[1]

10. When any married woman residing out of this State, unites with her husband in the execution of a power of attorney to convey real estate, she must acknowledge such execution, in the same manner as conveyances executed by married women residing out of the State.[2]

11. When a person has the power to do an act, in his own right, he may delegate it to an attorney; but an attorney cannot delegate his authority to a substitute, unless expressly authorized so to do. Whenever a substitute is regularly appointed, he must act in the name of the principal.

12. The authority of an attorney ceases when it is withdrawn by the principal; but where the letter of attorney forms part of a contract, and is security for money, or for the performance of any act which is considered valuable, it will be deemed irrevocable in law.[3]

13. The revocation of a letter of attorney takes effect, as to the attorney, from the time it is communicated to him; and as to third persons, from the time they have notice of it.

14. If a power of attorney is to be used in a different State or Territory from that in which the principal resides, it should be duly acknowledged or proved. Where the attorney resides, or is to transact business in a foreign country, the acknowledgment should be made before a Notary.

FORMS.

§ 913. *General Form of Power of Attorney.*[4]

Know all men by these presents: That I, A. B., of   , in the county of   , and State of New York, have made, constituted and appointed, and by these presents do make, constitute and appoint, C. D., of, &c., my true and lawful attorney, for me, and in my name, place, and stead,*[*set forth the subject matter of the power,*] giving and granting unto my said attorney, full power and authority, to do and perform all and every act and thing whatsoever,

---

[1] 2 R. S. (3d ed.,) 47, §§ 45, 46; 10 Paige, 346.
[2] 2 R. S. (3d ed.,) 47, § 47; Laws of 1835, chap. 275.
[3] 11 Johnson, 47 · 12 Id., 343; 6 Cowen, 489.

[4] For different forms of acknowledgments, to accompany powers of attorney, when necessary, see Chapter 1.

requisite and necessary to be done, in and about the premises, as fully, to all intents and purposes, as I might or could do if personally present, with full power of substitution and revocation, hereby ratifying and confirming all that my said attorney, or his substitute shall lawfully do, or cause to be done, by virtue thereof.

In witness whereof, I have hereunto set my hand and seal, the   day of   , in the year one thousand eight hundred and   .

Sealed and delivered in ⎫
   the presence of ⎬   A. B. [L. s.]
     G. H.   ⎭

------

§ 914. *Power of Attorney to Collect Debts.*

Know all men by these presents, &c.: [*as in* § 913, *to the* *, *and then add* :] and to my use, to ask, demand, sue for, collect and receive, all such sums of money, debts, rents, dues, accounts, and other demands whatsoever, which are or shall be due, owing, payable and belonging, to me, or detained from me, in any manner whatsoever, by E. F., of, &c., his heirs, executors and administrators, or any of them, [*or*, by any person or persons residing or being in the State of   ;] giving and granting unto my said attorney, &c., [*as in* § 913, *to the end.*]

------

§ 915. *Power to Collect Rents.*

Know all men by these presents, &c.; [*as in* § 913, *to the* *, *and then add:*] and for my use, to ask, demand, [*insert*, distrain for, *if necessary*,] collect and receive, all such rents, and arrears of rent, as now are or may be, or shall hereafter grow, due, or owing to me, from E. F., R: F., and L. M., of, &c., or any of them, as tenants or occupiers of any lands, tenements, or hereditaments, belonging to or claimed by me, situate in the county of   , in the State of   , or which may be due from, or payable by, any other person or persons whomsoever, as tenants, occupiers, lessees, or assignees, of any term or terms, of such lands, tenements, or hereditaments; or any of them, or any part or parcel of them ; and upon receipt thereof, to give proper acquittances and sufficient discharge thereof ; giving and granting unto my said attorney, &c., [*as in* § 913, *to the end.*]

------

§ 916. *Power to Receive a Legacy.*

Know all men by these presents : That whereas, L. M., late of   , deceased, by his last will and testament, did give and bequeath unto me, A. B., of, &c., a legacy of   dollars, to be paid unto me on the   day of   , 18 , of which said will G. H. and S. T., of, &c., are joint executors: Now, therefore, I, the said A. B., have made, constituted and appointed, and by these presents do make, constitute and appoint, C. D., of, &c., my true and lawful attorney, for me and in my name, and for my use and benefit, to ask, demand and receive, of and from the said G. H. and S. T., executors as aforesaid, the legacy given and bequeathed unto me by the said will of the said L. M., as aforesaid ; and upon receipt thereof by, or payment thereof to, my said attorney, to make, execute and deliver, a general release or discharge for the same; hereby ratifying, confirming and allowing, whatever my said attorney shall lawfully do in the premises.

In witness, &c., [*as in* § 913.]

---

§ 917. *Power to Receive Distributive Share of Personal Estate,
Executed by Husband and Wife.*

Know all men by these presents: That whereas, C. D., late of   , the father of the undersigned, E. B., deceased on the   day of   , 18 , at   aforesaid, leaving certain personal property belonging to him, the said C. D., which is to be divided among the heirs at law of the said C. D., according to the provisions of the statute relative to the distribution of the personal estates of intestates; and whereas, G. H. and S. T. have been duly appointed by the Surrogate of the county of   , administrators of the goods and chattels, rights and credits, which were of the said C. D., deceased : Now, therefore, we, the undersigned, A. B., and E. B., his wife, daughter of the said C. D., deceased, have made, constituted and appointed, and by these presents do make, constitute and appoint, E. F., of, &c., our true and lawful attorney, for us, and in our place and stead, and for our use and benefit, to ask, demand and receive, of and from the said G. H. and S. T., the distributive share of the personal estate of the said C. D., deceased, coming to us, in right of the said E., as one of the heirs at law of the said C. D., as aforesaid : and upon receipt thereof by, or payment thereof to, our said attorney, to make, execute and deliver, a good and sufficient receipt, release, or discharge, for the same; hereby ratifying, confirming and allowing, whatsoever our said attorney shall lawfully do in the premises.

In witness whereof, we have hereunto set our hands and seals, the   day of   , one thousand eight hundred and   .

Sealed, &c., [*as in* § 913.]
                                       A. B. [L. S.]
                                       E. B [L. S.]

§ 918. *Power to Take Charge of Lands, &c.*

Know all men by these presents, &c., [*as in* § 913, *to the *, and then add :*] to exercise the general control and supervision over the lands, tenements and hereditaments, belonging to me, and situate in the county of   ; to prevent, forbid and hinder, by all lawful means whatsoever, the commission of any trespass or waste upon the same, or any part thereof ; and, at my cost and charge, and under the advice of my counsel, R. F., Esq., of   , to sue for, collect, recover and receive, and compound for, any damages which may accrue by means of the commission of any trespass or waste upon the said lands, tenements and hereditaments, or any part thereof, by any person or persons whomsoever, giving and granting unto my said attorney, &c., [*as in* § 913, *to the end.*]

§ 919. *General Power to Transact Business.*

Know all men by these presents: That whereas, I, A. B., or have this day leased the premises known as No.   , in the of   , for the term of   years next ensuing after the day of   next, for the purpose of conducting. carrying on and transacting, at the place and number aforesaid, the business of a general commission merchant, and more particularly, the receiving, selling and vending, on commission, all kinds of dry and wet groceries: Now, therefore, I, the said A. B., have made, constituted and appointed, and by these presents do make, constitute and appoint, C. D., of   , aforesaid, my true and lawful attorney, for me and in my name, place and stead, to conduct, carry on and transact, the business aforesaid, at the place and number aforesaid; to receive on commission, sell and vend, all and every such goods, wares and merchandise, appertaining to the business aforesaid, as my said attorney may deem meet and proper; to make and execute, sign, seal and deliver, for me and in my name, all bills, bonds, notes, specialties, or other instruments in writing whatsoever, which shall be necessary to the proper conducting, carrying on and transacting, the business aforesaid ; and to do and perform all and every act and deed, of whatsoever name or nature, legally appertaining to the same, binding me as firmly and irrevocably by such deed or performance, as if I were myself present thereto consenting ; hereby ratifying, confirming and allowing, whatever my said attorney shall lawfully do in the premises.

In witness, &c., [*as in* § 913.]

§ 920. *General Custom House Power.*

Know all men by these presents, &c., [*as in* § 913, *to the* *, *and then add:*] to receive and enter at the custom-house of the district of , any goods, wares, or merchandise, imported by me, or which may hereafter arrive, consigned to me; to sign my name, and to seal and deliver, for me and as my act and deed, any bond or bonds which may be required by the collector of the said district, for securing the duties on any such goods, wares, or merchandise: Also, to sign my name to, seal and deliver, for me, and as my act and deed, any bond or bonds, requisite for obtaining the debenture on any goods, wares, or merchandise, when exported; and generally to transact all business at the said custom house, in which I am or may hereafter be interested or concerned, as fully as I could if personally present. And I do hereby declare that all bonds signed and executed by my said attorney, shall be as obligatory on me as those signed by myself, and this power shall remain in full force until revoked by written notice given to the said collector.

In witness, &c., [*as in* § 913.]

---

§ 921. *Power to Sell and Convey Real Estate.*

Know all men by these presents, &c., [*as in* § 913 *to the* *, *and then add:*] to enter into and take possession of all such lands, tenements, hereditaments, and real estate whatever, in the State of to or in which I am or may be in any way entitled or interested; and to grant, bargain and sell the same or any part or parcel thereof, for such sum or price, and on such terms, as to him shall seem meet; and for me, and in my name, to make, execute, acknowledge and deliver, good and sufficient deeds and conveyances for the same, either with or without covenants and warranty; and until the sale thereof, to let and demise the said real estate, for the best rent that can be procured for the same; and to ask, demand, [*insert* distrain for, *if necessary,*] collect, recover, and receive, all sums of money which shall become due and owing to me, by means of such bargain and sale, or lease and demise; giving and granting unto my said attorney, &c., [*as in* § 913 *to the end.*]

---

§ 922. *Power to Effect Insurance.*

Know all men by these presents, &c., [*as in* § 913, to the *, *and then add:*] to effect insurance on [*insert the property to be insured,*] with the Fire [*or*, Marine] Insurance company, in the city of , on such terms as to my said attorney shall seem meet and proper; and I hereby empower my said attorney to sign any application for said insurance, any representation of the condition and value of said property, articles of agreement, promissory, or premium note, and all other papers that may be necessary for that purpose; and also to cancel and surrender any policy he may obtain, and on such canceling, or the expiration thereof, to receive any dividend, return premium, or deposit, that may be due, and on such receipt full discharge to give therefor; giving and granting unto my said attorney, &c., [*as in* § 913, *to the end.*]

---

§ 923. *Substitution of an Attorney.*

Know all men by these presents: That I, C. D., of   , by virtue of the power and authority to me given, in and by the letter of attorney, of A. B., of   , which is hereunto annexed, do substitute and appoint E. P., of   , to do, perform and execute, every act or thing which I might or could do, in, by, and under, the same, as well for me, as being the true and lawful attorney and substitute of the said A. B.; hereby ratifying and confirming all that the said attorney and substitute, hereby made and appointed, shall do in the premises, by virtue hereof, and of the said letter of attorney.

In witness, &c., [*as in* § 913.]

---

§ 924. *Revocation of a Power of Attorney.*

Know all men by these presents: That whereas, I, A. B., of, &c., in and by my letter of attorney, bearing date the   day of   , in the year one thousand eight hundred and   , did make, constitute and appoint C. D., of, &c., my true and lawful attorney, for me, and in my name, to, &c., [*here copy the language of the letter of attorney,*] as by the said letter will more fully appear: Now, therefore, I, the said A. B., have revoked, countermanded, annulled, and made void, and by these presents do revoke, countermand, annul, and make void, the said letter of attorney, and all power and authority thereby given, or intended to be given, to the said C. D.

In witness, &c., [*as in* § 913.]

CHAPTER XXXVII.

RECEIPT AND RELEASE.

PRACTICAL REMARKS.

1. A receipt in full, though strong evidence, is not conclusive; and the party signing such receipt will be permitted to show a mistake or error therein, if any exist.[1]

2. Receipts for the payment of money, are open to examination, and may be varied, explained, or contradicted, by parol testimony.[2]

3. Where a receipt is given for money paid on a bond or contract, and an indorsement also made, the latter should mention the fact that a receipt was given for the same sum.

4. A release must be by an instrument sealed. The most beneficial release is one of all demands. The word "demand" is more comprehensive than any other, except "claim," and when it is used, all classes of actions and rights of action are extinguished.[3]

5. A release of one of several joint wrong doers or contractors, in general, discharges all; but where all are parties to the release, and those not in terms discharged, covenant in it to remain liable, they will not be discharged.[4]

6. A release of one of several joint, or joint and several obligors, discharges all.[5]

7. A covenant not to sue two joint debtors, is a release as to both; but a covenant not to sue one will not operate as a release to either.[6]

8. The competency of an interested witness may be restored by release, or payment. A release for this purpose may always be given

---

[1] 2 Hill, 291.
[2] 1 Johnson's Cas. 145; 2 Johnson, 378; 5 Id., 72; 7 Cowen., 334; 2 Hill, 291; 4 Id., 104, 107.
[3] 1 Denio, 527.
[4] 18 Wendell, 319; 1 Hill, 165.
[5] 3 Denio, 238.
[6] 8 Paige, 229.

where the party executing it has a present interest, or a present right to take effect *in future;* and it must be delivered to the witness himself, or to a third person, for the use of the witness, before his competency will be deemed to have been restored.[1]

FORMS.

§ 925. *General Form of Receipt on Account.*

$50.   Albany, May 1, 1847.

Received of C. D. fifty dollars, to apply on account.

A. B.

---

§ 926. *Receipt in Full.*

$110 10.   Albany, May 1, 1847.

Received of C. D. one hundred ten dollars and ten cents, in full of all demands against him.

A. B.

---

§ 927. *Receipt for Money paid by Third Person.*

$100.   Albany, May 1, 1847.

Received of C. D., by the hand of E. F., one hundred dollars, to apply on account of said C. D.

A. B.

---

§ 928. *Receipt for Money on Bond.*

$200.   Albany, May 1, 1847.

Received of C. D. two hundred dollars, to apply on his bond, dated the   day of   , 18   , being the same sum this day indorsed on said bond.

A. B.

---

§ 929. *Receipt for Interest Money.*

$140.   Albany, May 1, 1847.

Received of C. D. one hundred forty dollars, being the annual interest due on his bond, dated the   day of   , 18   , given to me, [*or,* to E. F.,] and conditioned for the payment of the sum of two thousand dollars, in three years from date, with annual interest.

A. B.

---

[1] 2 Johnson, 170 , 9 Id., 123 ; 4 Hill, 255.

§ 930. *Receipt to be Indorsed on a Bond or Contract.*

$140.   Albany, May 1, 1847.

Received of C. D. one hundred forty dollars, being the annual interest due on the within bond, and the same sum this day receipted by me to the said C. D.   A. B.

---

§ 931. *Release of all Demands.*

Know all men by these presents: That I, A. B., of the
of   , for and in consideration of the sum of   dollars, to me in hand paid by C. D., of   , have remised, released, and forever discharged, and by these presents do, for myself, my heirs, executors, administrators and assigns, remise, release, and forever discharge, the said C. D., his heirs, executors and administrators, of and from all and all manner of action and actions, cause and causes of action, suits, debts, dues, sums of money, claims and demands, whatsoever, in law or in equity, which I ever had, or now have, or which I or my heirs, executors, administrators, or assigns, hereafter can, shall, or may have, by reason of any matter, cause, or thing, whatsoever, from the beginning of the world to the date of these presents.*

In witness whereof, I have hereunto put my hand and seal, this
     day of   , one thousand eight hundred and   .

In presence of ⎱
G. H.   ⎰   A. B. [L s.]

---

§ 932. *Special Release.*

Know all men, &c., [*as in* § 931, *to the* *, *and then add:*] arising out of any dealings, or transactions, between myself and the said C. D., at my store in the city of   .

In witness, &c., [*as in* § 931.]

---

§ 933. *Release by Creditor Named in an Assignment.*

Know all men, &c., [*as in* § 931, *to the* *, *and then add:*] saving and excepting, however, and without prejudice to, all my rights, remedies, claims and demands, and the rights, remedies, claims and demands, of my heirs, executors, administrators and assigns, under a certain deed of trust, bearing even date herewith, and made and executed by the said C. D. to E. F., upon the trusts therein expressed and declared.

In witness, &c., [*as in* § 931.]

§ 934. *Release of Part of Mortgaged Premises.*[1]

This indenture, made this   day of   , in the year between A. B., of, &c., and C. D., of, &c., witnesseth: That whereas, the said C. D., by his indenture of mortgage, bearing date the day of   , A. D. 18   , did, for the consideration and for the purposes therein mentioned, convey to the said A. B. [*or*, to one E. F., by mortgage duly assigned to the said A. B.,] certain lands in   aforesaid, and of which the lands hereinafter described are part and parcel; and the said C. D., on the day of the date hereof, has paid unto the said A. B. the sum of   dollars, being part of the money secured by the mortgage aforesaid, as therein specified, on which payment the said A. B. hath agreed [*or*, and the said A. B., at the request of the said C. D., hath agreed] to release to the said C. D., his heirs and assigns, the lands hereinafter described, and to take and accept the residue of the said mortgaged premises as his security for the payment of the moneys remaining unpaid on the said mortgage: Now, therefore, the said A. B., in consideration of the premises, doth hereby grant, release, assign and make over, to the said C. D., and to his heirs and assigns, all that part of the said mortgaged lands, bounded and described as follows, viz: [*give description:*] with the hereditaments and appurtenances thereunto belonging, or in any wise appertaining: To have and to hold the lands and premises hereby released and conveyed, to the said C. D., his heirs and assigns, to his and their only proper use and behoof forever, free, clear, and discharged of and from the lien of the said mortgage.

In witness whereof, the said A. B. hath hereunto set his hand and seal, the day and year above written.

Sealed and delivered }
  in presence of   }
     G. H.

A. B. [L s.]

———

§ 935. *Release of Land by a Judgment Creditor.*[2]

In   Court.

A. B.
  against }   Judgment rendered the   day of   ,
C. D.   } 18   , in the   Court, in the county of
     : [*or*, before C. C., Esq., a Justice of the Peace in and for   county.]

Judgment perfected and docketed in   County Clerk's office, the   day of   , 18   : [*or*, Transcript filed and judgment docketed in   County Clerk's office, the   day of   , 18   .]

———

[1] A release of a lien on real estate, by mortgage or judgment, should be acknowledged and recorded in the county where the premises are situated.
[2] See note to § 934.

In consideration of   dollars, to me in hand paid, the receipt whereof is acknowledged, I do hereby remise, release and discharge, the following described land and premises, to wit: [*describe the premises:*] from all claim to, or interest in, the same, or any part thereof, which I may have, under and by virtue of the above mentioned judgment, and from all lien or incumbrance that has attached to the same by reason of the recovery of the said judgment, as free and clear, in all respects, as though said judgment had not been rendered.

In witness whereof, I have hereunto set my hand and seal, this   day of   , 18   .

Sealed and delivered }
  in presence of }   A. B. [L. S.]
     G. H.

---

§ 936. *Release of a Legacy.*

Know all men by these presents: That, whereas, A. B., of   , in the county of   , and State of   , by his last will and testament in writing, bearing date the   day of   , A. D. 18   , did, among other legacies therein contained, give and bequeath unto me, C. D., of   , in the county of   , and State of   , the sum, or legacy, of   dollars, and of his said will and testament did make and constitute E. F. the sole executor, [*or*, E. F. and G. H. joint executors:] Now, therefore, I, the said C. D., hereby acknowledge the receipt from the said E. F., executor, [*or*, E. F. and G. H., executors,] as aforesaid, of the said sum, or legacy, of   dollars, so given and bequeathed to me as aforesaid, and do acquit, release and discharge, the said E. F. [*or*, E. F. and G. H.,] of and from all legacies, dues and demands whatsoever, under or by virtue of the said last will and testament, or against, or out of, the estate of the said A. B.

In witness, &c., [*as in* § 931.]

---

§ 937. *Release from a Party to a Witness.*

Supreme Court. [*or*, Justice's Court.

A. B.,		A. B.,	
against	}	against	} Before G. H., Esq.]
C. D.		C. D.	

For value received, I do hereby release E. F., a witness offered [*or*, to be offered] by me, on the trial of this cause, of and from any claim or demand which I now, or may hereafter have, against him, by reason of the determination of this suit, or any matter, either di-

33

rectly or indirectly brought, or to be brought, in question, in this suit, either for or against me. And I do further release him from all demands connected with, or depending upon, the subject matter of this suit, or any part thereof, which I now or may hereafter have against him.

In witness, &c., [*as in* § 931.]

---

§ 938. *Release from a Witness to a Party.*

In Supreme Court.

> A. B.,
> *against* } [*or, as in* § 937.]
> C. D.

For value received, I do hereby release A. B., plaintiff in the above cause, of and from any claim or demand which I now, or may hereafter have, against him, by reason of the determination of this suit, or any matter, either directly or indirectly, brought or to be brought in question, in this suit, either for or against him. And I do further release him, &c., [*as in* § 937, *to the end.*]

CHAPTER XXXVIII.

SCHOOLS.

PRACTICAL REMARKS.

1. Common Schools in the State of New York are free to all persons residing in the district over five and under twenty-one years of age; and persons who are not residents may be admitted therein, with the consent, in writing, of the trustees, or a majority of them.[1]

2. The inhabitants of school districts entitled to vote at district meetings, when legally assembled, have power, by a majority of the votes of those present : To appoint a chairman for the time being; to adjourn from time to time, as occasion may require; to choose a District Clerk, three Trustees, a District Collector, and a Librarian, at the first meeting, and to supply vacancies whenever they occur; to designate a site for a district school-house; to lay such tax on the taxable inhabitants as the meeting shall deem sufficient to purchase or lease a suitable site for a school-house, and to build, hire, or purchase such school-house, and to keep the same in repair and furnish it with necessary fuel and appendages; to designate sites for two or more school-houses for their district, and lay a tax in the same manner as above provided, with the consent of the Town Superintendent; to levy a tax, not exceeding twenty dollars in any one year, for the purchase of maps, globes, black-boards and other school apparatus; to vote a tax for the purchase of a book in which to record the proceedings of the district; whenever the site of their school-house has been legally changed, to direct the sale of the former site or lot, with the buildings and appurtenances; in a district numbering more than fifty children, between the ages of five and sixteen years, and having over one hundred and twenty-five volumes in the district library, or numbering fifty children or less, between the above ages, and having

---

[1] Laws of 1849, chap. 140

over one hundred volumes, to appropriate the whole or any part of the library money belonging to the district for the current year, at a special meeting to be called for the purpose, to the purchase of maps, globes, black-boards, or other scientific apparatus for the use of the school ; to lay a tax, not exceeding ten dollars for each year, for the purchase of a district library, to consist of such books as the district may direct, and such further sum as they may deem necessary for the purchase of a book-case,—provided, however, that the intention to propose the tax be stated in the notice of the meeting; with the consent of the Town Superintendent, to unite their library moneys with those of an adjoining district, or districts, and purchase a joint library for the use of such districts, to be selected by the Trustees, or such person as they may designate; to direct the public money going to the teachers, to be divided into not exceeding two portions for each year, one of which is to be assigned and applied by the Trustees to each term during which a school shall be kept in the district, for the payment of teachers' wages; and to alter, repeal and modify, their proceedings from time to time, as occasion may require.[1]

3. The amount of tax which may be voted for the purchase or lease of sites for the school-house, for repairs, fuel, furniture, and appendages, is unlimited by law; but no tax for building, hiring, or purchasing a school-house, can exceed the sum of four hundred dollars, unless on the certificate of the Town Superintendent of the town in which the school-house is to be situated, that a larger sum, specifying the amount, is necessary; in which case a sum may be raised not exceeding the amount so certified. In districts composed of parts of several towns, the certificate of a majority of the Town Superintendents of such towns will be necessary.[2]

4. A majority of all the taxable inhabitants of any school district, to be ascertained by taking and recording the ayes and noes of such inhabitants attending at any annual, special, or adjourned school district meeting, may determine that a tax exceeding four hundred dollars, for building, hiring, or purchasing a school-house, be raised by installments; and it will then become the duty of the Trustees to raise the tax in accordance with such determination. The payment or collection of the last installment cannot be extended beyond five years from the time the original vote to raise the tax was taken; and no vote to levy any such tax can be reconsidered, except at an adjourned general or special meeting, to be held within thirty days thereafter, and the same majority will be requisite for a reconsideration as was necessary to levy the tax.[3]

5. The following are the qualifications of voters at district meet-

---

[1] Laws of 1847, chap. 480.
[2] Laws of 1847, chap. 480 ; 18 Johnson, 351 ; 5 Hill, 46.
[3] Laws of 1847, chap. 480.

ings: The voter must be a male, twenty-one years old, or upwards, and an actual resident of the district. In addition to the foregoing, he must possess one or other of the following qualifications: He must be entitled by law to hold land in this State, and must own or hire real property in the district, subject to taxation for school purposes—or he must be entitled to vote at town meetings of the town in which the district, or part of a district is situated, and must have paid a rate bill for teachers' wages in the district within one year preceding, or must own, personally, property liable to be taxed for school purposes in the district, exceeding fifty dollars in value, exclusive of what is exempt from execution.[1]

6. The Town Superintendent of Common Schools is elected at the time, and in the manner, provided by law for the election of other town officers, and holds his office for two years, commencing on the first Monday of November succeeding his election. He is required to perform all the duties, and is subject to the restrictions and liabilities formerly imposed by law on Commissioners and Inspectors of common schools, in addition to the other powers and duties conferred and enjoined upon him. It is his duty, on or before the first Monday of November succeeding his election, to execute to the Supervisor of his town, and file with the Town Clerk, a bond, with one or more sufficient sureties, to be approved by the Supervisor, in the penalty of double the amount of school money received from all sources during the preceding year; and whenever the Supervisor is of the opinion that the security of the Town Superintendent is not sufficient for the protection of the public, he may require further security. If the Town Superintendent fails to give such further security, within five days after the service of a written notice from the Supervisor upon him, his office will be vacant. A person appointed to fill a vacancy in the office of Town Superintendent, will hold his office, only till the first Monday of November, following the next annual town meeting, at which a successor to the incumbent must be regularly chosen by the electors.[2]

7. The Town Superintendent has the general supervision of the common schools in his town; visits and inspects each school legally organized, at least twice a year, and oftener if, in his opinion, it be necessary; examines and licenses teachers, and re-examines them and annuls their licenses whenever he thinks proper; receives and apportions the school moneys; regulates and alters school districts, (in conjunction with the Supervisor and Town Clerk, when required by the Trustees of any district interested;) prosecutes for, and col-

---

Laws of 1847, chap. 480
[2] Laws of 1847, chap. 480 Laws of 1849, chap. 382; Laws of 1850, chap 184.

lects all fines, penalties and forfeitures; and makes an annual report to the County Clerk, of the condition, &c., of common schools in his town. Vacancies in the office of Town Superintendent are to be filled by any three Justices of the Peace, of the same town, by warrant under their hands and seals.[1]

8. Town Superintendents are to be deemed qualified teachers, while they remain in office. They have power, also, to administer oaths in all cases relating to school affairs and controversies, but they cannot charge any fees therefor.[2]

9. The Town Clerk of a town is required to act as the clerk of the Town Superintendent. He receives all the estimates and apportionments of school money, and records the same; and receives, keeps, and files in his office, all reports made to the Town Superintendent by the Trustees of School Districts, and, when required, all the books and papers belonging to the Town Superintendent. He also notifies the Town Superintendent to make his annual report, when informed by the County Clerk that such report has not been made.[3]

10. Trustees of school districts are to be chosen by the inhabitants of the district entitled to vote, at their first meeting, and thereafter at any annual or special meeting legally convened, whenever a vacancy occurs. Each district elects one Trustee annually, who serves for three years, and until a successor be elected or appointed. Any person elected to fill a vacancy, holds the office only for the unexpired term. Where the office of Trustee becomes vacant by the death, refusal to serve, removal out of the district, or incapacity of the officer, and the vacancy is not supplied by a district meeting within one month thereafter, the Town Superintendent of the town may appoint any person residing in the district to fill the vacancy. The duties of Trustees are: To receive and apply the public money: to call annual and special meetings; to assess and provide for the collection of district taxes; to purchase and lease sites; to build, hire and purchase school-houses, repair and furnish them, and attend to the custody and safe-keeping of district property; to sell and execute conveyances of sites and houses when no longer required; to employ teachers and pay them; to make out and attend to the collection of tax lists; and account annually to the district, and report to the Town Superintendent. Trustees are also required to pay over all balances in their hands, to their successors; and the latter are liable for all lawful contracts made by their predecessors. Joint Trustees are responsible for their own acts, and not for the acts of each other, unless by express agreement; they are not answerable for mistakes of law, or mere errors of judgment, without any fraud or malice;

Laws of 1847, chap. 480; 1 Denio, 141   [3] Laws of 1847, chap 480.
[2] Laws of 1849, chap. 382

but they are liable for fraud or neglect. A contract made by all the Trustees, and signed by two, is binding; and where any official act is performed by two, the presence of the third will be presumed, until the contrary be shown.[1]

11. The Trustees of each school district are required, within thirty, and not less than fifteen days, preceding the time for holding the annual district meeting in each year, to prepare an estimate of the amount of money necessary to be raised in the district for the ensuing year, for the payment of the debts and expenses to be incurred by said district for fuel, furniture, school apparatus, repairs, and insurance of school-house, contingent expenses, and teachers' wages, exclusive of the public money, and the money required by law to be raised by the counties and towns, and the income of local funds, and to cause printed or written notices thereof, to be posted for two weeks previous to said meeting upon the school-house door, and in three or more of the most public places in said district. The Trustees are to present this estimate to the school meeting, and the voters present, of full age, residents of the district, and entitled to hold land in the State, who own or lease real property in the district liable to taxation for school purposes,—or who have paid any district tax (not rate bill) within two years preceding,—or who own any personal property, liable to be taxed for school purposes, in the district, exceeding fifty dollars in value, exclusive of such as is exempt from execution,—and no others, may vote upon such estimate, for each item separately. So much of the estimate as shall be approved by a majority of the voters present, must be levied and raised by tax on the district, in the same manner as other district taxes. If the Trustees neglect to prepare the estimate, or to give the notice required by law, the meeting may adjourn to such time as will enable them to prepare the estimate, and give the notice. If the voters of any district, at their annual meeting, refuse or neglect to raise by tax a sum of money, which added to the public money, and the money raised by the county and town, will support a school for at least four months in the year, keep the school-house in repair, and provide the necessary fuel, it will be the duty of the Trustees to repair the school-house, purchase the necessary fuel, employ a teacher for four months, and levy and collect the additional expense from the district, in the same manner as other district taxes are levied and collected.[2]

12. It is the duty of the Board of Supervisors of every county, at their annual meeting, to cause to be levied and collected from their respective counties, in the same manner as county taxes, a sum equal to the amount of State school moneys apportioned to such

---

[1] Laws of 1847, chap. 480; 9 Johnson, 380; Id., 114; 7 Wendell, 181; 9 Id., 17; 4 Hill, 168; 1 Denio, 214.

[2] Laws of 1849, chap. 140; Id., chap, 404.

county, and to apportion the same as the State moneys are apportioned; also, to levy and collect from each of the towns in their respective counties, in the same manner as other town taxes, a sum
equal to the amount of State school moneys apportioned to such
towns respectively.[1]

13. Every district tax must be assessed by the Trustees, the tax
list made out, and the proper warrant attached, within thirty days
after the district meeting at which the tax was voted. Immediately
after the expiration of the thirty days, the tax list and warrant must
be delivered to the Collector.[2]

14. Where no provision, by tax or otherwise, is made for the
necessary fuel for the school in a district, the Trustees may procure
it, and levy a tax upon the inhabitants to pay for the same. The
Trustees may also expend a sum, not exceeding ten dollars in any
one year, in the repair of the school-house, and collect the same as
a separate tax, or add it to any other tax to be collected.[3]

15. District Clerks are required to record the proceedings of the
district; to enter in the district book true copies of all reports made
by the Trustees to the Town Superintendent; to give notice of
special meetings called by the Trustees, to each inhabitant in the
district liable to pay taxes, at least five days before the meeting, by
reading the notice in the hearing of such inhabitant, or in case of his
absence from home, by leaving a copy thereof, or of so much thereof
as relates to the time and place of meeting, at the place of his abode,
at least six days before the time of the meeting; to affix a notice in
writing of the time and place for any adjourned district meeting,
when adjourned over one month, in at least four of the most public
places in the district, at least five days before the meeting; to give the
like notice of every annual meeting; to keep and preserve all books,
records and papers, belonging to his office, and deliver them to his
successor; within ten days after each annual or special meeting for
the election of officers, to forward to the Town Clerk the names of
the persons elected to the several offices; and to receive and keep
the District School Journal, and cause the same to be bound.[4]

16. It is the duty of the Collector of a school district, to collect the
moneys required by all warrants placed in his hands, within the time
required therein, and to pay the same over to the Trustees, taking
their receipt therefor. When required by the Trustees, the Collector
must execute a bond with sureties, one or more, to be approved by
them, in double the amount of any tax list to be collected by him.
He has the same powers as a Collector of a town, authorized to
collect town and county taxes, and may in like manner, seize any
property under his warrant, except the arms and accoutrements of a

---

[1] Laws of 1849, chap. 140.
[2] Laws of 1849, chap. 382.
[3] Laws of 1849, chap. 382.

[4] Laws of 1841, chap. 267; Laws of 1847,
chap. 480; 6 Wendell, 486; 11 Id., 604; 6
Hill, 646; 1 Denio, 214; 3 Id., 526.

person enrolled in the militia, required by act of Congress to be kept by such person. The jurisdiction of a Collector is unlimited, and extends to any other district or town in the same county, or in any other county where the district is a joint district, and composed of territory from adjoining counties.[1]

17. The Librarian of a district has charge of the library thereof, subject to the directions and instructions of the Trustees, to whom he is amenable, and by whom he may be removed for wilful disobedience of their directions, or for wilful neglect of duty. If the office of Librarian be vacant, the District Clerk discharges the duties.[2]

18. The Town Superintendent may accept the resignation of a school district officer, for sufficient cause. Vacancies, except in the office of Trustee, are to be filled by the Trustees, or a majority of them; the persons so appointed will hold their offices until the next annual meeting, and until others are elected in their places.[3]

19. The term of office of school district officers expires at the time of the annual meeting, and they do not hold over till others are elected to fill their places.[4]

20. The apportionment of a school tax must be made by all the Trustees, or by two, the other being present, otherwise the warrant will be void.[5]

21. Want of notice of any annual or special district school meeting will not invalidate the proceedings, except where the omission was wilful and fraudulent. The annual meeting, however, must be held at the time and place fixed at the previous annual meeting.[6]

22. Whenever a suit is commenced against the Trustees of a school district, in consequence of any official act by them performed, in pursuance of, and by the direction of such district, on the final determination thereof, or whenever, after the final determination of a suit commenced by or against any Trustees or other officers of a school district, a majority of the taxable inhabitants of any school district so determine, it will be the duty of the Trustees to ascertain the amount of all costs, charges and expenses paid by such officer, in the following manner, and to assess and collect the same as other district taxes are assessed and collected : The officer must serve a copy of his account, verified by oath or affirmation, upon the Trustees, together with a notice that on a certain day, to be therein specified, he will present such account to the Board of Supervisors of the county. It is the duty of the officer on whom the notice, &c., is served, to attend at the time specified. The Board of Supervisors will examine the account, and may adjourn from time to time for that purpose. The account of the officer, with his oath, is prima facie

---

[1] Laws of 1847, chap. 480; 5 Wendell, 170; 1 Denio, 233 ; 2 Id., 86.
[2] Laws of 1847, chap. 480.
[3] Laws of 1847, chap. 480.
[4] Laws of 1849, chap. 382.
[5] 4 Denio, 125.
[6] Laws of 1847, chap. 480; 3 Denio, 525.

evidence of its correctness. The Board may make an order directing the whole, or such part of the account as they think proper, excepting the same appears to have been occasioned by the wilful neglect or misconduct of the claimant, to be paid by the district. Within thirty days after service of a copy of the order on the Trustees, it is their duty to enter the same in the book of records of the district, and issue a warrant for the collection of the amount directed to be paid in the same manner as upon a tax voted by the district. The amount, when collected, is to be paid to the officer. This provision does not extend to suits for penalties, nor to suits or proceedings to enforce the decisions of the Superintendent.[1]

23. Where two school districts are consolidated into one, the new district succeeds to all the rights of property of the old districts. When a district is annulled, the Town Superintendent of the town in which the school-house is located, is required to sell the property of the annulled district at public auction, notices of which are to be posted, at least five days previous to the sale, in three or more public places in the town, one of which must be in the annulled district. The proceeds of the sale are to be first applied to the payment of the debts of the district, and the residue thereof apportioned among the taxable inhabitants of such district, according to their respective assessments on the last assessment roll of the town, or towns, within which the district is located.[2]

24. Appeals may be made to the State Superintendent, from any decision made by a school district meeting; from any official act, proceeding, or decision, of a Town Superintendent, and from a refusal to discharge any duty imposed upon him by law, or the regulations of the State Superintendent; from the decision, or act, of any officer required to perform any duty under the Common School Law; from any act or decision of Trustees of school districts, in relation to the libraries or the books therein; and in cases of disputes between districts and their officers, or between different districts.[3]

25. The person aggrieved by the act complained of, only, can appeal. Appeals may be made by Trustees, in behalf of their districts, whenever they are aggrieved. An appeal must be in writing, and signed by the appellant. Where Trustees make an appeal, it must be signed by all, or a reason must be given for the omission, verified by the oath of the appellant, or of some other person acquainted with such reason. A copy of the appeal, duly verified, and of all the statements, maps and papers, intended to be presented in support of it, must be served on the officers whose act or decision is complained of, or some one of them; or, where a district is concerned, on the District Clerk, or one of the Trustees, within

---

[1] Laws of 1847, chap. 172; Laws of 1849, chap. 389.
[2] Laws of 1849, chap. 382.
[3] Laws of 1847, chap. 480; 11 Wendell, 90; and Regulations of the State Superintendent.

thirty days after the making the decision, or the performance of the act complained of, or within that time after the appellant had knowledge of such act or decision, unless some satisfactory excuse be rendered for the delay.

26. The party on whom the appeal is served, must answer the same within ten days afer such service, either by concurring in tne appellant's statement of facts, or by a separate answer. Such statement or answer, must be signed by all the Trustees, or other officers, whose act, or decision, is complained of, or, if this be omitted, a good reason, on oath, must be given therefor. Where the parties concur in a statement, no oath will be required ; but all facts, maps, or papers, not concurred in, or agreed upon, and evidenced by their signatures on both sides, must be verified by oath. All oaths required in cases of appeal, may be taken before any Judge of a Court of Record, Commissioner of Deeds, or Justices of the Peace.

27. A copy of the answer, and of all the statements, maps and papers, intended to be presented in support of it, must be served upon the appellants, or some one of them, within ten days after service of a copy of the appeal, unless further time be given by the State Superintendent; but no replication nor rejoinder shall be allowed, except by permission of that officer, and in reference exclusively to matters arising on the answer which he may deem pertinent to the issue. Replications and rejoinders, when allowed, must be duly verified by oath, and copies thereof served on the opposite party. Proof or admission of the service of copies of the appeal, answer, and all papers intended to be presented in support thereof, or used on the hearing, must accompany the same.

28. When any proceeding of a district meeting is appealed from, and when the inhabitants of a district generally are interested in the matter of the appeal; or, where an inhabitant might be an appellant, had the decision or proceeding been the reverse ; any one or more of such inhabitants may answer the appeal, with or without the Trustees.

29. Where an appeal has relation to the formation or alteration of a school district, it must be accompanied by a map, exhibiting the site of the school-house, the roads, the old and new lines of districts, the different lots, the particular location and distance from the school-houses of the persons aggrieved, and their relative distance, if there are two or more school-houses in question ; also a list of all the taxable inhabitants in the district or territory to be affected by the question; the valuation of the property, taken from the last assessment roll; and the number of children between five and sixteen belonging to each person, distinguishing the districts to which they respectively belong.

30. When the copy of an appeal is served, all proceedings upon, or in continuation of, the act complained of, or consequent in any way

upon such act, must be suspended, until the case is decided. And where the Town Superintendent, or the Trustees of a district, have money in their hands, which is the subject of dispute and appeal, they must retain such moneys to abide the event.

31. Whenever a decision is made by the State Superintendent, and communicated to the Town Superintendent, respecting the formation, division, or alteration of districts, the latter must cause the decision to be recorded in the office of the Town Clerk. All other decisions communicated to him, or to the Trustees of a district, are to be kept among the official papers of the Clerk of the town or district; and the District Clerk is required to record all such as come to his hands, in the district book kept by him.

FORMS.

§ 939. *Town Superintendent's Bond, with Approval.*

Know all men by these presents: That we, A. B., C. D., and E. F., of the the town of   , in the county of   , are held and firmly bound unto L. M., Esq., Supervisor of said town, in the penal sum of   dollars, [*double the amount of school money received from all sources during the preceding year,*] to be paid to the said L. M. or his successor in office; to the which payment, well and truly to be made, we bind ourselves and our legal representatives, jointly and severally, firmly by these presents. Witness our hands and seals, this   day of   , 18   .

Whereas, the above bounden A. B. has been duly elected [*or*, appointed] Town Superintendent of Common Schools for the said town of   : Now, therefore, the condition of this obligation is such, that if the said A. B. shall faithfully apply, and legally disburse, all the school money which may come into his hands during his term of office as such Town Superintendent, and faithfully discharge all the duties of said office, then this obligation to be void ; else, to remain in full force.

Signed, sealed and delivered, }
    in presence of   }
        G. H.

A. B. [L s.]
C. D. [L s.]
E. F. [L s.]

I approve of C. D. and E. F., as sureties to the foregoing [*or*, within] bond. Dated the   day of   , 18   .

L. M. Supervisor of the Town of

§ 940. *Warrant of three Justices appointing Town Superintendent to fill a Vacancy.*[1]

Town of   , ss:

Whereas, A. B., duly elected Town Superintendent of Common Schools of said town, at the annual town meeting held therein, on the   day of   , 18   , has neglected to execute the bond required by law; [or, has removed from said town; or, has deceased; or, Whereas, the bond executed by A. B., duly elected Town Superintendent, &c., has not been filed and approved in conformity to law;] by reason whereof, the said office of Town Superintendent has become vacant:

Now, therefore, we, the undersigned, three of the Justices of the Peace of said town of   , in pursuance of the statute in such case made and provided, do hereby appoint C. D. Town Superintendent of Common Schools of said town of   , to hold the said office until a successor shall be duly elected or appointed.

Given under our hands and seals, this   day of   18 .

H. S. [L. s.]
C. H. [L. s.]
G. G. [L. s.]

---

§ 941. *Notice to the Town Superintendent, to give Additional Security.*

To Mr. A. B., Town Superintendent of Common Schools of the Town of   :

You are hereby notified, that in my opinion, the security heretofore given by you is not sufficient for the full protection of the public against the loss of the school money, likely to be intrusted to you; and you are therefore required to furnish satisfactory security within five days after the receipt of this notice, otherwise your office will become vacant.

Dated   , the   day of   , 18 .

Yours, &c.,

L. M., Supervisor of the Town of

---

§ 942. *Resolution Creating a New District.*

At a meeting held for the purpose of forming a new school district, in the town of   , at the office of the Town Clerk, [or, house of R. T.,] in said town, on the   day of   , 18 : Present, A. B., Town Superintendent of Common Schools:*

Resolved, That a new school district be formed, to consist of the

---

[1] The Justices making the appointment, must cause the warrant to be forthwith filed in the office of the Town Clerk, and immediately give notice to the person appointed.

present districts number one and number two, [*or*, the present district number one, and part of district number two; *or*, parts of districts number one and number two:] which said district shall be numbered   , and shall be bounded as follows: [*state the boundaries with as much precision as the case will admit.*]

The formation of the aforesaid district, involving an alteration of districts number one and number two, [*or, as the case may be,*] the consent of the Trustees of the said districts to such alteration has been presented to the Town Superintendent, and filed with the Town Clerk. [*If such consent has not been given, make the following entry:* The formation of the aforesaid district, involving an alteration of districts number one and number two, and the consent of the Trustees of district number one to such alteration not having been given, it is ordered that a notice in writing, of the said alteration, signed by the Town Superintendent, be served on one of the Trustees of the said district, by the Town Superintendent.]

S. G., Town Clerk of said town of   , and
Clerk of the Town Superintendent.

---

§ 943. *Consent of Trustees, to be Indorsed on a Copy of the Order.*[1]

We hereby consent to the alterations made in district number   , in the town of   , by the order of which the within is a copy. Dated   , the   day of   . 18 .

G. H., ⎫
L. M., ⎬ Trustees of District No.   .
E. F., ⎭

---

§ 944. *Notice to Trustees Not giving Consent, to be served with a Copy of the Order, on any one of the Trustees.*

The Trustees of district number   , in the town of   , will take notice, that an order was made this day by the Town Superintendent of common schools of the said town, of which the following [*or, within*] is a copy, by which certain alterations in the said district are made, as will appear by the said order; and that

[1] The consent of the Trustees should be given at a meeting of the whole, or of a majority, when all have been notified to attend. Where an alteration of several districts is made at the same time,—the Trustees of some of the districts consenting thereto, and those of the others, withholding their consent,—the alteration takes effect immediately as to those districts the Trustees of which signify their consent. (3 Denio, 114.)

such alterations will take effect after three months from the service of this notice. Dated , the day of , 18 .

> A. B., Town Superintendent of Common
> Schools of the town of .

---

§ 945. *Acknowledgment of Service of the foregoing, to be Indorsed on a Copy.*

I, G. H., one of the Trustees of school district number , in the town of , hereby acknowledge due service of a notice and copy order, of which the within is a copy, this day of , 18 .   G. H.

---

§ 946. *Notice of the First Meeting in a District, to Organize.*[1]

To R. F., a taxable inhabitant of District No. , in the Town of :

The Town Superintendent of common schools of the town of , having by an order, of which the following is a copy, formed a new district in the said town, to be numbered , consisting of the territory particularly specified in the said order; you are hereby required to notify every inhabitant of the said district qualified to vote at district meetings, to attend the first district meeting of the said district, which is hereby appointed to be held at the house of , in the said town, on the day of next, at six o'clock in the afternoon, by reading this notice in the hearing of each such inhabitant, or in case of his absence from home, by leaving a copy of this notice, or of so much thereof as relates to the time and place of such meeting, at least six days before the said time so appointed for the said meeting. Dated, &c.

> A. B., Town Superintendent of Common
> Schools, of the town of .

---

[1] A copy of the order forming the district, should be annexed to the above. The notice is required to be given within twenty days after the formation of the district. If it be necessary to give notice to the Trustees of the alteration of a district, then the notice for the first meeting should specify a day subsequent to the expiration of three months after the service of the notice on the Trustees, as the district cannot organize until after that time. The inhabitant serving the foregoing notice should keep a memorandum of the persons served with the same, specifying the time and the manner in which such service is made; and the memorandum, certified by him, should be delivered to the chairman, or clerk, of the district meeting, and read, that it may be known whether all the voters have been notified. The original notice and return should be filed with the district Clerk.

§ 947. *Notice of the Sale of a School-House, &c., by the Town Superintendent, where a District is annulled, and portions thereof annexed to other Districts.*

NOTICE.

Notice is hereby given, that I shall sell at public auction, the school-house and other property belonging to the former School District number   , in the town of   ., at said school-house, [*or, such place as the Town Superintendent may designate,*] on the   day of   `next, [*or, instant,*] at   o'clock in the   noon; said school district having been annulled according to law, and portions thereof annexed to other districts.

Dated   , the   day of   , 18   .

A. B., Town Superintendent of Common
Schools of the Town of   .

---

§ 948. *Apportionment of the Proceeds of the Sale of the Property belonging to an Annulled District.*

APPORTIONMENT OF PROCEEDS OF SALE OF PROPERTY BELONGING TO ANNULLED SCHOOL DISTRICT NUMBER   , IN THE TOWN OF   .

Town of   , ss: .

School District Number   , in said Town of   , having been annulled according to law, by my order dated on the   day of   , 18   , and the property of said district having been duly and regularly sold by me, at public auction, and the debts thereof paid out of the proceeds of such sale; I do hereby make the following apportionment of the residue of such proceeds, among the taxable inhabitants of said annulled district, number   , according to their respective assessments on the last assessment roll of the said town of   :

Names of Inhabitants.	Amount apportioned to each.	
	Doll's.	Cents.
John Doe, Richard Roe, &c., &c.,	25 · 1	01 90
	Total Am't.	

Dated, &c., [*as in* § 947.]

---

§ 949. *Resolution for the Alteration of a District.*

At a meeting, &c.: [*as in* § 942 *to the* *, *and then add:*]

Resolved, That districts number one and number two, in the said town of   , be altered as follows, viz: by setting off the farms and parcels of land occupied by J. B., T. J., and W. R., from district number one, in which they have heretofore been included, to district number two; so that the east boundary of district number one shall hereafter be the easterly line of the farms and parcels of land occupied by C. D., G. H., and S. T., and the west boundary of district number two shall be the westerly line of the farms and parcels of land occupied by the said J. B., T. J., and W. R.; the said J. B., T. J., and W. R., having consented to be set off as aforesaid.

The written consent of the Trustees of the said districts number one and two, having been presented to the Town Superintendent, is filed with the Town Clerk; [or, the consent of the Trustees of the said districts respectively; or, of said district number one; or, number two;] not having been given to the said alteration, it is ordered that a notice, in writing, of such alteration, signed by the Town Superintendent, be served on the Clerk, or some of the Trustees of each of the said districts; [or, of said district number one; or, number two.]

S. T., Town Clerk, &c.

§ 950. *Resolution for the Formation, or Alteration, of a Joint District, from two or more Towns.*[1]

At a meeting held for the purpose of forming a joint district from district number   , in the town of   , and district number   , in the town of   , [or, of altering joint district number   , situate partly in the town of   , and partly in the town of   ,] at the office, &c., on the   day of, &c.: Present, A. B. and G. H., Town Superintendents of Common Schools of the said towns:

Resolved, &c., [*as in* § 942, *or* § 949, *with such alterations as the circumstances of the case may require.*]

A. B., Town Superintendent of Common
Schools of the Town of   .

G. H., Town Superintendent of Common
Schools of the Town of

§ 951. *Certificate to Teacher, by Town Superintendent.*

Town of   , ss:

I hereby certify, that I have examined C. F., and do believe that he [or, she] is well qualified, in respect to moral character, learning

---

[1] The resolution should be signed in duplicate: one of them is to be recorded in each town.

and ability, to instruct a common school in this town, for one year from
the date hereof.

Given under my hand, at   , this   day of   , 18   .

A. B., Town Superintendent of Common
Schools of the Town of   .

---

§ 952. *Instrument Annulling Teacher's Certificate.*[1]

Town of   , ss:

Having inquired into certain complaints against C. F., heretofore
licensed as a teacher of common schools of said town, and being of
opinion that he [*or*, she] does not possess the requisite qualifications
as a teacher, in respect to moral character; [*or, as the case may be;*]
and having given at least ten days previous notice in writing to said
teacher, and to the Trustees of the district in which he is employed,
of my intention so to do; I have annulled, and hereby do annul, the
said certificate and license so granted as aforesaid.

Given under my hand, this   day of   , 18   .

A. B., Town Superintendent of Common
Schools of the Town of   .

---

§ 953. *Annual Report of the Town Superintendent, to be made to the County Clerk.*

To P. V., Clerk of the County of   :

I, A. B., Town Superintendent of common schools of the town of
          , in said county of   , in conformity to the statutes
in relation to common schools, do report: That the number of entire
school districts in said town, organized according to law, is   ;
and that the number of parts of school districts in said town, is   ;
that the number of joint districts, the school-houses of which are
situated, wholly or partly, in said town, is   ; that the number of entire districts from which the necessary reports have been
made for the present year, within the time limited by law, is   ;
and that the number of parts of districts from which such reports
have been made, is   ; that the number of schools for colored
children taught in said town, during the year aforesaid, for four
months or upwards, by a duly qualified teacher, was   .

---

[1] A note in writing, containing the name of the teacher, and the time of annulling the cer
tificate, or a duplicate of the instrument must be filed in the Town Clerk's Office.

And I do further certify and report, that the whole amount of money received by me, or my predecessor [or, predecessors] in office, for the use of common schools, during the year ending on the date of this report, and since the date of the last report, for said town, is $; of which sum the part received from the County Treasurer, is $: the part from the town Collector, is $; and that we have collected the sum of $ for penalties; [*If nothing has been collected for penalties, omit the reference to the same; and if money has been received from any other source, specify it here:*] that the said sum of money has been apportioned and paid to the several districts from which the necessary reports were received, for the purposes and in the proportions following, viz: the sum of $ for the payment of teachers' wages, and the sum of $ for the purchase of district libraries; that the sum of $ was apportioned by me to district number , for colored children in said district, between the ages of five and sixteen years, who have attended a school taught in district number , in said town, by a duly qualified teacher, for four months during the preceding year; and $ to district number , for colored children so attending in said district; and that I have deducted the said several amounts from the sums by me apportioned to the said districts number and , respectively. And I further certify, that during the year before mentioned, I have not collected any fines, penalties or forfeitures; [or, that during the year before mentioned, I have collected a penalty of $25, imposed on C. D., a Trustee of District number , in said town, for signing a false report; and that my costs and charges in such collection amounted to $; and that the balance of such penalty was by me added to the school money received by me and apportioned as above mentioned;] that the school books most in use in the common schools of said town are the following, viz: [*Specify the same as reported by the Trustees:*] And I further certify the tables following, to be true abstracts from the reports of the Trustees of the several districts, and parts of districts, as aforesaid.[1]

---

[1] The children of Indian 'parents, between 5 and 16 years of age, are not to be enumerated, unless attending school for at least three months, during the previous year; and it is the duty of the Town Superintendent, where a school is kept for the instruction of Indian children in the elementary branches, under charge of a competent teacher, for four months in the year, to apportion and pay over to the teacher, or teachers, on the written consent of the peace makers for the Indians residing on the reservation where the children attending the school reside, such part of the public money as shall be in proportion to the number of children instructed for an average period of three months. Satisfactory evidence must be furnished to the Town Superintendent, of the time, and the number of children taught, and the facts stated succinctly in his report. (Laws of 1846, chap. 45.)

PARTS OF DISTRICTS.	DISTRICTS.	DISTRICTS AND PARTS.	
No. 9. / No. 8. / No. 7. / No. 6. / No. 5.	No. 4. / No. 3. / No. 2. / No. 1.	Districts and parts of Districts from which Reports have been made.	
8 68	5 8 6 6	7 8 3 4	**Mo.** Whole length of time any school has been kept therein.
11 43	4 25	2 10	**Days.**
11 43	4 6 7 6	7 8 4 3	**Mo.** Length of time such school has been kept by licensed teachers.
27	10	2 16	**Days.**
116 29	11 16 17 9	10 15 22 14	**Dolls.** For Teachers' wages.	Am't of money rec'd by district.
58 78	80 72 35	80 30 02 80	**Cts.**	
	4 9 3	5 11 7 42	**Dolls.** For Libraries.	
	82 60 00 49	92 14 65 85	**Cts.**	
			No. of children taught.	
			No. of do. over 6 and under 16, in each district.	
			Dolls. Am't paid for teachers' wages, besides public moneys. **Cts.**	
			No. of children between 5 and 16, taught in colored schools.	
			Dolls. Am't of public money rec'd from children attending colored schools. **Cts.**	
			Dolls. Am't paid for teachers' wages, in colored schools, besides public money. **Cts.**	
			No. of times visited by Town Superintendent.	
			No. of pupils who have attended less than 2 mo.	
			Two mo., and less than 4.	
			Four mo., and less than 6.	
			Six mo., and less than 8.	
			Eight mo., and less than 10.	
			Ten mo., and less than 12.	
			Twelve months.	
			No. of select and private schools not incorporated.	
			No. of pupils attending.	
			No. of volumes in district library.	

Dated at　　　　　, this 1st day of July, A. D. 18　.

A. B., Town Sup't of Common Schools

of the Town of　　　　　.

' The annual report of the Town Superintendent is to be made between the first day of July and the first day of August in each year, and is to be dated on the first day of July. ﬀ is necessary for the Town Superintendent to include, also, in his report, the amount, ﬀ

§ 954. *List of Votes Taken, by Ayes and Noes, to be kept by the District Clerk.*[1]

Names of Voters.	On change of Site of School House.		On motion to build School House.		On resolution to raise tax of $.		On resolution to raise tax for Apparatus.	
	AYES.	NOES.	AYES.	NOES.	AYES.	NOES.	AYES.	NOES.
C. D.	1			1		●		
E. F.		1		1				
G. H.		1		1				
R. T.	1			1				
O. P.	1		1					
	3	2	1	4	16	14	23	15

§ 955. *Form of Minutes of Proceedings of District Meetings, to be kept by the Clerk.*

At a meeting of the legal voters of school district number   ,
in the town of   , held pursuant to adjournment, at   ,
on the   day of   , 18   , [*or, if it be an annual meet-ing, say:* At an annual meeting of, &c., held pursuant to appoint-ment and public notice, at, &c.; *if a special meeting, say:* At a special meeting of, &c., called by the Trustees of said district, and held pursuant to special notice, at, &c.,] G. H. was chosen chairman, and C. D. was present as District Clerk; [*or, if the Clerk is absent, say:* E. F. was appointed Clerk pro tem., the District Clerk being absent.]*

Resolved, Unanimously, [*or,* by a majority of two-thirds of the voters present; *or,* by a majority of the votes of those present; *or, as the case may be,*] that, &c. [*Here state with precision the pro-ceedings of the meeting.*]

§ 956. *Record of Proceedings where the subject of a Change of Site has been under Discussion.*

At a meeting of the taxable inhabitants of District No.   , in the town of   , held at the school-house, in pursuance of notice to all the legal voters therein, on the   day of   , 18   , A. B. was chosen, &c., [*as in* § 955, *to the* *, *and then add :*] The written consent of the Town Superintendent of common schools of

---

any, of money paid for teachers' wages, in addition to the public money paid therefor; the amount of taxes levied for purchasing school-house sites; for building, hiring, purchasing repairing and insuring school-houses; for fuel and supplying deficiencies in tax lists; for district libraries; or for any other purpose allowed by law; together with such other in-formation as the State Superintendent may require. · (Laws of 1847, chap. 480.)

[1] When the site is to be changed in a district not altered, the law requires the vote to be taken by ayes and noes. When votes are taken in this manner the names of those voting should be written in full.

the town having been read, stating, that, in his opinion, the removal of the site of the school-house in said district is necessary; and it having been moved and seconded, that the present site of the school-house in the said district be changed, and that [*here state the locality of the contemplated site*] be designated as the site of a school-house for the said district, and the question being taken by ayes and noes, it was carried, [*or*, it was lost,] two-thirds of all the taxable inhabitants of said district being present at such meeting voting for such removal, and in favor of such new site; [*or*, not voting in favor thereof.] Those who voted in the affirmative, were C. D., E. F., &c., &c.; those who voted in the negative, were O. P., S. T., &c., &c. Ayes,   ; Noes,   .[1]

C. D., District Clerk.

---

§ 957. *Declaration, to be made by a Challenged Person.*

I do declare and affirm, that I am an actual resident of this school district, and that I am qualified to vote at this meeting.

---

§ 958. *Resolution Authorizing the Sale of Former Site of School House, &c.*

Resolved, By a majority of the votes of those present, that the Trustees of this school district be directed to sell the former site of the school-house in said district, with the buildings thereon, and the appurtenances, at such price, and upon such terms, as they shall deem most advantageous to the district.

---

§ 959. *Resolution for Raising a Tax for the Erection of a School House.*

The certificate of the Town Superintendent of common schools of the town of   , having been obtained, stating that, in his opinion, a larger sum than four hundred dollars ought to be raised for building a school-house in the said district, namely: the sum of   dollars; therefore,

Resolved, That the said sum of   dollars be raised by tax upon the said district, [*insert*, to be paid in four equal annual installments of   dollars each, *if necessary*,] for the purpose of building a school-house therein.

---

[1] In stating the ayes and noes, the Christian names of the voters should be given.

§ 960. *Resolution for the Purchase of a Site, to be separate from the foregoing resolution.*

Resolved, That the sum of   dollars be raised by tax upon the said district, for the purchase of the site for a new school-house, heretofore designated by the legal voters thereof.

§ 961. *Order of Trustees for Teacher's Wages.*

To A. B., Esq., Town Superintendent of Common Schools of the Town of

Pay to C. F., a teacher duly employed by us, and qualified according to law,   dollars, that being the amount which he is entitled to receive out of the moneys in your hands applicable to the payment of teachers' wages, and apportioned to our district. Dated , this   day of   , 18 .

G. H.,) Trustees
L. M., } of District
E. F.,) No.

§ 962. *Order for Library Money.*

To A. B., Esq., Town Superintendent, &c.:

Pay to   , the sum of   dollars, that being the amount of the library money in your hands due to school district number , in said town. Dated, &c., [*as in* § 961.]

§ 963. *Account of the Trustees, and Inventory of District Property, to be Entered and Signed in their Book, at or before each Annual Meeting.*

G. H., L. M., and E. F., Trustees of School District No.   , in the Town of   , in account with said District.

Dr.   Cr.

DATES.		$	cts.	DATES.		$	cts.
18 . June 30.	To amount collected on tax list.	58	69	18 . July 1,	By paid for apparatus, as per voucher No. 1.	15	00
Sept. 15.	To do. do.	28	92	Sept. 10,	By do. do. teachers' wages do. do. No. 2,	37	02
				Dec. 15,	By do. do. for fuel, do. do. No 3,	9	50
				Jan. 13,	By do. do. for repairing school-house, do. do. No. 4,	13	23
				May 2,	By bal. on hand,	12	86
		87	61			87	61

STATEMENT OF MOVABLE PROPERTY, BELONGING TO DISTRICT
NUMBER , VIZ:

One stove and pipe ; one pail; two chairs; one broom; one map of the United States, &c., &c. [*Specify all the different articles, including the books belonging to the district.*]

We, the subscribers, Trustees of District number , in the town of , do hereby certify, that the preceding, from page to page , inclusive, contains a true and accurate account of all the moneys received by us, for the use of said district, and of the expenditure thereof ; and a correct statement and inventory of all the movable property belonging to said district.

Dated, &c., [*as in* § 961.]

---

§ 964. *Annual Estimate of Trustees.*

ANNUAL ESTIMATE.

The Trustees of School District Number , in the Town of , in the County of , estimate the amount of money necessary to be raised in said district for the ensuing year, exclusive of the public money, and the money required by law to be raised by the county and town, [*insert*, and the income of local funds, *if there be such funds,*] as follows:

For providing fuel,	- - -	$10 00
" " furniture,	- - -	3 00
" " school apparatus,	- -	5 00
" paying for repairs of school-house,	-	7 50
" " insurance of school-house,	-	3 30
" " contingent expenses,	-	5 00
" " teachers' wages,	- -	56 00
	Total,	$69 80

Dated, &c., [*as in* § 961.]

---

§ 965. *Notice to be Posted on the School House Door.*]

SCHOOL DISTRICT NOTICE.

Notice is hereby given, that the trustees of school district number , in the town of , have prepared their estimate of

---

[1] The law does not, in terms, require a copy of the estimate to accompany the notice, but it would be well to annex one thereto.

the amount of money necessary to be raised in said district for the ensuing year, for the payment of the debts and expenses to be incurred by said district for fuel, furniture, school apparatus, repairs and insurance of school-house, contingent expenses and teachers' wages, exclusive of the public money, and the money to be raised by the county and town; [*insert*, and the income of local funds, *if necessary:*] and that the said estimate will be presented to the annual meeting, to be held at the school-house, in said district, on the   day of   instant, [*or*, next.]

Dated, &c., [*as in* § 961.]

---

§ 966. *District Tax List, and Warrant for its Collection.*

List of taxes apportioned by the Trustees of district number   , in the town of   , on the taxable inhabitants of the said district, and corporations holding property therein, and upon real estate lying within the boundaries of such district, the owners of which are non-residents thereof, for the purpose of raising the sum of   , laid and charged on the said district, according to law:

NAMES OF INHABITANTS AND CORPORATIONS.	AM'T OF TAXES.	
	Dolls.	Cts.
H. G.,	10	10
C. D., Executor of the estate of E. D., deceased,	37	90
The Bank of ,	89	10
The manufacturing company,	32	04

Statement and description of unoccupied and unimproved lands of non-residents of said district, upon which a tax has been imposed as above stated :

Number & Description of Lots and Parts of Lots.	Quantity of land therein liable to taxation.	Valuation of such quantity.		Amount of tax.	
		Dolls.	Cts.	Dolls.	Cts.
Lot No. 69,	594 acres.	4000	00	50	00
Southwest quarter of lot No. 23,	2½ "	5	00	0	50
Tract not subdivided, [Or, Tract, the subdivision of which cannot be ascertained, bounded, &c.,]	5 "	50	00	3	12½
	" "	"	"	" ·	"

To the Collector of School District No.   , in the town of   , in the County of   :

You are hereby commanded to collect from each of the taxable inhabitants and corporations named in the foregoing list, and of the owners of the real estate described therein, the several sums men tioned in the last column of the said list, opposite to the persons and corporations so named, and to the several tracts of land so described, together with the per centage allowed by law for your fees; and in case any person, upon whom such tax is imposed, shall neglect or refuse to pay the same, you are to levy the same by distress and sale of the goods and chattels of the person or corporation so taxed, in the same manner as on warrants issued by the board of Supervisors to the Collectors of towns; and you are to make a return of this warrant within thirty days after the delivery thereof to you; and within that time to pay over all moneys collected, by virtue hereof, to the Trustees of the said district, some or one of them; and if any tax on the real estate of a non-resident mentioned in the said list, shall be unpaid at the time when you are required to return this warrant, you are to deliver to the Trustees of the said district an account thereof, according to law. Given under our hands, this   day of   , 18   .

> G. H.,
> &c., &c., } Trustees, &c.

---

§ 967. *District Collector's Bond.*[1]

Know all men by these presents: That we, O. P. and R. F., are held and firmly bound to G. H., L. M., and E. F., Trustees of school district number   , in the town of   , in the sum of [*insert double the amount to be collected*] dollars to be paid to the said G. H., L. M., and E. F., Trustees as aforesaid, or to the survivor, or survivors, of them, or their successors: to the which payment, well and truly to be made, we bind ourselves, our heirs, executors and administrators, firmly by these presents.

Sealed with our seals, and dated this   day of   , A. D. 18   .

Whereas, the above bounden O. P. has been chosen [*or*, appointed] Collector of the above mentioned school district number   , in the town of   , in conformity to the statutes relating to common schools: Now, therefore, the condition of this obligation is such, that if he, the said O. P., shall well and truly collect and pay over, the moneys assessed upon the taxable inhabitants of said district, member in a tax list dated the   day of   , and this day received by the said Collector, which assessment amounts to a total sum of   dollars and   cents; and shall, in all respects, duly and faithfully execute the said warrant, and all the duties of his office as Collector of such district, then this obligation shall be void; otherwise, to be in full force and virtue.

> Signed, sealed, and delivered,)
> in presence of   }   O. P. [L. S.]
> A. B.   R. F. [L. S.]

---

[1] The Collector's bond must be executed within the time allowed by the Trustees, which cannot be less than ten days.

§ 968. *Notice that Collector will receive Taxes.*

SCHOOL DISTRICT NOTICE.

Notice is hereby given, that the undersigned has received a tax list from the Trustees of School District Number , in the Town of , to collect the sum of dollars and cents, in said district; and that all persons who pay in their taxes to me within two weeks from this date, will be charged one per cent. as my fees for collection, and five per cent. will be required to be paid on all sums collected after that time. Dated , this day of , 18 .

O. P., Collector of School District No. .

§ 969. *Renewal of Warrant.*[1]

We hereby renew the within warrant, with the approbation of the Town Superintendent of Common Schools, this day of , 18 .

G. H., } Trustees of
&c., &c., } School District No. .

§ 970. *Return of Collector to the Tax List and Warrant.*

I, the subscriber, Collector of school district number , in the town of , do hereby certify and make return to the within tax list and warrant, that I have collected, by virtue thereof, the sum. of , as therein required, and that the sum of , assessed on the real estate of , a non-resident mentioned in the said list, remains unpaid.

Dated , the day of , 18 .

O. P., Collector.

§ 971. *Notice of Levy and Sale by Collector.*

SCHOOL DISTRICT COLLECTOR'S SALE.

By virtue of a tax list and warrant, issued by the Trustees of school district number , in the of , to me directed and delivered, I have levied upon and taken the fol-

---

[1] Warrants may be renewed as often as may be necessary, with the approbation of the Town Superintendent, but not otherwise. Applications for his approbation must state the facts and circumstances, and the reason why the warrant has not been collected, and must be verified by oath.

[2] The notice must be given at least six days previous to the sale. and copies must be posted up in three public places in the town in which the sale is to be made

lowing goods and chattels of R. T., [or, in the possession of R. T.,] viz: [specify the articles:] which I shall sell at public auction, at the house of L. M., in said town, on the   day of   next, [or, instant,] at ten o'clock in the forenoon of that day. Dated at   , the   day of   , 18   .

O. P., Collector of School District No.   .

---

§ 972. *Affidavit of Verification of the Account of a District Officer, Claiming to have Costs, &c., Reimbursed.*

County, ss:

A. B., of said county, being duly sworn, says, that he was Collector of school district number   , in the town of   , in said county, for and during the year immediately preceding the   day of   , 18   , and that on the   day of   , 18   , a suit was commenced against him in the Supreme Court of the State of New York, in favor of C. D., plaintiff therein, claiming to recover damages against this deponent for acts performed by virtue of or under color of his office; that such suit was decided in favor of the said C. D., [or, in favor of the deponent;] that the foregoing is a just and true account of costs, charges and expenses, incurred by this deponent, in and about the defence of the said suit, [*insert here, if the suit was decided in favor of the officer,* and not collected, or collectible of the plaintiff therein,] and that the same have been fully paid and discharged by this deponent.

Sworn to, [or, affirmed,] this   day of }   A. B.
of   , 18   , before me, }
G. H., Justice of the Peace.

---

§ 973. *Notice to Accompany the Copy of the Account served on the Trustees.*

To G. H., L. M., and E. F., Trustees of District No.   , in the Town of   :

You are hereby notified, that an account, and the verification thereof, of which the above [or, within] is a copy, will be presented to the Board of Supervisors of the county of   , at the house of R. F., in the town of   , on the   day of   next, at ten o'clock in the forenoon of that day; and that application will then and there be made, for an order to be entered requiring the amount of the said account to be paid by said school district number   ; or for such other order in the premises as the said board may see fit to grant.

Dated   , May 1, 1847.   A. B.

· · § 974. *Order of the Board of Supervisors, with Clerk's Certificate.*

At a meeting of the Board of Supervisors of the county of   ,
held at the house of R. F., in the town of   , in said county, on
the   day of   , 18   , a majority of the said Board being
present, it was ordered:

That the sum of   dollars, being the amount [or, part of the
amount] of an account for costs, charges and expenses, incurred and
paid by A. B., late Collector of school district number   , in the
town of   , in a suit commenced against him in the Supreme
Court of the State of New York, in favor of C. D., plaintiff therein,
for acts performed by the said A. B., by virtue of or under color of
his office, and in which judgment was rendered against the said A.
B., [or, *as the case may be*,] be assessed upon and collected of the
taxable inhabitants and property of said school district number   ,
in the same manner as other taxes of said district are by law assessed
and collected, and paid to the said A. B.

I certify the foregoing to be a correct copy from the minutes.

M. P., Clerk of the Board.

---

§ 975. *Notice to be Served on the Trustees with a Copy of the
Order.*

To G. H., L. M., and E. F., Trustees of School District No.   ,
in the Town of   :

You will please take notice, that the foregoing is a true copy of an
order duly made and entered by the Board of Supervisors of the
county of   , on the   day of   , 18   .

Dated, &c., [*as in* § 973.]

---

§ 976. *District Report, to be made by the Trustees Annually, and
transmitted to the Town Superintendent, between the first
and fifteenth day of January in each year.*[1]

To the Town Superintendent of Common Schools of the Town of   :

We, the Trustees of school district number   , in said town,
in conformity with the statutes relating to common schools, do certify
and report, that the whole time any school has been kept in our district during the year ending on the date hereof, and since the date of
the last report for the said district, is [*insert the whole time, though*

---

[1] See note to § 953, in regard to not enumerating Indian Children.

for a part of it the school may have been kept by a teacher not quali-fied;] and during said year, and since the date of said last report, such school has been kept by a teacher, [*or,* teachers,] after obtaining a certificate [*or,* certificates] of qualification according to law, [*insert the time with precision;*] that the amount of money apportioned to our district by the Town Superintendent of Common Schools during the said year and since the date of the said last report, except library money, is [*insert the whole amount, except as aforesaid, though received by predecessors in office, in whole, or in part;*] and that the said sum has been applied to the payment of the compensation of teachers employed in the said district, and licensed as the statute pre-scribes ; [*If the amount has not been expended, the reason should be particularly specified;*] that the amount of library money received in our district from the Town Superintendent of Common Schools during said year, and since the date of the said last report, is [*insert the whole amount, though received by predecessors, in whole, or in part;*] and that the said sum was, on or before the first day of Octo-ber last, applied to the purchase of a library for the district [*or,* a map of the State of New York, a terrestial globe, a black-board, &c., [*giving particulars,*] in pursuance of a vote of the district at a special meeting called and held according to law;] that the number of vol-umes belonging to the district library, and on hand on the last day of December last, is [*insert the number;*] that the number of children taught in said district during said year, and since the last report, is [*insert the same, from the teacher's list, or other authentic sources ;*] that of the said children, ten attended less than two months ; eight, two months and less than four ; four, four months, and less than six ; seven, six months and less than eight ; nine, eight months and less than ten ; two, ten months and less than twelve; fourteen, twelve months ; and that the number of children residing in our district on the last day of December last, who are over five and under sixteen years of age, is [*insert the number in the district, between the ages specified, on the last day of December:*] and that the names of the parents, and other persons, with whom such children respectively re-side, and the number residing with each, are as follows, viz :

Parents, &c.	*No. of Children*
Thomas Jones,	- 5
Richard Hoe, - -	- - 4

[*If a school for colored children has been taught in the district insert the following :* That the number of colored children between the ages of five and sixteen years attending a school taught in our district during the year aforesaid, by a licensed teacher, for at least four months, was twenty-four, of whom ten reside in said district : five attending from district number five; four from district number seven; two from district number six; and three from district number nineteen ; that the whole amount of public money received from the Town Superintendent of Common Schools of our town during the year aforesaid, for the use of said colored school, was $; and that the said sum has been applied to the compensation of the teacher thereof ; and that the amount paid to such teacher, over and above the public money so received, was $.]*

And we further report, that our school has been visited by the Town Superintendent   times, during the year preceding this report ; and that the sum paid for teacher's wages, over and above the public moneys apportioned to said district, during the same year, amounts to $: [*give the sum total of all the monæ, exclusive of public money raised during the year and applied to the payment of teachers' wages :*] that the school books in use in said district, during said year, are the following, viz : [*give the titles of all the text books used during the year;*] that there have been   private or select schools, not incorporated, taught in said district during the year aforesaid, and that the average number of pupils in attendance therein, was   [*State the number as near as can be ascertained.*] Dated at   , the first day of January, [*this is the day on which the report must be dated,*] A. D. 18 .

G. H.,
&c., &c., } Trustees. &c

---

§ 977. *District Report, where the District is Formed out of two or more Adjoining Towns.*[1]

To the Town Superintendent of Common Schools of the Town of   ;

We, the Trustees of school district number   , formed partly out of said town, and partly out of the adjoining town of   , do, in conformity with the statutes relating to common schools, certify and report:

That the school house in said district is situated in the town of   ; [*or*, on the line of the towns of   and   ;] that the whole time any school, &c., [*as in the preceding form to the**, *substituting* Town Superintendents *for* Town Superintendent, *and* Town Superintendents of Common Schools of said towns of   and   , *for* Town Superintendent of Common Schools of our Town; *and inserting the name of the town in which the districts mentioned are situate, in that part of the form relating to the school for colored children; and then continue as follows:*]

And we do further specify and report, that of the said sum of money so as above stated to have been apportioned to our district, to

---

1 The report should be signed in duplicate, and one copy sent to the **Town Superintendent** of each town out of which the district is formed.

be applied to the payment of teachers' wages, the sum of $
[*insert the precise amount,*] was for and on account of that part of
said district lying in said town of   , and the sum of $
for and on account of the other part thereof, lying and being in said
town of   ; that of the said sum of money, so as above stated
to have been received in our said district for the purchase of a district
library, the sum of $, [*insert the precise amount,*] was re-
ceived for and on account of that part of said district lying in said
town of   , and the sum of $ for and on account of
the other part thereof, lying and being in the said town of   ;
that of the said children as above stated to have been taught in our
said district, the number belonging to that part of said district lying
in said town of   , is   ; and that the number belonging
to the other part thereof, lying in said town of   , is   ;
that of the said children between the said ages of five and sixteen
years, so as above stated to reside in our district, the number residing in that part of said district lying in said town of   ,
is   ; and that the number residing in the other part thereof,
lying in said town of   , is   .

And we do further report, that our school has been inspected by
the Town Superintendents of the towns of   and   ,
once, [*or, as the case may be,*]; and by the Town Superintendent of
the town of   , separately   ; that the sum paid
for teachers' wages in said district, over and above the public money
apportioned to said district, during the same year, amounts to $,
[*insert amount of money raised, as in § 976,*] of which   dollars and   cents were paid by that part of the district lying
in the town of   , and   dollars and   cents by
that part lying in the town of   ; that the school books in
use in said district, &c., [*as in § 976, to the end.*]

Dated at   , this first day of January, A. D. 18   .

G. H., ⎫
&c, &c., ⎬ Trustees, &c.
          ⎭

---

§ 978. *Notice for Annual Meeting.*[1]

SCHOOL DISTRICT NOTICE.

Notice is hereby given, that the annual meeting for the election
of officers in district number   , in the town of   , and

---

[1] Notices of annual and special meetings must be given at least five days before the day
on which such meetings are appointed to be held; if the meeting is to be on Saturday, the
notice must be given on or before the previous Monday. In the case of annual meetings, or
special meetings which have been adjourned for a longer time than one month, the notice
must be posted up in at least four public places in the district; but notices of special meetings
must be personally served on each inhabitant liable to pay taxes.

for the transaction of such other business as the meeting may deem necessary, will be held at the school-house, in said district, on day, the   day of   instant, [or, next,] at six o'clock, P. M.
Dated,   , July 13, 1847.

          C. D., District Clerk.

---

§ 979. *Notice for Adjourned District Meeting.*

SCHOOL DISTRICT NOTICE.

Notice is hereby given, that a meeting of the freeholders and inhabitants of school district number   , in the town of   , authorized by law to vote therein, will be held at the school-house in said district, on the   day of   next, [or, instant,] at o'clock in the   noon, pursuant to adjournment. Dated, &c., [*as in* § 978.]

---

§ 980. *Notice for Special District Meeting.*

To the Clerk of District No.   :

The Trustees of District number   , at a meeting held for the purpose, have resolved that a special meeting be called at the school-house, on   day, the   day of   , 18   , at o'clock in the   noon of that day, for the purpose of choosing a Collector in place of E. F. removed, [*or, as the case may be,*] and for the transaction of such other business as the meeting may deem necessary.

You will, therefore, notify each inhabitant of the district entitled to vote therein, by reading this notice in his hearing, or, if he is absent from home, by leaving a copy of it, or so much as relates to the time and place of meeting, at the place of his abode, at least five days before such meeting. Dated, &c., [*as in* § 961.]

---

§ 981. *District Clerk's Notice of Officers Elected, to be Forwarded to the Town Clerk within Ten Days after the Election.*

To S. T., Town Clerk of the Town of   :

At an annual [or, special] meeting of school district number   , in said town, held at the school-house in said district, on the day of   , 18   , the following persons were elected to the respective offices hereinafter named, to wit: G. H., Trustee, to serve for three years; and E. F., Trustee, to fill the vacancy occasioned by the resignation [*or, as the case may be*] of R. T.; and C. D.,

District Clerk; O. P., Collector; and R. F., Librarian, for the ensuing year. Dated, &c., [*as in* § 978.]

---

§ 982. *Librarian's Receipt, to be Written at the Foot of each Catalogue of Books.*

I, C. O., do hereby acknowledge, that the books specified in the preceding catalogue, have been delivered to me by the Trustees of school district number   , in the town of   , to be safely kept by me, as Librarian of the said district, for the use of the inhabitants thereof, according to the regulations prescribed by the Superintendent of Common Schools, and to be accounted for by me, according to the said regulations, to the Trustees of the said district, and to be delivered to my successor in office.

Dated   , the   day of   , 18 .

C. O., Librarian.

---

§ 983. *Trustees' Certificate, to be Annexed to a Correct Copy of the Catalogue and Librarian's Receipt.* [1]

We, the subscribers, Trustees of school district number   , in the town of   , do certify, that the preceding is a full and complete copy of the catalogue of books in the library of the said district, now in possession of C. O., the Librarian thereof, and of his receipt thereon.

Given under our hands, this   day of   , 18 .

G. H.
&c., &c., } Trustees, &c.

---

§ 984. *Entry required to be Made by the Librarian, in each Book belonging to the District.*

No. 182. This book belongs to the library of school district number   , in the town of   .

---

§ 985. *Form of Keeping Librarian's Book.*

Time of Delivery.	Title and No. of Book.	To whom.	When Returned.	Condition.
1845. June 10.	History of France, 44.	Jno. Stiles.	20th June.	Good.

---

[1] The catalogue bearing the Librarian's receipt, is to be delivered to the Trustees, and the copy with the certificate of the Trustees, is to be given to the Librarian.

§ 986. *Weekly Roll to be kept by Teacher.*[1]

Attendance of Pupils in District School of District No.   :

Names of Pupils.	1st week.	2d week.	3d week.	4th week.	5th week.
J. Smith.	5 days.	4 days.	5 days.	6 days.	5½ days.

§ 987. *Teacher's Quarterly List, with Verification.*

A list of the scholars who attended the district school of district number   , in the town of   , during the quarter or term commencing the   day of   , 18   , and the number of days they respectively attended the same :

Time of entrance.	Name of Scholar.	No. of days' attendance.
Nov. 1, 1844.	John Thompson,	Seventy-eight, (78) days,
Dec. 1, "	Peter Barker,	Forty-three, (43) "
Dec. 4, "	James Thomas,	Forty, (40) "

County, ss:

C. F., being duly sworn, [or, affirmed,] deposes, that the foregoing is a true and accurate list of the names of the scholars who attended the district school of district number   , in the town of   , during the quarter commencing the   day of   , 18   , and the number of days they respectively attended.

Sworn [or, affirmed] to, before me, } 　 C. F., Teacher.
this   day of   , 18   . }

G. H., Justice of the Peace.[2]

§ 988. *Teacher's Abstract, to be Made at the End of each Quarter, for the Use of the Trustees.*

Abstract of the attendances of scholars at the district school of district number   , in the town of   , during the quarter commencing the   day of   , 18   :

Of scholars who attended less than two months, there were   :
　 " 　 " 　 two months, and less than four,   :
　 " 　 " 　 four months, and less than six,   :
　 " 　 " 　 six months, and less than eight,   :
　 " 　 " 　 eight months, and less than ten,   :
　 " 　 " 　 ten months, and less than twelve,   :
　 " 　 " 　 twelve months,   :

Dated   , the   day of   , 18   .

C. F., Teacher.

---

[1] The roll is to be continued as many weeks as there are in the quarter, and at the close thereof the attendance of each pupil summed up, and entered in the book provided by the Trustees, as in § 987. This roll is necessary to be kept under what is commonly called the "free school law," in order to enable the Trustees to make their annual report.

[2] The affidavit may be taken before a Justice of the Peace, Commissioner of Deeds, Judge of a Court of Record, or County Clerk.

§ 989. *Teacher's Account of Inspections, to be entered in the Book Provided by the Trustees, with the Verification.*

Account of Inspections of the School in District No.   :

November 1, 1841.   The school was inspected by A. B., Town Superintendent of Common Schools.

December 1, 1841.   The school was inspected.

County, ss:

C. F. being duly sworn, [*or*, affirmed,] deposes, that the foregoing is a true account of the days on which the school in District No.   , in the town of   , was visited and inspected by the Town Superintendents respectively, during the quarter commencing on the   day of   , 18   .

Sworn [*or*, affirmed] and subscribed,   }   C. F., Teacher.
this   day of   , 18   , before me, {
G. H., Justice of the Peace.

———

§ 990. *Appointment of a District officer to fill a Vacancy, by the Trustees.*

Town of   , ss:

Whereas, O. P. duly elected [*or*, appointed] to the office of District Clerk [*or*, District Collector; *or*, Librarian] of School District No.   , in said town, at the annual [*or*, a special] district meeting held in said district, on the   day of   , 18   , has removed from said district, [*or*, has deceased ; *or*, has failed to execute the bond required by law; *or*, *as the case may be*,] by reason whereof the said office has become vacant:

Now, therefore, in pursuance of the authority vested in us by the statutes relating to common schools, we do hereby appoint M. R., a resident of said district, to fill the vacancy occasioned by the death [*or*, removal : *or*, *as the case may be*] of the said O. P.

Given under our hands, this   day of   , 18   .
G. H.,   }   Trustees of
&c., &c., { District No.   .

———

§ 991. *Appointment of a Trustee to fill a Vacancy.*

Town of   , ss:

Whereas, G. H., duly elected [*or*, appointed] to the office of Trustee of School District No.   , in said town, at the annual [*or*, a special] district meeting held in said district, on the   day of   , 18   , has removed from said district, [*or*, has deceased; *or*, *as the case may be*,] by reason whereof the said office has become vacant:

Now, therefore, in pursuance of the authority vested in me by the statutes relating to common schools, I do hereby appoint R. F. to fill the vacancy occasioned by the removal [*or, death; or, as the case may be*] of the said G. H., until the next annual meeting in said district.

Given under my hand, this   day of   , 18   .

A. B., Town Superintendent of Common
Schools of the Town of   .

---

§ 992. *Form of an Appeal to the State Superintendent, with Affidavit Annexed.*

To the Hon. C. M., Superintendent of Common Schools of the State of New York:

The undersigned, E. F., a taxable inhabitant and legal voter in [*or, G. H., L. M., and E. F., the Trustees of; or, as the case may be*] school district number   , in the town of   , in the county of   , respectfully appeals [*or, appeal*] to you from the proceedings [*or, a decision*] of a district meeting [*state whether special or annual*] held in and for said district, on the   day of   , 18   , [*or, from a decision made by the Trustees of said school district, on, &c.; or, as the case may be,*] as follows, to wit: [*State the proceedings, decision, or act, complained of, giving dates, names, and details; and, if necessary, add the following:* And the undersigned states [*or, state*] the following facts and circumstances in support of the said appeal, to wit: [*State the reason for asking a reversal of the proceedings, or decision, complained of.*]

[*If the appeal has relation to the formation, or alteration of a school district, add the following:* And the undersigned also states [*or, state*] that the schedule hereunto annexed, marked "Schedule A," is a correct map, exhibiting the site of the school-house, the roads, the old and new lines of districts, the different lots, and the particular location and distance from the school-house of the persons aggrieved; [*or, if there are two or more school-houses in question, say:* and the particular location and distance from the school-houses of the persons aggrieved, and their relative distance therefrom; that the schedule hereunto annexed, marked "Schedule B," is a correct list of all the taxable inhabitants in the district or territory to be affected by the proceeding [*or, decision*] appealed from, and the valuation of the property taken from the last assessment roll, [*or, rolls, if the district, or districts, lie in different towns;*] and that "Schedule C," hereunto annexed, is a correct list of the number of children between five and sixteen years of age belonging to each person, with the districts to which they respectively belong.]

The undersigned, therefore, respectfully asks [*or, ask*] for a reversal of the proceedings [or, decision] appealed from, as aforesaid : [or, that the proceedings appealed from, as aforesaid, be annulled.]

Dated at   , the   day of   , A. D. 18   .

G. H.,
E. F., [or, L. M., } Trustees, &c.]
E. F.,

        County, ss :

E. F., of said county, being duly sworn, [or, affirmed,] says that he has read [or, heard read] the foregoing appeal by him signed, and that the facts and circumstances therein stated and set forth, are true, to the best of his knowledge, information and belief.*

Sworn [or, affirmed] to, this   day   E. F.
  of   , 18   , before me,
          S. T., Justice of the Peace.

---

§ 993. *Affidavit of Verification, by Trustees, or two or more Appellants.*[1]

        County, ss :

G. H., L. M., and E. F., being duly sworn, depose and say, and each for himself deposeth and saith, that he has, &c., [*as in the affidavit to* § 992, *to the end.*]

G. H.
L. M.
E. F.

---

§ 994. *Affidavit of Verification, where a Trustee, or Appellant, has not signed the Appeal.*

        County, ss:

G. H., of said county, being duly sworn, says, &c., [*as in the affidavit to* § 992, *to the* *, *and then add :*] and that the said appeal is not signed by L. M., one of the Trustees of the said school district number   , therein mentioned, for the reason that the said L. M. is confined to his bed by sickness, and has been so confined for the space of   days last past, [*or as the case may be.*]

Sworn, &c., [*as in* § 992.]

---

§ 995. *Statement, where Parties Concur as to the Facts.*

To the Hon. C. M., Superintendent of Common Schools of the State of New York :

We do hereby signify our concurrence in the following statement of facts, in relation to which a difference, or dispute, has arisen be-

---

[1] Although all the Trustees, or appellants, should sign the appeal, the affidavit may be made by one, where all the facts stated are within his knowledge.

tween the undersigned, E. F., of the one part, and the undersigned, G. H., L. M., &c., Trustees, &c., [or, *as the case may be*,] of the other part, to wit : that, &c., [*here state the facts.*]

The point [*or*, points] in relation to which the aforesaid difference, or dispute, has arisen, is [*state the points in controversy*,] and the same is [*or*, are] hereby respectfully submitted to your decision.

Dated at , the day of , 18 .

E. F.,
G. H., } Trustees, &c.
&c., &c.,

---

§ 996. *Notice to be served with Copy of the Appeal, &c.*[1]

To C. D., District Clerk of School District No. , in the Town of :

You will take notice, that the within is a copy of an appeal made by the undersigned, to the Hon. C. M., Superintendent of Common Schools of the State of New York, and of the statements, maps and papers, intended to be presented in support of it.

Dated, at , the day of , 18 .

E. F.

---

§ 997. *Affidavit of Service of Appeal.*

ounty, ss:

E. F., of said county, being duly sworn, says, that on the day of , 18 , he personally served a copy of the annexed appeal, and of the statements, maps and papers, accompanying the same, upon A. B., Town Superintendent, &c., [*or*, C. D., District Clerk; *or*, G. H., one of the Trustees, &c.,] by delivering the same to him, [*or*, by leaving the same at his dwelling-house, with a person arrived at years of discretion having charge thereof ; the said A. B. being absent from his place of residence.]

Sworn, &c., [*as in* § 992.] E. F.

---

§ 998. *Admission of Service.*

I hereby admit due service of a copy of the within appeal, statements, maps and papers, this day of , 18 .

A. B., Town Superintendent.

---

[1] The above notice should be directed to the District Clerk, or to the Trustees, where the appeal is made from the proceedings or decision of a district meeting ; in other cases, it should be directed to the officers, or officer, whose act is appealed from.

§ 999. *Form of Answer to Appeal.*

To the Hon. C. M., Superintendent of Common Schools of the State of New York:

The answer of A. B., Town Superintendent of the town of   , [*or*, of G. H., L. M., and E. F., Trustees of school district number   , in the town of   ; *or, as the case may be,*] in said county, to the appeal of E. F., of the said town, [*or, as the case may be,*] respectfully showeth:

That, &c., [*State the facts and circumstances relied on to support the proceedings or decision appealed from, and if there are any statements, maps, or papers, to be annexed, refer to them as Schedule A, Schedule B, &c., as in § 992.*]

The undersigned, therefore, respectfully asks, [*or*, ask,] that the said proceedings [*or*, decision] appealed from, as aforesaid, may be sustained.

Dated at   , the   day of   , 18   .[1]

A. B., Town Superintendent of Common
Schools of the Town of   .

----

[1] The forms of affidavits, notice and admission, heretofore given to accompany an appeal, may be used for an answer, by merely substituting, "answer" for "appeals" wherever it occurs.

CHAPTER XXXIX.

SERVICE AND RETURN OF PROCESS IN JUSTICES' COURTS.

PRACTICAL REMARKS.

1. A *long* summons must be served at least six days, and a *short* summons at least two days, before the time of appearance mentioned therein, by reading the same to the defendant, and, if required, by delivering him a copy. If the defendant cannot be found, the service must be made by leaving a copy of the summons at the defendant's last place of abode, in the presence of some one of the family, of suitable age and discretion, who must be informed of its contents. In computing the days, one day must be excluded, and the other included; so that a *long* summons returnable on the eighth day of the month, must be served as early as the second.[1]

2. The Constable serving a summons must return thereupon, in writing, the time and manner of service, and sign his name thereto. The return is conclusive upon the defendant, so far as the proceedings in that suit are concerned.[2]

3. A warrant is to be served by arresting the defendant and bringing him before the Justice who issued it; or, if he be absent, or unable to hear and try the cause, before the next Justice of the city or town.[3]

4. No civil process can be served on Sunday, nor can it be served, in any city or town of this State, on an elector entitled to vote therein, on the day of any general or special election, or town meeting.[4]

5. A *long* attachment is to be executed at least six days, and a *short* attachment at least two days, before the time of appearance

---

[1] 2 R. S. (3d ed.,) 327, § 16; 15 Johnson, 196; 10 Wendell, 422.
[2] 2 R. S. (3d ed.,) 327, § 17; 14 Johnson, 481; 2 Cowen, 218; 3 Wendell, 202; 17 Id., 51.
[3] 2 R. S. (3d ed.,) 328, § 22; 9 Cowen, 71.
[4] 1 R. S. (3d ed.,) 390, § 18; Id., 849, § 65; Laws of 1842, chap. 130, title I, §§ 4, 5; 3 Johnson, 257; 12 Id., 178; 15 Id., 177; 1 Cowen 75 8 Id., 27; 12 Wendell, 59.

mentioned therein.   The officer taking property on an attachment is liable for its safe keeping, and is bound to provide some suitable place for the purpose.   He is also required to serve a copy of the attachment and inventory on the defendant personally, if he can be found, and if not, to leave the same at his place of residence.   Where the defendant has no residence in the county, the copy and inventory are to be left with the person in whose possession the goods are found. Where a bond is given to the officer, the goods taken cannot be removed.[1]

6. On receiving an execution, it is the duty of the Constable to levy upon any property of the defendant liable to be taken, within a reasonable time.   In order to constitute a levy, the property must be taken into the actual or constructive possession of the Constable.[2]

7. The following property, when owned by a householder, is exempt from levy and sale on execution, viz: All spinning wheels, weaving looms and stoves, put up or kept up for use by the family; the family Bible, family pictures and school books, used by or in the family of such person; all books, not exceeding fifty dollars in value, kept and used as part of the family library; a seat or pew occupied by such person or his family, in any house or place of public worship; all sheep, to the number of ten, with their fleeces, and the yarn or cloth manufactured from the same; one cow, and two swine, and the necessary food for them; all necessary pork, beef, fish, flour, and vegetables, actually provided for family use, and necessary fuel for the use of the family for sixty days; all necessary wearing apparel, beds, bedsteads and bedding, for such person and his family; the arms and accoutrements required by law to be kept by such person; necessary cooking utensils; one table; six chairs; six knives and forks; six plates; six tea-cups and saucers; one sugar dish; one milk pot; one cream pot; six spoons; one crane and its appendages; one pair of andirons; one shovel and tongs; and the tools and implements of a mechanic, necessary to the carrying on of his trade, not exceeding twenty-five dollars in value.   In addition to the above, necessary household furniture and working tools and team owned by any person being a householder, or having a family for which he provides, to the value of not exceeding one hundred and fifty dollars, are exempt from levy and sale on execution.   The defendant cannot, however, avail himself of this last exemption, against an execution issued upon any demand for the purchase money of such furniture, or tools, or team, or any of the other articles above enumerated.[3]

8. The exemption act of 1842 does not operate retrospectively, so

[1] 2 R. S. (3d ed.,) 329, § 32; Laws of 1831, chap. 300; 6 Johnson, 9; 20 Wendell, 238.   [3] 2 R. S. (3d ed.,) 347; § 148; 2 Cowen, 421; 3 Wendell, 446; 10 Id., 349; 11 Id., 548; 14 Id., 23; 19 Id., 495; 23 Id., 466, 492; 2 Hill, 666.

[2] 2 R. S. (3d ed.,) 464, § 23; Laws of 1842, chap. 157; 14 Johnson, 434; 18 Id., 400; 1 Cowen, 114; 3 Wendell, 274; 11 Id., 44; 16 Id., 571; 19 Id., 475; 21 Id., 68; 25 Id., 370; 3 Hill. 469; 5 Id., 334.

as to affect pre-existing contracts. The question as to the *necessity* of the articles thereby exempted, is one of fact for the jury to determine, and not one of law.[1]

9. The lot and buildings thereon, occupied as a residence and owned by a debtor, being a householder and having a family, will be exempt from sale on execution, for debts contracted subsequent to the 1st of January, 1851, to the value of one thousand dollars, provided a description of the premises be recorded as required by law. (See Chapter xxiv.)[2]

10. The interest of a mortgagor of personal property before forfeiture, where he has not a right of possession for a definite period, is but a right of redemption, which is not the subject of levy and sale on execution.[3]

11 A Constable is protected in the execution of process, provided it appear regular on its face.[4]

12. The party justifying the taking of property under legal process, must show he was an officer, and had lawful authority to take property.[5]

13. A levy upon the property of the defendant is a satisfaction of the judgment, except the same be abandoned upon his request, or where he has not paid the debt, or been deprived of his property.[6]

14. Where different articles are taken on an execution, subject to a chattel mortgage, they ought all to be sold together.[7]

15. Property pledged may be taken on execution and sold ; but after the sale, it must be returned to the pledgee till the purchaser at the sale redeems.[8]

16. Where the defendant sues for property taken on an execution against him, and recovers, the original judgment is not satisfied.[9]

FORMS.

§ 1000. *Return to Summons Personally Served.*

Personally served, July 10, 1847, [*add, if necessary:* and copy left with defendant, at his request.] Fees, twelve and a half cents.

H. C., Constable.

---

[1] 6 Hill, 442; 1 Denio, 128, 462 ; 3 Id., 694; 1 Comstock, 129.
[2] Laws of 1850, chap. 260.
[3] 1 Comstock, 295.
[4] 5 Wendell, 170 ; 6 Hill, 311.
[5] 2 Comstock, 115.

[6] 12 Johnson, 207 ; 4 Cowen, 417 ; 7 Id., 13; 23 Wendell, 490 ; 2 Hill, 329 ; 2 Comstock, 451.
[7] 4 Denio, 171.
[8] 2 R. S. (3d ed.,) 464, § 21 ; 8 Wendell, 339 ; 23 Id., 653 ; 24 Id., 117 ; 6 Hill, 48; 1 Comstock, 129.
[9] 4 Denio, 165.

§ 1001. *Return to Summons Served by Copy.*

Served by copy, defendant not being found, July 10, 1847. Fees, twenty-five cents. H. C., Constable.

---

§ 1002. *Return where one or more of several Defendants are not Found.*

Personally served on A. B., one of the defendants within named, July 10, 1847; and C. D. and E. F., two of the defendants within named, were not found, and I have been unable to ascertain their last place of abode in the county. Fees, thirty-one cents.

H. C., Constable.

---

§ 1003. *Return where no Person of Suitable Age is Found at the last Place of Abode of the Defendant.*

The within named defendant was not found, nor any person of suitable age or discretion to be informed of the contents of the within summons, at his last place of abode.

July 10, 1847. H. C., Constable.

---

§ 1004. *Return to Warrant.*

The defendant arrested, and before the court in custody; plaintiff notified, [*or,* not notified.]

July 10, 1847. H. C., Constable.

---

§ 1005. *Return to Warrant where one or more of the Defendants are not Found.*

The within named defendant, A. B., arrested, and before the court, in custody; C. D. and E. F., the other defendants within named, not found ; plaintiff notified, [*or,* not notified.]

July 10, 1847. H. C., Constable.

---

§ 1006. *Return to an Attachment.*

By virtue of the within attachment, I attached and took into my custody the goods and chattels of the defendant, mentioned in an inventory, of which the annexed is a copy, on the 10th day of July, 1847; and immediately, on the same day, I made an inventory of the property seized, and served a copy of said attachment and inventory, duly certified by me, on the defendant personally; [*or*, I made an inventory of the property seized, and because the defendant could not be found in the county of   , I left a copy of said attachment and inventory, duly certified by me, at the last place of residence of the said defendant; *or*, with E. F., in whose possession I found the said goods and chattels, the said defendant having no place of residence in the said county of   .]

July 10, 1847.   H. C., Constable.

---

§ 1007. *Return to an Attachment where Bond is Given.*

By virtue, &c.; [*as in* § 1006, *to the end, and then add :*] but the said goods and chattels were delivered up to C. D., the defendant, [*or, to E. F.,*] upon receiving the bond herewith returned.

July 10, 1847.   H. C., Constable.

---

§ 1008. *Copy of the Inventory.*

Copy of an inventory of property this day seized by me, by virtue of the within [*or*, annexed] attachment, viz: [*enumerate the articles.*]

July 10, 1847.   H. C., Constable.

---

§ 1009. *Bond to Prevent the Removal of Goods Attached.*[1]

Know all men by these presents: That we, C. D. and E. F., of   , in the county of   , are held and firmly bound unto H. C., in the sum of   dollars, to be paid to the said H. C., or to his certain attorney, executors, administrators, or assigns; to which payment, well and truly to be made, we bind ourselves, our and each of our heirs, executors and administrators, jointly and severally, firmly by these presents.

Sealed with our seals, and dated the   day of   , 18 .

The condition of this obligation is such, that if certain goods and chattels, to wit: [*name the articles,*] which have been seized by the above named H. C., a Constable of the town of   , in the county of   , by virtue of an attachment issued by G. H., Esq., a Justice of the Peace of said county, in favor of A. B., against the above bounden C. D., shall be produced to satisfy any execution that may be issued upon any judgment which shall be obtained by

---

[1] The penalty of the bond should be double the sum sworn to by the plaintiff on his application for the attachment.

the plaintiff upon the said attachment, within six months after the date hereof, then this obligation to be void; else of force.

Sealed and delivered, ⎱
   in presence of   ⎰   E. F. [L. S.]
     R. F.

I approve of E. F. as surety in the foregoing bond.
  Dated the   day of   , 18 .   H. C., Constable.

---

§ 1010. Bond by Claimant of Property Attached.

Know all men by these presents: That we, L. M., E. F., and S. T., of, &c., are held and firmly bound unto A. B., &c., [as in § 1009, to the *, and then add:] Whereas, certain goods, to wit: [name the articles,] were, on this   day of   , 18 , seized by H. C., Constable, by virtue of an attachment issued by G. H., Esquire, a Justice of the Peace of the county of   , in favor of the above named A. B., against C. D.; and whereas, the above bounden L. M. claims the said goods as his property: Now, therefore, the condition of this obligation is such, that if, in a suit to be brought on this obligation within three months from the date hereof, the said L. M. shall establish that he was the owner of the said goods at the time of the said seizure; and in case of his failure so to do, if the said L. M. shall pay the value of the said goods and chattels, with interest, then this obligation to be void ; else of force.

Sealed, &c., [as in § 1009.]   L. M. [L. S.]
                                E. F. [L. S.]
                                S. T. [L. S.]

I approve of the sureties in the foregoing bond.
  Dated the   day of   , 18 .
           H. C., Constable, [or, G. H., Justice.]

---

§ 1011. Indorsement of Levy on an Execution.

July 10, 1847. The within execution levied on two cows, the property of the defendant.   H. C., Constable.

---

§ 1012. Indorsement on Execution, where Inventory is Attached.

July 10, 1845. The within execution levied on the goods and chattels of the defendant mentioned in the annexed inventory.
           H. C., Constable.

---

1 The penalty of this bond should be double the value of the property attached. The bond is to be executed to the plaintiff, instead of the Constable, and may be approved by the latter, or by the Justice.

§ 1013. *Inventory to be Attached to Execution.*

An inventory of goods and chattels this day levied upon, and taken into my custody, by virtue of the annexed execution, viz:

Two cows,	One lumber wagon,
Fifty bushels of oats,	One bedstead,
	&c., &c.

Dated the   day of   , 18   .

H. C., Constable.

---

§ 1014. *Bond to Indemnify Constable.*[1]

Know all men by these presents: That we, A. B. and E. F., &c., [*as in* § 1009, *to the* *, *and then add :*] Whereas, the said H. C., as a Constable of the county of   , by virtue of a certain execution issued by G. H., Esq., one of the Justices of the Peace of said county, against C. D., in favor of the said A. B., for   dollars damages, and   dollars costs, has seized [*or, is about to seize*] one lumber wagon, and one set of double harness, now or lately in possession of the said C. D., with intent to sell the same, in order to satisfy the said execution: Now, therefore, the condition of this obligation is such, that if the above bounden A. B. shall, at all times, and forever hereafter, keep the said H. C. harmless and indemnified, of, from and against, all damages, costs, charges, trouble and expense, of what nature soever, which he may be put to, sustain, or suffer, by reason of such levy and sale, or either, then this obligation to be void ; else of force.

Sealed, &c., [*as in* § 1009.]

A. B. [L. S.]
E. F. [L. S.]

---

§ 1015. *Receipt of Goods Taken on Execution.*

Justices' Court,
    A. B.
    against   }   .
    C. D.

Execution issued by G. H., Esq., one of the Justices of the Peace of the county of , for	$26 02
Constable's fees for collecting,	2 25
Amount,	$28 27

By virtue of the above described execution, H. C., one of the Constables of said county of   , has levied upon the following

---

* This bond will be valid, where there is any doubt as to the title of property, but not where the constable is aware that he is a trespasser.

goods and chattels, the property of the said C. D., viz: [*enumerate the articles taken.*]

July 10, 1847. Received of H. C., Constable, as aforesaid, the goods and chattels above mentioned, which I promise to deliver to him, at any time when he shall demand the same, at the dwelling-house of the above defendant, C. D., in the town of   , in the said county; or, in default thereof, I do hereby agree with the said H. C., to pay him the amount of the judgment above described, together with the fees for the collection thereof, as above specified.

E. F.

§ 1016. *Constable's Advertisement of Sale.*[1]

By virtue of an execution, [*or*, of several executions,] I have seized and taken one lumber wagon and one set of double harness, the property of C. D., which I shall expose to sale at public vendue, to the highest bidder, on the   day of   instant, [*or*, next,] at   o'clock in the   noon, at the house of R. P., in the town of   .

H. C., Constable.

§ 1017. *Return to an Execution Satisfied.*

The amount of the within execution levied of the goods and chattels of the defendant therein named.

July 10, 1847.

H. C., Constable.

§ 1018. *Return to Execution, Satisfied in Part.*

The within execution satisfied in part, to wit : for the sum of   dollars ; and no goods or chattels of the defendant found whereof the residue could be made.

July 10, 1847.

H. C., Constable.

§ 1019. *Return where Defendant is Committed.*

No goods or chattels of the within named C. D. found, and his body taken and conveyed to the common jail of the county.

July 10, 1847.

H. C., Constable.

§ 1020. *Return of no Property found.*

No goods or chattels of the within named C. D. could be found.

July 10, 1847.

H. C., Constable.

---

[1] The notice must be posted up in three public places in the town where the sale is to be held, five days previous thereto.

§ 1021. *Return where no Property, nor the Body of the Defendant.*
is Found.

No goods or chattels, nor the body of the within named C. D., could be found.

July 10, 1847.   H. C. Constable.

———

§ 1022. *Return of Part Satisfied, and no Body Found.*

The within execution satisfied in part, to wit : for the sum of dollars, and no more goods or chattels, nor the body of the within named C. D., could be found.

July 10, 1847.   H. C., Constable.

———

§ 1023. *Return where Goods remain Unsold.*

Levied on a lumber wagon, the property of the within named C. D., which remains in my possession, unsold, for want of bidders.

July 10, 1847.   H. C., Constable.

36

CHAPTER XL.

STRAYS.

PRACTICAL REMARKS.

1. Whenever any person, at any time, has any strayed horse upon his inclosed land,—or, between the first day of November in any year, and the first day of April thereafter, has any strayed neat cattle or sheep upon his inclosed lands,—he may, within ten days after the coming of any such stray thereon, deliver to the Clerk of the town within which such lands shall be, a note in writing, containing the name and place of abode of such person, and the age, color and marks, natural and artificial, of each stray, as near as may be. If this notice is not delivered, no compensation can be recovered for keeping any strays.

2. It is the duty of the Town Clerk to enter every such note in a book, which is to be kept open for inspection free of charge. The fees of the Clerk for the entry are to be paid by the person presenting the note.

3. The person delivering the note will be entitled to receive therefor nine cents each, for all neat cattle and horses, and three cents for each sheep described therein; and he may detain such strays, until such fees, and the fees of the Clerk, and all reasonable charges of keeping, be paid. The charges of keeping strays are to be ascertained by the fence-viewers of the town, as mentioned in the former part of this work. (See Chapter xix.)

4. If no owner appear to claim any stray, on or before the first day of May next, after the making of the entry as above prescribed, or if the owner refuse, or neglect, to pay the fees and charges, the person who delivered the note and kept the stray, may proceed to sell the same by public auction to the highest bidder; notice of which sale must be posted up in three public places in the town where the strays shall have been kept, at least twenty days previous thereto. Out of the moneys arising from the sale, the person making the same may retain the fees and charges above mentioned, and the like charges

for the sale as are allowed to Constables on sales under executions issued out of Justices' Courts. The residue of the money must be paid to the owner of the strays, if he demands the same; if not demanded within one year of the sale, he will be precluded from recovering such residue, and the same is to be paid to the Supervisor, for the use of the town, within thirty days after the expiration of the year.[1]

FORMS.

§ 1024. *Notice to be Delivered to Town Clerk by Person Keeping Strays.*

To C. D., Town Clerk of the town of   :

You will take notice, that on or about the   day of   , 18   , one chestnut horse, of the age of seven years, or thereabouts, and marked with a star in his forehead, strayed upon my inclosed land in the town of   , and now remains thereupon; and that I reside in the said town of   .

Dated the   day of   , 18   .   A. B.

---

§ 1025. *Notice of Sale where Stray is not Redeemed.*

PUBLIC NOTICE.

By virtue of the statute in such case made and provided, I shall expose to sale at public auction, to the highest bidder, on the day of   instant, [*or*, next,] at   o'clock in the noon, at the house of R. F., in   , one chestnut horse of the age of seven years, or thereabouts, and marked with a star in his forehead, the same being a stray found upon my inclosed land in the town of   , and remaining unredeemed according to law.

Dated the   day of   , 18   .   A. B.

---

§ 1026. *Receipt of Supervisor.*

Received of A. B.,   dollars and   cents, being the proceeds of the sale of a stray chestnut horse, after deducting therefrom the expenses of keeping and the sale thereof,—said horse having been advertised and sold at public auction, by the said A. B., as a stray, according to the statute, on the   day of   18   .

Dated   , the   , day of   , 18   .

L. M., Supervisor of the town of   .

---

[1] 1 R. S. (3d ed.) 401, § 17, et seq.

CHAPTER XLI.

SUPERVISORS.

PRACTICAL REMARKS.

1. Supervisors are chosen annually, by ballot, at the town meetings held in their respective towns. If the office at any time be vacant, it may be filled by a special town meeting, which it is the duty of the Town Clerk to call within eight days after the happening of the vacancy. If the vacancy is not supplied by the electors, the Justices of the Peace of the town may fill it.[1]

2. It is the duty of a person elected or appointed to the office of Supervisor, within ten days after receiving notice of his election or appointment, to take and subscribe the oath of office, before some Justice of the Peace, or Commissioner of Deeds, or the Town Clerk.[2]

3. The general powers and duties of Supervisors in the State of New York, are defined and prescribed by statute, as follows:

1. The Supervisor of each town shall receive and pay over all moneys raised therein for defraying town charges, except those raised for the support of Highways and Bridges, of Common Schools, and of the Poor, where poor moneys shall be raised.

2. He shall prosecute in the name of his town, or otherwise, as may be necessary, for all penalties of fifty dollars or under, given by law to such town or for its use, and for which no other officer is specially directed to prosecute.

3. He shall keep a just and true account of the receipt and expenditure of all moneys which shall come into his hands by virtue of his office, in a book to be provided for that purpose, at the expense of the town, and to be delivered to his successor in office.

4. On the Tuesday preceding the annual town meeting, he shall

---

[1] 1 R. S. (3d ed.,) 392, § 2; Id., 398, §§ 53, 54; Laws of 1838, chap. 172; Laws of 1840, chap. 238; 2 Hill, 369.
[2] 1 R. S. (3d ed.,) 395, §§ 29-31.

account with the Justices of the Peace and Town Clerk of the town, for the disbursement of all moneys received by him.

5. At every such accounting, the Justices and Town Clerk shall enter a certificate in the Supervisor's book of accounts, showing the state of his accounts at the date of the certificate.

6. The Supervisor of each town shall attend the annual meeting of the Board of Supervisors of the county, and every adjourned or special meeting of such Board, of which he shall have notice.

7. He shall receive all accounts which may be presented to him against the town, and shall lay them before the Board of Supervisors at their next meeting.

8. He shall also lay before the Board of Supervisors such copies of entries concerning moneys voted to be raised in his town, as shall be delivered to him by the Town Clerk.

9. Whenever the Supervisor of any town shall be required by the Surveyor General to cause a survey to be made of the bounds of his town, it shall be the duty of such Supervisor, within sixty days thereafter, to cause such survey to be made, and to transmit by mail, or otherwise, a map and description thereof to the Surveyor General, under a penalty for refusal or neglect, of fifty dollars. The expense of such survey and map will be defrayed by the several towns, whose bounds either wholly or in part shall be described thereby; such expense to be apportioned by the Board of Supervisors of the county.[1]

4. Besides these general duties enjoined upon the Supervisor, he is *ex-officio* a member and chairman of the Board of Excise of his town, and he is charged with various special duties in regard to highways, the poor laws, schools, and strays, all of which are pointed out in previous Chapters of this work devoted to those particular subjects. (See Chapters XVII, XXII, XXXV, XXXVIII, and XL.)

5. The Supervisor is also a member of the Board of Town Auditors, and is clothed with certain powers under the law authorizing the erection of town houses. (See Chapters XLIII and XLIV.)

6. The official bonds of Commissioners of Highways, Town Superintendents of Common Schools, Collectors, and sometimes Constable's instruments, are approved by the Supervisor.

7. The Supervisor, Town Clerk, and Assessors of a Town, are required to meet at such place as may be appointed by the Supervisor, or in his absence, or in case of a vacancy in his office, by the Town Clerk, on the first Monday of July in each third year after the first selection has been made in a town, for the purpose of making a list of persons to serve as jurors. When assembled for that purpose, it is their duty to select from the names of those assessed on the last assessment rolls of the town, suitable persons to serve as jurors, in making which selection they are to take the names of such persons only as are—

1. Male inhabitants of the town, not exempt from serving on juries.

---

[1] 1 R. S. (3d ed.,) 399, § 1, et seq.

2. Of the age of twenty-one years or upwards, and under sixty years old :

3. Who are at the time assessed for personal property belonging to them in their own right, to the amount of two hundred and fifty dollars. or who have a freehold estate in real property in the county, belonging to them in their own right, or in the right of their wives, to the value of one hundred and fifty dollars ; or, if residents of either of the counties of Niagara, Erie, Chautauquo, Cattaraugus, Allegany, Genesee, Orleans, Monroe, Livingston, Jefferson, Lewis, St. Lawrence, Steuben, or Franklin, who have been assessed on the last assessment roll of the town for land in their possession held under contract for the purchase thereof, upon which improvements owned by them have been made, to the value of one hundred and fifty dollars :

4. In the possession of their natural faculties, and not infirm or decrepit :

5. Free from all legal exceptions, of fair character, of approved integrity, of sound judgment, and well informed.[1]

8. Duplicate lists of the persons selected as jurors by the town officers before mentioned, with their respective occupations and places of residence, are to be made out and signed by such officers, or a majority of them; and within ten days after the first Monday in July, one of the said lists must be transmitted to the County Clerk, and the other filed with the Town Clerk. The jurors thus selected serve for three years.[2]

9. Grand jurors are annually selected by the Boards of Supervisors; but it is the custom for each Supervisor to present a list of those required from his town, with their respective occupations and places of residence, to the Clerk of the Board at an early day in the session.

10. The duties of Supervisors, in regard to the assessment and collection of taxes, are pointed out in Chapter XLII of this work.

11. The Supervisor, Assessors, and Town Clerk of a town, are required to meet on the first Monday of October in each year, to designate the place or places where the annual election shall be held, and to give notice thereof. They have power at such meeting to alter any district, in which case they must make a certificate of the alterations, and file the same in the office of the Town Clerk. Any alteration so made will not take effect till after the then next general election, except where a town has been altered, divided, or newly erected.[3]

12. When a new town is formed, it is the duty of the Supervisor, Assessors, and Town Clerk thereof, to meet at the office of the Town Clerk, on or before the first Tuesday in September preceding the first general election to be held in the town, and they may adjourn from time to time, but not beyond the first day of October. If their

---

[1] 2 R. S. (3d ed.,) 508, 509, §§ 12, 13, 14, 18. | [3] 1 R. S. (3d ed.,) 134, §§ 15, 16; Laws of
[2] 2 R. S. (3d ed.,) 508, 509, §§ 15, 17, 18, 19. | 1847, chap. 240.

town contains more than five hundred electors, it is their duty to divide it into a convenient number of election districts, as compact as may be; and if it contains less than five hundred electors, the division may be made in their discretion. An election district must not contain more than five hundred electors. Where a town is divided, a certificate of the division must be made and signed by the Board, and filed in the office of the Town Clerk.[1]

13. Vacancies in the Board of Inspectors of an election district are to be filled by the Supervisor, Town Clerk, and Justices of the Peace of the town, at a meeting to be called by the Supervisor, or in case of a vacancy in his office, or his absence, or inability, by the Town Clerk. Certificates of the appointment of persons to fill vacancies are to be filed in the office of the Town Clerk.[2]

FORMS

§ 1027. *Supervisor's Oath.*

I do solemnly swear, [or, affirm,] that I will support the Constitution of the United States, and the Constitution of the State of New York; and that I will faithfully discharge the duties of the office of Supervisor of the Town of   , in the County of   , according to the best of my ability.

Sworn and subscribed, this   D. E. L.
day of   , 18   , before me,
    R. F., Town Clerk of the Town of   .[3]

§ 1028. *Form of Keeping Supervisor's Book.*

D. E. L., Supervisor of the Town of   , in account with said Town:

DR.   CR.

Dates.		Dolls.	cts.	Dates.		Dolls.	cts.
May 1, 1850.	For am't rec'd of O. P., Collector of the Town, - -	189	50	May 2, 1850.	By paid for Supervisor's book, -	1	25
July 30, "	For amount of penalty collected of A. B. for (*state what for.*) &c., &c.	50	00	" " "	" " E. F., Commissioner of Highways, - - - - &c., &c.	150	00

[1] 1 R. S. (3d ed.,) 134, §§ 15–17; Laws of 1847, chap. 240.   [2] 1 R. S. (3d ed.,) 136, § 22; Laws of 1847 chap. 240.

[3] No fee can be charged for administering the oath. The certificate must be filed by the Supervisor in the office of the Town Clerk, within eight days after taking the oath.

§ 1029. *Certificate of the Town Clerk and Justices of the Peace on the Examination of the Supervisor's Accounts, to be entered in his book.*

Town of   , ss :

We, the undersigned, the Justices of the Peace and Town Clerk of the Town of   , do hereby certify that we have this day examined the within [*or, foregoing*] account of D. E. L., Supervisor of said town; and that we find the same in all respects correct and true, and that there appears at this date to be a balance of dollars and   cents due from the said Supervisor to the town of   , [*or, as the balance may be.*]

   Dated   , the   day of   , 18 .

   H. F.⎫
   A. W.⎬ Justices of the
   G. H.⎭ Peace.
   S. T.

   R. S., Town Clerk.

---

§ 1030. *Certificate of the Supervisor, to Accompany Copies of Entries in Town Clerk's Book.*

Town of   , ss :

I do hereby certify that the within are the copies of entries concerning moneys voted to be raised in the said town of   , delivered to me by the town clerk thereof.

   Dated   , the   day of   , 18 .

   D. E. L., Supervisor of said Town.

---

§ 1031. *Notice of Supervisor, calling Special Meeting of the Board of Excise.*

[*See* § 429 *in Chapter* XVII : *all the Forms used by the Commissioners of Excise may be found in the same Chapter.*]

---

§ 1032. *Appointment of Commissioner of Highways to fill Vacancy.*

[*See* § 491 *in Chapter* XXII : *all the Forms used by the Supervisor under the Highway Act, may be found in the same Chapter.*]

---

§ 1033. *Report of Supervisor, where all the Poor are not a County Charge.*

[*See* § 870 *in Chapter* XXXV : *the other Forms required by the Super-*

visor in performing his duties under the Poor Laws, may be found in the same Chapter.]

---

§ 1034. *Notice to Town Superintendent of Common Schools to furnish Additional Security.*

[*See* § 941, *in Chapter* xxxviii: *the other Forms required by the Supervisor under the School Law, may be found in the same Chapter.*]

---

§1035. *Receipt of Supervisor for Proceeds of the Sale of a Stray*

[*See* § 1026, *in Chapter* xl.]

---

§ 1036. *Affidavit verifying Account.*

[*See* § 1056, *in Chapter* xliii: *other Forms used by the Town Auditors may also be found in that Chapter.*]

---

§ 1037. *Approval of Sureties in a Bond.*[1]

I approve of the sureties named in the above bond.

Dated   , the   day of   , 18   .

D. E. L., Supervisor of the Town of   .

---

§ 1038. *List of Jurors.*

List of Jurors selected from the town of   , in the county of   , to serve for three years from the   day of   , 18   .

Names.	Occupation.	Residence.
R. F., [*write the name in full.*]	Farmer,	Near the gate on the Plank Road,
S. M.	Merchant,	Village of .
&c., &c.		

[1] The Official Bond of a Commissioner of Highways may be found in Chapter xxii, (§ 492); that of the Town Superintendent of Common Schools in Chapter xxxviii, (§ 939); that of the Town Collector in Chapter xlii,(§§ 1051, 1052); and the Instrument of a Constable in Chapter xxxi, (§ 804.) It is the duty of Supervisors to prosecute Commissioners of Highways or Town Superintendents, and their sureties, for breaches of their bonds, or neglect to make proper returns and pay over moneys, according to law. The Bond of the Collector, given to the Supervisor, must also be prosecuted by him.

Town of   , ss:

We, the undersigned, the Supervisor, Town Clerk and Assessors of the said Town, do hereby certify that the foregoing is a correct list of jurors duly selected by us from the said town, to serve for the ensuing three years.

Dated   , the   day of July, 18   .

D. E. L., Supervisor.

S. G., Town Clerk.

A. B.,)

B. J., } Assessors.

R. S.,)

§ 1039. *List of Grand Jurors from a Town.*

List of Grand Jurors selected by the Supervisor of the Town of   , from the qualified inhabitants of said town.

Names.	Occupation.	Residence.
A. B., [*write the name in full.*] C. D.,	Blacksmith. Cooper.	Village of . Corners.

I hereby certify that the foregoing is a list of grand jurors se lected by me from the qualified inhabitants of the town of   .

D. E. L., Supervisor of said Town.

§ 1040. *Tax Bill.*

[*The Tax Bill is a mere copy of the Assessment Roll, (§ 1046, in Chapter* xlii,) *with another column headed "Amount of Tax" added thereto; in which column the Supervisor inserts the amount of each person's tax, calculated by him according to the rate per cent., established by the Board. For other Forms required in the assessment and collection of taxes, see Chapter* xlii.]

§ 1041. *Notice of Election.*

ELECTION NOTICE.

Town of   , ss:

We, the undersigned, composing the Board of Town Officers of said town, do hereby notify the electors thereof, that the ensuing general election, [*or*, that a special election duly ordered by the Governor of this State,] at which are to be elected the following officers, viz: [*insert here a list of the officers to be chosen,*] will be held in election district number one, in said town of   , on the ·   day of November next, [*or,*   instant,] at the house of O. P., in said district; in election district number two, on the same day, at the house of R. F., in said last mentioned district; and in election district number three, on the same day, at the house of S. T., in said last mentioned district: And that the poll of the election will be opened in each district on the   day of   aforesaid, at sunrise, [*or, at the time determined by the board, to be not later than nine o'clock in the morning,*] and closed at sunset on that day.

    Dated   , the   day of   , 18   .

D. E. L., Supervisor.
S. G.,   Town Clerk.
A. B.,)
B. J., } Assessors.
R. S.)

---

§ 1042. *Alteration of an Election District.*

Town of   , ss:

    We, the undersigned, composing the Board of Town Officers of said town, do hereby certify that we have this day altered the election districts in said town; and that the said districts are now constituted and bounded as follows:

    Election district number one is bounded on the west, by the west line of the town; on the north, by a line passing along the centre of the main channel of the   river; on the east, by the centre of the   road; and on the south, by the south line of military lots number   and   .

    Election district number two is bounded, &c., [*describe the boundaries clearly and distinctly.*]

    Election district number three, comprises the remaining territory in said town, not included in either of the districts above described, and is bounded, &c., [*give the boundaries.*]

    Dated, &c., [*as in § 1041.*]

---

§ 1043. *Division of a New Town into Election Districts.*[1]

Town of   , ss:

    We, the undersigned, composing the Board of Town Officers of said town, do hereby certify that we have divided the same into three

---

[1] Within ten days after the meeting of the Board, and at least two weeks before the day of the ensuing election, the town clerk must put up copies of the certificate of division in at least four public places in each election district, and deliver one copy thereof to an inspector in each district.

[or, *as the number may be*] election districts, which are bounded and described as follows, viz:

Election district number one is bounded, &c., [*describe the districts as in* § 1042.]

Dated, &c., [*as in* § 1041.]

---

§ 1044. *Notice of Supervisor calling Meeting to fill Vacancy in Office of Inspector of Elections..*

To S. G., Town Clerk, [*or*, Justice of the Peace,] of the Town of   :

You are hereby notified to attend a meeting of the Supervisor, Town Clerk, and Justices of the Peace, of said town, appointed by me to be held at your office, [*or*, at the office of S. T., Esq.,] on the   day of   instant, for the purpose of filling a vacancy in the office of Inspector of Elections, in election district number   , in said town.

Dated   , the   day of   , 18   .

Yours, &c.,   D. E. L., Supervisor.

---

§ 1045. *Appointment of an Inspector of Elections to fill a Vacancy.*

Town of   , ss:

R. F. is hereby appointed an inspector of elections in and for election district number   , in said town, to fill the vacancy occasioned by the death of C. D., [*or*, by the removal of C. D. from the district· *or*, by the inability of C. D., on account of sickness, to attend at the ensuing general election.]

Given under our hands, this   day of   , 18   .

D. E. L., Supervisor.

S. G.,   Town Clerk.

H. F.,
S. T.,   } Justices of the Peace.
&c., &c. }

CHAPTER XLII.

TAXES.

PRACTICAL REMARKS.

1. All lands and personal estate, within this State, whether owned by individuals or corporations, individual bankers or banking associations, are liable to taxation, with the following exceptions, viz: All property, real or personal, exempted from taxation by the Constitution of this State, or of the United States; all lands belonging to this State, or to the United States; every building erected for the use of a college, incorporated academy, or other seminary of learning, every building for public worship; every school-house, court-house and jail; the several lots whereon such buildings are situated; and the furniture belonging to each of them; every poor-house, alms-house, house of industry, and every house belonging to a company incorporated for the reformation of offenders, and the real and personal property belonging to, or connected with the same; the real and personal property of every public library; all stocks owned by the State, or by literary or charitable institutions; the personal estate of every corporation not made liable to taxation on its capital; the personal property of every minister of the gospel, or priest, of any denomination, and the real estate of such minister or priest, when occupied by him, provided such real and personal estate do not ex the value of one thousand five hundred dollars; and all property exempted by law from execution. If the real and personal estate, or either of them, of any minister or priest, exceed the value of one thousand five hundred dollars, that sum must be deducted from the valuation of his property, and the residue will be liable to taxation. Lands sold by the State, though not granted, or conveyed, must be assessed in the same manner as if actually conveyed. The owner, or holder, of stock in any incorporated company, liable to taxation on its capital, cannot be taxed as an individual for such stock.[1]

---

[1] 1 R. S. (3d ed,) 441, 442, § 1, et seq.; Laws of 1847, chap. 419; 4 Paige, 401.

2. Every person must be assessed in the town or ward where he resides, for all lands owned or occupied by him in such town or ward. Land not owned by a person residing in the town where the same is situated, may be assessed in the name of the owner or occupant. Where a farm, or lot, is divided, by the line between two towns in the same county, or in adjoining counties, it must be assessed in the town where the occupant resides; if there be no occupant, then each part must be assessed in the town in which the same may lie.[1]

3. Every person must be assessed in the town or ward where he resides, for all personal estate owned or held by him, in his own right, or as trustee, guardian, executor, or administrator; but if any person possessed of personal estate resides, during any year in which taxes may be levied, in two or more counties or towns, his residence will be deemed and held by the assessors to be in the county and town in which his principal business may have been transacted.[2]

4. The real estate of incorporated companies, liable to taxation must be assessed in the town or ward where the same may lie. The personal estate of such companies must be assessed in the town or ward where the principal office or place of business is located; if there be no such office, then in the town or ward where the operations of the company may be carried on. In the case of toll bridges, the company owning any such bridge must be assessed in the town or ward where the tolls are collected; and where the tolls of any company are collected in several towns, the assessment must be made in the town or ward in which the officer authorized to pay the last preceding dividend, resides.[3]

5. The Assessors of any town or ward may divide the same into assessment districts, not exceeding the number of Assessors. Between the first days of May and July in each year, they must ascertain, by diligent inquiry, the names of all the taxable inhabitants, and the taxable real and personal property in such town, or ward, and enter the same in their assessment roll; and where any person is assessed as a trustee, guardian, executor, or administrator, he must be so designated. The lands of non-residents are to be entered in the same assessment roll, but separate from the other assessments.[4]

6. If any person liable to taxation will make affidavit that the value of his real estate does not exceed a certain sum, to be specified in such affidavit, or that the value of the personal estate owned by him, after deducting his just debts, and his property invested in incorporated companies liable to taxation, does not exceed a certain sum to be specified as aforesaid, it will be the duty of the Assessors to value such real or personal estate, or both, at the sums specified in

[1] 1 R. S. (3d ed.,) 443, §§ 1–4; 4 Wendell, 429.

[2] 1 R. S. (3d ed.,) 443, § 5; Laws of 1850, chap. 92.

[3] 1 R. S. (3d ed.,) 443, § 6; 4 Paige, 384; 10 Wendell, 186; 22 Id., 9, 23 Id., 103; 1 Hill, 616; 4 Id., 20.

[4] 1 R. S. (3d ed.,) 444, 445, §§ 7–11.

the affidavit. Trustees, guardians, &c., &c., may make a similar affidavit in relation to the value of property held in trust by them. All real and personal property, the value of which shall not be specified by affidavit as aforesaid, must be estimated at its full value, as the Assessors would appraise the same in the payment of a just debt due from a solvent debtor.[1]

7. It is also the duty of Assessors to ascertain the amount of rents reserved on leases in fee, or for one or more lives, or for any term exceeding twenty-one years. The rents are to be assessed as personal estate, to the person or persons entitled to receive them, at a principal sum, the legal interest on which will produce a sum equal to such rents. If the rents are payable in property or services, the Assessors must ascertain the value of such property or services, in money, and find the principal sum which will yield so much interest.[2]

8. The Assessors are to complete their assessment roll on or before the first day of September in every year, and to make one fair copy thereof, to be left with one of their number. They are then forthwith to cause notice of its completion, &c., as in the form hereinafter given, to be posted up at three or more public places in the town or ward. The Assessors are to meet at the time appointed to review their assessments, and are to be governed by the same rules as above specified. Any person considering himself aggrieved, may offer his own affidavit, or other testimony, in order to show that his assessment is erroneous.[3]

9. The affidavits above mentioned are to be made before the Assessors, or any one of them.[4]

10. After completing the review of the assessment roll, the Assessors are to sign the same, and attach thereto a certificate, as in the form hereinafter given. The roll thus certified is to be delivered by the Assessors in the city of New York to the city comptroller, on or before the twentieth of September, and in all other towns or wards, to the Supervisor thereof, on or before the first day of October in every year.[5]

11. The duty of Assessors, in determining the value of taxable property, is, in its nature, judicial, and they are not legally responsible for an error.[6]

12. Every person chosen or appointed to the office of Collector in a town, before he enters on the duties of his office, and within eight days after he receives notice of the amount of taxes to be collected by him, must execute to the Supervisor of the town, and lodge with him a bond with one or more sureties, to be approved of by such Supervisor.[7]

---

[1] 1 R. S. (3d ed.,) 446, §§ 15–17.
[2] Laws of 1846, chap. 327.
[3] 1 R. S. (3d ed.,) 446, 7, §§ 19–24; 10 Wendell, 195.
[4] 1 R. S. (3d ed.,) 447, § 25.

[5] 1 R. S. (3d ed.,) 447, §§ 26, 27; Laws of 1842, chap. 218.
[6] 3 Denio, 117.
[7] 1 R. S. (3d ed.,) 396, § 36.

13. The Collector or receiver of any town or ward, in addition to the surety above mentioned, is required, before he enters on the duties of his office, to give a bond with sufficient sureties, to be approved of by the Supervisor of the town, or ward, in which he resides, conditioned for the faithful payment to the treasurer of the County or City, of all commutation money received by him from all persons liable to do military duty, on or before the tenth day of August.[1]

14. Whenever any Town Collector receives any warrant for the collection of taxes, it is his duty immediately thereafter to cause notice of the reception thereof to be posted up in five public places in the ward or town, (except in the city of New York,) and that he will attend at certain times and places to receive the taxes. It is the duty of the Collector to attend, in accordance with his notice, and any person may pay his taxes at any time and place designated therein, within thirty days from the first posting of such notices.[2]

15. Where a Collector returns any tax imposed on reserved rents, as unpaid, it is the duty of the County Treasurer to issue his warrant to the Sheriff of any county in which any real or personal estate of the person liable to pay the tax, may be found, commanding him to collect the same of such real or personal estate, together with the sum of one dollar for the expense of issuing the warrant, and to pay over the money at a certain time to be specified, not less than sixty days from the date of the warrant.[3]

16. Whenever the Comptroller has rejected a tax returned in arrear in the first instance, or charged the same to a county to which it was before credited, on account of any inaccurate or imperfect description of the lands on which the tax was laid, the Supervisor of the town in which the lands are situated must, if in his power, add to the next assessment roll of the town an accurate description of such lands.[4]

FORMS.

§ 1046. *Assessment Roll.*

Assessment Roll of the Town of   , in the County of   ,
[or, of the   ward, in the city and county of   ,] for the year   :

Names of the taxable Inhabitants.	Quantity of land.	Value of real property.	Personal property.	Total.
John Doe,	100	1,500	500	2,000
R. Roe, Trustee of A. B.	250	3,500	1,000	4,500
James Jackson,	45	600		600

[1] Laws of 1847, chap. 290, 494.   [3] Laws of 1846, chap. 327.
[2] Laws of 1845, chap. 180.   [4] 1 R. S. (3d ed.,) 459, § 50.

LANDS OF NON-RESIDENTS.

Description of Tract.	Quantity of Land.	Valuation.
Lot No. 84,	600	3,000
Subdivision No. 2, Lot No. 86,	99	990
A tract of land situate on road leading from, &c., bounded and described as follows, to wit: [description,]	43	600

Dated the day of , 18 .

E. F.,
&c., &c., } Assessors.

---

§ 1047. *Notice of Completion of Assessment, &c.*

PUBLIC NOTICE.

Notice is hereby given, that the Assessors of the town of ,
[*or*, of the ward in the city of ,] have completed
their assessment roll, for the present year, and that a copy thereof
is left with the undersigned E. F., at his dwelling-house, in ,
where the same may be seen and examined by any of the inhabitants
of said town, [*or* ward,] during twenty days from this date; and that
the said Assessors will meet at the house of R. P., in said town, [*or*,
ward,] on the day of instant, [*or*, next,] at o'clock
in the noon, to review their assessments, on the application of
any person conceiving himself aggrieved.

Dated, &c., [*as in* § 1046.]

---

§ 1048. *Affidavit to Reduce Amount of Tax.*

County, ss:

A. B., of the town of , in said county, being duly sworn,
says, that the value of the real estate assessed to him on the assessment roll of said town, for the year 18 , described as [*give a brief
description*,] and valued on said roll at dollars, does not in
fact exceed the sum of dollars; [*or*, that the value of the
personal estate owned by him, after deducting his just debts, [*if necessary insert here*, and his property invested in incorporated companies liable to taxation,] does not exceed the sum of dollars;
or, that the value of his personal property is not equal to the amount
of debts owed by him.]

Sworn to, this day of , } A. B.
 18 , before me, }

   E. F., Assessor.

§ 1049. *Certificate to Attach to Assessment Roll.*

County, }
Town of   , } ss:

We do severally certify, that we have set down, in the above assessment roll, all the real estate situated in the town of   , in said county, [*or*, in the   ward, in the city of   ,] according to our best information; and that, with the exception of those cases in which the value of the said real estate has been sworn to by the possessor thereof, we have estimated the value of the said real estate at the sums which a majority of the Assessors have decided to be the true value thereof, and at which they would appraise the same in payment of a just debt due from a solvent debtor; and also, that the said assessment roll contains a true statement of the aggregate amount of the taxable personal estate of each and every person named in the said roll, over and above the amount of debts due from such persons respectively, and excluding such stocks as are otherwise taxable; and that with the exception of those cases in which the value of such personal estate has been sworn to by the owner or possessor, we have estimated the same according to our best information and belief.

Dated, &c., [*as in* § 1046.]

---

§ 1050. *Notice of Supervisor to Collector of Amount of Taxes.*

To H. C., Collector of the Town of   :

You are hereby notified that the amount of taxes to be collected by you in said town of   , for the current year, is   dollars and   cents.

Dated   , the   day of   , 18 .

Yours, &c.,

L. S., Supervisor.

---

§ 1051. *Collector's Bond to Supervisor.*

Know all men by these presents: That we, H. C., A. B., and C. D., of the town of   , in the county of   , are held and firmly bound unto L. S., Supervisor of said town of   , in the penal sum [*insert double the amount of taxes to be collected*] of   thousand dollars, to be paid to the said L. S., or his successor in office; to which payment, well and truly to be made, we bind ourselves, and our, and each of our heirs, executors and administrators. jointly and severally, firmly by these presents. Sealed with our seals, and dated the   day of   , A. D. 18 .*

Whereas, the above bounden H. C. has been duly chosen Collector of said town of   : Now, therefore, the condition of this obligation is such, that if the said H. C. shall well and faithfully execute his duties as such collector, then the above obligation to be void; else to remain in force.

H. C. [L. s.]

Sealed, signed and delivered } in presence of }
G. H.

A. B. [L. s.]
C. D. [L. s.]

I approve of the sureties named in the above bond.

Dated   , the   day of   , 18 .

L. S., Supervisor of the Town of   .[1]

---

§ 1052. *Collector's Bond under the Law Providing for the Enrollment of the Militia.*

Know all men by these presents: That we, H. C., A. B., and C. D., of the town of   , in the county of   , are held and firmly bound unto L. H., Colonel of the   regiment of the enrolled militia of the State of New York, in the penal sum [*insert such sum as the officer approving the bond may deem sufficient,*] of   dollars, to be paid to the said L. H., or his successor in office to which payment, &c., [*as in* § 1051 *to the* *, *and then add:*]

Now, the condition of this obligation is such, that, if the above bounden H. C., who is the collector of the town of   aforesaid, shall faithfully pay all moneys received by him in pursuance of the act entitled " An Act to provide for the enrollment of the militia, and to encourage the formation of Uniform Companies, excepting the First Military Division of this State"—passed May 13th, 1847, as amended by an Act passed December 15, 1847, into the treasury of the county of   , on or before the tenth day of August next, then the above obligation to be void; else to remain in force.

Sealed, &c., [*as in* § 1051, *with the approval annexed thereto.*]

---

§ 1053. *Notice of Collector.*

PUBLIC NOTICE.

Notice is hereby given to the taxable inhabitants of the town of   , [*or, of the*   ward, in the city of   ,] that I, the undersigned, the Collector of taxes in and for the said town, [*or,*

---

[1] The Supervisor must file the bond of the Collector in the office of the County Clerk within six days after its execution.

ward,] have received the warrant for the collection of the taxes for the present year; and that I will attend at my dwelling-house, [or, at the house of R. P.,] in said town, [or, ward,] on Thursday of each week, for thirty days from the date hereof, from nine o'clock in the forenoon until four o'clock in the afternoon, for the purpose of receiving payment of taxes.

Dated   , the   day of   , 18   .

H. C., Collector.

---

§ 1054. *Warrant of County Treasurer.*

To the Sheriff of the County of   , greeting:

The people of the State of New York command you to make of the goods and chattels of A. B., in your county, the sum of dollars, being the amount of a tax assessed to the said A. B., in the town of   , and county of   , under and in pursuance of the provisions of an act, entitled "An Act to equalize taxation," passed May 13, 1846, together with one dollar for this warrant; and if sufficient goods and chattels cannot be found in your county to make the said sums of money, you are required to levy the same of the lands and tenements, real estate and chattels real, of the said A. B., whereof he was seized on the   day of   , 18   . And you will pay over the moneys collected by virtue of this warrant, to the undersigned, the Treasurer of the county of   aforesaid, on or before the   day of   , 18   .

J. C. D., Treasurer of the County of   .

CHAPTER XLIII.

TOWN AUDITORS.

PRACTICAL REMARKS.

1. The Supervisor, Town Clerk, and Justices of the Peace, or any two Justices, of any town, constitute the Board of Town Auditors, for the purpose of auditing and allowing all claims payable by such town. The Board are required to meet annually, at the place of holding the last town meeting, on the last Thursday preceding the annual meeting of the Board of Supervisors of the county.[1]

2. Accounts for services and disbursements presented to the Town Auditors, must be made out in items, and accompanied with an affidavit, as in the form hereinafter given. The affidavit must be made by the person presenting, or claiming, the account, and must be attached to, and filed with the same.[2]

3. The board must annex to each account audited by them, a certificate in duplicate, specifying the name of the person in whose favor the same is drawn, the nature of the demand, and the amount allowed. One copy of the certificate is to be filed with the Town Clerk, and the other delivered to the Supervisor, to be presented to the Board of Supervisors, who will order the amount to be collected in the town.[3]

4. It is the duty of boards of town auditors, to make annually, brief abstracts of the names of all persons who have presented to said board accounts to be audited, with the amounts claimed by each, and the amounts finally audited; which abstracts are to be delivered to the Clerk of the Board of Supervisors and printed with the other statements required to be printed by him.[4]

5. The original accounts and affidavits presented to the board of town auditors are to be filed in the office of the clerk of the town.

---

[1] Laws of 1840, chap. 305; Laws of 1844, chap. 228.
[2] Laws of 1845, chap. 180, § 24; Laws of 1847, chap. 490.
[3] Laws of 1840, chap. 305.
[4] Laws of 1847, chap. 455

FORMS.

§ 1055. *Certificate of Town Auditors.*

County, } ss:
Town of   ,

We, the undersigned, composing the Board of Town Auditors of said town, do hereby certify, that we have this day audited and allowed to E. F., Commissioner of Highways of said town, by whom the foregoing account has been presented to us, the sum of dollars, as and for his services as such Commissioner, [*insert,* and the disbursements necessarily paid out by him in the execution of his duties, *if necessary*] up to, and including, the   day of instant; and that we find a balance of   dollars and   cents to be due by the said E. F, to the town of   [*or, as the balance may be.*]

Dated at   , the   day of   , 18   .

A. B., Supervisor.
C. D., Town Clerk.
G. H., } Justices.
&c., &c., }

---

§ 1056. *Affidavit to attach to an Account.[1]*

County, ss:

E. F., of said county, being duly sworn, says, that the items for services and disbursements mentioned in the foregoing account, by him presented [*or,* claimed,] are in all respects correct; that such disbursements and services have in fact been made or rendered, or are necessary to be made or rendered, at this session of the Board; and that no part thereof has been paid or satisfied.

Sworn to, this   day of   ,'}   E. F.
    18   , before me,   }
A. B., Chairman of the Board of Town Auditors of   .

---

§ 1057. *Abstract of Claims Audited by the Town Auditors.*

Abstract of the names of all persons who presented accounts to be audited to the Board of Town Auditors, of the town of   , on

---

[1] This form may also be used to verify accounts presented to the Board of Supervisors, or County Superintendents of the Poor. The oath may be administered by the chairman of the Board of Town Auditors, or Supervisors, or by any one of the County Superintendents.

the   day of   , 18 , with the amounts claimed by cach, and the amounts finally audited.

Names.	Title of Office, or nature of claim or services.	Am't claimed.	Am't audited.
John Brown,	Justice of the Peace,	50 50	40 50
John Doe.	Town Superintendent of Com. Schools,	60 00	60 00
Richard Roe,	For supplies to town Poor,	78 00	78 00
James Thompson,	Medical services,	100 00	85 00
&c., &c.	&c., &c.		
	Total,		

Town of   , ss :

   We do hereby certify that the foregoing abstract is correct.

     Dated   , the   day of   , 18 .

              D. E. L., Supervisor.

              S. G., Town Clerk.

              H. F.,

              S. T., } Justices of the

              &c., &c., Peace.

CHAPTER XLIV.

TOWN HOUSES.

PRACTICAL REMARKS.

1. The electors of any town in this State, in which there shall not be a town-house, may, at any annual town meeting, by resolution, vote a sum of money for the purchase of a site, and the erection of a town-house, not exceeding in the number of dollars, twice the number of electors in the town; provided that a notice of the intention to propose such a resolution be posted, within fifteen, and not less than ten, days, preceding the town meeting, in five of the most public places in the town.

2. Upon presenting the action of the town to the Board of Supervisors of the county, they may cause the sum voted to be collected with the other expenses of the town, or require the question to be again submitted to the electors at the next annual town meeting.

3. Conveyances for sites of town-houses are to be made to the towns. The sites are to be purchased, and the houses erected, by the Supervisor, Town Clerk, and Justices of the Peace. The Supervisor, Town Clerk, and the Justice residing nearest the town-house, have the right to control the same.

4. The electors of any town may vote such sum as may be necessary to repair or insure the town-house.[1]

———

FORMS.

§ 1058. *Notice of Intention to Propose Resolution.*

PUBLIC NOTICE.

Notice is hereby given, that a resolution will be proposed by the undersigned, at the next annual town meeting of the town of   ,

---

[1] Laws of 1847, chap. 197

to be held at⠀⠀⠀⠀, in said town, on the⠀⠀⠀⠀day of next, authorizing the sum of⠀⠀⠀⠀dollars to be raised for the purchase of a site for, and the building of, a town-house, in said town. Dated at⠀⠀⠀⠀, the⠀⠀⠀⠀day of⠀⠀⠀⠀, 18 .

A. B,

---

§ 1059. *Certificate to be Laid Before the Board of Supervisors.*

Town of⠀⠀⠀⠀County,⠀} ss:
⠀⠀⠀⠀⠀⠀⠀⠀⠀,

We, the undersigned, the Board of Canvassers, at the annual town meeting of the town of⠀⠀⠀⠀, held at the house of R. F., in said town, on the⠀⠀⠀⠀day of .⠀⠀⠀⠀instant, do hereby certify, that the following resolution was proposed at said meeting, and adopted by a majority of the voices of the electors present and voting thereupon:

"*Resolved,* that the sum of⠀⠀⠀⠀dollars be raised in the town of⠀⠀⠀·⠀⠀, and that the same be, and hereby is, appropriated for the purchase of a site for, and the building of, a town-house, in said town."

Witness our hands, this⠀⠀⠀⠀day of⠀⠀⠀⠀, 18 .

G. H.,
S. T.,⠀} Justices.
&c., &c.,

---

§ 1060. *Resolution of the Board of Supervisors.*

Resolved, That the sum of⠀⠀⠀⠀dollars be raised and collected in the town of⠀⠀⠀⠀, for the purchase of a site for, and the building of, a town-house, in said town, in accordance with the resolution adopted by the electors thereof at the last annual town meeting; [*or,* That the question of raising the sum of⠀⠀⠀⠀dollars in the town of⠀⠀⠀⠀, for the purchase of a site for, and the building of, a town-house, in said town, voted upon at the last annual town meeting held therein, be again submitted to the electors thereof, at the next annual town meeting.]

CHAPTER XLV

WILLS.

PRACTICAL REMARKS.

i. All persons except idiots, persons of unsound mind, and infants, may devise their real estate by a last will and testament duly executed. Such devise may be made to any person capable, by law, of holding real estate; but no devise to a corporation will be valid, unless such corporation be expressly authorized by its charter, or statute, to take by devise. Every devise of any interest in real property, to a person, who, at the time of the death of the testator, may be an alien, not authorized to hold real estate, will be void.[1]

2. Every male person of the age of eighteen years, or upwards, and every female of the age of sixteen years, or upwards, of sound mind and memory, and no others, may give and bequeath his or her personal estate in writing. No nuncupative or unwritten will, bequeathing personal estate, will be valid unless made by a soldier, while in actual military service, or by a mariner while at sea.[2]

3. Married women may devise real or personal property belonging to them in their own right, and not conveyed, given, granted, or devised to them by their husbands.[3]

4. Every last will and testament of real or personal property, or both, must be executed and attested, in the following manner:—

1. It must be subscribed by the testator, at the end of the will:

2. Such subscription must be made by the testator, in the presence of each of the attesting witnesses, or acknowledged by him to have been so made to each of the attesting witnesses :

---

[1] 2 R. S. (3d ed.) 118, 119, §§ 1-4; 4 Paige, 22; 3 Wendell, 166; 10 Id., 379.

[2] 2 R. S., (3d ed.) 121, §§ 18, 19; 1 Hoffman's Ch. Rep., 1; Id., 202.
[3] Laws of 1849, chap. 375.

3. The testator, at the time of making such subscription, or at the time of acknowledging the same, must declare the instrument so subscribed, to be his last will and testament.

4. There must be, at least, two attesting witnesses, each of whom must sign his name as a witness, at the end of the will, at the request of the testator.

5. The witnesses to any will must write opposite to their names their respective places of residence; and every person who may sign the testator's name to any will, by his direction, must write his own name as a witness to the will.

6. Whoever neglects to comply with either of the foregoing provisions, will forfeit fifty dollars, to be recovered by any person interested in the property devised or bequeathed, who may sue for the same. Such omission will not affect the validity of any will; nor will any person liable to the penalty aforesaid, be excused or incapacitated, on that account, from testifying respecting the execution of such will.[1]

5. No will in writing, (except in the cases particularly specified in the statute,) nor any part thereof, can be revoked, or altered, otherwise than by some other will in writing, or some other writing of the testator, declaring such revocation or alteration, and executed with the same formalities with which the will itself was required by law to be executed; or unless such will be burnt, torn, canceled, obliterated, or destroyed, with the intent, and for the purpose of revoking the same, by the testator himself, or by another person in his presence, by his direction and consent; and when so done by another person, the direction and consent of the testator, and the fact of such injury or destruction, must be proved by at least two witnesses.[2]

6. Marriage and the birth of a child, subsequent to the execution of a will, operate as a revocation, if there be no provision made for the wife and child. A will executed by an unmarried woman will be deemed revoked by her subsequent marriage. After born children, not provided for or mentioned in a will, or in a settlement, are entitled to such share of the estate of the testator as they would have had if no will had been made.[3]

7. Fraud will vitiate a will.[4]

8. Mere imbecility will not avoid a will. The term "unsound mind," in the statute concerning wills, has the same signification as *non compos mentis*.[5]

9. A sound disposing mind, or testable capacity, is any point above idiocy or lunacy.[6]

---

[1] 2 R. S. (3d ed.,) 124, §§ 32,33; 8 Paige, 489; 10 Id., 85; 26 Wendell, 331, 525; 1 Denio, 33; 1 Barbour's S. C. Rep., 526; 2 Id., 40, 200.

[2] 2 R. S. (3d ed.,) 124, § 34; 20 Wendell, 457; 1 Hill, 590.

[3] 2 R. S. (2d ed.,) 124, 5, §§ 35, 36, 41; 4

Kent's Commentaries, (2d ed.,) 520, et seq.; 4 Johnson's Ch. Rep., 505; 5 Paige, 590; 7 Id., 99; 1 Denio, 27.

[4] 1 Comstock, 214.

[5] 3 Denio, 37.

[6] 26 Wendell, 255; 3 Denio, 37; 2 Comstock, 498

10. Where the personal estate is not in terms exonerated by a will, it will be deemed the primary fund for the payment of legacies.[1]

11. No provision made in a will for a wife, will prevent her from having dower also, unless it be expressly declared to be in lieu of dower, and she assent thereto. A testamentary provision, where the intention is doubtful, though accepted, will not deprive her of dower.[2]

12. Lands purchased after making a will, will not pass by it, unless it be republished in the presence of the former, or any other two witnesses.[3]

13. A codicil is a supplement to a will, and must be attested in the same manner.[4]

14. A codicil to a will causes it to speak from the re-publication.[5]

15. The term "heirs," or other words of inheritance, are not necessary to the devise of an estate in fee. Where it is the intention to give an estate for life only, the words "during his natural life," or other words to the same effect, must be used.[6]

16. A will is valid, although it contain a devise or bequest to the witness; such bequest, however, is void.[7]

17. Three witnesses to a will of real estate are required in Vermont, New Hampshire, Maine, Massachusetts, Rhode Island, Connecticut, New Jersey, Maryland, South Carolina, Georgia, Alabama, Mississippi, Michigan, Wisconsin, and Iowa. Two witnesses only are necessary in New York, Delaware, Virginia, Ohio, Illinois, Indiana, Missouri, Tennessee, North Carolina, and Kentucky. In Pennsylvania, no subscribing witness is necessary, provided the authenticity of the will can be proved by two witnesses: and if a will be subscribed by witnesses, it may be proved by the oaths of other persons.[8]

18. After the lapse of sixty years from the date of a will, its execution may be shown, without proving that efforts have been made to procure the attendance of the subscribing witnesses, as their death may be presumed.[9]

---

[1] 1 Comstock, 120.
[2] 2 R. S. (3d ed.,) 27, §§ 9–11; 2 Johnson's Ch. Rep., 448; 2 Paige, 559; 8 Id., 325; 7 Cowen, 285; 5 Hill, 206; 2 Denio, 430.
[3] 2 R. S. (3d ed.,) 124,5, §§ 37–40; 7 Johnson's Ch. Rep., 258; 4 Kent's Commentaries, (2d ed.) 528.
[4] 6 Johnson's Ch. Rep., 376; 1 Hill, 590.
[5] 7 Hill, 346.
[6] 2 R. S. (3d ed.,) 33, § 1; 2 Johnson's Cas 484; 2 Hill, 554; 3 Id., 165; 5 Id., 410; 1 Denio, 165.
[7] 2 R. S. (3d ed.,) 125, §§ 42, 43.
[8] 4 Kent's Commentaries, (2d ed.,) 513, 614
[9] 7 Hill, 475.

FORMS.

§ 1061. *Will of Real and Personal Estate.*

In the name of God, amen: I, A. B., of the town of   , in the county of   , and State of   , of the age of   years, and being of sound mind and memory, do make, publish and declare, this my last will and testament, in manner following, that is to say:

First, I give and bequeath to my wife, E. B., the sum of   , to be accepted and received by her in lieu of dower; to my son, C. B., the sum of   ; to my daughter, M. B., the sum of   ; and to my daughter-in-law, S. B., widow of my son, R. B., deceased, the sum of   ; which said several legacies or sums of money, I direct and order to be paid to the said respective legatees, within one year after my decease.

Second, I give and devise to my son, C. B., aforesaid, his heirs and assigns, all that tract or parcel of land, situate, &c., [*describe the premises,*] together with all the hereditaments and appurtenances thereunto belonging or in any wise appertaining: To have and to hold the premises above described to the said C. B., his heirs and assigns, forever.

Third, I give and devise all the rest, residue and remainder, of my real estate, of every name and nature whatsoever, to my said daughter, M. B., and my said daughter-in-law, S. B., to be divided equally between them, share and share alike.

And *lastly*, I give and bequeath all the rest, residue and remainder, of my personal estate, goods and chattels, of what nature or kind soever, to my said wife, E. B., whom I hereby appoint sole executrix of this my last will and testament; hereby revoking all former wills by me made.

In witness whereof, I have hereunto set my hand and seal, this   day of   , in the year of our Lord one thousand eight hundred and   .   A. B. [L. S.]

The above instrument, consisting of one sheet, [*or*, two sheets,] was, at the date thereof, signed, sealed, published and declared, by the said A. B., as and for his last will and testament, in presence of us, who, at his request and in his presence, and in the presence of each other, have subscribed our names as witnesses thereto. [*Or*, The above instrument, consisting of one sheet, was, at the date thereof, declared to us by A. B., the testator therein mentioned, to be his last will and testament; and he at the same time acknowledged to us, and each of us, that he had signed and sealed the same; and we thereupon, at his request, and in his presence, and in the presence of each other, signed our names thereto as attesting witnesses.]

C. D., residing at   , in   county.
G. H., residing at   , in   county.

§ 1062. *Codicil to a Will.*

Whereas, I, A. B., of, &c., have made my last will and testament in writing, bearing date the   day of   , in the year of our Lord one thousand eight hundred and   , in and by which I have given and bequeathed to, &c., [*here set forth the bequest which the testator desires to change:*] Now, therefore, I do, by this my writing, which I hereby declare to be a codicil to my said last will and testament, and to be taken as a part thereof, order and declare that my will is, that only the sum of   be paid to my daughter-in-law, S. B., in full of the said legacy given and bequeathed to her; and that the remaining part of the said legacy be given and paid to my nephew, R. F.: And lastly, it is my desire that this codicil be annexed to, and made a part of, my last will and testament as aforesaid, to all intents and purposes.

In witness, &c., [*as in* § 1061, except that the attestation will *read,* " as and for a codicil to his last will," &c.]

---

§ 1063. *Nomination of Executors in a Will.*

And *lastly,* I do hereby nominate and appoint my sons, C. B. and M. B., [*or,* my friends, E. F. and L. M.,] to be the executors of this my last will and testament, hereby revoking all former wills by me made.

---

§ 1064. *Devise to Executors in Trust, with Power to Sell, &c.*

I give and devise all my real and personal estate, of what nature or kind soever, to E. F. and L. M., the executors of this my last will and testament, hereinafter nominated and appointed, in trust, for the payment of my just debts and the legacies above specified, with power to sell and dispose of the same, at public or private sale, at such time or times, and upon such terms, and in such manner, as to them shall seem meet; provided, however, that no part of my real estate, as aforesaid, shall be sold at public auction, until after the expiration of three years from the time of my decease.

---

§ 1065. *Disposition of the Tuition and Custody of Minor Children.*

And I do hereby dispose of and commit, the tuition and custody of my children, M. B., R. B. and F. B., and every of them, for such time as they or any of them respectively continue unmarried, and under the age of twenty-one years, unto my wife, E. B., provided she remains my widow; but if she shall die or marry, during the single life and nonage of any of my said children, I hereby dispose of and commit their tuition and custody to my executors, hereinafter nominated and appointed.

---

§ 1066. *Provision in a Will for a Child, Born After the Death of the Testator.*

I give and bequeath to my wife, E. B., the sum of   , in trust for any child, or children, by me begotten, which may be born of her subsequent to the time of my decease; which said sum of money is to be paid to such child, or divided equally between such children, when he, or she, or they, shall have arrived at the age of twenty-one years.

---

§ 1067. *Provision for Children Born After the Execution of a Will.*

I give, bequeath and devise, all the rest, residue and remainder, of my real and personal estate, to my children now living, or who may be living at the time of my decease, to be divided equally between them, share and share alike.

---

§ 1068. *The same, in Another Form.*

I give and bequeath to each and every of my children born subsequent to the execution of this my last will and testament, the sum of   dollars, to be paid in the same manner as the other legacies hereinbefore mentioned.

---

§ 1069. *Devise of an Estate for Life to one Person, and Reversion to Another.*

I give and devise all my real estate, of what nature or kind soever, to my wife, E. B., [*or*, to my friend, L. M.,] to be used and enjoyed by her, [*or*, him,] during the term of her [*or*, his] natural life; and from and immediately after her [*or*, his] decease, I give and devise the same to my friend, S. T., his heirs and assigns, forever.

§ 1070. *Devise to Trustees, During a Life, or Lives.*

I give, bequeath and devise, all my real and personal estate, of what nature or kind soever, to E. F. and G. H., the executors of this my last will and testament, hereinafter nominated and appointed, in trust, for the payment of my just debts, and the legacies and charges upon the said estate hereinafter specified, to be held and possessed by them, for the purpose aforesaid, for and during the natural life of L. M., of the town of   , and State of   , and for and during the natural life of E. M., infant son of the said L. M.; and from and after their decease, and the decease of each of them, I give, bequeath and devise, my said estate, to my son, C. B., his heirs and assigns: And I do hereby order and direct, that during the continuance of the said trust estate, as aforesaid, there shall be annually paid out of the net income and profits thereof, the sum of to my wife, E. B., in lieu of all dower, or right of dower, in and to my said estate; the sum of   to my son, C. B.; and the sum of   to my daughter, M. B.; and that the rest, residue and remainder, of the said net income and profits, shall be divided equally between my said executors, in lieu of compensation for their services in the execution of the said trust.

---

§ 1071. *Devise of an Annuity.*

I give, devise and bequeath, to my wife, E. B., and her assigns, for and during the term of her natural life, one annuity, or clear yearly rent, or sum, of   , free of all taxes and other deductions, to be issuing and payable out of the real estate above devised to my son, C. B., in equal half yearly payments, at   , on the   day of January and July, in each and every year as aforesaid; and I do hereby charge and subject the said real estate with and to the payment of the said annuity, yearly rent, or sum, of   , at the times and in the manner aforesaid; fully empowering and authorizing, my said wife and her assigns, provided the said annuity, or any part thereof, shall remain unpaid after the expiration of twenty days from the time when the same shall be due and payable as aforesaid, to enter into all and singular the premises charged with the annuity as aforesaid, and the rents, issues and profits thereof, to receive and take, until she and they be therewith and thereby, or by the person or persons then entitled to the immediate possession of the premises, paid and satisfied the same and every part thereof, and all the arrears then due and payable, together with her and their costs, damages and expenses, paid out and sustained, by reason of the non-payment thereof, or of any part therof.

APPENDIX.

ABANDONMENT.

In Marine Insurance, where there has been a constructive total loss, there may be an abandonment; that is to say, the insured may claim a total loss from the insurers, by relinquishing all interest in the thing insured, to them. The notice of abandonment may be either oral or in writing; if given orally, it must be express. No particular form is required, but the cause must be stated, in whichever form the notice is given. It must be made within a reasonable time after the loss. The abandonment must be entire, and cannot be either partial or conditional; it cannot be revoked. Where there has been in fact no loss, it may become of no effect. When legally made, the abandonment transfers title to the insurer, and the insurance must be paid. An abandonment may be made in the following cases: When from any cause there has been a total loss; when the part saved is of less value than the freight; where the damage exceeds one-half of the value of the insurance; where the property is captured, or detained by an indefinite embargo.

Ordinary Form.

New York, April 7, 1872.

—— ——, Sec.
    Ocean Marine Ins. Co.,
    We understand that the ship ——, on her voyage from —— to——, has been compelled by reason of ——, to seek the port of —— in distress. The cargo was landed, and more than one-half its value destroyed. We therefore hereby abandon to you [*here state the property abandoned, and its value*) insured by you under our policy No. ——, for $——, and shall claim for a total loss.

Your Obt. S'vts.
Signature.

Form where the vessel and cargo are abandoned, with power of attorney and covenant for further assurance.

To all to whom these presents shall come greeting:
    Whereas, we, ——, and ——, of the city of ——, in the State of ——, caused to be insured by the —— Insurance Co., [*here set out the contract of insurance*] as by a policy numbered ——, will more fully appear; and whereas the said ship, whilst she was sailing on her voyage from —— to ——, on or about the —— day of ——, 18—, last past, [*here set out in full the cause of the loss.*]

38

Now, THEREFORE, know ye, that we the aforesaid —— and ——, do hereby abandon to the said —— Insurance Co., such proportion of the said ship and cargo, and of our interest therein, as the said sum of —— dollars by them insured bears to the whole vessel and cargo.

And we do hereby constitute and appoint —— ——, our true and lawful attorney in our names, but for the use of said Insurance Co., and at their costs and charges, to claim, sue for, recover, and receive such proportion of the said vessel and cargo as is hereinbefore by us abandoned. And we, the said —— and ——, do hereby for ourselves, our executors and administrators, covenant and agree, to and with the said —— Insurance Co., that we, our executors and administrators, shall and will, at all times hereinafter, at the request, and at the costs and charges of the said —— Insurance Co., make, seal, execute, acknowledge, and deliver all and every such further and other conveyances and assurances for the better conveying and assuring to the said —— Insurance Co., the proportions of the said vessel and cargo hereinbefore by us abandoned, and all and every such further and other letter or letters of attorney for enabling the said —— Insurance Co., at their own charges, to ask, demand, sue for, and recover the said proportions of the said vessel and cargo, as to them, the said —— Insurance Co., shall seem reasonably necessary.

IN TESTIMONY WHEREOF, we have hereunto set our hands and seals, this — day of —, A. D. one thousand eight hundred and —.

Signature, [SEAL.]
Signature, [SEAL.]

ACKNOWLEDGMENT AND PROOF OF DEEDS, &c.

IN ALABAMA.

1. *Proof by a subscribing witness.*

STATE OF ALABAMA, ⎱
County of ——. ⎰

I HEREBY CERTIFY, [*here set out the name and title of the officer giving the certificate*] that ——, a subscribing witness to the foregoing——, known to me, appeared before me, this day, and, being duly sworn, stated that——, the grantor in the foregoing instrument, voluntarily executed the same in his presence, and in the presence of ——, the other subscribing witness thereto, on the day the same bears date: that he attested the same in the presence of the said ——, and of the said other witness; and that such other witness subscribed the same as a witness in his presence.

Given under my hand, this —— day of ——, one thousand eight hundred and ——. *Signature and title of officer.*

IN ARKANSAS.

1. *Grantor known to the officer.*

STATE OF ARKANSAS, ⎱
County of ——. ⎰ *ss.*

ON THIS —— day of ——, in the year of our Lord one thousand

eight hundred and——, before me, [*here set out the name and title of the officer, state that he is acting and duly commissioned,*] within and for the county of ——, in the State of Arkansas, appeared in person ——*, to me personally well known as the person whose name appears upon the within and foregoing [*here state the name of the instrument*] † as the party grantor, and stated that he had executed the same for the consideration and purposes therein mentioned and set forth, and I do hereby so certify.

IN TESTIMONY WHEREOF, I have hereunto set my hand as such [*Commissioner, Notary or Justice of the Peace,*] at the County of ——, on the ——day of ——, 18—.

Signature and title of officer.

2. *Grantor not personally known to the officer.*

[*The form is the same as in No. 1, with the exception that between the * and the* † *the following words should be inserted,*] who being personally unknown to me, was by the oaths of ——, and ——, witnesses duly sworn and examined by me as to his identity, proven to my satisfaction to be the identical —— whose name appears upon the foregoing [*name the instrument.*]

3. *By husband and wife, joint deed of wife's land.*

[*Follow form No. 1 to the *, then as follows*] to me personally well known as one of the parties grantor, and stated that he had executed the same for the consideration and purposes therein mentioned and set forth, and I do hereby so certify.

AND I DO FURTHER CERTIFY, that on this day voluntarily appeared before me ——, wife of the said ——, to me well known [*where the wife is not known to the officer, same as in form No. 2,*] to be the person whose name appears upon the within and foregoing [*name the instrument,*] and in the absence of the said husband, declared that she had, of her own free will, *executed the same, for the purposes therein contained and set forth, without compulsion or undue influence of her said husband.

IN TESTIMONY [*same as in form No. 1.*]

4. *By husband and wife, joint deed of husband's land.*

[*Follow form No. 1 to the †, where party is known to the officer ; if not, modify by using No. 2, then as follows,*] as one of the parties grantor, and stated that he had executed the same for the consideration and purposes therein mentioned and set forth.

AND I FURTHER CERTIFY, [*same as in form No. 3 to the *, continuing*] signed and sealed the relinquishment of dower therein expressed, for the purposes therein contained and set forth, without compulsion or undue influence of her said husband.

IN TESTIMONY [*same as in form No. 1.*]

5. *Proof by a subscribing witness.*

STATE OF ARKANSAS, ?
County of ——. }

BE IT REMEMBERED, that on this —— day of ——, 18—, before me [*set out the name and title of officer, state that he is acting and duly commissioned*] in and for the county aforesaid * personally appeared —— one of the subscribing witnesses to the foregoing [*name the instrument,*] to me personally well known, who being by me first duly sworn, on his oath stated that he saw ——, grantor in said deed, subscribe and seal said deed on the day of its date [*or, that the said* ——, grantor in said deed, acknowledged to him, on the —— day of —— 18—, that he had subscribed, sealed and executed said deed,] for the uses, purposes, and consideration therein expressed; and that he and ——, the other subscribing witness, subscribed the same as attesting witnesses, at the request of the said grantor.

IN TESTIMONY WHEREOF [*same as No. 1.*]

6. *Proof of handwriting.*

[*Follow form No. 5 to the* *, *continuing,*] personally came —— and ——, upon their oaths stated that the signatures of ——, the grantor in the within and foregoing [*name the instrument,*] and of ——, a witness thereto, are genuine, and are in the handwriting of said ——, grantor, and —— witness, respectively.

IN TESTIMONY WHEREOF, [*same as No. 1.*]

IN CALIFORNIA.

1. *Grantor known to the officer.*

STATE OF CALIFORNIA, ? ss.
County of ——. }

I HEREBY CERTIFY, that on this —— day of ——, 18—, personally appeared before me [*here set out the name and title of the officer*] in and for said county, †the within named —— ——,* to me personally known to be the person [*or persons*] described in, and who executed the [*within or annexed*] instrument, and who [*severally*] acknowledged that he [*or that they severally*] executed the same, freely and voluntarily, for the uses and purposes therein mentioned. [*Where the acknowledgment is taken out of the State, add,* IN TESTIMONY WHEREOF, *as in form* 1 *of Arkansas.*]
[SEAL.] *if he have one.*

Signature and title of officer.

2. *Where a wife joins.*

[*As in form No.* 1 *to the* *, *then*] and ——, his wife, to me personally known to be the persons described in, and whose names are subscribed to, the [*within or annexed*] instrument, as parties thereto, and severally acknowledged that they severally executed the same, freely and voluntarily, for the uses and purposes therein mentioned. And the said —— ——, wife as aforesaid, having been by me first

made acquainted with the contents of such conveyance, acknowledged on an examination had by me, apart from and without the hearing of her husband, that she executed the same freely and voluntarily, without fear or compulsion, or undue influence of her husband, and that she does not wish to retract the execution of the same. [*Where the acknowledgment is taken out of the State, conclude as directed in form No.* 1, *of this State.*]
[SEAL.] *if he have one.*

Signature and title of officer.

3. *Grantor not personally known to the officer.*

[*As in form No.* 1 *to the* *, *then as follows*] satisfactorily proved to me to be the person described in, and who executed the [*within or annexed*] instrument as a party thereto, by the oath of —— ——, a competent and credible witness for that purpose by me duly sworn; that he the said —— ——, acknowledged, [*continue as in form No.* 1.]

4. *Subscribing witness personally known to the officer.*

[*As in form No.* 1 *to the* †, *then as follows,*] —— ——, who is a competent and credible witness * and who is personally known to me to be the person whose name is subscribed to the [*within or annexed, name instrument*] as a witness thereto; * and said —— ——, being by me first duly sworn, stated on oath that he personally knew —— ——, who executed the [*within or annexed*] instrument, and that he knew him to be the person described in, and whose name is subscribed to the same, as a party thereto; and that on or about the —— day of ——, 18—, the said ——, in the presence of said ——, and in the presence of —— ——, the other subscribing witness, voluntarily executed the same [*or, to them acknowledged that he had freely and voluntarily executed the same*], for the uses and purposes therein mentioned; and that the said —— —— thereupon subscribed his name thereto as a witness thereof, at the request of the said —— ——, and that such other witness subscribed his name thereto, as a witness, in his presence. [*Conclude as in form No.* 2, *when taken out of the State.*]
[SEAL.] *if he have one.*

Signature and title of officer.

5. *Subscribing witness not personally known to the officer.*

[*As in form No.* 4, *substituting for the words between the stars in No.* 4, *as follows,*] and who is satisfactorily proved to me to be the person whose name is subscribed to the [*within or annexed*] instrument, as a witness thereto, by the oath of —— ——.

IN TERRITORY OF COLORADO.

1. *Where wife does not, and where she does join.*

TERRITORY OF COLORADO, } ss.
County of ——————, }

BE IT KNOWN, that on this —— day of ——, 18—, before me, the

subscriber, personally came —— ——, to me personally known as the same person described in, and who executed the [*foregoing or annexed*] instrument of writing, and acknowledged the execution thereof to be his free act and deed, for the uses and purposes therein mentioned. [*Where the wife joins, add*]: And at the same time personally appeared before me the within named —— ——, wife of the said —— ——, who being by me privately examined, separate and apart from her said husband, acknowledged that she signed, sealed and delivered the said instrument in writting as her voluntary act and deed, freely and without any threat, compulsion or fear of her said husband.

WITNESS my hand and official seal, the day and year first above written.

Signature, title, and seal of officer.

IN TERRITORY OF DECOTAH.

TERRITORY OF DECOTAH, ⎱ ss.
County of ————, ⎰

BE IT REMEMBERED that on this —— day of ——, 18—, before me, the subscriber, personally came —— ——, to me personally known as the same person described in, and who executed the foregoing [*give a name to the instrument*] and acknowledged the execution thereof to be his free act and deed, for the uses and purposes therein mentioned.

IN WITNESS WHEREOF, I have this —— day of ——, 18—, made this certificate and hereunto set my hand.

[SEAL.] *if he have one.*

Signature and title of officer.

IN DELAWARE.

Form No. 1.

STATE OF DELAWARE, ⎱ ss.
County of ————, ⎰

BE IT REMEMBERED, that on the —— day of ——, 18—, personally came before the subscribers, two of the justices of the peace for —— county aforesaid, † —— ——, and —— ——, his wife, parties to the [*above or annexed*] instrument, [*if indenture say so*] known to us personally, [*or where not*] proved on oath of —— ——, of —— ——, to be such, and severally acknowledged said [*instrument or indenture*] to be their act [*or deed*] respectively; and that the said —— ——, wife as aforesaid, being at the same time privately examined by us, apart from her husband, acknowledged that she executed the said —— willingly, without compulsion, or threats, or fear of her husband's displeasure.

WITNESS our hands, the day and year aforesaid.

Signatures and titles of officers.

2. *Of a deed of a corporation.*

[*As in above form No.* 1, *to the* †, *then as follows,*] —— ——, [*here give description of officer of such corporation,*] to us personally known, and who being by us duly sworn, deposes and says, that he resides [*give place of residence in full*] that he is [*state what official position gives him the right to execute the instrument, e. g., that he is president, &c.,*] that the seal affixed to to the [*within or annexed*] —— ——, is the corporate seal [*in the case of a bank*] of the president, directors, and company of the said bank, and was affixed to the said —— by order of said directors, for the uses therein expressed; and he by like order, did subscribe his name thereto, as president of said bank.

Signatures and titles of officers.

In District of Columbia.

1. *Where wife does not, and where she does join.*

District of Columbia, ss.

Be it remembered, that on the —— day of ——, 18—, before us, —— —— and —— ——, two justices of the peace for ——. ——, a party to a certain [*name the instrument*] bearing date the —— day of ——, 18—. and hereto annexed, personally appeared in our said county of —— ——, the said —— ——, being personally well known to us as the person who executed the said deed, and acknowledged the same to be his act and deed.

[*Where the wife joins, add.*] · And we do further certify that——, wife of the said ——, party to the aforesaid deed hereto annexed, personally appeared before us in our said county of ——, and said ——, wife as aforesaid, being well known to us as the wife of the said——, who executed the aforesaid deed, and being by us examined privately and apart from her husband, acknowledged the same to be her free act and deed, and that she had willingly signed, sealed and delivered the same, and that she did not wish to retract her act.

Witness our hands, the day and year first above written.

Signature and title of officer.

In Florida.

State of Florida, ⎫
County of ——, ⎬ ss.

On this —— day of ——, 18—, before me, [*here set out the name and description of the officer*] personally appeared ——, to me known to be the person described in, and who executed the foregoing (*name the instrument*) and acknowledged the execution thereof to be his free act and deed, for the uses and purposes therein mentioned. [Seal.] if he have one.

Signature and title of officer.

IN GEORGIA.

STATE OF GEORGIA, } ss.
County of ———, }

BE IT REMEMBERED, that on this —— day of ——, 18—, before me, the undersigned, [*here set out the name and title of the officer*] personally came ——, to me well known to be the person described in, and who executed the foregoing [*name the instrument*], and acknowledged the same to be his free act and deed.

Signature and title of officer.

Proof by subscribing witness.

STATE OF GEORGIA, } ss.
County of ———. }

PERSONALLY CAME before the undersigned [*here set out the name and title of the officer*] in and for said county, [*here set out the name, business and residence*] who being duly sworn, deposes and says, that he saw —— sign, seal and deliver the within deed [*or other instrument*] for the purposes therein mentioned; that deponent subscribed the same as a witness, and saw ——, do so likewise as a witness.

Signature of witness.

SWORN to before me this —— day of ——, 18—.

Signature and title of officer.

IN IOWA.

1. *Grantor personally known.*

STATE OF IOWA, } ss.
County of ——. }

THIS IS TO CERTIFY, that on this —— day of ——, A. D. 18—, before me [*here set forth name and title of the officer*] in and for said county * personally appeared ——, personally known to me, to be the identical person whose name is affixed to the foregoing deed, as grantor [*or as the fact is,*] therein named, and acknowledged the same to be his voluntary act and deed, for the purposes therein mentioned.

IN WITNESS WHEREOF, I have hereunto set my hand [*add where a seal is used*] and the seal of my office, on the day and year first above written.

[SEAL.] if he have one.

Signature and title of officer.

2. *Party not personally known to the officer.*

[*As in above form to the *, then as follows,*] personally came ——, and ——, both proven to me satisfactorily to be the same identical persons described in, and who executed the within conveyance, by the oath of —— subscribing witness thereto, who being by me first duly sworn, did depose and say that he resided in ——, in the county of ——; that be was acquainted with said —— and ——, that he knew them to be the same persons described in, and who executed the within conveyance; and thereupon they severally acknowledged, before me, that they executed the same as their voluntary act and deed, for the uses and purposes therein mentioned.

[*In witness, etc., as in form above.*]

IN KENTUCKY.

STATE OF KENTUCKY, } *ss.*
County of ——. }

BE IT REMEMBERED, that on this —— day of ——, 18—, before me [*here set out the name and title of the officer,*] in and for said county, at my office personally came ——, and —— his wife, to me known to be the persons described in, and who executed the within deed and severally acknowledged that they executed the same for the uses and purposes therein mentioned; and the said —— wife as aforesaid, on an examination by me, privately and apart from her husband, declared that she did freely and willingly seal and deliver, the said conveyance, which was then by me shown and explained to her, and that she did not wish to retract it, and acknowledged it to be her act, and consented that it might be recorded.

Witness my hand and seal, the day and year above written.

Signature, title and seal of officer.

IN MARYLAND.

STATE OF MARYLAND, } *ss.*
County of ——. }

ON THIS —— day of ——, in the year 18—, before me personally came —— ——, and —— ——, his wife, to me known to be the persons described in and who executed the within conveyance and severally acknowledged that they executed the same; and the said —— —— wife as aforesaid, being by me first privately examined, out of the presence and hearing of her said husband, declared that she doth execute and acknowledge the same freely and voluntarily, and without being induced to do so by fear or threats by her said husband, and then and there in my presence did sign and seal the same, out of the presence and hearing of her husband.

[SEAL.] *if he have one.*

Signature and title of officer.

IN MINNESOTA.

STATE OF MINNESOTA, } *ss.*
County of —— . }

BE IT REMEMBERED, that on the —— day of ——, 18—, before the undersigned came —— ——, and —— ——, to me known to be the identical person [*or persons*] described in, and who executed the foregoing [*or annexed,*] deed [*or other instrument*] and severally acknowledged that he [*or they*] executed the same freely and voluntarily, for the uses and purposes therein expressed.

Signature and title of officer.

IN MISSISSIPPI.

STATE OF MISSISSIPPI, } *ss.*
County of ——.

ON THIS —— day of ——, 18—, personally appeared before me the subscriber, [*here set out the name and title of the officer,*] the above [*or within*] named —— —— *, who acknowledged that he signed, sealed and delivered the foregoing deed [*or other instrument*] on the day and year therein mentioned, as his voluntary act and deed.

GIVEN UNDER MY hand [*and seal*] this —— day of ——, A. D. 18—. [SEAL.] *if he have one.*

Signature and title of officer.

2. *Where wife joins.*

[*Use the form above to the* *, *then as follows*] : and —— ——, his wife, who severally acknowledged that they signed, sealed and delivered, the foregoing [*or annexed*] deed, [*or other instrument*] on the day and year therein mentioned, as their voluntary act and deed, and the said —— ——, wife as aforesaid, upon a private examination before me, apart from her husband previously acknowledged that she signed, sealed and delivered the same as her voluntary act and deed, freely without any fear, threats or compulsion of her said husband.

[GIVEN, *conclude as in preceding form*].

IN MISSOURI.

STATE OF MISSOURI, } *ss.*
County of ——.

BE IT REMEMBERED, that on the ——day of ——, 18—, before me the subscriber personally came —— ——, and [*where the wife joins*] —— ——, his wife, personally known to be the person [*or persons*] described in, and who signed the above [*or annexed*] deed [*or other instrument,*] as the party [*parties*] thereto, and acknowledged that he [*or they*] [*severally*] executed the same for the uses and purposes therein mentioned, [*and where the wife joins, add*] and the said —— ——, wife as aforesaid, being examined by me apart from her said husband, and made fully acquainted with the contents of the above [*or annexed*] deed [*or other instrument*], acknowledged that she executed the same, [*and relinquished the dower in the real estate therein mentioned,*] freely and without fear, complusion or undue influence of her said husband. [SEAL.] *if he have one.*

Signature and title of officer.

IN NEW JERSEY.

STATE OF NEW JERSEY, }
County of ——, } *ss.*
Town of ——.

ON THIS —— day of ——, 18—, personally before me [*here set out name and title of officer,*] —— ——, [*where the wife joins*] and —— ——, his wife, to me known to be the person [*or persons*] described in, and who executed the above, [*or annexed,*] deed [*or other instrument, and having first made known to him [*or them*] the contents thereof, he [*or they*] [*severally*] acknowledged that he [*or they*] executed the same for the uses and purposes therein mentioned [*and where the wife joins add,*] and the said —— ——, wife as aforesaid, on a private examination, apart from her husband, acknowledged that she signed, sealed and delivered the same as her voluntary act and deed, freely and without any fear, threats or compulsion of her said husband.

Signature and title of officer.

[SEAL.] *if he have one.*

IN OHIO.

STATE OF OHIO, }
County of ——. } *ss.*

BE IT REMEMBERED, that on the —— day of ——, 18—, before me, [*here set out the name and title of the officer*] in and for said county, appeared personally, —— ——. [*and where the wife joins add, and* —— ——, *his wife,*] to me known, and [*severally*] acknowledged that he [*or they*] did [*severally*] sign, and seal, and acknowledge the within [*or annexed*] deed [*or other instrument*] as his [*or their*] free act and deed. [*In case the wife join add*] And the said —— ——, wife as aforesaid, on an examination separate and apart from her husband; I having first read over and made known to her the contents of the within [*or annexed*] deed, [*or other instrument*] did declare that she did voluntarily sign and acknowledge the same, and that she is still satisfied therewith.

[SEAL.] *if he have one.*

Signature and title of officer.

IN VIRGINIA.

STATE OF VIRGINIA, }
County of ——. } *ss.*

WE, —— —— and —— ——, two of the justices of the peace in and for said county, do hereby certify that —— ——, and —— ——, his wife, whose names are signed to the within writing of conveyance, personally appeared before us, in the county aforesaid, and severally acknowledged the execution of the said writing for the uses and purposes therein mentioned ; and the said —— ——, wife as aforesaid, being by us duly examined, privately and apart from her said husband, and having the writing aforesaid fully explained to her, she the said —— ——, acknowledged the said writing to be her act, and declared that she had willingly executed the same, and does not wish to retract it.

GIVEN UNDER our hands, this —— day of ——, 18—.

Signature and title of officer.
Signature and title of officer.

IN WEST VIRGINIA.

Use the above form. It must be remembered that one justice is sufficient to take the acknowledgment in this State.

IN WISCONSIN.

STATE OF WISCONSIN, } *ss.*
County of ——. }

I hereby certify that on this —— day of ——, 18—, before me [*here set out the name and title of the officer*] came the within [*or above*] named, —— ——, and —— ——, his wife, to me known to be the person described in, and who executed the within deed, and severally acknowledged the execution thereof.

[SEAL.] *if he have one.*

Signature and title of officer.

AFFIDAVITS.

1. *Ordinary Form.*

[*Where the instrument is used in an action or other legal proceeding, the title should be here inserted.*]

—— ——, of [*here set out residence and business of deponent,*] being duly sworn, [*or affirmed*] deposes and says * [*here set out at length the allegations.*]

Signature of deponent.

SUBSCRIBED and sworn to [*or affirmed*] before me this —— day of ——, 18—.

Signature of officer.

[*Where for any cause, [as where the affidavit is to be used out of the county or State,] it becomes necessary that the certificate of the County Clerk should be obtained in order to authenticate the affidavit, this should be obtained and attached to it.*]

2. *Of subscribing witness.*

[*Follow form No. 1 to the *, then as follows,*] that I have true answers made to such questions as have been put to me in regard to the execution of the deed of conveyance [*or other instrument*] shown to me. So help me God..

Sworn to &c., as in No. 1. *Signature of affiant.*

3. *Of a witness to obtain release from arrest.*

Tittle of cause.

County of ——, ss. —— ——, of ——, being duly sworn, says that he [*or she*] has been legally subpœnaed as a witness to attend before the [*here insert the name of the court*] in and for the county of ——, now in session at ——, [*or to be held, giving the time*] on the trial of an indictment against —— ——, on the part of —— —— ; and that he [*or she*] this deponent, has not been so subpœnaed by his own procurement, with intent to avoid service of process ; and further this deponent saith not.

Signature of deponent.

Sworn to before me this —— day of ——, 18—.

—— ——, Sheriff of —————— county.

4. *Bastardy ; affidavit of mother on her examination.*

COUNTY OF ——, *ss.*

——, of the town of ——, in said county, being duly sworn according to law, says, that on the —— day of——, last past, she was delivered of a bastard child, which is likely to become chargeable upon said county ; and that ——, of ——, is the father of such child.

Signature of affiant.

Subscribed and sworn to, &c., as in No. 1.

5. *Of arbitrators.*

COUNTY OF ——, *ss.*

We [*here set out the names of the arbitrators*], the undersigned arbitrators, appointed by [*here set out the names of the parties appointing*], do severally swear, that we respectively will faithfully and fairly hear and examine the matters in controversy between the above named parties, and will make a just award therein, according to the best of our understanding.

Signature of arbitrators.

Severally subscribed and sworn to before me, &c., as in No. 1.

6. *Of amount due on judgments.*

COUNTY OF ——, *ss.*

——, being duly sworn, says, that he is the owner and holder of the judgment mentioned in the foregoing copy of docket of judgment, and that there is justly due to this deponent this day, on said judgment the sum of —— dollars, and —— cents, together with interest on the same from the —— day of ——, 18—.

Signature of deponent.

Subscribed, &c., as in No. 1.

7. *Of personal service.*

[*If in an action, insert title.*]

COUNTY OF ——, *ss.*

—— ——, being duly sworn according to law, says, that he [*here set out residence and business*]; that on the —— day of ——, 18—, he served on —— ——, one of the defendants above named at [*here set out the place of service*], the within [*or annexed*] summons [*or notice*], by delivering a copy thereof to him personally, and leaving the same with him, [*or by tendering a copy thereof to him personally, and on his refusal to receive the same, deponent placed it in a conspicuous place at the same time saying to him: "I hereby deliver these to you."*] Deponent further says, that he knows the person so served, to be the person mentioned and described in the summons as defendant therein, [*or the person to whom said notice was addressed.*]

Signature.

Subscribed, &c., as in No. 1.

8. *To entitle a creditor to redeem.*

SUPREME COURT, —— *County.*

$$\left.\begin{array}{c} \text{——} \\ v. \\ \text{——} \end{array}\right\rbrace \quad \textit{Judgment recovered and docketed, the ——— day of —, 18—, at —— hours, P. M.}$$

Recovery..$575 50
Costs... 17 19
                                                  ————
                                                  $592 69
                                        —— ——, *Plff's Atty.*

COUNTY OF ——, *ss.*

—— ——, above named, a judgment creditor of —— ——, being duly sworn, says, that the true sum due on said judgment at the time of claiming the right to acquire the title of ——, the original purchaser at the sheriff's sale of the real estate of the said ——, in the sum of $592.69, and interest thereon from the —— day of ——, 18—.

Signature.

Subscribed, &c., as in No. 1.

9. *Of imprisoned, to obtain discharge.*

Title of action.

COUNTY OF ——————, *ss.*

—— ——, the defendant in this action, being duly sworn according to law, says, that he was committed to the jail of the said county on the —— day of ——, under and by virtue of an execution issued by —— ——, Esq., a Justice of the Peace of said county, upon a judgment rendered before him, in favor of —— ——, the above named plaintiff, against this deponent, for the sum of $——, damages and costs, on the —— day of ——, 18—, and that he, this deponent, has remained a prisoner on said execution from the time of such commitment until the time of making this affidavit, to wit, the —— day of ——, 18—; and this deponent further says, that at the time of such commitment he had, and still has, a family in the town of ——————, county of ————, and State of ————, for which he provides, [*where such is not the case, this clause is to be omitted*] and that at the time of such commitment he was not, nor has he been since, nor is he now, a freeholder, and further he says not.

Signature of affiant.

Subscribed, &c., as in No. 1.

10. *Of publication on foreclosure by advertisement.*

STATE OF ————, CITY AND COUNTY OF ————, *ss.*

—— ——, of [*here give residence, State, county, and city or town,*] being duly sworn, says, that he is the foreman in the office of the printer of the newspaper called the [*here set out the name of the journal*] a public newspaper printed and published in the county of —— where the premises described in the annexed printed notice of sale, or a part thereof, are situated. Deponent further says, that such notice of the mortgage sale, of which a printed copy is hereto annexed, was published for twelve weeks successively in said paper, at least once in each week, prior to the time specified in said notice, for the sale of said premises; said publication having been commenced on the —— day of ——, 18—, and continued for twelve weeks at least, successively, at least once in each week, in said paper.

Signature of printer.

Subscribed, &c., as in No. 1.

11. *Of resident alien, in order that he may hold real property in New York, [this must be filed in the office of the Secretary of State, in New York State.]*

STATE OF ——, } *ss.*
County of——. }

—— ——, of ——, being duly sworn according to law, says, that he is a resident in the State of ——, and has been since the —— day of ——, 18—, and intends always to reside in the United States, and to become a citizen thereof as soon as he can be naturalized, and that he has taken such incipient measures as the laws of the United States require, to enable him to obtain naturalization.

Signature of alien.

Subscribed, &c., as in No. 1.

12. *Of posting notice of sale.*

COUNTY OF ——, *ss.*

—— ——, being duly sworn says, that on the —— day of ——, 18—, he posted in three (3) public places in the town of ——, in said county, a notice of sale, of which the foregoing [*or annexed*] is a true copy.

Signature.

Subscribed, &c., as in No. 1.

13. *Of officer making a distress.*

COUNTY OF ——, *ss.*

—— ——, being duly sworn, says, that he is the sheriff of said county; that the property mentioned in the annexed inventory and affidavit was distrained by this deponent, under and by virtue of ——, that the amount of the penalty was $——, that the property sold for the sum of $——, that I have paid the said penalty out of the said proceeds; and that I have retained the expenses of the appraisal, certificate, notice, proof, and affidavits, and of the filing of the same, amounting to $——, and that the surplus, being the sum of $——, I have this day paid to the county treasurer.

Signature of sheriff.

Subscribed, &c., as in No. 1.

14. *Of service of subpœna.*

COUNTY OF ———, *ss.*

——— ———, being duly sworn says, that on the —— day of ——, 18—, at ——, in said county, he served the within [*or annexed*] subpœna on —— ———, therein named, by then and there showing to him the said —— ———, the said original subpœna, and at the same time giving to and leaving with him a copy of the same, and at the same time and place giving to [*or tendering*] him —— cts., his legal fees.

Signature of deponent.

Subscribed, &c,, as in No. 1.

15. *Of summoning jurors in plank road case.*

COUNTY OF ———, *ss.*

—— ——, sheriff of the above named county, being duly sworn, says, that he summoned the jurors named in the annexed precept, at the times and in the manner set opposite to their names respectively, to wit :

—— ——, personally, —— day of ——, 18—; —— ——, personally, —— day of ——, 18—; —— ——, by leaving at his residence a written notice containing the substance of the precept, with a member of his family of suitable age, on the —— day of ——, 18—, he not being found.

Signature of sheriff.

Subscribed, &c., as in No. 1.

16. *Of service of award.*

COUNTY OF ———, *ss.*

—— ——, of —— ———, one of the arbitrators named in the within [*or above*] award, being duly sworn, says, that on the —— day of ——, 18—, at ——, in said county, he served the within award, upon [*here set out the parties names upon whom service was made,*] by delivering to, and leaving with them [*or him*] a true copy of said original award.

Signature.

Subscribed, &c., as in No 1.

17. *Of delivery of execution to sheriff.*

Title of action.

COUNTY OF ———, *ss.*

—— ——, being duly sworn according to law, says, that he is the attorney for the plaintiff in this action; that judgment was perfected, and the roll thereof filed in the clerk's office of —— county on the —— day of ——, 18—, for —— dollars and —— cents, damages and costs, and a transcript thereof was filed and the judgment docketed in the clerk's office of —— county, on the —— day of —— 18—, as this deponent is informed and believes; that execution in due form of law was duly issued thereon, to the sheriff of said last mentioned county, by which said sheriff was commanded to make the said sum of —— dollars and —— cents, together with interest from the ——

day of —— 18—, at —— per cent, and his fees ; and to return said execution to the office of the clerk of —— county, within sixty days after the receipt thereof by him, the said sheriff; and that the said execution was received by said sheriff for execution, on the —— day of ——, 18—, as this deponent is informed and believes. That this deponent has made inquires at the office of the clerk of —— county, for said execution, and that he has learned that though the time for returning said execution has expired, said execution has not been returned ; and that the said judgment, nor any part thereof, has not been paid to the plaintiff, but that the whole thereof remains due and unpaid ; and that the said sheriff is in default in not returning the said execution, and in not paying over the said moneys.

—— —— *Plff's Att'y.*

Subscribed, &c., as in No. 1.

18. *Procure arrest and extradition.*

COUNTY OF ————, *ss.*

—— ——, of —— ——, being duly sworn according to law, says : That —— ——, is a fugitive from justice from the state of ——, where he stands charged on oath with felony, committed in that state, viz. [*here set out the crime committed,*] which said acts are by the laws of this said state of ——, a felony. That said charge was made, on or about the —— day of ——, 18—, by —— ——, before [*here set out court or magistrate*], a copy of which said charge is hereunto annexed. That the said —— —— has fled from the said state of ——, and has taken refuge in the state of ——, seeking to escape from the laws and justice of the said state of ——, AND DEPONENT PRAYS that the said —— may be arrested and held in custody by the proper authorities of the state of ——, until the proper authorities of the said state of —— shall have have sufficient time to require, in manner and form as the law directs, the body of said —— ——, from the executive, and authorities of the said state of ——, and until the said executive of the said above named state shall make his warrant for the surrender of the body of the said —— ——, to the end that he may be taken to the state of ——, and there dealt with as the laws of that state, and justice shall require.

Signature of affiant.

Subscribed, &c., as in No. 1.

19. *Of sheriff when liable as bail, to be exonerated.*

Title of action.

COUNTY OF ————, *ss.*

—— ——, being duly sworn according to law, says, that he is the sheriff of the above named county : that by reason of the refusal or neglect of the bail taken on the arrest of the defendant in this action, to justify when thereto required by the plaintiff's attorney, it was and now is claimed by the plaintiff herein, that this deponent, sheriff as aforesaid, became and is liable to the said plaintiff as bail in said action ; [*here should be set out what has been done, and the present state of the action]:* and this deponent further says, that before, &c., said defendant was indicted and tried, and committed at a court of, &c., in, &c., of felony, and sentenced to State prison, and that said defendant has been committed to, and now is confined in the said State prison at ——, under and pursuant to said conviction and sentence, [*or set out at length any other reason why he should be exonerated.*]

Signature of sheriff.

Subscribed, &c., as in No. 1.

20. *To be annexed to proxy, in order that an attorney may vote at an election held by a moneyed corporation.*

STATE OF ——, } *ss :*
  County of ——, }

—— ——, being duly sworn according to law, says, that the shares upon which I hereby offer to vote by —— ——, my attorney and duly authorized agent in the above proxy, do not in any way belong, and are not hypothecated to the [*here set out the name of the corporation holding the election*], and that they are not hypothecated or in any way pledged to any other person or corporation whatever ; that such shares upon which I propose to vote, have not been transferred to me, for the purpose of enabling me to vote thereon at the ensuing election, and that I have not contracted to sell or transfer them, upon any condition, agreement or understanding, in relation to my manner of voting at the said election.

Signature of stockholder.

Subscribed, &c., as in No. 1.

21. *To accounts rendered by officers to board of supervisors.*

COUNTY OF ——, *ss :*

—— ——, being duly sworn, says, that he is [*here set out the title of officer*]; and he further says that the the items of the annexed [*or above*] account are correct, and that the disbursements and services charged therein, have been in fact made and rendered, and that no part thereof has in any way been paid or satisfied.

Signature of officer.

Subscribed, &c., as in No. 1.

22. *To statement of unclaimed deposits or dividends.*

STATE OF ——, } *ss :*
  County of ——. }

—— ——, of said county being duly sworn according to law, says, that he is the [*here set out the title of the officer, together with the name of the corporaiton*]; and he further says that the above [*or annexed*] schedule of dividends or deposits remaining unclaimed in the said [*here set out the name of the corporation*], for the space of two [2] years next preceding the —— day of ——, 18—, is in all respects just and true, according to the best knowledge and belief of this deponent.

Signature of officer.

Subscribed, &c., as in No. 1.

23. *Of coroner, with statement to board of supervisors.*

COUNTY OF ——, *ss.*

—— ——, being duly sworn according to law, says, that he is one of the coroners in and for said county, that the foregoing [*or annexed*] statement and inventory of all the moneys and other valuable things found with or upon all persons on inquests have been held, by and before him, within the time specified by such statement and inventory, and of the disposition thereof, is in all respects just and true, to the best of his knowledge and belief; and he further says that the moneys and other articles mentioned in such inventory and statement, have been delivered to the treasurer of the county of ——, and to the legal representatives of the persons therein mentioned as therein stated.

Signature of coroner.

Subscribed, &c., as in No. 1.

24. *Of pre-emption claimant.*

STATE OF ——, }
County of ——. } *ss :*

—— ——, of ——, being duly sworn, says, that he claims the right of pre-emption, under the provisions of the act of Congress, entitled, "An act to appropriate the proceeds of the sales of the public lands, and to grant pre-emption rights," approved September 4th, 1841, to the —— quarter of section No. ——, of township No. ——, of range No. ——, subject to sale at ——; and he further says that he never has had the benefit of any right of pre-emption under this act; that he is not the owner of three hundred and twenty acres of land, in any State or Territory of the United States, nor has he settled upon and improved said land to sell the same on speculation, but in good faith to appropriate it to his own exclusive use and benefit; and he further says, that he has not directly or indirectly made any agreement or contract in any way or manner with any person or persons whatsoever, by which the title which he may acquire from the government of the United States, should enure in whole or in part to the benefit of any person except himself, or his lawful heirs.

Signature of claimant.

I —— ——, register [*or receiver*] of the land office at ——, in the above named State and county, do hereby certify that the above affidavit was taken and subscribed before me, at my office, this —— day of ——, A. D. 18—.

Signature and title of officer.

AGREEMENTS AND CONTRACTS.

1. *For the sale of goods, as they shall be appraised.*

ARTICLES OF AGREEMENT made between —— —— of ——, and —— —— of ——.

WITNESSETH:

It is hereby agreed by and between the said parties, that all and singular the household goods, furniture, and utensils, which are the property of the said —— ——, and contained in and belonging to the dwelling house now in the occupation of the said —— ——, [*or the property may be scheduled; if so, it should be here referred to and the schedule annexed*] shall at the joint and equal charge of the said parties, be appraised by —— ——, to he chosen by the said—— ——, and —— to be chosen by the said —— ——, on or before the —— day of ——18—, next; when the said—— —— and ——————, shall in writing by them signed give in their appraisement to the said parties; and in case the said appraisers shall differ in such valuation, then they shall and must choose a third indifferent person as an umpire, to determine the same whose valuation of the said disputed goods must be given within three days after his election, and shall be conclusive when it is signed and given or tendered to the said parties or either of them.

And the said —— —— doth covenant with the said—— ——, that, immediately after such valuation, made as aforesaid by the said —— and ——, or by such umpire as above provided for, he, the said ——, will make an absolute bill of sale, and give possession of all the said goods, furniture, and utensils, unto the said —— ——, at the price the same shall be appraised at as aforesaid. And the said —— —— doth hereby covenant with the said —— ——, that he the said —————— will accept the said goods at the said price, and at the time of executing such bill of sale, and delivering possession of the said goods, furniture and utensils, by the said —— ——, he the said —— —— will then pay to the said —— —— the sum in lawful money of the United States, for which the same shall be appraised as aforesaid.

IN WITNESS whereof, we have hereunto set our hands and seals, this —— day of 18—.

Signature, [SEAL.]
Signature, [SEAL.]

WITNESS.

2. *Agreement between two or more persons to unite in a purchase, each to pay a part of the price and charges.*

WHEREAS we, —— —— of the first part [*here give his business and residence*], and —— —— of the second part [*here give his business and residence*] [*and if others join add here as above*] are desirous to purchase [*here set out the property*] now owned and in the possession of —— ——. Now this agreement witnesseth, that we severally agree to and with each other, that if any one or more of us shall purchase the same, each of the others of us will pay his respective proportion of such purchase-money, and that all charges and expenses relating thereto shall be borne by us in equal proportions, and that any such purchase shall be for the joint and equal benefit of us all; it is provided, however, that the price to be paid for the said property shall not exceed —— dollars.

IN WITNESS WHEREOF, the parties to these presents have hereunto set their hands [*and seals*] this —— day of —— 18—.

Signatures [*and seals.*]

Signed [*sealed*] and delivered in the presence of

Signature of witness [*or witnesses.*]

3. *Giving the right to make and sell an article covered by letters patent.*

THIS MEMORANDUM OF AGREEMENT, made this —— day of ——, 18—, between—— ——, the patentee, of the first part, residing at ——, and ——, [*here set out his business and residence,*] of the second part, witnesseth.

Whereas, the said —— —— party of the first part, is the owner and proprietor of an invention for [*here set out a description,*] and of letters patent issued therefor by the United States of America, bearing date the —— day of ——, 18—; and whereas the said —— ——, party of the first part, and owner as aforesaid, for the considerations hereinafter set forth, hath agreed with the said —— ——, party of the second part, to license and authorize the said party of the second part, his executors, administrators and assigns, to make and vend the articles covered by said letters patent, [*here set out the length of time during which the permission is granted.*]

Now, in pursuance of the said agreement, and in consideration of the covenants and agreements hereinafter entered into on the part of the said —— party of the second part, and in consideration of —— dollars, lawful money of the United States, paid to the said —— : party of the first part, by the said —— ——, party of the second part, the receipt whereof is hereby acknowledged; the said —— ——, party of the first part, doth hereby give and grant unto the said —— ——, party of the second part, his executors, administrators and assigns, during [*here set out the length of time for which the right is sold,*] full, and free liberty, license, power and authority to make, vend or sell, either at wholesale or retail, [with full power to employ others under his immediate control] to make, within [*here set out the limits within which the manufacture and sale can be carried on*] the said invented and patented articles, and to receive to his and their own use all profits and advantages which shall or can be made by the making and selling of the said patented articles within the said limits, and that without any let, suit, trouble or hinderance of, from or by him, the said —— —— party of the first part, his executors or administrators, or any other person or persons claiming to hold and use such invention as aforesaid, from, by, under or in trust for him or them, by virtue of the said letters patent, or otherwise. And the said —— —— party of the second part is hereby authorized to empower any number of persons within the said district, not to exceed —— in number, to make and vend the said articles; these persons to have power to employ others to assist them in the manufacture under their immediate supervision, but not to grant rights to manufacture, to others.

And the said —— ——, party of the first part, for himself, his executors, administrators and assigns, hereby convenants to and with the said —— ——, party of the second part, his executors, administrators and assigns, that he, the said —— ——, party of the first part, his executors, adminstrators and assigns, will not at any time during the residue and continuance of said term, grant any license to any other person to make or vend the said patented articles within the aforesaid limits, without the special license and consent of the said —— —— party of the second part, his executors, administrators or assigns, first had in writing under his hand and seal.

And it is further agreed by and between the said parties, that in case any person or persons shall infringe the said letters patent within the said limits, the said —————— party of the second part, his executors, administrators or assigns, may at his or their option, in the name of the said —— —— party of the first part, his executors, administrators or assigns, and for the use and benefit of the said —— —— party of the second part, commence, sue and prosecute all such suits or actions, as shall be judged expedient against any person or persons who shall make such infringement; and the said —— —— party of the first part further promises to assist the said —— —— party of the second part in the prosecution of such action or actions with any evidence which it may be in his power to furnish.

And for the purpose of the prosecution of such actions as may be brought as aforesaid, the said —— —— party of the first part, constitutes and appoints the said —— —— party of the second part, his executors, administrators and assigns, the lawful attorney irrevocably of the said —— —— party of the first part at the costs, and to the use of the said second party, his executors, administrators and assigns, to commence and prosecute in the name of the said —— —— party of the first part all such suits and actions as aforesaid.

IN WITNESS WHEREOF [*as in form No. 2.*]

4. *Sale of good-will of trade or business with covenant in re-restraint.*

THIS MEMORANDUM OF AGREEMENT made the —— day of ——, 18—, between —— —— [*here give business and residence*] party of the first part, and —— —— [*here give business and residence*] party of the second part, witnesseth: That the said —— —— party of the first part for the consideration hereinafter specified, agrees to sell to the said —— —— party of the second part, and the said —— —— party of the second part hereby agrees to buy of the said —— —— party of the first part; all [*here set out the property to be purchased; it is recommended that a schedule be prepared, which should be here referred to here,*] at the invoice price of the said goods respectively; deduction is to be made for any depreciation in value to said goods, the furniture and fixtures are to be inventoried at their fair cash value. If the said parties cannot agree at the value of the property, the same shall be [*here insert clause as to appraisal as in form No. 1.*] Each party must pay an equal part of the cost of such inventory, which is to be delivered to the said —— —— party of the second part on or before the —— day of —— 18—.

It is also distinctly understood and agreed upon, by and between the said parties, that the good-will of the said business [*here describe the business, the location, and the length of time the same has been carried on*], is by these presents bargained and sold to the said —— ——, party of the second part, his executors, administrators, and assigns forever. In consideration whereof, the said —— —— party of the second part, agrees to pay, [*here set out the terms of payment, in full.*]

And the said —— —— party of the first part, further covenants and agrees to and with the said —— —— party of the second part, his executors administrators and assigns, that he will not at any time hereafter, engage directly, or indirectly, or concern himself, in carry- ing on or conducting the business of ——, either as principal or agent of another, within —— of the aforesaid premises, now occupied by him as aforesaid for such purpose. And it is expressly understood that the stipulations aforesaid are to apply to, and bind the heirs, executors, administrators and assigns of the respective parties; and in case of failure, the parties bind themselves, each unto the other, in the sum of —— dollars, as liquidated damages, to be paid by the failing party.

IN WITNESS WHEREOF, [*as in Form No. 2.*]

5. *Where the contract is executed by agents.*

THIS MEMORANDUM OF AGREEMENT, made this —— day of ——, 18—, between —— ——, [*set out business and residence*] of the first part, by —— ——, his attorney, and —— ——, [*set out business and residence*] of the second part, by —— ——, his attorney. WIT- NESSETH, that the said party of the first part, [*etc., as the case may be.*]

Signature. [*Seal.*]

By—— ——, *his attorney.*

Signature. [*Seal.*]

By —— ——, *his attorney.*

6. *Construction of a previous contract.*

THIS MEMORANDUM OF AGREEMENT, made this —— day of ——, 18—, between —— ——, [*set out business and residence,*] of the first part, and —— ——, [*set out business and residence,*] of the second part. WITNESSETH, whereas a difference has heretofore arisen be- tween the respective parties to these presents, in relation to their re- spective rights and obligations under a certain contract, made and entered into on the —— day of ——18—, between them; and the said parties hereto, having now come to a mutual understanding and agree- ment, respecting all the matters aforesaid, and purpose to set forth the same in these presents, as declaratory of their respective rights, duties and obligations from the date hereof, henceforward, for the government of themselves under the same.

NOW THIS INDENTURE WITNESSETH, that —— ——, party of the —— part, covenants, promises, and agrees to and with —— ——, party of the —— part, [*here set out the mutual understanding and agreement.*]

IN WITNESS WHEREOF, [*as in Form No. 2.*]

EXCISE.

1. *Order appointing a commissioner.*

STATE OF NEW YORK, ⎫ *ss :*
County of ——.　⎭

WE, —— ——, the county judge of said county, and —— ——, justice of the sessions in said county, do hereby certify that in accordance with the provisions of an act of the legislature of the said State, entitled "An act to suppress intemperance and to regulate the sale of intoxicating liquors," passed April 16th, 1857, that having met in the court house in the —— of ——, the place where the county courts are held in and for said county, on the —— —— of ——, 18—, and appointed ——, a reputable freeholder, a resident of said county, under and by virtue of said act, and he is hereby entitled to hold such office for six years from the —— day of ——, 18—; unless removed by death, or a competent tribunal for misfeasance in office.

WITNESS our hands and seals this —— day of ——, 18—, being the second Tuesday of May, 18—. [*Or whatever day it may be.*]
　　　　—— ——, County Judge,　　[SEAL.]
　　　　—— ——, Justice of Sessions. [SEAL.]

2. *Certificate of character.*

WE, the undersigned, are acquainted with the above named applicant, and believe him to be of good moral character.
　　　　　　　　　　　　　　　　Signatures.

3. *Justification of sureties to bond.*

STATE OF NEW YORK, ⎫
County of ——,　⎬ *ss :*
City and Town of.　⎭

—— ——, of ——, one of the subscribers to the foregoing bond, being duly sworn, says, that he is a resident and householder [*or freeholder*] within this State, and is worth the full sum specified by him in the foregoing bond, over all his debts and liabilities, and exclusive of property exempt by law from execution.
　　　　　　　　　　　　　　　　Signature.
Subscribed and sworn to before me this —— day of ——, 18—.
　　　　　　　　　　　　Signature of officer.

4. *Acknowledgment of sureties' bond.*

STATE OF NEW YORK, ⎫ *ss :*
County of ——.　⎭

I certify, that on this —— day of ——, 18—, before me personally came the above named, [*here set out the names of the obligors*] known to me to be the individuals described in, and who executed the foregoing bond, and severally acknowledged that they executed the same for the uses and purposes therein mentioned.
　　　　　　　　　　　　Signature of officer.

5. *Proof of signatures to petition.*

COUNTY OF ——, *ss:*

—— · ——, being duly sworn, says that he is the [*or one of the*] subscribing witness [*or witnesses*] to the above [*or annexed*] petition, and that the same was duly signed by the above petitioners, of his own knowledge.

Signature of witness.

Subscribed, &c., as in No. 1.

6. *Transcript of minutes to be filed in the office of town clerk.*

At a meeting of the board of commissioners of excise, held in the court house in the —— of —— in and for the county of ——, on the —— day of ——, 18—, the following named persons residing in the town of ——, in said county, intending to keep an inn, tavern or hotel in said town, were licensed to sell strong and spirituous liquors and wines therein for the ensuing year, beginning from the —— day of——, 18—, for the respective sum set opposite to their names.

—— —— .... $——
—— —— .... $——

And at a meeting of said board, duly organized as aforesaid, at the place aforesaid, on the —— day of ——, 18—, the following named persons, being store-keepers, were duly licensed to sell strong and spirituous liquors and wines, in quantities less than five gallons, but the same not to be drank at their respective places of business, viz. :

—— —— .... $——
—— —— .... $——
—— —— .... $——
.... $——

A copy from the minutes.

Signatures.
Commissioners of Excise.

FEES OF OFFICERS.

Assessors' fees.

For each day actually and necessarily devoted to the service of the town, one dollar and fifty cents. The compensation varies in cities; in some cities the assessor receives a salary.

Clerk of the polls' fees.

For each day actually and necessarily devoted to the purposes of election, one dollar and fifty cents may be charged.

County clerk's fees.

For searching the records of his office, or the records of mortgages deposited in his office by Loan Officers and Commissioners of Loans, or the dockets of judgments, for each year (5) five cents.

Entering satisfaction of a judgment when actually done (12½) twelve and one half cents.

Administering an oath or affirmation in cases where no fee is specially provided, together with the certificate, (12½) twelve and one half cents.

Clerk of the court of oyer and terminer and grand sessions.

The same fees may be charged as are allowed in civil cases for copies of papers filed in his office, for all copies of records, indictments and other proceedings.

Swearing a witness (6) six cents.

Entering or respiting a recognizance (12½) twelve and one half cents.

Calling and swearing a jury (19) nineteen cents.

Entering a sentence in the minutes kept by him, (12½) twelve and one half cents; and the like fee for every certified copy thereof, and for a transcript thereof for the Secretary of State.

Clerk of the board of registry.

For each day actually and necessarily devoted to the duties of election ($1.50) one dollar and fifty cents shall be charged.

Commissioners of excise.

For each days service actually performed ($3.00) three dollars.

Commissioners of highwawys.

In any town where there is but one such officer, the sum of $2.00 per day for each day actually and necessarily spent in the discharge of his official duties. In towns where there are more than one, $1.50 for each day as above.

Commissioners to loan U. S. deposit fund.

In the case of the sale of any lands the commissioners may charge for their services in preparing the notices of such sale, and in superintending the same ($5.00) five dollars.

Constable's fees, (laws of 1869, chap. 820.)

Constables shall hereafter be allowed for services rendered in civil actions the following fees :

For serving a warrant or summons...................... 25 cts.
For a copy of summons on request of defendant, or left at defendant's dwelling in his absence...................... 15
For serving an attachment................... 75
For copy of the attcahment, and inventory of the property seized, left at the last residence of the defendant........ 75
For serving an execution, for every dollar collected to the amount of fifty dollars.............................. 5 cts.
For every dollar collected over fifty dollars.............. 2½ cts.
For every mile traveled, (going and returning) to serve a summons, warrant, attachment or execution; the distance

to be computed from the place of the abode of the defendant, or where he shall be found, to the place where the precept is returnable.................................. 10 cts.

For notifying the plaintiff of the service of a warrant...... 25 cts.

For going to plaintiff's residence, or where he shall be found, to serve such notice, for each mile traveled, (*going and returning*) .... 10 cts.

For subpœnaing witnesses, not exceeding four.......... 25 cts.

For summoning a jury................................ 75 cts.

For summoning a jury to assess damages in proceedings relative to highways...............................$2 00

For serving affidavit, notice and summons, in action to secure possession of personal property...................... 50 cts.

For a copy of such affidavit, notice and summons left with defendant, his agent, or at the last place of abode of the defendant.. 50 cts.

For every mile traveled, (*going and returning,*) to serve such affidavit, notice and summons, the distance to be computed from the place where the precept is returnable, to the place of abode of the defendant, or where he shall be found, 10 cts.

For taking charge of a jury during their deliberations.... 50 cts.

In special proceedings.

For serving a summons................................ 25 cts.

For serving a warrant .... 50 cts.

For arresting and committing any person pursuant to process, 1 00

For every mile traveled, (*going and returning,*) in each case, 10 cts.

In criminal cases.

For serving a warrant............................... 75 cts.

For every mile traveled, (*going and returning,*)........ 10 cts.

For taking defendant into custody on a mittimus....... 25 cts.

For every mile traveled in taking the prisoner to jail, (*going and returning,*) .... 10 cts.

For taking charge of a jury during their deliberations... 50 cts.

For attending any court pursuant to a notice from the sheriff for that purpose, for each day............... 2 00

For each mile traveled, in going to, and returning from such court....................................... 5 cts.

Which fees shall be chargeable to the county, and shall be paid by the treasurer thereof, on the production of the certificate of the clerk, specifying the number of days, and the distance traveled. To entitle any constable or other officer, to the increased or additional travel fees, provided for in this Act, such constable or officer, shall show by affidavit that such travel was necessary on the process on which it was charged; that no more miles are charged for than was actually and in good faith traveled on the execution of such process, and that such constable or officer at that time, had no other official or private business on such traveled route, and that the charge for going and returning, was made only upon one process, which process shall be

attached to, or described in such affidavit, and such additional or increased travel fees shall not be allowed by any court or auditing
board, unless such court or auditing board shall be satisfied, that
the miles charged were actually and necessarily traveled on the process named, and on that process only.

Affidavit in above case.

———— County, *ss.*

—————————, being duly sworn, says, that he traveled ——
miles, going and returning, to serve the within process, the distance
being computed from the place of the abode of the *defendant*, or
where *he w* found to the place where the said process is returnable;
that such travel was necessary on such process; that no more miles
are charged for, than was actually and in good faith traveled in the
execution of such process, and that the deponent at the time had no
other private or official business on such traveled route, and that the
charge for going and returning, was made only upon one (the within)
process.

Signature.

Sworn to before me, this —— day, of —— 18—.

Officers signature.

General services.

For any services not provided for, that a constable may legally
render, the same fees may be charged as are allowed by law to
sheriffs; among others, as follows:

Putting any person entitled, into the possession of premises, (and
removing the tenant,) one dollar and twenty-five cents. Together
with the same traveling fees as upon an execution. Summoning a
jury to try the title to any personal property, and attending such
jury, one dollar and fifty cents.

A constable is not entitled to any fees for traveling to serve a
criminal warrant, unless the service is actually made, though the
party sought to be arrested could not be found.

Coroner's fees.

For viewing the body, the amount is to be fixed by the board of
supervisors.

Precept for summoning a jury...........................	50 cts.
Summoning the jury, and attending the same.............$1	50 cts.
Swearing the jury....................................	25 cts.
Subpœna...	25 cts.
Subpœnaing each witness..............................	25 cts.
Travel fee in subpœnaing witnesses, for each mile traveled..	10 cts.
Swearing each witness................................	10 cts.
Drawing inquisition, for each folio....................	25 cts.
Engrossing to sign, each folio........................	12½ cts.
Travel fees in returning inquisition to clerk's office, each mile..	10 cts.
Warrant for arrest of one charged with crime............	25 cts.

Examination of accused, each day......................$1 00
Every necessary adjournment.........................   25 cts.
Warrant of commitment...............................   25 cts.
Each recognizance of witness.........................   25 cts.
A reasonable compensation, and the actual expenses of
    digging up and reburying the body, on which an inquest
    is held.
In the city and county of New York, the following fees, and none
other can be charged.
For viewing each body, and holding an inquest thereon. $10 00
Summoning, and swearing jury........................   5 00
Making and filing inquest............................   5 00

Inspectors of elections.

For each day actually and necessarily devoted to the duties of the
office, $1.50, may be charged.

Jurors' fees.

In civil cases in justice's courts.
For attending to serve as a juror though not sworn......   10 cts.
For attending and trying a cause.....................   25 cts.

Justices' of the peace.—In civil cases.

For a summons......... ....   25 cts.
For a warrant, attachment or transcript of judgment, each.   25 cts.
For an adjournment..................................   25 cts.
For subpœna, including all the names inserted therein....   25 cts.
For administering an oath............................   10 cts.
For filing each paper necessary to be filed.............   5 cts.
For swearing a jury..................................   25 cts.
For swearing a constable to attend a jury.............   10 cts.
For trial of an issue of fact, in case of no appearance of the
    defendant.......................................   25 cts.
In case of appearance and answer.....................   75 cts.
For entering judgment...............................   25 cts.
For taking affidavit.................................   10 cts.
For drawing any bond................................   25 cts.
For receiving and entering verdict of jury.............   25 cts.
For venire..   25 cts.
For drawing affidavits, applications and notices in cases
    required by law, per folio.........................   5 cts.
For execution.......................................   25 cts.
For making return to an appeal......................$2 00
For warrant for the apprehension of any person charged
    with any violation of the laws concerning the internal
    police of the State................................   25 cts.
For warrant for the apprehension of any person charged
    with being the father of a bastard.................   50 cts.
For endorsing any warrant, issued from another county..   25 cts.
For summons for any offence relating to the internal police

of the state, or in any case of any special proceeding to recover the possession of lands or otherwise...........	25 cts.
For drawing a record or conviction for contempt, or other special cases......................................	50 cts.
For an execution upon any such conviction	25 cts.
For warrant of commitment for any cause...............	25 cts.
For a precept to summon a jury in special cases..........	50 cts.
For swearing such jury.............................	25 cts.
For hearing the matter concerning which such jury is summoned	50 cts.
For receiving and entering the verdict of such jury........	25 cts.
For a view of premises alleged to be deserted............	50 cts.
For hearing an application for a commission to examine witnesses	50 cts.
For every order for such commission, and attending, settling and certifying interrogatories	50 cts.
For taking deposition of witnesses upon an order or commission issued by some court in this or a foreign state or territory, per folio...................................	10 cts.
For making the necessary return, and certificates thereto..	50 cts.
For endorsement on affidavit in an action to recover possession of personal property...........................	25 cts.

In criminal cases.

For administering an oath.........................	10 cts.
For a warrant, (*but no justice of the peace shall be obliged to issue a warrant on any complaint for assault and battery, unless the person making such complaint shall pay the fee therefor,*)..............................	25 cts.
For a bond, or recognizance........	25 cts.
For a subpœna, including all the names incerted therein,	25 cts.
For a commitment for want of bail....................	25 cts.
For an examination of the accused, when such examination is required by law, for each day necessarily spent,	$1 00
For every necessary adjournment of the hearing or examination..	25 cts.

Overseers of the poor.

For each day actually and necessarily devoted to the duties of the office, $1.50 may be charged.

Printers' fees.

Not more than seventy-five cents per folio for the first insertion, and thirty cents for each subsequent insertion after the first, except for proceedings in surrogates' courts, or any notices required to be published relating to the estates of deceased persons; and in such cases not more than fifty cents per folio for the first insertion, and twenty-five cents per folio for each subsequent insertion after the first.

Sheriffs' fees.

For conveying a single convict to the state prison, for each
    mile from the county prison from which such convict shall
    be conveyed.. 35 cts.
For two convicts.. 45 cts.
   " three " .... 50 cts.
   " four   " .... 55 cts.
   " five   " .... 60 cts.

For all additional convicts, such reasonable allowance as the comptroller may think just, which said allowance, together with $1.00
per day for the maintenance of each convict whilst on the route to
such state prison, (not however exceeding $1.00 for every thirty miles
travel,) shall be in full of all charges and expenses in the premises.

For serving any process by which an action shall be com-
    menced in a court of law, when there shall have been no
    process previous thereto, on each defendant............. 50 cts.

In the city and county of New York, all sales of real estate under
the decree or judgment of any court of record (except sales in cases
of partition, and where the sheriff of such county is a party) shall
be made by the sheriff of such city and county; and in cases of foreclosure he shall be entitled to receive :

For receiving order of sale and posting notices of such
    sale.. $10 00
Attending sale... 10 00
Drawing deed 5 00
Attending an adjourning sale at request of plaintiff, or
    order of the court.. 3 00
But no more than three such adjournments shall be
    charged.
Making report of sale.. 5 00
Paying over surplus moneys............................... 3 00
For serving a writ of possession or restitution; putting
    any person entitled into possession of premises, and
    removing the tenant 1 25
Traveling fees, going only, each mile .... 06 cts.
Returning the writ... 12½ cts.
Fees on attachments against ships 1 00
Serving warrant 1 00
Returning same 1 00
Bringing up prisoner on habeas corpus, to testify or
    answer in any court... 1 50
Traveling each mile from the jail......................... 12¼ cts.
Attending such court with such prisoner, per day, be-
    sides actual necessary expenses 1 00
Making return to the writ................................... 12¼ cts.
Copy of process to annex to return, for each folio.... 12½ cts.
Return to writ of certioiari................................. 12½ cts.
Copy of process to annex to return, for each folio..... 12½ cts.
Service of attachment against defaulting witness; the
    usual allowance is .... 50 cts.
For the return... 12½ cts.

Travel fees from the place of arrest to the court where
the writ is returnable, for each mile............. 12¼ cts.

Supervisors' fees.

One dollar and fifty cents per day (except when attending the
board of supervisors) for each day actually und necessarily devoted
by them to the services of the town, in the duties of their respective
offices. The supervisors of Albany and Rensselaer counties are allowed $1.00 besides their travel fees, and no more.

Witnesses' fees.

For attending before a justice of the peace in a justices' court, or
a commission appointed by a justice of the peace, or before a justice
of the peace taking depositions to be used in courts in other states,
twenty-five cents for each days actual attendance.

GUARANTIES.

1. *That a note will be paid.*

For value received, the receipt whereof is hereby acknowledged,
I hereby guaranty the payment of the above note.
This —— day of ——, 18—.   *Signature.*
Witness.

2. *That a bond will be paid.*

In consideration of the sum of one dollar to me in hand paid the
receipt whereof is hereby acknowledged, I hereby guaranty the
payment of the above [or *annexed*] bond [or *other instrument.*]
                              Signature with or without a seal.
This —— day of ——18—.
Witness.

3. *Of collectibility.*

For value received, the receipt whereof is hereby acknowledged,
I hereby guaranty that the above [or *annexed*] [*here set out the name
of the instrument*] is good, [or *is collectible.*]
                                                  Signature.
This —— day of —— 18—.
Witness.

4. *Of rent.*

In consideration of the letting of the above described premises, and
for value received the receipt whereof is hereby acknowledged, I
guaranty the punctual payment of the rent, and the performance of
the covenants in the above agreement mentioned to be paid and performed by said lessee. This, without requiring any notice of non-
payment, or non-performance, or proof of notice or demand being
made, whereby to charge me therefore.
                                                  Signature.
This —— day of ——18—.
Witness.

5. *In consideration that legal proceedings shall be estopped.*

—— ——, having at my request, agreed to discontinue the proceedings instituted by them against —— ——, of —— ——, to enforce payment of —— —— dollars, due by him to them. I hereby in consideration thereof, guaranty the payment of that sum together with lawful interest and costs to date, within —— days from date.

Signature.

This —— day of ——, 18—.
Witness.

6. *That a contract will be performed.*

In consideration of the sum of one dollar to me in hand paid, the receipt whereof is hereby acknowledged, I hereby guaranty, and by these presents do promise and agree, to and with them, that the above named —— —— party of the —— part in the above contract, will well and truly, and faithfully on his part perform and fulfill every thing by the foregoing agreement on his part and behalf to be performed and fulfilled, at the times and in the manner above provided. And I do hereby expressly waive and dispense with any demand upon the said —— ——, and any notice of any non-performance on his part.

This —— day of ——, 18—. *Signature.*
Witness.

7. *General letter of guaranty.*

I hereby guaranty to any person advancing money or selling goods on credit to —— of ——, not exceeding the sum of —— dollars; the payment thereof, at the expiration of the credit given, always provided the said —— —— does not pay on demand.

This —— day of —— 18—. *Signature.*
Witness.
To Messrs.—— ——
    Residence.

8. *Special letter of Guaranty.*

To Messrs. —— ——, of —— ——.
DEAR SIR :
I will be responsible for the goods sold [*if desired, here limit the quality and kind,*] [*or money to be lent*] by you to —— ——, of —— ——, to an amount not exceeding in the aggregate the sum of —— ——dollars, [*or where it is desired to give a continuing guaranty say*] not exceeding an indebtedness of —— —— dollars at any one time.

This ——day of —— 18—. *Signature.*
Witness.

PAY AND BOUNTY.

The arrears of pay to which a deceased officer or soldier is entitled is payable to the following persons in the order named :

Where the deceased was married, payment will be made, 1st. to the widow; 2d. she being dead, to his child or children. If minors, the payment will be made to a guardian duly appointed.

Where the deceased was unmarried, 1st. to the father; 2d. he being dead, to the mother; 3d. they both being dead, to the brothers and sisters collectively; and lastly, to the heirs in general.

The bounty of $100 is payable to the following persons, in the following order, and to no other persons: 1st. to the widow; she being dead, to the children, share and share alike. There being no wife or children, such bounty shall be paid to the following persons, provided they are residents of the United States: 1st. to the father, provided that he has not abandoned the support of his family; 2d. to the mother; 3d. to the brothers and sisters collectively. Widows of commissioned officers, of three months volunteers, and of soldiers dying after being discharged, are not entitled to bounty. No money will in any case be paid to the heirs of a deceased soldier or sailor, against whom it is proven, that they have in any manner aided or abetted the late rebellion.

A soldier is not entitled to the bounty of $100 unless he has served for a period of two years, or during the war if sooner ended, unless he has been discharged by reason of wounds received in battle.

The proper officers before whom the application and deposition required should be sworn to, are a judge, a commissioner, a notary public, or a justice of the peace, duly authorized to administer oaths; the oath must be accompanied with the certificate and seal of a court of record, certifying to the fact that the said judge, commissioner, &c., was duly commissioned, and was acting in his official capacity at the time of the execution of the papers.

Payment will be made by an order from the accounting officers on any paymaster of the army. Such order will require the signature of the claimant on its face, and duly witnessed.

All claims for arrears of pay and bounty may be sent directly to the office of the Second Auditor of the Treasury Department, Washington, D. C.

No claim will be rejected on account of the form in which it is presented, if it substantially complies with the instructions, which will be furnished by the above officer.

All letters of inquiry in relation to a claim should specify the name of the deceased, and the company, regiment, and State to which he belonged; and in all cases, in order to secure an answer, the name, post-office, and State of the writer should be distinctly written.

The government pays all postages on such business communications, whether received or transmitted by the Second Auditor.

If the declarant, or any witness, signs by mark, the officer must certify that the contents of the paper were made known to the affiant before signing. In every case the declaration or affidavit must either be signed by the affiant's own hand, or else by mark (X); this mark must be witnessed. Signing by another's hand, when the party is unable to write, is wholly inadmissible.

The allegations made in the applicant's declaration must be sustained by the testimony of two credible and disinterested witnesses, to be certified as such by the officer before whom the testimony is taken. The applicant must also take and subscribe the oath prescribed in the recent amnesty proclamation of the president of the United States, filing such oath with the application for a new pension certificate, in the following form:

OATH.

I, [here insert the name of the party taking the oath], do solemnly swear [or affirm] in the presence of Almighty God, that I will henceforth faithfully support, protect, and defend the Constitution of the United States, and the union of the States thereunder; that I will in like manner abide by and faithfully support all laws and proclamations which have been made during the existing rebellion with reference to the emancipation of slaves, so help me God.

Signature of party taking the oath.

In cases where the applicant is an invalid pensioner, he must be examined by an army surgeon, or by a surgeon duly appointed by this office (*the pension office*), as to the continuance of his disability. If a widow, she must prove, by two credible witnesses, her continued widowhood. In the case of the guardian of a minor child, newly appointed, he must file evidences of his appointment as such.

With each and every application for pay and bounty due a *colored* soldier, the attorney presenting the same must file his oath [*or affirmation*] that he has no interest whatever in said pay or bounty, beyond the fees for the collection for the same as fixed and established by law. The failure to file such oath or affirmation will in every case result in the suspension of the application.

When application is made by *heirs* of deceased soldiers for the *additional* bounty, they should so state the fact in the application, and if possible, give the number of the certificate issued in any previous settlement made by the Second Auditor. Parents must apply jointly.

All declarations of claimants, residing within twenty-five miles of any court of record, must without exception, be made before such court, or before some officer thereof having custody of its seal. For the convenience of persons residing more than twenty-five miles distant from any court of record, officers qualified by law to administer oaths may be designated by the Commissioner of Pensions, before whom such declarations shall be executed. Claim agents are prohibited, under severe penalty, from receiving more than $10 (*ten dollars*) in all for their services in prosecuting any pension claim, or from receiving any part of such fee in advance, or any per centage of any claim, or of any portion thereof, for pension or bounty.

In all cases where a mark is substituted for a written signature, two disinterested witnesses are required.

1. *Form of declaration for an invalid pension.*

STATE (DISTRICT OR TERRITORY) OF —— } ss.
County of ——

On this —— day of——, A. D. 18—, personally appeared before me [*here set out the name and official character of the person ad-*

minstering the oath] within and for the county, state aforesaid, [*here set out the name of the applicant*] aged ——, a resident of ——, in the state of ——, who, being duly sworn according to law, declares that he is the identical —— who enlisted in the service of the United States at ——, on the —— day of ——, in the year ——, as a ——, in company ——, commanded by ——, in the —— regiment of ——, in the war of 1861, and was honorably discharged on the —— day of ——, in the year 18—; that while in the service aforesaid, and in the line of his duty, he received the following wound [*or other disability, as the case may be*] [*here set out in full, a particular and minute account of the wound or other injury, and state how, when and where it occurred, where the applicant has resided since leaving the service, and what has been his occupation.*]

Signature of Applicant.

Also personally appeared before me —— and ——, residents of [*state county and city or town*] persons whom I certify to be respectable and entitled to credit, and who being by me duly sworn, say that they were present and saw —— —— sign his name [*or make his mark*] to the foregoing declaration; and they further swear that they have every reason to believe, from the appearance of the applicant and their acquaintance with him, that he is the identical person he represents himself to be, and they further state that they have no interest in the prosecution of this claim.

Signature of witnesses.

Sworn to and subscribed before me this —— day of ——, A. D. 18—; and I hereby certify that I have no interest, direct or indirect, in the prosecution of this claim.

Signature and title of officer.

Applicants post office address —— ——.

2. *Application for an increase of pension.*

INSTRUCTIONS.—All applications for increase of pensions must be endorsed by the Pension Agent where payment has been made, and he must certify that he knows or believes, on information from others that the surgeons are reputable in their profession. The application must be accompanied with the pension certificate when sent to the Pension Office.

It is hereby certified, that, ——, formerly a —— of Captain —— Company in the —— regiment of ——, who, it appears by the accompanying certificate, was placed on the pension roll at the rate of —— dollars per month, on account, as he states, of having [*here state wound received, or disease contracted, for which the applicant alleges that he was pensioned*] while in the line of his duty, and in the said service, on or about the —— day of ——, in the year 18—, at a place called ——, in the state of ——, is not only still disabled in consequence of said injury, [*or disease contracted*] but, in our opinion, his disability to obtain his subsistence by manual labor, has increased since his last examination ——, so that it now amounts to [*one half, two-thirds, or total, as the case may be*] disability; the said increased disability, originating entirely from the injury [*or disease*] on account of which he was originally pensioned.

Signature of Surgeon.
Signature of Surgeon.

STATE OF——, } *ss.*
County of ——.

On this —— day of ——, A. D. 18—, personally appeared before me [*here set out the name and title of the officer,*] in and for the state and county aforesaid, Dr.—— ——, and Dr.——, who being duly sworn according to law, say that the above document by them signed is, to the best of their knowledge and belief, just and true.

Sworn to before me, this ——day of —— 18—.
[SEAL.] *if he have one.*

Signature and title of officer.

Pension agency ——
—— ——, 18 ——

I hereby certify that Dr. —— and Dr. ——, whose signatures appear above, are surgeons in actual practice, and reputable in their profession, as I [*here set out reasons for such opinion, and whether personal knowledge or otherwise*] and entitled to full credit and belief.

Pension agent.

3. *Application for a transfer.*

INSTRUCTIONS. — The oath to be taken before a duly qualified magistrate, whose official character and signature must be certified by the proper officer, under his seal of office. The county clerk, secretary of state, or some other officer, must certify, under his seal of office, that the officer who administered the oath is such officer as he purports to be, and that his signature is genuine.

The oath must be supported by the testimony of some respectable person as to the pensioner's identity. He must swear that the person who has taken the oath is the person described in the affidavit. The magistrate must certify that the witness is a person of veracity; and the affidavit must also be authenticated in the manner above described.

In every case where the clerk of the court, or other certifying officer, has no public seal of office, the certificate of a member of Congress, proving the official character and signature of the certifying officer, should be sent with the papers.

Mode of authenticating papers. — In every instance where the certificate of the certifying officer who authenticated the paper is not written on the same sheet which contains the affidavit, or other papers authenticated, the certificate must be attached thereto by a piece of tape or ribbon, the ends of which must pass under the seal of office of the certifying officer, so as to prevent any paper from being improperly attached to the certificate.

STATE OF ——, } *ss :*
County of——.

On this —— day of ——, A. D. 18—, before me [*here set out the name and title of the officer*] in and for the said county, personally appeared —— ——, who on her oath declares that she is the widow of —— ——, who formerly belonged to —— company, commanded by Captain —— ——, in the —— regiment of ——, commanded by Colonel —— ——, in the service of the United States; that her name was placed on the pension roll of the State of ——, whence she has lately removed; that she now resides in the—— of ——, city of ——, where she intends to remain, and wishes her pension to be there payable, in future. The following are her reasons for removing from —— to ——: [*here set out the reasons.*]

Sworn and subscribed to before me the day and year aforesaid.

[SEAL.]

Signature and title of officer.

Where the transfer is applied for by a man, the change in the above form will be readily made.

4. *Application for a new certificate.*

STATE OF ——, } ss :
County of ——. }

On this —— day of ——, 18—, before the subscriber [*here set out the name and title of the officer*] in and for said county, personally appeared —— ——, who on his oath declares that he is the same person who formerly belonged to —— company, commanded by Captain —— ——, in the —— regiment, commanded by Colonel —— ——, in the service of the United States; that his name was placed on the pension roll of the State of ——, that he received a certificate of that fact under the signature and seal of the secretary of ——; which certificate, on or about the —— day of ——, 18—, at or near ——, was [*here set out at length, the facts and circumstances attending the loss of the certificate.*]

Sworn to before me the day and year aforesaid.

[SEAL.]

Signature and title of officer.

STATE OF ——, } ss :
County of ——. }

On this —— day of ——, 18—, before the subscriber [*here set out the name and title of the officer,*] in and for said county, personally appeared —— ——, who on his oath declares that he well knows —— ——, who has executed the foregoing affidavit, to be the identical pensioner named therein.

Sworn to, &c., as above.

5. *Application for widow's pension.*

STATE OF ——, } ss :
County of ——. }

ON THIS —— day of ——, 18—, personally appeared before me the subscriber [*here set out the name and title of the officer, who must be authorized to administer an oath*], in and for the county and State aforesaid, —— ——, of ——, who being duly sworn, declares that her age is —— years, that she is the widow of —— ——, late of the county ——, and state of ——, who was a ——, in company ——, commanded by Captain —— ——, in the —— regiment of [*here state whether of a State, or the United States, and whether infantry or otherwise*], who died in the service of the United States at ——, in the State of ——, on or about the —— day of ——, 18—: that her maiden name was —— ——, and that she was married to said —— ——, deceased, on

or about the —— day of ——, 18—, at ——, in the State of ——, by
—— ——: that she has remained a widow since the decease of her said
husband, and knows that there is no record evidence of said marriage
[*in a case where there is record evidence, set it out.*]

This declaration is made by the said—— ——, wife as aforesaid, to
recover all arrears of pay and other allowances due said deceased from
the United States, and the bounty provided by the 6th section of the
act of Congress, approved July 22d, 1861. She also declares that she
has not in any manner been engaged in, or aided or abetted the rebellion in the United States.

AND SHE HEREBY APPOINTS, —— ——, of ——, as her lawful attorney, and authorizes him to present and prosecute this claim, and to
receive and receipt for any orders or moneys that may be issued or paid
in satisfaction thereof. The post-office address of the claimant is as
follows [*set it out.*]

Signature of claimant.

ALSO, personally appeared before me, the subscriber, —— ——, and
—— ——, of the county of ——, and State of ——, to me well known
as credible persons, who being duly sworn, declare that they have
been for —— years acquainted with the above named applicant,
and were well acquainted with the said —— ——, deceased, and that
he was a member of [*set out the co. and reg. as above*] and they further state that the said deceased recognized the said applicant as his
lawful wife, and that she was so recognized by the community in
which she resided; and that they have no interest whatever in this
application.

Signature of witnesses.

Sworn to before me this —— day of——, 18—, and I hereby certify that I have no interest direct or indirect, in the prosecution of
this claim.

[*Seal.*]
Signature and title of officer.

6. *Form of application for restoration to the pension rolls, by persons
whose name has been dropped under the act of Feb. 4th, 1862.*

STATE OF ——, }
County of ——. } *ss:*

On this —— day of ——, 18—, personally appeared before me [*here
set out the name and title of the officer*] in and for the said State and
county, —— ——, aged —— years, a resident of ——, in the State of
——, who being duly sworn, according to law, declares that he [*or
she*] is the identical —— ——, who was a pensioner on the roll of the
agency at ——, and whose pension certificate is herewith returned;
that he [*or she*] has resided since the *first day of Jan.* 1861, as follows,
[*here set out the place or places where the applicant has resided since
that date*]: that during this period, his [*or her*] means of subsistence
have been [*here set out the means by which a livelihood has been gained*]
and that he has not borne arms against the government of the United
States, or [*that she has not*] in any manner encouraged the rebels, or

manifested a sympathy with their cause; and that he [or she] was last paid his [or her] pension on the —— day of ——, A. D. 18—.

This application is made for the purpose of securing a restoration of his [or her] name to the pension rolls, and of obtaining a new pension certificate, such as he [or she] may be entitled to under existing laws, reference being made to the evidence heretofore filed in the Pension Office to substantiate his [or her] original claim.

Signature of applicant.

Also personally appeared —— —— and —— ——, residents of [*here give State, county and city or town*] persons whom I certify to be respectable and entitled to credit, and who, being by me duly sworn according to law, say that they were present and saw —— ——, sign his [or her] name, [or *make his or her mark*] to the foregoing declaration; and they further swear that they have every reason to believe from the appearance of the applicant, and their acquaintance with him [or her] that he [or she] is the identical person [*he or she*] represents himself [or *herself*] to be; and they further swear that they have no interest in the prosecution of this claim.

Signature of witnesses.

Sworn to and subscribed before me, this —— day of ——, A. D 18—; and I hereby certify that I have no interest, direct or indirect, in the prosecution of this claim.

[SEAL.]   *Signature and title of officer.*

7. *Application of father for arrears of pay and bounty.*

STATE OF ——, } ss :
County of ——. }

ON THIS —— day of ——, A. D. 18—, personally appeared before me [*here set out the name and title of officer*] in and for the county and state aforesaid, —— ——, who resides in [*here set out State, county and city or town*] aged —— years, who being duly sworn, declares that he is the father of —— ——, late of [*here set out late residence*] and who was a —— in —— company, commanded by —— ——, Captain, in the —— regiment of ——, commanded by —— ——, Colonel; who died in the service of the United States at ——, on or about the —— day of ——, 18—; leaving neither wife nor child.

This application is made to recover all arrears of pay and other allowances due the deceased from the United States, and the bounty provided by the 6th Section of the Act of Congress approved July 22d, 1861; and the applicant desires all communications and the certificate for pay, sent to him at —— post office, county of ——, and State of ——.

Signature of claimant.

ALSO personally appeared before me, the subscriber, —— ——, and —— ——, of [*set out residence of witnesses, State, county and city or town*], to me well known as credible persons, who being duly sworn according to law, declare that they have been for —— years acquainted with the above named applicant, and with said —— ——, deceased, who was [*here set out co. and reg. as above*]: and know said applicant to be the father of said deceased, and that the said deceased left neither wife nor child; and they further swear that they have no interest whatever, directly or indirectly, in this application.

Signature of witnesses.

Sworn to and subscribed before me, this —— day of ——, 18—.
[SEAL.]

Signature and title of officer.

I certify that —— ——, before whom the above declaration and affidavit were made is a ——, that he is duly authorized to administer oaths, that I am well acquainted with his signature, and that the above, purporting to be, is his.

IN WITNESS WHEREOF, I have hereunto set my hand and official seal, this —— day of —— 18—.
[SEAL.]

Signature of the clerk of the court.

8. *Application of mother, for arrears of pay and bounty.*

Form No. 7, should be followed with the following exceptions. That she is the mother. Leaving neither wife, child nor father [*if such is the fact.*] That the name of the father of said deceased was [*or is*] —— ——. Where such father is living, and has abandoned his family, set out the fact, together with time and place, state his habits. In the case of an abandonment by the husband, the witnesses should state their knowledge of that fact in their affidavit.

9. *Application of brothers and sisters for arrears of pay and bounty.*

Form No. 7, should be followed with the following exceptions: That they are the brothers and sisters. Leaving neither widow, child, father, mother, nor any other brother or sister than the present applicants. The witnesses in their affidavit, should state that no other brother and sister of the applicant are living. The name, age and residence of each of the claimants must be stated, and the names and residences of the guardians, if any.

10. *Guardian's form.*

Form No. 7, should be followed with the following exceptions: That he is the legally appointed guardian, as appears by the letters of guardianship hereto annexed, of, state the names and ages of all the wards. Leaving no widow. And that the above named minor —— —— is [*or are*] the only —— of —— deceased. The names and residences of the adult children should follow. The witnesses in their affidavit should state that the deceased soldier left surviving him no other minor child, or children, and should also make a statement as to the adult children, if any.

11. *Form of declaration to be made by a person who has never had a land warrant, or made a declaration therefor.*

STATE OF ——, } *ss.*
County of ——. }

ON THIS —— day of ——, 18—, personally appeared before me, [*here set out the name and title of the officer,*] in and for the county and State aforesaid,—— aged years, a resident of ——, who being duly sworn according to law, declares that he is the identical —— ——, who was a —— in —— company [*where the person was an officer, vary the form accordingly,*] commanded by Captain —— ——, in the —— regiment of ——, commanded by Colonel —— ——: in the war with Great Britain, declared by the United States on the 18th day of June, 1812, [*or other war describing it*] that he enlisted, [*or was drafted*] at ——, on or about the —— day of ——, 18—, for the term of —— years, and continued in actual service in said war for the term of ——, and was honorably discharged at —— on the —— day of ——, A. D. 18—. [*Where the claimant was discharged in consequence of disability incurred by the service in the line of his duty ; or, if he was in captivity with the enemy, he must vary his declaration so that the facts in the case may be set forth.*]

He makes this declaration for the purpose of obtaining the bounty land to which he may be entitled under the act approved ——. He also declares that he has not received a warrant for bounty land under this, or any other act of Congress, nor made any other application therefor.

Signature of the claimant.

We, —— —— and —— ——, residents of ——, in the State of ——, upon our oaths, declare that the foregoing declaration was signed and acknowledged by —— —— in our presence, and that we believe from the appearance and statements of the applicant that he is the identical person he represents himself to be.

Signature of witnesses.

The foregoing declaration and affidavit were subscribed and sworn to; before me on the day and year above written ; and certify that I know the affiants to be credible persons ; that the claimant is the person he represents himself to be, and that I have no interest in this claim.

[SEAL.] *if he have one.*

Signature and title of officer.

12. *Claim for compensation for property taken by United States forces.*

STATE OF ——, } *ss :*
County of ——. }

I, [*here state name of claimant,*] on oath, state that I am a citizen of the county and State aforesaid ; that I was, at the date the claim hereinafter set forth originated, and have been ever since, loyal to the United States ; that on or about the [*here set out the date the stores or property was taken*], at or near the town of [*here follows the place of taking, State and county being mentioned*] the following articles: [*If the articles taken pertained to the quartermaster's department, say "quartermaster's stores ;" if to the commissary department, say " commissary supplies." Quartermaster's stores and commissary supplies must not be put in the same claim.*] Were taken from me by [*name and rank, with company and regiment if possible, by whom the property was taken*] to wit : [*here set out at length a full description of the articles, as to quality, quantity, kind and value.*] That [*if no receipt or voucher was given, say for which no receipt or voucher was given, in case one was received, say for which the voucher attached was given, in such a case it must be forwarded with the claim*] for said property. That said property was actually taken by said officer for the use of, and used by the army of the United States ; that no payment has been made, or compensation received in any way, or from any source whatever, for the whole, or any part of said claim ; that it has not been transferred to any person or persons whomsoever ; and that the rates or prices charged are reasonable and just, and do not exceed the market rate or price of the articles at the time and place stated. And I do hereby appoint —— —— as my attorney to prosecute this claim for me, with full power of substitution and revocation, and to receive and receipt for the money or certificate issued in payment thereof.

The claimant's post office address is —— ——.

50c. *Int. rev. stamp.*

Signature and title of officer.

STATE OF ——, }
  County of ——. } *ss :*

This day personally appeared before the undersigned [*name and title of officer*] in and for the county and State aforesaid, —— ——, who subscribed and made oath to the foregoing affidavit, this —— day of ——, 18—.

5c. *Int. rev. stamp.*

Signature of claimant.

Oath of allegiance.

I [*name of claimant*] do solemnly swear [*or affirm*] that I will support, protect, and defend the constitution and government of the United States, and the union of States thereunder, against all enemies, whether domestic or foreign; that I will bear true faith, allegiance, and loyalty to said constitution and government; that I will faithfully support and abide by all acts of Congress passed, and all proclamations of the President made during the rebellion with reference to slaves, so long and so far as not modified or held void by Congress or by decision of the Supreme Court of the United States ; that I will faithfully perform all the duties which may be required of me by law ; and further that I do this with a full determination, pledge and promise, without any mental reservation or secret evasion of purpose whatever. So help me God.

Signature of claimant.

STATE OF ———, } ss :
  County of ——.

WE [*here must follow the names of two witnesses, with their residence,
State, county, city or town*] who being duly sworn according to law,
state, that on or about the —— day of ——, 18—: [*time when the
property was taken*] at or near [*place where property was taken.*]
Quartermaster's stores, [*or Comissary supplies* described and charged
for in the foregoing claim of —— ——, consisting of the following articles, to wit : [*here enumerate*] actually taken by —— ——, for the
use of the army of the United States, which stores were used by the
said army ; that the quantity charged for is correct, and that the
prices charged are reasonable and just, and do not exceed the market
rate or price of the articles at the time and place stated.
                              Signatures of the witnesses.
  Subscribed and sworn to before me, by —— ——, and —— ——,
this —— day of ——, 18—.
                              Signature and title of officer.

  5c. Int. Rev. stamp.

STATE OF ——— } ss :
  County of ——.

I CERTIFY THAT [*here set out the name and title of the officer before
whom the application was sworn,*] is duly authorized to administer
oaths and that I am well acquainted with his signature and that the
above which purports to be such is his, and I further certify that the
claimant —— ——, is a citizen of —— county in the State of ——.
  In witness whereof I have hereunto set my hand, and official seal,
this —— day of ——, 18—.
  [*Seal.*]   *Signature of the clerk of the court.*
  5c. Int. Rev. stamp.

*This certificate can only be made by a United States officer, civil or
                              military.*

  I —— ——, do certify that I am [*here set out rank or title*] that I
am well acquainted with [*name of claimant*] the claimant in the case,
and know that he was at the date the claim originated, and has been
ever since loyal to the United states, and that he is of good reputation
for veracity, and is entitled to be believed.   And I do further certify
that I am well acquainted with —— ——, and —— ——, the witnesses who subscribed the foregoing affidavit, and that they are also
of good reputation for veracity and entitled to be believed.
                              Signature and rank or title of officer.
  This certificate should be obtained, if possible; it is not however in-
dispensable.

to 562.

RECOGNIZANCES.

1. *Short form of memorandum.*

—— ——, bound in —— dollars.

—— ——, bound in —— dollars.

On condition that —— ——, be and appear at the next —— court in ——, to answer.

This —— day of ——, 18—.

2. *Formal recognizance.*

STATE OF ————,   } *ss* :
County of ——.   }

BE IT REMEMBERED, that I —— ——, of the —— of ——, in said county, acknowledge myself to be indebted to the people of the State of ——, in the sum of —— dollars, to be well and truly paid, if default shall be made in the condition following.

WHEREAS the said —— ——, [*here set out the circumstances authorizing the exaction of the instrument,*] Now, THEREFORE, the condition of this recognizance is this, that if the said —— ——, shall [*here set out at length what is to be performed by the person liable.*] Then this recognizance shall be void ; else to remain of full force.

Signature and seal.

Subscribed and acknowledged in open court this —— day of ——. 18—, before me.

Signature and title of magistrate or clerk of court.

SUBSCRIPTION PAPERS.

1. *For a Church, (the same may be modified for any other structure.)*

BE IT KNOWN, That we, the undersigned subscribers to this instrument, hereby agree to pay the sums set opposite to our respective names by us (in lawful money of the United States), for the purpose of erecting [*here set out with care the building that it is proposed to erect, and the place of its erection*]. The amount to be subscribed in cash is $ ——; the money is to be paid to [*here set out the names of the persons who are to receive it*]. [*Here make any statement as to how the building is to be erected and finished, and the purpose for which it is to be used*].

Signatures and amount subscribed.

Date of each signature.

2. *For the support of a Clergyman, [the same may be modified to suit other facts].*

BE IT KNOWN, That we, the undersigned subscribers to this instrument, being members of the —— religious society in the —— of ——, State of ——, and being desirous of raising a salary for the support of the Rev. —— ——, (*D. D.*) as a minister of the gospel in said society, do, for this purpose and for the consideration of one dollar, the receipt whereof is hereby acknowledged, received of the trustees of said society, before signing this instrument, promise, covenant, and engage, each one for himself [*and herself*], individually and severally, to and with the said trustees, and to and with each other, that we will each pay to the said trustees, or to such person as they shall appoint to receive the same, the sums of money respectively annexed to and set opposite to our names in this instrument, to be paid annually on or before the —— day of ——, in each and every year, in lawful money of the United States, so long as the said Rev. —— ——, (*D. D.*) shall administer the gospel in said society, and so long as we, the subscribers, shall reside within four miles of the meeting-house used and occupied by said society; these subscriptions are to be by the said trustees applied for the sole purpose of paying the salary of the Rev. —— ——, (*D. D.*) The first annual payment shall be made at the expiration of one year, after he shall be installed or ordained in and over the said society, and in each and every year thereafter.

It is further distinctly understood, that the said Rev. —— ——, (*D. D.*) shall be allowed in each and every year that he shall administer the gospel in said society, to be and remain away and absent from his duties as such minister for and during —— Sabbaths; and this fact shall furnish no excuse for withholding the above mentioned subscriptions.

It is further distinctly understood, that this instrument shall not be obligatory upon us in any manner, until the whole sum subscribed shall amount to the sum of —— dollars.

It is further distinctly understood, that any one of us may cease paying the sum subscribed by us, by giving notice of our intention one year in advance to the said trustees.

Signatures, and amounts subscribed.
Date of each signature.

TITLE, ABSTRACT OF.

This is an instrument, presenting in a clear, simple, and connected form, the history and substance of the various instruments which in any way affect the title to real property. A very complete form will be found in 3 Abb. Forms, 5; see also, 1 Preston on Abst. 36; Carwin's Manual. It is advisable to commence back at least sixty years from the date of the abstract. See also, Willard on Real Estate, 551.

INDEX.

41

REDEMPTION— PAGE.
    of real estate by judgment creditor, forms for,............ 167

REFEREES—
    fees of,.. 250
    see "HIGHWAYS."

RELEASE—
    lease and release,.. 173, 174
    release of dower,... 226
    of owner of land on laying out highway,.................. 299
    surrender of term of years,............................... 393
    surrender of lease,....................................... 394
    release of all demands,................................... 511
    special release,.. 511
    by creditor named in assignment,......................... 511
    of part of mortgaged premises,........................... 512
    by judgment creditor,.................................... 512
    of legacy,.. 513
    to restore competency of witness, different forms,........ 513, 514
    release of party to arbitration in pursuance of an award,......
    release by supervisor and commissioners to plank road company,.. 467

REVOCATION—
    of submission to arbitration,............................. 69
    of power of attorney,..................................... 508

SALE—
    see "BILLS OF SALE," ETC., "LANDLORD AND TENANT," and
    "SERVICE AND RETURN OF PROCESS."

SATISFACTION—
    of judgment,.. 24, 25
    of mortgage,.. 22, 23, 24

SCHOOLS—
    practical remarks,.. 515-524
    town superintendent's bond,.............................. 524
    notice of supervisor to furnish additional security,...... 525
    warrant appointing town superintendent to fill vacancy,... 525
    resolution creating new district,......................... 525
    consent of trustees,...................................... 526
    notice to trustees not consenting, and proof of service,... 526, 527
    notice of the first meeting in a district to organize,.... 527
    notice of sale of school house by the town superintendent,... 528
    apportionment of proceeds of the sale,.................... 528
    resolutions for the alteration, or formation, of districts,... 528, 529
    certificate to teacher by town superintendent,........... 529
    instrument annulling the certificate,..................... 530
    annual report of town superintendent,.................... 530
    list of votes to be kept by district clerk,.............. 533
    forms of minutes of proceedings of district meetings,.... 533
    declaration to be made by a person challenged at district meeting,.. 534
    resolutions relative to sale and purchase of sites, and erection of school house,... 534
    order of trustees for teachers' wages,................... 535
    order for library money,................................. 535
    account of trustees, and inventory of district property,... 535, 536
    annual estimate of trustees,............................. 536

INDEX TO APPENDIX.